KENT HISTORY PROJECT

9

Later Medieval Kent, 1220–1540

KENT HISTORY PROJECT

ISSN 1352–805X

Already published

Traffic and Politics: The Construction and Management of Rochester Bridge, AD 43–1993, ed. Nigel Yates and James M. Gibson

Religion and Society in Kent, 1640–1914, Nigel Yates, Robert Hume and Paul Hastings

The Economy of Kent, 1640–1914, ed. Alan Armstrong

Faith and Fabric: A History of Rochester Cathedral, 604–1994, ed. Nigel Yates with the assistance of Paul A. Welsby

Early Modern Kent, 1540–1660, ed. Michael Zell

Kent in the Twentieth Century, ed. Nigel Yates with the assistance of Alan Armstrong, Ian Coulson and Alison Cresswell

Government and Politics in Kent, 1640–1914, ed. Frederick Lansberry

The Archaeology of Kent to AD 800, ed. John Williams

Volumes in progress

Early Medieval Kent, 800–1220, ed. Jake Weekes, Andrew Richardson and Ian Coulson

LATER MEDIEVAL KENT, 1220–1540

EDITED BY

SHEILA SWEETINBURGH

THE BOYDELL PRESS

KENT COUNTY COUNCIL

First published 2010
The Boydell Press, Woodbridge, and
Kent County Council

ISBN 978 0 85115 584 5

The Boydell Press is an imprint of Boydell & Brewer Ltd
PO Box 9, Woodbridge, Suffolk IP12 3DF, UK
and of Boydell & Brewer Inc.
668 Mt Hope Avenue, Rochester, NY 14620, USA
website: www.boydellandbrewer.com

A catalogue record for this book is available
from the British Library

Printed in Great Britain by
CPI Antony Rowe, Chippenham and Eastbourne

Contents

Illustrations

Plates

Figures

Maps

Front cover
Seal of the Corpus Christi Fraternity, Maidstone. Reproduced with permission from Maidstone Borough Council, held at Centre for Kentish Studies. CKS–U1823/89

Tables

Notes on Contributors

Bruce Campbell is Professor of Medieval Economic History at The Queen's University of Belfast, where he has taught since 1973. His research currently focuses upon the economic history of late-medieval Britain and Ireland, with particular reference to human–environment interactions during the fourteenth century and trends in agricultural output and productivity from the thirteenth to nineteenth centuries. He is the author of *English Seigniorial Agriculture 1250–1450* (2000), with Ken Bartley, *England on the Eve of the Black Death: An Atlas of Lay Lordship, Land, and Wealth, 1300–49* (2006), three collections of essays in the Ashgate Variorum Series, and the online database *Three Centuries of English Crop Yields, 1211–1491* [URL http://www.cropyields.ac.uk]. He delivered the 2008 Tawney Memorial Lecture to the Economic History Society and is a Member of the Royal Irish Academy and Fellow of the British Academy.

Barrie Dobson was a lecturer at the University of York until he became Professor of Medieval History at the University of Cambridge in 1988. After his retirement in 1999 he returned to York, where he now lives. Among his various works on that city, his chapter on 'York Minster, 1215–1500' for a collaborative history of that cathedral was written shortly after his book on *Durham Priory, 1400–1450*. He also contributed a chapter to *A History of Canterbury Cathedral* (1995). Among his other publications are studies devoted to the medieval English Jewry, to the Peasants' Revolt of 1381 and to town government and finance.

Dr Gillian Draper, FRHS, FSA is an Associate Lecturer at the University of Kent, and Events and Development Officer for The British Association for Local History. Recent publications include *Rye: a History of a Sussex Cinque Port to 1660* (2009) and *The Sea and the Marsh: the Medieval Cinque Port of New Romney* (Pre-Construct Archaeology monograph 10, 2009).

Dr Elizabeth Edwards is Honorary Senior Research Fellow in the School of History, University of Kent, where she developed and taught on the regional and local history programmes from 1994 to 2007, specialising in the late medieval and early modern periods. She has contributed to *Archaeologia Cantiana* and *An Historical Atlas of Kent* and has edited volumes on various aspects of Kentish history.

Dr Peter Fleming is Principal Lecturer in Medieval History at the University of the West of England, Bristol. His University of Wales PhD thesis dealt with the gentry of fifteenth-century Kent, and he has published several articles on the social and political history of later medieval Kent. His other research interests include medieval urban history, with particular reference to Bristol, and migration. He is the co-author, with Madge Dresser, of *Bristol: Ethnic Minorities and the City, 1000–2001* (2007).

Dr David Grummitt is a Lecturer in British History at the University of Kent. He previously worked at the History of Parliament Trust and has completed biographies of all the MPs who sat for Kent and the Kentish towns and Cinque Ports in Henry VI's Parliaments. He has published extensively on Calais under English rule and the reign of Henry VII. He is currently preparing a new study of Cade's Rebellion of 1450.

Dr Karen Jones taught History in secondary schools in Canterbury for many years. Her PhD thesis (University of Greenwich) was based on Kentish sources and her book *Gender and Petty Crime in Late Medieval England* (2006) won the Women's History Network Book Prize for 2007.

Dr Rob Lutton is a Lecturer in Medieval History at the University of Nottingham and is the author of *Lollardy and Orthodox Religion in Pre-Reformation England: Reconstructing Piety* (2006).

Mavis E. Mate is an Emeritus Professor of History at the University of Oregon. She has written extensively on the agricultural and economic history of south-east England and two books on the position of women in Kent and Sussex. Recently, she worked with colleagues on a history of Sandwich.

Dr Malcolm Mercer is currently Curator of Tower History with the Royal Armouries at the Tower of London. He has previously worked as Senior Medieval Records Specialist at The National Archives and Senior Research Archivist at Canterbury Cathedral Archives. His research interests are focused primarily upon the political culture of Late Medieval and Early Modern England, and he has published widely on subjects including gentry behaviour during the Wars of the Roses, Kentish political society, and the Anglo-Irish political community.

Dr Sheila Sweetinburgh is an Associate Lecturer at the University of Kent, and a freelance documentary researcher, principally for Canterbury Archaeological Trust. She is the author of *The Role of the Hospital in Medieval England: Gift-giving and the Spiritual Economy* (2004) and has written numerous articles on medieval Kentish society.

Abbreviations

Arch. Cant.	*Archaeologia Cantiana*
BL	British Library, London
CCAL	Canterbury Cathedral Archives and Library
CChR	*Calendar of Charter Rolls* [1226–1517], 6 vols (London, 1903–27)
CCR	*Calendar of Close Rolls* [1272–1509], 47 vols (London, 1892–1963)
CFR	*Calendar of Fine Rolls* [1272–1509], 22 vols (London, 1911–62)
CKS	Centre for Kentish Studies, Maidstone
CPR	*Calendar of Patent Rolls* [1232–1509], 52 vols (London, 1891–1916)
EKA	East Kent Archives, Whitfield
FA	*Feudal Aids* 3, 1284–1431, Kent–Norfolk (London, 1904)
Hasted, *History*	E. Hasted, *History and Topographical Survey of the County of Kent*, 12 vols (1797–1801, repr. 1972)
HMC	Historical Manuscripts Commission: 5th Report (1876); 9th Report (1883); Canterbury (1882)
IPM	*Inquisition Post Mortem*
Letters and Papers	*Letters and Papers, Foreign and Domestic, of the Reign of Henry VIII*, ed. J. S. Brewer et al., 22 vols (London, 1862–1932)
LPL	Lambeth Palace Library
ODNB	*Online Dictionary of National Biography*
PCC	Prerogative Court of Canterbury
PRO	Public Record Office
TNA	The National Archives, Kew
Valor Eccles.	*Valor Ecclesiasticus*, ed. J. Caley and J. Hunter, 6 vols, Record Commission (London, 1810–33)
VCH Kent	*Victoria County History: Kent*, 3 vols (London, 1908–32)

Introduction

The further we go back in time, the greater the length of time that is seen to constitute a particular period. Although perhaps inevitable because of its remoteness from the present, this desire to elide long stretches of our history under a particular heading or timeframe can be problematic. The resulting homogeneity hides important differences across centuries, let alone decades, as experienced by our forebears. This volume, which was designed to cover the period 1220 to 1540, is a case in point because the world of the men and women of Kent in the early thirteenth century was radically different from that experienced by their descendents in the mid-sixteenth century, as it was for those who lived in the intervening three centuries. Not least, this period is bisected by the arrival of what is known as the Black Death, an international disaster that many historians believe led to the death of between a third and a half of the population over much of Europe. The centrality of this in the shaping of later medieval society (and beyond that, the early modern period) is reflected in historical titles, the events of 1348–50 acting as a watershed in studies such as *Before the Black Death*, edited by Bruce Campbell, and *The Black Death in England*, edited by Mark Ormrod and Philip Lindley. Moreover, the arrival of the plague, though the most important 'event', was not the only significant happening during these centuries. As will be discussed in the various essays here, other matters, be they particular events such as the 'Great Famine' of 1315 to 1322 or Cade's Rebellion of 1450; or the introduction of new ideas, as seen through the presence of 'Lollards' in the county, all contributed to the complex mix of continuity and change that characterise the history of Kentish society during this formative period.

As the organiser of this volume, my aim was to provide a collection that included essays across the timeframe from the translation of St Thomas of Canterbury's relics to the new shrine in the Trinity Chapel at Canterbury Cathedral in 1220 to the destruction of this same shrine in 1538. To achieve this objective, Professor Mavis Mate's two opening essays offer a valuable overview of the period, allowing the rest of the volume to follow a thematic approach. Even though many of the specialist chapters concentrate on the later Middle Ages, in part a reflection of the surviving primary evidence and the research interests of the contributors, the earlier period, what is sometimes called the high Middle Ages, is, indeed, represented here, not least in the contributions by Dr Elizabeth Edwards and Professor Bruce Campbell.

My second aim was to include essays that foregrounded the distinctive nature of Kent, such as its maritime heritage (surrounded on three sides by the sea) and its geographical position vis-à-vis its proximity to France and London, and the royal court. The former, in terms of shipbuilding, is considered by Dr Gillian Draper; and the latter by myself amongst others. Allied to this aim was the desire to look at a theme from differing perspectives and the three articles on the gentry community of Kent and its political activities during the fifteenth century, provided by Drs Peter Fleming, David Grummitt and Malcolm Mercer, highlight the value of such a collaborative approach. Where possible links among all the various articles have also been drawn, which, it is hoped, will aid readers to move beyond a compartmentalised view of medieval Kentish society. Similarly, I sought to provide a degree of thematic connection between this volume and its early modern successor, edited by Professor Michael Zell in 2000. Dr Karen Jones's essay on witchcraft is an important reminder of how social and cultural attitudes altered over time, while Dr Robert Lutton's contribution on heresy and heterodoxy underlines the need to consider lines of continuity, as well as change, regarding religious belief across what is in some ways an artificial division between the medieval and the early modern.

Working on a volume of this size, even though I have only been involved in its later history, means that I am grateful to a number of people. First, the various contributors have shown great patience and resilience as this volume has moved towards completion, even though at times this has been painfully slow, and for this and their professionalism I thank them heartily. In addition, Ian Coulson and Richard Eales have both been extremely helpful and supportive, Ian, in particular, having in many ways carried the burden of the whole project for probably far longer than he cares to remember. John Hills of Canterbury Christ Church University has very generously given of his time and considerable expertise to compile the two maps. Permission to include several plates in this volume has been kindly given by Jon Iveson of Dover Museum, the town councils of Sandwich and Maidstone, Pre-Construct Archaeology Ltd, and the Dean and Chapter of Canterbury Cathedral. Thanks are also due to Imogen Corrigan, Faversham Town Council, Cobham College, Kent Archaeological Society and Canterbury Archaeological Trust. Finally, to the long-suffering supporters of the Kent History Project, a single volume, however large, cannot do justice to three centuries of Kentish history. Yet, I believe, any gaps are compensated by the quality of the various essays produced by well-qualified experts, who have brought the results of their recent research to this penultimate volume in the series on Kent's history.

Sheila Sweetinburgh

1

The Economy of Kent, 1200–1500: An Age of Expansion, 1200–1348

MAVIS MATE

By the thirteenth century Kent had developed into a county with marked contrasts in wealth, population density, and land use. The northern plain, readily accessible to the sea, and with fertile, easily cultivated loams, had long been settled and already enjoyed a substantial population. Much of the land was devoted to grain products, although there were no common fields or large, nucleated villages, such as existed in the east midlands. Instead, land was held in severalty and settlement was concentrated in scattered hamlets. Across the middle of the county lay a narrow band – the Vale of Holmesdale – of fertile, well-watered land, where, likewise, in many places, settlement had occurred by the Roman period or earlier. On either side of this strip lay chalk downland, and stony, infertile Chartland, more suited to pastoral than arable husbandry. Clearance and colonisation there had taken place much later than in the more fertile areas, but these lands were well settled by 1200. At the western edge of the county, however, the dense oak forests of the Weald were still sparsely populated. Each summer people in other parts of Kent drove their pigs – sometimes as far as twenty miles – to feed on the rich mast under the trees. It has been estimated that as many as sixty thousand animals were accommodated at the end of the eleventh century. In the two centuries after the Conquest, some farms had been carved out of the forest, but the cold, clay soils were unrewarding and hard to work, and keeping livestock was the major occupation.[1]

Underlying all these differences, however, was one factor common to the whole area, the prevalence of gavelkind tenure. On the death of a tenant, his widow had the use of half of her former husband's lands, so long as she did not remarry, and all male heirs shared the inheritance equally. Partible inheritance encouraged the fragmentation of holdings, although this tendency was offset, to

1 The best introduction to the settlement history of Kent is A. Everitt, *Continuity and Colonization: The Evolution of Kentish Settlement* (Leicester, 1986). See also his article 'The Making of the Agrarian Landscape of Kent', *Arch. Cant.* 92 (1976), 1–31. For details on the Weald, see K. P. Witney, *The Jutish Forest* (London, 1976) and his article, 'The Woodland Economy of Kent, 1066–1348', *Agricultural History Review* 38 (1990), 20–39.

some extent, by the right of gavelmen to sell or give their land to whom they chose. One brother could sell his share to another. A man could make his holding more compact by buying or exchanging small portions – a half acre or acre – as well as larger parcels. When such a transaction took place, the new tenant did not have to pay an entry fine, but was expected to attend his lord's court, do fealty for his new property, and pay the lord a relief.[2] The court rolls, recording these transactions, clearly show the briskness of the land market throughout the thirteenth and early fourteenth centuries.

Although personally free, gavelkinders owed various labour services and rents for their land. The rents were usually paid in money or kind – hens, eggs, or ploughshares – or on some manors, goods such as honey or eels. In addition, tenants were expected to plough, sow, harrow or reap a limited number of acres, or perform certain other named tasks that varied from place to place. Below the gavelmen in status were cottars, who performed a much greater variety of tasks, and whose services consumed more of their time. Such men often found it hard to survive on the proceeds of their holdings and worked, whenever possible, as carpenters, thatchers, shepherds, pigmen and the like. Their wives might also bring in further income by brewing ale for sale, making cheese, or keeping chickens. At harvest time, they and/or members of their family could help reap, stook, or stack grain. Harvesters were usually paid by 'the sheaf' and given food and drink while they were working.[3]

All tenants found that their standard of living declined as the population expanded over the course of the thirteenth century and the size of the family holding shrank. For the first time, in parts of Kent – at Bexley, Gillingham, and Wrotham – substantial villages appeared, but, in other parts of the county – at Otford, for example – despite the increase in population, settlement remained in the form of scattered farms.[4] As land was shared out among heirs, each new family built a separate dwelling, and houses, farms and barns sprang up in the midst of fields. The pressure of population had also encouraged the bringing of new land into cultivation. New sea-walls, drainage channels, and water courses were constructed in the marshes to protect those areas of Romney Marsh that had been long reclaimed and to turn Walland Marsh into excellent pasture for sheep and cattle. As the thirteenth century progressed some marshland that had been long devoted to pastoral husbandry was ploughed up.[5] Wheat was sown in fields

2 F. R. H. Du Boulay, *The Lordship of Canterbury* (London, 1966), p. 145. The size of the relief varied from manor to manor.

3 Ibid.; F. R. H. Du Boulay, *Medieval Bexley* (Bexley, 1961). After the Black Death, harvesters on the estates of Christ Church Priory were clearly being paid every tenth sheaf, but in the thirteenth century they may have been paid at a lower rate. At Yalding in the 1350s they were paid every twelfth sheaf; MS TNA PRO SC 6/907/16.

4 A. R. H. Baker, 'Some Fields and Farms in Medieval Kent', *Arch. Cant.* 80 (1965), 152–74; D. Clarke and A. Stoyel, *Otford in Kent: A History* (Battle, 1975), p. 68.

5 J. Eddison, 'The Settlement of Romney Marsh: Some Aspects Reconsidered', *Arch. Cant.* 99 (1983), 47–58; N. Brooks, 'Romney Marsh in the Early Middle Ages', *The Evolution of Marshland Landscapes*, ed. T. Rowley (Oxford, 1987), pp. 24–94.

that had been well manured and marled, but elsewhere oats and beans were the main crop. Settlers were also moving into the High Weald. By 1240 some permanent farms had replaced temporary huts and shelters, but these forest clearings were at first still scattered and isolated. It was not until the end of the century that a new wave of pioneers entered the forest in larger numbers and began to settle in hamlets. On their small farms they planted fruit trees, grew oats and legumes, and kept animals. They also utilised the resources of the woods around them, manufacturing wooden objects, cutting wood into faggots and preparing charcoal. Gradually, the ready availability of fuel attracted industry to the area and small forges were set up. Men also worked as potters, tanners, and rope makers.[6]

The constant demand for fuel, however, saved the woods in northern Kent from a similar wave of colonisation. By the thirteenth century, most of them were being coppiced and cut on a regular basis (see Draper, this volume). They could then be used as cattle pasture as well as providing firewood to be carted or shipped to centres of population, especially London. Between 1260 and 1348 the price of faggots nearly trebled, making the woodland increasingly valuable.[7] On the Battle Abbey manor of Wye, for example, the serjeant in 1347 received £8 2s from the sale of faggots.[8] Timber, although less in demand, was needed for framing and roofing building. Thus, despite the pressure to bring all available land into cultivation, the trees survived.

Concomitant with the population explosion was an increase in the use of money and a growth in markets. The Crown, however, had long claimed the authority to regulate trade and in the thirteenth century was able to insist on its right to license new markets.[9] The resulting records clearly show the large number of markets existing in Kent on the eve of the Black Death.[10] Most families would have been able to travel to market and back in a single day and, in many places, there would have been a choice of markets within easy reach. Markets held within towns almost certainly attracted a greater volume of trade than smaller village markets. Faversham market, held four days a week, drew supplies of wheat and barley from the rich, agricultural lands of east Kent, and was visited regularly by London cornmongers as well as merchants from Picardy and Flanders. Maidstone benefited from its position as the last navigable place on the River Medway and in its markets products from the pastoral activities in the Weald were exchanged with those from the arable areas of the Vale of Holmesdale and north Kent. Sandwich, which around 1250 housed as many as forty different occupations, including inn-keepers, maltsters, bakers, tailors,

6 Witney, 'The Woodland Economy of Kent', pp. 20–39; J. Birrell, 'Peasant Craftsmen in the Medieval Forest', *Agricultural History Review* 17 (1969), 91–106.

7 Witney, 'The Woodland Economy of Kent', pp. 27–39.

8 MS TNA PRO SC 6/899/7.

9 R. H. Britnell, 'English Markets and Royal Administration before 1200', *Economic History Review*, 2nd series 34 (1981), 209–21.

10 B. McLain, 'Factors in Market Establishment in Medieval England: The Evidence from Kent, 1066–1360', *Arch. Cant.* 117 (1997), 83–101; M. Mate, 'The Rise and Fall of Markets in Southeast England', *Canadian Journal of History* 31 (1996), 60–85.

ship-masters, and merchants, in the late thirteenth century was focusing on the import of wine, and on the export of wool and grain.[11]

By far the most important town, dwarfing all others, was Canterbury. In the early thirteenth century it housed about two hundred shops and a wide variety of tradesmen and craftsmen. A small, but wealthy, Jewish community lent money to clients living in all parts of Kent and even in London.[12] The royal mint employed moneyers. Workers in the cloth and leather industries – weavers, saddlers, shoemakers, and glovers – manufactured goods that were sold throughout the region as well as in the town itself. Goldsmiths supplied monasteries and the better-off citizenry with chalices, cups, and plates. Innkeepers housed pilgrims and visiting merchants. Moreover, since Canterbury was an ecclesiastical as well as trading centre, it attracted priests, chaplains, and clerks, who served the parish churches and worked for the archbishop or the local monasteries. To cater for the everyday needs of this vast throng of people, there were cooks, bakers, brewers, taverners, and alehouse keepers. Below the solid citizens existed an unquantifiable mass of servants, apprentices, transient labourers, and beggars, whose number probably grew as the population expanded.[13]

Throughout the thirteenth and into the fourteenth century prices slowly but steadily rose.[14] The two major factors behind this long-term inflation were first the marked increase in population, which was exerting considerable pressure on sources of food production, and second, an increase in the silver supply. Between 1000 and 1300 the volume of silver circulating in England increased ten or fifteen times and the velocity of circulation probably increased as well. Then, between 1305 and 1310, a sudden influx of foreign silver into English mints nearly doubled the number of coins in circulation. The continued expenditure by the government after 1290 on war with Scotland and France also had an inflationary effect, since coins which in the past might have been hoarded or set aside for another day, were being used to pay taxes and then spent by the government to buy provisions and other necessities. Rising prices naturally increased the cost of all purchased goods, but also made possible substantial profits if one sold more than one bought.[15]

The prospect of greater profits encouraged landlords to make a major change in estate management. In the eleventh and twelfth centuries most manors had been leased out for a food farm or cash rent, or a combination of the two. Around 1200, however, lords began to take their estates in hand and exploit them directly.

11 T. H. Lloyd, *The English Wool Trade in the Middle Ages*, (Cambridge, 1977), pp. 50–1, 71. Nine Sandwich men worked alongside the Flemish merchants who dominated the trade.

12 For a full account of the Canterbury Jewry, see M. Adler, 'The Jews of Canterbury', *Jewish Historical Society Transactions* 7 (1915), 19–59.

13 W. Urry, *Canterbury under the Angevin Kings* (London, 1967).

14 D. L. Farmer, 'Prices and Wages', *Agrarian History of England and Wales, 1042–1350* (Cambridge, 1988), pp. 715–817.

15 M. Mate, 'High Prices in Early Fourteenth Century England, Causes and Consequences', *Economic History Review*, 2nd series 28 (1973), 1–16.

By appointing their own officials to run their estates, the expected profits from an expanding market might remain in their own hands, not in those of lessees.[16] Religious considerations, as the case of Christ Church Priory shows, sometimes also influenced decisions. The Christ Church estates, when leased, were put in the hands of one of the monks. But the time-consuming responsibility of managing the estates made it absolutely impossible for the monk-farmer to participate fully in the cathedral services. Moreover, after living for a long period of time outside the convent, the monks sometimes forgot their vows. One monk-farmer, for example, was accused of seducing young women.[17] A new prior, Thomas de Ringmere, summoned the monks home and his action was strongly supported by the next archbishop, John Pecham. Yet the switch to lay serjeants did not immediately produce additional revenues. It was not until the priorate of Henry de Eastry (1284–1331), under a new system of strict financial accounting for both annual revenues and arrears, that the priory's income grew.

The detailed records produced under this system of direct management clearly show the efficiency of Kent demesne agriculture (see Campbell, this volume). Manure was regularly carried from cattle and sheep barns on to wheat fields in the summer and early autumn and animals that had been pastured elsewhere were folded onto the fallow at night. Land was often further enriched by the widespread sowing of legumes – peas, beans, vetch – which added nitrogen to the soil. In addition, grain was sown at a high rate of seed, which generally produced high yields per acre. Even though a larger quantity of grain was needed for seed, there was still plenty left over for sale, as well as food for the household and other purposes, such as grain liveries to workers. Cropping patterns were extremely varied. Demesne fields might be sown in sections with different crops, thus reducing the risk of losing one's whole crop of wheat or barley, because of an outbreak of fungoid disease or hail.[18]

Animal husbandry seems to have been equally efficient. Lords – both lay and ecclesiastical – were willing to invest large sums to build up their sheep flocks on land that was not particularly fertile. John Cobham, for example, in 1290–91, spent £33 6s 8d on the purchase of 273 wethers (castrated rams) and five ewes, bringing the total flock on his Cobham manor to 590 animals.[19] In addition, dairy farming and cattle breeding became an increasingly important part of the demesne economy. Cows provided milk, butter, and cheese for the household or

16 E. Searle, *Lordship and Community: Battle Abbey and its Banlieu, 1066–1538* (Toronto, 1974); T. May, 'The Estates of the Cobham Family in the Later Thirteenth Century', *Arch. Cant.* 84 (1969), 211–29.

17 MS CCAL DCc Chart. Ant. M/368. M. Mate, 'The Farming out of Manors: A New Look at the Evidence from Canterbury Cathedral Priory', *Journal of Medieval History* 9 (1983), 331–43.

18 M. Mate, 'Medieval Agrarian Practices: The Determining Factors?', *Agricultural History Review* 33 (1985), 22–31. The theory of 'risk aversion' was first promulgated by D. McCloskey, 'The Persistence of the English Open Fields', in *European Peasants and Their Markets*, ed. W. N. Parker and E. C. Jones (Princeton, NJ, 1975), pp. 73–119; and ibid., 'English Open Fields as a Behavior towards Risk', *Research in Economic History* 1 (London, 1976), 124–70.

19 May, 'Cobham Family ', 223.

for sale, as well as providing new stock. By 1300, however, oxen were no longer the main draught animals, as lords switched to mixed teams of horses and oxen, or relied solely on horse power.[20] Nonetheless, young calves could be killed for food. With an expanding population the demand for cheese and beef rose and lords could lease out their cows at a high rate. The Christ Church monks, although they relied heavily on horses for draught animals, built up cowherds on many manors that had never contained cows before.

Since very little of the work needed to run the demesne was provided by tenant services, a lord had to hire full-time labourers: the *famuli*. They were paid a small money wage and given extensive grain liveries. The rates, especially for the ploughmen, were higher than those in many other parts of the country. Whereas ploughmen elsewhere often received one quarter of grain every twelve weeks, or at best, every ten weeks, in east Kent ploughmen were paid one quarter every seven weeks, and in the rest of Kent, one quarter every eight weeks. Such high rates – paid on the lay manor of Cobham, the archiepiscopal manors in Kent, and the Christ Church manors – resulted, perhaps, from the free status of the men concerned. Money wages were also higher than in other parts of England. The ready availability of such employment must have made it easier to survive at a time when the demand for land far exceeded the supply.

The expansion in population and production also led to an increased demand for mills. The earliest known watermill, dating from the eighth century, existed in Kent at Chart. At the time of Domesday, the county had a considerable concentration of watermills, but there were still areas where the number of mills was disproportionately low compared to the population.[21] The introduction of windmills, at the end of the twelfth century, added a new source of energy. Lords were prepared to sink money into mill construction and acquisition. When the Christ Church prior, Henry de Eastry, listed his accomplishments just before his death, he mentioned seven Kentish mills made anew or acquired.[22] Most mills were rented for grain, with quantities that tended to remain fixed, so their value obviously fluctuated with the rise and fall in grain prices. Moreover, mills, especially windmills, needed constant repair and these expenses ate into the revenues.

From the 1290s, for the next sixty years, the Kentish economy was buffeted by exogenous shocks, some of which were natural disasters, but some were man-made. First, in the 1290s the king laid an unprecedented burden of taxation on clergy and laity alike.[23] Purveyance, the compulsory purchase of goods to

20 J. Langdon, *Horses and Oxen and Technological Innovation*, (Cambridge, 1986), pp. 80–127.

21 R. Holt, *The Mills of Medieval England* (Oxford, 1988).

22 MS BL Cotton Galba E. IV, fol. 109.

23 For a good, general discussion of the burdens imposed by the various kinds of taxation, see the chapter by W. M. Ormrod, 'The Crown and the English Economy, 1290–1348', in *Before the Black Death: Studies in the 'Crisis' of the Early Fourteenth Century*, ed. B. M. S. Campbell (Manchester, 1991), pp. 149–83.

provide for royal troops, fell with particular severity on Kent. Grain, cheeses, and hay were all seized without payment at different times by 'men of the king'.[24] Although royal purveyors often received bribes to move away, they usually took something – even if it was just apples from the garden – before they left. Their activities caused acute shortages in Kent and pushed up prices. In 1295–96, in areas of Kent closest to the ports, the price of wheat was more than double the national average. The following year, even though the harvests were extremely plentiful, the price of wheat throughout the county, at 7s a quarter, was well above the national average of 6s 4d a quarter. People or institutions that had grain to sell were able to make substantial profits.[25]

The period 1305–15 was a time of rising revenues for the great lords, but one of increasing hardship for many peasants. A new surge in prices, caused partly by the disastrous harvest of 1306 and partly by the influx of silver, encouraged the further production of goods for sale. Large purchases maintained or expanded sheep flocks, and marling and the intensive use of legumes facilitated an increase in the area under cultivation, especially for wheat, the major cash crop. Grain was frequently shipped directly to London or to urban markets across the Channel. In many places the high revenues from sales were used to finance new construction at both the central and local level. In Kent, the Christ Church monks started work on the rebuilding of their choir and spent £234 5s 3d on new building within the city of Canterbury alone. On their manors, new mills, barns, and halls, many of stone, with elaborate tiled roofs, rose on all sides.[26]

In 1315 and 1316 heavy rain caused the wheat harvests to fail for two years in succession and much of England suffered widespread famine.[27] The chroniclers report tales of the unprecedented price of 40s a quarter for wheat and a resort to the consumption of cats, dogs, and horses. It is not known whether prices in Canterbury and other Kent towns ever reached the heights recorded by the chroniclers, but in the countryside the highest price received by the Christ Church monks was 24s a quarter for wheat in 1316. In Kent, however, barley and oats yields remained relatively unaffected, and although their prices rose, they did not soar to the same heights as that of wheat. On some Christ Church estates the *famuli* were paid in oats, or given mixed grain, instead of pure barley. On the archiepiscopal manor of Otford the grain livery was paid in money at the rate of 1s a week for ploughmen. Although the rates paid for mowing did go up – from 6d to 9d and in one place to ls ld an acre – this rise almost certainly did not begin to compensate for the increased cost of food. More smallholders, than usual, with

24 In 1295–96 the sheriff of Kent collected 4884 quarters of grain to provision the army in Gascony; M. Prestwich, *War, Politics and Finance under Edward I* (London, 1972), p. 121.

25 M. Mate, 'The Impact of War on the Economy of Canterbury Cathedral Priory, 1294–1340', *Speculum* 57 (1982), 763–6.

26 M. Mate, 'Property Investment by Canterbury Cathedral Priory, 1250–1400', *Journal of British Studies* 23 (1984), 1–21.

27 I. Kershaw, 'The Great Famine and Agrarian Crisis in England, 1315–22', *Past and Present* 59 (1973), 3–50.

limited resources, may have died. The tenant population, however, seems to have remained stable, with the vacant holdings being filled immediately.

In 1319–21 another blow fell when a devastating epidemic killed both cows and oxen. The loss of oxen was extremely serious, since on many manors just one or two animals were left at the end of the year, not enough to pull a plough. Wherever possible, local officials restocked, buying plough horses where no oxen were available, and in this way encouraged the trend towards the total reliance on horse power. Naturally, the purchase price of horses rose. Smallholders could not afford them and were forced to leave much of their land untilled. Fortunately, not all of Kent was equally afflicted. The north Kent marshes, which were a major centre of dairy farming, seem to have escaped entirely. Their animals could be used in rebuilding herds in areas where the disease had been most endemic. Rebuilding, however, seems to have been a slow process. On the Christ Church estates, despite the considerable resources at the disposal of the monks, most herds of cows in 1331 were still below the early fourteenth-century level, although above the low levels of 1321.[28]

At a moment when recovery might have been well underway, poor weather and animal disease returned. In 1331 many places in Kent suffered from drought and the yields of barley and oats collapsed. In 1334 sheep and cattle disease appeared again. At Boxley, belonging to Boxley Abbey, young animals were particularly devastated and, in 1334–35, 214 newborn lambs died out of 264 and 156 year-old lambs out of 216.[29] Finally, in 1339 drought returned. Peasant farmers suffered a great deal from the cumulative effects of these agricultural disasters. If their crops failed during a year of bad weather, they needed all the grain they could harvest for their own sustenance or for next year's harvest, and were not able, like the great landowners, to sell at higher prices. Furthermore, prices as a whole fell steadily throughout the decade of the 1330s, reaching their lowest level in 1337–39. The stock of silver which had built up in the early fourteenth century was slowly draining away with the natural wastage of the currency, heavy overseas expenditure by the Crown, a deteriorating balance of trade, and an exchange rate that favoured the export of silver.[30] This deflation, although it made purchases easier, also reduced income. Peasants, who relied on the sale of wool or grain to provide them with the revenues necessary to pay their rent or buy manufactured goods such as shoes or scythes, could not afford to let their stock sit in their barn or house until prices rose. They had to find buyers when they could.

The outbreak of the Hundred Years War caused further disruption. In 1338–40 French attacks, including the sack of Southampton, caused great panic and

28 M. Mate, 'The Estates of Canterbury Cathedral Priory before the Black Death, 1315–1348', *Studies in Medieval and Renaissance History,* new series 8 (1986), 3–31.

29 MS TNA PRO SC 6/886/9.

30 N. J. Mayhew, 'Numismatic Evidence and Falling Prices in the Fourteenth Century', *Economic History Review* 2nd series 27 (1974), 1–15. M. Prestwich, 'Currency and the Economy of Early Fourteenth Century England', in *Edwardian Monetary Affairs, 1279–1341*, ed. N. J. Mayhew, British Archaeological Reports 36 (1977), pp. 45–58.

necessitated the establishment of a defence force. To feed the force as well as men going overseas, royal purveyors once more sought grain and stock all across southern and eastern counties. But as far as can be ascertained, the burden of purveyance within Kent during these years was less than in the 1290s, during the first Anglo-French war, and considerably below the early years of Edward II's reign. Far more serious were the constant demands of the tax-collector which bit more steeply than earlier. The historian, J. R. Maddicott, believes that in the six years, 1336–41, 'the weight of taxation may have been greater than at any other time in the Middle Ages, greater even than in the years preceding the revolt of 1381'.[31] Taxes almost certainly consumed a higher proportion of disposable income among the peasantry than among either the gentry or the nobility. Tenants whose stock had survived the outbreaks of disease, or whose fields had not been touched by bad weather, could lose their grain or stock to the purveyor or be forced to sell to pay the tax-collector. Their resources might thus be totally depleted. Consequently those who had goods to sell could not always find a buyer. Prospective customers, even though they might need the goods, no longer had the means to purchase them.

It is impossible to estimate with any degree of accuracy how widespread and how serious this peasant distress was. In some places, in the 1330s, local serjeants had difficulty finding tenants and collecting rents, but elsewhere there were no problems. Likewise on some manors pasture revenues dropped, as tenants had so few animals they did not need to rent additional grazing, but on other manors, such as on the Christ Church manor of Lydden, the revenues and the number of animals accommodated remained high through the 1340s.[32] Harvests, moreover, in the period 1340–49, consistently produced more than the average of the earlier period 1290–1309. Disease attacks and purveyance did not affect all manors to the same extent. Furthermore, Lydden lay in close proximity to the major ports of Dover and Sandwich, so it is possible that many of the animals pasturing on its marshes belonged, not to peasants, but to urban butchers, who were fattening them before sale. Sandwich became the major assembly point for the siege of Calais.

There seems little doubt that for tenants with very little land, who relied primarily on outside employment for their income, the 1330s and early 1340s were hard times. The yearly *famuli* found that the total value of their grain liveries dropped with the falling grain prices. This would not matter if they used the grain primarily to feed themselves, but if they were accustomed to sell some of it, they would have received less. Building workers – carpenters, thatchers, tilers – may have faced extensive periods of unemployment, as lords like Christ Church Priory cut costs by concentrating on essential repairs and no longer embarked on new

31 J. R. Maddicott, 'The English Peasantry and the Demands of the Crown, 1294–1341', *Past and Present* Supplement 1 (Oxford, 1975), reprinted in *Landlords, Peasants and Politics in Medieval England*, ed. T. H. Ashton (Cambridge, 1987), p. 329.

32 MS CCAL DCc/Bedels rolls Lydden.

building projects. Even when they found work, some employers, like the monks of Boxley Abbey, took advantage of the low prices and fed their thatchers and carpenters during the working day, reducing their money wage accordingly. A thatcher and his boy, who had been paid four and a halfpenny a day in 1334–35, received just one and a halfpenny a day with their food in 1339–40. The men themselves might have eaten better, but they had less to take home to their families. The court rolls of Wye clearly show that a number of men with very small holdings were dying before their prime, leaving minor children as heirs. Other tenants were refusing or unable to pay their rents.[33]

When a tax was levied on moveable goods in 1334, it revealed the comparative poverty of the Weald and parts of Romney Marsh relative to northeast Kent.[34] In both areas dairy farming and cattle rearing were extremely important and they may have been particularly badly hit by the renewed outbreaks of murrain in 1334–35. In addition, people who supplemented their income by making such items as pots, wooden objects or gloves received a lower return on their goods when prices fell. Finally, the work of Flemish weavers, who had been established in 1332 in the area around Cranbrook, was hurt by royal manipulation of the wool trade. In contrast, farmers on the rich, arable lands in north-east Kent seem to have bounced back after the bad harvests with remarkable ease. Wheat and barley continued to be grown for the market and shipped to London via Faversham. Agriculture was still a profitable occupation and became even more so once prices began to rise in the mid-1340s.

The easing of the money supply after the introduction of a gold coinage and the minting of new silver pennies and halfpennies allowed prices to recover from the slump of the late 1330s.[35] In the case of wool, heavy export duties prevented prices from rising as high as they might otherwise have done, but the rise was sufficient to encourage at least some growers to rebuild their flocks. The Christ Church monks had almost the same number of sheep and lambs in 1347 as they did in 1303.[36] Grain prices also rose. The need to provision Calais after its capture stimulated the demand for grain and stock throughout south-eastern England. With higher prices came higher revenues from all goods sold in local or national markets. Peasants, however, who frequently sold their goods to itinerant corn- and woolmongers, not in the open markets, did not always get the best deal. With limited resources, rebuilding their sheep flocks and cow herds took longer.

33 MS TNA PRO SC 2/181/11–15.

34 R. E. Glasscock, 'The Distribution of Lay Wealth in Kent, Surrey and Sussex in the Early Fourteenth Century', *Arch. Cant.* 80 (1965), 63.

35 M. Mate, 'The Role of Gold Coinage in the English Economy, 1338–1400', *Numismatic Chronicle* 7th series 18 (1978), 126–31.

36 Mate, 'Estates of Canterbury Cathedral Priory', 3–31.

2

The Economy of Kent, 1200–1500: The Aftermath of the Black Death

MAVIS MATE

The Impact of Pestilence, 1348–c. 1400

The arrival of the Black Death in Kent in 1348–49 disrupted every aspect of society. At Rochester at least 50 per cent of the tenants of Rochester Priory may have died.[1] A monk there described the breakdown of normal life. The entire household of the bishop died and no one was left to serve him. Local clergy fled and their parishioners were deprived of spiritual services. In places corpses did not receive a proper burial and 'men and women carried their own children on their shoulders to the church and threw them into a common pit'.[2] Within the countryside mortality obviously varied from place to place. Some remote areas may have escaped relatively unscathed, but most places had probably lost a third to a half of their population by 1350. Then in 1361–62 a second, major epidemic struck Kent and pestilence returned again in 1374–75. Young children, with no immunity, may have been particularly hard hit. The population dropped even lower.

Survivors, however, were able to demand better working conditions, such as higher money wages or payment in better quality grain. The rate for mowing, for example, went up from 6d to 8d, 9d, or 10d an acre. On a number of manors tenants insisted on being paid for reaping and threshing with a money wage, instead of being paid by the sheaf or threshed bushel. The vigorous enforcement of the Statute of Labourers did succeed in dampening the general wage rise, but the spread between the highest and lowest wage became far greater than earlier in the century. By the mid-1350s rates had become very specific to a particular area. An institution such as Battle Abbey or Canterbury Cathedral Priory, with estates in more than one part of the county, did not adopt a common wage policy for all its estates, but paid the prevailing rate in each area. In north-west Kent wages were generally lower than elsewhere. A shepherd at Meopham was earning 5s 6d in the

1 A. F. Butcher, 'English Urban Society and the Revolt of 1381', in *The English Rising of 1381*, ed. R. H. Hilton and T. H. Aston (Cambridge, 1987), p. 95.

2 P. Ziegler, *The Black Death* (New York, 1971), pp. 161–4.

mid-1350s compared to the 6s and 7s prevailing on the east Kent manors and the 10s to 12s on some of the Romney Marsh manors. For the most part this differential remained unchanged until the mid-1370s, with men in north-west Kent receiving wages comparable or just slightly above those in other parts of the country, and workers on the marsh manors being paid considerably more.[3] But the gains in the marshes partly arose because the whole area was gradually depopulated. Soon after the Black Death families began to withdraw from lands that had earlier been colonised and churches on the Romney Marsh fell into ruins. By the beginning of the fifteenth century a number of settlements had disappeared.[4]

Of all the Kentish *famuli*, it was the unskilled labourer, such as the pigman, who, where he continued to be employed, eventually enjoyed the most marked improvement in his standard of living. So long as labour had been plentiful, pigmen had been in a poor bargaining position. In the early part of the century, pigmen on the marsh manors of Appledore and Dengemarsh were paid 4s a year, and received just a quarter of grain every sixteen weeks. By the 1370s they were receiving 12s a year in money and a grain livery of one quarter every eight weeks (at Appledore) and one quarter every six weeks (at Dengemarsh). In other places, however, serjeants, rather than pay higher wages, simply eliminated the position. More and more often pigmen were employed part-time, or the task of keeping the pigs was given to the cowman, or the demesne pigs were kept with those of the vill. It became harder for unskilled men to find permanent full-time positions, although the rewards were greater.

Kentish landlords, however, seem to have successfully maintained their rights through the 1370s and did not immediately commute or phase out any customary services that were still being worked in 1347. At Wye, belonging to Battle Abbey, in 1365/6 tenants reaped forty-seven acres, mowed twenty-eight acres, and were responsible for 542 'carrying services', transporting grain and malt from Wye to Battle.[5] On the east Kent manors of Christ Church, Canterbury, where it had been common for tenants to carry out their 'works', they continued to do so, and indeed, on some manors, where the services had been only partially worked before, they were fully performed thereafter. The payment of reapers with money was a temporary concession, and once the first shock of the pestilence was over, most of the threshing and the reaping was carried out as before by a combination of customary labour and payment in kind. On the archiepiscopal manor of Northfleet, in 1366/7, 102 acres were reaped by tenants fulfilling customary services. On the Christ Church manor of Meopham, in 1384, eighty acres of wheat were reaped by tenants and the rest of the reaping was done by the tenth sheaf.

3 M. Mate, 'Labour and Labour Services on the Estates of Canterbury Cathedral Priory in the Fourteenth Century', *Southern History* 7 (1985), 55–68.

4 At Midley, Hope All Saints, Eastbridge, Orgarswick, Blackmanstone, and Orlestone; M. Beresford, *The Lost Villages of England* (London, 1954), pp. 358–9.

5 MS TNA PRO SC 6/899/20.

Meanwhile, arable farming was hit once more by periods of severe drought and outbreaks of fungoid diseases (see Campbell, this volume).[6] In the early 1350s it scarcely rained for three years; in the 1360s and 1370s Kentish harvests were far worse than the national average. On the other hand, in the 1360s, grain, wool, and stock prices rose markedly. In the period 1365–74 oxen, cows, and even pigs sold for at least 25 per cent, and frequently 75 per cent, more than in the decade before the Black Death. Wool prices, during most of the seventies, stood at a higher level than at any time since the 1320s.[7] With the general rise in wages, some peasants were able to spend a smaller proportion of their income on grain and so had more money to spend on meat and dairy products, which earlier had been regarded as luxury items, thus causing an increase in demand. In addition, there was a general inflationary pressure brought about by an increase in the money supply with the issue of gold coins and new lighter weight silver coins. By the 1370s it seems clear that the quantity of money in circulation was substantially larger than it had been in the 1240s, even though the population was substantially smaller.[8]

These high prices helped to cushion any losses from bad harvests. People may have had less grain or wool to sell, but they received more for such goods as they could sell. Consequently, during the 1360s and early 1370s, many lords found it still worthwhile to manage their manors directly rather than to lease them out. The manor of Wye, for example, provided the house at Battle with grain, cheese, butter, and cider. Its tile-house, with seven furnaces, produced all the tiles needed for repair on manorial buildings, and the sale of wool from its wethers, ewes, and lambs brought in revenues of around £20 a year.[9]

The demands of the war effort exacerbated existing problems. War recruiters competed with lords for the services of labourers. Purveyors of grain and cattle for provisioning Calais drained east Kent of needed goods. In 1359–60, when the king stayed with his army in Kent before crossing to France, the demands of the purveyors became particularly harsh. Farmers also had to cope with the depredation caused by the armies of powerful lords. In 1371 the 'malicious men of Robert Knolles' destroyed much of the peas and vetch in the fields of Great Chart. Elsewhere, officials had to pay the head of Knolles's army to go away. Finally, French raids along the coast wreaked destruction and caused unrest. In 1380 'men from the galleys' set fire to the shops of Appledore, destroyed the hay, burned the bridge and dairy, and took five calves and two pipes of cider.[10]

6 In 1373 much of the barley on the Christ Church manor of Copton was destroyed by a harmful herb called 'yellowbothel'. M. Mate, 'Agrarian Economy after the Black Death: The Manors of Canterbury Cathedral Priory, 1348–91', *Economic History Review* 2nd series 37 (1984), 342–9.

7 D. L. Farmer, 'Prices and Wages, 1350–1500', in *Agrarian History of England and Wales, 1348–1500*, ed. E. Miller (Cambridge, 1991), pp. 431–525.

8 M. Mate, 'The Role of the Gold Coinage in the English Economy, 1338–1400', *Numismatic Chronicle* 7th series 18 (1978), 131–8.

9 MS TNA PRO SC 6/892/31–3; SC 6/892/11; SC 6/889/18–23. In addition the market and yearly fairs, in the early 1370s, produced revenues around £11 a year, SC 6/900/2–7.

10 Mate, 'Agrarian Economy', 349–50.

Trade was disrupted since ships were vulnerable to attacks by pirates and enemy forces. Fighting in Gascony, moreover, destroyed many of the vines and reduced the output of wine. Likewise the export of wool through the port dropped from a high of 1230 sacks in 1305 to 353 sacks in the 1360s. The war effort was clearly taking precedence over general trade. Sandwich remained the chief port for the forwarding of supplies to Calais and to the army operating in its vicinity. In 1359–60, men-at-arms and archers converged there from all over the southern counties, and large numbers of hurdles and bridges for the shipment of horses, plus tools, hand-mills, and cooking utensils for the use of the army were collected.[11] The six thousand carts that were brought into the town provide a clear measure of the scale of operations at this time. Trade with the Low Countries, however, was not so badly affected as that with Gascony and Italy, and small ships continued to leave Kent ports taking with them wheat, flour, malt, and oats, and bringing back onions and garlic. Coastal trade also flourished. The accounts of the wealthy fishmonger, Daniel Rough of New Romney, show him sending oysters, crabs, lampfreys, and trout to London, the eastern counties, and up the Thames to Wallingford. He brought back to Romney calves, pork, and bacon, all of which found a ready market.[12]

The revenues that were hardest to maintain were mill rents and those coming from fairs and markets. Over the country as a whole the number of grain mills had fallen by about 15 per cent by the 1370s, then the number stabilised for a few years before starting to shrink again.[13] Kent was no exception. On many of the Christ Church accounts, especially in the 1360s after the second outbreak of plague, were such comments as 'the mill could not be rented any dearer this year' or 'the mill stood vacant for lack of a tenant'. With the rise in wages and the price of raw materials, repairs became more expensive. When some mills collapsed, they were left in disrepair. Adisham had supported four mills in the early fourteenth century, but by the end of the 1360s two of the mills had disappeared. On the archiepiscopal estates, in 1399, the two windmills of Wingham were in poor condition, in ruins, and stood empty for lack of a lessee. The windmill at Gillingham and the two windmills at Bocton were also broken and untenanted and at Shoreham a watermill and a fulling mill were no longer in operation.[14] Revenues from fairs and markets likewise dropped as stalls stood vacant for lack of renters. At Sevenoaks, for example, the rents from shops and stalls in the market dropped from 20s to 6s 8d, and the markets and fair at Wye, which had produced revenues of around £11 in 1369–71, produced no more than £4 in the 1390s.

11 H. J. Hewitt, *The Organisation of War under Edward III, 1338–62* (Manchester, 1966); T. L. Richardson, *Medieval Sandwich and its World* (Sandwich, 2004), pp. 25–43.

12 K. M. E. Murray, ed., *Register of Daniel Rough, Common Clerk of Romney, 1353–1380*, Kent Records 16 (Ashford, 1945).

13 J. Langdon, *Mills in the Medieval Economy* (Oxford, 2004), pp. 26–31.

14 Mate, 'Agrarian Economy', 351–2; *Calendar of Inquisitions Miscellaneous 1392–99* (London, 1965), nos 318, 324, 326.

In the 1370s, in both town and the countryside, there was increasing tension between those in power and lesser men. Urban tradesmen and craftsmen had to pay high prices for any food that they bought, yet their rents remained unchanged, and wages were controlled. In Canterbury additional financial burdens were imposed when the town levied murage grants to pay for the repair of the town walls in anticipation of a French invasion. The subsequent prosecution of those who had taken stones from the city walls or who refused to pay taxes caused further tension that ultimately escalated into violence.[15] At the same time, the weight of lordship was increasingly resented in the countryside as seigniorial courts continued to levy dues such as fines on brewers and for failure to repair buildings. Local court rolls record sporadic violence against manorial officials. In 1380 a complaint was brought to the central court of King's Bench that Roger Manston and other malefactors had assaulted the estate steward of the abbot of St Augustine's, Canterbury, and prevented him from holding the abbot's court at Minster in Thanet.[16]

How much had peasants benefited from the changed economic situation after 1348? Full-time *famuli* employed on demesnes, received higher money wages, and, in many cases, larger or better quality grain liveries. Any goods, such as eggs or piglets, that were sold produced high revenues. A peasant with eleven acres of intensively cultivated land and with sufficient pasture for his animals could probably manage without too much difficulty, even in years of bad harvests such as those of 1368–70.[17] Yet in only a few places had rents fallen. Thus, although land was more readily available with the drop in population, smallholders could not always afford it, and it was picked up by gentry, townsmen, or better-off peasants. Families with just two or three acres had no option but to supplement the produce of their land with outside employment. Building workers, hired by the day – carpenters, tilers, thatchers, and the like – were able to demand a higher wage rate, but they may have faced longer periods of unemployment if people sought to reduce expenses by scaling down new building and delaying repairs on old ones. Thus, their yearly wages may not have increased at all. So too craftsmen, such as tailors, cobblers, and weavers, may have faced a declining demand for their services as the population dropped. Their income, like that of the building workers, may not have risen commensurately with the rise in prices. For these families the imposition of poll taxes to pay for the war would have brought considerable hardship.

When Essex villagers rose in revolt at the attempts to enforce payment of the

15 Butcher, 'English Urban Society', pp. 84–111.

16 C. Dyer, 'The Social and Economic Background to the Rural Revolt of 1381', in *The English Rising of 1381*, ed. R. H. Hilton and T. H. Aston (Cambridge, 1987), pp. 28–34.

17 In 1362 William Baker, who held eleven acres from the abbot of St Augustine's, fell into a pit. At the time of his death he had two acres sown with wheat, two acres sown with spring barley, two acres of oats, and one acre sown with vetch. He also owned five horses, sixty sheep, three young oxen, and eleven piglets. These goods were valued at £10 13s 6d; *Calendar of Inquisitions Miscellaneous 1348–77* (London, 1937), no. 831.

third poll tax, the men of Kent joined in. In June 1381 Canterbury Castle and town hall, as well as the houses of some of the leading citizens, were attacked and Maidstone gaol was assaulted. John Tebbe, who had served as MP for Canterbury, and held many high offices in the city, was killed. In the countryside rebels burned customals, rentals, and other records, and ransacked and pillaged the property of those who had served as royal or ecclesiastical administrators.[18] The disaffected came from a wide cross-section of Kentish society.

Faced with the difficulties of these years, great lords, unsure what policy to adopt, shifted back and forth between farming estates directly and leasing them out. The high prices that continued until the mid-1380s made demesne farming still profitable. Thus, the monks of Christ Church, Canterbury, who in 1377/8 had leased out nearly all their manors, took them back in hand when the leases ended. In the early 1380s they spent considerable sums on the purchase of new stock and £2000 on repairs and new construction. Yet within a few years wages, and thus expenses, began to rise. When grain and wool prices started dropping in the late 1380s the Christ Church monks returned to the policy of leasing.[19] Other lords followed similar policies. Yet even when the majority of estates were leased out, it was quite common to keep at least one manor, or part of a manor 'in hand', to serve as a home farm. The archbishop of Canterbury, for example, started leasing in the 1380s and by 1400 most of the demesnes were leased. Direct management, however, continued until 1443 at Otford, where he had one of his palaces.[20]

By 1400 the number of people in Kent remained at least a third, and perhaps more, below the level of 1348. Yet, except in the Weald, very little land was lying unused. Arable land was converted into pasture and in the marshes, at Appledore, the area under cultivation was actually increased by inning. The leasing of manors did not seriously affect agricultural practices. Peasants had been able to demand higher wages, but it was not until the late 1380s, when the Statute of Labourers lost its bite and prices began to fall, that the standard of living of the wage labourer began to improve significantly. Much of the land that came on the market was picked up not by the former landless, but by the better-off peasant. Moreover, the Peasants' Revolt notwithstanding, some tenants were still expected to reap and carry for their lord as earlier.

In the 1380s and 1390s, two periods of truce – 1383–85 and again in 1388–96 – allowed a modest trade revival. Alien merchants imported herrings, garlic, onions, haberdashery, and wine, plus occasional shipments of salt and Flanders

18 Butcher, 'English Urban Society', p. 106; Du Boulay, *Lordship of Canterbury*, pp. 175, 188–9; W. E. Flaherty, 'The Great Rebellion in Kent Illustrated from the Public Records', *Arch. Cant.* 3 (1860), 65–96.

19 Mate, 'Agrarian Economy', 352–4; M. Mate, 'The Farming Out of Manors: A New Look at the Evidence from Canterbury Cathedral Priory', *Journal of Medieval History* 9 (1983), 337–42.

20 The area under cultivation had contracted. In 1273–74, 277 acres were sown; in 1391–92, 168 acres were ploughed and in the last account, 1443–44, just 149 acres were sown; F. R. H. Du Boulay, 'Late Continued Demesne Farming at Otford', *Arch. Cant.* 73 (1959), 116–24. See also MS LPL ED 835; ED 871. The manor also housed around three hundred sheep.

tile. The wine trade revived and between 1379 and 1395 an average of 271 tuns of wine a year was brought in via Sandwich, although it never reached the level of the early fourteenth century.[21] Native shippers were more active than they had been earlier in the century and in 1390, a peak year for imports, several prominent Sandwich men were involved. One of them, Thomas Elys, who was mayor in 1370 and again in 1382, was able to endow both a hospital and a chantry.

The Great Slump of the Mid-Fifteenth Century

Over the course of the fifteenth century the inhabitants of Kent continued to face bad weather and further outbreaks of disease. According to the obituary record of Christ Church Priory, plague visited the city in 1413, 1419, 1420, and 1431.[22] Hard frosts gripped the country in 1434 and 1435, and if the chroniclers may be believed, many old people died from the cold and the scarcity of wood and coal.[23] In 1438 and 1439 the wheat harvests failed in many places.[24] Prices of wheat, rye, barley, and other foodstuffs rose markedly. People suffering from a lack of food frequently succumbed to a new outbreak of pestilence. At the same time, workers were constantly being attracted to London. With the renewal of the war effort under Henry V, soldiers were also recruited to fight in France. Many did not return, having died in battle or been killed by dysentery.

Money wages paid to demesne workers continued to rise, although the precise amount varied from manor to manor.[25] At Wye, the plough-man who had been earning 8s 4d a year in 1393–94 was being paid 26s 8d in 1410–11, and the shepherd who in 1393–94 had been paid 10s, was earning double in 1413–14.[26] Building workers, employed part-time on the estate, also earned more. An Otford carpenter, who in 1402 was being paid 4d or 5d a day, by 1427 was receiving 6d a day and a tiler with boy was being paid 7d a day in 1422–23 and 8d a day in 1427–28. Finally, in 1437–38, a year of famine and high prices, tilers were paid

21 M. K. James, *Studies in the Medieval Wine Trade* (Oxford, 1971).

22 J. Hatcher, 'Mortality in the Fifteenth Century: Some New Evidence', *Economic History Review* 2nd series 10 (1986), 19–38.

23 F. W. Brie, ed., *The Brut or The Chronicles of England*, Early English Text Society, original series 131, 2 vols (New York, 1906–08, repr. 1960), 2, p. 467; A. H. Thomas and I. D. Thornley, ed., *Great Chronicle of London* (London, 1938), p. 171; C. L. Kingsford, ed., *Chronicles of London* (Oxford, 1905), p. 137; J. S. Davies, ed., *An English Chronicle of the Reigns of Richard II, Henry IV, Henry V and Henry VI*, Camden Society, original series 64 (1856), p. 55; J. Gairdner, ed., *The Historical Collection of a Citizen of London*, Camden Society, new series 17 (1876), p. 178.

24 On the Christ Church home farm of Barton, where the wheat yielded on average four times the seed, the harvest of 1438 produced just over six bushels an acre (1.65 x seed); MS CCAL DCc *Caruca Bartona* 25. On the archiepiscopal manor of Otford the oats yield was normal, the barley yielded 83 per cent and the wheat yielded just half; MS LPL ED 83.

25 For a complete list of wages paid on the archiepiscopal manor of Otford and on the Christ Church manor of Barton, see M. Mate, 'Tenant Farming and Tenant Farmers', in *The Agrarian History of England and Wales, Volume III, 1348–1500*, ed. E. Miller (Cambridge, 1991), p. 691.

26 MS TNA PRO SC 6/902/3; SC 6/902/27.

9d and 10d a day.[27] The workforce in Kent, reduced by disease and emigration, and faced with competing demands for its labour, was able to secure higher wages than elsewhere.[28] At the same time rents began to fall. Smallholders used their additional earnings to add to what they had and many former landless were able to afford a smallholding.

Consequently, the pattern of land-holding was constantly changing as tenants sold, bought, exchanged, or leased small parcels. A detailed rental for Gillingham in 1447 reveals the existence of both enclosed fields or crofts and many relatively small, subdivided fields containing unenclosed parcels, usually marked by boundary stones. An individual tenant might have all his, or her, land entirely enclosed or entirely in open parcels, or in some combination of the two. These parcels might not be contiguous, but they were likely to be in one part of the township and not widely scattered.[29] By 1447 the tenant population had been reduced by two-thirds, as former holdings were picked up by existing tenants or outsiders moving into the area. The accumulation, however, had not occurred equally. A comparison of parcels in an earlier rental of 1288 with those of 1447 shows that, although some parcels had been enlarged, others had been reduced as inheritances were shared and land was sold. A quarter of all holdings in 1447 were still of two acres or less. The simultaneous process of both consolidation and fragmentation seems to have occurred everywhere, leading to considerable inequality of holding size. At Otford, in 1440, only 8 per cent of the tenant population held a hundred acres or more, whereas roughly 40 per cent held between one and five acres.[30] This constant shifting among tenants, plus the overall drop in population, made it extremely difficult to collect rents that had originally been set down in the early fourteenth century. In manor after manor the rent-collector was given a respite for rents that could not be collected either for lack of tenants, or because no one knew who was currently holding the original parcel. Arrears mounted.[31]

In the early fifteenth century the flow of trade through the port of Sandwich was transformed by the arrival of Italian merchants – first, the carracks of the Genoese and subsequently, the galleys of the Venetians. Both groups brought in oil, soap, wine, luxury fabrics, and fruit and nuts such as figs, almonds, raisins, and dates.[32] The Genoese also brought in woad for use in the Kentish cloth industry and took away some of the finished cloth. In addition, Hanseatic

27 MS LPL ED 838; ED 858; ED 863.

28 On the Winchester estates just a few carpenters were earning 5d a day by 1430. None was earning 6d. At Stratford on Avon, 5d was the normal rate for carpenters by 1427–28. T. H. Lloyd, 'Some Aspects of the Building Industry in Medieval Stratford upon Avon', *Dugdale Society Occasional Papers* 14 (Oxford, 1961).

29 A. R. H. Baker, 'Open Fields and Partible Inheritance on a Kent Manor', *Economic History Review* 2nd series 17 (1964), 1–23.

30 D. Clarke and A. Stoyel, *Otford in Kent: A History* (Battle, 1975), p. 90.

31 At Wye, in 1463/4, arrears that had been collecting for twenty years amounted to £401 9s 5d; MS TNA PRO SC 6/905/20. At Otford, in 1460/1, the regular yearly allocation for loss of rents was just under 31 per cent of the rents; MS LPL ED 1240; 1241; 1243.

32 MS TNA PRO SC 6/895/17.

merchants brought in all kinds of timber and merchants from the Low Countries imported red and white herrings, saffron and madder, and bricks.[33] As earlier, wine remained an important import, but there was considerable fluctuation between years, the high of 970 tuns imported 1439/40 offset by lower imports other years.[34] Overall, the early 1440s were years of great prosperity for the port. In 1439/40 when a special subsidy was levied on aliens, it was paid by ninety-eight householders and 101 non-householders. Among the householders were two resident Genoese, who served as factors and commission agents for their fellows. This prosperity had begun to crumble by the end of the decade as the Wantsum Channel became constricted through silting and its navigability lessened. The number of cloths exported, for example, dropped dramatically from a peak of 6665 exported in 1442/3 to an average of 425 cloths in the period 1445–50.[35]

The period 1445–65 was a time of bullion famine, deflation and a severe recession. The population had declined faster than production. More grain, stock, and wool were being produced than the market could absorb. Land dropped out of cultivation and was soon to revert to shrub and waste, and as thorns and brambles crept over former arable and pasture in the Weald the work of assarting was undone. As the export trade slowed, the surplus circulated at home. The aggregate volume of wool and cloth exports reached their lowest point in the late 1450s and early 1460s. This coincided with the nadir in the decline of national mint outputs.[36] Despite a marked drop in wool prices, producers had a hard time finding buyers for their crop.[37] Tenant farmers were particularly affected and large tenant flocks, geared towards production for the market, disappeared. Kent, where earlier in the century substantial flocks of sheep pastured on the northern and Romney Marshes, was particularly affected by this trade slump. In Wealden villages, such as Smarden and Pluckley, where perhaps a quarter of the male population was engaged in the cloth industry, workers began to worry about the security of their employment.[38]

As in the early fourteenth century low prices benefited people when they needed to buy goods, but hurt them when they sold goods in the market. Families, who received very little from the surplus grain or stock they sold, still had to pay fixed money rents or risk losing their land. They had less to spend on other goods – shoes, bread, ale, or meat – even though the cost of these goods had fallen. Thus a butcher or shoemaker might find that not only did he himself receive a lower price for his goods, but the demand for his goods had lessened. Moreover, in

33 MS TNA PRO E 122/127/18.

34 James, *Studies in Wine Trade*.

35 E. M. Carus-Wilson and O. Coleman, *England's Export Trade, 1275–1547* (Oxford, 1963).

36 J. Hatcher, 'The Great Slump of the Mid Fifteenth Century', *Progress and Problems in Medieval England*, ed. J. Hatcher and R. Britnell (Cambridge, 1996), pp. 237–72.

37 Mate, 'Pastoral Farming in Southeast England in the Fifteenth Century', *Economic History Review* 2nd series 11 (1987), 527.

38 I. M. W. Harvey, *Jack Cade's Rebellion of 1450* (Oxford, 1991), p. 19.

many places wages fell in tandem with prices, so that real wages did not in fact increase. The contraction in one area also spilled over and affected other areas. The farmer who could not sell his wool was likely to postpone rebuilding his barn. Carpenters and thatchers, as well as cloth-workers, could not rely on finding as much employment as they wished. Lords had difficulty in attracting lessees.

Misgovernment within the county brought additional hardship. Local officials of all kinds abused their office to extort money. Robert Est, as keeper of Maidstone gaol, wrongfully imprisoned people until they paid a fine for their release. In addition, he and others seized and detained goods and livestock until the owners paid to get them back.[39] These losses, coming at a time when people's ability to pay had lessened with the recession, produced a deep resentment that was ultimately to explode in rebellion. In January 1450, Thomas Cheyne, under the name 'Bluebeard', led a small uprising that was quickly suppressed. But in May and June, when Kentishmen found a new leader in Jack Cade (also known as Jack Mortimer), rebellion became widespread. In their manifesto they complained about the actions of officials, the seizures of purveyors and the enforcement of the Statute of Labourers. Even the capture and death of Cade did not end the resistance. In August, William Parmynter, a smith from Faversham, calling himself the second captain of Kent, encouraged former supporters of Cade to rise again. Harsh repression, including the hanging of thirty Kentishmen, restored some measure of order, but could not totally eradicate disaffection. In April 1451 men rose again and this time, according to the indictment, planned to depose the king, destroy the lords, and set up a dozen peers from among themselves to rule the kingdom.[40] As in the past, the authorities acted quickly; the leaders were hanged and resistance was quashed.

These men, however, were by no means the marginals of society. Five men who were hanged at Canterbury in February 1451 had tenements ranging in size from sixteen to one hundred acres. The wealthiest, described as a yeoman, and holding a hundred acres, owned six oxen, ten cows, one horse, a plough, two carts, some bedding (a blanket and three pairs of sheets), two brass pots, three platters, and ten pieces of pewter. The total assessed value of his goods was £21 15s.[41] Even someone, like John atte Wood, with a tenement of twenty acres, possessed four oxen, six cows, three horses, a plough, two carts, and some household goods – two candle sticks, four platter, and a great brass pot.[42] Such accumulations reveal in a very concrete way the high standard of living that some Kentishmen were able to achieve as a consequence of the better economic conditions resulting from the drop in population. But not everyone benefited. The

39 R. Virgoe, 'Some Ancient Indictments in the King's Bench, 1450–52', in *Documents Illustrative of Medieval Kentish Society*, ed. F. R. H. Du Boulay (Ashford, 1964), pp. 214–43. See also Harvey, *Cade's Rebellion*, pp. 36–43.

40 Virgoe, 'Ancient Indictments', pp. 243–56; Harvey, *Jack Cade's Rebellion*, pp. 64–159.

41 MS TNA PRO E 357/42.

42 Ibid.

relative affluence of families with land stood in sharp contrast to the situation of a labourer, possessing two geldings, two cows, two piglets, and one cart.

During the prolonged unrest, some tenants became more recalcitrant. In 1451, at Street, in southern Kent, the common fine, usually paid in the manorial court, could not be collected because 'of the insurrection of the people'.[43] On the archiepiscopal lands, after the appointment of Thomas Bourgchier, tenants resisted paying the customary recognition – palfrey money – on the enthronement of a new archbishop. Each year the amounts were carried forward as debts, and the loss of revenue to the archbishop was substantial.[44] Archiepiscopal tenants in the 1460s also refused to pay the common fine. Their bargaining position may have been strengthened since in 1457 a devastating outbreak of disease struck much of Kent. Sixteen Christ Church monks died that year, fourteen of them between 15 July and 25 September. This represents a crude death rate of 189 per thousand, the highest in the fifteenth century.[45] The city of Canterbury was equally affected and both the monks and city authorities found it impossible to collect the normal quota of rent for their city property.[46] The port of Sandwich was especially vulnerable when the French attacked, killing many of the townsmen, including the mayor, John Drury, looting silver and gold plate and setting fire to buildings. How much damage and loss occurred is not known, but trade was clearly disrupted and for several years most of Sandwich's revenues from the port were earmarked for the repair of the town's defences.

It was not until the 1480s and 1490s that pastoral farming became profitable again, after an expansion in the demand for meat, the growth of the Kentish cloth industry, and the revival of the international wool trade. The archbishop of Canterbury and Christ Church Priory once more thought it worthwhile to spend money maintaining breached sea-walls in the Romney Marshes, and also embark on land reclamation and enclosure. These lands were then leased to yeomen and husbandmen, who already had some land of their own. The lessees kept cattle as well as sheep, and sometimes paid part of their rent in kind, supplying wethers and other victuals to the households of the priory or the archbishop. Some of them also supplied meat to the garrison and burghers of Calais as well as providing wool for the local cloth industry. The Knatchbulls were a particularly successful yeoman family. In the early sixteenth century they became the principal lessees of the archbishop's marsh manors and were active in the Calais trade.[47] Small-

43 Harvey, *Cade's Rebellion*, p. 159.

44 MS LPL ED 1241 (bailiwick of Otford, £40); ED 1223 (bailiwick of Maidstone, £38 6s 8d).

45 Hatcher, 'Mortality in the Fifteenth Century', p. 28.

46 MS LPL ED 83; ED 84.

47 In 1513–14 Richard Knatchbull shipped 116 sheep in wool to Calais and his son William Knatchbull shipped 210 sheep; MS TNA PRO E 122/130/2. William leased the manor of Willop for seventeen years at the rate of £48 per annum, and the manor of Cheyne Court for fifteen years at £120 per annum; F. R. H. Du Boulay, 'Calendar of Archbishopric Demesne Leases, 1503–1532', *Documents Illustrative of Medieval Kentish Society*, nos 28 and 29.

holders also raised stock and helped to provision ships leaving local ports and supplied meat (often young lambs and calves) to small-town butchers.

Meanwhile, the spread of the new drink of hopped beer was helping to revive the economy, encouraging the import of hops and stimulating the demand for fuel, and for barley (the premier brewing grain). Beer lasted longer and travelled better than ale. Although first produced by aliens, or with alien help, male native beer brewers quickly adopted the new techniques and between 1460 and 1500 the brewing of beer spread throughout Kent and parts of Sussex. Large, commercial beer breweries were established in Woolwich, Gravesend, and Sandwich, as well as in Southwark and the City of London. By the mid-sixteenth century beer had become a major drink for the masses, and was even being exported to the Low Countries. In addition, large quantities of malted barley were shipped from Kent ports to London, Calais, and to other southeast towns such as Rye.[48] Prices paid for faggots and firewood rose. Agriculture, by 1530, in many parts of the county, had recovered from the contraction brought about by the recession, with land being brought back into cultivation, and tenants, as well as lords, keeping large flocks of sheep and cattle. New crops such as saffron were being cultivated and commercialised fruit-farming was just beginning.

Some rents from mills situated in or near towns recovered. The archbishop of Canterbury had two watermills at Maidstone, which were rented in the late fourteenth century for £8 3s 4d. In the early 1450s, just one mill was in operation, providing a rent of £3 a year.[49] By the sixteenth century, however, the archbishop was able to lease a grain mill for £7 6s 8d and a fulling mill for £5 6s 8d. Moreover, when the lease of the fulling mill was renewed in 1525, the new lessee was authorised to build another corn-mill either within the existing building or next to it.[50] Clearly, the economy must have seemed healthy enough to sustain this expansion. Rents for the mill at Otford followed a somewhat similar path. In mid-century the mill stood vacant, first for lack of a miller and then for lack of repairs. But when it was rebuilt, the new mill was rented for £4 a year, slightly above the 66s 8d that had been received in the early 1400s. In the late 1470s, however, the archbishop was willing to invest considerable capital: £41 15s 10d in building another mill.[51] The two mills, in the early sixteenth century, were rented for £6 a year.[52]

As land became more valuable, the split between large and small tenements grew. In east and north Kent local gentlemen, wealthy yeomen, clothiers, and townsmen bought up former tenant land. Sir Thomas Lovell, for example, held no land at Eastry from Christ Church Priory in 1481. Yet by the time of the next

48 Mate, *Trade and Economic Developments, 1450–1550: The Experience of Kent, Surrey and Sussex* (Woodbridge, 2006).

49 MS LPL ED 670; ED 1223; *Calendar of Inquisitions Miscellaneous 1392–1399*, p. 177.

50 Du Boulay, 'Calendar of Archbishopric Demesne Leases', pp. 273, 279, 292.

51 MS TNA PRO SC 6/1130/8. This sum included the purchase of a mill-stone for £4 at London.

52 Du Boulay, 'Calendar of Archbishopric Demesne Leases', p. 276. The archbishop agreed to repair the mills, dams, and buildings and to find millstones, except when the damage was done by the lessee.

rental, in 1511–12, he had built up a substantial holding of 224 acres. One Londoner and six men from Sandwich also held Eastry land.[53] In north Kent, with its closer proximity to the metropolis, the proportion of Londoners was naturally higher.[54] In many instances these men did not cultivate these lands directly with their servants, but rented them in smaller parcels to sub-tenants. In other cases, they lived on their land and built new two-storey houses, with fire-places, chimneys, and perhaps glazed windows. Many of these buildings have survived.[55] Yet unlike the rest of the country, very small holdings did not disappear in Kent, although the number diminished. In 1500 tenements of four acres, were still quite common, especially in the Kentish Weald.

As trade revived, more of it occurred outside the market place. Large-scale bakers and brewers, for example, found it easier to buy grain in bulk from producers, rather than in small lots in a market; urban butchers likewise bought surplus animals directly from local farmers and sold the slaughtered carcases in small lots from their permanent shop. At the same time the dominance of London became increasingly felt, as the export of wool and cloth and the import of wine, linen goods, and luxury fabrics were primarily channelled through the metropolis. London became the arbiter of taste and London goods, from specialist game and luxury gowns to ordinary belts and buckles became more desirable. Areas nearest the metropolis were obviously the most influenced. Families living in Greenwich, with its close association with the court, were more likely to own elaborate cushions and tables than families living in more remote towns.[56]

There was no common pattern to the experience of Kent towns. Maidstone and Faversham benefited from the presence of good oyster fisheries and the ease of water transportation in the Medway valley and along the Thames. Their merchants shipped grain, cattle, and firewood to feed and fuel the population of London and traded with south Essex, Sussex ports, and across the Channel (see Draper, this volume). Both grew in size and wealth. In contrast, Canterbury and Sandwich faced periods of contraction. Canterbury was hit by the drying up of its pilgrim trade, which affected the profits of the city's inns and other hostelries as well as the receipts at the shrine and cathedral altars.[57] The town was also hit with periodic outbreaks of disease.[58] Landlords like the priory and the city chamberlains were forced to reduce property rents 'for lack of takers'.[59] Without

53 MS CCAL DCc/Miscellaneous Accounts 33.

54 A. Brown, 'London and Northwest Kent in the Later Middle Ages: The Development of a Land Market', *Arch. Cant.* 92 (1976), 150.

55 S. Pearson, *The Medieval Houses of Kent: An Historical Analysis* (London, 1994).

56 E. E. Salter, 'Some Differences in the Cultural Production of Household Consumption in Three North Kent Communities', in *The Medieval Household in Christian Europe, c.850–1550*, ed. C. Beattie et al. (Turnhout, Belgium, 2003), pp. 391–407; C. T. Richardson, 'Household Objects and Domestic Ties', in ibid., pp. 433–47.

57 A good analysis of pilgrim traffic and the revenues received by cathedral altars can be found in B. Nilson, *Cathedral Shrines of Medieval England* (Woodbridge, 1998), pp. 171–84.

58 Hatcher, 'Mortality in the Fifteenth Century', 29.

59 A. F. Butcher, 'Rents and the Urban Economy: Oxford and Canterbury in the Later Middle Ages', *Southern History* 1 (1979), 40–3.

the presence of a substantial alien population, the economy of the city might have faltered more than it did.[60] Sandwich was hurt by the silting up of its harbour and the channelling of its trade in wool, cloth, and wine through London. Yet, on the other hand, trade with the Low Countries, whose ships had a shallower draft than the Italians, expanded. Merchants brought with them increasing number of hops, plus herrings and other salt fish and took out beer and grain, allowing the mayor and jurats to collect new taxes. Within the town new building was undertaken at least until the 1520s, as townsmen not only built for their own use, but also developed dwellings and shops as rental properties.

When taxation records from the early sixteenth century are compared with those of 1334, it appears as if lay wealth had increased fourfold during that time.[61] Yet neither the wealth, nor the population, was evenly divided. The lands of north-east Kent, and the area around Cranbrook, were the wealthiest and the most heavily populated. The wealth, however, was concentrated in the hands of the large landowners and the clothiers, and below them was a large group of labourers and smallholders who paid taxes at the lowest rate. When prices began to rise in the 1520s, these people found it harder to make ends meet; they particularly suffered when faced with unemployment and the high cost of food after a bad harvest. The 1520s – a decade that may have been as devastating in its impact as the 1430s had been earlier – saw heavy taxation and repeated outbreaks of disease and death.[62] All the Cinque Ports showed increasing concern for the maintenance of law and order and sought to control the activities of 'beggars and vagabonds'.

Nonetheless, by 1530 the overall economy within Kent was well on the way to recovery from the recession. It had been helped by the immigration of an alien population. In the fifteenth century, the process of beer brewing was first introduced by alien brewers: in the sixteenth century, the influx of French workers into the Weald helped to bring about the expansion of the Wealden iron industry, and the arrival of religious refugees later in the century encouraged the growth of 'new draperies' within cloth manufacturing. Moreover, at all times the foreign hatters, cappers, and brick makers used their specialised skills to produce much needed goods. Even when aliens carried out more traditional tasks such as shoemaking, their presence helped to offset the impact of population losses, and provided a critical mass of consumers and producers, thus helping to maintain the overall buoyancy of urban trade. Nevertheless, in 1530 labourers and artisans, who, in the aftermath of the Black Death, had seen some amelioration of their lot, faced little prospect of improvement in their economic position within Kentish society.

60 In 1524–25 the lay subsidy was paid by seventy-eight aliens out of a total of 783 taxpayers; MS TNA PRO E 179/124/188.

61 R. S. Schofield, 'The Geographical Distribution of Wealth in England, 1334–1649', *Economic History Review* 2nd series 18 (1965), 483–510.

62 In 1521 and 1522 a series of bad harvests coincided with an outbreak of plague. In 1527 the grain harvests failed again and the sweating sickness returned; *Letters and Papers Henry VIII* 4, part 1, nos 1266, 1305; 4 part 2, nos 4173, 4188.

3

Agriculture in Kent in the High Middle Ages*

BRUCE M. S. CAMPBELL

Prologue

Kent is renowned for its topographical diversity, which, over many centuries, has shaped settlement, land-use, and husbandry.[1] Throughout time, soils derived from the cold stiff clays of the Weald, the free-draining chalk of the North Downs, the deep rich loams of the coastal plain, and the fertile alluvium of the flood-prone coastal marshes have engendered contrasting agricultural responses, both in terms of the crops and animals produced and the techniques and intensity of their management.[2] In the Middle Ages, when all husbandry was organic and the maintenance of productivity largely depended upon effective on-the-farm recycling of soil nitrogen, potassium, and phosphorous, these internal agricultural contrasts were particularly deeply etched.[3] Yet, from a national perspective such

* This chapter is partly based upon the projects 'Feeding the City I' and 'The Geography of Seigniorial Land-ownership and Use, 1270–1349' funded by the Leverhulme Trust between 1988 and 1994 (I am grateful for the research collaboration of Derek Keene and John Power and for research assistance provided on the first project by James Galloway and Margaret Murphy and on the second by Ken Bartley). Detailed yield and other time-series data for the Kent demesnes of Christ Church Priory were collected in 2005 with the assistance of Marilyn Livingstone. This work was funded by a grant from the British Academy ('Harvest Failure and Success: Crop Yields on the Kent Manors of Christ Church Priory, c.1275–c.1375') as part of a wider ESRC-funded project ('Crops Yields, Environmental Conditions, and Historical Change, 1270–1430' – RES–000–23–0645). Work on the Christ Church Priory beadles' rolls was greatly facilitated by the staff of the Canterbury Cathedral Archives and Library (CCAL). The maps and graphs have been drawn by Gill Alexander with her customary patience and skill. Tom de Vesci provided a quiet haven at Knapton Cottage, Co. Laois, where the chapter was drafted. It is respectfully dedicated to my doctoral supervisor, Dr Alan Baker, Fellow Emeritus of Emmanuel College Cambridge, himself a distinguished historian of medieval Kent.

1 For example, S. W. Wooldridge and D. L. Linton, 'Some Aspects of the Saxon Settlement in South-East England Considered in Relation to the Geographical Background', *Geography* 20 (1935), 161–75; S. W. Wooldridge, 'The Anglo-Saxon Settlement', in *An Historical Geography of England before A.D. 1800: Fourteen Studies*, ed. H. C. Darby (Cambridge, 1936), pp. 88–132; J. Thirsk, 'The Farming Regions of England', in *The Agrarian History of England and Wales, Volume IV, 1500–1640*, ed. J. Thirsk (Cambridge, 1986), pp. 4, 55–64.

2 S. J. Fordham and R. D. Green, *Soils of Kent*, Soil Survey of Great Britain (England and Wales) (Harpenden, 1980).

3 R. S. Shiel, 'Improving Soil Fertility in the Pre-Fertiliser Era', in *Land, Labour and Livestock: Historical Studies in European Agricultural Productivity*, ed. B. M. S. Campbell and M. Overton (Manchester,

topographically derived variations were less remarkable than those that stemmed from the county's unusual institutional characteristics and the strength and penetration of the external commercial opportunities to which producers were early and for long exposed.[4] Collectively, these influences endowed Kentish agriculture in the High Middle Ages with a character all of its own. Moreover, that character became more pronounced from west to east, so that it was east Kent that most strongly embodied the distinctive agricultural attributes of the county (Figures 1 and 2).

Institutionally, one of the most striking features of Kentish agriculture was the insignificance of common rights and regulations with the result that the bulk of all land was held and worked in severalty.[5] Although by circa 1300 in the most crowded parts of the county there was much subdivision of holdings and parcellation of land, so that the properties of many petty producers comprised a scatter of unenclosed plots, common rights over these 'open fields' were virtually non-existent. Instead, individual producers bore the full costs of managing and policing their scattered parcels and supervising the pasturing of animals on the post-harvest stubble and half-year and full-year fallows. Significantly, common meadows appear to have been as unknown in the county as common arable, a feature shared in common with neighbouring parts of Essex to the north as well as Devon and Cornwall in the extreme south-west.[6] Nor does there appear to have been much common pasture. Indeed, in the absence of such pastures and rights over them, demesnes in the county were endowed with significantly greater quantities of several pasture than was the norm elsewhere, thereby conveying the misleading impression that Kent was one of the grassiest counties in England.[7] Instead, it was the county within which several property rights prevailed most extensively and, consequently, where individual decisions about rotations and resource management enjoyed fullest rein. Of course, husbandmen cannot have been indifferent to their neighbours and the practical benefits to be obtained from cooperating with them, but such cooperation was voluntary rather than obligatory with the result that there were fewer institutional curbs upon how they farmed their land than almost anywhere else in lowland England.

Kent was further unusual in the relative absence of villein tenure per se and, concomitantly, of labour rent.[8] On Kentish manors by the end of the thirteenth

1991), pp. 51–77; E. I. Newman and P. D. A. Harvey, 'Did Soil Fertility Decline in Medieval English Farms? Evidence from Cuxham, Oxfordshire, 1320–1340', *Agricultural History Review* 45 (1997), 119–36.

4 For national classifications of land use, husbandry, and agriculture, see B. M. S. Campbell and K. Bartley, *England on the Eve of the Black Death: An Atlas of Lay Lordship, Land and Wealth, 1300–49* (Manchester, 2006), pp. 197–249.

5 Campbell and Bartley, *Eve of the Black Death*, pp. 55–68; A. R. H. Baker, 'Field Systems of Southeast England', in *Studies of Field Systems in the British Isles*, ed. A. R. H. Baker and R. H. Butlin (Cambridge, 1973), pp. 377–419.

6 Campbell and Bartley, *Eve of the Black Death*, pp. 59–63.

7 Ibid., pp. 137–41.

8 E. A. Kosminsky, *Studies in the Agrarian History of England in the Thirteenth Century*, trans. R. Kisch, ed. R. H. Hilton (Oxford, 1956), pp. 137–40.

century the bulk of tenants, both free and servile, owed and paid their rents in money.[9] These rents were typically determined by custom rather than market competition and hence were often worth less than a full economic rent. Few lords, therefore, enjoyed rental incomes commensurate with the number of tenants or quality of land on their estates, nor did the predominance of free and semi-free tenants paying low and effectively fixed rents permit any immediate or obvious remedy to this situation.[10] Unable to raise to competitive levels the rents of their tenants, many lords must have endeavoured instead to maximise the returns to be obtained from the demesne lands over which they exercised direct control. They did so with such effect that, exceptionally, on many Kent manors demesne revenues exceeded rental income.[11] Without significant resources of servile labour to draw upon, these demesnes were worked primarily with hired labour, both permanent farm servants (the *famuli*) and casual labourers, of whom there was no lack.[12] This makes the violence of 'peasant' protest within the county in 1381 all the more remarkable.[13] What seems to have been at issue in 'free' Kent was not the oppressiveness of serfdom per se but the fact that it should have existed at all, coupled with imposition of government-imposed wage restraint upon a rural society long accustomed to selling its labour for wages and clearly enjoying the strengthened bargaining power consequent upon plague's brutal culling of the labour force. Until that demographic disaster, labour scarcity had not been a problem, since – where the coercive powers of manorial lords were so circumscribed, the occupying tenantry so comparatively 'free', tenurial barriers to the subdivision and subletting of land so weak, gavelkind tenures such a source of land division between heirs, and opportunities for reclaiming land from marsh or wood so extensive – household formation was relatively unconstrained. During the twelfth and, more particularly, the thirteenth centuries this fuelled the growth of population to such an extent that by the close of the latter century Kent was one of the dozen English counties with an average of one hundred or more people per square mile.[14] Moreover, on the evidence of the distribution of taxpayers, the most populous parts of north Kent supported population densities that were substantially higher.[15]

Where labour was so plentiful, mouths so many, and land so sought after, there were strong incentives to adopt relatively intensive forms of agriculture. Horticulture, systematic manuring, marling, and liming of soils, use of wheeled and swing ploughs, continuous cropping, legume cultivation, fodder cropping, hay making, stall and sty feeding of livestock, partial or complete substitution of

9 Campbell and Bartley, *Eve of the Black Death*, pp. 251–9.

10 B. M. S. Campbell, 'The Agrarian Problem in the Early Fourteenth Century', *Past and Present* 188 (2005), 21–4.

11 Campbell and Bartley, *Eve of the Black Death*, pp. 265–8.

12 K. Witney, trans. and ed., *The Survey of Archbishop Pecham's Kentish Manors 1283–85*, Kent Records 28 (Maidstone, 2000), pp. xvii–xx, xliv–xlvi; Campbell, 'Agrarian Problem', 37–9.

13 R. B. Dobson, *The Peasants' Revolt of 1381*, 2nd edn (London, 1983), pp. 123–47.

14 B. M. S. Campbell, 'Benchmarking Medieval Economic Development: England, Wales, Scotland, and Ireland, *circa* 1290', *Economic History Review* 2nd series 61 (2008), 926, 929.

15 Campbell and Bartley, *Eve of the Black Death*, pp. 328–34.

horses for oxen, specialist dairying, and the systematic coppicing of woodlands, were all practised in Kent by the close of the thirteenth century, placing the county in the vanguard of contemporary agricultural advance.[16] Such techniques were expensive and owed their adoption to more than just internal demand; commercial proximity to the great cities of London, Ghent, and Bruges, with populations respectively of 75,000, 80,000, and 50,000 circa 1300, was also a factor.[17] In the case of London, agricultural producers in west Kent enjoyed immediate access to the city's markets, while grain growers in north Kent via the transport artery provided by the Thames estuary were able to deliver corn cheaply to the metropolis.[18] Thanks to the navigable River Medway, grain and wood producers in mid-Kent were also within provisioning range of London and cornmongers from the metropolis regularly frequented the Rochester and Maidstone markets.[19] Further east, Faversham served as a major grain entrepôt and at Sandwich London cornmongers rubbed shoulders with dealers from the great cities of the Flanders and northern France.[20] Sandwich, in fact, was closer to Ghent and Bruges than it was to London, and at the close of the thirteenth century was at the peak of its medieval prosperity.[21] South of Sandwich, the Channel ports of Dover, Hythe, Romney, and Winchelsea were all closer in cost-distance to the continent than London and most plied a busy export trade in agricultural produce, including wood, across the Channel.[22] Finally, livestock rearers almost everywhere were within convenient droving distance of the capital. Throughout Kent, therefore, external urban demand acted as a selective stimulus to production and spur to specialisation and, more than in almost any other English county, shaped both what was produced and the manner of its production (see Mate, this volume).[23]

16 Ibid., pp. 105–9, 180–1; H. L. Gray, *English Field Systems* (Cambridge, MA, 1915), pp. 302–3; R. A. L. Smith, *Canterbury Cathedral Priory: A Study in Monastic Administration* (Cambridge, 1943), pp. 135–41; P. F. Brandon, 'Farming Techniques: South-Eastern England', in *The Agrarian History of England and Wales, Volume II, 1042–1350*, ed. H. E Hallam (Cambridge, 1988), pp. 312–25; J. L. Langdon, *Horses, Oxen and Technological Innovation: The Use of Draught Animals in English Farming from 1066–1500* (Cambridge, 1986), pp. 87–9, 134–9; K. Witney, 'The Woodland Economy of Kent, 1066–1348', *Agricultural History Review* 38 (1990), 20–39.

17 For London; B. M. S. Campbell, J. A. Galloway, D. J. Keene, and M. Murphy, *A Medieval Capital and its Grain Supply: Agrarian Production and its Distribution in the London Region c.1300,* Historical Geography Research Series 30 (n.p., 1993), pp. 9–11, 44–5; B. M. S. Campbell, *English Seigniorial Agriculture 1250–1450* (Cambridge, 2000), p. 405. For Ghent and Bruges; D. Nicholas, *Urban Europe 1100–1700* (Basingstoke, 2003), p. 20.

18 Campbell et al., *Medieval Capital*, pp. 48–52, 195–6.

19 Ibid., pp. 51–2, 60–1, 174–5.

20 Ibid., pp. 48–9, 51–2, 174–5, 180.

21 In 1290 Sandwich is likely to have been about the same size as Winchelsea, with a population of at least 3,000; Campbell, 'Benchmarking', Table 4.

22 B. M. S. Campbell, 'The Sources of Tradable Surpluses: English Agricultural Exports 1250–1349', in *Cogs, Cargoes and Commerce: Maritime Bulk Trade in Northern Europe, 1150–1400*, ed. L. Berggren, N. Hybel and A. Landen (Toronto, 2002), pp. 6–10; D. Sylvester, 'The Development of Winchelsea and its Maritime Economy', in D. and B. Martin, *New Winchelsea, Sussex: A Medieval Port Town*, Field Archaeology Unit Monograph 2, Institute of Archaeology, University College London (London, 2004), pp. 7–19.

23 Campbell, 'Sources of Tradable Surpluses', pp. 20–1; B. M. S. Campbell, 'Economic Rent and the

Land-Use and Husbandry

The characteristics of the county's seigniorial land-use and husbandry can be reconstructed during the half-century or so before the Black Death from the many extents attached to inquisitions post mortem [*IPM*s] (which document exclusively manors belonging to lay tenants-in-chief of the Crown) and those manorial accounts that survive for the estates of Christ Church Priory, the archbishop of Canterbury, Westminster Abbey, the king, and a handful of other lords.[24] In fact, for all the presence within the county of several high profile Church estates, especially in the country around the ancient ecclesiastical metropolis of Canterbury, the high density of surviving Kent *IPM*s demonstrates that it was lay tenants-in-chief – the vast majority of them comparatively minor lords possessed of only one manor – who clearly dominated landownership.[25] Substantial lay lords and large and valuable lay manors show up most strongly in eastern and south-eastern Kent, but even here they co-existed with many lesser manors with an annual value of less than £10. In north-central Kent lay land-ownership was dominated by such petty manors, each presumably managed directly by a resident lord of correspondingly humble means. It is therefore all the more unfortunate that estates of this class have rarely bequeathed any manorial records of their own.[26] Indeed, they can never have required the sophisticated administration and associated record keeping that were such a feature of the great estates of the Church and the higher aristocracy. Instead, for information on this most numerous class of lords, reliance has to be placed on the record of their activities created on behalf of the Crown by sheriffs, escheators, coroners, and tax collectors.

In westernmost Kent analysis of the wealth of detailed information contained in the *IPM*s reveals that land-use on lay demesnes closely resembled that of the immediately adjacent portions of Surrey, Middlesex, and Essex.[27] In central and eastern Kent, in contrast, it assumed a character all of its own (shared only with neighbouring portions of east Sussex), whose principal features were arable of superior quality and value combined with significant quantities of several pasture and wood (Figure 1). This was a type of land-use encountered almost nowhere else in the country, primarily because the bulk of all agriculturally productive land was held in severalty. In lieu of rights of common grazing over the fallow and access to communally managed pastures, demesnes were typically endowed with an above-average allocation of several pasture. This pasturage was, however, more notable for its quantity than its quality, for much was low in unit

Intensification of English Agriculture, 1086–1350', in *Medieval Farming and Technology: The Impact of Agricultural Change in Northwest Europe*, ed. G. Astill and J. Langdon (Leiden, 1997), pp. 235–41.

24 Campbell and Bartley, *Eve of the Black Death*, pp. 13–31; J. A. Galloway, M. Murphy, and O. Myhill, *Kentish Demesne Accounts Up to 1350: A Catalogue* (London, 1993).

25 Campbell and Bartley, *Eve of the Black Death*, pp. 29–34.

26 Manors in lay ownership account for only 6 per cent of those with surviving manorial accounts: Galloway et al., *Kentish Demesne Accounts*, pp. vi–vii.

27 K. Bartley and B. M. S. Campbell, '*Inquisitiones Post Mortem*, G.I.S., and the Creation of a Land-Use Map of Pre Black Death England', *Transactions in G.I.S.* 2 (1997), 333–46; Campbell and Bartley, *Eve of the Black Death*, pp. 205–8.

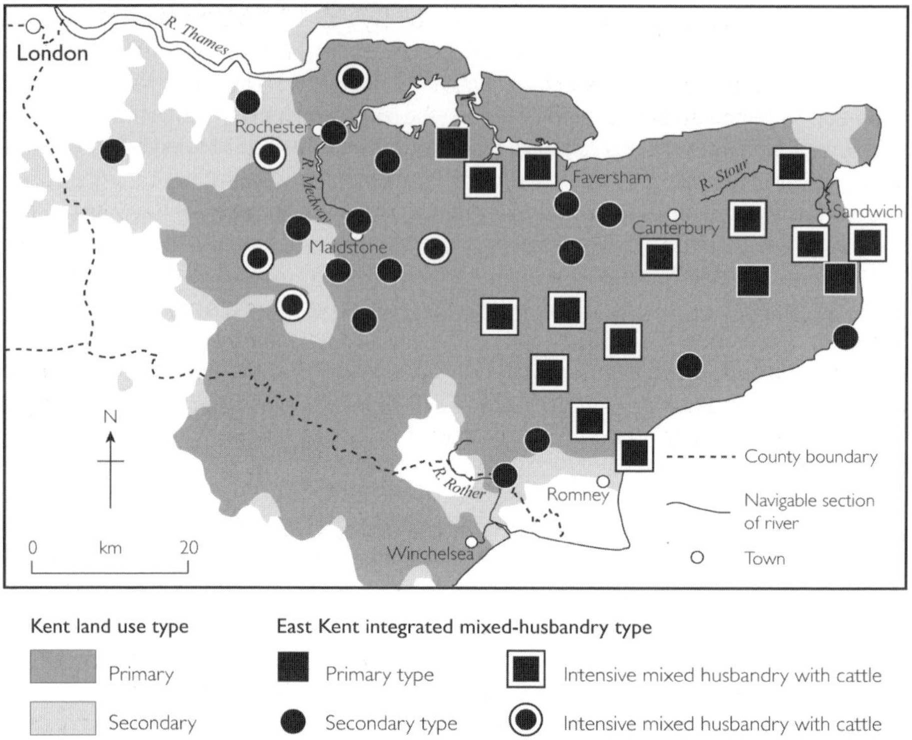

Figure 1: 'Kentish' land-use and agriculture

value with the result that the aggregate value of these grasslands was less impressive than their physical extent.[28]

Kent has never been a natural grassland county. Its climate, more continental – with colder winters and hotter, drier summers – than most of the rest of the country, was better suited to corn growing and during the harsh winter months of the year it was usually necessary to house horses, cattle, swine, and even sheep in stalls, byres, sties, and cotes.[29] That meant augmenting natural grazings with hay and a range of fodder crops – oats, various grain mixtures, and assorted legumes. Perforce, animal husbandry within the county was in part arable based. Hence the fact that in northern and eastern Kent grassland accounted for less than a fifth of demesne land-use by value whereas pastoral production contributed double that proportion to manorial revenues.[30]

28 Campbell and Bartley, *Eve of the Black Death*, pp. 137–41.

29 Manorial extents and inventories furnish much documentary evidence concerning the housing of livestock on Kent demesnes, although this information awaits systematic investigation.

30 Campbell and Bartley, *Eve of the Black Death*, p. 129; B. M. S. Campbell, 'Measuring the Commercialisation of Seigniorial Agriculture *circa* 1300', in *A Commercialising Economy: England 1086–1300*, ed. R. H. Britnell and B. M. S. Campbell (Manchester, 1995), pp. 143–5.

Meadow in Kent was circumscribed in supply but was by far the most valuable component of grassland on account of the strategic importance of the hay that it yielded. Yet although highly prized, it rarely exceeded 30 pence an acre – far less than the 48 pence an acre commanded by the most productive meadowlands elsewhere in England.[31] In fact, the most productive arable land in Kent often rivalled meadow of moderate quality in value. In northern and eastern Kent tillage valuations of at least 9 pence an acre – double the national average – were normal and valuations of 24 pence an acre not unknown. Indeed, on the Isle of Thanet and on the fringes of the Walland and Romney Marshes, where arable of superior quality, productivity, and profitability was juxtaposed with unusually abundant supplies of grassland, the unit values of arable and grassland approached parity.[32] This narrow, and occasionally non-existent, differential between the unit values of arable and grassland was general throughout, and almost unique to, Kent. It expressed the county's natural comparative advantage in arable production.

Nationally, agricultural land attained a peak unit value – matched but not exceeded by the more extensive reclaimed silt lands of west Norfolk and south-east Lincolnshire – in the Isle of Thanet and associated Ash Levels of east Kent.[33] Land was only marginally less valuable on the fringes of the Romney and Walland Marshes in south-eastern Kent, where fertile upland soils and reclaimed alluvium co-existed with extensive tracts of meadow and pasture painstakingly reclaimed from the coastal marshes (Figure 2). In these privileged environmental situations agriculture was capable of delivering sustained high levels of unit output. Individual enterprise was unencumbered by common rights and regulations and population densities were high, guaranteeing the labour force required to sustain the prevailing intensive methods of production. Thanet undoubtedly constitutes the Kentish extreme.[34] The equally distinctive agriculture of the Kent marshlands, in contrast, was a response to specific micro-environments. Nevertheless, the most striking attributes of these localities – agricultural land with a mean value per acre well above the national average and a narrower than average differential between the unit values of arable and grassland – were also present to a less pronounced degree throughout eastern and northern Kent, wherever good loam soils, several property rights, and favourable commercial opportunities justified adoption of intensive and productive systems of agriculture. The high profits and rents thereby secured are reflected in the high value placed upon agricultural land (Figure 2).

Nevertheless, not all agricultural land within the county gave such good returns. The infertile sands of central and western Kent were incapable of sustaining the more intensive forms of cultivation and the heavy clays of mid-Kent and the Weald were costlier and hence less profitable to cultivate. In

31 Campbell et al., *Medieval Capital*, pp. 140–1; Campbell and Bartley, *Eve of the Black Death*, pp. 172–3, 180–1.

32 Campbell and Bartley, *Eve of the Black Death*, pp. 185–8.

33 Ibid., pp. 191–5.

34 Ibid., pp. 191–5 (Figure 10.12).

both situations arable valuations were lower and the corresponding differential between the unit values of arable and grass, wider. Moreover, since heavy land promoted a greater reliance upon oxen for draught this further enhanced the value of hay meadows within the overall production system. It was, however, in the infertile and far less accessible Wealden interior of Kent that agricultural land of all types was least valuable and, by implication, least productive. Those who endeavoured to cultivate these most intractable of soils for profit laboured under a real environmental disadvantage. Here, tillage seems mostly to have been undertaken in order to satisfy purely local consumption needs and it was pastoral husbandry that tended to offer the better commercial prospects, with the result that grassland was invariably the more highly valued land-use and by a wider margin than was normal elsewhere in Kent.[35] Here, it would seem, pastoral husbandry enjoyed the greater comparative advantage.

The distinctive Kentish pattern of land-use and associated configuration of absolute and relative unit values thus described and depicted in Figures 1 and 2 has been established from a national analysis of approximately ten thousand *IPM*s. Linking information on the crops grown and animals stocked for a corresponding national sample of manorial accounts identifies a similarly unique Kentish system of agriculture – east Kent integrated mixed husbandry – whose complementary distribution is also shown in Figure 1.[36] This, too, was characterised by much secondary differentiation, as individual demesnes adapted their husbandry to specific local topographical and market conditions and the particular institutional requirements of the estates to which they belonged. The single most striking feature of this Kentish system of husbandry, as implied by the foregoing discussion of land-use and land values, was the close integration of crop and livestock production, with the arable providing fodder and seasonal pasturage to the animals and the latter supplying draught power and manure to the arable. Kent, therefore, was par excellence, a county of mixed-husbandry and its demesnes were mostly as generously stocked with animals as they were productive of crops. Indeed, the county's single greatest agricultural producer, Christ Church Priory, derived 44 per cent of its gross agricultural cash revenues from sales of animals and their products and 56 per cent from sales of crops, hay, and wood.[37]

With certain notable exceptions, Kent demesnes usually devoted 60 to 80 per cent of their cropped area to grain and the rest to legumes, mainly peas and vetches sown separately or as a mixture and some beans.[38] Vetches were, in fact, a feature of Kent, with a longer tradition of cultivation than almost anywhere else in

35 Ibid., pp. 187–8.

36 Ibid., pp. 231–5, 240, 246–9.

37 Campbell. 'Measuring the Commercialisation', p. 144.

38 For a comparative discussion of cropping patterns in Kent, see A. Smith, 'Regional Differences in Crop Production in Medieval Kent', *Arch. Cant.* 78 (1964 for 1963), 147–60; Campbell et al., *Medieval Capital*, pp. 111–39.

England.[39] Unlike peas, they were grown exclusively as a fodder crop and were the closest substitute for hay where the latter was scarce. Sowings of legumes were necessarily greatest where cropping was most continuous. This was both because of the heightened need for fodder where annual fallows and their temporary pasturage were foregone and the importance of sowing a nitrifying crop between successive courses of grain. Cropping tillage almost continuously – apart from the occasional relieving fallow intended to cleanse the arable of weed growth whenever the land became too 'dirty' to sustain further grain cultivation – was the most effective method available to medieval husbandmen of raising its productivity.[40] Much skill and experience were involved in tailoring rotations to prevailing soil conditions and the length and flexibility of those rotations would have been irreconcilable with a communally regulated system of cultivation. This same rotational flexibility is evident in the varying shares of the grain area occupied by the winter- and spring-sown grains. It was usual for slightly more winter than spring grain to be sown but the former might include some winter barley and winter oats (a crop rarely grown outside of Kent).[41] Wheat, the pre-eminent commercial bread grain, generally occupied at least half and sometimes the whole of the area devoted to winter grains. Rye, its closest substitute, was less frequently grown and invariably occupied a far smaller area.[42] Likewise, on a majority of demesnes, barley, the premier malting and brewing grain, was the most important spring grain.[43] Such prominence was rare in England at this date, except in eastern Norfolk where spring barley was grown on an even greater scale.[44]

Such a demanding cropping regime, in which all of the arable was potentially under the plough each year and some of it subject to repeated ploughings, naturally had significant draught requirements. Carting needs – of harvested grain, hay, marl, and manure – could also be considerable. Yet hay was often scarce and pasture of poor quality. The solution lay in partial substitution of oats- and grass-fed cart and plough horses for hay- and grass-fed oxen. Horses, moreover, worked faster and longer than oxen and were better suited to harrowing.[45] This early and, by English standards, relatively extensive use of horses for farm work echoed their prominence across the Channel in Flanders, where the intensity

39 C. R. J. Currie, 'Early Vetches: A Note', *Economic History Review* 2nd series 41 (1988), 114–16; B. M. S. Campbell, 'The Diffusion of Vetches in Medieval England', *Economic History Review* 2nd series 41 (1988), 195–8.

40 Campbell, *English Seigniorial Agriculture*, pp. 340–7.

41 Winter oats was sown on the marshland demesnes of Barksore, Ruckinge, Appledore, and Ebony, and also at Great Chart.

42 Before the Black Death rye was widely sown in modest quantities, as at Agney, Appledore, Cliffe, Eastry, East and West Farleigh, East Peckham Ebony, Ham, Lydden, and Westerham. Mixed with wheat, it was sown as maslin at Cliffe, East Peckham, Great Chart, Hollingbourne, and Orpington.

43 Winter barley was commonly sown on Kent demesnes, usually in conjunction with spring barley. The latter is described in the accounts as 'Palm' (i.e. Lenten) barley.

44 Campbell, *English Seigniorial Agriculture*, pp. 222–3; B. M. S. Campbell and M. Overton, 'A New Perspective on Medieval and Early Modern Agriculture: Six Centuries of Norfolk Farming *c.*1250–*c.*1850', *Past and Present* 141 (1993), 54–66.

45 Langdon, *Horses*, pp. 112–14.

of cultivation exceeded even that of east Kent. Keeping arable land productive nevertheless required more than draught animals alone since soils had to be manured regularly if their fertility was to be maintained. Maintenance of significant numbers of non-working animals was therefore a key requirement of any successful mixed-husbandry regime. Impressively, draught animals (horses and oxen) accounted on average for only about a quarter of total livestock units on these mixed-husbandry Kent demesnes. Furthermore, notwithstanding a strong land-use bias towards tillage and the inferior quality of much grassland, stocking densities on Kent demesnes were generally well above the national average.

Within the pastoral sector, cattle were the most important category of animal stocked. The demographic structure of these herds, with their emphasis upon adult females, indicates that they were functionally geared towards dairying rather than rearing or fattening. This was the most capital intensive and food productive form of pastoral husbandry. Close management of herds, with selective culling of barren cows and disposal of surplus calves, was essential if yields of calves and milk were to be maximised and a satisfactory return obtained upon investment. Sheep required less intensive management and greater resources of permanent grassland and hence were less widely stocked, showing up in greatest relative numbers where specific environmental opportunities, in the form of extensive downland or marshland pastures, promoted sheep farming, as at Boughton-under-Blean, Lyminge, and Northfleet.[46] Elsewhere, sheep generally took second place to cattle and rarely accounted for as large a share of livestock units. It was unusual, however, for demesnes not to keep a small flock of sheep alongside their dairy herd. Swine, too, were often stocked in significant numbers and, by tradition, were more important in Kent than in most of the rest of the country. In part, this was because of the abundance of several woodland and the pannage seasonally available within it, but swine also responded well to intensive methods of production and by the late thirteenth century most demesne herds were kept in sties and fed on legumes, inferior grain, and any other edible agricultural residues.[47] In this respect they were an integral component of this intensive and integrated mixed-husbandry system and it was a rare demesne on which they did not account for between a tenth and a fifth of all non-working livestock units.

Individual demesnes naturally tailored this mixed-husbandry system to their individual factor endowments. 'Cattle-based mixed husbandry' most closely approximates to the Kentish system of mixed-husbandry just described and was the most widely represented type of mixed-husbandry within the county (Figure 1). Demesnes practising this form of mixed-husbandry grew legumes in the greatest quantities, cropped their arable most intensively, employed a combination of oxen and horses for draught power, and stocked mainly dairy cattle and

46 Campbell, *English Seigniorial Agriculture*, pp. 107, 114, 445.

47 On the intensive sty-feeding of swine, see K. Biddick, 'Pig Husbandry on the Peterborough Abbey Estate from the Twelfth to the Fourteenth Century A.D.', in *Animals and Archaeology, Volume IV, Husbandry in Europe*, ed. J. Clutton-Brock and C. Grigson, BAR International Series 227 (Oxford, 1985), pp. 161–77; Campbell, *English Seigniorial Agriculture*, pp. 165–8.

swine.[48] It was not unknown, however, for Kent demesnes to stock virtually no animals at all beyond those essential to cultivation of the arable, usually because of the asset-stripping activities of lords, executors, and the Crown. Only perpetual institutions tended to escape this periodic selling off of herds and flocks with its undoing of years of painstaking pastoral management. Any long-term persistence of this state of affairs would have limited the recycling of soil nutrients and thereby jeopardised the sustainability of arable production. As most demesne managers in Kent were well aware, the productivity of the tillage depended upon proper attention being paid to the management of livestock. Their expertise lay in fusing the two activities into a single integrated enterprise.

The presence within intensive mixed-husbandry Kent of demesnes lacking a sufficient quota of non-working animals serves as a reminder that farm enterprise was always a function of more than environmental, economic, and technological factors alone. What type of landlord, what size of estate, and the position of the individual demesne within the overall estate production system were also important considerations. Church, lay, and royal estates differed in their capacities to invest in herds and flocks. Maintaining those herds and flocks was a further problem. Episcopal and lay estates were far more exposed to asset stripping than perpetual institutions, such as convents and colleges, which never died. Individual estate policy also exercised a bearing upon the choice of animals stocked and whether or not these were managed directly at demesne level, centralised and accounted for separately (as was sometimes the case with sheep), or leased out (as became increasingly the practice with dairy herds and poultry). More rarely, estate policy might determine the choice of crops grown. For instance, Christ Church Priory maintained its manor of Orpington as a key staging post between London and Canterbury and cultivated significant quantities of oats and vetches in response to the unusually heavy demand for fodder from priory officials and the many other horse borne travellers who visited this manor.[49] Its home manors of Chartham, Eastry, and Ickham similarly concentrated upon producing malting barley for direct delivery to the Priory.[50]

Land-Values and Yields

Whether the high value of agricultural land, especially tillage, in much of Kent was matched by correspondingly high crop yields can be tested using the detailed information on the quantities of seed sown and harvested recorded in consecutive manorial accounts and the calculations of yields sometimes recorded in the accounts by the medieval auditors.[51] In addition to the well-documented

48 Campbell and Barley, *Eve of the Black Death*, pp. 214–15, 221, 228–9.

49 MS CCAL DCc/Bedels rolls Orpington 1–45.

50 Campbell et al., *Medieval Capital*, p. 151; Campbell. 'Measuring the Commercialisation', p. 187.

51 On the calculation of yields from manorial accounts, see J. Z. Titow, *Winchester Yields: A Study in Medieval Agricultural Productivity* (Cambridge, 1972), pp. 5–9. Unusually, Christ Church Priory's

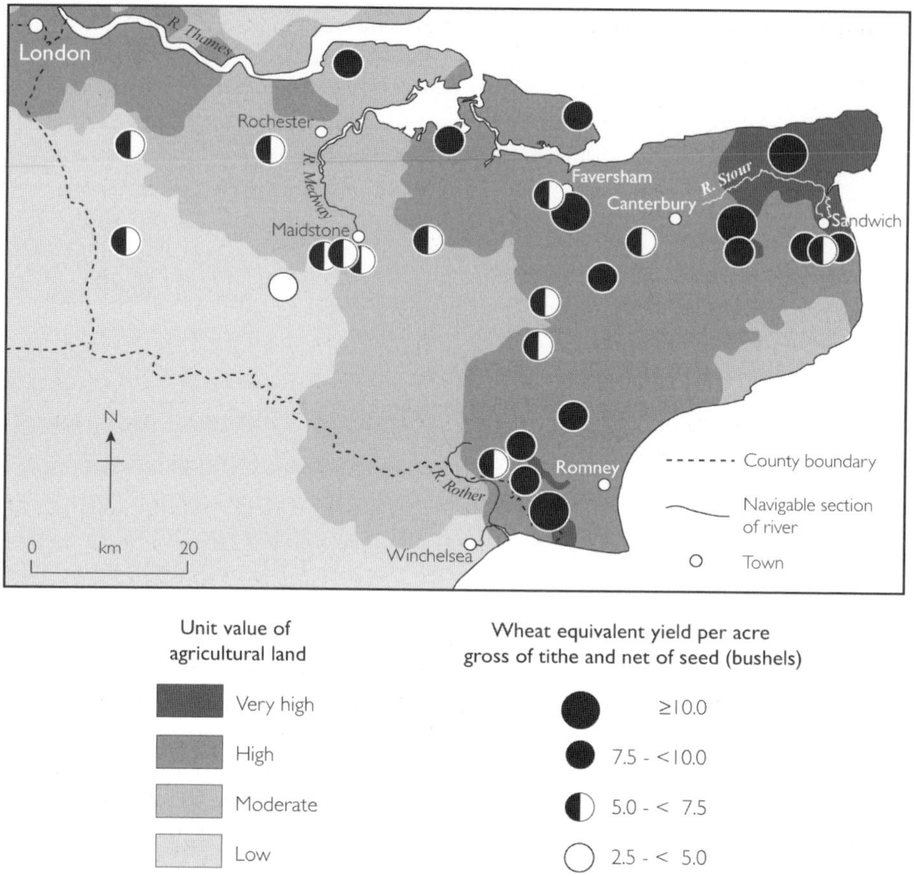

Figure 2: Kent unit land values and yields per acre

demesnes of Christ Church Priory, the demesne at Westerham belonging to Westminster Abbey has a good run of yield data.[52] The expectation, of course, from the unit valuations given in the *IPM*s, is that crop yields in Kent were well above the national average, especially in those parts of the county where the value per acre of arable land was high. Given that the national average value of arable land was a mere 4½ pence per acre, the many Kent valuations that were at least double that average are virtually inexplicable unless the land was at least twice as productive.

auditors calculated yields per acre rather than per seed and they often reported the acreage that had been sown the previous year. By assuming a constant seeding rate, these yields per acre can be converted into yields per seed.

52 The Westerham yields were calculated by the late Professor David Farmer, whose detailed research notes are preserved in the D. L. Farmer Papers at the University of Saskatchewan Archives, Canada. I am grateful to the staff of the University of Saskatchewan Archives for facilitating access to this material and to the Centre for Data Digitising and Analysis, The Queen's University of Belfast, for incorporating Professor Farmer's calculations into a database.

Table 1: Kent demesnes: mean yield per seed gross of tithe and net of seed, 1285–1348

Crop	Number demesnes	Demesne with highest mean	Max. mean	Mean mean	Min. mean	Demesne with lowest mean
Wheat	28	Monkton	4.30	2.47	1.60	E. Peckham
Rye	13	Ruckinge	4.08	3.26	1.37	Chartham
W. barley	13	Ruckinge	5.31	3.21	1.60	Hollingbourne
W. oats	2	Gt. Chart	2.22	2.07	1.91	Appledore
W. grains	*28*	*Ickham*	*4.72*	*2.82*	*1.80*	*Chartham*
S. barley	27	Ruckinge	3.61	2.01	0.92	Ebony
S. oats	28	Agney	2.64	1.67	0.93	E. Peckham
S. grains	*29*	*Ruckinge*	*3.05*	*1.84*	*1.25*	*Chartham*
All grains	*28*	*Ruckinge*	*3.54*	*2.32*	*1.53*	*Chartham*

Sources: D. L. Farmer Papers, University of Saskatchewan Archives; TNA, PRO SC6/893 (31-6) & 894 (1-8); Canterbury Cathedral Archives, beadles' rolls.

On the evidence of two hundred demesnes from across the whole of lowland England, the average ratio of seed harvested to seed sown gross of tithe but net of seed over the period 1285–1348 was 3.7 for wheat, 3.1 for rye and other lesser winter grains, 2.2 for barley, and 1.1 for oats.[53] Comparable figures for Kent are 2.5 for wheat, 3.3 for rye, 2.0 for barley, and 1.7 for oats (Figure 1).[54] For England, the mean return for all four grains was approximately 2.5, for Kent it was 2.3. On this evidence, yield ratios in Kent were broadly on a par with those in the country as a whole, not twice as great. Even at Ruckinge, the highest yielding Kent demesne of all, advantageously located on the edge of Romney Marsh where grain cultivation benefited from good soils and abundant supplies of draught power and manure, the mean grain yield ratio of 3.5 was only 50 per cent above the county and 40 per cent above the national averages.[55] Its grain yield ratio was, however, more than double that obtained on the Priory's home demesne at Chartham, a mere half dozen miles up the Stour valley from Canterbury in the heart of the east Kent intensive mixed-husbandry region.[56] Yield differences of this order of magnitude therefore certainly existed.

How is this discrepancy between the evidence of the *IPM* valuations and the yield ratios calculated from manorial accounts to be reconciled? The answer lies in four further aspects of arable productivity: the rate at which seed was sown (*alias* the seeding rate) (Table 2), the yield per acre (which was a product of the rate at which grain was seeded as well as that at which it yielded) (Table 3), the relative proportions and values of the grains cultivated (Table 3), and the frequency with which the land was made to yield a crop (Appendix 1).

Whereas average yields per seed in Kent may have deviated but little from the

53 For the demesnes and raw data from which these means are generated see: www.cropyields.ac.uk.
54 Calculated for the Kent demesnes within the national crop-yields database: www.cropyields.ac.uk.
55 MS CCAL DCc/Bedels rolls Ruckinge 3–22.
56 MS CCAL DCc/Bedels rolls Chartham 4–27.

Table 2: Kent demesnes: mean seed sown per acre (bushels), 1285–1348

Crop	Number demesnes	Demesne with highest mean	Max. mean	Mean mean	Min. mean	Demesne with lowest mean
Wheat	29	Adisham, Cliffe, Ham	4.02	3.82	2.80	Westerham
Rye	15	Chartham	4.80	3.83	2.52	Orpington
W. barley	17	Adisham	6.10	4.63	3.01	Meopham
W. oats	5	Ebony	8.05	7.15	5.75	Barksore
W. grains	*29*	*Ebony*	*5.10*	*4.21*	*2.88*	*Westerham*
S. barley	28	Monkton	6.72	5.24	3.72	Ebony
S. oats	28	Agney	8.03	6.37	4.04	Orpington
S. grains	*29*	*Monkton*	*6.96*	*5.80*	*4.03*	*Orpington*
All grains	*29*	*Ruckinge*	*5.61*	*5.01*	*3.54*	*Meopham*

Sources: D. L. Farmer Papers, University of Saskatchewan Archives; TNA, PRO SC6/893 (31-6) & 894 (1-8); Canterbury Cathedral Archives, beadles' rolls.

national average, the rates at which seed was sown were significantly higher. Typical seeding rates throughout the greater part of lowland England were around 2 bushels an acre for the winter grains and the winter-sown legumes (peas and vetches), and 4 bushels an acre for the spring-sown grains and for beans. With the exception of spring barley, in Kent even minimum seeding rates were heavier. Moreover, mean seeding rates on Kentish demesnes were two-thirds heavier than the standard national rates and maximum rates were typically twice as great. Normal rates on the most intensively managed Kent demesnes were 4 bushels an acre for the winter grains, peas and vetches, 6 bushels an acre for spring barley, and 8 bushels an acre for oats and beans.[57] Ruckinge, for instance, sowed wheat, rye, winter barley, and peas at 4 bushels an acre, spring barley at 4½ bushels, and winter and spring oats at 8 bushels.[58] Monkton likewise sowed winter grains at 4 bushels an acre but sowed spring barley at 6½ to 6¾ bushels and spring oats at 7 bushels.[59] By and large, as Mavis Mate has shown, seeding rates were a matter of local husbandry practice rather than estate policy, with the result that similar rates tended to prevail on neighbouring demesnes.[60] Comparably heavy seeding rates were employed in a few other parts of the country where cultivation was equally intensive, most notably in eastern Norfolk (another area distinguished by high unit valuations of arable land), but nowhere were they heavier.[61] Seed, of course, was a form of capital, consequently it was only worth investing it in quantity where this was justified by the prevailing level of economic rent and anticipated level of return. Heavy seeding rates also met a technological need, insofar as they were a means of smothering the weed growth that tended to become rampant

57 Campbell et al., *Medieval Capital*, p. 131; Campbell, *English Seigniorial Agriculture*, pp. 309–15.

58 MS CCAL DCc/Bedels rolls Ruckinge 3–22.

59 MS CCAL DCc/Bedels rolls Monkton 1–71.

60 M. Mate, 'Medieval Agrarian Practices: The Determining Factors?', *Agricultural History Review* 33 (1985), 25–6.

61 Campbell, *English Seigniorial Agriculture*, pp. 309–15.

Table 3: Kent demesnes: mean yields per acre gross of tithe and net of seed (bushels), 1285–1348

Crop	Number of demesnes	Demesne with highest mean	Max. mean	Mean mean	Min. mean	Demesne with lowest mean
Wheat	28	Monkton	17.25	9.43	5.59	E. Peckham
Rye	13	Ruckinge	16.32	12.07	6.53	Chartham
W. barley	13	Ickham	28.36	14.53	5.22	Meopham
W. oats	2	Appledore	14.95	13.85	12.75	Gt. Chart
W. grains	*28*	*Ickham*	*22.06*	*11.46*	*6.51*	*Meopham*
S. barley	27	Copton	16.08	10.61	4.06	Ebony
S. oats	28	Agney	20.40	10.75	6.04	E. Peckham
S. grains	*28*	*Agney*	*17.86*	*10.66*	*7.46*	*E. Peckham*
All grains	*28*	*Ruckinge*	*16.97*	*11.06*	*7.07*	*Meopham*
*WAGY in wheat equivalents**	*28*	*Copton*	*12.7*	*7.6*	*4.6*	*E. Peckham*

*WAGY = Weighted aggregate grain yield, i.e. weighted by the relative area occupied by each grain and the following relative grain prices: wheat 1.0; rye 0.83; winter & spring barley 0.76; winter & spring oats 0.43.

Sources: D. L. Farmer Papers, University of Saskatchewan Archives; TNA, PRO SC6/893 (31-6) & 894 (1-8); Canterbury Cathedral Archives, beadles' rolls.

when bare fallowing was infrequent. They are therefore one of the hallmarks of relatively continuous cropping.

Such above-average seeding rates automatically meant that Kent's mostly unremarkable yields per seed were translated into far more impressive yields per acre. Whereas the national average grain yield per acre gross of tithe but net of seed was around 7½ bushels, demesnes in Kent secured an average yield of 11 bushels – almost 50 per cent higher (Table 3). The highest yielding demesnes with the heaviest seeding rates performed even better: Ruckinge achieved a grain yield of around 17 bushels and yields per acre at Ickham and Monkton were scarcely inferior.[62] These were more than double the national norm. Maximum mean yields per acre of individual crops were usually even more impressive: 17¼ bushels for wheat at Monkton (a tiny glebe demesne belonging to Christ Church Priory), a remarkable 28½ bushels for winter barley and 22 bushels for winter oats at Ickham, and 20½ bushels for spring oats at Agney (Table 3). On this measure, therefore, Kent did enjoy a significant productivity advantage over the country as a whole. Nevertheless, the advantage was not universal. At 7 to 7½ bushels per acre, grain yields at Meopham in the Medway valley and East Peckham in mid-Kent barely matched the national average. Here, as nationally, heavy soils yielded but indifferently. Fine loam soils, as at Copton, Eastry, Ickham, and Monkton, invariably delivered better results and for less effort.

62 The manor and year-specific yields from which the averages cited in this paragraph are derived are given in http://www.cropyields.ac.uk.

Richly fertile silt and alluvium, alone among heavy soils, rewarded with generosity those who tilled them, as witnessed by the high yields obtained from reclaimed marshland at Agney, Appledore, and Ruckinge.

In the Middle Ages, given prevailing ploughing and drainage technology, only soils that were naturally retentive of nutrients, free draining, and comparatively light and easy to work were able to withstand the intensive methods of cultivation that raised output per arable acre to its highest levels. These were the soils that predominated in much or north and east Kent where the *IPM*s sometimes specify that arable land was cropped continuously. Thus, at Greenwich, Kingston, Sheldwich, Sibton, and Wilmington it is expressly stated that the arable could be sown annually without the loss of value that occurred when land was left fallow for a year.[63] The absence of communal rotations and pasture rights over fallows were a further pre-requisite for adoption of such long rotations. Replacing bare fallows with a crop, usually legumes, naturally raised the yield and value of the arable, especially when that crop replenished rather than depleted soil nutrient supplies. The root systems of peas, vetches, and beans all helped fix nitrogen in the soil, as well as supplying fodder to animals and food to humans. Collectively, they occupied a substantial share of the cropped area on most Kentish demesnes (Appendix 1). It was a rare demesne which devoted less than one tenth of its cropped area to legumes, most devoted at least a fifth, a good many a quarter, and a few a third; and this at a time when, nationally, legumes of all sorts probably occupied less than 10 per cent of the national demesne cropped area and were not grown at all on 30 per cent of demesnes.[64] The clear implication of their far greater prominence in Kent is that on many demesnes they were a straight replacement for fallows with the result that grain was sown on between two-thirds and three-quarters of the arable and legumes on the bulk of the remainder.

Further value was added to the harvest by specialising in those crops which commanded the highest relative market price. Price differentials between crops differed with distance from the market, while varying levels of economic rent meant that it usually made sense to produce the lowest-priced grains least able to bear the costs of transport closest to the market and higher-priced grains at a greater distance.[65] Nevertheless, across the greater part of lowland England, wheat generally commanded the highest price of all, followed by rye, barley, and then oats, whose price was usually less than half that of wheat. By devoting a majority of their winter-sown area to wheat and a majority of their spring-sown to barley – the two most important crops on Kent's mixed-husbandry demesnes – producers effectively maximised the market value of their harvests. The approximate effect of this strategy can be measured by expressing total grain output per acre in wheat equivalents, using relative sown areas and relative prices as the

63 MS TNA PRO C 135/81 (4); C 135/11 (12); C 135/56; C 134/82 (6).

64 Campbell et al., *Medieval Capital*, pp. 130, 135–6; Campbell, *English Seigniorial Agriculture*, pp. 228–30.

65 Campbell et al., *Medieval Capital*, pp. 111–44; Campbell, 'Economic Rent', pp. 235–43.

weights: this is the 'Weighted aggregate grain yield' given in Table 3 and Appendix 1.[66]

By dint of large-scale legume cultivation, the associated fodder cropping of animals and recycling of livestock wastes, careful attention to ploughing and preparation of the soil, heavy seeding rates, and lavish use of labour for weeding and harvesting, the most industrious and enterprising demesne managers in Kent transformed unexceptional yield ratios into impressive levels of grain output per acre. When expressed in wheat equivalents, the extent of the productivity differentials that existed both within the county and between Kent and the rest of lowland England become clear and the high value placed upon the most productive of Kent's arable soils becomes explicable. In fact, the weighted aggregate grain yields achieved on the demesnes at Copton, Ickham, Monkton, and Agney rival the exceptional yields obtained on a handful of Norfolk demesnes at that date.[67] As in Norfolk, the demesnes that achieved these impressive results enjoyed the triple benefit of intrinsically good soils, a freedom from communal constraints, and ready access via coastal entrepôts to national and international grain markets. In fact, for grain producers in Thanet and north-east Kent, proximity to the then thriving port of Sandwich – which was ideally placed to provision major cities on both sides of the North Sea – may have been commercially more advantageous than access to the regional focus of demand provided by Canterbury.[68] A combination of environmental conditions and commercial opportunities undoubtedly also explains the high yield levels achieved at Leysdown on the Isle of Sheppey, Barksore on the Medway estuary, Cliffe on the Isle of Grain, Eastry beside the Ash Levels, Ruckinge on the edge of Romney Marsh, and Appledore on the Isle of Oxney (Figure 2). But yields were also good at a scatter of locations further inland, notably at Ickham, Monkton, and Godmersham (Appendix 1).

Away from these favoured locations grain yields, like land values, subsided, and sank to their lowest on Westminster Abbey's demesne of Westerham on light soils in west Kent and Christ Church Priory's demesne of East Peckham in the clay-bound Wealden interior of the county.[69] On the latter demesne, in an area where arable land was valued at only 3 pence an acre, the weighted aggregate grain yield was barely a third that of the highest yielding Kent demesnes and below-average seeding rates and sowings with legumes denote employment of less intensive methods of production (Appendix 1), as was consistent with East Peckham's heavy soils and land-locked location. Low productivity was therefore

66 For other applications of this measure, see Campbell, *English Seigniorial Agriculture*, pp. 334–41, 375–85, and C. Thornton, 'The Level of Arable Productivity on the Bishop of Winchester's Estate in the Early Fourteenth Century', in *The Winchester Pipe Rolls and Medieval English Society*, ed. R. H. Britnell (Woodbridge, 2003), pp. 115–21.

67 Campbell, *English Seigniorial Agriculture*, pp. 334–40.

68 In 1290 Canterbury may have boasted a population of approximately 8800 and in normal years ought, therefore, to have been able to meet the bulk of its grain provisioning requirements from a hinterland of a dozen miles radius; Campbell, 'Benchmarking', 908; Campbell et al., *Medieval Capital*, p. 123.

69 For a discussion of cultivation methods and results at Westerham, see T. A. M. Bishop, 'The Rotation of Crops at Westerham, 1297–1350', *Economic History Review* 9 (1938), 38–44.

as much a feature of Kent's medieval agricultural geography as high, although well-documented examples are scarcer and, by contemporary standards, it was far less remarkable.

Continuity, Crisis, and Change

The patterns of land-use, systems of husbandry, and levels of productivity that have been described were the product of processes of agricultural expansion, colonisation, and technological advance whose inception may well have ante-dated the Conquest. It was, however, during the quarter century or so that preceded the Great European Famine of 1315–22 that the county's medieval population probably attained its maximum, labour became cheapest and most plentiful, the inflation of agricultural prices was most marked, competition for tenancies among smallholders became so intense as to verge upon land hunger, and the great cities of London, Ghent, and Bruges reached a peak of prosperity (see Mate, this volume).[70] Such circumstances underpinned the twin tendencies towards the substitution of labour for land and commercialisation of all branches of production. Thereafter, for the remainder of the Middle Ages, the story of Kentish agriculture is essentially one of a slow retreat from this peak of land exploitation combined with a progressive reorientation of production as, under the assault of plague and other diseases, the population shrank, prolonged hostilities with France played havoc with international trade, and the economic fortunes of the great cities waned and their gravitational draw weakened.[71] Of this long saga it is the pivotal point, spanning the crisis of the early fourteenth century – when producers reeled from the onslaught of exceptionally extreme weather, sea flooding, a devastating cattle plague, repeated outbreaks of mildew, and the human disaster of the Black Death and its subsequent manifestations – that is most fully documented by surviving sources.[72]

70 Population trends are controversial; for developments on a group of Essex manors, see L. R. Poos, 'The Rural Population of Essex in the Later Middle Ages', *Economic History Review* 2nd series 38 (1985), 515–30. For agricultural farm wages and living costs, see G. Clark, 'The Long March of History: Farm Wages, Population, and Economic Growth, England 1209–1869', *Economic History Review* 2nd series 60 (2007), 97–135. On the size distribution of free holdings on the estates of the archbishop of Canterbury in 1285, see Witney, *Survey*, pp. lxxi–lxxv. For a case study of extreme subdivision on one Kent manor, see A. R. H. Baker, 'Open Fields and Partible Inheritance on a Kent Manor', *Economic History Review* 2nd series 17 (1964), 1–23. Parallel developments at Leatherhead in Surrey are discussed in R. Evans, 'Merton College's Control of its Tenants at Thorncroft 1270–1349', in *Medieval Society and the Manor Court*, ed. Z. Razi and R. Smith (Oxford, 1996), pp. 199–259. On the waning of central London's economic fortunes after c. 1315, see D. J. Keene, *Cheapside before the Great Fire* (London, 1985), pp. 19–20.

71 M. Mate, 'Farming Practice and Techniques: Kent and Sussex', in *The Agrarian History of England and Wales, Volume III, 1348–1500*, ed. E. Miller (Cambridge, 1991), pp. 268–85; J. A. Galloway, 'London's Grain Supply: Changes in Production, Distribution and Consumption during the Fourteenth Century', *Franco-British Studies: Journal of the British Institute in Paris* 20 (1995), 23–34.

72 For the general difficulties of the period see, I. Kershaw, 'The Great Famine and Agrarian Crisis in England 1315–22', *Past and Present* 59 (1973), 3–50; B. M. S. Campbell, ed., *Before the Black Death:*

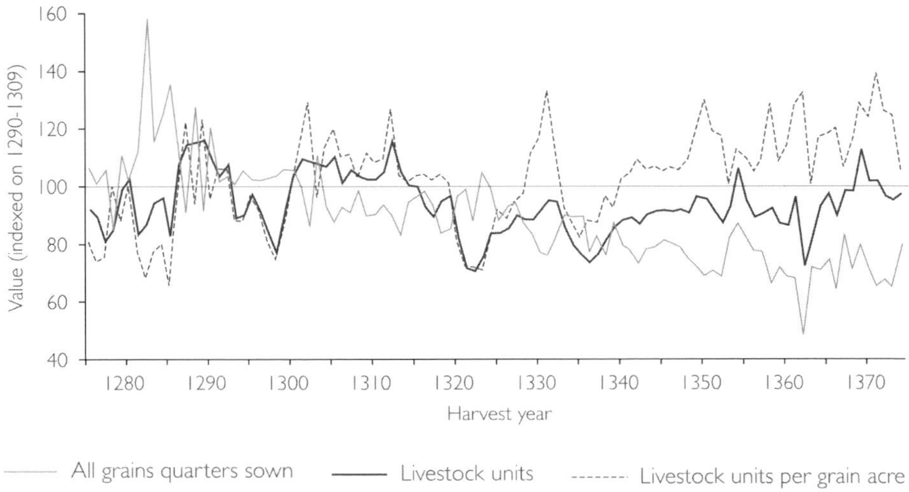

Figure 3: Kent demesne production trends, 1275–1374

When the first Kent manorial accounts become available in the 1270s it is plain that demesne agriculture within the county was already functioning at close to its maximum potential. All of the key technological innovations necessary to evolution of a fully integrated mixed-husbandry system had taken place and most of the demesnes that would adopt those methods had already done so. As measured by the quantities of grain sown, the scale of demesne cultivation attained on Christ Church Priory's estate in the early 1280s, immediately before Henry of Eastry became prior, was never again exceeded (Figure 3 and Appendix 2).[73] In fact, attempts under Henry of Eastry to bring more land into cultivation on the marshland manors of Appledore, Ebony, Lydden, and Barksore proved futile in the face of repeated sea flooding.[74] Loss of crops and land to the sea was repeatedly reported at Appledore between 1310 and 1328 and Barksore between 1323 and 1340; it was also a problem at Cliffe in 1326–27 and Ebony in 1327–28.[75] Nor, for the next hundred years, did livestock numbers expand beyond those stocked in the late 1280s (Figure 3 and Appendix 2). When, from the 1360s, stocking densities

Studies in the 'Crisis' of the Early Fourteenth Century (Manchester, 1989); M. Bailey, 'Peasant Welfare in England, 1290–1348', *Economic History Review* 2nd series 51 (1998), 223–51; Campbell, 'Agrarian Problem'.

73 Henry of Eastry was prior from 1285 to 1331; his managerial achievements are the subject of Smith, *Canterbury Cathedral Priory*. They have become more celebrated than those of his predecessors partly because they are far better documented.

74 Smith, *Canterbury Cathedral Priory*, pp. 173–89.

75 MS CCAL DCc/Bedels rolls Appledore 13–28; DCc/Bedels rolls Barksore 28–40; DCc/Bedels rolls Cliffe 30; DCc/Bedels rolls Ebony 37. It was not just crops that suffered from these inundations: in spring 1335 a sudden influx of the sea killed four cattle and between 250 and 320 sheep grazing on the Medway marshes at Barksore: DCc/Bedels rolls Barksore 36.

per grain acre eventually registered a modest improvement (Figure 3 and Appendix 2), this owed more to a reduction in the area under crop than an increase in the numbers of animals being carried.

What, in fact, is most striking about the broad parameters of production within the demesne sector between c. 1280 and c. 1380 is how much more pronounced continuity was than change. Remarkably, over a period when natural hazards and associated economic changes inflicted a succession of profound shocks upon both supply and demand, the basic contours of agricultural production within Kent remained essentially unaltered. Within the tillage sector, legumes were grown on much the same scale at the end of this period as they had been at the beginning. Wheat and barley also remained the dominant winter and spring crops throughout. Indeed, their importance was if anything enhanced as, from the 1300s, oats occupied a slowly shrinking share of the cropped area and then, from the 1360s, the cultivation of rye was either scaled down or abandoned altogether on many demesnes.[76] No contraction in the actual scale of arable cultivation is apparent until the 1320s, when a gradual decline set in which resulted in a 20 to 30 per cent reduction in the amount of seed being sown by the late 1370s (Figure 3 and Appendix 2). Since there was no significant reduction in seeding rates until the 1360s, and even then only a relatively small downward adjustment, this reduction in the aggregate amounts of seed sown was largely a product of a commensurate contraction in the sown area. If less demesne land was being cropped the likelihood is that there were modest gains in the amounts of land being fallowed, left untilled, or leased out piecemeal to other producers.

Figure 3 shows that livestock numbers over this same period fluctuated but did not rise (which implies that the shrinkage in the area under tillage was not to the benefit of the area under pasturage). There were, however, some shifts in the proportions of the different animals stocked. Oxen and especially draught horses were reduced in number, in line with the reduction in the tillage area, and working animals shrank from about a third to a quarter of all livestock units. Among non-working animals, swine declined in significance and sheep gained in importance (although less so than in many other parts of the country since the quality of Kentish wool was not highly rated). More significantly, cattle maintained their established prominence, since they integrated better than sheep into an intensive mixed-husbandry system and, by implication, demands for milk, meat, manure, and replacement draught oxen must have remained strong.

Levels of arable productivity, as measured by the ratio of the grain harvested to the seed sown, gross of tithe but net of seed, also held up remarkably well. It might be thought that by cropping the land so relentlessly demesne managers were courting disaster, but, as will be observed from Figure 4, annual fluctuations in yield apart, there is nothing in the long-term chronology of yields to suggest that arable land was either losing or gaining in its intrinsic fertility. On this

76 Campbell, *English Seigniorial Agriculture*, pp. 219–21.

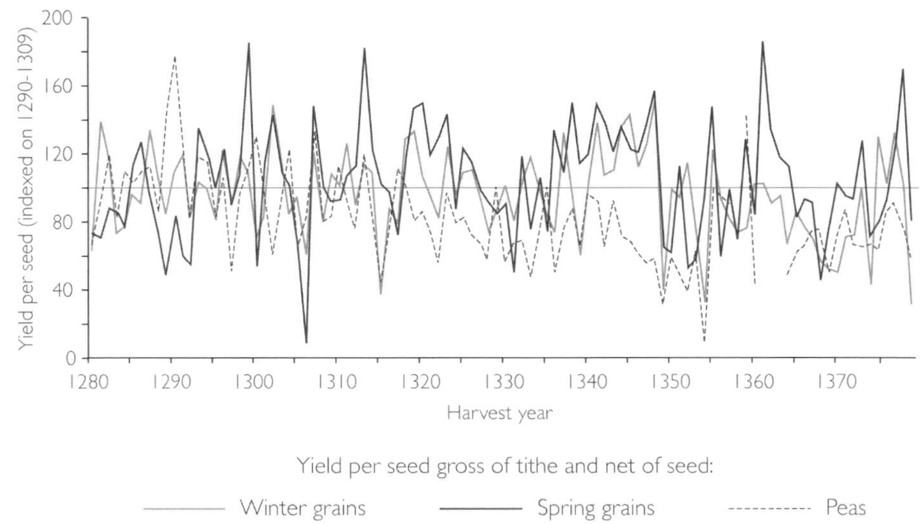

Figure 3: Kent yields per seed 1280–1379

measure, therefore, Kent's intensive mixed-husbandry regime met the key organic requirement of sustainability and thereby provides further evidence of the capacity of medieval husbandmen to maintain high levels of output from the land without jeopardising the fragile ecological equilibrium upon which that output rested.[77] Contending with short-term climatic and pathogenic shocks was a different matter, and bouts of adverse weather and outbreaks of rust and mildew frequently sent yields tumbling. In Kent a net grain yield of at least 10 per cent below average could be expected at least once every three years; a yield of at least 20 per cent below average once every five years; and a yield of at least 30 per cent below average once every seven years. In fact, yields of at least 40 per cent below average were not unknown, the worst harvest of all occurring in 1306 when the yield of spring grains was an outright disaster and that of winter grains very poor as a result of extreme weather abnormalities consequent upon a major tectonic and/or impact event in 1303–04 (Figures 4 and 5 and Appendix 2).[78] One-off harvest failures of this unprecedented order of magnitude may have been difficult to cope with, but back-to-back harvest failures were far more likely to result in famine.

Double harvest failures, when yields were consecutively at least 20 per cent below average, occurred in Kent in 1283–84, 1349–50 (coinciding with the Black Death and the bad weather which followed hard upon it), 1353–54, and 1368–70

77 B. M. S. Campbell, 'Agricultural Progress in Medieval England: Some Evidence from Eastern Norfolk', *Economic History Review* 2nd series 36 (1983), 26–46.

78 M. Baillie, *New Light on the Black Death: The Cosmic Connection* (Stroud, 2006), pp. 144–5.

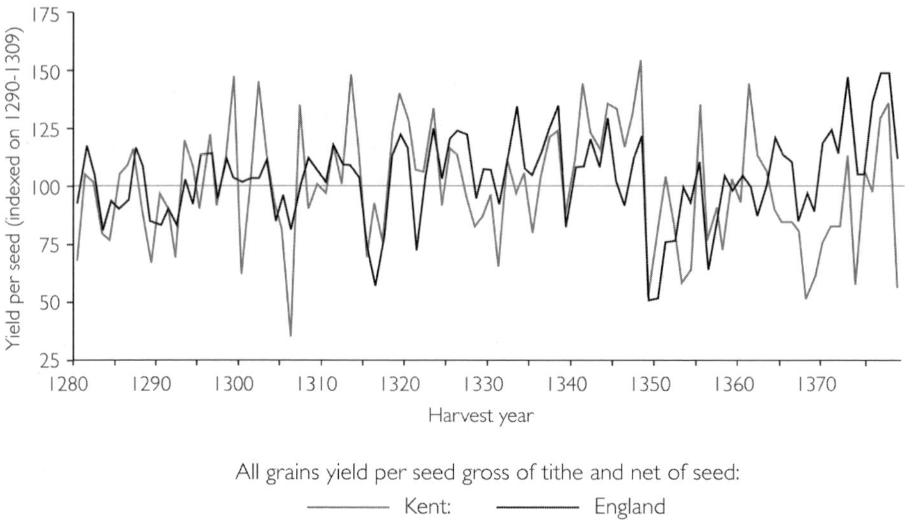

Figure 5: Kent and England grain yields per seed 1280–1379

(the only instance of a triple harvest failure) (Figure 4 and Appendix 2). The single longest run of below-average harvests was from 1364 to 1372, when not one of the nine harvests matched the average of the years 1290–1309 and the worst harvest of all, in 1368, fell short of that standard by more than 40 per cent (Figure 5). As Figure 4 demonstrates, for grain yields to sink so low required a failure of both the winter- and spring-sown crops and this was usually further compounded by a failure of the legume harvest. In such instances, the evidence of each crop corroborates the others in testifying to the impact of exceptionally unfavourable growing conditions. Years that were bad in Kent often show up as similarly so in the country as a whole but not always in equal measure (Figure 5). Thus, the 1306 crisis was more marked in Kent than almost any other region of the country. Conversely, in Kent the triple harvest failure of 1315–17 (which initiated the agrarian crisis of 1315–22) was alleviated by the relative resilience of barley and oats yields, to such an extent that the harvest of 1316, which everywhere else was so terrible, in Kent witnessed a modest recovery of yield. The post-famine yields of 1318–20 were far better in Kent than in the country as a whole, nor was the harvest of 1321 the outright failure that it was elsewhere. During this notorious run of years, therefore, Kent producers got off relatively lightly. But in 1331 they fared worse, in 1339 and 1349 no better, and in the 1360s and 1370s far worse than the national average (Figure 5).

On the yield evidence, the most difficult period of all for Kent producers were the twenty-five years ushered in by the Black Death of 1349 (Figures 4 and 5 and Appendix 2). The repeated bouts of heavy plague mortality certainly created massive problems for large-scale grain producers, as is witnessed by the recorded complaints of reeves of the difficulty of recruiting and retaining labour on demesnes, and of finding enough harvesters, problems rendered all the greater in

Kent since there were virtually no labour services to fall back on.[79] Labour supply and managerial difficulties were, however, only part of the problem, for continuing bad weather and associated mildew outbreaks repeatedly ruined crops and depressed yields.[80] Mildew is first recorded as having attacked the wheat crop on the Christ Church Priory estates at East Peckham and Meopham in 1336–37, the next recorded outbreak was at Mersham in Surrey in 1364–65, and the following year at Copton, Eastry, Great Chart, and Ickham, when it was 'general throughout the country'; it broke out again at Copton and Godmersham in 1366–67, at Adisham, Eastry, Great Chart, and Monkton in 1369–70, and repeatedly thereafter on these and other manors until at least 1374–75 (see Plate 1).[81] This would appear very much to have been a 'Kent' problem and would go some way towards explaining why wheat yields in the county were so poor in the 1360s and early 1370s.

The years immediately prior to the Black Death, in contrast, had delivered the longest unbroken run of above-average yields on record. Harvests had been good in 1336–38, failed badly in 1339, and then for nine consecutive years, commencing in 1340, were consistently 10 per cent or more above the 1290–1309 average (Figures 4 and 5 and Appendix 2). This extraordinary run of good harvests culminated in the bumper harvest of 1348, more than 50 per cent above average, which was immediately followed by the disastrous harvest of 1349, when the grain yield was almost 50 per cent below average. No two years on record present such a striking contrast but then no other two years straddle a disaster as great as the Black Death. Not until 1377–78 did bumper harvests return, when for two consecutive years yields rose to more than 20 per cent above average. Until then, for more than twenty-five years, harvests had mostly been deficient. This post-plague depression of yields is all the more remarkable given that, over the entire hundred-year period from 1280 to 1379, there were almost as many years when yields were 10 per cent or more above the 1290–1309 average, as there were when yields were at least 10 per cent below. Moreover, one in five

79 In 1349 the reeves at Agney and Ruckinge complained, respectively, that peas and vetches and winter barley were left un-harvested because of the lack of labourers; MS CCAL DCc/Bedels rolls Agney 49 and DCc/Bedels rolls Ruckinge 24. Presumably for much the same reason, livestock were fed un-harvested barley at Chartham and un-threshed wheat at Mersham; MS CCAL DCc/Bedels rolls Chartham 29 and DCc/Bedels rolls Mersham 22. The following year there were still insufficient reapers to harvest all the vetches at Mersham; MS CCAL DCc/Bedels rolls Mersham 23.

80 In 1350–1 excessive rain ruined harvests at Chartham, Great Chart, and Ickham; MS CCAL DCc/Bedels rolls Chartham 30–1; DCc/Bedels rolls Great Chart 54; DCc/Bedels rolls Ickham 42. Then in 1352–53 it was the turn of drought to create problems at Great Chart, Ickham, Meopham, and 'throughout the country'; MS CCAL DCc/Bedels rolls Great Chart 56; DCc/Bedels rolls Ickham 43; DCc/Bedels rolls Meopham 94. In 1356 summer drought was responsible for the failure of the barley and oats harvests at Ickham, while the wheat crop was choked with poppies; MS CCAL DCc/Bedels rolls Ickham 45–6.

81 MS CCAL DCc/Bedels rolls East Peckham 41; DCc/Bedels rolls Meopham 81; DCc/Bedels rolls Mersham 29; DCc/Bedels rolls Copton 27, 29, 32, and 33; DCc/Bedels rolls Eastry 99, 103, and 106; DCc/Bedels rolls Great Chart 65, 70, 73, and 76; DCc/Bedels rolls Ickham 50, and 53–4; DCc/Bedels rolls Godmersham 23; DCc/Bedels rolls Adisham 34 and 36; DCc/Bedels rolls Monkton 90; DCc/Bedels rolls Agney 55; DCc/Bedels rolls Hollingbourne 49–50.

of all harvest delivered yields that were at least a fifth or more above that standard of productivity. For instance, yields were particularly good in 1299, 1302, 1313, 1319, 1341, 1348 of course, and 1361. The problem was that insofar as good and bad harvests more or less balanced each other out, they only did so in the long term. In the short to medium term they occurred with such irregularity and unpredictability that they must have created major difficulties for producers and consumers alike.[82]

Fortunately, for grain producers recovery from a bad harvest could be swift, since it was botanically entirely possible for yields to return to normal or better within a year. The three good harvests of 1318–20 that followed the three famine years of 1315–17 are clear evidence of this. Only if supplies of seed corn were seriously depleted might aggregate grain output take longer to recover. Making good the destruction wrought by livestock epidemics, in contrast, took far longer, since it took time to reproduce and rear up to maturity the replacement animals, especially in the case of horses, oxen, bulls, and cows which took several years longer than sheep or swine to reach adulthood. Only by resorting to the market to purchase replacement animals could individual producers accelerate the restocking process. That, however, required considerable capital resources. The great cattle plague which struck herds throughout Kent in 1319 and 1320 (Figure 6 and see Plate 2) therefore dealt a major blow to the county's mixed-husbandry economy. Within the space of a single accounting year numbers of oxen and cattle on the county's demesnes were, on average, halved (Figure 6) and the painstaking herd management of more than a generation undone.[83] Once signs of infection manifested themselves, or in anticipation of disease, reeves hastily sold animals off for whatever money they might make, for once bovines became infected with rinderpest (the likely cause of the plague) they became worthless.[84] Crisis selling therefore reinforced the disease-induced collapse of bovine numbers on the county's demesnes. Then, once the plague had passed, most demesnes immediately set about restocking. This would have been a slow task if reliance had been placed upon breeding alone but Christ Church Priory had the capital resources to accelerate the process by purchasing additional animals.[85] Oxen, vital for draught power, were given priority (except when substituted with horses) and their

82 Bailey, 'Peasant Welfare'.

83 Kershaw, 'Great Famine', 24–9. Norfolk demesne managers lost on average 50–60 per cent of their cattle in the same year. The cattle plague was a national disaster and by 1321 it had broken out in Ireland, with equally devastating result it would seem: M. Lyons, 'Weather, Famine, Pestilence and Plague in Ireland, 900–1500', in *Famine: the Irish Experience, 900–1900: Subsistence Crises and Famine in Ireland*, ed. E. M. Crawford (Edinburgh, 1989), pp. 321–74. For a pioneering study of the cattle plague based on chroniclers' accounts, see T. P. Newfield, 'A Cattle Panzootic in Early Fourteenth-Century Europe', *Agricultural History Review* 57 (2009), 155–90.

84 Cattle were sold off for fear that they would sicken and die at Ebony, Great Chart, Mersham, and Ruckinge; MS CCAL DCc/Bedels rolls Ebony 32; DCc/Bedels rolls Great Chart 32; DCc/Bedels rolls Mersham 9; DCc/Bedels rolls Ruckinge 8.

85 M. Mate, 'The Estates of Canterbury Cathedral Priory before the Black Death, 1315–1348', *Studies in Medieval and Renaissance History* new series 8 (1986), 7–8.

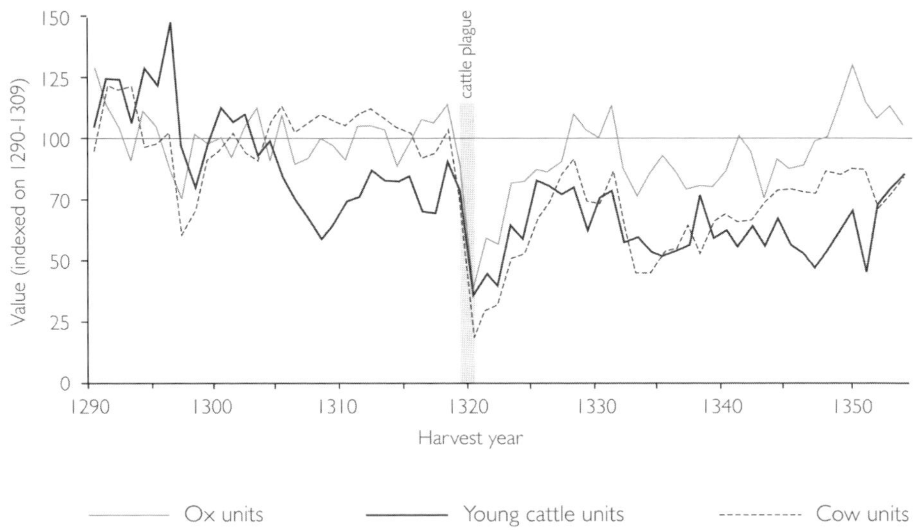

Figure 6: Impact of the 1319–20 cattle plague in Kent

numbers would soon have been restored to the pre-plague level but for a second and lesser outbreak of cattle plague in 1333–34.[86] Numbers of bulls, cows, immature and juvenile cattle, however, recovered more slowly, not least because of the growing tendency to lease out dairy herds for cash possibly as a means of evading mounting tax liabilities on movable goods (Figure 6).[87]

From the final decade of the thirteenth century, therefore, a succession of hazards beset agricultural producers in Kent and continued to do so for virtually the whole of the following century. By any standard the fourteenth century was an exceptionally difficult period. Much remains to be learnt about the precise impact of these events on the county's economy and population. Nevertheless, the demesne sector proved to be sufficiently resilient for the overall scale and composition of its production to survive in relatively unaltered form until almost the end of the fourteenth century, at least as exemplified by such major estates as those of Christ Church Priory and Westminster Abbey. As the fourteenth century drew to a close what changed was not what was produced on demesnes but who produced it, insofar as estate owners increasingly opted for a policy of leasing out their demesnes rather than managing them directly.[88] By the opening of the fifteenth

86 Ibid., 16. The cattle herd at Great Chart was particularly badly affected in 1333–34; MS CCAL DCc/Bedels rolls Great Chart 40.

87 Smith, *Canterbury Cathedral Priory*, pp. 157–65.

88 M. Mate, 'The Farming Out of Manors: A New Look at the Evidence from Canterbury Cathedral Priory', *Journal of Medieval History* 9 (1983), 331–44; F. R. H. Du Boulay, 'Who were Farming the English Demesnes at the End of the Middle Ages?', *Economic History Review* 2nd series 17 (1964–65), 443–55.

century the era of direct demesne exploitation was effectively over in Kent with the result that manorial accounts record the receipt of rents rather than the production of crops and animals.

Epilogue

Demesne producers, of course, enjoyed greater command over land and capital than the county's far more numerous occupying tenantry and farmed on a far greater scale and often with different objectives in terms of the relative primacy accorded production for sale versus consumption. Certainly, such great and perpetual institutional producers as Christ Church Priory were better able to weather economic and environmental hazards than the plethora of petty producers who must have cultivated well over two-thirds of all the land in the county and for whom a major back-to-back harvest failure or heavy mortality of cattle or sheep may well have spelled economic ruin. Indeed, great lords may actually have profited from the high prices which were the invariable accompaniment of such difficulties. Yet their experience is not wholly unrepresentative of agriculture within the county. With the peasants they shared a common labour force and agricultural technology, supplied much the same markets, and were informed by the same prices. They also cultivated similar soils and had to cope and contend with the same weather, pests, parasites, and pathogens. Moreover, it made little economic sense for lords to manage their demesne lands directly, unless they were able to obtain at least as good a return as they would from leasing them for competitive rents to tenants. Much can therefore be learned from analysis of the economic activities of Christ Church Priory and other well documented seigniorial producers, provided that it is remembered that Kent contained many other classes of producer whose activities, as yet, remain largely obscured from view.[89] Rescuing the agriculture practised on the estates of lesser lords and the myriad holdings of the occupying peasantry from this obscurity is therefore the major challenge confronting historians of this most remarkable medieval English county.

[89] Rectory accounts recording tithe receipts are one source that capture the grain output of all classes of producers. Tithe receipts at Monkton, Eastry, and Birchington are currently the subject of research being undertaken by Dr Ben Dodds of the University of Durham.

Appendix 1: Kent demesnes indicators of land productivity and cropping intensity, 1285–1348

Manor	Mean *IPM* value per arable acre (pence)	[1]Weighted aggregate grain yield per grain acre (bus.)	All grains seed sown per acre (bus.)	Total grain acreage	Legumes as % cropped area	[2]Livestock units per 100 grain acres	[3]Working horse units as % working units	[4]Cattle units as % non-working units
Copton (in Preston)	7	12.7	5.0	104	29	12	100	
Ickham	13	12.1	5.3	331	26	36	47	45
Monkton	16	11.6	5.5	13	37			
Agney	12	10.6	5.4	103	28	137	65	65
Eastry	11	9.6	5.3	216	24	34	48	48
Ruckinge	12	9.4	5.6	70	22	117	26	85
Leysdown	8	9.1	4.9	18	39		22	
Barksore	7	8.3	5.1	46	31	213	27	35
Godmersham	6	8.3	5.0	123	27			
Cliffe	5	8.3	5.0	198	26			
Adisham	11	7.9	5.5	254	14	28	60	28
Fairfield	12	7.7	5.5	33	23			
Appledore	11	7.7	5.5	78	5	36	51	63
Ebony (with Stone)	11	7.4	5.5	139	10	75	64	58
Lydden	8	6.9	5.2	47	33	290	63	40
Ospringe	7	6.9	4.7	220	24	25	73	77
Chartham	6	6.8	5.2	131	25	58	82	63
Great Chart	7	6.6	5.6	155	22	70	22	73
Loose	4	6.5	4.7	74	27	32	39	47
East Farleigh	4	6.4	4.8	143	24	38	39	50
West Farleigh	4	6.2	4.9	149	26	44	34	58
Meopham	4	6.0	3.5	225	15	33	51	41
Westwell	5	5.8	5.1	164	22	63	28	58
Orpington	3	5.8	3.6	156	20	41	37	42
Hollingbourne	4	5.5	5.1	162	26	54	42	59
Ham	9	5.5	5.3	13	29	525		33
Westerham	2	5.0	3.7	178	8	59	27	69
Elverton		4.8	5.0	39	28	31	100	
East Peckham	3	4.6	4.7	86	17	40	34	56
Average	8	7.6	5.0	126	24	87	49	54

[1] Weighted by the relative area occupied by each grain and the following relative grain prices: wheat 1.0; rye 0.83; winter & spring barley 0.76; winter & spring oats 0.43. This expresses the yield in wheat equivalents, gross of tithe & net of seed.

[2] Horses x 1.0; oxen, bulls, & cows x 1.2; immature cattle x 0.8; sheep & swine x 0.1.

[3] Cart & plough horses + oxen

[4] All livestock other than cart horses, plough horses, & oxen.

Sources: D. L. Farmer Papers, University of Saskatchewan Archives; TNA, PRO SC6/893 (31-6) & 894 (1-8); Canterbury Cathedral Archives, beadles' rolls.

Appendix 2: Kent demesnes: crop yields, total seed sown, livestock units, and animal ratios, 1280–1379

Harvest year	Yield per seed gross of tithe & net of seed:				Indexed on 1290–1309:		
	Wheat	Spring barley	Spring oats	All grains indexed on 1290–1309[1]	(A) Total seed sown	(B) Total livestock units[2]	Stocking density (A)/(B)
1280	2.04	1.70	1.30	68	102	102	100
1281	3.38	2.78	0.53	105	112	84	74
1282	1.97	1.98	0.98	102	158	87	54
1283	1.95	1.45	1.26	80	116	94	81
1284	2.70	2.31	0.98	77	125	96	76
1285	2.58	2.29	1.52	105	135	83	61
1286	2.68	2.44	1.59	109	113	107	94
1287	3.49	2.59	1.16	116	91	115	125
1288	2.99	1.91	0.84	89	127	115	90
1289	2.19	1.35	0.83	67	92	116	125
1290	2.65	0.91	1.64	96	120	110	91
1291	2.13	1.21	0.89	90	102	104	101
1292	2.42	1.35	1.05	69	103	107	103
1293	1.91	1.60	2.09	119	101	89	87
1294	2.45	2.15	1.42	108	105	90	85
1295	2.33	1.45	1.62	90	102	97	94
1296	2.59	1.28	2.05	122	102	91	88
1297	2.52	1.03	1.61	91	103	84	81
1298	3.32	1.71	1.54	113	103	77	74
1299	2.38	2.90	2.13	147	106	92	86
1300	2.14	0.93	1.41	62	105	104	97
1301	2.31	1.91	1.64	99	100	109	109
1302	3.21	2.04	0.87	145	86	108	125
1303	2.64	2.24	1.43	113	111	108	97
1304	2.16	1.46	1.72	93	93	107	114
1305	2.15	1.49	1.25	81	88	110	125
1306	1.89	0.76	0.75	35	93	101	108
1307	2.53	2.06	1.89	134	91	105	114
1308	2.18	1.93	1.34	90	98	103	104
1309	2.81	1.40	1.56	100	90	103	113
1310	2.26	1.76	1.55	97	90	102	112
1311	2.95	1.59	1.53	117	93	105	112
1312	2.43	2.88	0.99	101	90	115	127
1313	2.83	1.76	1.23	147	83	105	125
1314	3.02	2.13	1.68	115	94	100	106
1315	1.73	1.65	1.81	70	96	100	103
1316	2.60	1.63	1.50	92	98	93	94
1317	2.52	1.21	1.21	76	93	90	95
1318	3.20	1.40	1.52	124	84	95	112
1319	3.33	2.26	1.87	140	85	97	112
1320	2.82	2.16	1.75	128	96	82	84
1321	2.02	1.93	1.07	106	98	71	72
1322	2.39	2.31	1.72	106	88	71	79
1323	2.53	2.17	1.97	133	104	76	72
1324	2.45	1.81	1.05	92	99	84	84
1325	2.90	1.68	1.66	116	88	84	94
1326	2.70	2.04	1.50	113	93	86	92

1327	2.65	1.45	1.61	95	94	90	95
1328	2.35	1.48	1.09	83	87	89	101
1329	2.79	1.62	1.38	87	83	89	106
1330	3.09	2.07	1.31	96	77	91	117
1331	2.13	0.49	1.38	66	76	95	124
1332	3.04	1.52	1.85	111	81	94	115
1333	3.28	1.25	1.17	97	90	86	94
1334	2.78	1.36	1.69	105	89	80	88
1335	2.43	2.06	1.29	80	90	76	84
1336	2.18	2.36	2.04	104	77	73	94
1337	2.91	2.03	1.20	121	82	76	92
1338	3.19	2.45	2.02	124	76	81	106
1339	1.73	2.75	1.39	88	87	86	97
1340	2.93	2.09	1.68	112	79	88	110
1341	2.88	2.47	1.84	143	78	89	113
1342	2.59	2.12	2.06	122	73	87	117
1343	2.97	2.36	1.66	116	78	90	114
1344	3.32	2.32	1.77	135	79	92	115
1345	3.08	2.30	1.52	133	81	92	112
1346	3.03	1.95	1.83	117	80	91	112
1347	2.89	2.23	1.88	131	79	92	116
1348	3.14	2.57	2.02	154	75	91	121
1349	1.90	0.97	1.58	53	72	97	133
1350	2.19	0.95	1.36	80	69	95	137
1351	2.37	1.34	2.10	103	71	91	128
1352	3.48	0.48	1.42	83	69	87	126
1353	2.25	1.12	1.09	59	83	93	111
1354	1.77	1.42	1.93	64	87	106	121
1355	2.22	2.06	2.13	134	82	95	115
1356	2.77	0.94	1.35	77	78	90	114
1357	1.99	1.59	1.63	90	77	90	116
1358	1.80	0.36	1.94	72	66	93	138
1359	1.81	1.81	1.86	102	71	87	122
1360	2.47	1.67	1.19	93	68	86	125
1361	2.94	No data	2.84	143	68	96	141
1362	1.86	1.25	1.90	112	49	72	147
1363	2.33	1.77	1.84	106	72	81	113
1364	2.33	2.21	1.51	89	71	93	130
1365	1.43	1.32	1.40	84	74	97	131
1366	2.47	1.88	1.30	85	64	90	139
1367	2.09	1.89	1.51	81	83	98	118
1368	2.67	0.98	1.25	52	71	98	137
1369	1.24	1.13	1.33	62	79	113	141
1370	2.27	1.58	1.70	76	72	102	141
1371	2.08	1.59	1.63	83	65	102	154
1372	1.09	1.62	1.42	83	67	96	141
1373	2.29	1.65	2.04	113	65	95	144
1374	1.32	1.46	1.24	58	80	97	121
1375	1.72	1.19	1.22	105	84	109	128
1376	2.23	1.75	1.15	98	73	106	144
1377	3.21	1.58	2.30	129	69	123	177
1378	2.62	2.28	2.30	135	71	137	192
1379	1.18	1.69	1.46	57	65	160	243

[1] Includes rye, maslin, winter barley, and winter oats.

[2] Horses x 1.0; oxen, bulls, & cows x 1.2; immature cattle x 0.8; sheep & swine x 0.1.

Sources: see Appendix 1.

4

Timber and Iron: Natural Resources for the Late Medieval Shipbuilding Industry in Kent*

G. M. DRAPER

Introduction

The significance of the maritime economy of late medieval Kent has been emphasised by recent archaeological work. This chapter offers a new historical contribution to this subject and period, presenting the results of research among a wide variety of source materials. Maritime Kent from 1500 has received much more study than that of earlier centuries, but important points of comparison and contrast between the medieval and early modern periods can now be made, challenging the suggestion that 'the sixteenth and seventeenth centuries saw the origins and development of a shipbuilding and repair industry on the Thames and Medway estuaries'.[1] The county's ports and the Thames were major points of entry and departure for late medieval England. Proximity to the continent and the long Channel coastline made Kentish coastal settlements the base for cross-Channel commerce and for defence. These activities were to a large extent integrated with local coastal trade and fishing operations, partly because of the relatively small size of the late medieval vessels which operated out of the ports. The vessels which provided the ship service of the Cinque Ports to the monarch for two weeks a year were generally those otherwise used for commerce or fishing. Two major changes occurred in this over the period: larger vessels were built and demanded by the monarch for warfare and the harbours and shipbuilding facilities of the Cinque Ports were increasingly unable to supply such vessels, due to siltation and damage by French raids. The building of vessels for royal and other use was transferred to Smallhythe, although it was not until the

* Comments, information and pointers on this chapter from Dr Sheila Sweetinburgh, Dr Alan Tyler, Terry Burke, Jo Kirkham and Roger Nixon, members of the Romney Marsh Research Trust, are gratefully acknowledged.

1 J. Andrewes, 'Industries in Kent, c.1500–1640', and J. Bower, 'Kent Towns, 1540–1640', in *Early Modern Kent 1540–1640*, ed. M. L. Zell (Woodbridge, 2000), pp. 128, 279–314; T. Lawson, 'Maritime Kent 1500–1700, in *An Historical Atlas of Kent*, ed. T. Lawson and D. Killingray (Chichester, 2004), p. 91.

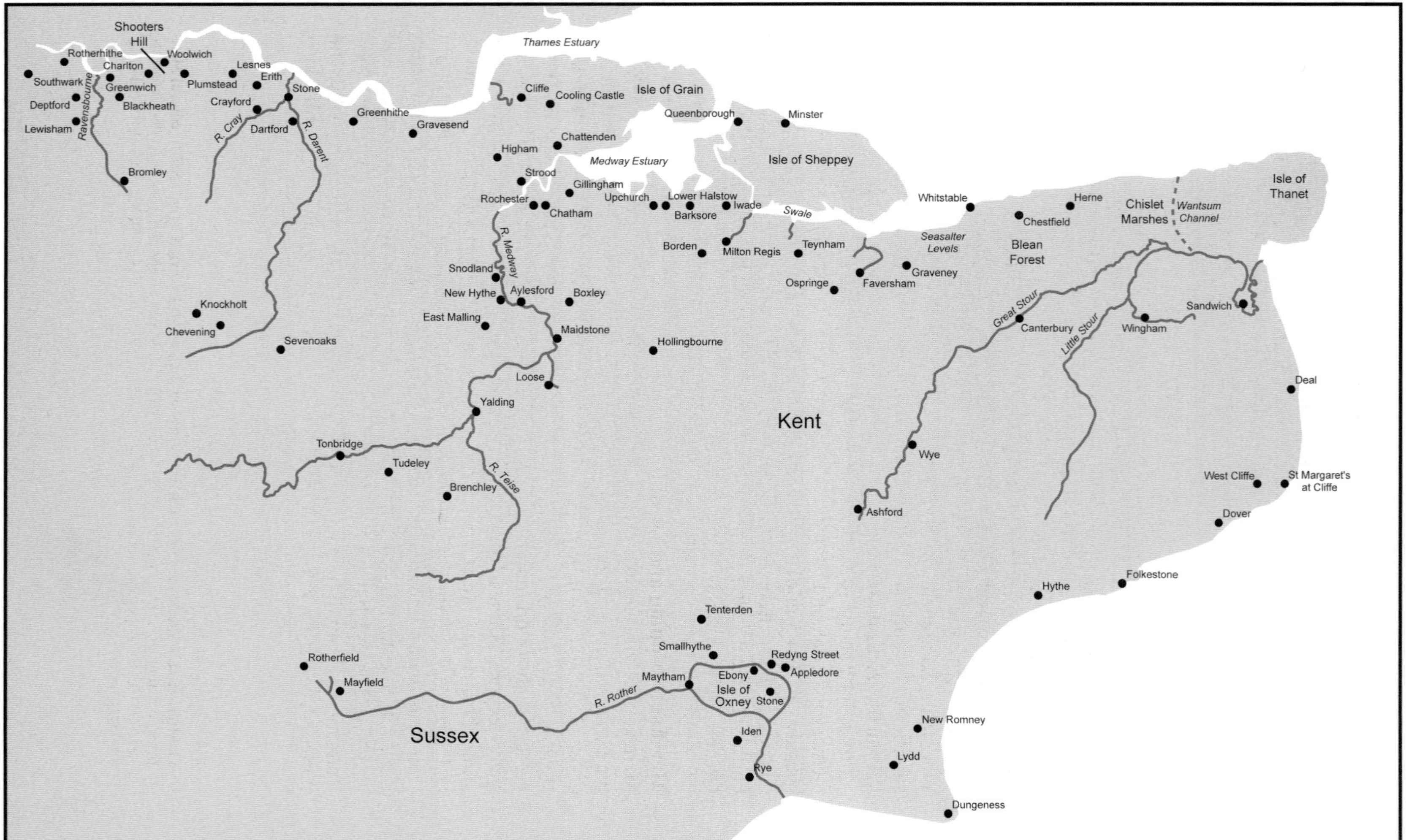

Map 1: Late Medieval Kent

sixteenth century that the royal dockyards were developed on the Thames and Medway. Against this background of change, an economy continued to exist in coastal and riverine settlements which was heavily based on various kinds of fishing, and made a major contribution to local and more distant trade, including with London.

This chapter therefore reviews the maritime economy of Kent between c. 1350 and 1500 and in particular considers the provision of resources for the building of vessels. It focuses on two localities, the ports and shipbuilding area of south-eastern Kent, and the north Kent river courses and estuaries, an area until recently less studied (see Map 1). These two localities were in different ways centres for merchant activity, fishing, ferrying, the transport of goods and people, and royal ship service. All of these activities demanded the construction and maintenance of vessels, both large and small. At most places, maritime activity was long term and has to be examined as such, for example at Greenwich, Whitstable, Sandwich, and New Romney. Smallhythe was exceptional in being a significant shipbuilding location only in the late Middle Ages. Nautical activity in late medieval Kent and the supply of wood and iron are subjects which have received little study. Nevertheless, this chapter suggests that deed, lease and testamentary material, and an analysis of maritime occupational by-names in the lay subsidy of 1334/5 allow significant points to be made. The chapter also briefly considers the extremely important interrelationships between London and north-west Kent in the supply and transport of materials, using the examples of Greenwich, Knockholt, and Southwark.

Merchant Shipping and Trade

Merchant activity and the vessels used for it are investigated from the examples of the Cinque Ports and the Medway ports. Vessels mentioned in the Patent and Close Rolls and town records of the Cinque Ports included barges, balingers, crayers, cogs, galleys, carracks, and tarrits. The larger types of late medieval vessels such as dromonds, hulks, and great cogs did not use the Cinque or Medway ports. Barges, balingers, and crayers were shallow-draught vessels operating along rivers, around the coast and sometimes as far as Gascony. Carracks and tarrits were larger deep-draught cargo or merchant vessels importing a variety of luxury goods from more distant places such as Genoa. Such vessels were able to enter Sandwich haven in the fourteenth and fifteenth centuries, and also Rye (Sussex), but not New Romney where the harbour was silting up.[2] New Romney was a small merchant port which was at its peak in the late twelfth and thirteenth centuries. In the early fourteenth century its townsmen were still taking

2 G. Milne et al., 'The Fourteenth-Century Merchant Ship from Sandwich: A Study in Medieval Maritime Archaeology', *Arch. Cant.* 124 (2004), 255–7; M. Mate, *Trade and Economic Developments, 1450–1550: The Experience of Kent, Surrey and Sussex* (Woodbridge, 2006), p. 86; MS TNA PRO E 199/42/311373/4 (1373/4).

part in the wine trade, although probably as shippers rather than merchants *per se*. For example, four brothers of New Romney were participating in the Bordeaux wine trade in 1309 using 'a ship called Seynte Marie Bot'. They did so in conjunction with four merchants including two of Périgord.[3] Both townsmen and alien merchants or shippers transported goods across the Channel in the mid-fourteenth and early fifteenth centuries. Nieuport, Sluys, Bruges, Amiens, Boulogne, Calais, and Dunkirk were 'most frequently mentioned' as destinations of alien or Romney merchants and shippers. In 1356 one S. Walop, a New Romney freeman, delivered victuals (corn, suet, sacks, and tubs) to C. Mistlelyn of Nieuport which were intended ultimately for Calais.[4] In 1414 thirty-nine tuns of Bordeaux wine were specified as being transported, and separately forty tuns of wine and one tun of oil; in 1417 fifty-three tuns and one pipe of wine from Bordeaux.[5] The vessels carrying this wine and oil may have been built at New Romney. The building and repair of vessels at New Romney is known from historical and archaeological evidence between c. 1250 and c. 1450. Split, bent, and distorted iron roves, nails, and complete rovenails found at New Romney demonstrate that ship breaking and/or dismantling for repair took place on, or very close to the beachfront, which lay on the north-east side of the town. The abandoned unused rove strips and cut-off nail tips also indicate that either the repair or new building of clinker vessels occurred at this location. The wrecking of merchant ships, whether or not it was deliberate, also occurred frequently on the coast near New Romney, Lydd, and Dungeness, thus creating part of the need for ship repair.[6] It can however be noted that in 1401 the New Romney town barge was constructed at Smallhythe, suggesting that shipbuilding, at least of larger vessels, was already being transferred there.[7] In 1398 the town of New Romney paid the large sum of £5 6s 8d to John Tymberden for purchase of a house on the 'quay of St Nicholas' in the town centre.[8] Tymberden's by-name (surname) suggests that this quay may have been used for the shipping of timber and firewood grown and felled in one of the nearby Wealden dens, firewood being a fourteenth-century export of New Romney.[9]

Sandwich was an important Cinque Port for the export of wool and wool-fells by the end of the thirteenth century, with the vessels used for trade generally

3 *Calendar of Chancery Warrants Preserved in the Public Record Office, 1244–1326* (London, 1927), p. 293.

4 K. M. E. Murray, trans. and ed., *The Register of Daniel Rough, Common Clerk of Romney 1353–1380*, Kent Records 16 (1945), pp. xlvi–ix, 96, 97, 181.

5 H. Riley, 'Manuscripts of the Corporation of New Romney', HMC V, part 1, pp. 533–54.

6 D. Goodburn, 'Ship Construction and Breaking at the Southlands School Site', in *The Sea and the Marsh; The Medieval Cinque Port of New Romney*, G. Draper and F. Meddens, Pre-Construct Archaeology monograph 10 (London, 2009), pp. 97–101..

7 P. Bellamy and G. Milne, 'An Archaeological Evaluation of the Medieval Shipyard Facilities at Small Hythe', *Arch. Cant.* 123 (2003), 354.

8 HMC V, p. 535.

9 In 1352 Sir Richard de Totisham at New Romney 'freighted a certain ship, whereof Lypyn Monfort is master, with 18 thousand [*sic*] of firewood to be conveyed (with the aid of God) and delivered at Calais within the week, for 4d a thousand'; Murray, *Rough's Register*, p. 249.

being the same as those used for ship service.[10] At Sandwich a discussion of vessels for ship service took place between the townsmen, the king and also the townsmen of New Romney in 1354/5.[11] A fourteenth-century English merchant ship which had been abandoned in a silted creek at Sandwich has recently been analysed. The parent trees from which the timbers and logs of this clinker built vessel came 'indicate that the surviving framing elements were predominantly drawn from large mature wood-pasture or possibly hedgerow trees with low branches or limbs'.[12] This ship is likely to have been locally built rather than being a foreign trader. The location of its discovery suggests that Sandwich harbour was no longer in active use, and thus perhaps that shipbuilding was no longer occurring there. The Sandwich ship was probably c. 20 m to c. 30 m in length, and of the sort involved in the Anglo-Gascon wine trade, although its size was limited by the nature of the tidal estuary at Sandwich.[13] By way of comparison two sea-going trading vessels which operated also along the rivers and around the coast of Kent may be considered. They were c. 16 m to c. 19 m long and built mainly of oak. These were found respectively near New Romney and near Maytham on the River Rother and appear to be of sixteenth-century date and to have originated in the Low Countries (see Plate 3).[14] The size of rovenails found at New Romney indicates that it was coastal and estuary traders or small ships c. 11–20 m long, as well as small boats (up to c. 10 m long), which were repaired or built there in the high and late Middle Ages.[15]

In the late fifteenth century merchant activity was based on the River Medway as well as in the Cinque Ports. A vessel called 'The Thomas of New Hythe' is noted in the correspondence of the important Cely family of wool merchants as transporting Cotswold fells from New Hythe to Calais in 1481.[16] This was New Hythe (Newhethe) on the west side of the Medway and in the north of East Malling parish. The vessel 'The Anthony of Snodland' is also known in 1492. These two vessels assisted members of the Cinque Ports confederation in providing their royal ship service at a period when the harbours of the Cinque Ports such as New Romney and Sandwich were largely silted up and useless for vessels of any size.[17] A century earlier, New Hythe on the Medway had been important as a loading place for timber, including for the repair of Rochester Castle in 1367–69. Early modern sources demonstrate that vessels were built at New Hythe. It is also very likely that shipbuilding occurred there in the later Middle Ages from the evidence of the 1334/5 lay subsidy (see below). The existence of 'The Thomas of Maidstone', known in 1481, indicates the role of that

10 R. Pelham, 'Some Aspects of the East Kent Wool Trade in the Thirteenth Century', *Arch. Cant.* 44 (1932), 218–28.
11 Murray, *Rough's Register*, pp. 89–91, 160.
12 Milne, 'Ship from Sandwich', 227, 249.
13 Ibid., pp. 255–7.
14 Draper and Meddens, *New Romney*, pp. 40–1.
15 Goodburn, 'Ship Construction', in Draper and Meddens, *New Romney*, p. 99.
16 C. Sinclair Williams, 'Maritime East Malling', *Arch. Cant.* 88 (1973), 52.
17 HMC V, p. 548; Milne, 'Ship from Sandwich', 257.

town as a port on the Medway. This vessel is likely to have been under thirty tuns in order to pass under Aylesford Bridge.[18]

Fishing

Fishing of all kinds took place along the coast, rivers, and creeks of Kent, all requiring vessels of different sizes. Some of the fish caught in the Medway is known to have been transported to London by boat; for example, one Richard Clements of New Hythe, on the Medway, apparently caught fish and landed them just below the Tower of London.[19] Finds of fish hooks, lead net weights and fish bones demonstrate that both deep-sea trawling and coastal fishing took place at New Romney. Marine molluscs, mainly oyster but also common cockle, mussel, and common whelk, were also found. The north Kent coast was well known for its shellfish. Whitstable was a major focus of estuarine and perhaps more distant fishing, including oysters. Shellfish and wet fish were evidenced from finds at Chestfield in the thirteenth century. Chestfield was associated with Whitstable and lay approximately 2 km inland of the latter. It was an estuarine street settlement similar to Smallhythe. Roads extended south from the north Kent coast on which Whitstable lies to settlements such as Chestfield, and were used for the transport of salt and seafood. These roads continued southwards into the Forest of Blean as drove roads, along which swine were driven for pasture. The woods south of Whitstable were part of the Forest of Blean. They were valued from the Anglo-Saxon period as swine pastures and until the early fourteenth century to provide faggots for fuel for the extensive saltworks in the area, including those on the Chislet Marshes, east of Herne, and on the Seasalter Levels, west of Whitstable. The Forest of Blean would also have provided timber for boat building on the north Kent coast.[20] The hundred of Whitstable, which lay to the east of Graveney and to the south of Whitstable itself, was also wooded and would similarly have supplied timber. In 1356 a grant was made from Adam le Heir, a citizen of London by licence of the king, to Thomas de Wolton of Eastbridge Hospital, Canterbury, ‘of certain tenements, lands, rents, pastures, [and] woods in the hundred of Whitstable and Swalklyne, for the master and his successors to hold for life’.[21] Whitstable remained an important location for fishing with ‘various and constant’ fishing disputes in the fifteenth and sixteenth centuries.[22] Furthermore, the fish wives of Whitstable had their own fish market at Canterbury from the late fifteenth century (see Sweetinburgh, this volume).[23]

18 Sinclair Williams, ‘Maritime East Malling’, 51–3.

19 Sinclair Williams, ‘Maritime East Malling’, 53.

20 T. Allen, ‘Swine, Salt and Seafood: A Case Study of an Anglo-Saxon and Early Medieval Settlement in North-East Kent’, *Arch. Cant.* 124 (2004), 124–5, 131.

21 MS CCAL U 24/Box4/E/4.

22 Allen, ‘Swine, Salt and Seafood’, 131.

23 MS CCAL CC/FA 2, fol. 199; HMC Canterbury, p. 223.

Men from Lydd and Folkestone participated in North Sea fishing, mainly for herring, and also in more local coastal waters.[24] The Lydd fisherman had fishing cabins on Dungeness by or before the mid-fourteenth century and they still had a chapel there in the early sixteenth century. Participation in North Sea fishing had fallen considerably by the late sixteenth century. Fishermen from Folkestone like those of Lydd also had cabins or lodges by the seaside.[25] In the late fourteenth and fifteenth centuries men brought fish caught at Dungeness to the fish quay area in New Romney, sometimes attempting to sell it at night or before the market officially opened. Ripiers also transported fish to inland towns in Kent and to London by the 1340s. Fish from coastal waters and landed in the Cinque Ports such as New Romney, and Rye, Sussex, was transported on horseback to London and inland towns such as Maidstone, Ashford, Tonbridge, and Sevenoaks. The route to the latter two towns would have used Twyford Bridge (known by 1381) across the Medway near Yalding.[26] Ripiers are also known at Hythe and Dover by the mid-fifteenth century. The nature of fishing and fishing settlements at Dover has been revealed by recently published archaeological and historical investigation. Simple timber houses and other buildings dated between 1150 and 1250 have been excavated, some of which belonged to seafaring families, probably including some Dover Portsmen who provided ship service. These buildings lay at Townwall Street, near to St James' church, and near Woolcomber Street and Russell Street. This was on the eastern seaward flank of the town near the beachfront and about 300 m from central medieval Dover. The beachfront provided a sizeable area for fishing and related activities, as at New Romney, and the earliest buildings may have been seasonally occupied and linked to those activities. From c. 1175 there was an intensification of settlement in this part of Dover, occupying land either previously not required for permanent habitation or unavailable due to coastal change. One building may have been a smoke house for curing fish. The building of the town wall in the late thirteenth or fourteenth century, probably for both defence and protection against marine erosion, cut off the ready access between the waterfront and the town. The Dover fishers caught a variety of fish in the fourteenth and fifteenth centuries in a series of seasons or 'fares'. As elsewhere herring was the most important catch. Fish processing took place on the beachfront (the Townwall site) and there was a conveniently placed fish market by, and probably before, the late fifteenth century. As at New Romney, vessels used in fishing and also other maritime activities including ship service were frequently described as *batella* and *navis*. Some fishermen were members of the town elite and served as civic officers in the late fourteenth and fifteenth

24 L. Barber and G. Priestley-Bell, *Medieval Adaptation, Settlement and Economy of a Coastal Wetland: The Evidence from around Lydd, Romney Marsh, Kent* (Oxford, 2008), 18, 23–4, 226–7, 228–39.

25 S. Sweetinburgh, 'Strategies of Inheritance among Kentish Fishing Families in the Later Middle Ages', *The History of the Family* 11 (2006), 95–6.

26 Draper and Meddens, *New Romney*, p. 46; LPL 358a Courtenay (will of John Burgeys); G. Draper with contributions by D. Martin, B. Martin and A. Tyler, *Rye: A History of a Sussex Cinque Port to 1660* (Chichester, 2009), ch. 8.

centuries. This suggests a contrast with New Romney and a longer-continued importance of fishing in the Dover economy, since at New Romney fishermen were replaced by men described as vintners as the town elite during the fifteenth century.[27]

Ferrying and Transport

Transport for people and goods was needed across and along the Thames, and to the Isles of Sheppey, Grain and Thanet. Small ferries and transport boats also sailed up the many creeks entering the Swale and the Thames estuary such as those at Ospringe and Faversham. From west to east, crossings of the Thames are known or indicated at the following places by the record of ferries on early maps, by place-names incorporating *hithe* and by the landscape evidence of road patterns and causeways leading to the embarkation points: Rotherhithe (some testamentary material considered Rotherhithe to be in Kent), Greenwich, Upper Woolwich/Charlton, Woolwich, Erith, Dartford, Greenhithe, Gravesend, and Higham.[28]

Ferry embarkation points also provided opportunities for travellers, including pilgrims, not only to cross the Thames but also to sail up or down the river.[29] This alternative route to Watling Street and other land routes is attested by the number of pilgrim badges that have been found in the mud of the river. The settlements along the Thames, themselves, offered opportunities for devotion and almsgiving for pilgrims as they travelled towards Canterbury or onto ports such as Dover or New Romney. At the latter, pilgrims gathered in the late fourteenth and early fifteenth centuries to embark for more distant destinations such as Rome and Jerusalem.[30] Places of pilgrimage along the Thames included the ancient site of the Minster on the north coast of the Isle of Sheppey, and the cultic site at Lesnes which was new in the late fourteenth century.[31] A track or road led from the Thames edge across the reclaimed marsh running on a wall or causeway to Lesnes Abbey.[32] Pilgrims could equally reach the places of pilgrimage at Rochester, Strood, and Chatham by boat. Travel by boat avoided the notorious danger spots

27 K. Parfitt, B. Corke and J. Cotter, *Townwall Street, Dover: Excavations 1996*, Canterbury Archaeological Trust (Canterbury, 2006), pp. 6, 393, 395, 397–8, 401, 403, 417.

28 P. Thornhill, ‘A Lower Thames Ford and the Campaigns of 54 B.C. and A.D. 43’, *Arch. Cant.* 92 (1976), 120–3.

29 F. Hull, *Ordnance Survey Historical Guides: Kent*, George Philip, London and the Ordnance Survey (Southampton, 1988), p. 37.

30 Draper and Meddens, *New Romney*, p. 47.

31 D. Webb, ‘Pilgrimage’, in *An Historical Atlas of Kent*, ed. T. Lawson and D. Killingray (Chichester, 2004), pp. 46–7. Also the tomb of ‘St Robert’ of Newington, local tradition being that those who crawled through the aperture above the tomb-base would be closest to these holy relics; D. Webb, *Pilgrimage in Medieval England* (London and New York, 2000), pp. 157–8.

32 Hull, *Kent*, map 2. Cf. Erith, Higham near Cliffe, and Smallhythe/Wittersham on the Rother, Thornhill, ‘A Lower Thames Ford’, p. 123; T. Burke, ‘Wittersham Walk, 4 September 2004’, *Romney Marsh Irregular* (the newsletter of the Romney Marsh Research Trust) 26 (2005), 21–2.

on Watling Street at Shooters Hill to the south of Greenwich and Lesnes, the poor state of the road around Strood and the 'haunt of brigands' at Blean Forest near Canterbury which Chaucer noted.[33] Pilgrims could make their journeys partly by road and partly by boat, landing at places on the Thames such as Gravesend, Milton Regis, and Queenborough, or on creeks running into the Thames such as Ospringe and Faversham. The medieval hospitals of Kent, some taking in pilgrims, were clustered around these places as well as along Watling Street (see Sweetinburgh, this volume).[34]

The ferry embarkation points along the Thames, and in the other rivers and creeks were in addition likely to be hythes or quays which also served as landing places for goods.[35] The transport of foodstuffs to London from the manors of northwest Kent from such quays was very important and this is one aspect of the maritime economy considered through a case study of Greenwich. Greenwich is well documented and the medieval development of Deptford ('West Greenwich') counterbalances suggestions that shipbuilding here, as Woolwich and Chatham, was a new sixteenth-century development.

Greenwich: A Case Study

Greenwich was a medieval settlement and port on the Thames. As such it demonstrated the mixed or non-specialised characteristics of such ports and its role must be examined in that context.[36] Greenwich developed from the tenth century becoming 'a leading port on the River Thames for trade between Flanders and Britain'.[37] St Peter's Abbey, Ghent, held land both at Greenwich and Lewisham with the port (*portus*) recorded in Domesday Book under Lewisham but it was undoubtedly located at Greenwich.[38] Lewisham Priory was the 'alien' house belonging to St Peter's. By 1086 there were up to thirty-five houses at Greenwich plus a grange, the small manorial administrative centre, of Lewisham Priory. This lay adjacent to a quay.[39] The grange and the quay lay in the marshy area where the River Ravensbourne joined the Thames at Deptford Creek. The significant

33 Webb, 'Pilgrimage', pp. 46–7.

34 S. Sweetinburgh, 'Medieval Hospitals and Almshouses', in *An Historical Atlas of Kent*, ed. T. Lawson and D. Killingray (Chichester, 2004), pp. 44–5.

35 See R. James, G. Draper and D. Martin, 'Archaeological and Historical Landscape Survey, Smallhythe Place, Kent, NGR TQ 893 300, commissioned by the National Trust', Archaeology South-East Project no. 1967, April 2005, pp. 52–7.

36 See G. Milne, 'Joining the Medieval Fleet', *British Archaeology Magazine* 61 (2001) (unpag.); Draper and Meddens, *New Romney*.

37 J. Mills, 'The Priory at Lewisham' (unpublished Diploma in Local History dissertation, University of London, 1986) (copy at Lewisham Local Studies Library), pp. 10–11, maps on pp. 14A, 30A; M. Egan, 'The Church in Medieval Greenwich', *Arch. Cant.* 123 (2003), 234, map 1, 235.

38 Domesday Book has a reference to a port at Dover but not, for example, to ports at Woolwich or at Deptford. Also early markets are not recorded for either place. At this period Greenwich appears to have had the market functions in this locality; P. Morgan, ed., *Domesday Book: Kent* (Chichester, 1983), 8,1; D10.

39 Egan, 'Greenwich', 233–4; Mills, 'Lewisham', map on p. 14A.

income of forty shillings from the port recorded under St Peter's lands in Lewisham in Domesday Book 'would probably have arisen from the dues paid at a small quay in the eastern part of Greenwich located in the area later known as Billingsgate'.[40] The Billingsgate area lay on the east of Deptford Creek, and references to repairing a marshland wall in sources of the early fourteenth century at 'Est Grenewich' (below) would be compatible with an associated quay here. In fact, Lewisham Priory's quay at East Greenwich was in use in the late thirteenth century, and contemporary verbal evidence was that this had been the case from about 1260.[41] The priory took a once-yearly toll of 1.5d on firewood being taken there on the highway 'from Kent'. Firewood from Lewisham Priory's own woods at Lewisham was loaded there (see below).[42]

As well as its property and quay in Billingsgate or East Greenwich, St Peter's apparently also had land at Deptford, which lay on the left bank of Deptford Creek and was known in the early fourteenth century as West Greenwich.[43] At that period Deptford was a shipbuilding location, 'possibly from as early as 1326'.[44] A 'ferour' is known at Deptford ('West Greenwich') in 1335 among the records of the London Bridge estates.[45] Ferours were specialist iron workers usually found working in the central parts of medieval towns across England including, in Kent, Tonbridge. Their role was associated with blacksmithing, castles, and market sites and possibly here at Deptford/West Greenwich with the production of iron fittings for vessels.[46] The royal ship 'Trinity Royal' was built at Greenwich in 1413–16, with timber and boards shipped out from the Weald via Smallhythe.[47]

Within Greenwich town centre there were the site or sites of a Saxon church and a later parish church among a sub-rectangular grid plan of streets and buildings near the Thames. Watling Street ran west to east to the south of Greenwich. Creek Street and Greenwich Church Street, in the modern town centre, are suggested to have possibly represented the reach of high water in medieval

40 Mills, 'Lewisham', p.14; Billingsgate at Greenwich must be distinguished from the nineteenth-century market in Lower Thames Street on the north side of the medieval London Bridge.

41 Mills, 'Lewisham', pp. 44–5.

42 For comparison, in 1349 John Boton of Strood held a tenement 'upon the quay of Stroodmill' (*cayam de Strodemelle*). The mill is equated with a watermill used to grind corn next to the end of Rochester Bridge; presumably the quay was next to the mill and used for loading and unloading grain; A. Arnold, 'A Fourteenth-Century Court Roll of the Manor of Ambree, Rochester', *Arch. Cant.* 29 (1911), 89–153.

43 Lewisham Local History Library, M/163 (a microfilm copy of the demesne accounts, 1332–36). Later sources also record that West Greenwich was an alternative name for Deptford, in particular the strand area. For example, a quitclaim of William Dallets, blacksmith of Deptford, notes that Deptford was 'alias West Greenwich'; MS Cambridgeshire County Records Office Huntingdon Thornhill Collection 148/2/755 (1586). Deptford Strand specifically was known otherwise as West Greenwich; MS London Metropolitan Archives LD O/581/001/1–2, 1654; an inquisition post mortem on Richard Guildford of the Guilford family of Kenardington was taken at Deptford alias West Greenwich; MS Surrey History Centre LM/1550, 22 October 1586.

44 Lawson, 'Maritime Kent', p. 91, n. 3, with reference to *VCH Kent* 2, p. 337.

45 MS Corporation of London Records Office Bridge House Estates CLA/007/EM/02/D/042.

46 G. Draper, 'Historical Report for the Pre-Construct Archaeology Excavation at the Former Stock and Cattle Market, Bank Street, Tonbridge, Kent', unpublished April 2006, pp. 25–7.

47 Dr Helen Clarke, pers. comm.

Greenwich. With regard to the development of the foreshore and quayside, by 1558 there were a big jetty, a wall with a ramp down to the foreshore, and an open area, possibly a landing and market area. These were in the centre of Greenwich adjacent to the houses and church. Combe, to the east of Greenwich, was a vill or manor and an early chapel of Greenwich. At the side of the Thames towards Combe was the manorial hall and guest house of the alien priory of St Peter's, which is known in 1396. This was 'the first house as one approached Greenwich by river from Flanders'. In fact, much of St Peter's 125 acres of demesne, as well as its tenant land, lay within the marshland on the Greenwich peninsula where the Thames looped northwards at Blackwall Reach.[48]

Against this background the maritime activity at Greenwich in the later Middle Ages can be examined. By 1328 Greenwich had become a significant port and was 'required to provide all its vessels of forty tons or more' to the king's seagoing defences.[49] The surname (by-name) seaman, seafarer, and schipman are found in Blackheath hundred, including Woolwich, Deptford, and Greenwich in 1334/5. These occupational by-names are concentrated in riverine and coastal parts of Kent and are not found as widely as others are (see below). In 1349 two Greenwich fishermen were accused of using nets with too small a mesh. In 1370 sixty acres of Lewisham Priory's (St Peter's) lands at Greenwich were submerged by the Thames, 'a frequent hazard before effective river walls and embankments were finally constructed'.[50] This was an ongoing problem. Between 1332 and 1336 the serjeant of the priory had organised the 'conserving and mending the wall of the marsh next to the Thames' at East Greenwich (Estgrenwich), receiving a payment in kind of sixteen quarters and one bushel of grain, undoubtedly from the agricultural lands of this estate. Such walls could effectively provide quaysides for the loading of vessels, and at this period the Lewisham/Greenwich estate provided wheat to London and delivered it there by boat (*navigium*). This may have been from a quay in the central rather than the marshland area of Greenwich. A major focus of the manorial economy at Lewisham in 1332–36 was corn and stock. Beans, oats, peas, and rye were sown as well as wheat presumably for local use rather than supply to London. Notably too, the Lewisham Priory estate produced large quantities of faggots of wood, most of which was undoubtedly also transported to London, as were 6150 baueyns (bundles of brushwood) made in Lewisham at Westwode at 4s 7d a thousand, total value 52s 2.5d, in 1335. Another hundred shillings' worth of 'faggots de Westwode' were also produced in 1335.[51] The baueyns may have had a specialised use in the construction of riverside walls.[52]

48 Egan, 'Greenwich', map 1, 235–7; Lewisham Local History Library, M/163.

49 Egan, 'Greenwich', 234.

50 Ibid., 237, 246.

51 In the demesne accounts there is also reference to the mill of Slagrave on this estate, perhaps a tide mill such as existed at Faversham; Lewisham Local History Library, M/163. Though earlier, there is also a reference to a similar mill at Dover; Morgan, *Domesday: Kent*, D, 10.

52 See O. Harris, 'Marshmen at Work: Dover Harbour, 1583', *Romney Marsh Irregular* 28 (2006), 15. Bavins, lighter than ordinary faggots, were required for 'arming' a wall defending the artificial harbour

As noted, part of St Peter's estate appears to have included Deptford (West Greenwich), a shipbuilding location. Shipbuilding would have required timber as would the quays, walls, and revetments along the side of the Thames. It can be envisaged that Westwood in Lewisham, like other woods in north-west Kent (see below) supplied timber as well as firewood. This use of wood from Westwood and transported to London via Greenwich was paralleled by tree felling in the valleys of Darent and Cray for London coopers at an 'early' period, and 'later, from the time of Henry VII, to build new and larger ships'.[53] People carrying out the trade of cooper or barrel-maker in Kent were found along the long navigable rivers of Kent and at New Romney in 1334/5.[54] The distribution pattern was quite distinctive, with the trade clustered between Deptford, Dartford, and Chevening to the west of the rivers Ravensbourne, Cray, and Darent; to the east of the Medway between Chatham and Loose; to the west of the Teise in the hundred of Brenchley; along the lower Rother in the hundred in which Smallhythe lay; and either side of the rivers Great and Little Stour and the Wantsum Channel.[55] Coopering is a specialised craft requiring carpentry skills and possibly for this reason was carried out where there were also carpenters building vessels too.[56] The barrels which coopers produced were used for the preservation of fish, for example, at New Romney.[57] Well-seasoned English oak was used for barrels in the late Middle Ages, and the Lord Mayor of London made an ordinance in 1488 against 'green and sappy' timber being used.[58]

In the early modern period there was a quay at Deptford as well as at East Greenwich, the nature and use of the quay probably reflecting earlier arrangements because Deptford Wharf was known as a 'Woodwarfe'. Its lessee leased this wharf and its appurtenances, including 'a messuage on its mouth end and three lighters and one corkboat for the carriage of wood and coals. He had free liberty of stowage in the parish of Deptford, Kent, and ingress, egress, and way and passage to stowage.' The lessor reserved 'all the timber rights and trees there growing'.[59] Another lease demonstrates the close links between the growing of timber, Deptford and East Greenwich. It concerned Barnsfield along the highway between Deptford Bridge and East Greenwich, with the timber reserved to Robert Walthew of East Greenwich, esquire.[60] These early modern leases replicate the

begun about 1500. An entry in the Pipe Rolls of 1353 indicates that bavins were loppings of oaks ('Talwode'); MS TNA PRO Pipe Roll 32 Edw.III m.36/1 dorso.

53 A. Brown, 'London and North-West Kent in the Later Middle Ages: The Development of a Land Market', *Arch. Cant.* 92 (1976), 145–6.

54 H. A. Hanley and C. W. Chalklin, 'The Kent Lay Subsidy Roll of 1334/5', in *Documents Illustrative of Medieval Kentish Society*, Kent Records 18, ed. F. R. H. Du Boulay (Ashford, 1964), pp. 71–172.

55 Shallow-draught river craft and coasting vessels of good burden were used on the lower Rother and Great Stour to distribute imported goods and carry Wealden cloth to the ports, T. L. Richardson, *Medieval Sandwich and its World* (Sandwich, 2004), pp. 59–61.

56 R. Filmer, *Kent Town Crafts* (Meresborough, 1982), pp. 7–11.

57 Draper and Meddens, *New Romney*, pp. 25–6.

58 K. Kilby, *Coopers and Coopering* (Princes Risborough, 2004), p. 22.

59 MS Cambridgeshire County Records Office Huntingdon Thornhill Collection 148/2/772 (1656).

60 MS Cambridgeshire County Records Office Huntingdon Thornhill Collection 148/2, 763.

close connections between West Greenwich and East Greenwich seen in Lewisham Priory's accounts of 1332–36. It is likely, therefore, that the lands recorded in the deeds and leases of 1575 to 1686 derive from the landholdings of Lewisham Priory, before the confiscation of its lands as an alien priory in 1413–15; and indeed that they also mirror the maritime economy and organisation of the earlier period.

Merchants and Places beyond Greenwich

From the mid-fourteenth century administrative officials from London and rich merchants, members of the very wealthy London guilds, bought property alongside the Thames and lower Medway at some distance from London, for example, in Borden, and near Chatham and Gillingham. Less wealthy ones bought at Woolwich, Greenwich, and Dartford. Notably, this buying-up of property increased greatly from about 1340 onwards.[61] These merchants would have needed transport by boat to London. A hythe or quay is known at Dartford in 1334/5, recorded in the name of William Puttenhethe. This may have been a quay near where pots were cast or thrown and/or transported.[62] Hithe street ran north from the market place in Dartford High Street.[63] It has to be envisaged again that the hythe or quay at Dartford functioned both for the transport of people and for the loading and unloading of goods. Tenants at Stone, to the north of Dartford, where the rivers Cray and Darent joined, 'had to keep in readiness a boat and a mariner to go on the lord's business wherever he sent them and this included London'.[64] The name of John le Ost at Dartford is notable in the context of merchants, suggesting that men there were 'hosting' alien merchants or carriers from Flanders as people did at New Romney and at other ports in the late fourteenth century. The connections between London and places along the rivers of north Kent are clear in the names of men such as John de London who was taxed in Dartford. The links between the members of the London merchant guilds and places such as Dartford and Greenwich lay in their involvement in the same areas of economic activity, above all the catching and selling of fish, the retailing of food, the leather trades, and shipbuilding. Crafts and trades associated with maritime activity, and particularly ship or boat building, are also evidenced at Dartford: ropemaking, barrel-making, tanning, and fishing, as well as petty retailing.[65]

61 Brown, 'London and North-West Kent', 150.

62 In Vill de Dertford; Hanley and Chalklin, *Lay Subsidy*, 142–3; 'Putten' meant throw, Middle English Dictionary, Michigan, http://ets.umdl.umich.edu/m/ med/.

63 P. Lee, *Nunneries, Learning and Spirituality in Late Medieval English Society: The Dominican Priory of Dartford* (York, 2001), p. 10.

64 Brown, 'London and North-West Kent', 148.

65 Brown 'London and North-West Kent', 150–1; Watergate [Street] is also recorded in a by-name at Dartford; Hanley and Chalklin, *Lay Subsidy*, 142–3; Draper and Meddens, *New Romney*, pp. 38–9.

Wood and Timber and the Building of Vessels

Brown noted the significance of wood production in north-west Kent in the late Middle Ages. This occurred very largely in places with access to river transport for the wood to the Thames via the Kent rivers, for instance, Sandling manor which lay in parishes on or close to the Cray.[66] Similarly, the existence of woods, mainly now lost, can be detected in place-names on the 1905–08 six-inch to one mile Ordnance Survey maps, for example 'Hydeswood' at Bromley on the Ravensbourne (see Mate, this volume). The production of wood may have been both to supply London with firewood and also shipbuilding along the Thames with timber. An important pointer to this is the use of the occupational by-name 'carpenter' in fourteenth-century sources. It is notable that New Romney's 'Table of Maletolts' (a customary trading tax) distinguished between carpenters of ships and those of houses.[67] In the period when Smallhythe was a shipbuilding location between the mid-fourteenth and mid-sixteenth centuries, the by-name carpenter referred to carpenters working on ships rather than houses.[68] The use of the term carpenter to refer to those working on vessels in fourteenth-century Kent is confirmed by the lay subsidy of 1334/5. Analysis of by-names in this subsidy demonstrates conclusively that the occupation 'carpenter' referred overwhelmingly to riverine or coastal areas of Kent and must therefore have applied to men primarily who were carpenters of ships rather than houses. Carpenters were found in the hundreds which included Deptford, Greenwich, Woolwich, Gravesend, Milton Regis, Ospringe, Faversham, and the Isle of Sheppey.[69] Carpenters were also found at Deal, and in the hundreds containing, or adjacent to, the towns of Dover, Hythe, New Romney, Folkestone, and Lydd, members of the Cinque Port confederation in south-east Kent. There were also carpenters in the hundreds containing the towns of Wye and Wingham on the Great and Little Stour rivers in east Kent, in the latter named in close association with a man surnamed coggere. This was a rare reference to people presumably named from the vessels known as cogs, coggers, or cogge-ships.[70] One other person surnamed coggere lived in the hundred of Hoo, and one in the Lydd/Dungeness area, where a cog apparently involved in wrecking and piracy is known in 1360.[71] Cogs were wide, spacious shallow-draught transport vessels with one sail which could also be rowed short distances. This early ship-type underwent significant development over the medieval period and could be used in military expeditions.[72] After the thirteenth

66 Brown, 'London and North-West Kent', 150–2.

67 This table was recorded in the *Register of Daniel Rough*, the mid- to late-fourteenth-century town clerk, but probably originates before the thirteenth century.

68 James, Draper and Martin, 'Smallhythe', pp. 29–30.

69 The prior of Christ Church Canterbury complained that 'royal shipbuilding at Woolwich and Erith competed with local needs for timber in north Kent', Mate, *Trade and Economic Developments*, p. 48 n. 2 citing *Letters and Papers, ... from the time of Henry VIII*, Addenda, pt 1, p. 10.

70 Hanley and Chalklin, *Lay Subsidy*, pp. 77, 86, 89, 90, 92, 95, 97, 100, 105, 112, 129, 137, 148, 149, 151, 152, 156, 157, 161, 164, 165, 167, 168.

71 *CPR 1358–61*, pp. 482–3, 516.

72 P. Ákersson, 'The Cog', http://www.abc.se/~pa/mar/cog.htm; Middle English Dictionary, Michigan.

century, quays and even cranes would have been needed to load and unload goods from cogs.[73] A reference occurs in the mid fifteenth century to such a quay and crane at Cliffe on the Thames, to the north-east of Gravesend, and opposite Tilbury.[74]

Other maritime occupational surnames are similarly associated with hundreds bordering the river estuaries. Nine men with the by-name Seaman or Seman were listed in the lay subsidy.[75] They were all taxed in towns, hundreds, or bailiwicks in north Kent from London eastwards along the Thames side or the Swale and Medway estuaries. They lived on the Isle of Thanet, in the bailiwick of Key in Milton Regis, or in the hundreds of Blackheath, Little, and Teynham. Blackheath hundred included Woolwich, Deptford, and Greenwich. Adjacent Little hundred was bounded to the north by the Thames and to the east by the River Cray and Dartford; it included Lesnes, Plumstead, Erith, and Crayford. Teynham hundred was immediately west of Faversham, and at Teynham itself a river creek, Conyers Creek, joined the Swale, across which lay the Isle of Sheppey.[76] There were seamen living in towns such as Rochester and Faversham. At Rochester, Roger Seman lived in the part of the city outside the walls: an area next to the River Medway.[77] Moreover, if the listing of the people paying the lay subsidy in this year was partly organised on a topographical basis within the towns, hundreds, and bailiwicks, it points to the physical proximity in the mid-fourteenth century of seamen and those involved in trades linked to maritime activities. Roger Seman, for example, was listed near Clement le Chaundeler, chandlers being involved in the supply of wax including for waterproofing vessels, and Roger de Southwyk' (Southwark), a shipbuilding location.[78]

In addition to those named as seaman or seafarer, four schipmen or shipmen are found in Faversham, Hythe, and the hundred of Shamwell which comprised Cliffe at Hoo and the west bank of the lower Medway including Strood.[79] As a member of the Cinque Ports confederation, Faversham (on Faversham Creek) supplied a ship of no more than forty tuns towards the ship service of Dover.

73 O. Crumlin-Pedersen, 'The Vikings and the Hanseatic Merchants: 900–1450', in *A History of Seafaring, based on Underwater Archaeology*, ed. G. Bass (London, 1972), p. 190.

74 MS CCAL DCc Bedels' rolls Cliffe 91, c. 1425–75.

75 Hanley and Chalklin, *Lay Subsidy*, pp. 72, 73, 75, 97, 99, 105, 130, 137, 139, 164. A family surnamed Seman were among the wealthy and influential shippers and ship owners at New Winchelsea, the new royal port in East Sussex, involved in 'fishing, overseas trade and naval service'; D. Sylvester, 'Shaping the Urban Landscape of Maritime England: The Interests of the King and Barons in the 1292 Founding of New Winchelsea', in *Maritime Topography and the Medieval Town*, Studies in Archaeology and History 4, ed. J. Bill and B. Clausen (Copenhagen 1999), p. 157.

76 One Emma Sefare (Seafarer) was taxed in the hundred of Larkfield which included the River Medway below Rochester, Hanley and Chalklin, *Lay Subsidy*, p. 115.

77 See the map of John Speed, 'Theatres of the empire of Great Britaine: presenting an exact geography of the Kingdomes of England, Scotland, Ireland and the Iles ajionyng: divided and described by John Speed' (London, 1627), first published in 1611, and based on a rather earlier survey.

78 Clement le Chaundeler was listed as having taxable property in the areas of Rochester both within and outside the city walls, Hanley and Chalklin, *Lay Subsidy*, pp. 130, 160.

79 Hanley and Chalklin, *Lay Subsidy*, pp. 99, 131, 153. There was also a Schyppere on Thanet; ibid., p. 72.

Ships of between sixty and a hundred tuns were demanded from the Cinque Ports in 1588, but Faversham agreed only to provide a vessel, or the cost, of one of forty tuns.[80] The small size of vessels which members of the Cinque Ports were willing or able to build or fund meant that they were largely irrelevant to the sixteenth-century navy.[81]

In the fifteenth century the association of carpenters and shipmen with coastal parishes is also indicated by a bond of 1474 between Christ Church Priory and John Whytton of West Cliffe parish, Kent, carpenter, Simon Palmer, shipman, and Robert Harneys, shipman, both of St Margaret's at Cliffe parish, which lay north of Dover.[82] Similarly in the mid-fifteenth century, Thomas Smyth, a shipman, resided at Dover and also at Calais, where he was a 'wolleporter', a role connected with regulation of the wool market.[83]

Simon (or Seman) Carpenter of Southwark had two leases, dated 1394 and 1406, of all the oaks in Christ Church Priory's woodland at Knockholt on the North Downs.[84] The River Ravensbourne would have provided transport for timber from close to Knockholt to the Thames and thus to Southwark. The connections between Southwark, Rochester, Chatham, and Gillingham are pointed up by the 1334/5 lay subsidy.[85] At Southwark archaeological evidence for boatbuilding on the waterfront exists in the later medieval centuries.[86] The master of the hospital of the Blessed Thomas, Southwark, and Saint Mary's Priory, Southwark, paid two very large sums in the lay subsidy in Blackheath hundred.[87] St Mary's was the riverside priory, now Southwark Cathedral, which was situated across the Thames from the Vintry and Queenhithe, London. There was a river stair at St Mary's, an important embarkation point in the fifteenth century.[88] The large sums which the hospital and the priory paid in Blackheath hundred indicates that they held property in the part of Kent between Deptford and Woolwich along

80 Vessels of a minimum size of forty tuns had been required by the king much earlier from the Cinque Ports and other English ports, for example for the voyage to Gascony which Edward I made in 1296/7; MS TNA PRO C 47/2/63/1; C 47/2/16/9; C 47/2/10/17.

81 F. F. Giraud, 'Cinque Ports. Notes from minute books of the corporation of Faversham', *Arch. Cant.* 28 (1909), 28–74.

82 MS CCAL DCc Chart. Ant. M/267/2.

83 R. Virgoe, 'Some Ancient Indictments in the King's Bench', in *Documents Illustrative of Medieval Kentish Society*, Kent Records 18, ed. F. R. H. Du Boulay (Ashford, 1964), p. 248.

84 In one of the leases Simon was also granted all the wood and underwood. Certain reservations were placed on the largest oaks, which were marked with Carpenter's agreement, possibly with the intention that he or someone else would be paying specially for those; MS CCAL DCc Chart. Ant. O/119, O/120.

85 Roger de Suthewyk' and Mar' de Suthewyk' (Southwark) are listed in Chatham and Gillingham hundred, and Roger also at Rochester, Hanley and Chalklin, *Lay Subsidy*, pp. 128, 130.

86 G. Milne, *The Port of Medieval London* (Stroud, 2003), p. 170. A. K. McHardy, ed., 'Ecclesiastical Property in the City of London, 1392: Queenhithe Ward', in *The Church in London 1375–1392*, London Record Society (London, 1977), pp. 52–3. URL: http://www.british-history.ac.uk/report.asp?compid=36027 (accessed 2 February 2006).

87 Hanley and Chalklin, *Lay Subsidy*, pp. 136, 137.

88 The Vintry was the 'Anglo-Norman wine-importing quarter'. Queenhithe had a series of clay and timber revetments from the late ninth century; later timber-faced revetments incorporated reused ship timbers and a 'long sequence of later waterfront activity'. Masonry waterfront warehousing was first introduced in these places in the twelfth century; Milne, *Medieval London*, pp. 17, 23, 75–7, 85–6.

the Thames, and in the wooded land to the south including the Lewisham area. They were probably involved in similar economic activity to that of Lewisham Priory, including the transport and supply of foodstuffs, wood, and timber to London.

The strong evidence of maritime activity in the part of Kent near London in the mid-fourteenth-century lay subsidy continues in the fifteenth century and beyond in testamentary material. For example, between 1438 and 1560 Dartford wills include those of carpenters, smiths, shipmen and a waterman, fishmongers, tanners, and chandlers. At nearby Erith there were mariners and shipwrights, and a large number of boat and barge-owners in Gravesend.[89]

Maritime Activity in the Remote Marshlands of Kent Bordering the Thames and Lower Medway

This section reviews maritime activity and the supply of wood for vessel building in places more distant from London, including Milton hundred to the south-west of the Isle of Sheppey, Cliffe at Hoo, and also the Chatham area. Milton hundred was bordered by the Swale to the north and east. Close to this channel the hundred contained the settlements of Iwade, Barksore, Upchurch, and Lower Halstow.[90] This locality was remote marshland deeply penetrated by small creeks. The marshland was protected in places throughout the high and later Middle Ages by walls which often had to be renewed. For example, in 1434 a wall had to be built, or repaired, at Barksore which was thirty-nine rods long, only one foot high but five feet wide, with a foreland seven feet wide and a hedge on each side. Economic activity in this locality was based on fishing including shellfish. Rents for land here were paid in the fourteenth century in lambs, cheeses, and iron hoops, perhaps for barrels for fish. Small boats would have been needed here which were able to use the creeks and the Swale, including ferrying across to Sheppey. Archaeological and historical evidence indicate that settlement here began or was renewed between the mid-twelfth and mid-thirteenth centuries, and that connections with Sheppey by land route and boat were important.[91] Finds of coins, buckles, and a silver button may suggest a temporary importance of the route from Iwade to Sheppey in the high and later Middle Ages. These high-quality items were found in a medieval holloway at Iwade leading to Sheppey, presumably dropped by travellers. The holloway was 'possibly part of the route linking the mainland with the Isle of Sheppey'. Medieval Sheppey had high-status associations including the Minster church rebuilt in the thirteenth

89 Lee, *Dartford*, pp. 11–12.

90 Iwade was a 'street' settlement of the type found in coastal and riverine areas of Kent, like Seasalter, Chestfield, Smallhythe, and Redyng.

91 B. Bishop and M. Bagwell, *Iwade: Occupation of a North Kent Village from the Mesolithic to the Medieval Period*, Pre-Construct Archaeology monograph 3 (London, 2005), p. 104; MS CCAL DCc Barksore Bedels' rolls; DCc Chart. Ant. B/335, B/336, B/337, B/412; DCc MSSB/A/80.

century and Queenborough Castle built in the fourteenth. Between the thirteenth and the late fourteenth or early fifteenth century there may have been a relatively important moated dwelling near this holloway at Iwade which was subsequently abandoned.[92]

It is possible that the marshes to the north of Iwade (Chetney Marsh) had some woodland when medieval settlement began there, evidenced in the place-name element *ced* which is said to be 'Celtic' for wood.[93] However, charter evidence suggests that by the mid-thirteenth century wood for boat building may have come from Hollingbourne on the North Downs approximately nine miles to the south-west of Iwade, that is in parallel to the supplying of wood from the Downs for the building of vessels in places such as Greenwich, Deptford, and Southwark.[94] Hollingbourne was linked to Iwade by a route passing, near Watling Street, through Keystreet (that is the street leading to the quay) wood, Keystreet Hill woods and various other small woods where timber may also have been obtained.[95] Iwade was, of course, a small settlement in contrast to those near London. Even though this route may have been well used while Queenborough on Sheppey was flourishing, the basis of Iwade's economy was seasonal grazing on the marshes to the north and the exploitation of fish, wild fowl, and shell fish, particularly oysters. The creeks which penetrated the salt and fresh marshes allowed this exploitation, requiring the use of small boats, with timber obtained as suggested.[96]

The other two places with the 'wood' place-name element *ced* in Kent, like Chetney Marsh near Iwade, are Chattenden and Chatham. Chattenden lay three miles to the south of Cliffe at Hoo, which itself had access to the Thames through the marshes via Cliffe creek. Cliffe was a very ancient place, the location of Great Councils in the eight and ninth centuries. It was a manor of Christ Church Priory, was known as a 'town', and gave access from the Thames to nearby Higham Priory and Cooling Castle. Cliffe had 'port' facilities until 1520 when a fire destroyed them and as such is likely to have been a place where vessels were built, demanding timber. Chattenden was a small remote settlement, the element *den* in its name indicating woodland pasture. Chattenden was surrounded by other areas of woodland: Timberwood, Rathey Hill Wood, Bury Court Wood, Lodge Hill

92 Bishop and Bagwell, *Iwade*, pp. 101–4.

93 Bishop and Bagwell, *Iwade*, p. 7. The marshlands of Kent were not bereft of trees in this period. Romney Marsh had adequate resources of wood and timber, including oaks, at least to construct and maintain its very extensive sea-defence and reclamation walls between the twelfth and late fifteenth centuries. Carts and boats were hired to transport timber across the marsh for this purpose. Nevertheless, by the early sixteenth century there was an acute shortage of timber on Romney Marsh; A. Reeves, 'The Testimony of Trees', *Romney Marsh Irregular* 24 (2004), 21–2; Barber and Priestly-Bell, *Coastal Wetland*, pp. 20–1.

94 Two of the witnesses of this mid-thirteenth-century charter were Roger de ywede (Iwade) and Simon cockel (cockle). The charter records the grant by a local man to Christ Church Priory of eight acres of wood in two parcels lying in the priory's wood called snocherst in the vill of Hollingbourne with all the grantor's rights in the paths leading to the woods, MS CCAL DCc Chart. Ant. H/16.

95 Hull, *Kent*, map 12. Peter atte Kayestreete is listed; Hanley and Chalklin, *Lay Subsidy*, p. 132.

96 Bishop and Bagwell, *Iwade*, p. 95.

Wood, Cart Wood, and Cliffe Wood, known as an old wood. Their location is shown as still wooded on the earliest Ordnance Survey map (1801).[97] The names of the woods, particularly Cliffe Wood, suggest that it was here that timber was obtained for building the small vessels which were required locally.

Similar evidence indicates that the vessel building near medieval Chatham suggested by the lay subsidy was supplied with timber and wood from the North Downs, although the place-name element *ced* may suggest that Chatham, itself, was a wooded area at an early period. From the earliest Ordnance Survey map, surveyed in the 1790s, it can seen that routes ran north and north-west to the lower Medway estuary at Chatham from extensive areas of woodland near the crest of the North Downs, some in monastic hands. These woodlands included Monk Wood, Bridge Wood, Tunbury Wood, Malling Wood, Great and Little Cowbeck Woods, Shawsted Wood, Parke Wood, King's Frith Wood, Limb's Frith Wood, and Lord's Wood. It included too Boxley (Abbey) Wood, also known as Monkdown Wood, on the edge of which Boxley grange was located.[98] The names of several of these woods demonstrate their medieval existence.

Smallhythe

The 'port' at Smallhythe was an area of shipbuilding, ship repair and ship breaking on the former northern Rother course around the Isle of Oxney, interpreted as such on the basis of findings of hammerscale, iron rove nails, spikes, and rivets, and part of a small ship's timber.[99] These probably dated to the fourteenth century.[100] Smallhythe existed as a settlement by the mid-thirteenth century, but maritime activity is known to have taken place there from the early fourteenth century on 'the common foreland' or Foreland Marsh. This is an important piece of land immediately to the south and east of the large timber-framed house, Smallhythe Place. Just to the south of the area of medieval shipbuilding and metal-working was a wharf associated with a family of shipmen.[101]

A major factor in the subsequent rise of Smallhythe, evidenced in the Patent and Close Rolls from 1326 onwards, was the diversion of the main course of the Rother round the north of Oxney after the Knelle Dam was constructed to the west of the isle in c. 1330. From the 1330s the main channel of the Rother flowed around the north side of the Isle of Oxney. It passed, from west to east, south of Tenterden at Smallhythe, Redyng (Street), Ebony, and Stone on its way towards

97 Hull, *Kent*, maps 4 and 5; http://hoo-peninsula.biography.ms/ (accessed 1 April 2005).

98 Hull, *Kent*, p. 8, map 11 and modern OS map on opposite page.

99 T. Taylor, T. and M. Aston, *Time Team 99: The Site Reports* (London, 1999), p. 41; Bellamy and Milne, 'Small Hythe', 367, 375–6.

100 H. Clarke, 'Early Harbours along the Rother', *Romney Marsh Irregular* 16 (2000), 12.

101 For this and what follows, see James, Draper and Martin, 'Smallhythe', and especially pp. 8–9, 56–7. Dr Helen Clarke and the Small Ports Project of the Romney Marsh Research Trust contributed important information.

Appledore. It then turned south, down the west side of Walland Marsh via the Appledore Channel, and out to sea near Rye, Sussex. During the later medieval period shipbuilding, ship breaking and repair in the Smallhythe area did not take place in large, fixed localities but where ships could be built or repaired on a protected waterline, and the ships subsequently launched into the water down a slipway. Any remains on the ground may be nothing more than slight depressions of a size and shape to accommodate boats and ships under construction. There would also have been landing stages with at least two functions. One was as a boarding point for ferries across the Rother. The other was for offloading goods such as the ones known to have been sold at Smallhythe in the sixteenth century, and also sold farther afield, particularly in Tenterden town centre. These hythes would have been lightweight constructions of wood.

Roberts noted that timber came from the Weald for shipbuilding in the early fifteenth century (c. 1430).[102] However, the role of Smallhythe men, and of Christ Church Priory as landowner in growing and using timber, can be more closely identified and at an earlier date. By the late fourteenth century, and probably from much earlier, the brushwood and timber of the dens local to Tenterden and Smallhythe was being systematically exploited.[103] Local tenants had the rights to the brushwood; the feudal lords, often ecclesiastical houses, had the rights to the timber. In the 1380s and 1390s Christ Church Priory recorded several new leases of its dens around Tenterden. The leases noted that the timber rights of the priory had been invaded by recent tenants and the new leases asserted the priory's rights to the timber. It is likely that the growth of shipbuilding at Smallhythe since the 1330s had increased the demand for timber and its felling by local people.[104] The leases confirm the rights of the tenants to brushwood, and it is notable that this commodity is recorded as being loaded onto a ship at Smallhythe for provisioning London.[105]

The priory leases describe groups of local men leasing the various dens of the priory around Tenterden. It appears that these groups of men had strong connections with each other and with a specific den; one group, specified as being of Smallhythe, had the lease of one particular den, Hockenden. The other dens were leased by men described as of Tenterden. These documents include important early references, from 1338 onwards, to families known to have been involved in the maritime economy of Smallhythe in the fifteenth century, such as Gilbert de Brickenden, the Haymes, and the Blossom families (see Lutton, this volume).

The requirement that members of the Cinque Ports confederation, including

102 H. Roberts, *Tenterden: The First Thousand Years* (York, 1995), p. 50.

103 The growing use of timber and underwood in the eastern Weald with access to river transport can be traced back at least to the twelfth century; K. Witney, ed., *The Survey of Archbishop Pecham's Manors, 1283–5*, Kent Records 28 (Maidstone, 2000), p. xxxiii.

104 Some of the leases are dated 1381 and the possible relationship of these new leases to the Peasants' Revolt should be borne in mind; MS CCAL DCc Chart. Ant. I/115, I/124, I/126, B/280, B/281, C/392.

105 Roberts, *Tenterden*, p. 49. It can be noted that in 1364 a London merchant and ship owner had £74 and goods stolen from a ship at Smallhythe; *CPR 1364–67*, p. 73.

Tenterden from 1449, provide boats and ships for royal transport and defence provided a reason for them to be built locally at Smallhythe. As the royal requirement for naval ships commissioned directly by the king from the fifteenth century increased, Smallhythe continued to be a good location for their construction since it was close to their point of use in the Channel. The primary materials for shipbuilding were timber and iron and these could easily be obtained close to Smallhythe and brought there by river, road, or track. Timber and board were prepared at Smallhythe for shipbuilding at Greenwich in c. 1430, and transported by sea from Smallhythe to Greenwich.[106] In 1512 timber was felled in the Weald, prepared in the Smallhythe shipyards and taken by sea to Greenwich for the building of the great ship *Henri Grace à Dieu*. This is presented, no doubt correctly, as part of the decline of Smallhythe as a shipyard in the later fifteenth century, partly because of silting of the Rother.

Much of the iron used at Smallhythe would have come from the small medieval iron industry in the Weald of Kent and Sussex.[107] However, at busy times in the shipyard, this was supplemented by other sources. In 1390 iron was brought from London to Smallhythe via Calais. The re-use of material was a feature of the medieval iron industry and in 1512 old anchors were shipped from Plymouth to Smallhythe where they were remade. However, in the late fifteenth century Smallhythe, as the archaeological evidence also demonstrates, did process iron. Nails and other iron objects were bought by Mote Manor in Iden, Sussex, from a manufactory at Smallhythe.

Supplies of Iron for Medieval Shipbuilding in Kent

The names of two men are significant in understanding iron supplies from the Weald for shipbuilding, both along the Thames and at Smallhythe. The first is John Maghfeld (Mayfield, Sussex) who was taxed alongside shipmen, a seaman and smiths at Faversham in 1334/35.[108] The second is Gilbert Maghfeld, a successful ironmonger and London merchant, who imported grain, cloth, wine, fur, spices, and dyes, including Lombardy woad, in the late fourteenth century.[109] It is clear that men who originated from Mayfield were involved with the supply

106 Roberts, *Tenterden*, p. 50.

107 It 1544, when the iron industry of the Weald was much more extensive, iron from the Weald was delivered to Smallhythe from Bodiam by lighters. The information in this paragraph was provided by Dr Helen Clarke.

108 John Maghfeld appears among the Liberty of the Cinque Ports at Faversham, as do the shipmen and the seaman; Hanley and Chalklin, *Lay Subsidy*, pp. 97–100. The smiths appear also in the other part of the listing for the hundred of Faversham: 'The Parish of Mayfield otherwise Maghfield'; MS East Sussex Record Office QDP/50/1.

109 Thomas Croft/Craft was a 'London merchant' on the 'staff' of Gilbert Maghfeld; Milne, *Medieval London*, pp. 133–4. A man of this name (perhaps Thomas Croft, junior?) appears as the last witness to a deed of 1454 concerning the transfer of a tenement and lands in Maghfeld to John Reed of Hastings; MS East Sussex Record Office SAS-DB/14B.

of iron and/or had connections with those working iron for shipbuilding. Men from Mayfield had links too with Tonbridge, a centre of iron-making and metal-working in fourteenth-century Kent.[110]

Mayfield together with Rotherfield (Sussex) were centres of the Wealden iron industry.[111] The Wealden iron industry is known by 1277 and again in 1300, and probably there were smiths and forges in both the Kent and Sussex Weald. Iron was made at Tudeley and worked at forges there or nearby, perhaps by and certainly in Edward III's reign. Tudeley forge is known to have been active until 1363, and was then disrupted by the Black Death and subsequent plague outbreaks.[112] Recent archaeological excavation demonstrates that iron-making and metalworking took place in the area outside Tonbridge Castle gates, near the medieval market place and at a site along East Street, Tonbridge.[113] Iron was made at Tonbridge Castle and its forge in 1323–35, including the production of seven thousand iron nails and seven thousand iron clenches for shipbuilding made there in 1325, and sent to Porchester, Hampshire, presumably via the Medway. Furthermore, the Tonbridge forge at this time was quite a substantial operation with the many tools, listed in a castle inventory, including a branding iron for the king's cattle and other tools indicating that the forge was mainly used for farriery.[114] This is confirmed for the period 1334/5 by the occupational names Ferour and Neylere in the lay subsidy.[115] The evidence of the bailiffs' and rent collectors' accounts of Tonbridge Castle in 1384/5 and 1403/5 demonstrate that there were two workshops outside the castle barbican associated with ferours (farriers and blacksmiths). These two workshops were merged into one unit and were vacant for lack of a tenant in this period.[116] This may well reflect the ongoing economic and human damage to Tonbridge's iron industry caused by plague, with iron-making in the High Wealden centres taking over by the end of the fifteenth century. The blast furnace and finery forge appear to have been brought to the central High Weald by French ironworkers after 1496.[117] The early decades of the sixteenth century saw an increase 'in the number of furnaces and forges associated with the Wealden iron industry' in north-east Sussex and in Kent, rather than the commencement of that industry.[118]

110 Draper, 'Tonbridge', pp. 23–4.

111 D. Crossley, 'Iron and Glass Industries', and M. Howard, 'Tudor and Stuart Great Houses', in *An Historical Atlas of Sussex*, ed. K. Leslie and B. Short (Chichester, 1999), pp. 55, 63.

112 *VCH Kent* 3, pp. 384–5.

113 S. Holden, 'An Archaeological Assessment of Land at Tonbridge Stock and Cattle Market', Pre-Construct Archaeology Ltd, unpublished December 2005; E. Wragg, C. Jarrett and J. Haslam, 'The Development of Medieval Tonbridge Reviewed in the Light of Recent Excavations at Lyons, East Street', *Arch. Cant.* 125 (2005), 119–50.

114 *VCH Kent* 3, p. 386.

115 Hanley and Chalklin, *Lay Subsidy*, p. 116.

116 MS CCAL FX 21, 2, 2v; FX 23; FX 25.

117 Crossley, 'Iron and Glass Industries', pp. 62–3.

118 R. Spain, 'Medieval Watermills', in *An Historical Atlas of Kent*, ed. T. Lawson and D. Killingray (Chichester, 2004), p. 62.

Conclusions

Nautical activity along the coast and rivers of medieval Kent has recently begun to receive attention from archaeologists and it is time for historians to respond by exploring the documentary sources. This chapter has attempted a short review of the maritime economy and in particular the supply of natural resources. The latter must be understood in terms of the size of vessels and the ways in which they were used in the Middle Ages. Overall, it is clear that the widespread use of boats and small ships around Kent prompted the local building and repair of vessels, although notably the Tonbridge iron-making industry also supplied ship nails beyond Kent. It is an important point that the naval dockyards which were significantly developed in early modern Kent at Deptford, Woolwich, and Chatham had medieval precursors. The later Middle Ages was the period in which the ship service of the Cinque Ports decreased in significance to the monarch. The size of vessels which could be built or based in the Cinque Ports was crucial. Their service, embedded in a feudal system of mutual dependence between Ports and king, was replaced by a more pragmatic system of supplying vessels from maritime trading places along the Medway; New Hythe, Snodland, and Maidstone being particularly important. Such places could not, however, supply vessels of sufficient size for the royal navy, and ships built at Smallhythe helped fulfil this need in the fifteenth century.

Although the focus of this book is Kent, this chapter has noted that the maritime economy of the county must be understood in terms of the riverine and human connections with London (see Mate, this volume). The human connections were formed by both individuals and ecclesiastical institutions. Monastic houses of different kinds were crucial in exploiting their landholdings in Kent to benefit from growing trade and demand from London. These houses, as well as individuals such as Simon Carpenter of Southwark who leased their lands, were notable in managing woodland to supply timber and wood for shipbuilding and repair. This chapter has demonstrated that, as well as the exploitation of Wealden timber, the woodlands of the North Downs were utilised for boat and shipbuilding along the north Kent estuaries and at London in the late Middle Ages. Relatively small quantities of iron were required and some were provided by re-using material or bringing it in from places beyond Kent. Nevertheless, it is clear that the iron industry of the Sussex and Kent Weald played a significant part in supply, with individuals such as the Mayfields drawing on local resources to facilitate their wider enterprises.

5

The Religious Houses of Kent, 1220–1540

BARRIE DOBSON AND ELIZABETH EDWARDS

Between the foundation of St Augustine's Abbey by Augustine himself in 598 and the surrender of the even greater Benedictine monastery of Canterbury Cathedral to Henry VIII in 1540, the county of Kent, like western Christendom at large, witnessed the most remarkable and sustained attempt ever made to reject the things of this world for those of the next. As in the case of all mass idealistic movements, it need occasion no particular surprise that medieval Christian monasticism often failed to attain its objectives and that by its very nature it proves highly resistant to conventional historical analysis and explanation. Nevertheless, in retrospect it seems hard to deny that the years around 1220, the date at which this cursory survey of the religious houses of late medieval Kent begins, marked a genuine turning point in their history.

Most of the religious foundations in Kent were already established by the beginning of the thirteenth century, the majority as a result of the nationwide expansion in the twelfth century, although Kent had proved completely resistant to the intoxicating enthusiasm for the Cistercian order which swept northern England and Wales during the anarchy of Stephen's reign, with the solitary exception of Boxley Abbey two miles north of Maidstone.

Apart from the pre-Norman foundations under the aegis of Ethelbert, principally those at Canterbury and Rochester, and several smaller houses which were re-dedicated in the twelfth century, the earliest Norman foundations were the Benedictine nunneries of St Mary at Malling in the 1090s and St Sepulchre in Canterbury in 1100.[1] Thereafter the rapid twelfth-century growth in the number of religious houses established the monastic landscape for the next three hundred years, give or take a few short-lived experiments. Thus, before the arrival of mendicant friars, grey, black and Austin, in Canterbury from the 1220s, and the establishment of the Carmelite friaries at Aylesford (1240–41), Lossenham (1242), and Sandwich (1272), the dominant rule in the monastic houses of Kent

1 For example, St Sexburga's, at Minster in Sheppey, originally founded c. 670, was in effect re-established in 1130 as a Benedictine nunnery dedicated to St Mary and St Sexburga.

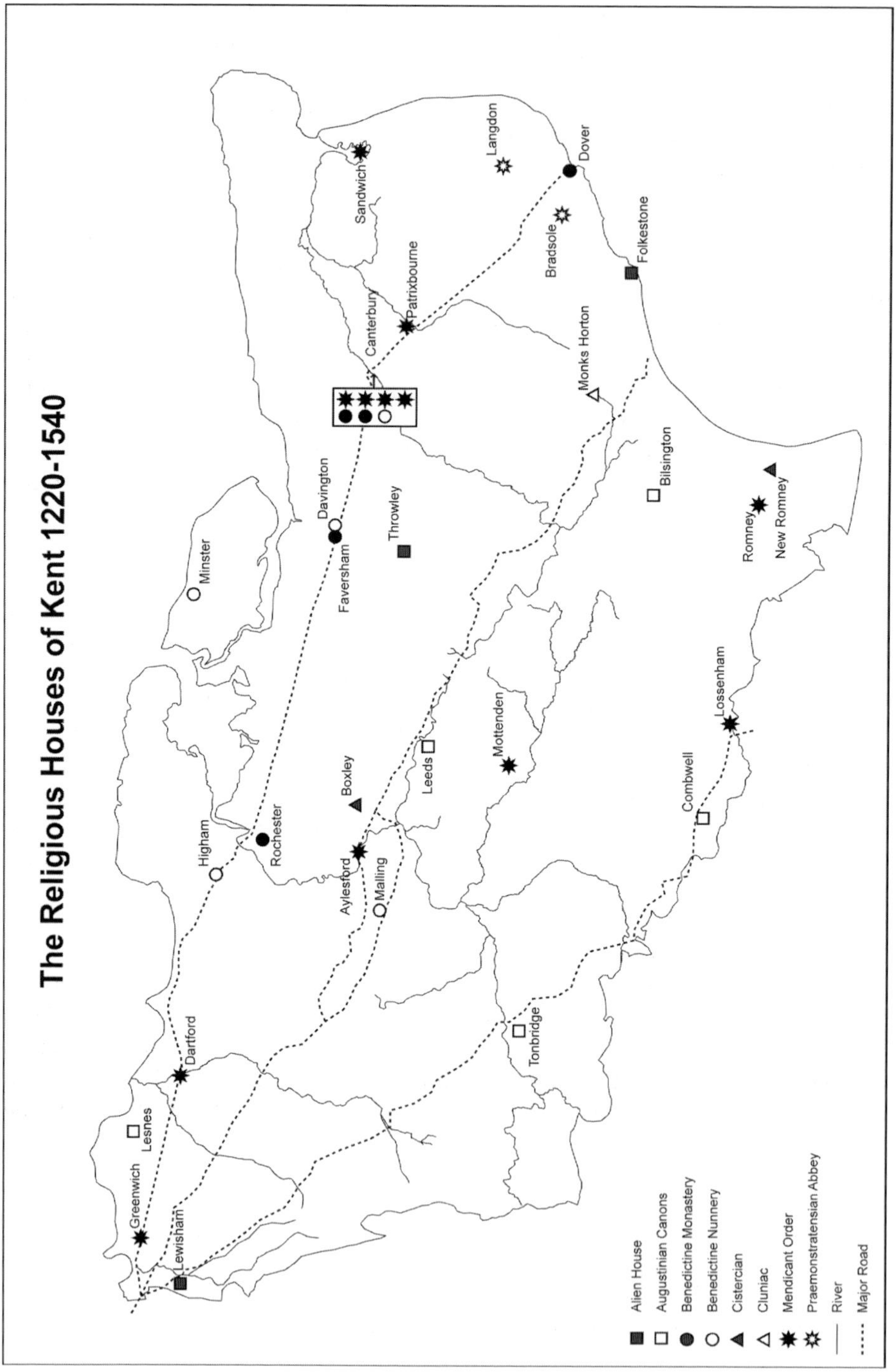

The Religious Houses of Kent 1220-1540

was Benedictine, and these remained the wealthiest foundations until the Dissolution. There was also a significant number of Augustinian houses of regular canons and nuns.[2]

Pope Honorius III in 1219 informed Archbishop Stephen Langton that 'the happy church of Canterbury can sing a new song to the Lord' on the grounds that it had now been 'made beautiful by the precious blood of the martyr Thomas and is visited by multitudes of people who come there from every nation under heaven'.[3] On Tuesday 7 July in the following year the fifty-year-old mortal remains of Thomas Becket were at last translated from the sombre cathedral crypt to their spectacular new resting place in the chapel of the Holy Trinity (see Plate 4). Among those reported to have attended what was perhaps the grandest state occasion of its sort in the entire course of medieval English history were not only Archbishop Langton and the young Henry III but also numerous lay magnates, almost the whole of the English episcopal bench and nearly every abbot in England.[4] Although not at all a monk himself, Becket's martyrdom could soon be presented as a victory for English monasticism in general and for Canterbury Cathedral in particular.

Thus was inaugurated not only the most lavishly adorned and legendary shrine in the country, but also the Jubilee of St Thomas, thereafter held at Canterbury every half-century until 1470. The translation of Becket's relics undoubtedly did more than any event since his assassination fifty years earlier to enhance the astonishing popularity of his cult and the unchallengeable primacy of his cathedral as 'the chief of all the churches of England'.[5] On the other hand, the increased fame and prosperity of the monks of Christ Church Canterbury, as custodians of the shrine of St Thomas, were not to be shared by the religious orders of Kent as a whole. By the 1220s many of the latter were no longer lords of the ascendant at all. Of the twenty-six regularly constituted houses of monks, regular canons or nuns in late medieval Kent, only two were created after 1220: a mysterious little Cistercian dependency of Pontigny at New Romney from 1264 to c. 1439 and an isolated priory for seven Augustinian canons founded at Bilsington six miles south of Ashford in 1253.

Much more significant for the future of the religious life in the county, within a few months of the translation of Becket's relics a small group of Dominican friars passed through Canterbury on their way to establish the first of all English mendicant convents at Oxford. Under the impact of mendicant ideology, that last remarkable Italianate invasion of English religious and cultural life before the

2 Dom D. Knowles, *The Religious Orders in England: The End of the Middle Ages*, 2 vols (Cambridge, repr. 1961), 2, p. 361. Knowles saw a growing lack of a clear distinction between orders by the fifteenth century, partly because of changes within their houses, but also because they were joining together against common enemies, although the gulf between monks/canons and friars remained.

3 B. Dobson, 'The Monks of Canterbury in the Later Middle Ages', in *A History of Canterbury Cathedral*, ed. P. Collinson, N. Ramsay and M. Sparks (Oxford, 1995), p. 135.

4 Dobson, 'The Monks of Canterbury', p. 69.

5 Ibid., p. 68.

Renaissance, the pursuit of spiritual perfection in Kent was to take an entirely unanticipated turn. Moreover, by 1300 there were also clear signs that the traditional patterns of Kentish monasticism were being compelled to adjust to the changed religious priorities of the laity, priorities which most often found institutional expression in the form of private chantries and secular chantry colleges. In south-east England, as elsewhere, it was not the shortcomings of the monks and nuns themselves but rather the gradual transformation of religious attitudes outside the cloisters which eventually contributed to the complete and humiliating collapse of the greatest of all monastic experiments.

Fundamentally, the history of the religious houses of late medieval Kent was in many ways similar to monastic fortunes in other regions of the English realm. Admittedly, the monastic map of the county does reveal some uncommon and distinctive features. The fact that Kent was the only county in the kingdom with two episcopal sees and two cathedrals, both served by communities of Benedictine monks, was inevitably the occasion for intense if periodic jurisdictional conflicts between the churches of Canterbury and Rochester.[6] However, as nearly thirty miles separated the two cathedrals and as, especially after 1220, the former so unquestionably surpassed the latter in wealth and prestige, such conflict could usually be contained. A more dangerous source of tension was the propinquity at Canterbury itself of two of the greatest and most self-regarding monasteries of medieval England, the communities of Christ Church, Canterbury, and of St Augustine's Abbey. There too however, a more or less effective, if never fully amicable, *modus vivendi* was gradually achieved between the two chapters. Apart from the three monastic colossi of St Augustine's Abbey and the cathedrals of Canterbury and Rochester, there were fewer major Black monk houses in Kent than the size and agricultural wealth of the county might have led one to expect. For reasons not altogether easy to understand, no significant new religious foundation had been made in Kent during the so-called tenth-century 'monastic reform movement'. The country was still something of a monastic *tabula rasa* as late as 1148, when King Stephen and Queen Matilda founded, and were later buried in, the county's fourth largest Benedictine house, the abbey of St Saviour at Faversham.

By contrast, there was no shortage within the dioceses of Canterbury and Rochester of patrons and benefactors willing to found or endow convents of the less prestigious, and less expensive, religious orders of the twelfth century. In addition to four small and badly documented alien priories, of which Folkestone Priory was always the most considerable, between 1119 and 1193 Kent followed a national trend by acquiring five houses of Augustinian and two of Praemonstratensian canons.[7] Only the Augustinian priory at Leeds and the

6 Only eight English cathedrals were also monastic foundations, seven Benedictine including the two in Kent, and one Augustinian (Carlisle).

7 Alien priories: Folkestone, Lewisham, Patrixbourne and Throwley. Augustinian: Combwell, Leeds, Lesnes, Tonbridge, St Gregory's, Canterbury. Praemonstratensian: St Radegand's Abbey, Bradsole and Langdon Abbey, the latter two both near Dover.

Benedictine nunnery at Malling were of any national significance. Much more noticeable, as R. C. Fowler commented a century ago, was the large number of friaries in the county, although their influence should not be exaggerated. There were only a dozen mendicant convents in the county; and the only town to possess more than one such house was Canterbury itself, while the attempt to establish a friary in Maidstone failed.[8] Nevertheless, several of the Kent friaries undoubtedly did add a dynamic radicalism to the county's religious scene, and much the most spiritually innovative and intriguing religious houses in Kent on the eve of the Dissolution were probably the Dominican nunnery at Dartford founded by Edward III in 1346 and the comparatively new community of Observant friars at Greenwich (1482).[9]

At the other end of the religious spectrum lay the late medieval appetite for elaborate collegiate chantry foundations, in addition to the smaller, private chantries (see Lutton and Sweetinburgh, this volume). As they needed to be handsomely endowed to survive at all, it is no surprise that of the five Kentish examples, the colleges of Maidstone, Wingham and Wye were all founded by archbishops of Canterbury, while that at Cobham was endowed by Lord John Cobham, the most powerful military leader in Kent during the last part of the reign of Edward III, and Bredgar also by a local landowner. At Ashford a college of priests was also established in the late fifteenth century as a rebuilding and refoundation by John Fogge.[10] A much more remarkable feature of the religious scene in Kent was the presence of considerably more than thirty hospitals. Although often notoriously difficult to identify and to investigate with any degree of precision, there seems little doubt that there were more hospitals, however defined, within the 1440 square miles of the county of Kent than in any comparable area of England (see Sweetinburgh, this volume).

However that particular phenomenon should best be explained, the patterns of the monastic colonisation of Kent seem to have been more similar to those found elsewhere in England than is often supposed. No doubt the close proximity of Dover and Sandwich to Calais and Boulogne had some significance in exposing the religious houses of the county to continental visitors, to wine from the upper Seine valley and to the intermittent dangers of coastal attack. However, the most important determinant of the highly uneven monastic settlement of Kent was the very variable quality and fertility of the soil to be encountered in different regions of the county. To the late Ernest Hemingway's axiom that 'wherever you see a medieval cathedral, you are in grain country', Kent is certainly no exception. According to the lay subsidy return of 1334/5, as for centuries before, the most striking feature of the geographical distribution in medieval Kent was the

8 *VCH Kent* 2, pp. 198–9.

9 P. Lee, *Nunneries, Learning and Spirituality in Late Medieval English Society: The Dominican Priory of Dartford* (York, 2001); *VCH Kent* 2, pp. 194–8.

10 G. M. Draper, '"There hath not bene any grammar scole kepte, preacher maytened or pore people releved, other then … by the same chauntreye": Educational Provision and Piety in Kent, c.1400–1640', in *Pieties in Transition: Religious Practices and Experiences, c.1400–1640*, ed. R. Lutton and E. Salter (Aldershot, 2007), p. 84.

comparative poverty of the Weald, in particular, and parts of the Romney Marshes relative to the north-east.[11] The environment of the Weald remained so hostile to human settlement that it seems to have been the only area in southern England which escaped monastic influence more or less completely, apart from the house of Trinitarian Friars at Mottenden on its northern fringes. By contrast, the long campaign waged by the canons of Bilsington Priory and others to drain Romney Marsh and Walland Marsh was ultimately effective, providing them with profitable holdings but offering little scope for the founding of new religious establishments of any size in the area. The community of Franciscan friars at New Romney survived for little more than a generation. It accordingly followed that many of the religious houses of Kent were sited within a few miles to the north or south of Kent's most famous road, leading from London and Greenwich, through Dartford, Rochester, Ospringe (Faversham) and Canterbury to either Dover or Sandwich. This was of course the arterial route regularly traversed, like the lower Thames estuary itself, by the monks of Kent and their servants during their incessant journeys in search of rents, provisions and the favour of kings, archbishops and royal clerks at Westminster (see Draper, this volume). Smaller clusters of foundations centred around the upper Medway valley and Maidstone, the ancient road and river routes to Rye, and a few miles inland from the south coast (see Map 2).

Religious communities with a dominant role in education and spiritual guidance were, like other influential institutions, from the Crown to the local governments influenced by more than geography. They served many masters and none, in that they were always liable to be subject to jurisdictional conflicts between the papacy, the Crown and the archbishops, but also because their establishment had a degree of autonomy within their own walls. The demands of lay patrons could interfere with their independence and the interests of property rights and finance often rose to high prominence in their affairs. Ownership of manors and their accompanying lands gave them responsibilities and incomes within the wider county and interests in trade both within the south-east and continental Europe. The lands of the major Benedictine houses were extensive within the county but most houses had connections and some manors in other counties; and in the case of Christ Church Priory in France as well. The monastic houses were, therefore, forces to be reckoned with in the economy and the wider social infrastructure, in addition to the political connections of the more senior prelates. Their educational role, which began as purely clerical, went through several shifts in nature during the three hundred years from 1220 and laid the foundation for some of the post-Reformation establishments.

All their roles were therefore subject to external influences throughout the period, whether it was the papal schisms and the periodic attempts to cleanse the Church, echoed from time to time in the findings of visitations, the new

11 H. A. Hanley and C. W. Chalklin, 'The Kent Lay Subsidy Roll of 1334/5', in *Documents Illustrative of Medieval Kentish Society*, Kent Records 18, ed. F. R. H. Du Boulay (Ashford, 1964), pp. 67–8.

spirituality of the mendicant orders, the development of more secular studies within the universities, the shifting trade patterns, their relationships with kings, popes, archbishops, lay patrons and the local community, or the socio-economic changes arising from the Black Death and subsequent plague outbreaks.

This major trauma to European society in the middle of the fourteenth century stimulated changes to wage labour, rents and incomes, having a direct impact on management of properties and the employment of the laity and secular clerks. So with 1220 identified as a turning point in the fortunes of Christ Church coinciding with the influx of the Italian friars, and the late-thirteenth-century relaxation of the rule of St Benedict, another turning point must be seen in the reaction to, and gradual recovery from, the effects of the Black Death during the late fourteenth and early fifteenth century.[12] While some of the changes in the later fourteenth century were already underway before the 1340s and were merely accelerated by the plague, others were clearly a result of the demographic changes in society occasioned by the widespread deaths.

At Rochester the number of monks fell by just over a third (from 35 to 21), and never recovered, with only sixteen monks at the Dissolution in 1540.[13] Christ Church Canterbury on the other hand suffered relatively few losses in the late 1340s, but later plague outbreaks in the 1360s and 1370s did have a short-term effect on their numbers.[14] Numbers at Christ Church had fallen to around thirty in the late thirteenth century during Archbishop Winchelsey's dispute with Edward I after which steps were taken to increase recruitment.[15] Wider interests in the Christ Church manors were also affected by the rate of mortality and led to some changes in agrarian policy from arable to pasture in manors on the north Kent marshes and Essex (see Campbell, this volume).[16] In smaller houses any decrease in numbers could be critical and at St Mary's, Malling, numbers dropped to four nuns and four novices, with the quick succession of three abbesses dying within three weeks.[17] Within the Benedictine houses the revisions to practices initiated nationally from 1277 had by the mid-fourteenth century led to 'a centralised system headed by a single General Chapter empowered to enforce the customary legislation, to levy subsidies, and to subject each house to regular visitation'.[18] Nevertheless, it should be noted that Christ Church never attended any meetings

12 J. G. Clark, 'The Religious Orders in Pre-Reformation England', in *The Religious Orders in Pre-Reformation England*, ed. J. G. Clark (Woodbridge, 2002), p. 12.

13 A. Oakley, 'Rochester Priory, 1185–1540', in *Faith and Fabric: A History of Rochester Cathedral 640–1994*, ed. N. Yates and P. Welsby (Woodbridge, 1996), pp. 51–2.

14 B. Dobson, 'The English Monastic Cathedrals in the Fifteenth Century', *Transactions of the Royal Historical Society* 6th series 1 (1991), 156. Christ Church numbers averaged about eighty monks throughout the whole period but dropped to forty-six in 1376.

15 Dobson, 'The Monks of Canterbury', pp. 116–17.

16 M. Mate, 'Agrarian Economy after the Black Death: The Manors of Canterbury Cathedral Priory, 1348–91', *Economic History Review* 2nd series 37 (1984), 341–2 citing the contrasting examples of the loss of income in the Chatham manors from high mortality in the fishing industry and the immediate recovery of income at Meopham in 1350 after a drop during the plague year of 1349.

17 A. Maycock, *Malling Abbey: A History of St Mary's Abbey West Malling* (West Malling, 1975), p. 13.

18 Clark, 'Religious Orders', p. 11; Knowles, *Religious Orders* 2, pp. 3–4.

until forced to do so in the late fourteenth century.[19] This system persisted for the next two hundred years, by which time Renaissance and humanist ideas were spreading throughout the universities and courts of Europe and infiltrating the very heart of the monastic movement.

Alongside the more dramatic changes the growing effectiveness of the Statute of Mortmain curtailed the expansion of monastic estates, and religious houses became landowners earning income through leasing to tenant farmers.[20] This trend had already begun in the larger houses particularly Christ Church, Rochester and Faversham before the fourteenth century, despite the policy of leasing having been forbidden by Archbishops Pecham and Winchelsey in 1283 and 1299 (see Campbell and Mate, this volume).[21] Hicks summarises the results of the changes in landholding and labour resulting in rising land values and falling rental incomes, with patronage coming more in the form of cash, 'in kind', and moveable bequests rather than landed property, together with other 'unseen costs', all compounded by the need to pay high wage rates.[22] The establishment of private chantries illustrates well the acceleration of change after 1350. The majority of foundations by private benefactors had taken place before 1300 but saw a major decline after 1350, as the cost of chantry priests rose (see Lutton, this volume).

The rest of this study will look at the monastic houses of Kent within this broad landscape in order to chart their individual shifting fortunes in matters spiritual and temporal leading to their demise in the early sixteenth century. Most extant evidence relates to the foundation and early establishment of the religious houses and of course to the Dissolution period in the early sixteenth century. The fifteenth century is therefore relatively poorly served by historians, Christ Church Canterbury excepted, and the evidence is loaded with the records of various visitations, which naturally tended to report on the negative rather than the positive. The most common complaints arising from the evidence of visitations were: negligence over divine services; misuse and abuses of privileges;

19 W. A. Panton, ed., *Documents Illustrating the Activities of the General and Provincial Chapters of the English Black Monks, 1215–1540,* 3 vols, Camden Society, 3rd series 45; 47 (1931–37).

20 J. O. Moon, 'The Art of Managing Canterbury Cathedral Priory in the Middle Ages 1270–1414' (unpublished research paper, 2007), pp. 7–8, argues that the ongoing disputes between the Crown and Christ Church over the granting of land was not solved by the Statute of Mortmain, but that 'it is highly probable that an ordinance of 1228 and the writs of alienation of 1256 which afforded unequal protection to the Crown and tenants-in-chief were the real causes for concern and were again raised by Archbishop Winchelsey' in his disputes with Edward I.

21 E. D. Jones, 'The Crown, Three Benedictine Houses, and the Statute of Mortmain, 1279–1348', *Journal of British Studies* 14 (1975), 1–28; T. A. M. Bishop, 'Monastic Demesnes and the Statute of Mortmain', *English Historical Review* 49 (1934), 303–6; Clark, 'Religious Orders', p. 13; Oakley, 'Rochester Priory', pp. 37–40.

22 M. A. Hicks, 'The Rising Price of Piety in the Later Middle Ages', in *Monasteries and Society in the British Isles in the Later Middle Ages*, ed. J. Burton and K. Stöber (Woodbridge, 2005), pp. 96–9.

sales of timber; grants of corrodies; dilapidations; visiting women; and as the fourteenth and fifteenth centuries progressed, increasing evidence of individualism with monks shunning communal eating and obedientiaries gradually setting up separate households within the community.[23] Such evidence does confirm the traditional view of religious houses in a state of decline, far from the spirituality of their founders, rife with corruption and with buildings in decay. The growing influence and impact of secular ideas and education, and demands of patrons, together with the foundation of separate, secular chantry colleges, necessarily encouraged change in the spiritual economy and were reflected in the similar results of the contrasting policies of Wolsey and Cromwell, and the appointment of Thomas Cranmer as archbishop in 1533. The new Protestant foundations at Canterbury and Rochester do, in contrast, demonstrate a resilience of many of the earlier monastic forms and structures, and the evidence of the visitations of some of the smaller houses as late as the 1490s shows a fairly buoyant situation, with decline only becoming fully evident in some cases in Archbishop Warham's visitations in 1511 and the pre-surrender audits in the 1530s. The case of the quasi-survival of Greenwich friary may be considered as further evidence that the final demise of monasticism in Kent was the result of knife-edge circumstances, usually outside the control of the religious themselves. Debates over the Reformation will of course continue for as long as there are historians of the period eager to engage with the evidence, and, apart from Christ Church Canterbury, and to a lesser extent Rochester, the houses of Kent provide a very localised view of events.[24]

Before the events of the sixteenth century much of the everyday life of the religious houses was parochial and guided by their immediate interests.[25] The work of libraries and nascent schools, interpretations of the scriptures and obedience to the Church's discipline, continued at times strictly, at others with laxity, but always within the confidence of the system. Liturgical and musical traditions were increasingly affected by secular practices.[26] The struggles to maintain incomes and numbers, and the management of properties and manors led to the apparent dominance of less spiritual activities. Quarrels over jurisdiction, property rights and authority often resulted in litigation between houses and their overlords and neighbours, both temporal and spiritual.

The granting of corrodies in response to the demands of patrons from the Crown to local benefactors was a continual drain on resources, particularly of the smaller houses. At Rochester corrodies for lay people with wealth seeking

23 Oakley, 'Rochester Priory', p. 30; Dobson, 'Monastic Cathedrals', 158.

24 See for example, N. P. Tanner, *The Ages of Faith: Popular Religion in Late Medieval England* (London, 2009). For a full discussion on the Reformation in Kent and its impact, see M. L. Zell, 'The Coming of Religious Reform' and 'The Establishment of the Protestant Church', in *Early Modern Kent 1540–1640*, ed. M. L. Zell (Woodbridge, 2000), pp. 177–206 and 207–44, and for the suppression of the religious houses in particular, pp. 196–200.

25 Clark, 'Religious Orders', p. 8, confirms the view that for much of their time the focus of the monks' interests was within their own enclosed communities with little involvement in public affairs.

26 Ibid., p. 9.

Table 4: The Religious Houses of Kent 1220–1540

	Founded	Dissolved	Notes
Benedictine monasteries			
St Augustine's Abbey, Canterbury	598	1540	
Christ Church Priory, Canterbury	598	1540	
St Andrew's Priory, Rochester	*c.*600	1540	
St Martin's Priory, Dover	1136	1535	Originally Augustinian
St Saviour's Abbey, Faversham	1147/8	1538	Originally Cluniac
Benedictine Nunneries			
St Mary's Abbey, Malling	1090[1099]	1538	
St Sepulchre's Priory, Canterbury	1100	1536	
St Mary's and St Sexburga's Priory, Minster, Sheppey	1130	1535/6	
St Mary's and St Sulpice's Priory, Higham/Lillechurch	1148	1525	
St Mary Magdalen's Priory, Davington	1153	1535	Deserted
Cluniac			
St John the Evangelist's Priory, Monks Horton	Early 12thC	1536	Originally cell of St Pancras, Lewes. Independence granted by Edward III
Cistercian			
St Mary's Abbey, Boxley	1146	1538	
Augustinian Canons			
St Gregory's Priory, Canterbury	1070+	1536	
St Mary's and St Nicholas' Priory, Leeds	1119	1538/40	Formerly Praemonstratenstian
St Thomas the Martyr's Abbey, Lesnes	1178	1524	
St Mary Magdalen's Priory, Tonbridge	1192	1525	
St Mary Magdalen's Priory, Combwell	1227	1536	Founded 11C as abbey
St Mary's Priory, Bilsington	1253	1536	
Praemonstratensian Canons			
St Mary's and St Thomas the Martyr's Abbey, Langdon	1189	1506	Decayed
St Radegand's Abbey, Bradsole	1192/3	1536	
Mendicant Orders			
Franciscan Friars, Canterbury	1224/6	1538	Observant Friars 1496
Franciscan Friars, Romney	Before 1241	Before 1300	
Dominican Friars, Canterbury	1236	1538	
Dominican Nuns, Dartford Priory	c.1356	1539	
Carmelite Friars, Aylesford	1240-1	1538	
Carmelite Friars, Lossenham	1242	1538	
Carmelite Friars, Sandwich	1272	1538	
Austin Friars, Canterbury	1318	1538	
Trinitarian Friars, Mottenden	Before 1235	1538	
Friars of the Sack, Canterbury	Before1274	1314	
Observant Friars (Strict), Greenwich	1482	1538&1559	Refounded by Mary 1555
Alien Houses			
St Peter and St Paul, Lewisham (Ghent)	1081	1415	
St Mary and St Easwith Priory, Folkestone (Lonley/Lorlay)	1095	1535	
St Bertin, Throwley (St Omer)	mid-12thC	1424	
Patrixbourne (Beaulieu)	Late 12thC	1409	
New Romney (Pontigny)	1264	1439	

provision for their old age within the monastery were common practice.[27] The corrodies claimed by the Crown at Faversham and Leeds in the late thirteenth and early fourteenth centuries were probably manageable because of the wealth of the houses, but at Langdon the exploitation of corrodies was more of a burden.[28] They were also seen as a problem at Malling, where the bishop of Rochester intervened from time to time to restrict the number granted (see Sweetinburgh, this volume).[29]

Throughout the fifteenth century the identified characteristics of the larger monastic foundations were echoed in the experiences of the smaller houses. Recruitment to houses was frequently through the convent's educational provision and highly localised, as evidenced by the patronyms of monks which were most often their place of birth. Once within the monastic system, monks in the larger Benedictine houses were increasingly exposed to university education. More and more the monks were burdened with the elaborate round of liturgical observances, exacerbated by the increasing demands of communal and private masses. To these duties were added the further responsibilities of a fully developed obedientiary system with a large proportion of the monks having administrative roles.[30] Employment of lay clerks as teaching masters, as well as other members of the laity to keep the basic functions of the houses running, in turn increased.

On the whole the friars, with their dedicated role within the secular communities and their late establishment relative to the monastic houses tended to encounter fewer disputes, the early problems of the Canterbury Carmelites friars with the prior of Christ Church over property being a fairly rare example.[31] This was possibly because they were fulfilling a need and were not seen as a direct threat by the major monastic foundations, but were rather adding a further useful dimension to the role of the religious in the local community. Or it may have been because, apart from within Canterbury, they were not established alongside older houses of monks or canons.

The Benedictine Monastic Houses

Christ Church Priory, Canterbury

No monks of late medieval Kent travelled the road to London more assiduously than those of Christ Church Priory. As the owners of a large complex of estates and rents dispersed throughout south-east England, they were the most

27 Oakley, 'Rochester Priory', p. 30.
28 *VCH Kent* 2, pp. 139, 163 and 172.
29 Maycock, *St Mary's Abbey*, p. 12.
30 Dobson, 'Monastic Cathedrals', 158.
31 S. Sweetinburgh, 'The Austin Friars in Late Medieval Canterbury: Negotiating Spaces', in *Monasteries and Society in the British Isles in the Later Middle Ages*, ed. J. Burton and K. Stöber (Woodbridge, 2005), pp. 201–2.

formidable landowners in Kent with the possible exception of their archbishop. Accordingly the prior and chapter of Christ Church were in many ways the largest business corporations that late medieval Britain had to offer. For that and other reasons, the Christ Church monks form the best documented religious house in the country. Apart from its remarkable library, the convent's unrivalled collection of charters, registers, account rolls, estate records and letters (many of which still survive at Canterbury) make it possible to scrutinise monastic life at a depth unchallenged even by such other exceptionally well documented monasteries as Westminster Abbey and Durham Cathedral.[32] To that extent Christ Church must always seem the grandest but least typical religious house of medieval England, and Kent.

Not unnaturally therefore, Christ Church nearly always housed more monks than any other English religious house. As the surviving remains of the Romanesque cathedral church and its precinct still demonstrate, by 1200 the monks of Canterbury were already among the largest group of Benedictines in Angevin England. During the single most serious crisis in their entire history, their five-year exile (1209–13) during the Interdict of King John's reign, sixty-four of the Christ Church monks had to seek shelter in the abbey of Saint Bertin and other religious houses in the north of France.[33] By that date, Thomas Becket had been assassinated before the altar of St Benedict in his cathedral on 29 December 1170, and within a few months of his martyrdom was the most venerated of all archbishops of Canterbury. A generation later, during the long reign of Henry III (1216–72) and especially after the translation of the saint's body to the new chapel of the Holy Trinity at the east end of the cathedral on Tuesday 7 July 1220, the convent had not only recovered but also enhanced its prosperity and prestige.[34]

For the rest of the thirteenth century the Christ Church monks were, ironically enough, most often at risk from the hands of their own archbishops.[35] Minor jurisdictional conflicts about the archbishops' alleged usurpation of the convent's long cherished liberties could easily escalate into outright hostility. Perhaps the extreme case is that of Edmund of Abingdon (archbishop 1234–40) who was alleged to have visited the Roman Curia in 1238 to air the possibility that the Benedictine monks of Christ Church ought to be replaced by a 'prebendal church of secular canons'.[36] Despite their corporate self-confidence, the monks of Christ Church were always in fact aware that they stood to suffer in any conflict between their archbishop and the Crown. Thus Archbishop Robert Winchelsey's prolonged and savage dispute with Edward I at the close of the thirteenth century allegedly reduced the monastery's numbers to as few as thirty. In July 1297 that

32 Dobson, 'The Monks of Canterbury', pp. 69–153; B. F. Harvey, *Westminster Abbey and its Estates in the Middle Ages* (Oxford, 1977); R. B. Dobson, *Durham Priory 1400–1450* (Cambridge, 1973).

33 W. Stubbs, ed., *The Historical Works of Gervase of Canterbury*, 2 vols (London, 1880), 2, p. 100.

34 Dobson, 'The Monks of Canterbury', p. 70.

35 Ibid., p. 160, argues that this might have been mitigated if more archbishops had been monks or friars.

36 Ibid., pp. 73–4; Knowles, *Religious Orders* 1, p. 261.

archbishop thought it necessary to write from his palace at Charing to his prior and chapter urging them to recruit thirty new novices to restore 'the ancient and proper number of monks there'.[37] Significantly enough, Winchelsey, who died in 1313, was the last archbishop of Canterbury willing to suffer exile from the realm because of his principled opposition to the English Crown.

At the same time the archbishops also became more ready to compromise in their dealings with the monks of their cathedral. The proximity of the prior and chapter to the most powerful ecclesiastic in the realm naturally sometimes strained relations between the archbishops and the monks, but both parties normally handled contentious issues with enough delicacy to avoid unseemly friction. Unlike many other members of the English episcopal bench most archbishops of Canterbury visited their palace near their cathedral quite often, between intervals of residing at Lambeth or one of their Kent manor houses. There were other reasons why the relationship between the archbishops and the Christ Church chapter became increasingly cordial in the fourteenth and fifteenth centuries. The Canterbury monks were well aware that a generous archbishop was the most munificent patron they could hope to have. To judge from the letters written to their titular abbots by the priors of fifteenth-century Christ Church, the former were now regarded less as lords and masters than as founts of possible patronage, as 'their good lords', to use the ubiquitous contemporary secular phrase. All the more traumatic for the convent was the succession in 1533 to the benevolent, long-lived and conservatively minded Archbishop William Warham (1503–32) of a revolutionary new prelate, Thomas Cranmer, who had no respect for the monastic way of life at all.[38]

As ordained in the rule of St Benedict itself, the key to the material and spiritual welfare of a Benedictine monastery was the managerial skills of its abbot. Nowhere was this more true than in the case of the cathedral chapter of Canterbury, whose prior acted as a much more effective pastor and leader of his brethren than did their titular abbot, the archbishop. With hardly an exception, the Christ Church chapter was exceptionally fortunate in its priors. Despite occasional external pressures from royal government and the archbishop himself who wished to interfere in the choice of the most influential head of a religious house in the country, the monks of Canterbury rarely rebelled against the authority of priors who had, after all, normally been elected from the ranks of the community. Admittedly the strains of the office led two thirteenth-century priors into abrupt and obscure retirement, John Chartham, probably to become a Carthusian, in 1238, and Thomas Ringmere in 1285 to the Cistercian abbey at Beaulieu.[39] By

37 Dobson, 'The Monks of Canterbury', p. 116.

38 Ibid., p. 151.

39 '*Dominus Thomas de Ryngmere qui tunc fuit prior Ecclesie Christi Cantuar' resignavit Prioratum et habitum nigrum exuens habitum album Cistersiensem induit apud Bellum Locum Regis in diocesi Wyntoniensi..*'; MS BL Cotton Galba E. IV, fol. 109v and T. L. Hogan, 'The Memorandum Book of Henry of Eastry', 2 (unpublished PhD thesis, London, 1966), p. 1124. Ringmere did not seek permission to leave the Black monks and Archbishop Pecham, a Franciscan reformer, excommunicated

contrast, Ringmere's successor, the famous Henry of Eastry was head of his house for no less than forty-six years. So long a term of office is more or less impossible to trace elsewhere among late medieval English monasteries; and of Eastry's sixteen successors as prior, only four, namely Master Robert Hathbrand (1238–70), Dr Thomas Chillenden (1391–1411), Dr William Sellyng (1472–94) and Master Thomas Goldstone (1495–1517) served in the supreme office for more than twenty years. Of the many great advantages of such long terms of office, perhaps the most important was that they enabled the priors to enjoy the benefits of extremely close collaboration with successive archbishops of Canterbury. Eastry himself acted as a valued counsellor to four successive archbishops, and his surviving personal letters, especially to Archbishop Walter Reynolds (1313–27), reveal him as a masterly exponent of cautious diplomacy in national political as well as ecclesiastical affairs.

The long priorate of Henry of Eastry also gives the historian the first opportunity to analyse the convent's remarkably burdensome administrative methods and routines in their full complexity.[40] Much of Eastry's time and responsibilities were spent in matters relating to the priory's many manors and properties in Kent and beyond (see Campbell, this volume). He had continued the policy of his predecessors in the acquisition of lands, but he made a greater investment in urban property in Canterbury, London, Southwark and Sandwich and the priory was able to exploit the potential of property owned by Jews before their expulsion in 1290.[41] Prior Eastry and some of his relatively long-serving successors were also able to undertake building works which remain as a visible memorial to the 'financial competence and organizational skills of the successive priors of Christ Church'.[42]

Uniquely among the monastic houses of Kent, Christ Church also held property in France. The Cistertian abbey of Pontigny, where Becket had stayed in exile, granted the archbishop and monks of Canterbury a 'substantial estate', with land at Quincieux and quarters in Lyons Cathedral, the dean of Lyons founding a chapel dedicated to St Thomas. Despite growing local discontent with Canterbury and the outbreak of the Hundred Years War when the property was seized, the monks were still in possession and maintaining their rights in 1350, and they clung on until the Dean and Chapter of Lyons finally took possession in the early fifteenth century.[43] French support for the cult of St Thomas extended beyond the

him for six years. In 1292 Ringmere asked to return but again Pecham refused permission and threatened him with being an apostate and also instructed the bishop of Winchester to ensure that no one gave Ringmere any assistance. We are grateful to John Moon for this and other references from recent research into the administration of Christ Church Priory; *VCH Kent* 2, p. 120.

40 For a full discussion on the priorate of Henry of Eastry and the role of the prior in the community, see Dobson, 'The Monks of Canterbury', pp. 84–99.

41 M. Mate, 'Property Investment by Canterbury Cathedral Priory 1250–1400', *Journal of British Studies* 23 (1984), 3–5; M. Jurkowski and N. Ramsay, ed., *English Monastic Estates, 1066–1540: A List of Manors, Churches and Chapels*, Part One, List and Index Society Special Series 40 (2007), pp. 212–17.

42 Dobson, 'The Monks of Canterbury', p. 98.

43 N. Vincent, 'English Monasteries and their French Possessions' (unpublished paper), pp. 12–19.

grant of lands and Christ Church had privileges which gave them pecuniary advantages. In honour of Becket, Louis VII had granted wine to Christ Church in the 1170s from vineyards at Poissy near Paris, which continued, but often only after petitioning, into the fourteenth century.[44] Christ Church was also granted exemptions from tolls by the Counts of Boulogne and Flanders and after 1170 from tolls on the Seine from Paris to Rouen, probably associated with the Wine of St Thomas, but this freedom from tolls was not renewed once the Hundred Years War began. It is possible that the original grant in 1096 was also partly for purposes linked to the wool trade, but by Prior Eastry's time this was in all probability redundant and certainly by the early fourteenth century freedom from tolls had more to do with the cult of St Thomas than any original trade grant.[45] Moon suggests that it is 'possible that such grants were only made in return for a customary payment from the archbishop or archbishop elect', as evidenced in the *sede vacante* register of 1293 when Archbishop Winchelsey paid forty marks to receive 'quittance from tolls for all his lifetime'.[46]

By the fourteenth century the other three major Benedictine houses, St Andrew's, Rochester, St Augustine's Canterbury and St Saviour's, Faversham were not in the same league as Christ Church, but were each of local significance throughout the later Middle Ages. Both Rochester and St Augustine's were in anomalous positions in relation to the dominant Christ Church, the former as the cathedral priory of a second bishopric in the County, and the latter as the next door neighbour to the archbishop's priory.

St Andrew's Priory, Rochester

Like Canterbury, Rochester was run by the prior with the bishop as abbot essentially absent, and similarly their de facto head was therefore not in a position to take part in the political nation as a member of the House of Lords. Whereas only two monastics were made archbishop between the thirteenth century and the Dissolution, the second, Henry Deane, not until 1501, at Rochester seven bishops were monastics.[47] Issues of authority for Christ Church were with the archbishops, the Crown and the papacy, but within Kent they were subject to no other house, with jurisdiction over others which they would extend wherever possible, often resulting in litigation when their own masters might have to intervene. At

44 Vincent, 'English Monasteries', pp. 9–10; J. O. Moon, 'The European Connection: Aspects of Canterbury Cathedral Priory's Temporalities Overseas' (paper given to 'Canterbury: A Medieval City' conference at University of Le Havre, March 2009), p. 2. Christ Church Priory sold wine in France and moved cash to England, often via their links with Florentine merchants such as the Bardi.

45 Within the first ten years of his priorate Eastry organised manors into food farms and revenue farms and sold all of the Kent wool clip to Italian merchants; Hogan 'The Memorandum Book of Henry of Eastry', 1, pp. 97 and 101.

46 Moon, 'The European Connection', pp. 3 and 10–14.

47 Dobson, 'Monastic Cathedrals', 160; Clark, 'Religious Orders', p. 7. Dobson sees this as a limitation on Christ Church's political muscle, while Clark, less convincingly, considers it is evidence of the prominence of monastics.

Rochester disputes with the archbishop over the choice of bishop in 1235 were eventually settled in favour of Rochester by the Pope. The contrast to Christ Church goes far deeper, as in wealth Rochester was one of the two 'most financially insecure' monastic cathedral foundations in England.[48] After Henry II's abortive attempt to 'demonachise' Rochester at the end of the twelfth century, a quarrel between the bishop and the monks persisted over the 'rights of presentation to benefices' (which brought in fees); the bishop's hospitality allowance (*xenium*), which was seen as an abuse by monks; and corruption in the appointments of priory servants. The 1329 visitation of Simon Meopham identified twenty-five complaints about Bishop Hamo and nepotism in the appointment of servants, reflecting the essentially localised, internal interests of the monks. These quarrels were exacerbated because of the poverty of the Rochester diocese and its dependence on the personal wealth of the bishop.[49]

In the thirteenth century in order to counteract the shortage of direct finances and meet the cost of fabric and shrines, the priory began leasing property in Rochester, together with the acquisition of shares in the Goldhawk mill on the River Darenth, and like Canterbury, in the second half of fourteenth century adding to their property portfolio with acquisitions in London and Lambeth.[50]

Relations with the laity were seriously strained in the late thirteenth and early fourteenth centuries by the lack of a church for the parish of St Nicholas (see Sweetinburgh, this volume). An altar was erected in the nave of the cathedral for the parishioners, much to the annoyance of the monks who in 1327 locked them out. Eventually a compromise was reached with the offer of a purpose built oratory in a corner of the nave until a dedicated church was eventually built and consecrated in 1423.[51]

St Augustine's Abbey, Canterbury

The dissolution of St Augustine's and later use of the abbey fabric and site have in contrast to the survival of Christ Church and its library and archives, left very little evidence of the achievements and experiences of the monks in the later Middle Ages (see Plate 5). William Thorne's *Chronicle of Saint Augustine's Abbey* mainly covering the years 1272 to 1397 gives a welcome, if somewhat biased, view through a narrow window in the thousand-year panorama from its illustrious foundation by Augustine in 598 to its surrender in 1540.[52] At the beginning of our period the papal decision that St Augustine's should not be subject to Christ Church was disputed by the archbishop and became a continuing theme,

48 Dobson, 'Monastic Cathedrals', 157–8. The Augustinian foundation at Carlisle was the other.

49 Oakley, 'Rochester Priory', pp. 30–4.

50 Ibid., pp. 38–9; Jurkowski and Ramsay, *English Monastic Estates*, pp. 226–8.

51 *VCH Kent* 2, p. 123.

52 There is a valuable translation: A. H. Davis, trans., *William Thorne's Chronicle of Saint Augustine's Abbey, Canterbury* (Oxford, 1934).

despite attempts to heal divisions.[53] In 1233 one of the attempts to reach agreement over a wide range of spiritual and jurisdictional issues was solved thus:

> Let all know who shall inspect or hear the present writing, that whereas there has been long controversy between the lord Edmund by God's grace archbishop of Canterbury, primate of all England, Master S. de Langton, archdeacon of Canterbury, of the one part and lord Robert, abbot, and the convent of the blessed Augustine on the other, with regard to the church of Chistlet, and the right of punishment over the men and clerks of the same abbot and convent who are evil-doers in the diocese of Canterbury outside the boundaries of their monastery, which include an almonry outside their gate; as well as on the ordination of vicarages in chapels looking to the church of Menstre, and the ringing of bells, which they say was accustomed to be done in their churches on the arrival of the said abbot, and the confinement of anchorites, and the annual payments which in divers churches in their patronage the said abbot and convent have from ancient times received, and about the churches of Middleton and Faversham, as well as about the custody of churches vacant in their patronage and the keys and the income at a time of vacancy, and sequestrations and sending to take corporal possession, and procurations and the blessing of the abbot having to be done by the archbishop in the monastery of St Augustine without exaction of 'profession'; that all subject of dispute may be removed for the future and those hitherto in dispute may be set at rest, to ensure everlasting peace on the points noted above, at length this agreement has been amicably reached, that the said archbishop, having inspected the agreement formerly made between his predecessor Richard, of good memory, and Roger, then abbot of St Augustine, with the consent of the convents of both, which agreement was attested word for word under the seals of the same and under the seal of the illustrious Henry, formerly king of England, has now for himself and his convent, just as his said predecessor had done before, renounced with the consent of the said archdeacon, all impugnment of the privileges of St. Augustine. Also the same archbishop, having inspected the sentence of Pope Alexander … he for himself and his successors agrees for the future, to grant the blessing to the abbots-elect of St Augustine in the same monastery, without exaction of profession, when he shall be requested to do so. But when the said archbishop shall come to bless the elect as above said, he shall be received by the convent with a procession and bell-ringing, not as the Ordinary, but as the servant of the lord pope, specially sent to do this by reason of the privileges of the said monastery …[54]

In this instance the abbey achieved its aims with cognisance paid to the status of the archbishop and Christ Church only insofar as they were answerable to the papacy. The other issues within this case were dealt with similarly with the

53 See for example, *VCH Kent* 2, pp. 174–5, 180, and 197.
54 Thorne, *Chronicle*, pp. 197–8.

authority of the archbishop and archdeacon recognised in spiritual matters, but the local rights and privileges of St Augustine's upheld. Such disputes continued to be solved with similar compromises, but in the long term never really went away.

Like Christ Church, St Augustine's also had a considerable property portfolio in the city, in addition to the lands granted directly to the abbey, and from time to time came into conflict with the civic authorities over rights and jurisdiction.[55] In 1268 a case was brought to determine which institution had the right of *Infangenthef* in the area immediately outside the gates of the convent. Although an agreement was reached on this occasion the proviso at the end that future disputes should come to trial by a jury acknowledged the inbuilt problems of property rights within Canterbury.

Barker-Benfield concludes that throughout its history until the Reformation, St Augustine's never really outgrew its original purpose as a burial church and keeper of holy relics, while Christ Church established its formidable local and national role. But within this somewhat limited role grew a magnificent monastic library and a complementary contribution to medieval intellectual history, with Abbot Thomas Findon (1283–1310) expanding the library and building on the early work of Abbot Hadrian and Archbishop Theodore in the late seventh and early eighth centuries.[56]

St Saviour's Abbey, Faversham

The abbey of St Saviour's at Faversham was the last Benedictine monastery to be founded in Kent – by King Stephen and his wife Matilda in the 1140s. A charter of Henry III in 1227 described Faversham as Cluniac, subject to the Benedictine Rule, but the abbey was definitely recognised as a Benedictine foundation by 1288.[57] It was subject to the authority of St Augustine's Abbey rather than Christ Church as was the neighbouring parish church of St Mary of Charity (see Sweetinburgh, this volume).[58]

Faversham, a busy port and market, was an important location both for coastal traffic to the north Kent coast and London, and on the parallel main road with access to the north-south routes to Maidstone and beyond (see Draper and Mate, this volume). The local civic authorities had strong interests in maintaining their trade and their own authority and the abbey at Faversham had continual problems with the town. From its very foundation tenants who 'had held lands directly from the crown resented paying dues, rights and services to the Abbot as Lord of the Manor'.[59] The monks found the costs of litigation were so high that in order to

55 Ibid., pp. 250–7; Jurkowski and Ramsay, *English Monastic Estates*, pp. 217–19.

56 *St Augustine's Abbey, Canterbury Catalogue*, ed. B. C. Barker-Benfield, *Corpus of British Medieval Library Catalogues 13*, 3 vols (2008), vol. 1, 'Introduction', pp. xlix–l.

57 *VCH Kent* 2, pp. 137–8.

58 Jurkowski and Ramsay, *English Monastic Estates*, p. 217.

59 D. Harrington and P. Hyde, *The Early Town Books of Faversham c.1251 to 1581* (Folkestone, 2008), pp. xliii–xliv; *VCH Kent* 2, pp. 138–9.

reach a compromise some townspeople were able to purchase land to mitigate manorial imposts and limit monastic interference in town affairs. In 1229 Faversham was granted the status of a limb of the Cinque Ports acquiring liberties which in theory gave the townspeople greater independence from the abbey, but the disputes continued and, as with St Augustine's trials with the Canterbury civic officers, settlement of one dispute did not preclude further conflicts. In the 165 years from 1258 to 1413 on twenty occasions disputes between the abbey and the town had to be taken to litigation.[60] After a long dispute the abbey was able for a short time in the reign of Henry III to assert its rights over the town by insisting on nominations for mayor being submitted to the abbot.[61]

From the thirteenth century onwards, generally each monk was provided with an income as 'wages' for the purchase of necessaries, and by the later Middle Ages such sums could be considerable, allowing a surplus to accumulate.[62] However, during the 1511 visitation the monks of Faversham Abbey were complaining that stipends were paid in kind and not in money.[63]

St Martin's Priory, Dover

If Faversham Abbey appears to have operated fairly autonomously and without serious identifiable problems with its mother house, the case for Dover Priory was in complete contrast and its conflicts with Christ Church are an exemplar of the problems for smaller houses. In the twelfth century, while the priory was still under the rule of St Augustine, the question of jurisdiction by king or archbishop was raised, and privileges were granted by the king. When the canons regular replaced the canons secular under the 'personal ownership' of the archbishop, St Martin's effectively came under the jurisdictional authority of Christ Church which was of course run by the prior in the absence of the abbot archbishop. The consequent tensions between St Martin's and Christ Church Priory led to an appeal to the papacy and eventually Christ Church prevailed. Under the influence of Archbishop Theobald, in 1142, Dover Priory converted to the rule of St Benedict, confirmed in a charter of Henry II granting the priory to Christ Church and the archbishop. However, when the papal confirmation of the changes was made a gloss was added to the terms and Christ Church was specifically excluded from authority over Dover, with more power vested in the archbishop.[64] Grants of charters confirming the subjection of St Martin's to Canterbury were re-enacted regularly by the Crown, but did not avoid further tensions and disputes, despite Pope Gregory X's 1261 confirmation that it was the archbishop and not the prior

60 Harrington and Hyde, *Faversham*, p. xlvii.
61 E. Jacob, *The History of Faversham* (1774), p. 9.
62 B. F. Harvey, *Living and Dying in England 1100–1540: The Monastic Experience* (Oxford, 1993), p. 153.
63 K. L. Wood-Legh, ed., *Kentish Visitations of Archbishop William Warham and his Deputies, 1511–12*, Kent Records 24 (Gloucester, 1984), p. 34.
64 C. R. Haines, *Dover Priory: A History of the Priory of St Mary the Virgin, and St Martin of the New Work* (Cambridge, 1930), pp. 60–77.

at Canterbury who had jurisdiction over Dover, after what was seen as further interference by Christ Church.[65] By 1350 in theory the disputes were finally settled with the archbishop's ordinance confirmed by the king that the priors of Dover should 'do canonical obedience' to the prior of Christ Church during an archiepiscopal vacancy. This 'most notorious and long-standing [of Christ Church's] *cause célèbres*' was also an expensive drain on its finances.[66] Haines believed this resolution of the issues in effect made Dover no more than a cell of Canterbury, despite the assertion that Dover 'shall be, as they have always been, free in every respect from the jurisdiction of the Canterbury chapter'. Consequently, beyond brief biographies of the subsequent priors, he gave no more history of the priory from 1356 until the Dissolution period.[67]

St Martin's Priory, or St Martin's of the New Works as it was strictly called, took over the rights cited from the old St Martin Le Grand's church in Dover in the 1130s, and as a result the latter reverted to being a parish church. St Martin's links with the church of St Mary the Virgin in Dover bestowed the benefit of tithes from the fisheries, and in a Henry I charter also granted a 'moiety of the issues of port' of Dover and one-third of the toll of Saturday market.[68]

The Benedictine Nunneries

Efforts have been made recently to address the apparent neglect by historians of female religious houses since Eileen Power's 'broad sweep' survey of 1922, which may have been just too early to stimulate more work.[69] Nuns were of course subject to the same requirements under the rule of St Benedict as their male counterparts, and in 1298 as part of the wider reform movement Pope Boniface VIII attempted to enforce strict enclosure on female convents. This does not appear to have been very effective and nuns continued to enjoy the benefits of external patronage and other interaction with the external world.[70]

Of the five medieval female Benedictine convents settled in north Kent before 1153, the only nunnery of major national standing was St Mary's at West Malling, with a community of approximately thirty nuns by the early fourteenth century. The liberties and charters granted provided an annual income of £100 by 1291 which had risen to £245 by 1535, with the bulk of its revenue coming from the manors of East and West Malling, and its properties in Southwark, Essex and Great Cornard in Suffolk.[71] In contrast to the decay and abandonment of the

65 John 1199, Henry III 1237, Edward II 1315, Richard II 1380, Edward IV 1461 and Henry VII 1504. *VCH Kent* 2, p. 133.
66 Dobson, 'The Monks of Canterbury', p. 96.
67 Haines, *Dover Priory*, pp. 109–10 and 268; *VCH Kent* 2, p. 134.
68 Haines, 'Appendix I to Chapter VII', *Dover Priory*, pp. 429–34; *VCH Kent* 2, p. 134.
69 E. Power, *Medieval English Nunneries: c.1275 to 1535* (Cambridge, 1922). Lee, *Nunneries*, pp. 1–6.
70 Clark, 'Religious Orders', pp. 12–23.
71 Jurkowski and Ramsay, *English Monastic Estates*, p. 225.

convent at Davington, the nuns of Malling, having recovered from their drop in numbers following the arrival of the Black Death, were still in good heart in 1538 and put up some resistance before surrendering.[72]

The other four female Benedictine houses in Kent did not rise to any great significance, only St Sepulchre's gaining small notice at the end of its days when it housed the Maid of Kent, Elizabeth Barton, during her challenges to Henry VIII over his divorce (see Lutton, this volume). In common with monks and canons, the nuns of all the Benedictine convents were frequently exhorted to wipe out laxity and immorality.

One of the earliest post-Conquest foundations, St Sepulchre's had been founded by Anselm c. 1100 within the boundaries of St Augustine's but on land belonging to the archbishop. By 1244 it was necessary to formalise the relationship between St Sepulchre's and St Augustine's, by a charter excluding the priory from benefiting from any possessions within the bounds of the abbey.[73] Despite its location the priory did not attract many recruits and by the 1511 visitation only five nuns were left.[74] The situation at Davington Priory was even worse as it was deserted by the time of its surrender in 1535 with the last nun left alive after the death of the prioress leaving of her own accord. In its early years there had been some tensions between the priory and Faversham Abbey over possessions, but the archbishops generally decided in favour of the nuns and protected their rights.[75] In his *History of Faversham*, Jacob alleged that at its foundation the priory was, like St Saviour's Abbey, originally Cluniac, and that the priory was always short of funds and never able to support the twenty-six nuns for which it was founded.[76]

The priory of St Mary's and St Sulpice's at Higham/Lillechurch was originally a cell of the Cluniac priory of St Sulpice in Brittany, but was founded as an English priory during the reign of Stephen. Like Davington it always struggled with recruits and was dissolved in 1525 because of falling numbers and 'immorality'.[77] The only house of nuns which maintained its numbers into the sixteenth century was the priory of St Mary and St Sexburga at Minster in Sheppey, but throughout its history it had like other female houses been subject to severe criticism at times. Both Archbishops Pecham and Winchelsey exhorted the convent to enforce strict adherence to appropriate enclosure and silences as part of the late-thirteenth-century reforms.[78]

It was not, therefore, until the foundation of the Dominican Priory of nuns at Dartford in the mid-fourteenth century that, apart from the house at Malling, any real impact was made by female religious in Kent (see below p. 104).

72 Maycock, *Saint Mary's Abbey*, pp. 8–14.
73 Thorne, *Chronicle*, p. 215.
74 *VCH Kent* 2, p. 142.
75 Jacob, *History of Faversham*, pp. 28–9.
76 Ibid., pp. 112–16.
77 *VCH Kent* 2, pp. 145.
78 Ibid., pp. 149–50.

Cistercians, Cluniacs and Alien Houses (under the rule of St Benedict)

The foundation of St Mary's Abbey, Boxley, by the Fleming, William of Ypres in 1146 created the one English Cistercian house in Kent, under its mother house the Cistercian Abbey in Citeaux in Normandy.[79] Boxley suffered its share of criticisms in visitations, but maintained its wealth throughout its existence and was subject to providing Crown corrodies, albeit not always willingly. Despite its isolation from the major Cistercian houses in England the abbey played a full part in their activities and when the abbot of Citeaux was declared a schismatic in 1395 Pope Boniface IX authorised the abbot of Boxley, *inter alia*, to convene a chapter in London and to undertake visitations of English Cistercian houses.[80] Earlier, in a late-twelfth-century dispute between a local landowner and the alien priory at Throwley, the abbot of Boxley, together with the abbot of Faversham, acted as arbitrator.

In contrast the alien Cistercian house of New Romney, a cell of Pontigny, had a very low profile, with few if any resident monks, despite its auspicious beginnings in 1264 arising from the refuge Pontigny gave to Becket during his exile. New Romney survived slightly longer into the Hundred Years War than the other Kentish alien houses (Folkestone Priory excepted), and was not confiscated until 1439 when it was granted to All Souls College at Oxford.[81] However, its survival may have been due in large part to its failure as a priory and the financial advantage to the Crown of taking possession and letting it out to farm locally. In the early stages of the war in the fourteenth century alien houses were taken into the possession of the Crown together with their revenues, which could no longer be sent abroad.[82] The national wave of suppressions of alien houses during the war under Henry V's Act of Dissolution of 1414 accounted for the three alien houses at Lewisham, Patrixbourne and Throwley, although the possessions of Patrixbourne and part of Throwley were granted to the Praemonstratensian abbey at Langdon.[83]

The priories at Lewisham and Folkestone, both of which had their origins in pre-Conquest times but had been refounded in the late eleventh century, were, like the other alien houses, taken into the Crown's possession during the Hundred Years War. Nonetheless, unlike New Romney, they were 'let out to farm' to the priors rather than to local landowners. This did not prevent Lewisham being confiscated in 1415, but Folkestone, as the only alien house in Kent to be more than a small cell, was granted to Westminster Abbey in 1390 subject to the payment of appropriate tithes and taxes.[84] This seems to have saved the priory

79 Ibid., p. 153. Harrington and Hyde, *Faversham*, p. xli; William of Ypres had come to England in 1138 or 1139 and had served as King Stephen's man in Kent for the next ten years or so until the accession of Henry II. He held manors from the king in Faversham and in addition to founding Boxley Abbey made grants to local churches; R. Eales, 'William of Ypres, Styled Count of Flanders (*d.* 1164/5)', *ODNB*.

80 *VCH Kent* 2, p. 154.

81 Ibid., p. 239.

82 Knowles, *Religious Orders* 2, p. 159.

83 Clark, 'Religious Orders', p. 7; *VCH Kent* 2, pp. 239–40.

84 Knowles, *Religious Orders* 2, pp. 161–2.

which was restored to its own prior in 1399 on payment of a tax of six marks annually to the king. Before the end of the war it was no longer designated an alien house, and survived as an English Benedictine house until its suppression in 1535.[85]

Monks Horton was founded as a cell of the priory of St Pancras at Lewes in Sussex, close to the Roman route from Canterbury to Lympne, and with direct access to the ancient routes now designated 'Pilgrim's Way' and North Downs Way. As a Cluniac house it was at times in the Hundred Years War treated as an alien house although the prior remained in charge, and eventually it was made a *prioratus indigena*. The prior had been able to prove that Monks Horton did not pay dues to a religious house abroad, and when Lewes was made a native English house in 1373, the first to receive this favourable treatment, Monks Horton's continuance as the only Cluniac house in Kent was secured.[86] Nevertheless, it was not a success story and after the visitation in 1279 recorded the optimum number of thirteen monks, that figure was never reached again, and even the default number of eight became beyond their reach (see Plate 6).[87]

The Houses of Augustinian Canons

The earliest Augustinian house in Kent, St Gregory's Priory, Canterbury, was founded by Lanfranc in the late eleventh century as a 'guild of clerks', but they were replaced by regular canons from Merton Priory in 1133.[88] Study of the foundation of the houses of Augustinian canons in Kent does not paint a picture of a coherent group of houses, nor the 'quasi-establishment' foundation of the Benedictine convents. Two of the houses were originally Praemonstratensian with subjection to the rule of St Augustine remaining common to both strands of canons regular. The priory of St Mary and St Nicholas at Leeds, although its 'goodly church parallel to many cathedrals' has long since vanished, was the most impressive, and was founded for Augustinian canons by the local Crevequer family in 1119. It remained the only Augustinian house of any major standing in Kent and was favoured by the Crown with grants for a royal chantry and corrodies claimed for servants of the monarch in the fourteenth century.[89] On paper, Leeds was still the fourth richest and largest monastic community in the county on the eve of the Dissolution, but in 1537 debts amounting to well over £1000 offset the net value of the house as at 1535 of just over £362.[90] The priory held extensive manors throughout the wider mid-Kent region, as well as one in Essex and one in Surrey, and was not immune from disputes with other houses.[91] In 1278 a

85 *VCH Kent* 2, pp. 236–8.
86 Knowles, *Religious Orders* 2, p. 159.
87 *VCH Kent* 2, pp. 151–2.
88 M. Sparks, 'St Gregory's Priory, Canterbury: A Re-assessment', *Arch. Cant.* 118 (1998), 77–90.
89 *VCH Kent* 2, pp. 162–3.
90 Ibid., p. 164.
91 Jurkowski and Ramsay, *English Monastic Estates*, pp. 223–4.

disagreement with Christ Church Priory over rights to common pasture in Harbledown and Blean was settled not by litigation deciding for one party, but by a compromise partition.[92]

The original (Praemonstratensian) foundation of St Mary Magdalen at Combwell was as an abbey in the twelfth century under the jurisdiction of Bayham in east Sussex. By 1220 it became clear that numbers were remaining low and it was reduced to the status of a priory. Ten years later after a visitation by the abbot of Bayham, the priory was charged with abandoning the principles of Prémontré and the matter was referred to the archbishop who agreed that thenceforward the priory should be subject to the rule of St Augustine. Throughout the fourteenth century Combwell remained a weakened house with serious failings identified in visitations of 1369 and 1387, and by the time of Archbishop Warham's visitation in 1512 the priory was severely in debt and barely managing to maintain its basic functions.[93]

The other two twelfth-century Augustinian foundations, the abbey of St Thomas the Martyr, Lesnes, and St Mary Magdalen's Priory at Tonbridge were both established in the last part of the century. Tonbridge Priory held manors in both Suffolk and Cambridgeshire, but most of its properties were within its own hinterland, whereas Lesnes Abbey had a smaller, but more widespread portfolio of properties evenly spread throughout Kent, Essex, Cambridgeshire, Surrey and London.[94] In the fifteenth century both houses were accused from time to time of corruption, but the most dramatic event in Tonbridge's history before its dissolution was the fire in 1337 which destroyed all the main buildings. Rebuilding took place with the powerful incentive of indulgences granted to those in the Rochester diocese who assisted in the works.[95] Both convents were suppressed by Wolsey in his attempt to acquire funds and resources for the establishment of his college at Oxford, although the original intention at Tonbridge was for a much larger, but abortive, scheme with a grammar school in the town to provide scholars for Oxford.[96]

The final Augustinian house of regular canons, St Mary's Priory, Bilsington, was founded by the will of the provost of Beverley in 1253 and was unencumbered in its foundation charters by subjection to the jurisdiction of any other house, having the freedom to appoint its prior without licence. This grant was confirmed by Edward I in 1276, yet, as is the way with jurisdictional authority, restrictions were imposed on their liberties. As a result, the new priors had to be 'presented' to the king, their appointment confirmed by the archbishop. And of course the convent was subject to visitations by priors of other Kentish Augustinian houses in the normal way. By the early sixteenth century Bilsington too

92 *VCH Kent* 2, p. 163.
93 Wood-Legh, *Kent Visitations*, p. 48.
94 Jurkowski and Ramsay, *English Monastic Estates*, pp. 227–8 and 224.
95 Oakley, 'Rochester Priory', pp. 52–3; *VCH Kent* 2, p. 167.
96 *VCH Kent* 2, pp. 167–8.

was in debt, but had managed to hold off its creditors for a short time by persuading the prior of Leeds to endorse outstanding bills.[97] The priory survived for another twenty years until its final surrender in 1536.

The Houses of Praemonstratensian Canons at St Mary's and St Thomas the Martyr's Abbey, Langdon, and St Radegund's Abbey, Bradsole

These two Praemonstratensian abbeys outside Dover, both subject to the jurisdiction of Bayham Abbey, had slightly different fortunes. In the early part of the period the reputation of these houses was high and it was the abbot of Bradsole who acted as one of the intermediaries of a dispute in 1311 between the abbot of Prémontré and the English houses. Throughout the fifteenth century Langdon was very prosperous and generally well-run with only minor misdemeanours identified at visitations. Nevertheless, between 1494 and 1497 Langdon was beginning to decay and fall into debt, which by 1500 had increased sixfold. By 1506 and at the 1530s surrender audit the house was 'in utter decay and [about to] tumble down'.[98] Decline at Bradsole set in slightly earlier with the need for repairs noted in the 1491 visitation and clear signs of a decline in standards and apostasy by 1497, yet it remained a going concern until its dissolution in 1536.

The Mendicant Orders

With their houses in towns usually close to gates and major thoroughfares, friars were near to the everyday economic life of markets, and rivers. Although this may have been in part a deliberate response to their given role within the communities, it may have been more a matter of chance, a result of their being the last of the religious establishments and necessarily ending up on the urban fringes where there were still vacant plots of land.[99] Friars as mendicants with the emphasis on lack of possessions and an evangelical preaching role were in their early days a very different breed from their brothers in houses of monks and canons. Although the distinction remained clear throughout the later Middle Ages, nevertheless as the period progressed the friars began to embrace many of the practices and were to serve in many of the roles associated with claustral orders; and the poverty of the orders was often very healthily offset by the grants and gifts from wealthy patrons.[100]

97 Ibid., p. 156.
98 Ibid., p. 171.
99 Sweetinburgh, 'Austin Friars', pp. 197–8.
100 Knowles, *Religious Orders* 2, pp. 144–56.

Franciscans

Henry III did relatively little for the Greyfriars compared with what he was to do for the Blackfriars a few years later.[101] The only successful establishment of Franciscans was at Canterbury with a rather later abortive attempt to establish a friary at Maidstone in 1331 and the very short-lived friary at Romney which was established some time before 1241 when Henry III granted £100 from the revenues of the archbishop for buying clothes and may have lasted at least fifteen years.[102] Nevertheless the Franciscans made their mark and the 'Franciscan lectors at Christ Church, Canterbury in the late thirteenth and early fourteenth century are proof of the respect in which they were held by the monks who put them in charge of teaching their novices'.[103]

The reformed branch of Franciscans was formally recognised in 1415 as either Observants or Strict Observants and their adherence to the simpler life was still in evidence in the early sixteenth century when they instigated a change to cheaper material in 1502, six years after the Franciscans at Canterbury had reinvented themselves as Observant friars.[104] The Observant friars at Greenwich had been founded by Henry VII, a few years before the change of the Canterbury friars in 1496, and they remained strong under the patronage of the Tudor dynasty. Their church was used by the royal family for baptisms, and marriages until the time of the royal divorce. Katherine of Aragon had great sympathy for the order, some sources alleging that she was a member herself. Although Elizabeth was christened at Greenwich, the friars suffered persecution from the king's officials and in 1534 were expelled from their house and forced to flee with their brethren from the other English Observant houses. The resilience of the order and its royal patronage led to its reinstatement in 1555 by Mary until the accession of Elizabeth in 1558.[105]

Dominicans

The Dominican foundations were also well-supported by the Crown and Henry III gave the Dominicans in Canterbury an island in the Stour and many sums of money. But donations also came from wealthy citizens of Canterbury. Although they were not exempt from getting into disputes with Christ Church Priory over rents in 1294, six years later their standing was confirmed by Archbishop Winchelsey who licensed six Dominican friars to hear confessions in the Canterbury diocese.[106] Property disputes with St Augustine's were also not unknown

101 *VCH Kent* 2, p. 190.

102 Evidence citied in *VCH Kent* 2, p. 199 suggests that Richard of Devon spent the last fifteen years of his life as a pensioner at the Romney friary.

103 J. Greatrex, 'Recent Perspectives in Monastic History', in *The Religious Orders in Pre-Reformation England*, ed. J. G. Clark (Woodbridge, 2002), p. 39.

104 *VCH Kent* 2, p. 195.

105 Ibid., pp. 197–8.

106 Ibid., pp. 177–8.

and in the later fourteenth century they were in dispute with the abbey over damage to their buildings when the abbot had the level of the millpond raised.[107]

The priory of Dominican nuns at Dartford was also a royal foundation 'exempt from archiepiscopal and diocesan jurisdiction', with a definitive role in its establishment to provide for the mendicant friars of King's Langley, Buckinghamshire, from the incomes of its properties granted by the king.[108] The convent was exempted from taxes in 1356.[109] Although the prior of King's Langley was originally expected to conduct visitations, by the mid-fifteenth century Dartford was no longer under the friary's jurisdiction and maintained its independence thereafter until 'Henry VII assumed authority over the English Church and severed the English Dominican province from the continental order'.[110] The strength of the community persisted after the Dissolution with the nuns setting themselves up as a distinct community within the secular society.[111]

Carmelites

Aylesford Priory was one of the first Carmelite establishment in England set up by the authority of the bishop of Rochester in 1240, but later in 1369, under the bequest of John de Ringer for a chantry at Aylesford, submitted to the 'jurisdiction and supervision of the archbishop of Canterbury'.[112] Aylesford remained remarkably free of tensions with either Rochester or Canterbury. The next Carmelite house to be established within a year of Aylesford was Lossenham, which having been founded under the patronage of the Aucher family remained dependent on them and other Kentish landowners for the rest of its existence. But despite their patronage Lossenham was in a very poor state at the Dissolution.[113] The very small house of Carmelites at Sandwich was not established until some thirty years later in 1272, and by the end of the fifteenth century most of its lands were let out as smallholdings, a common feature of the Sandwich area.[114] The activities of these Kent Carmelites are lost in the shadows and they seem not to have played any significant part in the academic disputes and attacks on Lollardy at the end of the fourteenth century, which exercised the wider English Carmelite colony.[115]

Austin Friars

Under a papal directive of 1256 the Austin friars changed from an eremitical order to one serving in urban communities.[116] They were established initially in

107 Ibid., pp. 178–9.
108 Their privileges were agreed in 1321; Lee, *Nunneries*, p. 22.
109 Ibid., pp. 17–24.
110 Ibid., pp. 38–9.
111 Ibid., p. 132.
112 *VCH Kent* 2, pp. 202–3.
113 Ibid., p. 203.
114 Ibid., pp. 204–5. E. Deighton, 'The Carmelite Friary in Sandwich', *Arch. Cant.* 114 (1994), 317–27.
115 Knowles, *Religious Orders* 2, pp. 144–8.
116 Sweetinburgh, 'Austin Friars', p. 201; J. Röhrkasten, 'The Mendicant Orders in Urban Life and Society: The Case of London', in *Religious and Laity in Western Europe, 1000–1400: Interaction, Negotiation, and Power*, ed. E. Jamroziak and J. Burton (Turnhout, 2006), p. 337.

1318 in the suburbs outside the Westgate in Canterbury, but during the next decade moved to St George's parish encroaching on property owned by Christ Church Priory. This led to early conflict over property which the friars exacerbated by the construction of an oratory for celebrating divine service without the archbishop's approval. Peace was restored by an agreement in 1326 with the friars undertaking to make a payment to the priory for loss of revenue.[117] The Austin friars added relatively late to the large number of religious houses within the city and in the suburbs immediately beyond the walls, increasing the complexity of property ownerships within the walls of Canterbury. Both the civic authorities and Christ Church Priory were beneficiaries of the pilgrimages to the shrine of St Thomas, but the spiritual economy also led to interdependence of the various religious institutions, even while running into disputes over property rights.[118] It was the Austin friars who, having managed to establish fairly good relations with the city, housed the Crown officials arbitrating in the dispute between St Augustine's and the corporation over property rights in 1476, on receipt of payment.[119] Yet by 1538 at the surrender the Austin friars, like so many other houses were seriously in debt, though still having extensive assets in the form of buildings.[120]

Other Mendicant Orders

Two other orders of friars set up in Kent: the Trinitarians who survived successfully until the Dissolution retaining significant numbers and property until the end and the Friars of the Sack who lasted less than forty years in Canterbury at the turn of the fourteenth century.[121] It can only be supposed that location and patronage accounted for such different fortunes. As one of the late mendicant orders in Canterbury and numbering less than five, the Friars of the Sack would always be at a disadvantage dependant on the poorest of handouts. In contrast the Trinitarians had chosen a comparatively rich part of the north Weald close enough to the routes across the Downs and the river routes near Maidstone. The friary was never short of patrons and at the Dissolution a large part of its property was acquired by the patrons of Lossenham, the Aucher family.[122]

Chantry Colleges and Education

The story of monastic scholarship and education in Kent can be charted through a similar chronology to the fortunes of the religious houses and the increasing

117 *VCH Kent* 2, p. 199.

118 Sweetinburgh, 'Austin Friars', p. 201, suggests that the interdependence and the need for compromises to be reached in disputes may have led to formalised litigation.

119 Ibid., p. 205.

120 *VCH Kent* 2, p. 201. A. Hicks and M. Houliston, *The Whitefriars Excavation*, forthcoming.

121 S. Sweetinburgh, 'Monastic Houses', in *An Historical Atlas of Kent*, ed. T. Lawson and D. M. Killingray (Chichester, 2004), p. 42; *VCH Kent* 2, pp. 205–8.

122 *VCH Kent* 2, p. 207.

influence of the laity already identified. The mid-thirteenth century saw a 'resurgence of monastic learning', after the decline of cloister schools for secular clerks.[123] The almonry school at Christ Church was established some time between 1291 and 1325, but from time to time encountered difficulties in finding suitably qualified masters. In one instance the shortage of masters led to a case of the poaching of a qualified master from Christ Church by the corporation of Kingston-upon- Thames, which resulted in the prior, in a fit of pique, refusing to send on his baggage.[124] Concurrently, monks were increasingly forming the core of scholars at the universities, Oxford from 1227 and Cambridge by 1400, when it has been suggested that the 'monk-scholar' was 'at his peak'.[125] From 1331 monks from Christ Church regularly studied at Oxford, originally at Gloucester College, but after the establishment of Canterbury College, by royal licence in 1361, at their own college.[126] By this time the *scriptoria* were in decline, but the libraries of the major houses continued to be developed, and in hindsight the inevitability of changes in intellectual interpretations through extra-claustral exposure to a wider range of ideas is obvious.[127] Many monks spent several years at the universities and when they returned to their mother house they brought their skills and ideas with them. Taken alongside the growing influence and interest of the laity in the religious houses, and the relaxation of the Benedictine Rule, the change of approach to education and theology gradually infiltrated the whole system over the next two hundred years (see Lutton and Sweetinburgh, this volume).

As liturgical and obedientiary responsibilities took more of the time of the resident monks, and university study much of the best years of others, the time available for education at the more mundane and social level was squeezed out of their role, and led to the employment of secular clerks as masters for the almonry schools. Clark has recently argued that this can also be seen as a growing formalisation of schooling, perhaps under the influence of lay patrons, removing the 'moral, educational high ground' from the parish priests.[128]

Long before the sixteenth century monks in Kent would have been exposed to the ideas of Wyclif and the Lollards and the growing European influence of the Renaissance and humanism. By 1500 there is evidence that the monks at Canterbury College were showing great interest in humanism.[129] But not all aspects of the new learning were embraced immediately and it was not until the early 1530s

123 J. G. Clark, 'Monasteries and Secular Education in Late Medieval England', in *Monasteries and Society in the British Isles in the Later Middle Ages*, ed. J. Burton and K. Stöber (Woodbridge, 2005), pp. 147–8.

124 Ibid., p. 157. There is also reason to believe that there may have been some schooling offered at St Gregory's Priory from an early date, Sparks, 'St Gregory's Priory', 82–3.

125 Clark, 'Religious Orders', p. 20.

126 Dobson, 'The Monks of Canterbury', pp. 99–109. *VCH Kent* 2, p. 118.

127 The Franciscan friars in Canterbury had a very respectable collection in their library from as early as the 1230s which was added to regularly until the Dissolution, *VCH Kent* 2, p. 192.

128 Clark, 'Monasteries', pp. 148–51.

129 Clark, 'Religious Orders', p. 20 and ibid., 'Monasteries', p. 148.

Table 5: Late Medieval Chantry Colleges in Kent

College	Founded	Founder
Wingham	1287	Archbishop Pecham
Cobham	1362	Lord John Cobham
Maidstone	1375	Archbishop Boniface
Bredgar	1392	Robert of Bredgar
Wye	1432	Archbishop Kemp (founded while he was still Archbishop of York)
Ashford	Late C15	rebuilt and refounded by John Fogge

that St Augustine's monks started printing, rather late in the day catching up with secular practices. At the same time the standard of education for the novices and young monks was seen to be in decline with a widening gulf between those exposed to university education and those dependent on whatever education could be garnered in their houses. Archbishop Warham's visitation in 1511 to Christ Church Priory noted that the novices and junior monks had no teacher of grammar and many did not know or understand what they were reading in the Latin mass.[130] The situation was similar in the small Augustinian house at Combwell where the visitation the following year found it too had no teacher of grammar.[131] Clark and Lee both suggest that, while the evidence is not conclusive, the level of literacy among nuns may have been more consistent.[132] This may have been a reflection of the nature of the recruits to female convents, their associated patronage and the greater effectiveness of controls on their activities.

We have seen how the changes in the mid-fourteenth century accelerated the decline in funding for private chantries, and it was these same changes which were to influence the later fourteenth- and fifteenth-century fortunes of the secular chantry colleges, together with the growing interest of the wealthy lay patrons in the control of education and the increasing use of secular masters.[133] The foundation of separate colleges of secular clerks and master with private chantry responsibilities for schools can be seen as a transitional phase with practices and systems drawn from the earlier monastic foundations and university colleges, but with a hint of the future demise of the monastic establishment (see Plate 7).[134]

130 Wood-Legh, *Kent Visitations*, p. xiv.

131 *VCH Kent* 2, p. 160.

132 Clark, 'Religious Orders', p. 21; Lee, *Nunneries*, pp. 167ff.

133 Hicks, 'The Rising Price of Piety', pp. 96–9.

134 P. Burnham, *The College at Wye: A Historical Guide* (2007), p. 3.

Conclusion

By 1540 all the monastic houses of Kent had surrendered to the Crown, some fighting to the last, others succumbing without significant protest, and one or two surviving in a shadowy existence of the monastic system, while the two New Foundations of Dean and Chapter at Canterbury and Rochester with their associated grammar schools, marked the new order of the Church in England. Tonbridge and Lesnes had fallen to Wolsey's ambitions, Bradsole and Higham had decayed before that, while Davington was in its death throes. Archbishop Warham's visitations of 1511 and 1512 and the surrender audits of 1535 generally provide a clear picture of the state of the religious houses on the eve of the Dissolution and individual stories can be told from these sources, to which can be added the visual remains and further histories of buildings, and studies of the fortunes of displaced monastics. The exploitation of properties, lands and fabric by the Crown and favoured aristocracy are well recorded, and the fineness of the line between the winners and losers can be seen in the case of Leeds Priory. The penultimate prior of Leeds was Arthur Sentleger, and after the Dissolution the priory was granted to his brother Anthony in fee.[135]

In a brief survey of this nature it is not possible to do justice to the individual experiences of the diverse religious establishments in Kent. The dominance of Christ Church Priory with its extant wealth of evidence and visual memorials should not detract from the local importance of the smaller houses, whose buildings and place within the community provided a permanent feature of Kentish life for upwards of five hundred years, and were to continue to provide part of the landscape thereafter.

The large Benedictine houses' success compared with the relative struggles to attract numbers and appropriate financial support in the smaller houses; the initial breath of fresh air of the mendicants and their gradual adjustment to a more mainstream role; and the growing influence of secular patrons in the maintenance of houses and the practices of liturgy, education and music, all contributed to continually evolving institutions. The monastic system had reinvented itself in response to changes, both spiritual and temporal throughout its entire existence, and further reform and rationalisation may well have been in the offing in the sixteenth century, but the wholesale suppression and dissolution of the English religious houses was unprecedented and, until the 1530s, unpredictable.[136]

135 *VCH Kent* 2, p. 164.

136 Zell, 'The Coming of Religious Reform', p. 179.

6

The Hospitals of Medieval Kent*

SHEILA SWEETINBURGH

From soon after their disappearance in the mid-sixteenth century, medieval hospitals were the focus of antiquarian research as part of a general interest in religious houses. Such studies are particularly important for their preservation of now lost documents and without this material the task of investigating the medieval hospital would be more difficult. Nevertheless, it was Rotha Mary Clay's work on English medieval hospitals in the early twentieth century that was the groundbreaking study, to be followed by Mary Seymour's national survey written in 1946.[1] Using these studies, county gazetteers produced in the Victoria County History series, the work of Knowles and Hadcock and extant documentary sources, modern historians have shown a renewed interest in the medieval hospital.[2] This has led to the production, and sometimes publication, of individual and regional hospital studies, as well as national and international studies, the latter frequently drawing on these local and regional works. This article on Kent's medieval hospitals may be seen as part of the growing corpus of regional studies of which probably Nicholas Orme and Margaret Webster's on Devon and Cornwall, Patricia Cullum's on Yorkshire, E. M. Phillips's on Norfolk and Suffolk, Miri Rubin's on Cambridge and Carole Rawcliffe's on London and Norwich are the most notable.[3] One interesting aspect of this literature is the

* I should like to thank the Marquess of Salisbury, the President and Fellows of Magdalen College, Oxford, and the Master and Fellows of St John's College, Cambridge, for allowing access to their manuscript collections for the hospitals of Maidstone, New Romney and Ospringe, respectively.

1 R. M. Clay, *The Medieval Hospitals of England* (London, 1909, repr. 1966). M. Seymour, 'The Organisation, Personnel and Functions of the Medieval Hospital in the Later Middle Ages' (unpublished M.A. thesis, University of London, 1946).

2 W. Page et al., ed., *The Victoria Histories of the Counties of England* (London, 1900–). D. Knowles and R. N. Hadcock, *Medieval Religious Houses: England and Wales*, 2nd edn (London, 1971), pp. 250–324; Knowles and Hadcock, 'Additions and Corrections to Medieval Houses: England and Wales [Hospitals]', *English Historical Review* 72 (1957), 76–85.

3 N. Orme and M. Webster, *The English Hospital, 1070–1570* (New Haven, CT and London, 1995). P. H. Cullum, 'Hospitals and Charitable Provision in Medieval Yorkshire' (unpublished D.Phil. thesis, University of York, 1990). E. M. Philips, 'Charitable Institutions in Norfolk and Suffolk c.1350–1600' (unpublished PhD thesis, University of East Anglia, 2001). M. Rubin, *Charity and Community in Medieval Cambridge* (Cambridge, 1987). C. Rawcliffe, 'The Hospitals of Later Medieval London', *Medical History* 28 (1984), 1–21; Rawcliffe, *The Hospitals of Medieval Norwich*, Studies in East Anglian History 2 (Norwich, 1995).

differing approaches adopted to try to assess the place of the hospital within medieval society. For the purposes of this publication, a modified form of the structure used by Orme and Webster for their national survey in *The English Hospital, 1070–1570* has been adopted as a way of setting Kentish hospitals comparatively.

It is neither feasible nor sensible to consider medieval hospitals without considering their close relative the almshouse, which may have first appeared in Kent in the fourteenth century. To date over seventy hospitals and almshouses have been identified as existing in Kent at some point during the period 1080 to 1540.[4] But there were certainly others, especially small leper houses and poorly endowed 'maisonsdieu', a type of almshouse first characterised by Cullum as ephemeral establishments that might last no longer than the lifetime of a single occupant.[5] References to the latter are primarily to be found in testamentary records, making it difficult to verify whether the testator's wishes came to fruition, though in some cases there are confirmatory documents in Churchwardens' accounts and later wills.[6] The identification of leper hospitals presents different problems. Where their existence is dependent on a single entry in the royal records it is conceivable that a few may have been wrongly identified and, at the very least, such records indicate first known rather than foundation dates.[7] Nonetheless, compared to some counties the records for Kent are good, yet like any set of sources they are patchy and only a few hospitals are well documented.

Between the Conquest and the Reformation, hospitals and almshouses were established at irregular intervals in Kent, and, as a way of providing a backdrop for the later sections on hospital function, resources and management, the first section comprises a brief foundation chronology. Instead of a conclusion there is

4 S. Sweetinburgh, *The Role of the Hospital in Medieval England: Gift-giving and the Spiritual Economy* (Dublin, 2004), pp. 68–126; S. Sweetinburgh, 'Medieval Hospitals and Almshouses', in *An Historical Atlas of Kent*, ed. T. Lawson and D. Killingray (Chichester, 2004), pp. 44–5.

5 I should like to thank Terry Lawson for this reference to a leper hospital at Pluckley; MS BL Add. 29794, m. 3. P. H. Cullum, ' "For pore people harberles": What was the Function of the Maisonsdieu?', in *Trade, Devotion and Governance: Papers in Later Medieval History*, ed. R. G. Davies and P. McNiven (Stroud, 1994), pp. 36–54.

6 The vicar at Holy Cross, Canterbury, intended that his tenements near to the city wall should be used to house poor women and these same women (or their successors) were remembered, in 1523, by Richard Wilkinson when he left 2d to each of them; MS CKS PRC 32/6, fol. 26; PRC 17/16, fol. 40. In the adjoining parish of St Peter, Henry Swerder (1504) wished his executors would establish an almshouse of three messuages. His wish was fulfilled and the establishment was managed by the local churchwardens; MS CKS PRC 32/8, fol. 68.

7 Presumably 'the howse of lazaris', noted in the Lydd chamberlains' accounts of 1458, was an early leper hospital; MS EKA Ly/2/1/1/1, fol. 56; A. Finn, ed., *Records of Lydd* (Ashford, 1911), p. 185. Similarly, the spital house called the 'Bekyn' at Faversham was probably an old establishment in 1516, the date of the only known reference; MS CKS PRC 32/12, fol. 33. At the same time it is not always clear whether envisaged new foundations ever came to fruition, such as Sir Anthony Woodville's bequest for an almshouse to be established at Rochester; L. Pidgeon, 'Antony Wydevile, Lord Scales and Rivers: Family, Friends and Affinity, Part 2', *The Ricardian* 16 (2006), 43, citing MS TNA PROB 11/8, fol. 316v. I should like to thank the author for drawing my attention to this reference.

a postscript because many of these institutions were able to cross the Catholic/Protestant doctrinal divide, highlighting the importance of continuity regarding charitable provision in sixteenth-century Kentish society.

Foundation Chronology

Charity and hospitality may have been offered at the county's monastic communities before the Conquest, but it was probably not until Archbishop Lanfranc's ambitious ecclesiastical building programme that Kent gained its first hospital.[8] The twin foundations of St John's and St Nicholas' Hospitals were established c. 1084, the former to house thirty poor men and thirty poor women just outside Canterbury's Northgate, the latter for a similar number of lepers living in wooden houses at Harbledown, a village on the London to Canterbury road.[9] Each hospital had its own chapel, the one at St John's staffed by priests from a neighbouring institution that became a house of Augustinian canons, St Gregory's Priory, in the twelfth century.[10] Lanfranc's contemporary at Rochester, Bishop Gundulf, was unable to emulate his friend to the same degree, but as part of his own building plans he did establish St Bartholomew's Hospital to house both the leprous and the poor outside Rochester's Eastgate at Chatham.[11]

These episcopal initiatives were emulated by certain monastic houses at Canterbury and Dover, leading to a concentration of hospitals at Canterbury, and to a lesser extent at Rochester and Dover, by the mid-twelfth century.[12] Perhaps in

8 M. Rule, ed., *Eademeri Historia Novorum in Anglia*, Rolls Series (London, 1884), pp. 15–16.

9 The location of leper and non-leper hospitals vis-à-vis the local community, especially regarding issues of segregation or non-segregation of the leprous, have been discussed by a number of historians; Cullum, 'Hospitals in Yorkshire', p. 21. R. Gilchrist, 'Medieval Bodies in the Material World: Gender, Stigma and the Body', in *Framing Medieval Bodies*, ed. S. Kay and M. Rubin (Manchester, 1994), pp. 47–9. Orme and Webster, *English Hospital*, pp. 41–8. C. Rawcliffe, 'The Earthly and Spiritual Topography of Suburban Hospitals', in *Town and Country in the Middle Ages: Contrasts, Contacts and Interconnections, 1100–1500*, ed. K. Giles and C. Dyer (Leeds, 2005), pp. 251–74. C. Rawcliffe, *Leprosy in Medieval England* (Woodbridge, 2006). P. Richards, *The Medieval Leper and his Northern Heirs* (Cambridge, 1977). A. E. M. Satchell, 'The Emergence of Leper-Houses in England' (unpublished D.Phil. thesis, University of Oxford, 1998). Sweetinburgh, *Role of the Hospital*, pp. 24, 28, 79–80.

10 M. Hicks and A. Hicks, *St Gregory's Priory, Northgate, Canterbury: Excavations, 1988–1991* (Canterbury, 2001), p. 371.

11 Like Lanfranc, Gundulf rebuilt his cathedral, as well as a number of ancillary buildings, and he was also involved in the construction of Rochester Castle and Malling Abbey; M. Ruual, 'Monks in the World: The Case of Gundulf of Rochester', in *Anglo-Norman Studies* 11, ed. R. A. Brown (Woodbridge, 1989), p. 248. From its inception the hospital may have accommodated fifteen brothers and sisters because it was said to house nine brothers and seven sisters in 1342; *CCR 1341–43*, p. 408.

12 The Benedictine monasteries of St Augustine's Abbey, Canterbury, and St Martin's Priory, Dover, were the mother houses of the leper hospitals of St Lawrence and St Bartholomew, respectively; MS CCAL Lit. C 20, pp. 9–10, 34; MS Bodleian Rawlinson B 335, not numbered. St James' Hospital, located close to the boundary of the liberty of Canterbury, was founded on land given by Godefrid de Malling; MS BL Add. 32098, fol. 1. The first master there was a local physician, Master Feramin, who seems to have been a member of Becket's household before serving at Christ Church Priory. Probably as a result of this connection, and as a means of protecting 'his' hospital, he sought archiepiscopal approval for his request to the prior that St James' should come under the patronage of Christ Church; MS CCAL DCc/Register B, fol. 426; J. B. Sheppard, ed., *Literae Cantuarienses: The Letter Books of*

response to such developments, certain leading townsmen and their knightly contemporaries sought to establish leper hospitals, and less frequently houses for the poor, in their own towns, apparently resulting by 1200 in a plethora of small establishments close to Watling Street and at the Kentish Cinque Ports.[13] Consequently, Gervase's total of eight hospitals in the county by this date is far too low.[14] There were at least twice that number, the majority accommodating lepers, while others catered for the poor and/or infirm and the growing numbers of poor pilgrims and travellers.[15] An example of the latter is Bishop Granville's foundation of St Mary's Hospital at Strood, the house established in 1192 to shelter the local poor and infirm, and pilgrims frequently on their way to Becket's shrine at Canterbury.[16] St Bartholomew's Hospital at Dover and St Stephen and St Thomas' Hospital at Romney initially seem to have accommodated pilgrims and the infirm poor respectively, though within a short time both had apparently become *leprosaria*.[17]

Hospital foundations may have increased in frequency during the early thirteenth century, their location following the pattern established in the previous century: the episcopal cities of Rochester and Canterbury, the Cinque Ports and at various settlements bordering the Canterbury to London road.[18] There were three exceptions: the archiepiscopal hospital of St Peter and St Paul at Maid-

the Monastery of Christ Church, Canterbury, 3 vols (London, 1887) 3, p. 75; E. Holland, trans., *The Canterbury Chantries and Hospitals in 1546. A Supplement to Kent Chantries*, Kent Records 12 supplement (Ashford, 1934), pp. 36–7.

13 P. H. Cullum, 'Leperhouses and Borough Status in the Thirteenth Century', in *Thirteenth Century England* 3, proceedings of the Newcastle upon Tyne Conference 1989, ed. P. Coss and S. Lloyd (Woodbridge, 1989, 1991), pp. 37–46.

14 He lists four (or five because he counts St Gregory's for St John's) in Canterbury: St Lawrence's, St James', St Nicholas', St Thomas'; and one each at Bapchild 'Bakechilde', Blean: St John's, Dover and Rochester; W. Stubbs, ed., *The Historical Works of Gervase of Canterbury*, 2 vols (London, 1880) 2, p. 418.

15 Canterbury: St Nicholas and St Katherine's (first known c. 1195), Maynard's (first known c. 1200); Milton by Gravesend: St Mary the Virgin (first known c. 1175); New Romney: St Stephen and St Thomas (first known c. 1180); Saltwood near Hythe (first known 1169); Sandwich: St Bartholomew's (first known c. 1180), Shooter's Hill (founded 1170s); Stroud: St Mary's (founded 1192); Sutton at Hone: Holy Trinity (first known c. 1200); Tong: St James' (first known c. 1182).

16 C. Johnson, ed. and trans., *Registrum Hamonis Hethe Diocesis Roffensis AD 1319–1352* (Oxford, 1948), p. 1.

17 St Bartholomew's; MS Bodleian Rawlinson B 335, fols 5v, 7v. MS Magdalen College Oxford Deeds Romney 42, 60, 61, 62; A. F. Butcher, 'The Hospital of St Stephen and St Thomas, New Romney: The Documentary Evidence', *Arch. Cant.* 96 (1980), 18.

18 Canterbury: St Thomas' or Eastbridge (the amalgamation of St Thomas, and St Nicholas and St Katherine's occurred c. 1200), St Mary's or the Poor Priests' (founded c. 1218); Chestnuts: leper hospital (first known 1256); Dartford: St Mary Magdalen's (first known 1256), St Bartholomew's (first known 1315); Dover: St Mary's or the Maison Dieu (possibly founded c. 1203); Hythe: St Bartholomew's (first known 1276); New Romney: St John's (first known 1269); Ospringe: St Mary's or the Maison Dieu (possibly refounded c. 1230), St Nicholas' (first known 1241); Otford: leper hospital (first known 1228); Sandwich: St John's (first known 1287), St Anthony's or the Maldry (first known 1315); Sittingbourne: Shamele (first known 1216), St Thomas' (first known c. 1255); Strood: St Nicholas' (first known 1253); Swainestrey in Murston: Holy Cross (first known 1225), St Leonard's (first known 1232).

stone, and two dubious hospitals, one said to be at Ivychurch on Romney Marsh and the Trinitarian friars at Headcorn, who may have sheltered the poor.[19] It is conceivable that the Maidstone hospital may have aided pilgrims travelling to Canterbury, but the early charters indicate that its benefactors believed they were aiding an institution for the poor.[20] Whether they were local paupers is unclear, but it seems these thirteenth-century founders and benefactors generally preferred to assist lepers and poor sick folk from the neighbourhood, rather than itinerants. This apparently growing desire to provide some institutional care may indicate feelings of collective responsibility among the county's leading townsmen towards their less fortunate neighbours, which may in turn reflect their increasing pursuit of greater civic autonomy, especially at the Cinque Ports.[21] Nevertheless, poor pilgrims could find accommodation at some hospitals, and a few institutions specifically catered for them. Two of the most important pilgrim hospitals were under royal patronage, the houses dedicated to St Mary at Ospringe and Dover.[22]

By the early fourteenth century the great wave of hospital building was over. Only a few new institutions were established in Kent, the county continuing to mirror national trends.[23] Of these a couple were leper hospitals, the last founded at Boughton under Blean in 1384.[24] As in the past, the founders of the fourteenth-century hospitals were often prosperous townsmen or senior churchmen, their establishments generally either at one of the Cinque Ports or close to Watling

19 MS Marquess of Salisbury Hatfield Deeds Maidstone 110/21. Clay mentions a hospital at Ivychurch but nothing else is known about it; Clay, *Medieval Hospitals*, p. 298. The connection between the friars at Mottenden and the medieval hospital seems very slim, though Orme and Webster do include the order in their study; *English Hospital*, p. 73.

20 MS Marquess of Salisbury Hatfield Deeds Maidstone 110/20; 110/31; 68/13; 180/14; 181/16.

21 J. P. Croft, 'The Custumals of the Cinque Ports c. 1290–c. 1500: Studies in the Cultural Production of the Urban Record' (unpublished PhD thesis, University of Kent, 1997). Sweetinburgh, *Role of the Hospital*, pp. 188–90.

22 S. Sweetinburgh, 'Royal Patrons and Local Benefactors: The Experiences of the Hospitals of St Mary at Ospringe and Dover in the Thirteenth Century', in *Religious and Laity in Northern Europe 1000–1400: Interaction, Negotiation and Power*, Europa Sacra 2, ed. E. Jamroziak and J. Burton (Turnhout, 2007), pp. 111–29.

23 E. Prescott, *The English Medieval Hospital 1050–1640* (Melksham, 1992), p. 23.

24 Thomas atte Herst dedicated his leper hospital to Holy Trinity, the house also accepting travellers on a short-stay basis; *CPR 1381–85*, p. 448. The other late leper hospital, founded in 1316, was Simon Potyn's hospital of St Katherine; J. Thorpe, ed., *Registrum Roffense* (London, 1769), p. 546. W. Dugdale, *Monasticon Anglicanum*, 6 vols (London, 1823–30), 6 part 2, p. 764. Even though some lazar hospitals continued to house the leprous; St Nicholas' at Harbledown; MS CCAL U 39/2/K; J. Duncombe and N. Battely, *The History and Antiquities of the Three Archiepiscopal Hospitals at or near Canterbury viz. St Nicholas at Harbledown, St John, Northgate and St Thomas of Eastbridge, with some Account of the Priory of St Gregory, the Nunnery of St Sepulcre, the Hospitals of St James and St Laurence and Maynard Spittle* (London, 1785), p. 210. A number of *leprosaria* had become little more than chantry chapels: St Stephen and St Thomas' at New Romney; *CPR 1361–64*, p. 481; *Literae Cantuariensis* 2, pp. 437–41; MS Magdalen College Oxford Deeds Romney 2, 15, 56; Butcher, 'Hospital of St Stephen and St Thomas', 20–2. Yet in the sixteenth century there were still said to be lepers in Kent, though probably only a small number; K. Wood-Legh, ed., *Kentish Visitations of Archbishop William Warham and his Deputies, 1511–12* (Gloucester, 1984), pp. 115–16; MS CCAL CC/J/Q/307/XIV. Rawcliffe, *Leprosy in England*, pp. 348–51.

Street.[25] St John's Hospital at Sevenoaks is one of the few exceptions, and though probably a far earlier foundation, its existence may suggest that there were other medieval hospitals in west Kent.[26]

The late fifteenth and early sixteenth centuries witnessed at upsurge in the number of new foundations, yet many were probably relatively short-lived maisonsdieu.[27] Kent, unlike some counties, did not gain any well-endowed almshouses on the scale of Ewelme or those founded at Coventry or Bristol.[28] Instead, even the best endowed institutions were far more modest, probably a reflection of the size of the county's urban settlements, the more moderate wealth of even the leading merchants and the low level of landholding in the county among leading members of the English aristocracy, though the almshouses belonging to the Corpus Christi Guild at Maidstone demonstrate the value of a communal undertaking.[29] Of the Kentish endowed almshouses or bedehouses, where the inmates were expected to pray daily for the souls of founders and benefactors, the last medieval foundation was the house dedicated to Holy Trinity at Dartford. The original licence had been issued in 1453 but it was not until 1500 that William Milett, a leading local citizen, was able to implement his patron's instructions and establish a place for five almsmen.[30] Though small by national standards, it was still larger than most Kentish maisonsdieu, which frequently accommodated one or two people, possibly in a single tenement or part of one.[31] As in Yorkshire and Wiltshire testamentary records are the principal sources, and to date only part of

25 Bishop Hamo of Rochester founded two hospitals in his natal town of Hythe: St Andrew's (later St John's) in 1336 and St Bartholomew's in 1342, the latter apparently incorporating an existing hospital in the town at some point in the fourteenth century; *CPR 1334–38*, p. 264; *CPR 1340–48*, p. 427. Thomas Elys of Sandwich was instrumental in the establishment of the town's fourth hospital (c. 1392), his house for the poor dedicated to St Thomas the Martyr; *CPR 1391–96*, p. 109. The archiepiscopal hospital at Meopham may date from this period; Clay, *Medieval Hospitals*, p. 298. Knowles and Hadcock, *Medieval Religious Houses*, pp. 344, 366, 389.

26 Several hospitals are only known through their later history: Sevenoaks; *CPR 1338–40*, pp. 46, 411; *CPR 1354–58*, pp. 14, 90, 246; Sevenoaks (and Otford); R. Clarke, *The Medieval Hospital of St John the Baptist, Sevenoaks* (Sevenoaks, 1971), pp. 2–3, 10–11; A. Everitt, *Continuity and Colonization: The Evolution of Kentish Settlement* (Leicester, 1986), pp. 296, 298; Gravesend, *CPR 1370–74*, p. 130; Sutton at Hone, *IPM Edward I* 4, no. 331; Queenborough, Hasted, *History* 6, p. 244.

27 S. Sweetinburgh, 'The Role of the Hospital in Medieval Kent, c.1080–c.1560' (unpublished PhD thesis, University of Kent, 1998), p. 21. Though she did not include Kent among her south-eastern counties in her study of almshouse foundation for this period, her results show similar trends; M. K. McIntosh, 'Local Responses to the Poor in Late Medieval and Tudor England', *Continuity and Change* 3 (1988), 220–3.

28 Orme and Webster, *English Hospital*, pp. 136–46; Prescott, *English Hospital*, pp. 48–65.

29 As well as a guild hall (comprising hall, cloister, kitchen, bakehouse and pantry), the guild had several almshouses and was a major institution in the life of fifteenth-century Maidstone; MS CKS U 1823/89, box 4; U 1823/1 04. P. Clark and L. Murfin, *History of Maidstone: The Making of a Modern County Town* (Stroud, 1995), pp. 35–7.

30 *CPR 1452–61*, p. 114; MS TNA PRO PROB 11/12, fol. 138.

31 For example, in 1476 Alice Berd, a widow from Gravesend, stipulated that the son of her executor, Thomas Sent, should have her tenement except for a small low chamber. This was to be the lodging place of a pauper and when the pauper died another was to be chosen by Thomas and his heirs forever; MS CKS DRb/Pwr4, fol. 205. I should like to thank Dr Paul Lee for this reference.

the county's records have been investigated.[32] Yet even this incomplete search has revealed a more widespread distribution across Kent compared to the earlier hospitals. For example, there were almshouses in Wealden towns such as Cranbrook and Goudhurst, though generally they were concentrated in the county's northern and eastern urban settlements.[33]

Function

Through their hospitals, founders and patrons wished to provide spiritual and material benefits for those who entered the house short-term, for the resident community, and for themselves, their ancestors and successors. To achieve these ends the hospital fulfilled a number of functions which may be classified under the headings: worship, charity and a miscellaneous collection of other works. Hospitals were often engaged in more than one activity, and the balance at a particular institution might change over time, as it appears to have done more broadly across the county, but for the purposes of this article a summary of the diverse functions found at the county's hospitals has been given.

Relatively few Kentish hospitals adopted the rule of St Augustine, but some, such as St Bartholomew's at Dover, and St Lawrence's and St James' at Canterbury, apparently lived under a modified rule of their Benedictine mother house.[34] St Mary's at Ospringe was under the order of Holy Cross, while those under civic patronage were lay communities served by one or more secular priests.[35] Even though it had been forbidden by Pope Gregory IX, St Mary's Hospital at Dover followed the Augustinian Rule after 1239, and almost a century later Bishop Hamo introduced this rule at St Mary's Hospital, Strood, to try to combat certain irregularities that had occurred there.[36] At the same time he initiated a more rigorous devotional regime, as well as placing the hospital under the authority of Rochester Priory.

Nonetheless, the hospital's spiritual role was of prime importance, and founders sought to provide at least one priest and, if possible, a chapel where he might celebrate the divine service daily, attended by members of the hospital's community. As a result initially some early Kentish hospitals may have resembled the classic model: the sick-poor or pilgrims lying in their beds in the hall

32 Cullum, 'Hospitals in Medieval Yorkshire', pp. 330–1. A. D. Brown, *Popular Piety in Late Medieval England: The Diocese of Salisbury, 1250–1550* (Oxford, 1995), pp. 182–5. McIntosh, 'Local Responses to the Poor', 209–45.

33 P. W. Fleming, 'Charity, Faith, and the Gentry of Kent 1422–1529', in *Property and Politics: Essays in Later Medieval English History*, ed. A. Pollard (Gloucester, 1984), p. 45.

34 MS Bodleian Rawlinson B 335, fols 1–5; J. Lyon, *The History of the Town and Port of Dover*, 2 vols (Dover, 1813–14) 1, pp. 53–6. MS CCAL Lit. C 20, pp. 1–8, 22–7. Duncombe and Batterly, *Three Archiepiscopal Hospitals*, pp. 431–4.

35 Drake, 'Hospital of Ospringe', 36; Frohnsdorff, *Maison Dieu*, pp. 13–15.

36 *Calendar Papal Letters 1198–1304*, pp. 154, 181. Johnson, *Registrum Hamonis*, pp. 4–5.

(nave) with a chapel (chancel) at the east end of the building.[37] Moreover, with regard to the chapel, sometimes local townspeople were also expected to join the brothers and sisters at their devotions, especially where the hospital had parochial responsibilities, as at the Canterbury hospitals of St Lawrence and St Nicholas, or civic affiliations, as at St Bartholomew's Hospital in Sandwich.[38] In the chapel the priest brothers, with the rest of the hospital community, were duty bound to pray daily for the well-being of the house's founder while living and for his soul after death. Some founders extended this provision, as Simon Potyn did at Rochester, the inmates also expected to pray for the prosperity of the king and for the realm.[39] At St Bartholomew's, Dover, the brothers and sisters had an even greater list of beneficiaries because they were to pray for the peace of the Church, for the king and queen of England, for the prior and convent of St Martin at Dover, for the burgesses of the town on land and at sea and, most particularly, for all the deceased benefactors of the hospital.[40]

These seven services were the cornerstone of monastic life and so were appropriate for the medieval hospital.[41] At St Lawrence's Hospital, Canterbury, the 1294 revised regulations state that all the brothers and sisters should attend church together saying their beads.[42] Only those who were sick or who had leave of absence from the warden were allowed to miss these services. In contrast, civic patrons seemingly placed greater emphasis on the material needs of their hospital's community: the inmates required to work on the hospital's home farm or in the community's brewhouse or bakehouse. However at St Bartholomew's and St John's Hospitals, Sandwich, the devotional duties of the brothers and sisters increased in the later fifteenth century, thereafter the inmates expected to say daily two psalters of Our Lady and attend divine service at their respective chapels, a level of spiritual observance which was similar to that required by Simon Potyn at his hospital of St Katherine, Rochester.[43] To facilitate such observances some Kentish hospitals and almshouses stipulated that new brothers and sisters should know their *Pater Noster*, *Ave Maria* and *Credo* before entry.

37 Prescott, *English Hospital*, pp. 7–22. St Mary's Hospital, Chichester, is a fine example of the classic layout; Orme and Webster, *English Hospital*, pp. 86–8. Yet this was not always the case and neither of Canterbury's earliest hospitals followed this pattern; P. Bennett, 'St John's Hospital and St John's Nursery', *Arch. Cant.* 108 (1990), 226–31. Generally pragmatism and flexibility seem to have been adopted by founders and patrons in Kent, hospital layouts often becoming increasingly complex over the Middle Ages, in part a reflection of cultural changes and the varying requirements of those involved.

38 Holland, *Canterbury Hospitals*, p. 44. The tithes belonging to St Lawrence's came into lay hands after the hospital was dissolved; MS CCAL U 160.

39 Thorpe, *Registrum Roffense*, p. 546.

40 MS Bodleian Rawlinson B 335, fol. 1v. Lyon, *Dover*, 1, p. 54.

41 Orme and Webster, *English Hospital*, pp. 50, 52.

42 MS CCAL Lit. C 20, pp. 1, 22.

43 MS EKA Sa/LC 1, fols 16–22; Sa/LC 2, fol. 70v; W. Boys, *Collections for an History of Sandwich in Kent, with Notices of the other Cinque Ports and Members and of Richborough* (Canterbury, 1792), p. 574. Thorpe, *Registrum Roffense*, p. 546.

These houses included Bishop Hamo of Rochester's two early fourteenth-century hospitals at Hythe, and William Milett's Dartford almshouse.[44] Yet this basic level of proficiency was presumably considered normal or could be readily acquired because hospital authorities often included the saying of these prayers among the duties to be undertaken daily by the hospital community, as at St Lawrence's and St John's at Canterbury, and St Bartholomew's at Dover.[45]

Notwithstanding its importance, the building of a chapel had potentially serious implications for the diocese because it was outside the parochial system, necessitating a negotiated agreement between the holder of the advowson of the local parish and the hospital authorities or its patron. In 1235 the abbot of St Augustine's Abbey, Canterbury, who held the parish church of Faversham, did agree to the building of a chapel at St Mary's Hospital in Ospringe; that is within the parish of Faversham (see Edwards, this volume).[46] Ten years later he was also prepared to grant the right of burial at the hospital chapel for those brothers who 'wore the habit' and sick people who died there, but only on condition that the priest brothers did not perform the sacraments on behalf of local parishioners.[47] Furthermore, the hospital was to give all the gifts and offerings it received in the fulfilling of these services to the parish church of Faversham. A similar provision was employed at *leprosaria* concerning mortuary fees due to the local parish priest for the burial of lepers. Such burial practices were implemented in response to directives from the Papal Curia in the late twelfth century, though this segregation of the dead, as for the living, at many early Kentish houses may predate papal initiatives because a chapel was seemingly provided at an early stage.[48]

The development of doctrinal ideas concerning purgatory during the thirteenth century led to the foundation of chantries, and, in addition to the parish church, religious houses, including hospitals, were seen as suitable institutions by wealthy senior clerics and laypeople in the pursuit of salvation.[49] In broad terms, chantries were generally linked to leper hospitals but some were associated with houses for the poor and for pilgrims, though the three priests at St Bartholomew's, Sandwich, formed an exceptionally large institution.[50] Often the chantry was in or

44 Johnson, *Registrum Hamonis* 1, p. 393; MS EKA hbarth 5 (trans. provided by A. F. Butcher). MS TNA PRO PROB 11/12, fol. 138.

45 MS CCAL Lit. C 20, pp. 1, 22. Duncombe and Battely, *Three Archiepiscopal Hospitals,* pp. 203, 255. MS Bodleian Rawlinson B 335, fol. 2v.

46 C. Drake, 'The Hospital of St Mary of Ospringe Commonly called Maison Dieu', *Arch. Cant.* 30 (1914), 37.

47 Ibid., 40, 70–1; M. Frohnsdorff, *The Maison Dieu and Medieval Faversham* (Faversham, 1997), p. 37.

48 For the national picture, Rawcliffe, *Leprosy in England*, pp. 259–62.

49 A. D. Brown, *Church and Society in England, 1000–1500* (Basingstoke, 2003), pp. 126–7.

50 They may have been part of the original foundation, and the evidence points to their presence by the early fourteenth century at the latest. According to the custumal they were pray for certain named individuals but a contemporary chronicle seems to imply that the hospital and chantry had been founded by and for the commonalty; MS EKA Sa/LC 1, fol. 19v; H. Cannon, 'The Battle of Sandwich and Eustace the Monk', *English Historical Review* 108 (1912), 669, citing the *Polistorie de Jean de Cantorbery*.

near the hospital's chapel, as at St Thomas', Canterbury, where a chapel within the hospital housed the Bourne chantry.[51] At others, however, the master was expected to make the necessary provisions at a local parish church: Henry de Cantuaria's chantry in the oratory next to St Dunstan's church was the responsibility of the master of the Poor Priests' Hospital, Canterbury.[52] Such provisions mark a shift in the role of these charitable institutions and the consequent balance between hospital and chantry, a position exacerbated by growing financial difficulties. Leper hospitals were particularly affected, and some became little more than chantry chapels. How far the leper population had actually fallen is unclear, but the decline was seen as a legitimate excuse for those seeking to convert hospitals to chantries. Nevertheless, even though the Brenchley family's appropriation of St Stephen and St Thomas Hospital, New Romney, was seen as reasonable, several decades later there were still sufficient lepers at St Nicholas' Hospital, Canterbury, to cause difficulties recruiting a suitable priest.[53]

For those of more limited means, hospitals could offer other spiritual services: a place in a bede or obit roll, a chance to join a confraternity, an offer of indulgences or an opportunity to visit relics. Few records survive regarding the production of bede rolls at Kentish hospitals, the only ones so far discovered were at Lanfranc's hospitals of St John and St Nicholas, and St Mary's and St Bartholomew's Hospitals at Dover.[54] Evidence concerning confraternities is almost equally sparse and again this seems to have been on offer to benefactors of the Lanfranc hospitals, and also to those who supported St Mary's Hospital, Strood.[55] Alternatively, the guild of Corpus Christi at Maidstone had its own almshouses in the town, and in Canterbury the city's clerks formed the fraternity of Corpus Christi at St Thomas' Hospital (see Sweetinburgh, this volume).[56] Some houses were able to offer papal and episcopal indulgences, either to those who visited the hospital, as at St Andrew's, Hythe, and St Bartholomew's, Dover, or to those who made donations to the hospital's proctors, such as those from St John's and St Nicholas', Canterbury.[57] Relics were also viewed as spiritual assets,

51 Hussey, *Kent Chantries*, pp. 62–3.

52 *CPR 1330–34*, p. 10.

53 MS Magdalen College Oxford Deeds Romney 29, 30; MS CCAL DCc/ChAnt/W/214. *CPR 1361–64*, p. 481; Butcher, St Stephen and St Thomas', 21–3. Other hospitals that suffered a similar fate include St James' at Tong and St John's, Sevenoaks; *CCR 1339–41*, p. 183; *CPR 1354–58*, pp. 14, 90. MS CCAL U 39/2/K.

54 MS CKS PRC 32/7, fol. 70. MS CKS PRC 32/4, fol. 109. MS Bodleian Rawlinson B 335, fol. 37. Rawcliffe, *Leprosy*, p. 151.

55 MS CKS PRC 17/7, fol. 213. Thomas Petite of Canterbury may have sought such a gift at St Nicholas' Hospital when he bequeathed 2s 7d for the repair of the hospital's clock; MS CKS PRC 17/7, fol. 64. Thorpe, *Registrum Roffense*, p. 632; Johnson, *Registrum Hamonis* 1, p. 1.

56 MS CKS PRC 17/15, fol. 101. In 1484/5, for example, the fraternity paid 6s 8d towards repairs on its almshouses in Puddynglane; MS CKS Md/G12; Clark and Murfin, *Maidstone*, p. 56.

57 In 1368, Archbishop Langham granted an indulgence of forty days to the Hythe hospital for those who visited and aided the house; A. Wood, trans. and ed., *Registrum Simonis Langham, Cantuariensis Archiepiscopi*, Canterbury and York Society (Oxford, 1956), p. 192. MS Bodleian Rawlinson B 335, fols 5–7v. Duncombe and Battely, *Three Archiepiscopal Hospitals*, pp. 203, 253–6.

and St Mary's, Ospringe, had an extensive collection, while its namesake at Dover had the bowels of St Richard of Chichester, who had died at the house during a preaching crusade in 1253.[58]

Like piety, charity was a cornerstone of the hospital's work, and the principal groups aided were those housed long term, the short-term inmates who either left or died, those seeking overnight accommodation and those who received relief at its gate. Kentish hospitals were most likely to aid the first group, though some houses had the flexibility to care for several categories. Generally, the long-term inmates were lepers or poor and/or infirm persons, who, in the twelfth and thirteenth centuries, probably entered the hospital without paying. However, by the fourteenth century certain houses had seemingly introduced an entry fee and even though others legislated against the entry of fee-paying corrodians, the very presence of such statutes may indicate that the charging of fees was relatively widespread (see Edwards, this volume).[59] Furthermore, hospitals under the patronage of the king or the archbishop were expected to house the patron's aged retainers. For example, one of Archbishop Winchelsey's servants, Stephen de Wengham, lived at St Peter and St Paul's Hospital in Maidstone at the institution's expense from 1306 until his death.[60] Like the fee-paying residents, these people were known as corrodians and their presence might become a considerable burden on the hospital.[61] Even more of a problem was the level of exploitation of this system at the royal hospitals by the three Edwards, who were particularly ruthless in their use of the Dover and Ospringe establishments. Even when certain masters complained bitterly, claiming that they were poverty stricken as a result of the king's actions, he continued to place men in their custody.[62]

Some hospitals, such as St John's and St Nicholas', Canterbury, specifically forbade the entry of cripples, the blind, the feeble, the old and the impotent, but it is not known how strictly this was enforced.[63] Furthermore, the records show that

58 J. Adair, *The Pilgrims Way: Shrines and Saints in Britain and Ireland* (London, 1978), p. 47. The master at the Ospringe hospital carried off many of its treasured relics in the early fifteenth century; *CPR 1416–22*, p. 208. T. Tanner, *Saint Edmund's Chapel, Dover, and its Restoration* (Dover, 1968), p. 8.

59 For example, when the ordinances were written up, apparently for the first time in 1301, for the civic hospitals of St Bartholomew and St John in Sandwich, they included notes about entry fees; MS EKA Sa/LC 1, fols 18, 21v. Croft, 'Custumals of the Cinque Ports', p. 348.

60 R. Graham, trans. and ed., *Registrum Roberti Winchelsey, Archiepiscopi Cantuariensis AD 1294–1313*, Canterbury and York Society, 2 vols (Oxford, 1952) 1, p. 507.

61 For example, Archbishop Islip was said to have granted two concurrent corrodies, thereby exerting extra pressure on the house's resources; *Calendar Inquisitions Miscellaneous*, 3, p. 361.

62 For the master at Ospringe the constant presence of such corrodians was especially taxing, Edward III being a particularly ruthless exponent of the system, placing three concurrent corrodians there during the second and third decades of the fourteenth century; Rigold, 'Two Kentish Hospitals', 36. Sweetinburgh, *Role of the Hospital*, pp. 114–15; Sweetinburgh, 'Royal Patrons', p. 127.

63 These exclusions were included in the revised statutes drawn up by Archbishop Winchelsey in 1299; Graham, *Registrum Winchelsey* 2, p. 828. Orme and Webster reproduce some of the most well-known lists of excluded persons at particular hospitals; *English Hospital*, p. 58.

St Bartholomew's at Chatham did house a few infirm persons in the fourteenth century, though the nature of their ailments is less certain.[64] In addition, many of the corrodians, like the lepers and other long-term residents, probably suffered from ill health before they died, possibly becoming bedridden. Nevertheless, there is very little evidence of formal medical provision at the county's hospitals.[65] It is not clear whether any of the brothers were actually using the books of surgery known to have been at St Bartholomew's, Sandwich, in the early sixteenth century.[66] Similarly, even though Simon Bredon, a noted physician, was master at St Peter and St Paul's Hospital, Maidstone, from 1358 until his death in 1372, there is nothing to indicate that he practised there.[67]

Instead, care for the sick and the elderly, both the resident population and the sick poor who only stayed for a short time, was probably undertaken by the hospital sisters. Little is known from the documentary sources about such activities, but at St John's Hospital, Sandwich, three rooms were set aside at the back of the place to accommodate the sick and women in child birth.[68] On occasion, some of these may have been pilgrims, and at the pilgrim hospitals such sick people were allowed to stay longer than their able-bodied fellows.[69] Initially, the pilgrims who stayed at Dover and at Ospringe were looked after by the hospital sisters, but by the later Middle Ages the sisters had disappeared, and at Dover the poor were cared for by the wife of one of the lay brothers in the early sixteenth century.[70] At St Thomas' Hospital, Canterbury, the system was similar. Healthy pilgrims, who stayed overnight, and the sick, who stayed slightly longer, were all under the care of an elderly woman (she was to be at least forty years of age). She was given 4d daily to cover their board and lodging.[71]

64 In an inquisition dated 1342, it was said that there were 'enclosed places for the care of the sick' at St Bartholomew's Hospital, Chatham, who were presumably the responsibility of the nine brothers and seven sisters living there; E. Greenwood, *The Hospital of St Bartholomew, Rochester* (Rochester, 1962), p. 19; *CCR 1341–43*, p. 408.

65 For the national situation, E. Hammond, 'Physicians in Medieval English Religious Houses', *Bulletin of the History of Medicine* 32 (1958), 105–20. V. Bullough, 'A Note on Medical Care in Medieval English Hospitals', *Bulletin of the History of Medicine* 35 (1961), 74–7. C. Rawcliffe, 'Curing Bodies and Healing Souls: Pilgrimage and the Sick in Medieval East Anglia', in *Pilgrimage: The English Experience from Becket to Bunyon*, ed. C. Morris and P. Roberts (Cambridge, 2002), p. 115. Cullum, 'Hospitals of Yorkshire', pp. 61–2, 168–9.

66 Robert Ferrar, a brother at St Bartholomew's, entrusted his executor with his two books of surgery so that they might be copied for the benefit of the hospital after his death; MS CKS PRC 17/21, fol. 106.

67 A. Emden, *A Bibliographical Register of the University of Oxford to AD 1500*, 3 vols (Oxford, 1957–59), 1, p. 257.

68 MS EKA Sa/Ch 10J A1.

69 A papal indulgence granted to St Thomas' Hospital, Canterbury, in 1363, specifically mentioned women in childbirth; *Calendars of Entries in the Papal Registers Relating to Great Britain and Ireland* 4, p. 36.

70 Rigold, 'Kentish Hospitals', 35–6. In the 1530s the cost of providing for the poor at the Dover hospital was said to be yearly £40; *Valor Eccles.* 1 p. 56.

71 *Literae Cantuarienses* 2, p. 256. Alice was the 'custodian of the house of paupers' at St Thomas' Hospital in 1475, and fifty years later Rauf Cocker and his wife were employed to care for the poor people who came to the hospital; MS CKS PRC 32/2, fol. 324; Hussey, *Kent Chantries*, p. 65.

Even more difficult to gauge is the provision available for those given alms at the hospital gate. In some cases this may have comprised casual distributions of cash and food, yet many hospitals, like monastic houses, gave out doles either on a frequent basis as liveries or on specific anniversaries or feast days. The latter were often linked to the obits of the hospital's founder or benefactors and at St Mary's, Dover, the poor received special hospitality on at least seven days annually. Among these special annual distributions was one on the feast day of the Nativity of Our Lady, when two quarters of wheat bread, a quantity of ale and two oxen or four barrels of white herring were given to the poor for the souls of all the house's founders; and another on 17 March, when fifteen poor people received dinner for the soul of Beatrice Walkyn.[72] Nonetheless, there was nothing in Kent to rival the alms given at Cardinal Beaufort's refoundation of St Cross' Hospital at Winchester or the doles given at St Leonard's Hospital at York, but for the individual hospital the proportion of its revenue used in this way might be considerable and some Kentish institutions continued to aid the poor at their gate until their dissolution in the mid-sixteenth century.[73]

Like the monasteries and secular colleges, a few hospitals provided educational facilities. Probably the most important in this regard are the three hospitals dedicated to St Mary at Dover, Ospringe and Strood. Even though far more is known about the books owned by monastic houses, some work has been undertaken concerning English hospital libraries (see Edwards, this volume).[74] Evidence from Kent is extremely sparse but some hospitals may have had extensive libraries and perhaps the largest was at St Mary's, Dover, which had at least 117 volumes.[75] As might be expected of the handful of known titles all were liturgical or theological works, providing suitable material for those seeking to enter holy orders.[76] Yet few at these hospitals had a degree, and the brothers at Ospringe do not appear to have received a university education whilst staying at their sister institution in Oxford.[77]

Interestingly, hermits rarely envisaged Kentish hospitals as suitable abodes. Of the few examples, there was a chapel and hermitage at the small hospital in

72 *Valor Eccles.* 1, p. 56.

73 Orme and Webster, *English Hospital*, p. 63.

74 C. Rawcliffe, 'Written in the Book of Life: Building the Libraries of English Medieval Hospitals and Almshouses', *The Library* 7th series 3 (2002), 127–62.

75 MS BL Stowe MS 850. This is as large as any of the hospital libraries cited by Orme and Webster; *English Hospital*, pp. 64–5.

76 The lending of books also took place: the parson at Eastbridge in Romney Marsh lent several books to Robert Yong, a brother at St Mary's Hospital, Dover; MS CKS 32/15, fol. 371.

77 In the mid-thirteenth century, the connection between Ospringe and Oxford may have meant some of the Ospringe brothers received their education at Oxford, but the evidence is circumstantial; Orme and Webster, *English Hospital*, p. 65. From Emden, the only master at Ospringe who may have been educated at Oxford is Thomas Assby, but the dates do not fit unless he was a pluralist; for Strood, three perhaps four of the masters had studied at Oxford; for Dover, John Thompson's (last master) appointment to the mastership appears to have been a political decision; Emden, *Register of Oxford to 1500*, 1, pp. 56, 129, 496; 2, p. 1298; A. Emden, *A Biographical Register of the University of Oxford, AD 1501–1540* (Oxford, 1974), p. 571.

Sittingbourne in the mid-thirteenth century and another hermit was perhaps the last resident at St Mary's Hospital, Ospringe, when it was just known as the 'spetill house'.[78] Instead these religious men and women apparently preferred to live in churchyards, at religious houses, in Dover Castle, on the top of cliffs or in the walls of Canterbury. For the hospitals this was a missed opportunity because the presence of a recluse added to its reputation and status, and such holy persons often received visitors who might offer alms towards the work of the house.[79] Other 'visitors' could include those seeking sanctuary, and one of the few hospitals offering this right was St John's at Canterbury.[80]

Hospitals were also expected to aid the community more broadly, including the maintenance and provision of bridges and ferries, and as locations for the holding of markets or fairs.[81] In 1349, at the request of John Gybon, Edward III gave custody of the ferry between Sandwich and Stonar to St Bartholomew's Hospital, the master taking responsibility for its leasing to a local ferryman.[82] The master of St Thomas' Hospital, Canterbury, was duty bound to maintain the city's Eastbridge, though on more than one occasion he was indicted for failing to repair it.[83] An even more difficult task fell to the master of St Mary's, Strood, who was responsible for a section of Rochester Bridge.[84] The importance of this commitment may be gauged by the provision of a chapel and other buildings near the Strood end of the bridge by the hospital's founder. These were intended to produce rents and offerings for the benefit of the bridge and the hospital more generally.[85] This connection was even stronger during the late fourteenth century when Walter de Basing, the master at St Mary's, was for many years also master of the king's works at Rochester, which included the bridge.[86] Nevertheless, this relationship became more onerous after a new bridge was built further downstream and a new chapel, on the Rochester side, became the main recipient of the

78 *VCH Kent* 2, p. 228. Knowles and Hadcock, *Medieval Religious Houses*, p. 392. Drake, 'Hospital of Ospringe', 57.

79 Orme and Webster, *English Hospital*, pp. 66–7.

80 *VCH Kent* 2, p. 211.

81 Archbishop Boniface expected to aid his hospital and his town of Maidstone when he acquired the right to hold a market at the new hospital there in 1261; and the fair held on the eve of St Luke's feast day at St Bartholomew's Hospital, Sandwich, was presumably for a similar purpose; Clark and Murfin, *Maidstone*, p. 25; Boys, *Sandwich*, p. 17.

82 *CPR 1348–50*, p. 341. The hospital register contains details of agreements with two ferrymen from the late fourteenth century; MS EKA Sa/Ch 10B A1.

83 *CPR 1385–89*, p. 523; MS CCAL CC/A/A/13; CC/A/A/14.

84 H. Smetham, *History of Strood* (Chatham, 1899, reprinted 1978), pp. 133–4; N. Brooks, 'Rochester Bridge, AD 43–1381', in *Traffic and Politics: The Construction and Management of Rochester Bridge, AD 43–1993*, ed. N. Yates and J. Gibson (Woodbridge, 1994), p. 38 (the particular perils of crossing Rochester Bridge, pp. 35–6).

85 Though less hazardous than the ferry, the bridge crossing was notorious and stories like the divine rescue of 'the harper of Rochester' were probably well-known in the Medway towns, drawing alms from grateful travellers; Brooks, 'Rochester', pp. 35–6.

86 A. Harrison, 'Excavations on the Site of St Mary's Hospital, Strood', *Arch. Cant.* 84 (1969), 140, 149, 156–8.

offerings given by grateful travellers.[87] An allied area of responsibility held by various hospitals was town wall maintenance and the provision of defences against foreign invasion and incursions by the sea, all of which might involve considerable expense in terms of men and materials.[88]

Resources

In general terms, the wealthier the founder, the greater the hospital, consequently, there were few wealthy institutions in Kent compared to the national picture.[89] Using the *Valor Ecclesiasticus* and chantry certificates as a guide to comparative wealth, only two Kentish hospitals enjoyed a net value of their possessions in excess of £100 (St Mary's, Dover, and St Nicholas, Canterbury), though St John's Hospital, Canterbury, was close at over £91. Considerably less prosperous were five hospitals having net assets valued between £31 and £52. Yet these were far richer than the other six hospitals for which there are figures, the highest being £12 for St Thomas, Sandwich and the lowest £4 for St John's Hospital at Hythe.[90] Thus, it is hardly surprising that in 1533 the penultimate master at St Mary's Hospital, Dover, warned his fellow brethren of the likely danger to the house 'for it is named very rich'.[91]

The most important assets of any hospital were its site and buildings, and whether the hospital comprised a great hall and chapel with ancillary buildings or a single room or cottage for a selected pauper, such provisions were often the largest item of expenditure for founders.[92] Furthermore, some founders became the first master, as at the Poor Priests' Hospital, Canterbury, where Alexander of Gloucester continued to live in his stone house in which he had established his hospital.[93] In Kent, the largest and most elaborate hospitals were either under royal patronage: those dedicated to St Mary at Dover and Ospringe; or archiepiscopal, in particular, Lanfranc's hospital for the poor at Northgate, Canterbury.[94]

87 Brooks, 'Rochester', pp. 44, 49–50, 71.

88 For example, in 1528 the master and brothers at St Bartholomew's Hospital, Sandwich, initially refused to pay their contribution towards repairing the wharf at Davygate; MS EKA Sa/AC 3, fol. 10v. St Mary's Hospital, Dover, held the Romney Marsh manors of Honychilde and Eastbridge which meant the master was involved in the payment of marsh scotts. On occasion this led to disputes between the master and the hospital's tenants, as had happened in the late thirteenth century; *CPR 1281–92*, p. 407.

89 Orme and Webster, *English Hospital*, p. 84.

90 Sweetinburgh, 'Hospital in Kent', p. 39.

91 *Letters and Papers Henry VIII* 6, p. 413.

92 In other cases the whole house was used. In 1507, Johanna Lull left her house in Faversham to be an almshouse for poor, old and needy people under the supervision of Elizabeth Knyght, her servant. After five years Elizabeth was to receive the house, as well as the bedding and other goods there; and in return she was to pray for the soul of her former mistress; MS CKS PRC 17/13, fol. 339.

93 P. Bennett, 'The Poor Priests' Hospital – the Chapel', *Arch. Cant.* 98 (1982), 218.

94 M. Walcott, 'Inventories of (i) St Mary's hospital or Maison Dieu, Dover, (ii) Dover priory', *Arch. Cant.* 7 (1868), 272–80. Frohnsdorff, *Maison Dieu*, pp. 17–20. Bennett, 'St John's Hospital', 226–8.

Clearly patronage was extremely important, but hospital type might influence founders: Lanfranc's wooden huts for the lepers, and stone buildings for the poor.[95] Yet some leper hospitals were grander from their inception, which meant that St James' and St Lawrence's in Canterbury became desirable residences for members of Canterbury's aspiring gentry families in the late sixteenth century, and the leper hospital at New Romney was seemingly an impressive place before it became a chantry in the 1360s.[96] However for contemporaries, possibly the most visible contrast was between the different types of almshouse, William Milett's cottages for five poor people at Dartford and the single room in Alice Berd's tenement at neighbouring Gravesend.[97] Thus, the hallmarks of hospital building in Kent were variation and pragmatism, rather than an adherence to a particular style or ideology, and even on seemingly greenfield sites there were often restrictions, such as the presence of marshy ground.[98]

As time went on, and where funds allowed, hospital authorities frequently sought to add further buildings or adapt existing ones, as well as beautifying the chapel, often at the request of benefactors.[99] Some hospitals had gatehouses, but less frequently were enclosed by walls, such boundaries demarcating the house's jurisdiction, keeping out undesirables and offering a point of contact between the hospital and the outside world. At St John's, Canterbury, one of the hospital's alms boxes could be lowered from the porter's window in the gatehouse when travellers passed by, and the same gatehouse offered some protection in the late fifteenth century when the city's mayor attacked the place during a dispute over jurisdiction.[100]

A desire for privacy may have influenced the move away from dormitories to the provision of individual rooms by the later Middle Ages, and by this time the residents might also be allowed to keep some of their own possessions.[101] The accommodation was even more elaborate at certain hospitals, the brothers and

95 Rule, *Eademeri*, pp. 15–16.

96 MS CCAL U 160. MS EKA U 88/T57; MS CKS U 806/T85. *CCR 1354–60*, p. 587; *CPR 1350–54*, p. 303; Shepherd, *Literae Cantuarienses* 2, pp. 437–41.

97 MS CKS DRb/Pw4, fol. 205. I should like to thank Dr Paul Lee for drawing my attention to this reference and to all subsequent references in wills from the diocese of Rochester.

98 For St John's Hospital, Canterbury; K. Parfitt, 'St John's Hospital Reredorter, Canterbury', *Arch. Cant.* 109 (1991), 300. At St Bartholomew's Chatham, the existing road structure and steeply rising ground restricted the hospital builders; J. Hayes, D. Williams and P. Payne, 'Report of an Excavation in the Grounds of St Bartholomew's Chapel, Chatham', *Arch. Cant.* 98 (1982), 188.

99 For example, according to an inventory made in 1535, as well as the chapel and living quarters, the Maison Dieu at Dover had three stables, a granary, a brewhouse, a bakehouse and at least one barn; Walcott, '*Maison Dieu*', 279.

100 It is feasible that such a collecting box still survives among the hospital's possessions. MS CCAL U 13/1. MS BL Add. 32,311, fols 63–64. At its sister hospital, the 'custodian of the gate' in 1479 was Nicholas Glover; MS CKS PRC 32/2, fol. 465. This incident, in 1489, involved the mayor entering the house of John Belle, at the hospital's gate, and that of Thomas Curtes in the hospital, from which he took a kettle and a cooking pot; MS CCAL DCc/BB 9/2.

101 For example, John Godewyn of St Katherine's Hospital, Rochester, bequeathed to his daughter all 'his stuff' at the hospital; MS CKS DRb/Pw5, fol. 184.

sisters at St John's, Canterbury each having their own kitchen and other rooms, though communal meals remained an important aspect of hospital life.[102]

After buildings, land and property constituted the most important assets at many Kentish hospitals.[103] Nonetheless, the extent of such assets varied tremendously, dependent on the initial endowment and the level of gifts donated by subsequent benefactors. Both royal hospitals had extensive landholdings but were very different in character. St Mary's at Dover received most of its land from Hubert de Burgh, and his overlord, Henry III, with additional benefactors from among the Kentish aristocracy, but generally not from the local townsmen. As a result it had relatively little urban property in Dover. Instead, much of its land was in the town's hinterland, and in Romney Marsh and the Isle of Sheppey, with further holdings in London. At Ospringe the local townsfolk and their neighbours from Faversham followed their sovereign's lead. Consequently, St Mary's at Ospringe was an extensive property holder in the locality, and it also had a considerable acreage in Staple and Wingham.[104] Although the presence of the king may have made these hospitals atypical, at most twelfth- and early thirteenth-century foundations (the majority of Kent's hospitals and discounting the later almshouses) the build up of their estates occurred during the first century of their existence, so predating the Statute of Mortmain of 1279. However, the statute seems to have had much less impact than was thought at one time, hospital authorities apparently paying the necessary fee or finding other ways to circumvent it.[105]

Although the wealthy and those of high status might donate large landholdings, the patronage of churches or other substantial assets, most grants comprised small pieces of land or rents. These were useful but might be difficult to manage successfully because they were often scattered across a number of manors and parishes. To try to overcome such problems, especially where the hospital community was engaged in direct farming, the authorities seem to have adopted a policy of consolidating their holdings by seeking out adjacent property. The apparent success of this strategy in the thirteenth century may suggest that less prosperous peasants saw the release of their land or rents to the hospital as a way of generating much needed cash. Furthermore, in a world before mortgages, certain peasants negotiated their continuing use of the land for life, effectively becoming tenants on what had once been their own land.[106] Yet for all their

102 Margaret Fryer (1523), a sister at St John's, apparently had her own hall in the hospital because she left money for a chimney to be constructed there after her death; MS CKS PRC 32/13, fol. 150.

103 For example, in 1277 the brothers at St Mary's Hospital, Strood, complained that some of their houses near the wharf had been badly damaged when Rochester was besieged; *VCH Kent* 2, p. 216.

104 Sweetinburgh, 'Royal Patrons', pp. 115–16, 119–22.

105 S. Raban, 'Mortmain in Medieval England', in *Landlords, Peasants and Politics in Medieval England*, ed. T. Aston (Cambridge, 1987), pp. 205–7, 224–6. The prior at St Nicholas's Hospital at Canterbury had to seek a royal pardon in 1412 because the house had illegally accepted a considerable number of land grants; *CPR 1408–13*, p. 406.

106 S. Sweetinburgh, 'Supporting the Canterbury Hospitals: Benefaction and the Language of Charity in the Twelfth and Thirteenth Centuries', *Arch. Cant.* 122 (2002), 237–58.

success in obtaining such assets, hospitals were often claiming poverty by the early fourteenth century, and thereafter financial difficulties frequently hampered the efforts of many hospital authorities.[107]

Some benefactors gave what amounted to an annuity, either from rents for land, mills or other industrial activities, but most of the cash hospitals received from donors came in the form of offerings and gifts.[108] For example, hospitals were predominantly sited close to major thoroughfares, offering opportunities to collect alms from passing travellers, and those by bridges and fords may have been even more successful.[109] At Sandwich one of the brothers at St John's was sent to gather alms at the three parish churches on Sundays, possibly after high mass, and at Christmas the brothers also collected bread from local householders.[110] Nor did hospital authorities confine their alms gathering to the immediate neighbourhood. Several hospitals, including St Bartholomew's at Dover, had permission to send out proctors, often to collect within the diocese but some had permission to roam further afield.[111] It is unclear how successful such measures were except that the master at St Thomas' Hospital, Canterbury, complained bitterly on several occasions during the early fourteenth century about false proctors taking alms which belonged to the hospital.[112]

Fortunately, one important category of gift does show up in the record books. The writing of wills became increasingly common in Kent from the mid-fifteenth century and some hospitals were relatively well favoured. Looking first at the

107 Sweetinburgh, *Role of Hospital*, pp. 83–4, 93–4, 99–100, 112–16. An inquiry held in 1342 found that St Bartholomew's Hospital, Chatham, had various assets but that after it had paid dues to certain religious houses there was insufficient income to sustain its charitable work; Greenwood, *Hospital of St Bartholomew*, pp. 16–19.

108 For example, Simon de Chelesfeud gave an annual rent of 20s 3d from his tenements to St Mary's Hospital at Strood in 1273; MS Medway Archives DRc/T 589. The hospital also held rights in several properties in Aylesford, including a half share in a mill; MS Medway Archives DRc/T 574/1–4, T 576/2–3. In addition, hospitals might receive tithes or other offerings if they held the advowson of a local church. St Mary's Hospital held the local church of St Nicholas in Strood and when the parishioners set up an alms box there in 1330 the master objected on the grounds that it was diverting revenue away from the hospital, a position that was upheld by the bishop; Johnson, *Registrum Hamonis*, p. 244.

109 The bridge chapel associated with St Mary's Hospital and Rochester Bridge has already been noted, and another hospital close to a crossing point on the Medway was the hospital of St Peter and St Paul at Maidstone. Rawcliffe, 'Suburban Hospitals', pp. 263–7. For the Maidstone hospital, the advantage of such a location may have been enhanced by the offer of indulgences for those aiding the establishment; MS Marquess of Salisbury Hatfield Deeds Maidstone 110/19.

110 MS EKA Sa/LC 1, fols 20–1v.

111 The register records two of the hospital's proctors: Andrew Durant who went out for one year in 1330 and John de Chellesfelde who collected alms for two years in the following decade; MS Bodleian Rawlinson B 335, fols 97v–8v. Elsewhere, as at St John's, Canterbury, it was customary for some of the brothers to travel across the country twice a year gathering alms. They carried with them letters under the hospital's seal detailing a number of papal and episcopal indulgences and the promise that the hundred brothers and sisters would say thirty thousand *Pater Nosters* and *Ave Marias* for the benefit of the hospital's benefactors; Duncombe and Battely, *Three Archiepiscopal Hospitals*, pp. 203, 255. Only once are the hospital authorities known to have used a female proctor: Marina Swetman in 1465; Duncombe and Battely, *Three Archiepiscopal Hospitals*, p. 255.

112 *CPR 1307–13*, p. 499; *1313–17*, p. 87; *1321–24*, p. 122.

Rochester diocese, hospitals in the Medway towns were the most popular, and men such as Thomas Shemyng, a Rochester draper, were generous benefactors.[113] In 1523 he bequeathed 6s 8d to St Bartholomew's Hospital, Chatham and the same amount to St Nicholas' Hospital, Rochester. Interestingly, he did not mention St Mary's, Strood, preferring to aid St Katherine's at Rochester. He left 6s 8d to be spent on the chapel at St Katherine's but it was the poor inmates who received the greatest consideration, including a provision that his assigns would reorganise the house, setting up partitions as had been before and ensuring that there were two beds with bedding in each cubicle.

In the Canterbury diocese there were two groups of favoured hospitals, three in Canterbury itself: St John's, St Nicholas' and Maynards spital, all of which survive to this day; and two of the Sandwich hospitals: the leper hospital at Each End dedicated to St Anthony and St John's, though interest in these latter houses died away at the beginning of the sixteenth century.[114] St Anthony's may have disappeared at this time and St John's was apparently experiencing financial difficulties, the hospital subsequently declining still further when the civic authorities used it to lodge beggars as part of their policy on vagrants in the 1520s.[115] Consequently, status and reputation were important assets for any hospital. To be seen as an honest hospital was a key attribute, and the reputation of St James' Hospital, Canterbury, was not helped by the complaint made in 1511 that Richard Welles's wife had set up a beer stall in the precinct.[116] This was not the first irregularity because the community at St James' had been in trouble a century earlier, on that occasion the brothers and sisters had been admonished for talking in church and for allowing certain sisters to assist at divine service; and in the late twelfth century it had excited papal disapproval when healthy women sought admittance at the expense of the leprous.[117] Thus, if a hospital was to be successful, or at least survive, it needed to husband carefully all its resources, a process that often involved its patron which meant that in general terms those under local patronage were frequently better placed.[118]

Management

Patronage of a hospital brought the right to choose the master or, where this had been ceded to the community, to ratify or reject the chosen candidate.

113 MS CKS DRs/Pwr7, fol. 291.

114 Sweetinburgh, *Role of Hospital*, pp. 117–26, 205–7, 209–10.

115 MS EKA Sa/AC 2, fol. 326.

116 Wood-Legh, *Kentish Visitations,* p. 12.

117 *VCH Kent* 2, pp. 209–10; Duncombe and Battely, *Three Archiepiscopal Hospitals*, pp. 431–3; Shepherd, *Literae Cantuarienses* 3, pp. 75–6.

118 Personal knowledge was also important, and Joan Denys (1442) was sufficiently confident in the reformed St James' Hospital to bequeath several gifts to the place for the benefit of her soul. These included £20 to Dom. Edmund, the chaplain, so that he would travel to Rome and there celebrate the divine service for a year for her soul; MS CCAL DCc/Chart. Ant. W/241.

Consequently, the hierarchical relationship between patron and hospital varied, and one of the markers of this variation was who held the hospital's seal and any restrictions placed on its use by the master, brothers and sisters. According to the revised statutes (1342), St Thomas' Hospital, Canterbury, would not have a common seal, instead the archbishop, as patron, would control the house's property.[119] This was not the case at St Bartholomew's, Chatham, where the master held the common seal, allowing the community to alienate the hospital's landholdings if they so wished.[120] At its namesake in Sandwich the situation was more complex. The master held the hospital's seal but charters involving the hospital's property state that the transaction was undertaken by the mayor and jurats in the name and with the assent of the brothers and sisters, suggesting that those at the hospital had limited autonomy.[121]

Nevertheless, the master was the public representative of his house, appearing in court to defend the rights of his establishment, or acting in some other official capacity. Disputes over tithes often involved court appearances, as in the case concerning Stodmarsh which was heard at Wye in 1397 by the commissary general, William Hunsden.[122] In this instance the master of St Lawrence's Hospital was the victor, Hunsden deciding in his favour against the master of another Canterbury hospital, the Poor Priests'. Several masters at St Mary's, Dover were required to oversee the maintenance of Dover Castle on behalf of the Crown, while the penultimate master was a warden of the harbour in the early sixteenth century.[123] Henry VIII appointed John Thompson, his successor, to manage the construction of the new harbour to Thompson's own specifications, a plan which had its critics and added to the hospital's vulnerability in the late 1530s.[124]

Yet in many ways Thompson was exceptional. Apart from the well-known problems caused by a succession of poor administrators during the early fourteenth century at Ospringe and Strood, charges of abuse or mismanagement were less frequent in Kent compared to some counties.[125] Furthermore, where abuses had occurred often steps were taken to rectify them more quickly: in the late twelfth century the master's petition led to St James' Hospital, Canterbury coming under the patronage and so protection of Christ Church Priory.[126] The

119 Shepherd, *Literae Cantuariense* 2, p. 253.

120 Greenwood, *Hospital of St Bartholomew*, p. 15. Similarly, at its namesake in Dover the master held the common seal, but he was not allowed to alienate the hospital's property without permission from Dover Priory; Lyon, *Dover* 1, p. 55.

121 MS EKA Sa/Ch 10B A1.

122 MS CCAL Lit. C 20, p. 31.

123 *CPR 1367–70*; *1370–74*, p. 1. MS BL Egerton MS 2109, fol. 25.

124 *Letters and Papers Henry VIII* 9, no. 734; 10, nos 146, 214, 347, 614, 640, 985; 11, nos 275, 289, 745, 1254; 12(2), nos 982, 1108, 1229, 1230.

125 Frohnsdorff, *Maison Dieu*, pp. 21–22, 25–26. Johnson, *Registrum Hamonis*, pp. 4–5, 104, 122, 124–5, 156–7, 909. Clay, *Medieval Hospitals*, pp. 212–24; Seymour, 'Hospital in Later Middle Ages', pp. 109–27, 136–47, 163–72.

126 MS CCAL DCc/Register B, fol. 426; Shepherd, *Literae Cantuariensis* 3, pp. 75–6, 77.

type of patron is probably significant, and unlike some counties aristocratic patronage was extremely rare. Moreover, the king was a minor player in terms of the number of houses under royal patronage, and most hospitals were either under the Church – the episcopacy or a local monastic house – or the local town council. As a result the mastership was far less likely to be given to one of the patron's clients, possibly as a sinecure; rather patrons were generally concerned to appoint someone capable whom they could monitor closely. Additionally, unlike some of the extremely wealthy and prestigious hospitals nationally, many in Kent were small, modest institutions, making such appointments less attractive, though nepotism and pluralism did occur at two archiepiscopal hospitals in the later Middle Ages.[127]

Even though some hospitals aided the sick-poor and pilgrims, the primary recipients at many Kentish hospitals of their founder's largesse were the resident brothers and sisters. Occasionally, those at the county's almshouses were also known as brothers and sisters, but more often the terms almsfolk or bedesfolk were used, the latter closer to a job description, while most simply referred to them as the poor people living in the almshouse. These people were too poor to have servants, but there were servants at some hospitals: a shepherd at St Bartholomew's, Sandwich, general agricultural labourers at St Mary's, Strood; and the warden's personal servant at St Lawrence's, Canterbury.[128]

Kentish hospitals also varied considerably in size, ranging from St John's and St Nicholas', Canterbury, which each housed a hundred inmates in 1276, to the tiny house at Sittingbourne and its single priest-brother.[129] Nevertheless, most hospitals accommodated between twelve and fifteen resident inmates, though the almshouses were smaller. Generally, brothers outnumbered sisters, in part a reflection of the presence of priest brothers at the hospitals, and only two hospitals primarily housed women: St James' and St Lawrence's at Canterbury. At the latter Abbot Thorne, as patron, tried to stop the admittance of sisters in 1275, but he met with little success and the sisters were still there in the sixteenth century.[130] Some hospitals stipulated the division between the sexes in their ordinances, yet in reality by the fifteenth century there seems to have been some flexibility. Consequently, gender was just one of the selection criteria applied by hospital authorities.[131] The other criteria were age and life-cycle stage, health, domicile, reputation and status, and poverty. Although it is possible a few hospitals sheltered orphans, the evidence is very slim and there is nothing comparable to the great hospital of St Leonard, York.[132] Some of the sisters may have entered as

127 Maidstone hospital: Emden, *Register of Oxford to 1500*, 1, p. 257; 2, pp. 1173, 1375. Orme and Webster, *English Hospital*, p. 78. St Thomas', Canterbury: Emden, *Register of Oxford to 1500* 1, pp. 229, 412; 2, p. 1032.

128 MS EKA Sa/Ch 10B F1. MS Medway Archives DRc/F 44. MS CCAL Lit. C 20, p. 5.

129 *CChR 1257–1300*, p. 199. *VCH Kent* 2, p. 227.

130 Woodruff, 'Register of St Laurence', 33.

131 S. Sweetinburgh, 'Joining the Sisters: Female Inmates of the Late Medieval Hospitals in East Kent', *Arch. Cant.* 123 (2003), 17–39.

132 Cullum, 'Hospitals in Yorkshire', pp. 191–2.

young women, like William Gybbe's daughter, blind Helen and Joan (1413), the daughter of John Ive, whose father paid 26s for her to join St John's Hospital, Romney, but probably the vast majority were middle aged or old.[133] Very few ages at all are recorded in medieval documents; nevertheless evidence from Sandwich suggests that the majority were at least reasonably elderly when they joined the community. Again, merely indicative, but most of the men were still apparently married, but for the women widowhood may have provided a spur to seek institutional aid.[134]

Similarly, it is difficult to ascertain a policy regarding illness or infirmity but hospitals probably assessed each case on its merits rather than operating a blanket system. Patrons also considered the needs of the hospital community, so the ability to work was a major concern, which may have meant Brother Bukke's ploughing skills stood him in good stead when he applied to join St Bartholomew's in Sandwich in the early sixteenth century.[135] Yet in the mid-fourteenth century among the brothers and sisters at its namesake in Chatham were those suffering from blindness, epilepsy and leprosy.[136] Whether this meant they were totally incapacitated is not clear and the authorities may have found work of some kind for them.[137] The catchment area of the Canterbury hospitals in the late Middle Ages, especially St John's and St Nicholas', stretched as far as London, but this, like that for the royal hospitals, was somewhat artificial because the corrodians were selected by the archbishop or were members of his household.[138] In terms of the county as a whole, the Sandwich hospitals probably provide a more accurate picture, and of these St Bartholomew's accommodated brothers and sisters from the other Cinque Ports, and from as far away as Maidstone.[139] However, it seems likely most came from the town itself or its hinterland, allowing inmates to maintain contacts with their previous home area. Such proximity also meant a prospective inmate and his/her family were aware of the status and reputation of the local hospitals and similarly the hospital authorities would be aware of the candidate's fame and conversation.[140] As a result, it was often members of the middling sort or their poorer neighbours who became brothers and sisters at Sandwich, the destitute receiving a few days respite in the 'harbinge' at the back of St John's hospital if they were fortunate.

133 MS CKS PRC 32/14, fol. 210. *CCR 1234–37*, p. 48. HMC V, appendix, p. 539. *VCH Kent* 2, p. 225.

134 Sweetinburgh, 'Joining the Sisters', 20–4.

135 MS EKA Sa/Ch 10B F1.

136 *VCH Kent* 2, p. 216.

137 Although only suggestive, it is interesting to note that on one occasion one of the brothers at St John's Hospital, Sandwich was expected to leave because of his 'grete debilitie and seckenesse of bodie'; MS EKA Sa/Ch 10J A1.

138 For example, the corrody granted to John Edryke from Fulham; E. F. Jacob, ed., *Register of Henry Chichele, Archbishop of Canterbury AD 1414–1443*, Canterbury and York Society, 3 vols (Oxford, 1938–47) 3, p. 105.

139 At his death, Brother Simon Bertyn had considerable lands and tenements in the Maidstone area; MS CKS PRC 32/15, fol. 127.

140 William Gybbe's desire that his daughter should enter an honest hospital was of prime importance for both his daughter's and the hospital's reputation; MS CKS PRC 32/14, fol. 210.

Furthermore, a few very prosperous citizens were able to gain access to a local hospital. One of these was Robert Smyth who resided at St John's Hospital in Canterbury. According to his will, dated 1476, he had a considerable acreage of land in several parishes in north-east Kent and a number of tenements, including one with a dovecote and garden, many of which he was renting out.[141] He made a very large number of cash bequests to individuals and institutions, including 10s to the hospital and a further 6s 8d towards the chapel there. John Rooper, from the important St Dunstan's parish family, was even wealthier, and in his will (1527) he focused his attention of the chapel at St John's where he had presumably prayed daily.[142] He directed his executors to see to the construction of a great window behind the altar of Our Lady in the Lady Chapel to be glazed with images according to the design he had had devised. He also instructed his executors that if his heirs failed, a sizeable proportion of his extensive lands was to be used to build a chantry chapel at St John's, staffed by two secular priests.

For such prosperous men, their hospital experiences were in many ways atypical of those at most Kentish hospitals. Instead, the brothers and sisters, especially those in the smaller, less wealthy hospitals or in houses operating a stricter quasi-monastic regime, probably lived a relatively austere life as part of what might be considered a lay fraternity. Consequently, at many Kentish hospitals and almshouses the chapel may have been the dominant feature in the life of the community. In some cases the community did not have its own chapel, the brothers and sisters from St Bartholomew's at Hythe, for example, walked to the town's parish church, and Milett's almsfolk similarly attended services daily at Dartford parish church.[143]

Milett was also concerned about the behaviour of his almsfolk, and, like other founders and patrons, he laid down strict rules whereby any found to be scolders of their neighbours, fighters or chiders or having other vices were to be warned up to three times and then expelled if they continued.[144] At some hospitals new brothers and sisters had to take an oath on entry before the assembled community, promising among other things to obey the hospital rules.[145] Those who broke the rules might be punished, though the level of discipline imposed varied considerably among hospitals and over time.[146] In earlier centuries corporal punishment

141 MS CKS PRC 32/2, fol. 350.

142 MS CKS PRC 32/15, fol. 8.

143 Sweetinburgh, *Role of Hospital*, pp. 103–4.

144 MS TNA PRO PROB 11/12, fol. 138.

145 This might involve an elaborate ceremony, as at St Bartholomew's, Dover, after which the community retired to the refectory for a feast; MS Bodleian MS Rawlinson B 335, fols 1–2v; Rawcliffe, *Leprosy*, pp. 302–3.

146 The master at St Bartholomew's, Sandwich, was dismissed because he shut the hospital gates against the prior of Christ Church's commissioner when he made an official visitation to the hospital in the early fourteenth century; C. E. Woodruff, 'Some Early Visitation Rolls Preserved at Canterbury', *Arch. Cant.* 33 (1918), 81–2. At St Lawrence's Hospital, Canterbury, discipline was administered at the weekly meeting in the hospital's chapter house; MS CCAL Lit. C 20, pp. 2, 5, 24, 25. If any were found to have broken the rules at St Katherine's Hospital, Rochester, the prior was to speak to the local

had been more commonly used, but by the sixteenth century some were apparently able to flout regulations with impunity.[147]

Presumably most of the brothers and sisters spent their time running the hospital when they were not at their beads. For some this meant helping on the hospital farm, the brothers at St Bartholomew's, Sandwich, did much of the ploughing, harvesting, hedging and managing the house's livestock, and the inmates at its counterpart in Dover were also involved in cultivation and livestock rearing. Elsewhere, time was spent managing the hospital's scattered estates, while others seemingly principally depended on begging or municipal doles of confiscated commodities. Whether such activities ensured an adequate food supply for the hospital community is difficult to ascertain because the allowances listed in the various hospital ordinances may only indicate an ideal situation.[148] Yet the fragmentary evidence from the Kentish sources does point to a hospital population, at least by the later Middle Ages, which generally comprised the aged middling sort, such people may have thought that a 'guaranteed' level of board and lodging was a more attractive proposition than trying to establish maintenance agreements with kinsfolk or others. Moreover, the apparently greater desire among the laity for a more contemplative spiritual existence may have increased the attractiveness of hospital life, though at least a few managed to continue to run their business affairs from inside the hospital's gates.

Hospitals and the Reformation

Compared to certain counties, Kent escaped relatively lightly regarding the destruction of its hospitals, though there are a few notable exceptions: the Dover hospitals of St Bartholomew and St Mary, and the college/hospital of St Peter and St Paul, Maidstone.[149] This is probably due to the relatively high proportion that were under lay or archiepiscopal control, their generally modest scale and worth, and the earlier disappearance of more vulnerable houses, often appropriated by founders of institutions outside the county.[150] Many of the early, small leper hospitals had also disappeared by the sixteenth century, some through an absence

vicar, as one of the governors, who would then dismiss the offender. The miscreant was only allowed to take his/her clothing and his/her bed; Thorpe, *Registrum Roffense*, p. 546.

147 William Baldock at St Bartholomew's, Sandwich had a long record of dissent and insubordination yet still managed to remain there until his death in 1532; MS EKA Sa/AC 2, fols 279v, 363; AC 3, fol. 26v.

148 Sweetinburgh, 'Joining the Sisters', 29, 31.

149 Orme and Webster, *English Hospital*, pp. 150–66.

150 Holy Cross hospital at Swainestrey granted to New College, Oxford; R. Griffin, 'The Lepers' Hospital at Swainestrey', *Arch. Cant.* 34 (1920), 63–78. St Stephen and St Thomas' Hospital, Romney, granted to Magdalen College, Oxford; Butcher, 'Hospital of St Stephen and St Thomas', 17–26. St Mary's Hospital, Ospringe, granted to the college of St John the Evangelist, Cambridge; M. Underwood, 'Index of the Archive of St Mary's Hospital, Ospringe, held at St John's College, Cambridge' (Cambridge, unpublished).

of inmates or adequate resources, and even those that had become little more than chantry chapels apparently often suffered the same fate.

Consequently, by the early 1530s most of the hospitals in west Kent had gone, but there may have been a number of new almshouses. The eastern part of the county was better served, especially at the episcopal cities and Cinque Ports. Nevertheless, there had been some early casualties and Archbishop Warham's 1511 visitation noted signs of impending crisis.[151] Yet how far factors such as religious dissent should be seen as having a bearing on hospital survival in Kent is difficult to ascertain.[152] In certain towns, such as Canterbury and Sandwich, there were small vocal dissenting minorities in the late 1530s, but they were matched by those who fiercely defended Catholic orthodoxy, and for the majority the parish church and its fraternities probably remained the primary or exclusive focus of their devotional practice (see Lutton and Sweetinburgh, this volume).[153] Thus, neglect and lack of interest may have been far more significant than outright hostility and may explain some of the apparent anomalies in terms of the chronology of destruction.

The first casualty was St John's Hospital, Sevenoaks, though this archiepiscopal hospital was probably little more than a chantry chapel when it was surrendered to the king in 1538.[154] St Mary's at Strood was the first major house to be dissolved. Its subordination to Rochester Priory may have been significant, and even though it had continued to receive testamentary support from the surrounding communities, the frequent absences of its last pluralist master may have been similarly damaging.[155] The other casualty in this first wave of destruction was St Bartholomew's Hospital, Dover, its demolition in 1540 the work of a local entrepreneur who seems to have exploited his civic office holding to considerable advantage.[156] In patronage terms, its counterparts at Canterbury (St Lawrence's and St James') survived this first wave, and it is conceivable local civic support was a major contributory factor. St Mary's at Dover was in a far weaker position: it was the richest hospital in the county; unlike the penultimate

151 The ancient leper hospital of St James at Canterbury did not have a viable community, and there were also other difficulties; Wood-Legh, *Kentish Visitations*, pp. 11–13.

152 P. Clark, *English Provincial Society from the Reformation to the Revolution: Religion, Politics and Society in Kent 1500–1660* (Hassocks, 1977), pp. 3–33. For a more recent analysis, see E. H. Shagan, *Popular Politics and the English Reformation, Cambridge Studies in Early Modern British History* (Cambridge, 2003), chapters 4, 6; R. Lutton, *Lollardy and Orthodox Religion in Pre-Reformation England* (Woodbridge, 2006).

153 *Letters and Papers Henry VIII* 18 part 2, pp. 299, 311. Interest in religious matters did not stop at the hospital gate: at St Bartholomew's Hospital in Chatham, Thomas Batman, the former prior, was twice accused of being a heretic (1524 and 1525), and on the latter occasion he was imprisoned in the bishop's palace; J. F. Davis, *Heresy and Reformation in the South-East of England, 1520–1529* (London, 1983), pp. 41–2.

154 *Letters and Papers Henry VIII* 13 part 1, 1519 section 68.

155 Smetham, *History of Strood*, p. 138. In the period 1470–1530, nineteen testators from Rochester diocese are known to have made bequests to St Mary's Hospital (I should like to thank Dr Paul Lee for this information).

156 Haines, *Dover Priory*, pp. 50–1. Sweetinburgh, *Role of the Hospital*, p. 176.

master his successor had made many enemies in the locality; and his use of the hospital to store materials for the new harbour works, which were under his management, meant that it was a very short step for the Crown to turn its hospital into a victualling yard (see Plate 8).[157] Other casualties in the 1540s were St John's Hospital at New Romney and the college at Maidstone, both houses becoming private property.[158] The same fate later befell the two quasi-monastic hospitals in Canterbury: St James' and St Lawrence's; and St James' Hospital at Tonge similarly disappeared into gentry hands.[159]

Nonetheless, a considerable number of the county's hospitals and almshouses survived the mid-sixteenth-century doctrinal changes, as well as the problems of poverty and decay, and in the later decades of the century they were joined by new almshouses. Together these new and old charitable institutions were a vital part of the Elizabethan poor relief system, their patrons and benefactors sharing many of the ideals and attitudes of their medieval predecessors.[160]

157 MS EKA Do/ZZ 02/01, no. 3. Sweetinburgh, *Role of the Hospital*, pp. 181–2.

158 MS CKS PRC 32/22, fol. 116; EKA NR/TL/1; NR/TQ/1. *VCH Kent* 2, p. 232. The Corpus Christi Guild's hall at Maidstone became the town's grammar school; Clark and Murfin, *Maidstone*, p. 38.

159 MS EKA U 88/T57. MS CCAL U 160. *CPR 1550–53*, p. 181. *VCH Kent* 2, pp. 212, 224.

160 Canterbury as a case study: S. Sweetinburgh, 'The Poor, Hospitals and Charity in Sixteenth-Century Canterbury', in *Pieties in Transition: Religious Practices and Experiences, c.1400–1640*, ed. R. Lutton and E. Salter (Aldershot, 2007), pp. 63–73. For larger studies: C. Daly, 'The Hospitals of London: Administration, Reformation and Benefaction, c.1500–1572' (unpublished D.Phil. thesis, University of Oxford, 1993). S. Cavello, 'The Motivations of Benefactors: An Overview of Approaches to the Study of Charity', in *Medicine and Charity Before the Welfare State*, ed. J. Barry and C. Jones (London and New York, 1991), pp. 46–62. For a more negative view on the national situation: P. Horden, 'Small Beer? The Parish and the Poor and Sick in Later Medieval England', in *The Parish in Late Medieval England*, Harlaxton Medieval Studies 14, ed. C. Burgess and E. Duffy (Donington, 2006), pp. 343, 354, 356–7, 359.

7

Kentish Towns: Urban Culture and the Church in the Later Middle Ages

SHEILA SWEETINBURGH

Recent scholarship has estimated that perhaps 20 per cent of the population in England lived in towns in 1377, and though this proportion may have dipped in the fifteenth century, it had probably returned to about 20 per cent by 1524.[1] This may seem surprising to many, but as will be explained below, this is because certain small places displayed characteristics that historians consider to be features of towns. As a result, the widespread topographical distribution of England's urban settlements by the thirteenth century meant that the townmen's rural neighbours were indeed just that, for very few people lived any great distance from a market town. Such close proximity between rural and urban was especially noticeable in Kent: Christopher Dyer has estimated that, in terms of area of land in the county per town, Kent was among the most densely urbanised in the late medieval period.[2] Yet the nature of these towns requires some qualification because England, unlike the Low Countries, was not a land of great cities; and nowhere in Kent was in the same league as Norwich, York or Bristol, let alone London. In fact London's dominance, especially of south-east England, had a profound effect on urban development in north-west Kent, while the towns and ports further east were still effectively within the capital's hinterland, providing, in addition, stopping places en route to continental Europe.[3] As a result, Derek Keene considers there were eight principal towns in late medieval Kent: the two episcopal cities, the head ports of the Cinque Ports federation, Tenterden and Tonbridge. The former had been well established by the time of the Conquest, whereas Tonbridge was established by the Clare family under the Norman kings

1 D. M. Palliser, 'Introduction', in *The Cambridge Urban History of Britain, 600–1540*, ed. D. M. Palliser (Cambridge, 2000), p. 4.
2 C. Dyer, 'Small Towns 1270–1540', in *The Cambridge Urban History of Britain, 600–1540*, ed. D. M. Palliser (Cambridge, 2000), p. 507.
3 D. Keene, 'The South-East of England', in *The Cambridge Urban History of Britain, 600–1540*, ed. D. M. Palliser (Cambridge, 2000), p. 579.

and Tenterden later still.[4] Keene then adds Maidstone, Lydd, Sevenoaks and Ashford as having some significance as urban centres by 1300. However, probably several towns from both of these groups would only qualify as small towns under Dyer's categorisation because they had fewer than two thousand inhabitants.[5]

The lower end of the population scale regarding small towns is notoriously difficult, but broadly Dyer used three hundred persons as his lower limit.[6] For the later Middle Ages, historians have generally employed the 1377 poll tax returns to try to estimate population. Such figures are extremely valuable, the taxpayers listed on a vill by vill basis, though the total absence of the Cinque Ports does detract from their usefulness for Kent.[7] Nonetheless, using the generally recognised multiplier for the named Kentish vills, there were seventy-one having a population in excess of three hundred (discounting Canterbury and Rochester). Looking from west to east, there were places close to London and/or the Thames such as Greenwich, Lewisham, Erith, Bexley, Southfleet and Dartford; settlements further south at Sevenoaks, Shoreham Sundridge and Westerham; in the lower Medway area: Chatham, Strood, Cobham and Cliffe; further inland: Aylesford and Brenchley; a cluster around Maidstone: Boxley, Leeds, Headcorn, Hollingbourne and Stockbury; a large Wealden group: Tenterden, Rolvenden, Benenden, Biddenden, Sandhurst, Shadoxhurst, High Halden, Staplehurst, Goudhurst, Marden, Bethersden and Smarden; to the north of the Romney Marshes: Appledore, Kenardington, Woodchurch and Aldington; those close to Faversham and Sheppey: Rainham, Milton Regis, Eastchurch, Throwley, Teynham and Boughton; those around Ashford: Willesborough, Mersham and Charing; the north-east Kentish settlements: Whitstable, Herne, Chislet, Reculver and Sturry; and those to the south: Eastry, Woodnesborough, Northbourne and Alkham. Yet not all of these were small towns, being instead large market or industrial villages, and, by employing other criteria to determine their urban status, Dyer calculated that there were forty-five small towns in late medieval Kent.[8]

As Dyer discusses, population alone is not considered a sufficient determinant of urban status in medieval society, but exactly what is remains open to debate. One of the problems is the use of the term 'vill' in contemporary documents for both urban and rural settlements, and even the word 'town' was used to describe a wide range of settlements.[9] Nor is the presence of a market charter an indication of urban status because often seigniorial ambition was not in itself a guarantee of success and, as Bradley McLain has shown, it is the markets known to have

4 Ibid., p. 546.

5 Dyer, 'Small Towns', p. 505.

6 Ibid., p. 506.

7 C. C. Fenwick, ed., *The Poll Taxes of 1377, 1379, 1381, Part One: Bedfordshire to Leicestershire*, Records of Social and Economic History, new series 27 (Oxford, 1998), pp. 386–415.

8 Dyer, 'Small Towns', p. 507.

9 Ibid., p. 505.

existed before 1200 that were most likely to survive and prosper over the medieval period.[10] Furthermore, where the town ended and the countryside began was similarly difficult to determine, a situation made even more problematic by the frequent movement of people, who as workers, traders, migrants and visitors crossed and re-crossed these in some ways ephemeral boundaries.[11] Nevertheless, even if not all towns had received grants of borough status, probably almost all were commercial, administrative or religious centres of their locality, though this is not seen by historians as the definitive characteristic. Instead, occupational diversity is generally considered to be the critical feature; that is the notion that small towns usually had between twenty and forty separate non-agricultural occupations.[12] For England, contemporary documents such as court rolls may provide some information, but historians often draw heavily on the 1334/5 lay subsidy returns.[13] Unfortunately, the Cinque Ports were exempt and the Kentish records are listed by hundred rather than by vill, which means these sources are generally of little use for this type of study. Yet where occupational information is obtainable, it does provide evidence concerning the town's economy: levels and types of manufacturing and trade (see Draper, this volume).[14]

Other secondary literature on Kentish towns is quite patchy. The county is reasonably well served in terms of antiquarian scholarship, consisting mostly of single town studies, and Edward Hasted's survey of the county remains essential

10 B. A. McLain, 'Factors in Market Establishment in Medieval England: The Evidence from Kent 1086–1350', *Arch. Cant.* 117 (1997), 83–103. T. Lawson, 'Markets in the Medieval Period', in *An Historical Atlas of Kent*, ed. T. Lawson and D. Killingray (Chichester, 2004), pp. 50–1. See also the Centre for Metropolitan History's gazetteer of markets and fairs: http :// www. ihrinfo. ac.uk/ cmh/ gaz/ gazweb 1. html.

11 G. Rosser, 'Urban Culture and the Church 1300–1540', in *The Cambridge Urban History of Britain, 600–1540*, ed. D. M. Palliser (Cambridge, 2000), p. 337.

12 Dyer, 'Small Towns', pp. 505–6. See also R. Hilton, *The English Peasantry in the Later Middle Ages* (Oxford, 1975), pp. 76–94.

13 H. A. Hanley and C. W. Chalklin, 'The Kent Lay Subsidy Roll of 1334/5', in *Documents Illustrative of Medieval Kentish Society*, Kent Records 18, ed. F. R. H. Du Boulay (Ashford, 1964), pp. 71–172. Court rolls often record bakers and brewers under the assize of bread and ale. To these may be added regrators, those selling outside the market place, tanners and butchers, and in some cases petty disputes between individuals: debt, trespass, detention of chattels that occasionally include occupational details. The rolls for the small town of Appledore, for example, provide some occupational information; S. Sweetinburgh, 'Women, Household and Community: Appledore and Hythe c.1400–1470' (unpublished M.A. dissertation, University of Kent, 1993), pp. 54–62, 66–7, appendix 2. Though useful, those for the larger town of Maidstone are fairly limited in terms of its size; P. Clark and L. Murfin, *The History of Maidstone: The Making of a Modern County Town* (Stroud, 1995), pp. 28–31. As well as being the largest town in the county, Canterbury's records are very good in this respect and for details regarding occupation throughout the late Middle Ages, its 'intrantes' and freemens' lists are exceptional; J. M. Cowper, ed., *Intrantes: A List of Persons Admitted to Live and Trade within the City of Canterbury, 1392–1592* (Canterbury, 1904). J. M. Cowper, ed., *The Roll of the Freemen of the City of Canterbury from AD 1392 to 1800* (Canterbury, 1903).

14 For those interested in this aspect of Kentish society, see Gillian Draper's chapter in this volume, Mavis Mate's survey chapters, her monograph on south-east England and Derek Keene's regional chapter in the first volume of the *Cambridge Urban History of England*; M. E. Mate, *Trade and Economic Developments, 1450–1550: The Experience of Kent, Surrey and Sussex* (Woodbridge, 2006); Keene, 'South-East of England', pp. 545–82.

reading.[15] Early twentieth-century works such as Murray's history of the Cinque Ports federation offer considerable insights into the development of individual towns as well as the federation as a whole, but many of these ports and other Kentish towns have yet to be the subject of modern scholarly works.[16] Nonetheless, there has been a growth in the publishing of individual town histories in recent years, including a few multi-disciplinary studies, but details concerning the medieval period remain relatively sparse. In addition, there are some notable gaps in this modern secondary literature and the lack of a detailed history of medieval Canterbury is perhaps the most glaring omission. Yet rich archival sources are available, especially for Canterbury and the Cinque Ports (the head ports and limbs such as Fordwich and Lydd), in part a reflection of their importance from at least the late Anglo-Saxon period. Consequently, this chapter draws disproportionately on certain towns, mostly Keene's urban centres rather than Dyer's small towns.[17]

According to Susan Reynolds a town can be defined as 'a permanent and concentrated human settlement in which a significant proportion of the population is engaged in non-agricultural occupations … A town therefore normally lives, at least in part, off food produced by people who live outside it … *the inhabitants of towns normally regard themselves, and are regarded by the inhabitants of predominantly rural settlements, as a different sort of people*' [italics added].[18] The latter part of her definition underlines the significance of urban culture, a theme that has become increasingly popular among historians over recent decades. But what does Reynolds mean when she talks about the distinctiveness of urban culture? And can we get beyond the ideas of those in authority who seemingly sought to control daily town life; that is, can we get beyond the prescriptive to some sort of 'reality'? Gervase Rosser believes that we can,

15 Hasted, *History*. For example: W. Somner, *The Antiquities of Canterbury*, with an intro by W. Urry (Wakefield, 1977 [1703]); W. Boys, *Collections for an History of Sandwich in Kent, with notices of the other Cinque Ports and Members and of Richborough* (Canterbury, 1792); J. Lyon, *The History of the Town and Port of Dover*, 2 vols (Dover, 1813–14); E. Jacob, *The History of Faversham* (1774); J. Russell, *The History of Maidstone* (1881, repr. Rochester, 1978); W. Shrubsole, *The History and Antiquities of Rochester and its Environs* (printed and sold by T. Fisher, 1772); H. Smetham, *History of Strood* (Chatham, 1899, repr. 1978); J. Dunkin, *The History and Antiquities of Dartford with Topographical Notices of the Neighbourhood* (London, 1844); R. Pocock, *The History of the Incorporated Town and Parishes of Gravesend and Milton in the County of Kent, Selected with Accuracy from Topographical Writers and Enriched with Manuscripts hitherto un-noticed* (printed by R. Pocock, 1797); C. E. Woodruff, *A History of the Town and Port of Fordwich with a Transcription of the Fifteenth-Century Custumal* (Canterbury, 1895).

16 K. M. E. Murray, *Constitutional History of the Cinque Ports* (Manchester, 1935). Two new historical monographs that break new ground; H. Clarke, S. Pearson and M. E. Mate, *Sandwich: 'The Completest Medieval Town in England'. A Study of the Town and Port from its Origins to 1600* (Oxford, 2010); G. M. Draper and F. Meddens, *The Sea and the Marsh: The Medieval Cinque Port of New Romney*, Pre-Construct Archaeology monograph 10 (London, 2009). For Maidstone, see n. 13.

17 Among Dyer's 'small towns' would be places such as Wingham; E. W. Parkin, 'Wingham, a Market Town', *Arch. Cant.* 93 (1977), 61–79.

18 Palliser, 'Introduction', p. 5, citing S. Reynolds, 'The Writing of Medieval Urban History in England', *Theoretische Geschiedenis* 19 (1992), 49–50.

seeing the available evidence as offering 'testimony to creative processes of appropriation and reinterpretation ... [because] the practice of urban life never corresponded to the abstract schemata of official lawcodes and moral ordinances'.[19] Moreover, he considers that whatever the crossovers between urban and rural modes of behaviour, and he cites several examples including the practice in sixteenth-century Canterbury of sprinkling holy water on the roof-tops as a protection against lightning, contemporaries perceived the distinction, one of the defining characteristics of urban culture being 'its repeatedly asserted difference from, and control of, the rural world outside'.[20] For Rosser, the way forward is to examine certain criteria which he considered were distinctly urban to try to uncover ideas about late medieval British urban culture. Rather than employ all these criteria, this chapter uses those that seem especially pertinent to the situation in Kent: the politics of urban space; memory, time and history; the Church in the town; and finally urban culture on the eve of the Reformation.

The Politics of Urban Space

Leaving aside their defensive qualities, town walls were a powerful marker of urban identity.[21] Even though very few Kentish towns were walled, for their leading citizens the presence of a wall, gates, and often a ditch provided tangible reminders of the difference between themselves and those of the surrounding countryside.[22] Such differences might be expressed in terms of health/disease: each night the Rochester 'borsholders' of the seven boroughs were expected to search for newcomers and those who might have infectious diseases because such persons were viewed as a danger to the well-being of the city.[23] Not that judicially the town stopped at the wall, for example at Sandwich the liberty was far larger

19 Rosser, 'Urban Culture', p. 336.

20 Ibid., p. 338.

21 J. M. Steane, *The Archaeology of Power: England and Northern Europe AD 800–1600* (Stroud, 2001), pp. 194–5, 202–5; O. Creighton and R. Higham, *Medieval Town Walls: An Archaeology and Social History of Urban Defence* (Stroud, 2005), pp. 166–8. See also; C. Coulson, 'Battlements and the Bourgeoisie: Municipal Status and the Apparatus of Urban Defence in Later Medieval England', in *Medieval Knighthood* 5, Papers from the Sixth Strawberry Hill Conference 1994, ed. S. Church and R. Harvey (Woodbridge, 1995), pp. 119–95. For those interested in defence, see for example: S. Frere, S. Stow and P. Bennett, *Excavations on the Roman and Medieval Defences of Canterbury* (Canterbury, 1982). C. Flight and A. C. Harrison, 'The Southern Defences of Medieval Rochester', *Arch. Cant.* 103 (1986), 1–26. D. Renn, 'Refortification at Rochester in the 1220s: A Public/Private Partnership?', *Arch. Cant.* 124 (2004), 343–63.

22 A. Ward, 'Castles and Other Defensive Sites', in *An Historical Atlas of Kent*, ed. T. Lawson and D. Killingray (Chichester, 2004), p. 55.

23 F. Smith, *A History of Rochester* (1928, reprinted Rochester, 1976), p. 164. Ideas about pollution might also find expression in the provision of communal latrines and a common water supply, as at Sandwich and Dover; MS EKA Sa/FAt 5; FAt 6; FAt 9; FAt 10; Sa/AC 1, fol. 87v. MS BL Add. 29810, fol. 63v. Canterbury ordinances governing the removal of filth from the streets specifically made the connection between pollution and dishonour; MS CCAL CC/AB 1, fol. 6.

than the area enclosed within the town wall.[24] Nevertheless, possibly as a measure of the wall's perceived significance (not least because it was patrolled at night) the ward boundaries at Sandwich were described in terms of the town gates.[25] At Canterbury, several of the civic wards extended beyond the wall, especially along the main roads out of the city at Wincheap, Northgate and Rithercheap.[26] For the city's clerks those living outside the wall were said to be of the suburbs, yet this seems to have been more than a technicality because in the Early Modern records, at least, the inference appears to have been that those outside were rural folk.[27]

Dover, too, in terms of civic jurisdiction, controlled areas outside the town wall, but it is perhaps here that it is possible to envisage more fully the symbolic significance of the separation of town and country.[28] Even though its early history is unclear, by the late fourteenth century every three years the civic authorities were sending a great candle that was as long as the circumference of the town to St Thomas' shrine at Canterbury.[29] Very little information survives regarding the rituals involved in this corporate gift-giving to England's premier saint but continental examples from the twelfth century would seem to suggest that it was either offered as an act of gratitude or to invoke the saint's aid on the town's behalf against outside enemies.[30]

A more common indicator of the symbolic value local townsmen placed on their town wall is the displaying of a gate or walled town on the town seal. The reverse of Dover town seal commemorated St Martin, the town's saint from its ancient minster church (see below), who is shown dividing his cloak for the benefit of the beggar as he passes through a gate of a triple towered town.[31] The seals of Canterbury and Rochester highlighted the castle rather than the walled town *per se*, though Rochester's seal provides a more realistic image of the keep and drawbridge (see Plate 9).[32] Presumably all of these were intended to incorporate ideas of urban

24 MS EKA Sa/LC 1, fols 105–7; Boys, *Sandwich*, pp. 533–8. H. Clarke, 'The Liberty of Sandwich, Kent, c.1300, and its implications for earlier topography', in *Early Medieval Art and Archaeology in the Northern World*, ed. S. Reynolds and L. Webster (forthcoming).

25 MS EKA Sa/AC 2, fols 199–9v. The wards, through the constables, were responsible for the night watch.

26 W. Urry, *Canterbury under the Angevin Kings* (London, 1967), map 1a. Urry postulated that the ward system (named after the gates) may have its origin in the Assize of Clarendon (dated 1166). In 1395 the civic authorities sought a royal charter to confirm the city's liberty; MS CCAL CC/A/A/16.

27 That is, not withstanding the frequent presence of town fields, such persons were cited as being engaged in rural occupations within the constructs of the narratives produced by deponents in the ecclesiastical courts; C. T. Richardson, *Domestic Life and Domestic Tragedy in Early Modern England* (Manchester and New York, 2006), p. 36.

28 In the fifteenth century, twenty wards were listed for Dover; MS BL Add. 29615, fols 161v–62.

29 P. Rowe, 'The Customary of the Shrine of St Thomas Becket, a Translation of the Customary with Notes' (unpublished M.A. dissertation, University of London, 1990), p. 91 citing MS BL Add. 59616, fol. 9.

30 S. Sweetinburgh, 'Mayor-Making and Other Ceremonies: Shared Uses of Sacred Space among the Kentish Cinque Ports', in *The Use and Abuse of Sacred Spaces in Late Medieval Towns*, ed. P. Trio and M. de Smet (Leuven, 2006), pp. 180, 181–5. H. van der Velden, *The Donor's Image: Gerard Leyet and the Votive Portraits of Charles the Bold* (Turnhout, 2000), pp. 240–1.

31 G. Pedrick, *Borough Seals of the Gothic Period* (London, 1904), plate 23; Steane, *Power*, p. 227.

32 Pedrick, *Seals*, plates 9, 28; Steane, *Power*, p. 230.

independence, so emphasizing the division between the town and the hostile world beyond its gates. Spatial elements were occasionally employed by other Kentish towns, and even though the majority of the Cinque Ports had a ship on their common seals, the Lydd town seal comprised a church and a ship sailing near by.[33]

Whether those living in Tonbridge envisaged the wall that surrounded the town and castle in the same way is less certain, possibly it was instead seen as a manifestation of seigniorial lordship.[34] Additionally, the royal licence to the men of Tonbridge in 1318 to collect tolls for its maintenance was issued at the request of Hugh de Audele Jr, a further reminder of the town's subordinate status.[35] In contrast, at Kent's other walled towns (except Rochester) the civic authorities were able to petition the Crown for murage grants on their own behalf.[36] For the size/wealth of these towns, the authorities often spent significant sums, as at Dover in 1368/9, and at Sandwich a century later; the wall and gates offering opportunities for display in addition to their defensive function.[37]

Yet even though the town defences might provide ways of displaying civic pride and could be powerful symbols of urban autonomy, at times their upkeep was a serious drain on the citizenry.[38] Moreover, some townsmen apparently viewed the town wall, gates and ditch as a hindrance. Encroachments in the town ditch, whether through the construction of buildings, the grazing of animals or the dumping of rubbish were a frequent occurrence at several towns including Canterbury and Sandwich.[39] Also at Sandwich the wards and town institutions were expected to repair the town wall, but on occasion the civic authorities

33 Pedrick, *Seals*, plate 17.

34 Creighton and Higham, *Town Walls*, p. 72.

35 *CPR 1317–21*, p. 133. The townsmen elected two of their number to the offices of alderman and bailiff, who received 8d from the customary dues; J. F. Wadmore, 'Tonbridge Castle and its Lords', *Arch. Cant.* 16 (1886), 35. See also: E. Wragg, C. Jarrett and J. Haslam, 'The Development of Medieval Tonbridge Reviewed in the Light of Recent Excavations at Lyons, East Street', *Arch. Cant.* 125 (2005), 121–22, 134, 135–40.

36 Rochester never received a murage grant, instead other means had been employed to fund the city's defences; Renn, 'Refortification at Rochester', 343–63. First murage grants: Canterbury: 1378, Dover 1324, Sandwich 1321; H. Turner, *Town Defences in England and Wales: An Architectural and Documentary Study AD 900–1500* (London, 1971), pp. 148, 155, 158, 164. *CPR 1324–27*, p. 51; *CPR 1321–24*, p. 14.

37 In that year Dover spent almost £70; MS BL Add. 29615, fol. 13; between 1462/3 and 1472/3 Sandwich spent over £100 per year on at least six occasions; Turner, *Town Defences*, pp. 164–5. Prior to that in 1458, and following the French raid on the town the previous year, the authorities agreed to construct a brick barbican at Fishergate; MS EKA Sa/AC 1, fol. 105v.

38 Some towns in the later fifteenth century were still spending considerable sums, partly funded by individual gifts: the reconstruction of Newingate at Canterbury was funded by the city and by citizens such as William Bigge; MS CCAL FA 7, fols 12v–13, 25, 29; MS CKS PRC 17/1, fol. 343. By the sixteenth century (and earlier in some places) the town defences were becoming a serious financial burden. At Dover on several occasions the authorities resorted to using boulders gathered from the rear of the castle and from under the cliff; MS BL Add. 29616, fols 132–2v, 133v, 163v.

39 Some grazing was allowed, not least because it provided revenue, but at Canterbury the authorities (1424–25) only permitted tenants to graze sheep on the slopes of the city ditch, and no-one was allow to let ducks or geese swim there; HMC Canterbury, p. 211. At Sandwich, for example, a Breton was fined 6s 8d for breaking the town wall; MS EKA Sa/FAt 16. In 1496 the mayor and aldermen of Canterbury

encountered resistance to the performing of allotted tasks; and similarly at Canterbury bridge repairs were sometimes neglected, the culprits presented at the civic courts.[40] The situation at Rochester was different but the local communities, which had been responsible for looking after sections of the old bridge, were expected after 1381 to continue their maintenance of the newly-built bridge, working with the bridge wardens as the wardens and commonalty of Rochester Bridge. Though some were active on the bridge's behalf, Richard Britnell considers that the archbishops of Canterbury became increasingly involved in the fifteenth century because, as a body, the commonalty were generally desultory.[41] In addition, certain townsmen sought to use the town gates to display unofficial bills and other notices, as happened at Canterbury in 1460, and although from a later period, the presentment of John Blye for illegally walking his bear on Canterbury's wall is indicative of the conflicting interests that might be expressed in spatial terms.[42]

Nevertheless, the vast majority of Kent's towns were neither walled nor had free-standing gates. Yet their inhabitants were presumably aware of other markers of urban space. The division of the town into wards has already been noted for Canterbury and Sandwich, and several of the other Cinque Ports such as Hythe and New Romney used a similar system.[43] Elsewhere, some towns were divided into boroughs, and at Maidstone, for example, the town boroughs were seen as a distinct part of the archiepiscopal manor, having a separate town court.[44] Consequently, even those towns that were under outside lordship, having little or no self-autonomy, were often viewed in judicial terms as discrete entities, and for the townsmen the regular perambulations of such boundaries presumably gave them a sense of communal identity. They also provided a temporal element into this civic ritual because, as at Rochester, these rituals were often undertaken at the same time each year.[45] Perambulations generally used physical features in the

instigated a considerable number of measures to counter the problems of unclean streets, markets and other places within the city; MS CCAL CC/AC 1/14.

40 The organisation of the building of town walls by ward in Sandwich was in place by at least 1436, such regulations repeated later in the century, but they were not always adhered to; MS EKA Sa/AC 1, fols 29, 30, 98. In 1388 the master at St Thomas' Hospital, Canterbury, was summoned for failing to repair the Eastbridge; *CPR 1385–89*, p. 523; MS CCAL CC/A/A/13 and 14.

41 R. H. Britnell, 'Rochester Bridge, 1381–1530', in *Traffic and Politics: Rochester Bridge AD 43–1993*, ed. N. Yates and J. M. Gibson (Woodbridge, 1994), pp. 95–8.

42 J. S. Davies, *English Chronicle of the Reigns of Richard II, Henry IV, Henry V and Henry VI*, Camden Society, original series 64 (1856), pp. 91–4; C. Ross, *Edward IV* (London, 1974), p. 25. MS CCAL CC/J/Q/380/4.

43 At Hythe the wards were called west ward, market ward, middle ward and east ward; MS EKA H1055; 1058. The situation at New Romney was less stable and by the later fifteenth century the number of wards had shrunk from their peak of fourteen wards [including Old Romney]; M. Teichman-Derville, 'The Annals of the Town and Port of New Romney: With Some Extracts from the Records of the Town', *Arch. Cant.* 41 (1929), 167.

44 Clark and Murfin, *Maidstone*, p. 22.

45 Though the dating is later, it seems likely that it was an earlier feature of civic life: the mayor expected to make his perambulation in 'the perambulation week', accompanied by 'his brethren and such citizens and freemen's sons as the mayor shall appoint'; Smith, *Rochester*, p. 60.

landscape but some towns employed other markers to separate themselves from the countryside. Spatial elements within civic election rituals seem to have been especially important at the Cinque Ports (see below), and sometimes these were recorded in detail in the town's custumal: at New Romney the common horn 'shall be blown three times at every corner of the town' (see Plate 10).[46] Bells, too, might be used and a fifteenth-century Sandwich ordinance adds that the bell of St Clement's church 'shall be tolled for half an hour immediately before the mayoral election'.[47] Employing aural markers of urban space presumably strengthened feelings of distinctiveness among the portsmen, as well as indicating to those outside the town that they were not part of that 'privileged' community. Visible markers linked to crime and punishment were also deemed appropriate, a graphic reminder of the bounds of the city authorities' jurisdiction being the placement of Canterbury's gallows at the boundary of the liberty at what is now Hollow Lane.[48]

As well as the political use of space to delineate differences between town and countryside, the leading citizens of some of the larger Kentish towns employed spatial markers within their towns, dividing them into wards or boroughs, building crosses at important road junctions and market places, and naming streets and lanes. For example, at Ashford there was a market house for the collection of tolls and by 1500 a middle row had been built there.[49] Yet it was probably only at Canterbury that the naming of streets/areas incorporated trades, ethnicity and family: *Merceria*, Jewry and 'Planas'.[50] The location of markets and fairs was also a significant aspect of the topographical layout of the town. Yet, this too might become the subject of negotiation, as occurred in the late fifteenth century when the city authorities in Canterbury wanted to provide the fish wives of Whitstable with a 'new' market place in St Margaret's Street.[51] Though primarily commercial spaces, market places might be utilised by the town governors to make proclamations, and as civic spaces they could be used to hold civic celebrations, such as midsummer bonfires and plays.[52] However, at times this use of

46 MS EKA NR/LC 1, fol. 2.

47 MS EKA Sa/AC 1, fol. 169v.

48 MS CCAL CC/FA 12, fol. 75.

49 A. Ruderman, *A History of Ashford* (Chichester, 1994), p. 18.

50 MS CCAL DCc/Rental 133, the 'Planas' referred to an area where Susanna de Planaz had held land in twelfth-century Canterbury (the area at the junction between The Parade and St Margaret's Street). Even after the expulsion of the Jews in 1290, the area retained its name and today one of the lanes is still called Jewry Lane. Similarly, Mercery Lane and Butchery Lane are still part of Canterbury's street plan, as is Hawks Lane, named after the Haute family.

51 MS CCAL CC/FA 2, fol. 199; HMC Canterbury, p. 223. A petty sessions case from 1376/7 indicates the contentious nature of such changes to the commercial topography of the city; MS CCAL CC/J/B/1/176.

52 Many rural, as well as urban communities, put on religious plays in Kent, but the level of civic involvement and the importance placed on the town's play can be gauged from the town archives of New Romney and Lydd; J. M. Gibson, and I. Harvey, 'A Sociological Study of the New Romney Passion Play', *Research Opportunities in Renaissance Drama* 39 (2000), 203–21; J. M. Gibson, ed., *Kent: Diocese of Canterbury*, Records of Early English Drama, 3 vols (Toronto and London, 2002).

urban space might be contested: the public bonfires to celebrate midsummer feast days, such as that of St John the Baptist, becoming a contentious issue in mid-sixteenth-century Canterbury; and almost a century earlier Edward IV had appropriated one of the city's proclamation sites – the Bullstake – to execute the city's mayor following the failure of the Fauconberg Rising in 1471.[53] Similarly, halls, quays and gaols could become contested spaces where others, such as the king, members of the aristocracy and certain monasteries sought to establish their right to hold or control areas of the town. At Faversham the abbey had an extensive walled precinct to the east of the market. However, as overlord it was the abbey's presence in the town through its authority over the market, hallmoot and gaol that was most galling to the local townsmen (see Edwards, this volume). The abbot's gaol, in particular, became an extremely contentious issue when the townsmen were forced to build a new one on what was seen as town land after their defeat in the king's court in 1258.[54]

For some Kentish townsmen the construction of a guild, court or town hall offered them a way of underlining their authority in the town.[55] Even though many of the Cinque Ports used the local parish churches for civic occasions throughout the medieval period (see below), town buildings associated with local governance had apparently been established in a few towns by Henry III's reign.[56] Further buildings were constructed or adapted in the late fourteenth century (at Dover and perhaps Sandwich) and during the succeeding century (including those at Lydd, New Romney, Milton Regis, Canterbury, Fordwich and probably Ashford).[57] The presence of such a focal point in the political landscape of the town might be strengthened by the undertaking of processions, which linked together significant parts of the town. The known examples relate to rituals at Canterbury, Rochester and some of the Cinque Ports, often associated with civic elections or saints' feast days.[58] At Canterbury, for example, the civic church of St

53 Gibson, *Kent*, 1, pp. 187–9. 'Warkworth's Chronicle', in *Three Chronicles of the Reign of Edward IV*, with an Introduction by K. Dockray (Gloucester, 1988), p. 21. C. Richmond, 'Fauconberg's Kentish Rising of May 1471', *English Historical Review* 337 (1970), 673–92 (p. 684); M. Connor, 'The Political Allegiances of Christ Church Priory 1400–1472: The Evidence of John Stone's Chronicle', *Arch. Cant.* 127 (2007), 401.

54 D. Harrington and P. Hyde, *The Early Town Books of Faversham c.1251 to 1581* (Folkestone, 2008), p. xlix.

55 Even though Robert Tittler is primarily concerned with the early modern town hall, many of his findings are pertinent to the later Middle Ages; R. Tittler, *Architecture and Power: The Town Hall and the English Urban Community c.1500–1640* (Oxford, 1991).

56 The 'speech house' at Canterbury; Urry, *Canterbury*, p. 91; but also perhaps a guild hall, pp. 129–30. Fordwich, Faversham, Sandwich, Dover and New Romney had old 'guild halls', that at Faversham gave its name to the green (Yeldhall Greene); that at Sandwich to a street; Urry, *Canterbury*, p. 241; Harrington and Hyde, *Faversham*, p. lv; MS CCAL DCc/Reg. H, fol. 15. P. Morgan, ed., *Domesday Book: Kent* (Chichester, 1983), D, 8. Draper and Meddens, *The Sea and the Marsh*, p. 43.

57 Dover: MS BL Add. 29615, fol. 7. Canterbury: MS CCAL CC/Woodruffs/56A/7. E. W. Parkin, 'The old Court Hall, Lydd', *Arch. Cant.* 98 (1982), 107–20. The building referred to as the 'Cage' in fifteenth-century Ashford appears to have been a market or court hall; W. R. Briscall, 'The Ashford Cage', *Arch. Cant.* 101 (1984), 57–68.

58 St George's feast day was marked by the civic authorities in several towns, including Folkestone,

Plates

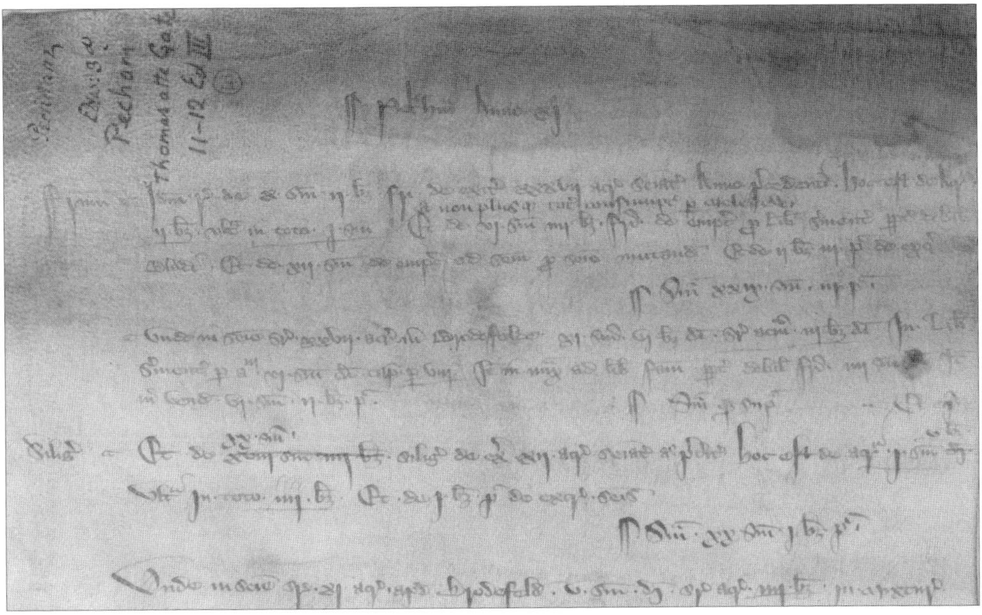

1. Extract from Peckham Bedels roll 41 showing the impact of ‘mildew’ (meledew) on the wheat harvest in 1337. Reproduced with permission from Canterbury Cathedral Archives, CCA–DCe–BR/Peckham/41

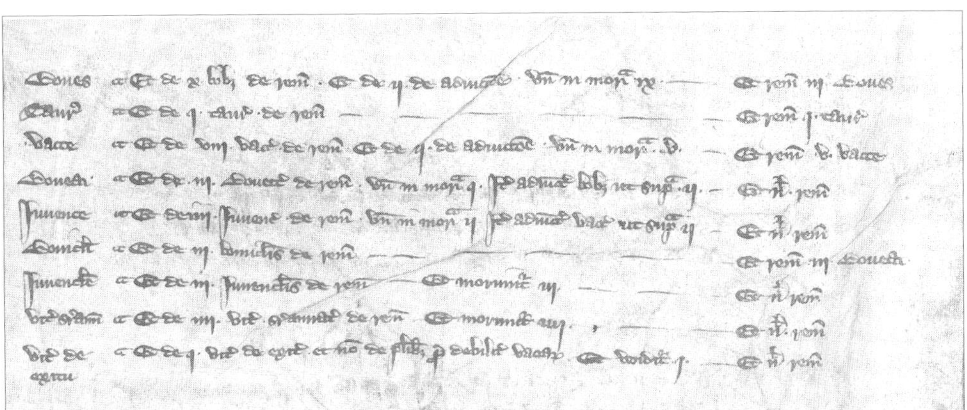

2. Extract from Meopham Bedels roll 65 (1319/20) showing the impact of cattle plague upon bovine numbers. Reproduced with permission from Canterbury Cathedral Archives, CAA–DCc–BR/Meopham/65

3. Remains of an early post-medieval vessel found in one of the former stream channels of the River Rother at Maytham Wharf. Reproduced with permission from Pre-Construct Archaeology Ltd

4. Artist's impression of St Thomas' Shrine, Holy Trinity Chapel in Canterbury Cathedral. Reproduced with permission from Canterbury Archaeological Trust

5. Remains of the great Benedictine abbey dedicated to St Augustine, Canterbury

6. Remains of the only Cluniac monastery in Kent at Monks Horton.
Reproduced with permission from Kent Archaeology Society

7. Cobham College continues to function as a charitable establishment. Photograph taken by Ian Coulson

8. The buildings at St Mary's Hospital, Dover survived as a royal victualling store after the Dissolution. Reproduced with permission from Dover Museum

9. Rochester and Dover seals showing Rochester Castle and St Martin outside the town gate, respectively

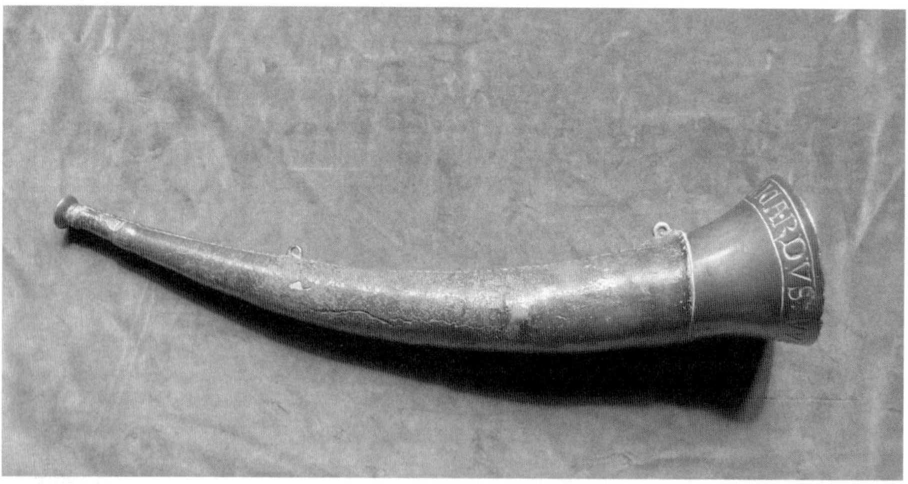

10. An early example of a moot horn from Faversham. Photograph by Ian Coulson

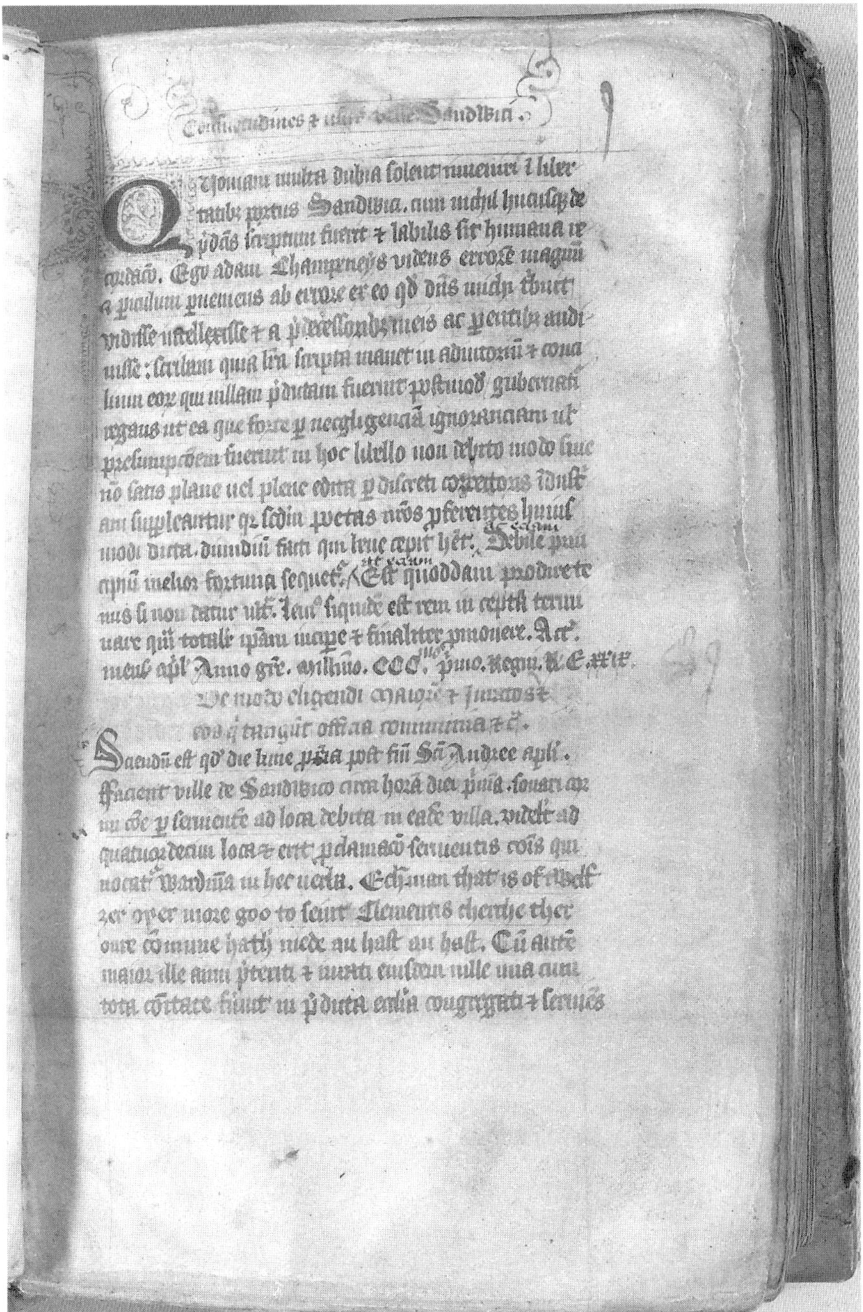

11. The first page of the earliest surviving copy of Sandwich's custumal showing Adam Champney's preamble. Reproduced with permission from Sandwich Town Council, held at East Kent Archives, EKA–Sa/LC/1

12. Misericord from Minster-in-Thanet showing the association of women with the Devil. Photograph taken by Imogen Corrigan

Mary Breadman was close to the guildhall, where the bailiff (later mayor) and aldermen attended Mass, and to the civic inn, the Red Lion (next to the guildhall), which they patronised on ceremonial and other occasions.[59] This idea of civic processions seems to have been especially favoured at Sandwich because, in addition to the annual mayor-making procession from St Clement's church to the new mayor's house, the town officers with the commonalty undertook an annual pilgrimage from St Peter's church to St Bartholomew's Hospital to commemorate the town's deliverance by the saint in 1217.[60] For the civic authorities at Rochester their agreement with the prior at Rochester Cathedral meant that the town sergeants at mace were allowed to proceed before the mayor when the town officers attended special cathedral services.[61] However, the civic authorities were not the only ones who valued these occasions. The procession announcing the arrival of the royal justices in eyre at Canterbury and Rochester, or less frequently at Maidstone, East Greenwich, Dartford, Sevenoaks and the Lowry of Tonbridge, provided a highly visual opportunity for the Crown to highlight its judicial power in the county.[62]

For the civic authorities, events such as mayor-making were seen as symbolic demonstrations of their authority over and responsibility for the local populace, which they were then expected to enact through the courts for the benefit of their town. Even though in many ways the town courts of Canterbury, Rochester and the Cinque Ports operated in parallel to those of the manor and view of frankpledge, they also exercised judicial rights normally the preserve of the higher royal courts. As a consequence it is possible to examine a wider range of cases compared to medium and small towns more generally in England, even though on an individual town basis the surviving court records for Kent are often patchy. Such records seemingly reveal civic attitudes towards the poor, 'criminals' (those seen as transgressing moral and communal boundaries designed to protect the urban community as a whole), and aliens. Looking first at the poor,

Dover and Sandwich; MS EKA Fo/FC 1/1, fol. 8; MS BL Add. 29618B, fol. 304v; MS EKA Sa/AC 1, fol. 262v. There was also a St George play at Lydd; S. Dimmock, 'The St George Play in Early Tudor Lydd', unpublished paper given at the University of Bristol (1996). Gibson, *Kent* 2, pp. 678, 681, 682, 685, 686, 687.

59 Court halls, like inns, could also be used for festivities such as the watching of plays or entertaining dignitaries. For example, at the Sandwich court hall in 1515 the mayor and his brethren saw a play, perhaps an interlude, enacted by the 'children of St Augustine's Abbey'; MS EKA Sa/FAt 21.

60 MS EKA Sa/LC 1, fol. 3; Boys, *Sandwich*, p. 431. MS EKA Sa/LC 1, fol. 15v; Boys, *Sandwich*, p. 17. This latter procession may have included an effigy, perhaps a giant puppet, of the villain in 1217: Eustace the monk, because there is a single reference in the civic records, dated 1489/90, for 10d spent on painting 'Stace monkes hedde'; MS EKA Sa/FAt 9. Something similar may have taken place as part of the Becket festivities in the city of Canterbury in the later fifteenth and early sixteenth centuries. The participants said to have included the marching watch, 'giants', the mayor and aldermen in scarlet or armour, and those involved in the St Thomas pageant; MS CCAL CC/AB 1, fols 5v–6; HMC Canterbury, p. 241. References to probably similar devices do occur for the same period: London had Gog and Magog and Norwich had Snap the dragon; G. Rosser, 'Myth, Image and Social Process in the English Medieval Town', *Urban History* 23 (1996), 22–3.

61 Smith, *Rochester*, p. 77.

62 Russell, *Maidstone*, p. 16.

while ongoing research by scholars has yet to reveal the whole picture nationally, from her detailed investigation of Kentish borough court records Karen Jones concluded that, even though the economic status of defendants was only very rarely mentioned, in terms of those indicted for offences against property probably the majority were people of limited means.[63] In part this may reflect the greater opportunities for petty theft in more densely populated urban spaces, but at Fordwich it is interesting that the civic authorities conducted an aggressive campaign against hedgebreakers during the late fifteenth and early sixteenth centuries, a crime more frequently associated with rural manor courts.[64] It apparently coincided with the peak of presentments for assault and scolding and, as Jones remarks, may have been part of a 'control wave' against the disorderly poor.[65]

Although often seen as disruptive, the courts were not the only means utilised by the civic authorities to control the poor. Again the evidence comes from the Cinque Ports where the town officers aided the poor by providing municipal doles of money or grain, introducing price regulations concerning essential commodities, prohibiting the hoarding of foodstuffs, creating or modifying civic hospitals and almshouses, relaxing certain local taxes and seeking to control potentially undesirable or disruptive groups. At Dover, for example, ad hoc civic gifts of small sums of money were given occasionally to known poor people and the town seems to have established several small almshouses.[66] The authorities at Lydd adopted a more regulated approach, especially during times of dearth. The chamberlains' accounts indicate that grain was given to those of the town known to be suffering from hardship, and such people might also be exempted from paying local taxes.[67] The measures at Sandwich were more complicated because as well as the poor *per se*, the mayor and jurats also introduced regulations to control prostitutes. One of their first priorities was to ensure a sufficient supply of basic commodities at reasonable prices but as conditions worsened in the mid-1520s the Sandwich magistracy also sought to control beggars, especially those entering the town.[68] These people were only allowed to beg if they had a licence and they were expected to reside in the 'harbinge': three rooms at the back of St John's

63 K. Jones, *Gender and Petty Crime in Late Medieval England: The Local Courts in Kent, 1460–1560* (Woodbridge, 2006), p. 40.

64 This clustering is probably significant but the presence of a generally 'rural' crime may also be connected to the area of the town's liberty which extended well into the countryside surrounding its urban centre.

65 Jones, *Gender*, p. 56.

66 There were at least two almshouses under civic jurisdiction by 1500; MS BL Egerton 2107, fols 14v, 58v.

67 For example, in 1460 the town paid 8d to deliver poor men's corn at Christmas; MS EKA Ly/FAc 1, fol. 60; A. Finn, *Records of Lydd* (Kent, 1911), p. 191.

68 In 1507, for example, the authorities sought to control the availability and quality of candles in the town, and the following year it was all grain types; MS EKA Sa/AC 2, fols 153, 165v. The authorities introduced two ordinances in 1523 concerning beggars and vagabonds; MS EKA Sa/AC 2, fols 326, 328.

Hospital while they remained in the town.[69] The hospital could be used in this way by the civic authorities because it was under their governance, a fairly common feature of the Cinque Ports, although there is no evidence to suggest that other ports followed suit.

The idea of confining potentially disruptive groups had previously been employed at Sandwich when the town brothel was established in 1474.[70] It was never a large institution, possibly accommodating four women, but was presumably considered sufficient to control the trade and also to generate an income for the benefit of the reputable community.[71] Though apparently successful in these terms, the court records do indicate that occasionally certain prostitutes were prepared to challenge the authorities.[72] Nor were they the only people willing to confront the local urban magistracy because various Kentish town court records include indictments brought against individuals for moral and communal crimes, such as not undertaking assigned public duties; failing to observe street, market and other ordinances; verbally and physically attacking office holders, and causing disquiet among their neighbours.[73] Nevertheless, the fact that certain townsmen were prepared repeatedly to confront town officers would seem to indicate the complexity of urban society, as well as a degree of fragility.[74]

It is far more difficult to ascertain whether such attitudes were to be found elsewhere in Kent because many of the county's small towns were governed through manorial courts. However, if Jones's findings for Maidstone are indicative – she found a greater diversity of reported criminal cases compared to rural Kent – it is possible that other urban communities did see the need to control those viewed as disruptive.[75] Yet Maidstone may in some ways represent a special case because the leading townsmen apparently established an alternative means of protecting their community. The Corpus Christi Guild was the most important fraternity in

69 In Paris, beggars found that churchyards were lucrative sites and in Norwich lepers seems to have preferred the market place; B. Geremek, *The Margins of Society in Late Medieval Paris*, translated J. Birrell (Cambridge, 1987), pp. 187–9; C. Rawcliffe, *The Hospitals of Medieval Norwich*, Studies in East Anglian History 2 (Norwich, 1995), p. 52. However at Sandwich, traditionally St Mary's churchyard had been used by the local lepers for this purpose; MS CKS PRC 17/6, fol. 70.

70 Jones, *Gender*, pp. 162–5. Nationally, this was a rare civic innovation; R. Karras, *Common Women: Prostitution and Sexuality in Medieval England* (Oxford, 1996), p. 35. Prostitutes brought before the Canterbury courts were fined, though interestingly the only reference to the use of 'ray hoods' to denote such women states that the two 'unthrifty quenys' concerned were to be banished; HMC Canterbury, p. 239.

71 MS EKA Sa/AC 1, fol. 217v; Sa/AC 2, fols 35–5v.

72 MS EKA Sa/AC 2, fols 81, 91.

73 There was considerable overlap concerning such matters between the civic and ecclesiastical courts in late medieval Kent; Jones, *Gender*, p. 201.

74 In Sandwich during the late 1520s, for example, there were serious factional disputes, leading to a time of considerable unrest in the town. Among those who insulted the mayor in 1528 was John Pascall. To Roger Manwood's face he called him 'a false harlot, a poller and a traitor'. Promptly jailed, Pascall was required 'to cry pardon and forgiveness' from the mayor at the fish market on the following Saturday at 9 o'clock; MS EKA Sa/AC 3, fol. 9v.

75 Jones, *Gender*, p. 17.

Maidstone, having its own hall and almshouses by the fifteenth century, its members drawn from the town's leading citizens, local gentry and senior churchmen, though there were some from the middling sort but not from the poor because members were expected to contribute a minimum of 3d annually (see Sweetinburgh, this volume).[76] The almshouses offered shelter for old, infirm or otherwise incapacitated members, but the main communal activity seems to have been the annual patronal Mass and feast.[77] In other parts of the country where a town was subject to outside lordship, such as Bury St Edmunds and Stratford upon Avon, these fraternities were used by the leading citizens as quasi-civic organisations. It is feasible that the one at Maidstone was employed to serve a similar purpose, thus providing an alternative means of 'managing' the local community for the benefit of its respectable townspeople.[78]

Other people who exercised the collective mind of the civic authorities were the different categories of 'outsider', their position vis-à-vis the town a matter of concern with respect to taxation, trading restrictions and similar issues, but presumably also regarding the treatment they received from local townsmen. Pilgrims and other short-term visitors were drawn to Canterbury, but Becket's shrine was only one of a number of sacred sites in the county (see Draper, this volume). Nevertheless, the towns on the road from London to Canterbury, and the seaports, especially Dover, were presumably extremely crowded during the jubilee years of St Thomas, and around the time of his annual feast days.[79] In 1420 the civic authorities at Canterbury, apparently in response to the problems of overcrowding at the previous jubilee, undertook a survey to assess the capacity of all the houses in the city to take in visiting pilgrims.[80]

Pilgrims were not the only people who moved in large numbers across the county. Sandwich, in particular, acted as an embarkation point for troops crossing to fight in France, though Southampton became increasingly important in this respect. The arrival of these often large bodies of troops offered trading and other opportunities but was also a logistical challenge. Such events were occasionally recorded in the Sandwich Year Books: in 1475 it was decreed that all householders must provide two beds to accommodate this major influx.[81] In compari-

76 Clark and Murfin, *Maidstone*, p. 36.

77 Ibid., pp. 36–7. There was both a wine cellar and an ale cellar at the fraternity hall; MS CKS Md/G 20.

78 In 1546 it was said that 'the master and brethren of the guild were wont to meet together [at the guild house], and there consider and talk over the ordinary business of the same town of Maidstone'; A. Hussey, ed., *Kent Chantries*, Kent Records 12 (1932), pp. 188–9. Clark and Murfin, *Maidstone*, pp. 32–3, 35. Though presumably far smaller, it is not clear what status the fraternity of the Gilde at Dartford enjoyed; 'Inquisition Post Mortem of the Lands and Tenements of Sir William de Fortibus', *Arch. Cant.* 3 (1860), 249.

79 As early as 1226 a letter patent had been directed to the Cinque Ports which stated that foot passengers and those on horseback were only to leave the realm via Dover; *CPR 1225–32*, p. 25. In the jubilee year of 1320 the offerings as Becket's shrine amounted to £670 13s 4d; C. Woodruff, 'Financial Aspects of the Cult of St Thomas of Canterbury', *Arch. Cant.* 44 (1932), 18–19.

80 W. Urry, 'The Jubilee of St Thomas, 1420: Billeting and Rationing Problems in the Fifteenth Century', *Canterbury Cathedral Chronicle* 42 (1947), 23–7.

81 MS CCAL Sa/AC 1, fol. 223. It was not only the troops who stayed in Sandwich, though Edward III

son, the arrival of the Westermen at Lydd to join the local fishermen was far less disruptive and some of these boat masters were regular visitors, thereby building up strong links with the fishermen of Dungeness.[82] Nevertheless, the civic authorities stipulated that the Westermen should be under the governance of local men, a system that allowed the town to regulate their activities and to collect fish taxes.[83] Of those from overseas, the records primarily mention men (very rarely women) from France, the Low Countries and the German States, but there was a small Genoese community at Sandwich in the 1440s (see Mate, this volume).[84] Compared to London, open hostility seems to have been rare, and some groups might receive preferential treatment, as the Lombards did at Sandwich in 1479.[85]

For the civic authorities throughout Kent, migration, even if only on a seasonal or short-term basis was vital because as producers and consumers the migrants aided the local economy. Nonetheless, the mid-fifteenth-century economic crisis seems to have meant that some civic authorities sought to protect the economies of the local townsmen, and at certain towns the later decades of this century witnessed falling rent rolls, presumably a reflection of the demographic conditions.[86] The authorities at Canterbury had introduced a type of licensing system in the late fourteenth century, whereby immigrants were allowed to trade in a particular ward provided they paid an appropriate fee. The records indicate that a small minority managed to remain in Canterbury for decades, though not necessarily in the same ward, annually paying their fee, but some barely lasted a year.[87] Nevertheless, for the town officers this system offered a means of raising revenue from migrants outside the freeman body, which was in addition to the sums received from those seeking to become freemen by redemption. Together such sums helped to offset the town's declining income from municipal rents, some town property remaining 'in hand' for considerable periods.[88] It is difficult to know

may have preferred Eastry, staying at the latter for several weeks and only the former for a few days before embarking for France in 1342; MS TNA PRO E 36/204, p. 63. I should like to thank Dr Michael Baron for this reference.

82 Such men came from ports like Sidmouth and Burport; MS EKA Ly/FAc 3, p. 60.

83 Finn, *Lydd*, pp. 210, 243, 244, 280. Though the system was abused by the collector of taxes in 1467; idem, p. 323. A later letter of 1528 refers to an unenforced statute of 10 Edward IV, where it was stated that no West Country fisherman not being a freeman of Lydd be allowed to sell his fish at the Stade market until the Lydd fishermen had sold the majority of their fish, subject to a penalty of 40s; MS EKA Ly/8/1/8. There were also strict regulations about renting cabins at the Ness to these West Country fishermen; MS EKA Ly/FAc 3, pp. 177, 185, 187.

84 J. Wallace, 'The Overseas Trade of Sandwich, 1400–1520' (unpublished M.Phil. thesis, University of London, 1974), pp. 352–65.

85 According to the ordinance passed that year, 'no alien stranger keep ostes upon pain of losing their goods except Lombards to whom is granted licence for people of their language and nation'; MS EKA Sa/AC 1, fol. 429.

86 J. Hatcher, 'The Great Slump of the Mid-Fifteenth Century', in *Progress and Problems in Medieval England*, ed. R. Britnell and J. Hatcher (Cambridge, 1996), pp. 237–72. A. F. Butcher, 'Rent and the Urban Economy: Oxford and Canterbury in the Later Middle Ages', *Southern History* 1 (1979), 37–44.

87 Cowper, *Intrantes*. For an assessment of these people in the Whitefriars area during the later Middle Ages, see A. Hicks and M. Houliston, *The Whitefriars Excavation* (forthcoming).

88 Rent arrears were also a growing problem from the late fifteenth century; MS CCAL CC/FA 5, fols 153,

whether other, smaller Kentish towns were able to develop a similar two-tier system, but some, at least, were able to collect fees from migrants seeking to enter the freedom.[89] The level of recording of new freemen varies considerably among the Cinque Ports, but at New Romney between the years 1433 and 1523 the town clerk listed nearly four hundred freemen of whom 218 had come from places more than six miles away.[90] It is not clear what was happening at Queenborough, but the civic rather than the ecclesiastical authorities were seemingly able to offer sanctuary to outsiders, a form of refuge that may have attracted migrants from other towns, as well as those from the countryside.[91] Regulations detailing how and when non-freemen might trade in markets were a common feature of late medieval civic ordinances, and those found guilty of contravening such customs were duly fined.[92] Other measures adopted for the protection of the local populace included regulations regarding the duties of the town porters at Faversham; and at Hythe, for example, the foreign butchers were listed separately by the town clerk who compiled the local tax or maletote returns.[93] Thus the urban authorities of Kent initiated various regulations that were apparently primarily intended to protect their interests and those of the commonality, which might include measures to attract those seen as desirable strangers but to keep out, if at all possible, those envisaged as disruptive to the common good.[94] Such ordinances were part of the political topography of urban society, yet just how different townspeople responded to Johanna Cokeis's expulsion from Sandwich after she had been led through the town along the designated route for malefactors must remain open to conjecture (for some reason the town clerk noted the route when he recorded her case in the town book).[95]

162. However, compared to the first decades of the fifteenth century, there were fewer intrants in the last decades of the century.

89 Compared to Canterbury, Sandwich had a simpler system in place, the fees for trading recorded in the treasurers' rolls.

90 Furthermore, almost half of these had travelled over fifty miles; A. F. Butcher, 'The Origins of Romney Freemen, 1433–1523', *Economic History Review* 2nd series 27 (1974), 20–2.

91 MS CKS Qb/AZ, fol. 230.

92 At New Romney in 1413, for example, John son of Roger Payne was fined 20d for buying fresh herring and then retailing to freemen and others at a higher price against the custom; Teichman-Derville, 'Annals', 159. Regulations regarding the rights of Canterbury's freemen to retail wine were introduced in 1473; MS CCAL CC AC/1/9.

93 The Faversham regulations (1448) related to the carriage of ale and beer, the loading and unloading of ships and the administration of local justice; F. F. Giraud, 'Faversham: Regulations for the Town Porters, 1448', *Arch. Cant.* 20 (1893), 219–21. For example, in 1467/8 five foreign butchers were listed; MS EKA H 1058, fol. 21. Detailed lists of the maletotes due from merchants and others survive from some ports; that for New Romney is preserved in a fourteenth-century register; K. M. E. Murray, trans. and ed., *Register of Daniel Rough, Common Clerk of Romney 1353–1380*, Kent Records 16 (Ashford, 1945), pp. 28–35.

94 The civic authorities did not want to see work being put out to those outside the town, a problem that occurred at Canterbury in 1500 due to the activities of certain cloth makers; MS CCAL CC/AC1/34.

95 MS EKA Sa/AC 1, fols 130–30v.

History, Memory and Time

The value leading townsmen placed on the antiquity of their town has been investigated for a number of towns in England and elsewhere in Europe.[96] Some of these foundation myths and legends were recorded in town chronicles, which drew on ideas and personages from the classical civilisations of Greece and Rome, as well as from the biblical past. In Kent neither the civic authorities at the episcopal towns nor those from the Cinque Ports engaged in this form of chronicle writing, though Faversham's earliest town book does include a chronicle but no explicit references to the town's ancient past.[97] Yet its inclusion does indicate an awareness of the importance of longevity, precedent, and memory, as well as the chronicle's significance in the production of the town's history, even if it does not suggest that it should be compared directly to such works as Ricart's *Kalendar* from Bristol.[98] Nor was such an awareness unique to Faversham among townsmen in Kent, and for the Cinque Portsmen, in particular, custumals appear to have served the same purpose, seen as repositories of the town's history and memory.[99] Other town documents were also treasured as records relating to the distant past, being seen as further indicators of the town's longevity. Probably the most important of these were charters, their perceived value to the leading townsmen demonstrated through their inclusion in the custumal itself.[100]

Among the charters of Henry II and his predecessors are a few granted to certain ports which refer to the rights enjoyed by these towns in exchange for what became known as Ship Service. As well as authenticating their privileged status, the charters, when considered with other documents, also indicate their antiquity.[101] In addition, subsequent *inspeximus* charters underlined the continuing relationship of these towns with the Crown, which was strengthened by the general charter to the Cinque Ports of 1278.[102] Furthermore, being able to display the town's charter collection, the power of the written word reinforced by the presence of the king's seal, would have heightened the town's sense of its own history. And also, this may have been understood by others, particularly those from the limbs of the head ports whose own history was strengthened by association.[103] Such relationships were valued during the Middle Ages but perhaps were

96 For example: Rosser, 'Myth, Image and Social Process', 5–25. Moreover, the value of recording more recent events in town books was similarly understood, as at Bristol and the production of 'The Great White Book'; P. Fleming, 'Conflict and Urban Government in Later Medieval England: St Augustine's Abbey and Bristol', *Urban History* 27 (2000), 321–43.

97 Harrington and Hyde, *Early Books*, pp. 48–54. J. P. Croft, 'The Custumals of the Cinque Ports c.1290–c.1599: Studies in the Cultural Production of the Urban Record' (unpublished PhD thesis, University of Kent, 1997), pp. 260–70.

98 L. T. Smith, ed., *The Maire of Bristowe is Kalendar by Robert Ricart*, Camden New Series 5 (London, 1872), pp. 3, 6–28. M. Merry, 'Ricart's *Kalender*: Urban Ideology and Fifteenth Century Bristol' (unpublished M.A. dissertation, University of Kent, 1994).

99 Croft, 'Custumals', p. 29.

100 Ibid., pp. 47, 210–12.

101 Murray, *Cinque Ports*, pp. 12–16, 231–5.

102 Ibid., p. 237. Eighteen years earlier, Henry III had granted liberties in common; ibid., p. 236.

103 For example, the men of Faversham seemingly saw the value of such a connection to Dover in their

especially significant in the thirteenth century when many town officers were actively engaged in the struggle for greater autonomy.[104] Nevertheless, towns continued to collect charters from late medieval kings to safeguard their privileged status, thereby cementing their relationship with the Crown and forming part of the community's collective memory. Thus, even though the careful preservation of these town charters may relate primarily to the legal rights and privileges they gave to the citizens, the Cinque Ports were not the only Kentish towns that valued their charters as markers of their town's history.[105]

Custumals, whether civic or manorial, often contained details about landholding, but those covering towns frequently included clauses concerning market and trade regulations, and also items regarding the governance of the community, its rights and responsibilities and copies of important charters.[106] When considering history and memory, of particular significance are those clauses (in addition to the charters) relating to civic elections (principally found in the Cinque Port custumals), and the preamble of the Sandwich custumal. Regarding the latter, Justin Croft's detailed investigation of the surviving copies of the Sandwich custumal has led him to believe that when Adam Champneys wrote down the custumal in 1301, he composed the preamble to highlight the authenticity of the town's claims regarding its right to self-governance (see Plate 11).[107] Champneys was well aware of the power of the written word but also wished to draw attention to the collective memory of his predecessors, though rhetorically (at least) he was prepared to accept that such oral testimony might be flawed. By so doing he was following in the footsteps of other thirteenth-century clerks, employing the written word to defend the town's customs by underlining their ancient usage (the past) and their stability (present and future).[108]

As one of the earliest Kentish custumals, the Sandwich document is particularly important, but in some ways it is the proliferation of Cinque Port custumals and their similar format that is noteworthy in the context of collective memory and urban identity. Unlike most other custumals, those from the Cinque Ports generally have as their first item the election procedure of the town officers.[109]

continuing dispute with the abbot of Faversham; Harrington and Hyde, *Early Books*, p. xlix. As did the men of Tenterden through their link to Rye, the oldest surviving town book having copies of Edward IV's charter to the Cinque Ports and Henry VI's charter to the men of Tenterden; A. H. Taylor, 'The Municipal Records of Tenterden', *Arch. Cant.* 32 (1917), 286–7.

104 G. H. Martin, 'The English Borough in the Thirteenth Century', in *The Medieval Town: A Reader in English Urban History 1200–1540*, ed. R. Holt and G. Rosser (London and New York, 1990), pp. 29–48.

105 Ashford's 'Customary Booke' contains a copy of the market grant dated 1243; Ruderman, *Ashford*, p. 115. Even today Faversham's charters are still held in the town, and it also has a rare copy of *Magna Carta*.

106 On the breadth of issues covered by town custumals; M. Bateson, ed., *Borough Customs*, Seldon Society, 2 vols (London, 1904, 1906).

107 J. P. Croft, 'An Assault on the Royal Justices at Ash and the Making of the Sandwich Custumal', *Arch. Cant.* 117 (1997), 18–21.

108 M. T. Clanchy, *From Memory to Written Record, England 1066–1307*, 2nd edn (Oxford, 1993), especially chapters 5, 7–9.

109 Croft, 'Custumals', p. 23.

The rituals they describe were viewed as time-honoured events, and this symbiotic relationship between writing and dramatic performance (custumal and mayor-making) would have been a powerful reminder of the special nature of the ports and portsmen.[110] The level and type of detail recorded varies, but among the common elements most custumals mention the use of a parish church. Though the Church's spiritual role in the town is considered below, that is what many may consider as its primary function, at this point it is worth examining its use for secular events. It seems highly likely that many of the Cinque Ports (head ports and limbs) had at least one parish church by the time of the Conquest and some of these were substantial buildings. As ancient sacred places they were eminently suitable spaces for the holding of civic rituals. Consequently, when the leading citizens of several of these ports sought greater autonomy during the thirteenth century, which often included the privilege of having a mayor as the senior civic officer, the employment of the parish church as the location for such annual rituals as mayor-making was a clear demonstration of the sanctity of the procedure.[111]

The linking of pragmatism and symbolism by the civic authorities seems to have extended beyond their use of the town's ancient parish church because the timing of such civic elections at some coastal towns was apparently tied to one of the most ancient and traditionally important occupations: fishing (for example, the beginning and end of the herring season). Thus, where a large proportion of the local townsmen were, or probably more significantly had been, fishermen who regularly spent part of the year deep-sea fishing this might represent a practical decision. At Dover civic elections were held at the feast of the Nativity of Our Lady (8 September) and according to Domesday the 'King's truce' was to operate in the town from Michaelmas (29 September) until the feast of St Andrew (30 November).[112] Yet such times may also have had symbolic meanings because some ancient dues were paid in fish, fish therefore taking on ideas of contested lordship. At Sandwich mayor-making was to take place on Monday after the feast of St Andrew the Apostle (end of the deep-sea herring season) and, according to Domesday, the town was to provide forty thousand herring annually to Christ Church Priory as its overlord.[113] Faversham's elections were to be held the day after Michaelmas, nationally by far the most common choice by royal and seigniorial accountants being linked to the agricultural year. Yet at Faversham it may additionally have been linked to fishing: the end of the grayling season and the beginning of the herring season.[114]

110 Ibid., pp. 24–7.

111 Sweetinburgh, 'Mayor-Making', pp. 170–6.

112 MS BL Stowe 850, fol 133. Though conjecture, the King's truce may imply that in the late eleventh century a significant proportion of the Dover men were away fishing; Morgan, *Domesday: Kent*, D, 4.

113 Morgan, *Domesday: Kent*, 2.2.

114 Both species of fish were important in the town's economy, and the leading townsmen used them as prestigious gifts in their long-running dispute with the abbot of Faversham, though at times the warden of the Cinque Ports demanded the 'gift' as a perquisite of his office. At least initially, however, the gift

Gifts of fish were not the only means employed by Kentish townsmen to mark specific events in their town's history. The great Dover candle (see above) was presumably instigated to mark either a thanksgiving offering to St Thomas for his deliverance of the town or as a means of seeking the saint's aid on a particular (now unknown) occasion. The feast day of St Bartholomew is still celebrated in Sandwich at St Bartholomew's Hospital by the civic authorities, though they no longer process from St Peter's church as their medieval forefathers did in honour of the saint who 'saved' the town in 1217.[115] A description of the annual procession is recorded as part of the town's custumal (within the section for St Bartholomew's Hospital), the earliest extant version dating from the late fourteenth century; the details remaining unchanged in the fifteenth-century custumal (see Sweetinburgh, this volume).[116] According to these documents, the mayor, jurats and commonalty (free barons, householders and indwellers) carried wax tapers, some playing musical instruments (the town waites?), the laity followed by the clergy from the town's three parishes, making in total 140 persons. The clergy, too, carried wax tapers and sang psalms as they processed from St Peter's church at the centre of the town to St Bartholomew's Hospital beyond the town wall. Once there the St Peter's clergy celebrated Mass at the hospital's chapel and the day concluded with a feast. By enshrining the initial event and its subsequent commemoration within the written word, the civic authorities were establishing the place of the divine in the town's past and present, and their responsibility to ensure this relationship continued without interruption into the future.

Whereas repetition, and so stability and continuity, had been the focus of the compilers of the late fourteenth- and fifteenth-century versions of the Sandwich custumal regarding the St Bartholomew's day procession, this was not always the case. According to Croft, the introduction of 'new' material into an existing custumal may relate to the perceived need by the civic authorities to respond to specific events or to periods of profound change in the town's history.[117] For example, he considers that the late fifteenth-century Hythe book (MS 1061), which includes the town's custumal, was produced in part as a response to the political uncertainties in the aftermath of Edward IV's death and especially Richard III's usurpation of the throne.[118] Thus custumal writing was a temporal

of herring had probably been seen as especially appropriate with respect to the warden; Harrington and Hyde, *Early Books*, p. lxx. The grain harvest was extremely important, Faversham acting as a major market centre; Harrington and Hyde, *Early Books*, p. liii.

115 For a near contemporary account of the battle of Sandwich in 1217, see H. Cannon, 'The Battle of Sandwich and Eustace the Monk', *English Historical Review* 108 (1912), 667 n. 144, citing the editor's paraphrase *L'Histoire de Guillaume le Marechal,* ed. P. Meyer (1901), for the text: II, lines 17501–68. For a recent new edition with full translation: A. J. Holden, ed., *History of William Marshal*, Anglo-Norman Text Society, 3 vols (London, 2002–2006). Matthew Paris provides an illustrated account of the battle; MS Cambridge Corpus Christi College 16, fol. 56. S. Sweetinburgh, *The Role of the Hospital in Medieval England: Gift-Giving and the Spiritual Economy* (Dublin, 2004), pp. 189–90.

116 MS EKA Sa/LC 1, fol. 15v; Sa/LC 2, fol. 9v. Boys, *Sandwich*, p. 17.

117 Croft, 'Assault', 31.

118 J. P. Croft, 'Hythe MS 1061: The Making of an Urban Register' (unpublished M.A. dissertation, University of Kent, 1992).

process requiring the town clerk and others to consult, discuss, read, copy and amend it and other town documents in order to re-establish the town's identity, as articulated through precedent and shared responses.[119]

Time-keeping, as a facet of urban culture, might also be articulated in the later Middle Ages through other civic processes, including the writing up of the various court proceedings, the listing of local tax assessments and the measurement of time itself. Though not a new concept because divine service punctuated the day outside as well as inside the monastery, the employment of clock time for such matters as markets, curfew and assemblies was presumably directly related to the introduction of mechanical clocks in the later fourteenth century.[120] Unlike the Low Countries where municipal clocks and free-standing bell towers were an increasing feature of the great cloth cities, public clocks in England were apparently predominantly located in parish churches.[121] The late fourteenth-century evidence for England, as at York, points to this being an urban phenomenon and Kent appears to follow this trend, though so far the earliest Kentish civic or parochial public clocks appear to date from the fifteenth century. There were probably others across the county but of the known clocks there was at least one in Sandwich, at St Mary's church, another at the church of St Martin le Grand in Dover, at St Lawrence's church in New Romney, others at Hythe, Lydd, Faversham, Wye, Chislehurst, Dartford and Lenham parish churches, and several in and around Canterbury.[122] It is difficult to gauge what they were like but interestingly there seems to have been a shift over the same period in terms of the recording of time from 'of the bell' to 'of the clock' which may be significant.[123] Presumably most or all of these clocks were in the west or central tower, making them the responsibility of the churchwardens. In many towns there was a considerable cross-over of personnel between the parish and the civic; and such links are known to have been even closer at Lydd, Faversham and Dover. The civic authorities at Lydd lent money to the churchwardens and the wardens gave an account of their financial dealings before the assembled bailiff and jurats.[124] At Dover the connection

119 Similarly the production of early town books, as at Faversham; Croft, 'Custumals', pp. 233–34; Harrington and Hyde, *Early Books*, p. lxiii.

120 G. Dohrn-van Rossum, *History of the Hour: Clocks and Modern Temporal Orders*, trans. T. Dunlap (Chicago and London, 1996), pp. 30–3, 35–40, 109–13, 128–72, 245–51.

121 Ibid., 197–202. Dohrn-van Rossum looks almost exclusively at continental Europe; a rare British example he uses is Edward III's installation of clocks at his residences in the late 1360s, including one at Queenborough; ibid., p. 135. R. A. Brown, 'King Edward's Clocks', *Antiquaries Journal* 39 (1959), 283–6.

122 Sandwich, St Mary's; MS CCAL U 3/11/5/1, p. 172, in this instance (1464), the churchwardens called on local expertise: a man from Wingham. Dover, St Martin's; MS BL Add. 29616, fol. 8v. New Romney, St Lawrence's; Teichman-Dervile, 'Annals', 170. Hythe; Mackeson and S. Robertson, 'Hythe Churchwardens' Accounts in the Time of Henry IV', *Arch. Cant.* 10 (1876), 244, 248. Lydd; Finn, *Lydd*, p. 332. Faversham; Harrington and Hyde, *Early Books*, p. 89. MS CCAL U 3/174/5/A/1, fol. 5v. Lenham, Dartford, Chislehurst; L. L. Duncan, ed., *Testamenta Cantiana: West Kent* (London, 1906), pp. 12, 19. A. Hussey, ed., *Testamenta Cantiana: East Kent* (London, 1907), p. 191. Canterbury, St Andrew's, St Nicholas' Hospital; MS CKS PRC 17/1, fol. 114; PRC 17/7, fol. 64.

123 Dohrn-van Rossum, *Hour*, pp. 202–15.

124 Finn, *Lydd*, pp.329, 331. Harrington and Hyde, *Early Books*, p. 93.

between the civic authorities and the clock at St Martin le Grand's was apparently even closer because the town employed the sexton to maintain the clock.[125] Thus through their role as guardians of the town's time (pieces), the civic authorities could be said to have placed a temporal and spatial 'boundary' around the town.[126]

The Church in the Town[127]

The religious environment of the town was frequently richer than that of the countryside.[128] The Benedictine and Augustinian houses were in or very close to towns, some, as at West Malling, had fostered the lay community at its gate, the institution providing the impetus for the local settlement to become a small market town. Hospitals too, were generally in or close to towns, even the leper houses; while the friars saw the town as their principal preaching arena, and, as mendicant communities, also needed towns to ensure their survival (see Edwards and Sweetinburgh, this volume).[129] Nonetheless, some Kentish towns did not have a single monastic establishment, and even the episcopal city of Rochester only had the cathedral priory and a few hospitals within its environs. Consequently, Canterbury was exceptional in Kent, having in total three Benedictine houses, an Augustinian priory, four friaries (at various times) and seven hospitals; as well as Becket's great shrine, other saintly repositories and numerous chantry chapels, where priests said Mass daily for the souls of the founders and other beneficiaries.[130]

Parochial chantries were generally a later medieval development, and even though they were founded in rural parish churches as well as urban ones, the largest were established in towns.[131] Furthermore, most chantry colleges were urban institutions, the colleges contributing to a significant increase in the number of secular priests resident in the town. As part of the endowment the

125 MS BL Add. 29810, fol. 17.

126 An obvious reminder was the curfew bell. At Faversham, for example, the town regulations of 1506 state that the 'couerfewe' was to be rung 'at 8 o'clock for a quarter of an hour with a bell as of old time has been accustomed'; Harrington and Hyde, *Early Books*, p. 89.

127 As well as specific articles on the parish church(es) in individual towns: M. Egan, 'The Church in Medieval Greenwich', *Arch. Cant.* 123 (2003), 233–51; essays on particular Kentish urban parish churches can also be found in edited volumes: J. Thirsk, ed., *Hadlow: Life, Land and People in a Wealden Parish 1460–1600* (Maidstone, 2007), chapter 12; and single author monographs: D. Gardiner, *Historic Haven: The Story of Sandwich* (Derby, 1954), chapter 16.

128 There were a few rural monastic houses: Cistercian and Praemonstratensian, but from the testamentary evidence their presence in the countryside seems to have added little to the spiritual life of the surrounding parishes.

129 S. Sweetinburgh, 'Monastic Houses', in *An Historical Atlas of Kent*, ed. T. Lawson and D. Killingray (Chichester, 2004), pp. 42–3.

130 M. Lyle, 'Canterbury 1500–1700: Two Centuries of Upheaval', in *An Historical Atlas of Kent*, ed. T. Lawson and D. Killingray (Chichester, 2004), pp. 68–9.

131 Of those that were at parish churches, probably the largest was Thomas Elys' chantry of three priests at St Peter's church, Sandwich; Hussey, *Chantries*, p. 264.

priests were expected to undertake educational activities, and probably to teach, and there may have been chantry schools at Wye, Ashford, Maidstone, Bredgar and Cobham.[132] Similarly, many of the other smaller chantry foundations may have provided some schooling, though opportunities were perhaps more extensive in towns due to the greater concentration of these institutions. Such provisions greatly extended those already available in some towns, education having previously been the almost exclusive preserve of the religious houses (see Edwards, this volume). Again Canterbury offered the greatest provision because as well as the religious houses, the city also had a long-established grammar school.[133] In Dover the local priory apparently had had a virtual monopoly of schooling in the town, but some form of education may have been available at St Mary's Hospital by the early sixteenth century.[134] Yet by this time parish officials might be involved: at Sandwich there was a schoolmaster at St Mary's church in the late fifteenth century, the parish clerk at St Clement's church was expected to teach the children pricksong each week under the provisions of Henry Pyham's will (1497), and Boys reported that one of Elys' chantry priests at St Peter's parish church was expected to teach, though the copy of the foundation document does not mention it.[135] In the west of the county, Sevenoaks 'gained' a grammar school in the 1430s, though, as Gillian Draper has highlighted, how far the school at Sevenoaks can be seen as a 'new' type of endowed grammar school is open to question, perhaps having its origins in the thirteenth-century chantry at the local parish church.[136]

For the laity the parish church was at the centre of their devotional practices. Most small Kentish towns had a single parish church, sometimes with peripheral chapels, but a few often ancient, larger towns did have a number of parish churches. In part this reflects patterns of lordship and the location of the ancient minsters and their daughter churches, the resulting parochial topography of the county becoming fixed to a reasonable extent by the eleventh century (quite a large number of chapels came into being during the period 1100 to 1300, many were later abandoned, but some did become full parishes).[137] Thus, for example,

132 G. M. Draper, '"There hath not bene any grammar scole kepte, preacher maytened or pore people releved, other then … by the same chauntreye": Educational Provision and Piety in Kent, c.1400–1640', in *Pieties in Transition: Religious Practices and Experiences, c.1400–1640*, ed. R. Lutton and E. Salter (Aldershot, 2007), p. 85. For Wye College, see E. W. Parkin, 'The Medieval Origins of Wye College', *Arch. Cant.* 102 (1985), 209–31. For Cobham College: J. M. Gibson, 'The Chantry College of Cobham', *Arch. Cant.* 125 (2005), 83–118.

133 Somner, *Canterbury*, appendix pp. 33–4.

134 The priory's monopoly is recorded in a document about the dispute between the town and the archdeacon in 1284; C. R. Haines, *Dover Priory: A History of the Priory of St Mary the Virgin, and St Martin of the New Work* (Cambridge, 1930), pp. 350–1; MS Cambridge Corpus Christi College 59, fol. 27.

135 MS CCAL U 3/11/5/1, p. 67. MS CKS PRC 17/6, fol. 291. Boys, *Sandwich*, p. 186; MS EKA Sa/AC 2, fols 166v–67.

136 Draper, 'Scole', pp. 87–9. For the national picture see; N. Orme, *Medieval Schools: From Roman Britain to Renaissance England* (London and New Haven, CT, 2006).

137 T. Tatton-Brown, 'The Churches of the Canterbury Diocese in the Eleventh Century', in *Minsters and*

there were six parishes at Dover, including three which had altars in the earlier minster church of St Martin le Grand, and three parishes at New Romney.[138] Canterbury was again exceptional, but some of the parishes were very small and, as elsewhere, some had disappeared as early as the thirteenth century.[139] A few of these Canterbury parish churches were located above the town gates, though only St Mary Northgate survived into modern times.[140] In contrast, the towns of Ashford and Tenterden each comprised a single parish.[141] Yet townsmen in these communities could still enrich their spiritual lives, the testamentary evidence indicating a proliferation of fraternities, altars, lights and images at Ashford parish church.[142] Tenterden, too, like some other Wealden towns (Bethersden, Biddenden and Cranbrook), had a considerable number of lights and altars, and in general terms rural parishes had fewer.[143] As a result only a proportion of the county's urban dwellers lived in settlements that had several parish churches and/or local religious house(s). So diversity in terms of the spiritual life of the townspeople was generally greatest in the older towns, providing opportunities for the leading citizens, in particular, to join several fraternities in their and possibly neighbouring parish churches, as well as becoming members of confraternities at local religious houses, hearing sermons given by friars and residing in local hospitals. For example, a harmonious relationship between religious house and town seems to have existed at Dartford; and while Elizabeth Cressener was prioress the priory appears to have been actively engaged in ensuring that the various services for its lay benefactors were undertaken properly.[144] Nevertheless, religious houses, as holders of the advowson of the parish church(es) in a town, were not always seen as enriching the spiritual lives of the local inhabitants. At Faversham, in 1301, the townsmen badly damaged the parish church when the long-running dispute over exemption between the archbishop of

Parish Churches: The Local Church in Transition, ed. J. Blair (Oxford, 1988), pp. 105–18. For an assessment of the development of the Church in Kent, see A. Everitt, *Continuity and Colonization: The Evolution of Kentish Settlement* (Leicester, 1986), chapters 8–10.

138 Dover: St Martin, St John and St Nicholas; St Peter; St Mary and St James (fishermen's church). New Romney: St Martin; St Nicholas and St Lawrence.

139 Yet if Canterbury was exceptional in Kent (in total twenty-two parish churches), in national terms it had far fewer ecclesiastical establishments compared to cities such as York and Norwich; T. Tatton-Brown, 'Medieval Parishes and Parish Churches in Canterbury', in *The Church in the Town*, ed. T. R. Slater and G. Rosser (Aldershot, 1998), pp. 236–71.

140 For example: St Edmund Ridingate; St Michael Burgate; St Mary Quenegate; Holy Cross Westgate.

141 Yet within parishes there might be a chapel which could be a focal point for the local community. Smallhythe chapel was built in the early sixteenth century within the parish of St Mildred's, Tenterden; R. Lutton, *Lollardy and Orthodox Religion in Pre-Reformation England* (Woodbridge, 2006), pp. 103–29. Others in the county include Gravesend parish and St George's chapel; P. Lee, 'Orthodox Parish Religion and Chapels of Ease in Late Medieval England: The Case of St George's Chapel in Gravesend', *Arch. Cant.* 119 (1999), 55–70.

142 Hussey, *Testamenta: East*, pp. 6–8.

143 Ibid., pp. xxi, 14–15, 18–19, 86–9. Urban parish churches were also more likely to have lights/altars dedicated to 'newer' saints, such as St Erasmus; ibid., p. 413.

144 P. Lee, *Nunneries, Learning and Spirituality in Late Medieval English Society: The Dominican Priory of Dartford* (York, 2001), pp. 101–2.

Canterbury and St Augustine's Abbey, which held the advowson, led to the suspension of the incumbent, the installation of a monk in his place and what appears to have been an unseemly episode at the deathbed of a local parishioner.[145] Yet by the later fifteenth century, and possibly earlier, the abundance of altars, lights and images might suggest that the townspeople of Faversham viewed the parish church as 'theirs', perhaps reflecting a lessening of the influence of a religious house that was not 'of the town', because the comparative testamentary evidence from Dover appears to suggest the parishioners there continued to envisage the town's parish churches as under the authority of Dover Priory.[146]

Furthermore, compared to their rural counterparts, Kentish townsmen seem to have been quicker and more willing to embrace new cults, perhaps one of the most important from the later fifteenth century being the Mass of the Holy Name of Jesus (commonly called the Jesus Mass).[147] The first known reference concerns a testator from Sandwich in 1466, implying that the Mass had been celebrated there for some while.[148] Its arrival in the county may reflect continental and London influences, and a growing awareness among townspeople, more generally, of the ideas surrounding lay piety; but it would be wrong to draw too great a distinction between rural and urban parishes because of the many strong inter-connections (see Lutton, this volume).

Parochial fraternities were an important part of lay spirituality in most Kentish communities.[149] However, in some towns certain parish guilds may have become pseudo-civic organisations. At Hythe, it appears that the fraternity of Assumption of Our Lady at St Leonard's parish church was patronised by the jurats and their wives, and by those of the 'middling' sort. As the senior fraternity, the guild chaplain celebrated services for members in the Lady Chapel, including intercessory masses, and on the principal feast day conducted Mass there, the service followed by a fraternal feast in the large room above the south porch.[150] For the senior guild members, including several widows, their patronage of this important chapel could be demonstrated through gift-giving.[151] This fraternal use of the town's

145 R. Graham, 'The Conflict between Robert Winchelsey, Archbishop of Canterbury and the Abbot and Monks of St Augustine's, Canterbury', *Journal of Ecclesiastical History* 1 (1950), 44–5. Harrington and Hyde, *Early Books*, p. lv.

146 Hussey, *Testamenta: East*, pp. 119–20. During the early decades of the sixteenth century, however, Dover testators were generally providing greater support for their parish churches; Sweetinburgh, *Hospital*, pp. 151–2, 169.

147 Of the twenty-eight parishes known to have celebrated the Jesus Mass in Kent, fewer than ten were rural parishes; ibid., pp. xxi; Lutton, *Lollardy*, pp. 69–77; R. Lutton, 'Geographies and Materialities of Piety: Reconciling Competing Narratives of Religious Change in Pre-Reformation and Reformation England', in *Pieties in Transition: Religious Practices and Experiences, c.1400–1640*, ed. R. Lutton and E. Salter (Aldershot, 2007), pp. 27–9.

148 MS CKS PRC 17/1, fol. 256.

149 Interestingly, there are very few references to parochial fraternities at any of the Dover churches, and parishes in the town's hinterland show a similar pattern; Sweetinburgh, *Hospital*, p. 161.

150 MS EKA Hy/Z4/4.

151 Alice Stevyn (1487) gave her mother's silver ring to the image of Our Lady of the Assumption and

sacred space might have offered a sense of stability and cohesion, which may have been viewed as especially important by the leading townsmen in the politically turbulent later fifteenth century.[152] It is conceivable that the fraternity of St George at St Clement's church in Sandwich was a more overt example of such an organisation. The spatial layout of the church was apparently modified to accommodate this important fraternal altar, and temporal adjustments were also made: the weekly St George Mass included choral singing.[153] Moreover, these devotional activities included an annual procession, and from 1481 this was subsidised by the town, the treasurers paying 6s 8d annually.[154] A third example is the Corpus Christi Guild (see above), which celebrated its patronal services in the north choir aisle (site of the altar of Corpus Christi) of All Saints' church, Maidstone.[155] Such examples are probably not isolated instances but apart from testamentary materials the evidence for religious fraternities is generally scarce in Kent, making it difficult to assess the socioeconomic composition of the membership and the specific form of their activities.[156]

There are early references to guild merchants in Kent, though there is little evidence concerning craft fraternities before the late fifteenth century and nothing to suggest that any Kentish towns had a highly organised craft guild structure similar to that of York, Chester or London at any stage during the medieval period.[157] Yet individually a few guilds did become well established in their respective towns in the late Middle Ages.[158] The guild of the cordwainers and cobblers at Canterbury, for example, held their patronal services at the Austin friars before processing to their hall to dine; and the senior members also regulated the occupational activities of the membership in the city.[159] Through this combination of piety and charity by and on behalf of the craft members, the guilds were a link between the Church and the civic authorities. Consequently, their

Agnes Downe (1480) bequeathed 6s 8d towards the large window in the Lady Chapel; MS CKS PRC 32/3, fol. 174; PRC 32/2, fol. 521.

152 Croft, 'Register', pp. 23–7.

153 MS CKS PRC 17/6, fol. 291.

154 MS EKA Sa/AC 1, fol. 262v. At Canterbury the exact relationship between the corporation and the Corpus Christi guild is unclear, but the guild's assets were sold off by the city in 1537–38; HMC Canterbury, p. 240.

155 Hussey, *Testamenta: East*, p. 206.

156 Apart from guild accounts themselves, one possibly useful source of evidence is churchwardens' accounts, and those for St Dunstan's parish to the west of Canterbury include some accounts relating to the fraternity of the Shaft. However, extant fifteenth-century churchwardens' accounts are relatively rare in Kent compared to some counties. Only one of the 547 parochial guild returns made to the Crown in the late fourteenth century came from Kent: the fraternity of St John at St John's church, Canterbury; MS EKA Hy/Z4/4.

157 There are a very few earlier references to occupational guilds: the smiths in Canterbury c.1200 and the ferrymen at Dover in the fourteenth century; Urry, *Canterbury*, p. 131. Statham, *Dover*, pp. 66–7. Only at Canterbury do the guilds appear to have been strong enough to put on plays (linked to the feast of Corpus Christi) but it is not clear how these would have compared to the northern play cycles; Gibson, *Kent*, 1, pp. 139–40; MS CCAL CC/AB 1, fols 5v–6.

158 For example, the ordinances of the Sandwich cordwainers' guild; MS EKA Sa/Ago 1.

159 CCAL, MS CC/Woodruffs/54/2.

emergence in the late fifteenth and early sixteenth centuries was, perhaps, part of the response by the leading citizens to the increasingly challenging economic conditions and the perceived need to establish additional protective measures to safeguard the town.[160]

Conclusion: Urban Culture on the Eve of the Reformation

Though the chronology of urban decline varied across the county, by the early 1520s most Kentish towns were experiencing considerable economic and social problems, a situation that was apparent to contemporary writers such as John Leland and others (see Mate, this volume).[161] Often this seems to have resulted in a greater polarisation of society, an increasingly prosperous tiny minority who may have become economically and socially isolated from the middling sort and their poorer neighbours.[162] Moreover, the physical shrinkage of the town probably also contributed to the difficulties experienced by the civic authorities who found that they were facing a rise in the number of poor people at a time when urban revenues were falling.[163] At the same time the Wealden cloth towns such as Cranbrook, which had developed in part because such settlements were not encumbered by urban trade regulations, were not immune from social problems either because growing numbers of migrants sought employment opportunities in shipbuilding, cloth, iron and other industries (see Draper, this volume).[164]

Politically, too, conditions were changing, and the late fifteenth and early sixteenth centuries brought greater autonomy for certain towns, especially those which had been under varying degrees of royal or ecclesiastical lordship.[165] Edward IV granted considerable privileges to Canterbury and Rochester, and

160 Interestingly, the late sixteenth century witnessed a further growth in the number of craft fraternities, possibly again primarily at the instigation of the civic authorities, though central government may also have been involved.

161 This picks up the points about urban decay that Jacqueline Bower raised in her essay of early modern Kentish towns; J. Bower, 'Kent Towns, 1540–1640', in *Early Modern Kent*, Kent History Project, ed. M. L. Zell (Woodbridge, 2000), pp. 141–2.

162 As Spencer Dimmock has shown for Lydd, local yeomen and gentry farmers could dominate small town society, their wealth derived from agrarian activities at the expense of their poorer tenants and neighbours; S. Dimmock, 'English Small Towns and the Emergence of Capitalist Relations, c.1450–1550', *Urban History* 28 (2001), 5–24.

163 W. K. Jordan, *Social Institutions of Kent 1480–1660: A Study of the Changing Pattern of Social Aspirations*, Kent Archaeological Society (Ashford, 1961).

164 For the development of Kentish industry in the sixteenth century, especially in the central Weald, see J. Andrewes, 'Industries in Kent, c.1500–1640', in *Early Modern Kent*, ed. M. L. Zell, Kent History Project (Woodbridge, 2000), p. 106. In contrast, Canterbury's cloth industry was in disarray and to combat such problems the civic authorities in 1506–7 commissioned the production of a number of broadcloths to aid 'poor spinners' and others; MS CCAL CC AB/1, fols 7–8.

165 However, it was also a time of political tension and Canterbury was not the only town that experienced discord among the various constituents of the civic authorities. To combat this the mayor and senior aldermen sought royal approval to change the governmental structure from a mayor and six aldermen and a common council of thirty-six to a mayor and twelve aldermen with a smaller common council of twenty-four. Henry VII agreed, issuing a charter to Canterbury in 1498; MS CCAL CC/A/A/44.

Sandwich gained control of the balliwick in 1530.[166] As noted above, the abbot of Faversham's control over the town had waned considerably by this period.[167] The dissolution of the religious house at Faversham, as at Dover, marked the final end of ecclesiastical lordship over the secular authorities, who as individuals and/or collectively took the opportunity to dismantle physically most of the monastic complex.[168] Nevertheless, greater autonomy did not necessarily halt the decline or bring greater prosperity to the town as a whole, and raising sufficient revenue continued to be a pressing issue in many east Kentish towns, and may have contributed to what has been called a flight from office.[169]

The religious beliefs of Kentish townspeople at this time remain a contentious issue (see Lutton, this volume) but the testamentary evidence from across the county does seem to indicate that in broad terms there was much less support for religious houses, including friaries, compared to other parts of the country. Proximity was an issue but did not necessarily equal support because corporately, and as individuals, many townsmen were apparently unwilling to aid the local monastery where questions of lordship had been disputed (often for centuries).[170] The level of support for the urban parish at this time is also problematic because of the heavy reliance on testamentary evidence but the range of cults and the arrival of new liturgical feasts, such as the Jesus Mass, even if not celebrated widely across the county, would seem to suggest a substantial interest in theological issues among townspeople.[171]

Drawing these issues together, their impact in cultural terms may be seen in several ways, though the individual experiences of the different Kentish towns

[166] During the later 1520s there was considerable disagreement between the town officers and the king's bailiff. This was finally resolved in 1530 when the town paid £100 to Sir Edward Ringley, the bailiff, the civic authorities retaining control of the bailiwick during Ringley's lifetime; EKA, MS Sa/AC 3, fol. 98v; Sa/FAt 29. Pearson, Clarke and Mate, *Sandwich*, p. 132.

[167] Harrington and Hyde, *Early Books*, p. lxxxiii.

[168] *Letters and Papers Henry VIII* 10, no. 146. A copy of a petition sent to the king and archbishop describing who had profited from the destruction of Dover's religious buildings 'to the prejudice of the king's profit'; MS CCAL Lit. C 16, fols 52–3.

[169] For such problems at Sandwich; Sweetinburgh, *Hospital*, p. 205. At Canterbury, too, there were difficulties; MS CCAL CC AC/1/74. After the Dissolution, the mayor and aldermen of Canterbury purchased from the Crown property in Canterbury previously held by St Augustine's Abbey in an attempt to revive the city's fortunes.

[170] The degree to which individuals engaged in such pious activities varied considerably and most studies have used testamentary materials to try to gauge this. Looking at the Rochester diocese, only about one in eight testators remembered religious houses at their death, the friars favoured over the monasteries; Lee, *Nunneries*, pp. 67–80. The towns of east Kent were not dissimilar, though the testators of Canterbury and Sandwich were far more likely to aid the local religious houses.

[171] For a detailed analysis of piety through testamentary giving in west Kent: P. Lee, 'Monastic and Secular Religion and Devotional Reading in Late Medieval Dartford and West Kent' (unpublished PhD thesis, University of Kent, 1998), chapter 5. Generally, most townspeople across the county considered their primary concern should be their local parish. Yet there were variations between towns: almost three out of four testators at Folkestone gave to named lights in their parish church, whereas it was one in three at Hythe; Sweetinburgh, *Hospital*, pp. 116–26, 169. The Wealden towns also showed considerable variation; Lutton, 'Geographies', pp. 14–16, 24–9, 37–9. So far a systematic study of testamentary giving in Kentish towns in the later Middle Ages has yet to be undertaken, but such a study would be extremely useful, shedding light on regional and local patterns over time.

were extremely varied. Nevertheless, for example, the foundation of small almshouses (maisonsdieu) was fairly widespread, seemingly part of the response by the civic authorities and prosperous citizens to the growing numbers of poor people in the county (see Sweetinburgh, this volume). Probably prompted by greater lay involvement in the organisation of the parish and the town, piety and charity appear to have been significant aspects of early sixteenth-century urban culture. However, it is important to remember that the far greater abundance of testamentary and other records may not always denote change, just greater visibility. Another area where the growth in record keeping and documentary survival may be significant is leisure: those caught playing cards, tennis and other prohibited activities brought before the courts. How far this was a 'new' development in this period is more difficult to ascertain, but its presence in urban society may still be important, like the provision of schooling and the evidence, however slight, of book ownership. In addition, the apparently greater desire (and ability) to regulate urban living, whether through civic ordinances regarding common latrines and street paving, or nuisance cases about dung hills may denote changing attitudes among town officials. Yet this level of regulatory control did not go unchallenged, and the pre-Reformation period seems to have been a time of complex and fluid networks and alliances as townsmen in Kent sought to overcome the difficult conditions of Henrician England.[172]

[172] Though published over thirty years ago, Peter Clark's discussion regarding such issues in Kentish society during this turbulent period continues to be a useful starting point; P. Clark, *English Provincial Society from the Reformation to the Revolution: Religion, Politics and Society in Kent, 1500–1640* (Hassocks, 1977), chapters 1–2.

8

Heresy and Heterodoxy in Late Medieval Kent

ROB LUTTON

The history of heterodoxy and heresy in Kent in the later Middle Ages is overwhelmingly dominated by Lollardy. Before the early fifteenth century, heresy, in the sense of heterodox religious beliefs and practices that were defined and detected by the Church as unorthodox, was not a concern in the county. In common with the rest of England, and in contrast with continental Europe, the first systematic prosecutions of heresy began only after the condemnation in 1382 of the ideas of the Oxford University master John Wycliffe and his followers. From this point onward the investigation of heresy was driven by an awareness among the ecclesiastical hierarchy that Wycliffe's ideas were gaining a clerical and lay following outside the university. It was given added impetus by the perception that the radical potential of those ideas made heresy a social and political, as well a religious, problem.[1] Kent saw its first heresy investigations in the third decade of the fifteenth century. The heretical network that was uncovered marked the first visible phase of a continuum of radical religious dissent in Kent from the later Middle Ages to the early twentieth century.[2]

What we cannot conclude from this is that there was no heterodoxy in Kent before Lollardy. There was almost certainly no organised movement or body of belief deemed heretical by Church and state, but there is very little way of knowing what lay people believed and what constituted orthodox religion in the parishes of Kent, prior to the upsurge of documentary evidence pertaining to lay piety from around the middle of the fifteenth century (see Sweetinburgh, this

1 I. Forrest, *The Detection of Heresy in Late Medieval England* (Oxford, 2005), pp. 11–27; A. Hudson, *The Premature Reformation: Wycliffite Texts and Lollard History* (Oxford, 1988), pp. 60–119; P. McNiven, *Heresy and Politics in the Reign of Henry IV* (Woodbridge, 1981); M. Aston, 'Lollardy and Sedition, 1381–1431' (first published in *Past and Present* 17 (1960), 1–44), in Aston, *Lollards and Reformers: Images and Literacy in Late Medieval Religion* (London, 1984), pp. 1–47.

2 For Lollard heresy in Kent, see J. A. F. Thomson, *The Later Lollards, 1414–1520* (Oxford, 1965), pp. 173–91. On the continuity of dissent, see A. Everitt, 'Nonconformity in Country Parishes', in *Land, Church and People, Essays Presented to Professor H. P. R. Finberg*, The Agricultural History Review 18, supplement, ed. J. Thirsk (1970), 178–99, esp. 188–93.

volume). From this date, last wills and testaments for both Kent dioceses survive in significant and increasing numbers. Together with churchwardens' accounts, they add exponentially to the evidence of lay religion. These increasingly abundant documentary sources may mark the growing importance of the parish in lay religion and provide evidence of increasing engagement by many parishioners with the cult of saints and their images, with the Mass as an intercessory rite and with the liturgy.[3] It is less clear that this engagement was universal, however. Recent research on lay piety in Kent suggests that the development of orthodox religion in the fifteenth century in some places was fitful and that not all of its key elements were uniformally popular.[4] This may mean that we should think of orthodoxy in Kent as more heterogeneous than homogeneous and that heterodoxy, in the sense of divergence from the norm, was relatively common, but went undetected. These ideas, and the evidence brought together here that documents heterodoxy where and when it was detected, begs the question: where did orthodoxy end and heterodoxy begin?[5]

Despite the best efforts of a number of bishops and archbishops to eradicate it, Lollardy survived in a relatively healthy state into the early sixteenth century in Kent. I begin below with an assessment of its impact from the early fifteenth century and then go on, in the second part of the chapter, to deal with its second major manifestation in the early sixteenth. There were, however, numerous suspects investigated for heresy who held and voiced erroneous beliefs that were either only partly inspired by Lollardy or were independent from it. I assess the possible origins and significance of these beliefs in the third part of the chapter. Finally, I attend to the significance of heresy and heterodoxy in Kent and its legacy in relation to the Reformation and later radical religious dissent and Nonconformity.

Early Lollardy

Lollard heresy came relatively late to Kent. It appears first to have been disseminated in the 1420s by Wycliffite priests. Thomas Drayton was a notorious heretic who had been involved in Sir John Oldcastle's revolt in 1414 and an associate of the Oxford academic and Wycliffite William Taylor in Bristol. In 1422 he took up the rectory of Snave on Romney Marsh, eight miles from Tenterden. He was called before convocation in 1425 to answer charges of heresy and denied any heretical activity since his first abjuration in 1420. Nevertheless, after being made to abjure again he was brought under the watchful eye of Archbishop Henry

3 See, for example, A. D. Brown, *Popular Piety in Late Medieval England: The Diocese of Salisbury 1250–1550* (Oxford, 1995); N. P. Tanner, *The Church in Late Medieval Norwich* (Toronto, 1984).

4 R. Lutton, *Lollardy and Orthodox Religion in Pre-Reformation England: Reconstructing Piety* (Woodbridge, 2006).

5 For a recent thoughtful discussion of these issues in relation to medieval Europe as a whole, see J. H. Arnold, *Belief and Unbelief in Medieval Europe* (London, 2005), passim, esp. pp. 191–231.

Chichele a few weeks later when he exchanged Snave for the living of Herne near Canterbury. There is no direct evidence that he had taught heresies to his parishioners in Kent. The same can be said of Richard Wyche, the veteran Lollard priest who was martyred in 1440 and held the benefice of Leaveland, north of Ashford, in the 1430s, but his influence cannot be ruled out.[6] There is no doubt, however, that William White's heretical teaching had an impact in the county. He was probably academically trained and may have written more than one heretical text. Although there is no evidence that the two men knew each other, it was perhaps not coincidental that he was apprehended for preaching without a licence as chaplain in the parish church of Tenterden only a few months before Drayton's arrival in Snave. Among other errors, White admitted to teaching in Gillingham and Tenterden against the Eucharist, the mendicants, and the temporal possessions of the Church. He moved to Norfolk in 1425, the year Drayton was called before convocation.[7]

Whether on his own or with the help of others, White rapidly succeeded in establishing a significant heretical network in Kent that survived his departure. It was uncovered three years later, in May 1428, when Chichele began a major campaign to eradicate heresy from the south-east of England. A total of twenty-three individuals were summoned, the majority men, including White, but also three married couples. Most were from seven Wealden parishes, especially Tenterden, together with three from New Romney. Only four of those named seem to have been captured in May but Bartholomew Cornmonger, a Lollard teacher, who knew the heretic Ralph Mungyn with Lollard connections in Oxford and London, was captured between 22 June and 31 July. He reportedly turned informer, giving up the names of many of his fellow dissenters. Chichele apprehended more than thirty suspects in the summer of 1428, some of whom were hanged on charges of sedition or condemned to perpetual imprisonment.[8] This must have been a major blow to Lollardy in Kent. All the indications are that a sizeable heretical network had been established in only a few years. From the start Lollardy was rooted, predominantly, in the Weald, that part of the county that appears to have had an enduring proclivity for religious dissent from the later Middle Ages onwards, but White had also taught heresies in Gillingham, and there are indications that heresy was embedded in the Medway valley by 1425.

6 E. F. Jacob, ed., *Register of Henry Chichele, Archbishop of Canterbury AD 1414–1443*, Canterbury and York Society, 3 vols (Oxford, 1938–47), 1, pp. 207, 227 for Drayton's moves to Snave and then Herne; 3, pp. 107–9 for his trial; Thomson, *Later Lollards*, pp. 149–50, 173–4, 177; Hudson, *Premature Reformation*, p. 125; Aston, *Lollards and Reformers*, pp. 29, 30.

7 Jacob, *Reg. Chichele*, 3, p. 85; Thomson, *Later Lollards*, p. 173; M. Aston, 'William White's Lollard Followers' (first published in *Catholic Historical Review* 68 (1982), 469–97) in Aston, *Lollards and Reformers*, pp. 71–100, at p. 87; J. F. Davis, 'Lollard Survival and the Textile Industry in the South-East of England', in *Studies in Church History* 3, ed. G. J. Cuming (1966), p. 197; W. W. Shirley, ed., *Fasciculi zizaniorum Magistri Johannis Wyclif cum tritico*, Rolls Series (1858), pp. 418–21 cf. J. Foxe, *Actes and Monuments of these Latter and Perillous Dayes* (London, 1583), p. 662.

8 Jacob, *Reg. Chichele*, 1, p. cxxxvii; 4, pp. 297–301; 3, pp. 198–9, 202–4; Aston, *Lollards and Reformers*, pp. 29, 78–80; Thomson, *Later Lollards*, p. 175; Foxe, *Actes and Monuments*, pp. 642–3.

There were cases in Rochester, West Malling and Addington in 1425 and 1426 that included mention of suspect English and Latin books and views against pilgrimages and the veneration of the cross. Thomas Halle of Rochester, examined by Bishop Langdon in 1425 appears to have offended on more than one occasion.[9]

Some of those suspects who evaded capture in 1428–29 may have gone into hiding in Kent, and at least one fled to London, but others exploited what seem to have been long established links with a well-organised Lollard network in East Anglia. Six or seven men were named as leaders or members of the heretical network in East Anglia uncovered by Bishop Alnwick's investigations into heresy in the diocese of Norwich in 1428–31. Four of them, including William White, were executed in 1428 or 1429. Most of them were probably literate and may have been itinerant. It is likely that there had been contact and possibly movement between the East Anglian and Kent groups for a number of years. At least two of those men who had fled the Weald for East Anglia were being sought back in Kent during Alnwick's purge.[10] Early Lollardy in Kent did not develop in isolation after its introduction by peripatetic priests from outside the county but appears to have been part of a larger regional network that had links with heretics in London and possibly with the continent. It is only because of these connections that there can be reasonable certainty that the Kent suspects were Lollards. The record of Alnwick's trials leaves little room for doubt that the beliefs taught in East Anglia and so, presumably in Kent also, were Wycliffite in origin albeit at the extreme end of the spectrum in terms of denial of the efficacy of the sacraments.[11]

There is every reason to believe that Lollardy was not extinguished in Kent by Chichele. Abjurations in 1431 by John and Thomas Glover of Wittersham, Richard Herberd of Hadlow (who admitted concealing heretical English books) and a man from Brenchley, and the arrest in 1436 of John and Robert Boydon of Strood, demonstrate that there was no geographical divide between the heretical networks of the Medway valley and the Weald (Map 1).[12] John Boreham, priest for some twenty years in the Sussex parish of Salehurst, just over the county border, was found to possess four vernacular gospels in 1438.[13] The tendency of the authorities to combine accusations of heresy with charges of sedition, unruliness and criminality in relation to the Tenterden revolt of 1438, Cade's rebellion

9 MS CKS Rochester Diocesan Registers, III, Register Langdon, fols 31v, 76r; Thomson, *Later Lollards*, p. 174. For Thomas Halle, see Forrest, *The Detection of Heresy*, p. 172.

10 Jacob, *Reg. Chichele*, 1, pp. cxxxvii, cxxxix; N. P. Tanner, ed., *Heresy Trials in the Diocese of Norwich, 1428–31*, Camden 4th Series 20 (London, 1977), pp. 29–30, 33 n. 14, 39, 41, 45 n. 44, 47, 60, 71, 73, 81, 85–6, 93–4, 140, 146, 152, 165, 176, 179, 209; Hudson, *Premature Reformation*, pp. 123–4, 139–40; Thomson, *Later Lollards*, pp. 121–2, 175–6; Aston, *Lollards and Reformers*, pp. 29, 79, 81, 86–7.

11 Tanner, ed., *Heresy Trials*, pp. 10–22; Davis, *Heresy and Reformation*, p. 4.

12 MS CKS Rochester Registers, III, Langdon, fols 93v–94v, 116v. On Herberd, see Forrest, *The Detection of Heresy*, pp. 185–6.

13 Thomson, *Later Lollards*, pp. 179–80.

of 1450, and disorders in the Weald in the 1450s makes it treacherously difficult to distinguish between cases of actual heresy, more widely held anticlerical views and outright false charges.[14] Accusations of heresy had been part and parcel of the official rhetoric of oppression since the first years of the Lancastrian regime and had intensified after Sir John Oldcastle's revolt of 1414. Kent had no apparent involvement in the Oldcastle rebellion and neither was the county part of the Lollard rising of 1431, and yet it was reported that large numbers of heretics were planning to gather together '... to the destruction of the English church ...' on the feast of St John the Baptist (24 June) in 1428. Whether or not this is to be believed, that John Glover of Wittersham, who abjured heresies in 1431, was pardoned for his part in Cade's revolt suggests that unrest and revolt, particularly where they involved criticism of clerical abuses such as pluralism and clerical wealth, may have coincided with Lollard opinions or sympathies.[15]

In addition to those cases that mixed charges of heresy with those of sedition, in 1450 a Tenterden woman was charged with holding erroneous opinions concerning offerings in churches and at saints' shrines and eating meat at Lent. In 1454 and 1455 less clear-cut accusations of heresy were made against two men from East Sutton and Wittersham, respectively, and in 1469 the Canterbury monk William Selling preached against heretical views on the sacraments at the abjuration of an unnamed offender. This, and evidence given in the 1511–12 trials, suggests Archbishop William Bourchier was conducting an anti-heresy drive at this time. Three cases in the early 1470s in Willesborough, Hackington and Ringwould appear to be less clearly Lollard-inspired but suggest that heterodox views on subjects such as the sacrament of confession and burial in consecrated ground were widespread.[16]

As yet, precious little biographical evidence has been discovered that would shed light on the social standing, economic activities and local office-holding of these early Kent Lollards. That which does survive suggests that at least some belonged to moderately substantial and enduring families.[17]

14 J. A. F. Thomson, 'A Lollard Rising in Kent: 1431 or 1438?', *Bulletin Institute Historical Research* 37 (1964), 100–2; F. W. Brie, ed., *The Brut or The Chronicles of England,* Early English Text Society, original series 131, 2 vols (New York, 1906–8, reprinted 1960), 2, p. 472; Thomson, *Later Lollards*, pp. 177–82; *CCR 1435–41*, pp. 117–18, 313; *CPR 1436–41*, p. 398.

15 Aston, *Lollards and Reformers*, pp. 1–47, at p. 78; Thomson, 'Lollard Rising in Kent', 100–2; I. M. W. Harvey, *Jack Cade's Rebellion of 1450* (Oxford, 1991), pp. 25, 29–30; M. Jurkowski, 'Lollardy in Coventry and the Revolt of 1431', in *The Fifteenth Century VI: Identity and Insurgency in the Late Middle Ages*, ed. L. Clark (Woodbridge, 2006), pp. 145–63; Thomson, *Later Lollards*, p. 175.

16 MS CCAL X.I.I, fols 19v, 67r, 68r, 73r; 1463–74; Y.I.II, fols 91r, 199v, 302r; Thomson, *Later Lollards*, pp. 180–3; N. Tanner, ed., *Kent Heresy Proceedings, 1511–12*, Kent Records 26 (Stroud, 1997), p. 11.

17 Lutton, *Lollardy and Orthodox Religion*, pp. 173–4. A survey of the surviving manorial evidence may well produce more evidence; see, for example, M. Jurkowski, 'Lollardy and Social Status in East Anglia', *Speculum* 82 (2007), 120–52.

Later Lollardy

In 1496 Christopher Payn, a cordwainer of Tonbridge, admitted that he had associated with heretics for five to six years, had favoured and received them in his house and had lent them books containing heresies including '… there is no purgatorie but in this world … that prestes have no power to consecrate cristes bodie and that all the workis of holy chirch be nought'. The following year Moises at Hale from Bridge was charged with not believing in the Eucharist and in 1498 a heretic priest was burnt at Canterbury.[18] These cases were but the tip of an impending iceberg. Archbishop William Warham's major investigation of heresy in the diocese of Canterbury in 1511–12 demonstrates that heterodoxy in Kent had enjoyed something of a revival from the last decade or so of the fifteenth century. Some suspects had learnt their heresy at least twenty or thirty years earlier, with more converts being added over the previous decade. A total of fifty-three individuals were named in the trial records and a handful of others were presented to the archdeaconry visitations of parishes in 1511–12.[19]

The geographical continuities between the networks uncovered in 1428 and early sixteenth-century heresy are striking. The majority of suspects were from the Weald, in particular the market towns of Tenterden and Cranbrook and their neighbouring parishes, and Staplehurst. In the Medway valley, a cluster of eight lived either in Maidstone or nearby parishes. Five came from Great Chart, Ashford and Godmersham, all on the road between Tenterden and Canterbury. Five suspects had lived or were still living in Canterbury itself.[20] The Harwodes of Rolvenden and the Buckhersts of Staplehurst may have been the descendents of individuals involved in heresy and unrest in the 1420s and 1430s but the 'survival' of heresy in certain areas, as opposed to 'reinfestation', need not have been dependent upon direct familial continuities.[21]

The trial proceedings mention neither Lollardy nor Wycliffe but, notwithstanding the distorting effect of the focused list of questions put to suspects, the abjurations and the content of the depositions by witnesses against those who refused to abjure confirm that they shared a body of belief that fell within the mainstream of Lollardy, even if they differed in their views on some subjects.[22] The three areas where there was greatest congruence concerned the Eucharist,

18 MS CKS Rochester Registers, IV, Savage, fol. 16v; MS CKS PRC 3/1, fol. 101v; Thomson, *Later Lollards*, p. 184; Hudson, *Premature Reformation*, pp. 140, 157, 457.

19 Tanner, *Kent Heresy Proceedings*, pp. ix, 12, 20–1, 41, 48, 54, 55, 66, 87, 95, 100, 108; K. L. Wood-Legh, *Kentish Visitations of Archbishop William Warham and his Deputies, 1511–12*, Kent Records 24 (Gloucester, 1984), pp. xxiv, 72, 207–11.

20 Tanner, *Kent Heresy Proceedings*, pp. xxiii–xxiv.

21 Jacob, *Reg. Chichele* 4, pp. 298–9; *CCR 1435–41*, pp. 117–18; Tanner, *Kent Heresy Proceedings*, pp. 116–22, 123, 124; Lutton, *Lollardy and Orthodox Religion*, pp. 156–7. The terms are Anne Hudson's; idem, *Premature Reformation*, at p. 21.

22 For summaries, see Tanner, *Kent Heresy Proceedings*, pp. xii–xv and Lutton, *Lollardy and Orthodox Religion*, pp. 157–61 cf. Hudson, *Premature Reformation*, pp. 468–72; On the implications of the ways in which bishops questioned heresy suspects, see A. Hudson, 'The Examination of Lollards', *Bulletin Institute Historical Research* 46 (1973), 145–59; J. H. Arnold, 'Lollard Trials and Inquisitorial Discourse', in *Fourteenth Century England*, 2, ed. C. Given-Wilson (Woodbridge, 2002), pp. 81–94

pilgrimage and devotion to images. Forty-four out of fifty-three suspects abjured or were reported as adhering to an extreme anti-sacramentarian view that conceived the Eucharist as '... but materiall brede and not the body of criste' and a memorial only. As Robert Reynold put it, '... a thing made in mynde and for the remembraunce of criste for the people, for crists owne body was in heven and his worde was in erthe'.[23] Forty held the common Lollard opinions that pilgrimages '... to holy and devoute places bee not profitable nother meritorious for mannys soule', and '... that images of seynts be not to be worchipped'. A number of suspects expressed the belief that pilgrimages were a waste of '... labor and money thereabout' and the five suspects who refused to abjure were charged with holding that those who went on pilgrimage and venerated relics committed idolatry. Images that '... ought not to be worshipped bicause they were made with manys hands and ... were but stocks and stonys', as Joan Riche of Wittersham expressed it, included the crucifix and representations of the Virgin and other saints.[24]

Despite these commonly held beliefs there was greater variation on other subjects. Fifteen believed that confession should not be made to a priest but whilst Stephen Castelyn held that '... confession was to be made oonly to god by mynde' the Grebills held to the Donatist and Wycliffite view that confession was 'good and profitable' only when made '... to a preest beying the folowar of peter and being pure and clene in life ...'[25] Only twelve suspects admitted the charge that they believed prayers should not be made to saints but to God directly, and ten held that holy bread and holy water remained the same after the priest's benediction as before it. Heterodox opinions on the other sacraments were abjured by a minority only: the efficacy of ordination, matrimony, baptism, confirmation and extreme unction was denied by between nine and eleven suspects but only five individuals abjured or were reported as holding heretical opinions on all seven sacraments. All were examined in the first few days of the proceedings between 19 April and 5 May 1511.[26] After 5 May and up to the end of the proceedings on 5 June 1512 opinions on the sacraments apart from the Eucharist and confession were abjured in only two out of thirty-one cases. This suggests that the archbishop and his deputies may have been more concerned in the early stages of the proceedings to thoroughly examine suspects on a wider range of questions and as the trials progressed they were content to secure abjurations on a smaller number of key articles. This is a salutary reminder that the abjurations should not be treated as an exhaustive record of suspects' opinions, even in those areas of belief

and idem, 'Inquisition, Texts and Discourse', in *Texts and the Repression of Medieval Heresy*, ed. C. Bruschi and P. Biller (York, 2003), pp. 63–80.

23 Tanner, *Kent Heresy Proceedings*, pp. xxv, 53; Lutton, *Lollardy and Orthodox Religion*, pp. 158–9.

24 Tanner, *Kent Heresy Proceedings*, pp. 27, 65, 67, 87, 90, 4, 51, 2, 9, 17, 44, 46, 85; Hudson, *Premature Reformation*, p. 302.

25 Tanner, *Kent Heresy Proceedings*, pp. 62, 63, 19; Hudson, *Premature Reformation*, pp. 294–7.

26 Namely William Carder, Christopher and John Grebill senior, William Riche and Thomas Mannyng: Tanner, *Kent Heresy Proceedings*, pp. 8–13, 27–30, 37.

upon which other suspects abjured.[27] This is indicated also by the fact that seven suspects examined between 19 May and 16 August 1511 abjured '… other damnable opinions and heresies …' that otherwise went unrecorded.[28] Occasionally views on which suspects were not questioned nevertheless came to light. For example, William Baker deposed that John Browne of Ashford had '… said that there was no purgatory but oonly in this world, and aftir that a man was decessid he shulde goo straight to heven or to hell', this being the only instance of denial of purgatory in the proceedings.[29]

The trial proceedings provide a considerable amount of information on the demography of heresy and the practices of suspects. Seventeen women and thirty-six men, all lay people, are named in the proceedings. The density of family relationships was as high as that among the very stable Lollard networks in the Chilterns, with as many as two-thirds being related to at least one other suspect.[30] Their ages, where mentioned, ranged from twenty to seventy-four with eight older than sixty. This, and the number of households where heresy spanned two generations adds to the impression that the groups detected in 1511 were mature and well-established. Family relationships played an important part in the dissemination of heterodox ideas but worked alongside other mechanisms of transmission. John Grebill senior of Benenden, for example, with the help of the Lollard teachers John Ive and William Carder, taught his wife heretical views in the 1480s. He then taught his sons Christopher and John junior the same beliefs from the age of seven. However, as they reached their mid-teens they had reservations and were only finally convinced by the teaching and books of John Ive and William Carder. The Grebills also had a daughter described by one deponent who visited the house to discuss heresies as 'a distrawght yong woman', implying either that she was unwell or less than comfortable with her family's convictions. Her mother, Agnes Grebill, more than sixty years old in 1511, was obstinate to the last, even when her husband and sons gave evidence against her, and paid with her life.[31]

The relative secrecy of the household provided the safest place to meet, talk about and teach prohibited beliefs, and read the scriptures or other suspect books together in English. Nine different households in Tenterden, Benenden, Ashford, Canterbury, Bearsted and Maidstone were mentioned as providing regular meeting places. Heretical conversations were reported as taking place before the

27 On this see Tanner, *Kent Heresy Proceedings*, p. xiv.

28 Ibid., p. 68.

29 Ibid., p. 46.

30 Lutton, *Lollardy and Orthodox Religion*, pp. 162–3; S. McSheffrey, *Gender and Heresy: Women and Men in Lollard Communities* (Philadelphia, 1995), pp. 156–60; D. Plumb, 'A Gathered Church? Lollards and their Society', in *The World of Rural Dissenters, 1520–1725*, ed. M. Spufford (Cambridge, 1995), pp. 132–63; R. G. Davies, 'Lollardy and Locality', *Transactions Royal Historical Society* 6th series 1 (1991), 193–7; N. Evans, 'The Descent of Dissenters in the Chiltern Hundreds', in *World of Rural Dissenters*, ed. M. Spufford (Cambridge, 1995), pp. 288–308.

31 Tanner, *Kent Heresy Proceedings*, pp. 11–13, 16–24, at p. 22; Lutton, *Lollardy and Orthodox Religion*, pp. 163–5.

fire in the hall or kitchen of the house, and sometimes over a meal or drink, on more than one occasion.[32] It appears that only a minority of suspects could read biblical or other prohibited material in English. That thirteen suspects were given penances that included the surrender of suspect books does not prove that they owned any.[33] What is more certain is that book-owning heretical teachers played a vital role in persuading, encouraging and instructing others. William Carder of Tenterden, a weaver by trade, was the most influential. He had been 'techer and reder' to John Ive as early as the late 1470s, who himself went on to teach others. John Grebill senior told how Carder had been born in Lincolnshire but that his parents had been 'of the same secte' and his mother had fled the Weald some forty years earlier for fear of persecution. He may, therefore, have provided a direct familial connection to the Lollard networks of the early fifteenth century. Carder was responsible, either directly or indirectly, for converting more than twenty suspects to heterodox opinions, he may have provided the main link between the Wealden and Maidstone groups and the trial proceedings portray him as someone who took every opportunity to pass on his heterodox views. He had discussed heterodox beliefs at alehouses, in his own house, at church, in John Grebill senior's house while Carder worked at his loom, and in other suspects' houses '… where they might be secretly togider'.[34]

Heretical conversations between other suspects that speak of evangelical opportunism took place while walking or 'goyng by the waye', '… at Tenterden upon seynt Marks day, at a feyre kept there …', and '… in a garden at Charte …'[35] Saints days and major festivals when social visits, not to mention pilgrimages, were made, provided occasions for numerous meetings.[36] They also allowed for other sorts of heretical activities, such as William Baker's decision after a heretical discussion at Edward Walker's house in Maidstone on May Day 1509 not to go to the Rood of Grace at Boxley but to give his intended offering to a poor man instead.[37] Meetings in homes seem to have involved no more than seven individuals at any one time and were informal in character. Although some individuals seem to have had seniority, there was no discernable organisational hierarchy or system of discipline.[38] The movement of teachers between those towns and villages where heretics lived, travelled to conduct business and had familial and kinship connections, ensured that the heretical network linked the southern Weald with Maidstone and Canterbury. Thirty-two of the fifty-eight suspects in

32 Tanner, *Kent Heresy Proceedings*, pp. xx, 4–6, 10–12, 18–22, 45–8, 52–5; Lutton, *Lollardy and Orthodox Religion*, p. 165.

33 Tanner, *Kent Heresy Proceedings*, p. xxv.

34 Ibid., pp. xx–xxi, 1–7, 8–15, 52–6, at p. 11; Lutton, *Lollardy and Orthodox Religion*, pp. 165–7.

35 Tanner, *Kent Heresy Proceedings*, pp. 4, 5, 46, 47.

36 For discussion of revolt and religious dissent in the context of the feast of Corpus Christi, see M. Aston, 'Corpus Christi and Corpus Regni: Heresy and the Peasants' Revolt', *Past and Present* 143 (1994), 3–47.

37 Tanner, *Kent Heresy Proceedings*, p. 53.

38 Hudson, *Premature Reformation*, pp. 449–50.

the proceedings or visitation returns of 1511–12 were interconnected by kinship or through conversations and meetings, and yet there is no evidence that these linked groups and households conceived of themselves as a single congregation or ever intended to gather as such.[39]

In addition to the apparent lack of involvement by clergy, early sixteenth-century Lollardy differed from that of the early fifteenth century in Kent by having no apparent connections with heretics outside the county and no tendency to violent rebellion against the Church. In fact, there are indications of considerable ambivalence towards the Church, or at least to church attendance. As was the case elsewhere in England, full-blown separatism does not appear to have been a feature of Lollardy in Kent.[40] For example, the Grebills appear to have attended church because they confessed to having '... brought home holy brede diverse tymes ... and ete it, and had noon other regard unto it but as to other brede' and Carder had talked about heresy in church.[41] The disruption of church services is suggested by the Tenterden visitation return for September 1511 which presented that 'Johan Frank with diverse other eville disposid persones use in the tyme of divine service to be in the churcheyard comenyng & talkyng and many other use to sitt stille in the churche atte processione tyme.' When questioned, Franke admitted to sometimes walking '... in the churchyard during divine service and sometimes between matins and high mass, but not habitually', and was ordered to be in church during services. Franke had abjured heresies on 16 August 1511 and among other penances was confined to the immediate locality. He may have been related to Robert Franke of Tenterden who was imprisoned for his errors.[42] While the many who sat still in church during processions may have been committed Lollards this alleged dissent may equally have been driven by lay conflict with parochial clergy or wider disquiet with aspects of orthodox ritual practice.

Levels of commitment to heterodox beliefs varied widely between individuals. William Carder, Agnes Grebill, Robert Harryson and Edward Walker all refused to abjure and so were handed over to the secular authorities to be burnt. John Browne of Ashford confessed to having abjured twelve years previously and so

39 For a contrary view on the limitations imposed by geography, see Davies, 'Lollardy and Locality', 206–7. For discussion of the organisational aspects of Lollardy in the Chilterns that places greater emphasis on collective identity, see Plumb, 'A Gathered Church?', passim, together with Patrick Collinson, 'Critical Conclusion', in *World of Rural Dissenters*, ed. Spufford, pp. 395–6. On the importance of leaders in creating Lollard networks, see McSheffrey, *Gender and Heresy*, pp. 15–16 and on kinship see Plumb, 'A Gathered Church?', passim; Davies, 'Lollardy and Locality', 195, 212 and M. Spufford, 'The Importance of Religion in the Sixteenth and Seventeenth Centuries', in *World of Rural Dissenters*, p. 13.

40 For open defiance by Lollards at the elevation of the host in Amersham in the Chilterns and for comments on the 'semi-sectarian' nature of Lollardy, see P. Collinson, 'Night Schools, Conventicles and Churches', in *The Beginnings of English Protestantism*, ed. P. Marshall and A. Ryrie (Cambridge, 2002), pp. 222–4.

41 Tanner, *Kent Heresy Proceedings*, pp. 19–20.

42 Wood-Legh, *Kentish Visitations*, pp. 207–10; Tanner, *Kent Heresy Proceedings*, pp. 90–1, 110–11.

suffered the same fate. Browne claimed to have been taught his heresies by John Riche whom 'as he thynketh' had been burnt at Halden.[43] Efforts to maintain secrecy are mentioned numerous times in the proceedings and Browne was certainly aware of the dire consequences of detection: Joan Harwode told how after she and her husband had discussed heresies in their house in Rolvenden with Browne '... the said John Browne as hir said husband commaunded and charged this deponent never to utter to any persone upon payne of hir lif of their forsaid communicacion ayenst the sacrament of the aulter, everyche of theym saying that it shuld cost theym all their lyves and be brent if it were uttred'.[44] The brutality with which heresy and unrest had been repressed in Kent in the fifteenth century would not have been forgotten by the early sixteenth.

Understandably, most suspects abjured and the carefully nuanced penances imposed on them demonstrate that different individuals were perceived as representing different levels of threat to orthodoxy. The seven who were sentenced to perpetual imprisonment in a religious house probably constituted the most committed after the five who were burnt, but a further thirty-one were confined to their parish or locality as well as receiving various humiliating and symbolically charged penances.[45] In immediate terms, Warham's investigations of 1511–12 stripped the heretical network of its leadership and exposed it to close scrutiny, and yet the effective enforcement of penances designed to prevent relapse into heresy or reinfestation depended on the ongoing cooperation of parochial and municipal office-holders, courts and clergy, and this was far from guaranteed.

The evidence suggests that the orthodox in Kent were reluctant to incriminate their heterodox neighbours. Although we do not know how Warham first broke open early sixteenth-century Lollardy, all the witnesses named in the trials were suspects rather than outsiders to heresy. There were no presentments for unorthodoxy to the archdeaconry visitations of parishes in the Tenterden area, for example, from 1498 to 1516.[46] At Tenterden itself, out of fourteen separate visitations from 1498 to 1523, the only presentments for heresy were in 1511–12: of three women, one of whom, Agnes Roche, 'commenly knowene as heretike', was deceased, and one man, John Franke, already mentioned. In 1511–12 there were only two further cases in the entire archdeaconry of Canterbury.[47]

One possible reason for the lack of presentments of unorthodox beliefs was the degree to which, in common with Lollards elsewhere in England, the heterodox

43 Tanner, *Kent Heresy Proceedings*, pp. 25, 58, 49, at p. 48.

44 Ibid., p. 45.

45 Ibid., pp. xv–xvii, xxv; N. P. Tanner, 'Penances Imposed on Kentish Lollards by Archbishop Warham, 1511–12', in *Lollardy and the Gentry in the Later Middle Ages*, ed. M. Aston and C. Richmond (Stroud, 1997), pp. 229–49.

46 Thomson, *Later Lollards*, p. 190.

47 MS CCAL X.8.2, pt. 2, fol. 13r; Z.3.1, fol. 41r; Z.3.37, fol. 83r; Z.3.2, fols 4r, 136v, 4v, 25v, 55r, 9r, 82v; Z.3.3, fols 15v, 51v, 83v; Z.3.4, fols 20r, 48v, 68r, 94v, 108r. See Wood-Legh, *Kentish Visitations*, pp. 207–10 for Tenterden, p. 211 for John Bayly of Rolvenden (and see below), and p. 72 for John Hale of St George's parish, Canterbury, accused of burying the heretic John Ive in the churchyard.

were integrated into local social and political life and were of relatively high social status.[48] The Grebills, for example, owned a house and at least fifty acres of wood and pasture in Benenden; and the Lynches of Tenterden and High Halden, were of moderate wealth and status. Vincent Lynche of Halden, one of the suspects in 1511, served as *parochianus* – an officer who made presentments to visitations – in Tenterden in 1501 and 1506.[49] Stephen Castelyn and William Pellond, both imprisoned in 1511–12, belonged to well-established middling-to-prosperous Tenterden families engaged in farming, crafts and trade, that grew in wealth and status in the early sixteenth century and became involved in parochial and municipal office-holding. Stephen Castelyn's uncle served as *parochianus* in 1505, 1506 and 1519 and his cousin was a churchwarden in the 1520s. The Pellonds were members of the urban franchise by the early 1530s. These sorts of connections may go some way to explaining the apparent protection that Lollardy received prior to and perhaps after the trials of 1511–12.[50]

That this protection may also have had something to do with the nature of orthodoxy in Tenterden, and perhaps in other places in Kent that indicate a long-term propensity for heterodoxy, is suggested by the sort of piety that families like the Castelyns and Pellonds demonstrate in their wills. They were representative of an increasingly significant number of will-makers in Tenterden who appear to have lacked engagement with the cult of saints and devotion to images, ignored the religious orders, gave only infrequently to secular clergy and very rarely endowed priests to sing masses for their souls. In the early sixteenth century, in particular, there was a marked decline in these elements of testamentary giving; the only aspects that remained steady or increased in frequency being arrangements for funerals and subsequent commemorations of the dead, and the Jesus Mass, a new devotion that arrived in the parish in 1513 (see Sweetinburgh, this volume). The reasons for these changes in Tenterden's religious culture can probably only partly be ascribed to the long-term influence of Lollardy, and they may reflect pious sensibilities that were sympathetic to the Kentish Lollards' anti-sacerdotalism and criticism of the cult of saints if not their extreme anti-sacramentalism.[51]

If the longevity and success of Lollardy in Tenterden can be explained partly

48 See, for example, Plumb, 'The Social and Economic Status of the Later Lollards', in *World of Rural Dissenters*, ed. Spufford, pp. 103–31 and idem, 'The Social and Economic Spread of Rural Lollardy: A Reappraisal', in *Voluntary Religion*, Studies in Church History 23, ed. W. J. Sheils and D. Wood (Oxford, 1986), pp. 111–29 and, more recently, Jurkowski, 'Lollardy and Social Status', passim and 'Lollardy in Coventry', passim.

49 MS TNA PRO C 1/336, 24–7; E 179, 125/324. MS CKS PRC 17/16, fol. 152; 17/17, fol. 294. MS CCAL Z.3.2, fols, 105v, 26r; Z.3.3, fol. 16r. See, also, Lutton, *Lollardy and Orthodox Religion*, pp. 175–8 and on *parochiani*, see ibid., p. 123.

50 Tanner, *Kent Heresy Proceedings*, 12, 52–4, 62–4, 106–7; 113–14; MS CCAL, Z.3.2, fols, 4v, 25v; Z.3.3, fol. 51v; Z.3.4, fols, 20r, 68r; MS CKS, Te/C1, fols, 116r, 141r. See also Lutton, *Lollardy and Orthodox Religion*, pp. 133–43, 178–180.

51 Lutton, *Lollardy and Orthodox Religion*, pp. 39–102, 130–48, 178–81, 186–7.

by the nature of its orthodoxy, can the same be said for other places in Kent that were home to the heterodox? Much detailed work remains to be done on the relationship between orthodoxy and heterodoxy in Kent but recent research comparing testamentary piety in the parishes of Cranbrook and Tenterden and surveys of the testamentary evidence for the towns of Sandwich, Dover, New Romney, Hythe and the city of Canterbury, suggest that Tenterden may have been exceptional. From the mid-fifteenth century to 1535, Cranbrook, also to some extent a Lollard centre, was much more similar to these other towns in terms of features in its testamentary giving that might be described as conventionally orthodox. This was true, particularly, of bequests to secular clergy and devotion to saints' images in the form of gifts to lights in the parish church. Cranbrook was, however, a large and exceptionally wealthy semi-urbanised parish and other less wealthy Wealden parishes, as well as those in Maidstone's immediate hinterland, the Medway Valley or other places where Lollardy was present such as the town of Ashford, might display features and changes more similar to those found in Tenterden. Also, not everyone in Cranbrook was enthusiastically orthodox in a conventional sense. Large topographically complex parishes, with urban cores, large populations and considerable disparities in wealth and status like Cranbrook and Tenterden were able to sustain a surprising degree of religious diversity.[52]

A number of theories have been put forward to attempt to explain why certain areas such as the Weald of Kent were breeding grounds for dissent and Nonconformity. Perhaps the least convincing among these is the argument that the Weald was isolated and so relatively free from ecclesiastical control or scrutiny. The Weald had ancient ties with the great religious houses of east Kent, contained a number of influential gentry families involved in national as well as regional government and was closely linked to London and the rest of Kent through trade. Furthermore, this would not explain why the Medway valley also sustained heresy. More certain, at least in the Weald, is the likelihood that scattered and fragmented settlement in large parishes discouraged church attendance and fuelled independent religion, and a relative lack of manorial structure lessened incentives for the expression of corporate identity. In Cranbrook, for example, it is likely that it was especially those families living in outlying hamlets that were less engaged in corporate devotional practices.[53] Also, industrialising areas such

52 R. Lutton, 'Geographies and Materialities of Piety: Reconciling Competing Narratives of Religious Change in Pre-Reformation and Reformation England', in *Pieties in Transition: Religious Practices and Experiences, c.1400–1640*, ed. R. Lutton and E. Salter (Aldershot, 2007), pp. 24–34, 37–9.

53 For the argument that the Weald, at least, had an 'absence of effective ecclesiastical policing' in this period see Clark, *English Provincial Society*, p. 31 a view shared to some extent by Everitt and Hill: Everitt, 'Nonconformity in Country Parishes', pp. 178–99 and idem, *Continuity and Colonization: The Evolution of Kentish Settlement* (Leicester, 1986), pp. 221–2; C. Hill, 'Lollards to Levellers', in Hill, *Collected Essays of Christopher Hill II: Religion and Politics in Seventeenth-Century England* (Brighton, 1986), pp. 89–116. On the Weald's connectedness, see Lutton, *Lollardy and Orthodox Religion*, pp. 29–31, 35–7, 46–7. On scattered settlement and Nonconformity in Cranbrook, see P.

as the Weald, that sustained wood-pasture agriculture and handicrafts were characterised by partible inheritance and small enclosed farms. As a result, the family, as opposed to the village or the hamlet, comprised the most important 'co-operative working unit' and dominated social and religious life.[54] It is not difficult to see how this would have created the sort of fragmented conditions in which heterodoxy could develop. At Tenterden, these tended to ensure that the moral and material concerns of family and kin dominated pious sensibilities to the exclusion of engagement with aspects of conventional parochial religion, and may have lent a certain cultural relevance to Lollardy with its emphasis on household-centred reading and discussion and rejection of priesthood and the sacramental basis of the Church.[55]

What remain striking but mysterious geographic continuities might be explained by further detailed investigation of the social, economic and cultural features and settlement patterns of areas that were host to heterodoxy, dissent and Nonconformity in the late medieval and early modern periods. In addition to the factors outlined above, trade connections, the growth of literacy and processes of urbanisation may all have played their part in fostering and sustaining heterodoxy.[56] Given the emerging picture of considerable diversity in orthodox religion in Kent, it is essential that any future investigation of heterodoxy also includes due attention to the diverse nature and development of orthodoxy in the county in the late medieval period. For example, there is evidence that, compared to the Weald, devotion to the saints and conventional orthodox religion remained strong in the early sixteenth century in Dartford and other towns and villages in the diocese of Rochester.[57]

Collinson, 'Cranbrook and the Fletchers: Popular and Unpopular Religion in the Kentish Weald', Collinson, in *Godly People: Essays in Protestantism and Puritanism* (London, 1983), p. 425.

54 J. Thirsk, 'Industries in the Countryside', in *Essays in the Economic and Social History of Tudor and Stuart England*, ed. F. J. Fisher (Cambridge, 1961), pp. 70–88, at p. 86; Spufford, 'Importance of Religion', pp. 40–64, esp. 41–2 n. 128; M. L. Zell, *Industry in the Countryside: Wealden Society in the Sixteenth Century* (Cambridge, 1994), passim; Brown, *Popular Piety*, pp. 219–22; D. Underdown, *Revel, Riot and Rebellion: Popular Politics and Culture in England, 1603–1660* (Oxford, 1985), pp. 4–8, 73–105, 206–7, 275–9.

55 Lutton, *Lollardy and Orthodox Religion*, pp. 143–7, 186.

56 On trade connections and dissent, see Spufford, 'Importance of Religion', pp. 40–64 and Clark, *English Provincial Society*, p. 31. On literacy, see A. Hudson, '"Laicus Litteratus": The Paradox of Lollardy', in *Heresy and Literacy, 1000–1530*, ed. P. Biller and A. Hudson (Cambridge, 1994), p. 235; M. D. Lambert, *Medieval Heresy: Popular Movements from the Gregorian Reform to the Reformation*, 3rd edn (Oxford, 2002), pp. 277–8 and McSheffrey, *Gender and Heresy*, pp. 143, 148 but see also R. N. Swanson, 'Literacy, Heresy, History and Orthodoxy: Perspectives and Permutations for the Later Middle Ages', in *Heresy and Literacy*, ed. Biller and Hudson, pp. 279–93. On urbanisation, see Lutton, *Lollardy and Orthodox Religion*, pp. 143–8, 186–7; Collinson, 'Critical Conclusion', p. 390; Brown, *Popular Piety*, pp. 219–22.

57 P. Lee, 'Monastic and Secular Religion and Devotional Reading in Late Medieval Dartford and West Kent' (unpublished PhD thesis, University of Kent, 1998), pp. 144–97.

Other Heterodox Beliefs

Heterodoxy in late medieval Kent was not confined to ideas derived from John Wycliffe. From early in the fifteenth century there is evidence of beliefs that indicate either the influence of other, perhaps continental strands of thought, or the presence of indigenous heterodoxy. For example, in 1431 Thomas Hellis of Brenchley held '… that a prest being in synfullyf or hath be may not do the sacrament of holy chyrche' including the consecration of the elements. This was in accordance with moderate Lollard views but he also believed that however much a man sinned he would not be damned; that adultery was not a sin but '… prive purchasse & commune solace'; '… that men & wymmyn devout in devyn service lifting her handis & heve yen to goddis blessyd bodi & ymage prayng and about the chyrch walkyng in here prayers beth to be blamed & laughed to scorn and beth ypocryetes'; and that women who fast in Advent and before Pentecost and then receive absolution and communion should be 'rebukyd as evylleverys and to be withdrawe fro the devocion and luve of god'. J. F. Davis attributes these wilder beliefs to the influence of antinomian continental ideas that have been associated with the Free Spirit heresy. It is now clear that the Free Spirit heresy was a creation of the late medieval Church in response to the perceived threat of lay mysticism. Over-zealous ecclesiastical interrogators who went looking for Free Spirit heresy were liable to find it and this may, in part, explain the tone of Hellis's views. Although the influence of continental ideas in Kent, so closely connected as it was with northern Europe, may have been significant, there is no firm evidence of this before the 1520s. Hellis's views suggest a hotchpotch of beliefs including an idiosyncratic personal morality and scepticism. His scathing disdain of the more demonstratively devout orthodox, speaks of indigenous dissent from the more flamboyant fashions of orthodoxy, including reverence for the sacrament of the altar.[58]

Further eccentric views outside the usual body of Lollard beliefs resurfaced in the early sixteenth century. John Moress, otherwise called John Wever, of Rochester, was accused in 1505 of asserting erroneous views in various parts of the city. He abjured having had '… divers doubtes of holy scripture', and had '… comynid erronosly of the fallyng of lucifer and Adam & eve …'. He had also said that '… criste whan he suffred a goode fridaye a pon the cross he dyed nat in perfict charite … for as moche as he redemyd nat the one as well as he did the other …' (a reference to the penitent and impenitent thieves with whom Christ was crucified). Even more idiosyncratic was his declaration, in many places, that '… ouer blessid lady she is but a sakk And the son of god desired the father to cum in to myddelherth to take a sakk uppon his bakk'.[59] Denigrations of the importance of Mary such as this have been attributed to the influence of continental

58 MS CKS Rochester Registers, III, Langdon, fols 93v–94v; Davis, *Heresy and Reformation*, p. 3. On the Free Spirit heresy, see Lambert, *Medieval Heresy*, pp. 204–7, 273.

59 MS CKS Rochester Registers, IV, Fisher fol. 41v; Davis, 'Lollardy and the Reformation in England', *Archiv für Reformationsgeschicte* 73 (1982), 224; Thomson, *Later Lollards*, p. 186.

ideas concerning the celestial flesh but they are better identified as part of an indigenous tradition of disregard for the role of Mary and the saints in general in salvation.[60] His use of the term 'myddelherth' indicates the popular currency of a Middle English literary term, denoting the earth or 'world of people', the 'worldly' as opposed to the spiritual realm. In its apparent eccentricity, Moress's cosmology is reminiscent of Menocchio, the miller of Friuli, but it should not be assumed that he was alone in holding such ideas.[61]

Simon Piers of Waldershare, apparently unconnected to the other suspects tried in 1511, abjured the related but subtly different belief 'That almighty God our lorde Jhesu Crist, very God eternal withoute begynnyng and very man incarnate, taking flesshe and bloode of the most pure and glorious virgyn our lady seynt Mary, was God and man incarnate at the begynnyng of the worlde and before he was conceived and borne of his said blissed moder and virgyn Mary.'[62] This also had its own continental parallels and Piers's name suggests Dutch origins but a definite continental connection remains unestablished.[63] John Buckherst of Staplehurst who was examined, with his wife and six other suspects from the same parish, at the very end of the trials in June 1512, mixed standard Lollard denials of the Eucharist, priesthood, images, pilgrimages and blessed bread and water with the more extreme beliefs that '… Crist was not incarnatt nor borne of our lady the Virgin Mary, nor deed suffer passion for the redempcion of mannys soule, nor dide aryse from deth to lyve the third day aftir his passion'. This group does not appear to have been part of the Lollard network more widely uncovered in 1511. Whether or not they had had contact with Lollards, John Buckherst may have reached his own particular position by way of a process of sceptical questioning and debate rather than through the direct influence of Lollard teachers or books.[64]

Cases of scepticism and unbelief as opposed to more formulated doctrinal or cosmological positions, document the verbalisation of what may have been widely held sentiments. Henry Potter of West Malling was charged in 1513 with having said to numerous people '… I willnat beleve that a man that departeth the world shalt a rise a gene at the daie of dome till I see it' and in 1509 Christopher Morthrop of Strood had said '… that a man hathe no sowlle but a breth'.[65] There were scattered cases in the east and west of the county of scepticism toward the

60 Davis argues that this and other cases are evidence of the influence of continental ideas: Davis, 'Lollardy and the Reformation', 224 and idem, *Heresy and Reformation*, p. 3. But see the dissenting A. Hope, 'Martyrs of the Marsh: Elizabeth Barton, Joan Bocher and Trajectories of Martyrdom in Reformation Kent', in *Pieties in Transition*, ed. Lutton and Salter, p. 52.

61 See 'middel-erd/erthe', in *Middle English Dictionary*, ed. H. Kurath and S. M. Kuhn (Ann Arbor, MI, 1952–). C. Ginzburg, *The Cheese and the Worms: The Cosmos of a Sixteenth-Century Miller*, trans. J. and A. Tedeschi (London and Henley, 1980).

62 Tanner, *Kent Heresy Proceedings*, p. 59.

63 Thomson, *Later Lollards*, p. 189.

64 Tanner, *Kent Heresy Proceedings*, pp. 116–24, at p. 117; Thomson, *Later Lollards*, pp. 189–90; Davis, *Heresy and Reformation*, pp. 37–8.

65 MS CKS Rochester Registers, IV, Fisher, fols 62r, 24r.

power of the sacraments, of the special status of priests and of the need for burial in holy ground in the late fifteenth century.[66] John Bayly of Rolvenden, presented to the parochial visitation in 1511, had allegedly criticised pilgrimage and the cult of relics. It was reported that Bayly's wife had made a pilgrimage on Relics Sunday, the feast of St Thomas the Martyr, and on returning home, when he asked her where she had been, she answered, 'At pilgrymage at the reliques for the parson declarid and said for every foote that a man or a woman sett to the reliques ward he shal have great pardone.' John responded, 'he said soo bicause he wille have folks money', to which his wife replied, 'Nay, for the parson said that when the churche was brennyd the silke with the reliks closid and the fyre had noo power on theym.' To this John declared, 'Whan I shalle see theym bifore me putt betwene ij faggots brennyng & they not perysshed, then wille I beleve that they bene holy relics.' Bayly successfully purged himself of the charges but it is likely he had questioned the motives behind this miraculous story.[67]

John Bayly was not the only individual charged with speaking against the clergy or the claims and privileges of the Church. In 1507 Richard Gavell of Westerham abjured having said '... that the feaste of the holy appostell Saint Thomas ys nat to be sanctified nor to be kept holydaye in the churche ...', '... that it is nat necessarye to any man to take holy water of the prestes hand' and '... that the oblacions and offeryng dayes that be ordenyd by the church ar nat necessary for they war only lymyted & ordenyd by prestes & curates by theire owne covetnosse myndes and singular avayles'. Also, he had persuaded Joan Harries, a fellow parishioner, to withdraw her offering. When excommunicated he had denied that priests or bishops had the power to curse and declared: 'Syrs thow my lorde of Canterbury hath accorsid me I trust yet I am not accorsid of god And therfor syrs fere ye not to company or ete & drynke with me for all that.' He had often left the church for the alehouse during divine service and the sermon on Sundays and holy days. His hostility may have arisen out of a personal conflict with his priest. On one occasion at sermon time in the alehouse he had said: 'Now the prest standeth in the pulpet and he doth no thing but chide and brawell ffor I loke more one his dedes thane of his wordes whate so ever he saith thair.'[68] The evidence of tithe disputes in the diocese of Canterbury in the sixteenth century indicates not only that there was widespread opposition to payment of tithes to parish clergy but that there were traditions of resistance that stretched over a number of generations in particular areas including the Weald. Opposition to the payment of tithes may have gone hand in hand with anticlerical attitudes, denials of the special status of priests and resistance to all ecclesiastical dues.[69]

Thomas Cooper of East Sutton was charged in 1454 for making various

66 Thomson, *Later Lollards*, pp. 181, 183, 185.

67 Wood-Legh, *Kentish Visitations*, p. 211. On scepticism, belief and unbelief, see Arnold, *Belief and Unbelief*.

68 MS CKS Rochester Registers, IV, Fisher, fols 47r–47v; Thomson, *Later Lollards*, p. 186.

69 P. Simpson, 'The Continuum of Resistance to Tithe, *c*.1400–1600', in *Pieties in Transition*, ed. Lutton and Salter, pp. 93–108.

statements including that he would no more wish to hear the Mass of a bad priest than that of a barking dog. He had also questioned the value of Christian burial and the solemnity of the feast of the dedication of his parish church. Lollardy may have been the source of these opinions but they could equally reflect a moralising sensibility that had led to unorthodox statements.[70] On occasions the authorities distinguished between anticlericalism and heresy. For example, the Wealden rioters of 1452 were reported as saying that bishops should not have any power because priests should own no more possessions than a chair and candlestick for examining their books, but were not accused of heresy but of speaking as or like heretics and Lollards. However, only four years later those accused of disorder in the Weald were described as Lollards but the only evidence supporting this was the charge that they had threatened to kill all pluralists and to castrate all other priests – sentiments that might well have been held by the orthodox.[71]

One final, and less common, category of charges that further demonstrates the blurred boundary between heterodoxy and orthodoxy concerns magical practices and beliefs. John Boreham, priest of Salehurst, Sussex, who was in trouble with Bishop Praty in 1438 for possession of vernacular scriptures and for allegedly teaching Lollard heresies in his house, admitted a number of charges concerning the use of charms to heal people of fevers and to find stolen goods and confessed to owning books of incantations (see Jones, this volume).[72] Without further details of the contents of these books and charms it is impossible to know if his interests went beyond the bounds of the very widely disseminated semi-magical devotional literature that in other circumstances did not raise suspicion of unorthodoxy.[73] John Crayer of River, near Dover, seems to have combined hostility to images with magical practices. He was charged in 1503 with having thrown down an image of the cross and had said that if a man wishes to abstain for three Sundays in the year from hearing Mass or the gospel of Saint John and from holy bread and water, he will obtain all the riches he desires.[74]

The Significance and Legacy of Heterodoxy

Assessments of the significance of heterodoxy in Kent have rested largely on the extent to which the county's early positive response to evangelical reform and Protestant doctrine from the 1520s onwards was influenced by the presence of Lollard heresy, as well as the degree to which the Kentish Lollards can be seen as the forerunners of radical opponents of magisterial Protestantism, and later

70 MS CCAL X.I.I, fols 67r, 68r; Thomson, *Later Lollards*, p. 181. For similar cases in the 1520s, see Davis, *Heresy and Reformation*, pp. 7–8.

71 Thomson, *Later Lollards*, pp. 180–1, 182.

72 Ibid., pp. 179–80.

73 See, for example, E. Duffy, *The Stripping of the Altars: Traditional Religion in England, 1400–1580* (New Haven, CT and London, 1992), pp. 266–98.

74 MS CKS PRC 3/1, fol. 180v.

Puritanism and Nonconformity. One way in which to measure Lollardy's contribution to these developments is to look for direct continuities between Lollardy, Protestantism and later radical dissent. To date the evidence is limited. John Foxe's infamously manipulated account of the martyrdom of John Browne of Ashford in 1511 emphasises how the Lollard's dissenting beliefs had rubbed off on his children. John's son, Richard, had been due to burn the day after Mary I's death and his daughter, Alice, told Foxe the story, passed on to her by her mother, of her father's execution.[75] The merchant Richard Harman may have moved from Cranbrook to Antwerp by the time of John Browne's martyrdom. In Antwerp he became an associate of Tyndale and probably exported his English New Testament and other Protestant books to the Weald, something for which he received letters of support from two Cranbrook men in 1528.[76] Less likely is the possibility that Joan Bocher, who may have helped bring Tyndale's New Testaments to England and was martyred for her radical opinions regarding the celestial flesh by the Edwardine Protestant regime in 1550, had been a Lollard living in Essex in the 1520s and 1530s. Instead, paradoxically, the evidence suggests that she was related by blood or marriage to William Knell of Kent who was executed for treasonous words in support of the papacy in 1538 and that her embracing of radical Protestantism was a personal decision forged in opposition to the traditionalism of her kinsfolk.[77]

It is unlikely that substantial additional evidence of direct continuities between Lollardy and Protestantism in Kent will be found. For those who have long stressed the doctrinal and social contrasts between the two this is only to be expected.[78] More recently historians have emphasised instead the influence of Archbishop Cranmer and his promotion of evangelical preaching with the cooperation of a sympathetic group of magistrates to explain the early growth of Protestantism in Kent.[79] There is much more agreement that Lollardy's contribution to the Reformation in Kent, particularly in the Weald, was in providing a radical strand of dissent that emerged in the form of the hotter sort of Puritanism and Nonconformist sects in Elizabeth's reign that developed into religious separatism

75 Foxe, *Actes and Monuments*, pp. 805, 1292–3. On Foxe's treatment of his sources, see P. Collinson, 'Truth, Lies, and Fiction in Protestant Historiography', in *The Historical Imagination in Early Modern Britain: History, Rhetoric, and Fiction, 1500–1800*, ed. D. R. Kelley and D. Harris Sacks (Cambridge, 1997), pp. 37–68 and idem, 'Truth and Legend: The Veracity of John Foxe's Book of Martyrs', in *Clio's Mirror: Historiography in Britain and the Netherlands*, Britain and the Netherlands 8, ed. A. C. Duke and C. A. Tamse (Zutphen, 1985), pp. 31–54.

76 Collinson, 'Cranbrook and the Fletchers', p. 402; Clark, *English Provincial Society*, p. 31; Hope, 'Martyrs of the Marsh', p. 50.

77 The theory that Joan Bocher had been a Lollard was advanced by J. F. Davis in his 'Joan of Kent, Lollardy and the English Reformation', *Journal of Ecclesiastical History* 32 (1982), 225–33. For a recent persuasive reinterpretation of the evidence for her heretical career and background, see Hope, 'Martyrs of the Marsh', pp. 43–4, 48–55.

78 See, for example, Clark, *English Provincial Society*, pp. 31, 77, 101 and more recently; R. Rex, *The Lollards* (Houndmills, 2002), pp. 133–9.

79 D. MacCulloch, *Tudor Church Militant: Edward VI and the Protestant Reformation* (London, 1999), p. 112 and Rex, *The Lollards*, p. 122.

under the very different conditions of the early seventeenth. However, in common with other dissenting areas such as the Chilterns, where the geographic continuity of dissent is equally suggestive of the development of one type of radicalism into another, actual continuities within families or instances of identifiable individuals who form a link between different stages or strands of dissent remain elusive.[80]

It is easier to demonstrate continuities in ideas between Lollardy and later radical Protestantism. Recent research on Cranmer's investigations into heresy in Kent in 1543 shows how members of the early evangelical conventicles held radically iconoclastic views which point to a Lollard legacy of attitudes to images, combined with newer Protestant teachings.[81] Fifteen years later the heresies of the Wealden Marian martyrs suggest the merging of at least three different bodies of thought: anti-sacramentarian Lollardy, evangelical emphasis on the supreme authority of Scripture and the stubborn endurance of belief in the value of prayers for the dead.[82]

The sheer strength of the geographic continuities between pre- and post-Reformation dissent in the Weald and Medway valley means that historians will continue to search for evidence of links between different radical sects but there may be more potential in exploring the nature of orthodoxy in these districts in comparison with the east of the county and the north-west part of the diocese of Rochester. What this may reveal is that there was a significant heterogeneity to late medieval orthodoxy in Kent and that culturally some areas were more disposed to dissenting and heterodox ideas. The evidence suggests that this was the case in Tenterden, where families drawn to Lollardy were also quick to embrace evangelical Protestantism, whereas in neighbouring Cranbrook the religious picture was more mixed, with a much stronger tradition of conventional orthodox devotion but a significant radical minority. In Tenterden heterodoxy, expressed by some in outright doctrinal unorthodoxy and dissenting behaviour, was, for most, part of the respectable religious mainstream and involved a deliberate but quieter disengagement from the cult of saints, the religious orders and

[80] For the possibility of continuities, see Clark, *English Provincial Society*, pp. 59–61, 101, 177; Rex, *The Lollards*, pp. 140–41; Collinson, 'Cranbrook and the Fletchers', pp. 399–428 and Lutton, 'Geographies and Materialities of Piety', pp. 14–16, 18–23. On the Chilterns, see Spufford, 'The Importance of Religion', pp. 23–37 and Evans, 'Descent of Dissenters', pp. 288–308. On Nonconformity and separatism in Kent, see R. J. Acheson, 'The Development of Religious Separatism in the Diocese of Canterbury, 1590–1660' (unpublished PhD thesis, University of Kent, 1983); T. Freeman, 'Dissenters from a Dissenting Church: The Challenge of the Freewillers, 1550–1558', in *Beginnings of Protestantism*, ed. Marshall and Ryrie, pp. 129–56; M. Reynolds, 'Religious Denominations in the 17th Century: The Compton Census', in *An Historical Atlas of Kent*, ed. T. Lawson and D. Killingray (Chichester, 2004), pp. 83–5.

[81] A. Ryrie, *The Gospel and Henry VIII: Evangelicals in the Early English Reformation* (Cambridge, 2003), pp. 223–38.

[82] Foxe, *Actes and Monuments*, pp. 1688, 1858–9, 1954, 1970; Davis, *Heresy and Reformation*, pp. 38, 107–29, 149, 222; M. L. Zell, 'The Establishment of a Protestant Church', in *Early Modern Kent, 1540–1640*, ed. M. L. Zell (London, 2000), p. 209 and further references in Lutton, 'Geographies and Materialities of Piety', pp. 21–22, nn 37–9.

the Mass as an intercessory rite, and an embracing of new, Christocentric, devotional forms.[83]

In the Weald and Medway valley, and perhaps in other parts of Kent, it seems that there was a propensity to question the sacerdotal and sacramental basis of the claims of the Church, its cultic life and even some of its more fundamental doctrines. This tendency to heterodoxy appears to have given rise to a variety of scepticism and doctrinal views, changes in the nature of orthodox piety, anti-clerical opposition to tithes and Church dues and the ready reception of Lollardy and Protestantism. This suggests that dissent was a cultural phenomenon that pre-dated Lollardy, and that orthodoxy in these parts of Kent was an ideal to which the Church could only aspire.[84]

83 Ibid., chs 2 and 5 and pp. 196–210 and idem, 'Geographies and Materialities of Piety', passim.

84 For the suggestion that 'anti-catholic and specifically anti-sacramentarian sentiment' in the Kentish Weald 'may have had older, indigenous origins', see Collinson, 'Cranbrook and the Fletchers', p. 402.

9

Witchcraft and Magic in Kent, 1396–1543

KAREN JONES

There can have been few late medieval peasants or townspeople who did not at some time in their life have to appear before the local ecclesiastical courts, either as suitors, defendants or oath-helpers. In the diocese of Canterbury, the courts met frequently in the city and regularly in the remoter parts of their jurisdiction: in the early sixteenth century the archdeacon's court, presided over by the archdeacon's official, met fortnightly in Canterbury, held sessions in the deanery of Sandwich, and went on circuit to five rural deaneries in the west of the diocese fourteen times a year. Meanwhile the consistory court, presided over by the archbishop's commissary, but dealing with much the same types of disciplinary cases, met eighteen or nineteen times a year in Canterbury and also had sessions in the south of the diocese.[1] Their records, though not easy to use, are thus among the best sources for the social history of this period, and Kent is fortunate in having substantial quantities of these surviving for the later Middle Ages. As well as dealing with probate and inter-party litigation, the Church courts exercised discipline over considerable numbers of men and women. The disciplinary or *ex officio* part of the courts' business was conducted in the following way: a defendant summoned to the court would have the accusation read out to them. If they denied their guilt, they would be given the chance to clear their name by compurgation.[2] A person who admitted their offence, or failed in compurgation and so was judged to be guilty, was usually required to perform public penance. In some times and places this involved being publicly beaten, but in the diocese of Canterbury in the fifteenth and early sixteenth centuries it usually consisted in the sinner's having to walk in front of the cross in the procession at the parish church, with bare feet and shins, head bare for a man, and covered with an untied kerchief for a woman, carrying a candle. This form of public humiliation might be

1 B. L. Woodcock, *Medieval Ecclesiastical Courts in the Diocese of Canterbury* (Oxford, 1952), pp. 32–5.

2 That is, to find a given number of neighbours who would swear that the accused was a person whose oath could be relied upon.

prescribed for a number of Sundays, depending on the judge's view of the gravity of the offence. The overwhelming majority of those who were summoned to the disciplinary proceedings were men and women accused of sexual offences and marital irregularities. A few, however, were accused of witchcraft.

This was not the high-profile witchcraft which in the Middle Ages usually involved members of the political elite; it was the efforts of ordinary people to utilise supernatural forces for their own ends. Nearly a hundred such cases can be found in the surviving records of the archdeaconry and consistory courts in the diocese of Canterbury between the late fourteenth century and the Reformation. In this essay I shall consider these cases in the context of the ideas about witchcraft which developed during the fifteenth century and earlier, and which would later underpin the far greater numbers of prosecutions in the Early Modern period. Use of the word 'witchcraft' for the late medieval period may need some justification. Modern writers have tended to use the words 'magic' or 'sorcery' for medieval witchcraft and to refer to practitioners of 'white' magic as 'cunning folk', reserving 'witches' for people alleged to have done harm, and almost exclusively for women. But it is likely that throughout the fifteenth and sixteenth centuries, the English word 'witchcraft' covered all varieties of magic. Chaucer in the late fourteenth century, enumerating the offences which the archdeacon punished in his court, gave 'wicchecraft' as the only kind of sin involving magic, while he listed separately the three main kinds of sexual sin: 'fornicacioun', 'bauderye' and 'avoutrye'.[3] That a 'witch' still meant a practitioner of either good or bad magic as late as the 1580s is clear from the eminent Kentish sceptic Reginald Scot: 'at this daie it is indifferent to say in the English toong: she is a witch; or, she is a wise woman'.[4] The ecclesiastical court act books were kept almost exclusively in Latin during this period; they usually describe offences involving the supernatural as either *sortilegium, incantationes* or *ars magica* and these terms appear to be used interchangeably.[5] Before the fourteenth century they had had discrete meanings: the change in their use may reflect the way different kinds of magical offences had, in learned theory, been amalgamated into diabolic witchcraft.[6]

This amalgamation of different offences or sins involving the supernatural resulted from the development of the idea of the witch that was to receive widespread acceptance in the late sixteenth and seventeenth centuries, the peak period of witch persecutions. By that time, witches were expected to be mainly if not exclusively female and to derive their powers from the devil. The stereotype of the witch evolved during the late Middle Ages through a fusion of three traditions. As far back as the fourth century some theologians had argued that magic could only be performed through the use of diabolic power: over subsequent

3 'The Frere's Tale', W. Skeat, ed., *The Complete Works of Geoffrey Chaucer* (Oxford, 1954), p. 582.
4 R. Scot, *The Discoverie of Witchcraft* (1584) (New York, 1972), p. 62.
5 That is, 'sorcery', 'enchantments' or 'incantations', 'magic art'.
6 E. Peters, *The Magician, the Witch and the Law* (Philadelphia, 1978), p. 169.

centuries the idea developed that magicians, usually male scholars, obtained their supernatural powers by making pacts with the devil. The practitioners of late medieval occult sciences such as alchemy and divination, and necromancy (which required literacy) were largely male clergy; they were considered to be equal partners with the devil in the pact. Meanwhile, in folk tradition, cunning folk, sorcerers or witches, male and female, were considered either to possess innate supernatural powers, or to use charms and curses which had inherent power in themselves.[7] A third tradition, that heretics were sects of secret, nocturnal, sexually promiscuous devil-worshippers, had developed by the early thirteenth century (see Lutton, this volume). Towards the end of the Middle Ages, penitential emphasis was shifting from the seven deadly sins to the Ten Commandments; the prohibition of idolatry in the First Commandment became linked to sorcery and superstition and was emphasised in sermons and confessors' manuals.[8] In 1398 the theological faculty of the University of Paris ruled that *maleficium* – harm done by supernatural means – was accomplished through an overt or tacit pact with the devil.[9] Theologians were soon elaborating this theme and the devil-worshipping stereotype thus began to be transferred to witches, or, put another way, witchcraft was being redefined as a kind of heresy. Over the next few decades theologians and canonists abandoned the Church's earlier notion of magic as illusory and elaborated the idea of witches flying by night, attending the witches' sabbat and sealing a pact with the devil by copulating with him.[10] At the international ecclesiastical councils of the early fifteenth century, the attention of scholars, political and legal authorities was drawn to the assorted traditional beliefs and practices of what might now be termed cunning folk: many of these were condemned as superstition, sorcery or witchcraft. The councils facilitated the spread of ideas throughout Europe, and, particularly at the council of Basel (1431–39), new ideas about the diabolical character of these practices were discussed.[11] Varying sorts of offences, which had previously been considered as the separate offences of magic, sorcery, divination, necromancy and 'natural magic' had by this time come to be regarded as a single type of crime, based on alliance with the devil, and as such, a particularly terrible kind of heresy. Edward Peters writes '[e]very individual manifestation of "magic" became simply one of many tips of a giant iceberg – the "new" conspiracy directed by

7 B. P. Levack, *The Witch-hunt in Early Modern Europe* (London, 1987), pp. 7–8; S. Brauner, *Fearless Wives and Frightened Shrews: The Construction of the Witch in Early Modern Germany* (Amherst, 1995), p. 8.

8 E. Peters, 'The Medieval Church and State on Superstition, Magic and Witchcraft: From Augustine to the Sixteenth Century', in *Witchcraft and Magic in Europe: The Middle Ages*, ed. K. Jolly, C. Raudvere and E. Peters (London, 2002), p. 229.

9 R. Kieckhefer, *European Witch Trials: Their Foundations in Popular and Learned Culture, 1300–1500* (London, 1979), p. 22.

10 K. Jolly, 'Medieval Magic: Definitions, Beliefs, Practices', in *Witchcraft and Magic in Europe: The Middle Ages*, ed. K. Jolly, C. Raudvere and E. Peters (London, 2002), p. 24; Levack, *Witch-hunt in Early Modern Europe*, pp. 27–46; Brauner, *Fearless Wives*, p. 7.

11 Peters, 'Medieval Church and State', p. 227.

Satan to destroy the human race'.[12] Kieckhefer considers that '[t]he full force of the new composite notion of witchcraft' came in the years from 1435–1500, with trials for diabolical sorcery taking place in parts of continental Europe, principally in France, Germany and Switzerland.[13] However, in fourteenth- and fifteenth-century trials, the original charge was usually sorcery, and the diabolical element was superimposed on this by the educated personnel of the courts; the common people had not accepted the new theories of witchcraft.[14]

Although the witches of classical antiquity were women, those of fourteenth- and early fifteenth-century Europe were not particularly expected to be female. But once the activities of unlettered peasants had been classed as identical with those of elite magicians the nature of the imagined pact with the devil changed, and the witch or magician was considered by theologians to be subordinate to the devil, rather than their being equal partners as formerly. At this point it was easier to conceive of witches as female.[15] And once ritual coupling became part of the stereotype, it made sense to assume that witches were female: in popular imagination the devil was male, and women had long been believed to possess insatiable lust.[16] Moralists also tended to see women as especially prone to magic and superstition because of their supposed moral and intellectual weakness.[17] An illustrated poem, *Le Champion des Dames*, written about 1440, contained a section on female sorcerers in which a group of old women are described as going to the witches' sabbat and paying homage to the devil in the form of a goat. A marginal illustration showed for the first time women riding on broomsticks to the sabbat.[18] Further treatises, sermons, trials and visual representations of witches followed so 'knowledge' of the threat of diabolic witchcraft spread more rapidly as the fifteenth century advanced. The invention of printing accelerated the process. Nevertheless, in the fifteenth century, attempts to instigate a moral panic about diabolic witchcraft, and about women as its chief practitioners, were met with considerable scepticism. The notoriously misogynist text *Malleus Malificarum* (1487) was aimed at those who remained incredulous, and in particular aimed to convince them that most witches were women.[19] Despite this, when discussing real life witch trials the authors of the *Malleus* had to use examples of male witches because there had been so few trials of women.[20] Although the *Malleus* is sometimes regarded as a trigger of the great witch-craze, its publication and those of other late fifteenth-century works on witchcraft did not immediately give rise to an epidemic of trials; in fact from about 1500 the numbers of trials for

12 Ibid., pp. 231–2.
13 Kieckhefer, *European Witch Trials*, p. 23.
14 Ibid., p. 79.
15 Levack, *Witch-hunt in Early Modern Europe*, pp. 7, 34–5; R. Kieckhefer, *Magic in the Middle Ages* (Cambridge, 1990), p. 198.
16 J. B. Russell, *Witchcraft in the Middle Ages* (London, 1972), pp. 145, 182–3.
17 Kieckhefer, *Magic in the Middle Ages*, p. 187.
18 Peters, 'Medieval Church and State', p. 236.
19 Ibid., pp. 239–40.
20 Brauner, *Fearless Wives*, p. 34.

witchcraft in Europe diminished. Literature and illustrations of witchcraft continued to be produced in the first half of the sixteenth century, but it was not till after this that a further and greater outbreak of witch persecution arose.[21]

In England in the early fifteenth century there was even less inclination than in mainland Europe to prosecute for diabolic witchcraft. The canonist William Lyndwood in his *Provinciale*, completed in 1433, warned that sorcery, incantations and superstition constituted infractions of the First Commandment, and that vain things must not be mixed with sacred words, which might serve for the invocation of demons.[22] This stops somewhat short of the belief that all magic is the result of a pact with the devil. The evidence from Canterbury suggests, as we shall see, that the expectation that evil witches were most likely to be female evolved during the fifteenth century independently of the notion of the diabolic pact: there seems to have been no such expectation at the beginning of the century. A writ of Henry IV in 1406 ordering the bishop of Lincoln to tackle the problem of magic or witchcraft enumerated *sortilegii*, *magici*, *incantatores*, *nigromantici*, *divinatores*, *arioli*, using the masculine forms of all the Latin nouns.[23] Similarly, the English didactic text *Dives and Pauper*, which dates from around the same time, deplored the prevalence of witchcraft 'amongys men and women'.[24] However, all these texts show that there was some preoccupation with witchcraft in early fifteenth-century England. It was evidently based on practices which were actually current, and which had been prosecuted in the lower echelons of the Church courts for some time. In a stray document recording *ex officio* business in the diocese of Rochester in 1363–64, Philip Russell of East Greenwich is recorded as having done penance for sorcery because he had put a toad in a bag round the neck of a sheep to cure scabies.[25] Why were cases like this being heard in the Church courts? Keith Thomas considered that when witchcraft was prosecuted in late medieval England, 'it was because it was thought to involve harm to others, not because it was seen as a Christian heresy'.[26] But Philip Russell was practising *beneficial* magic. He may have said prayers or 'incantations' over the sheep while applying this supposed remedy, although there is nothing to indicate this. If he had used prayers he would have been mixing sacred words and 'vain things',

21 Peters, 'Medieval Church and State', pp. 242–4.

22 R. Houlbrooke, 'Magic and Witchcraft in the Diocese of Winchester, 1491–1570', in *Cross, Crown and Community: Religion, Government and Culture in Early Modern England*, ed. D. J. B. Trim and P. J. Balderstone (Oxford, 2004), pp. 119–20.

23 G. L. Kittredge, *Witchcraft in Old and New England* (Cambridge, MA, 1929), p. 59 and note.

24 P. H. Barnum, ed., *Dives and Pauper*, Early English Text Society, 2 vols (Oxford, 1976), 1, p. 165.

25 S. L. Parker and L. R. Poos, 'A Consistory Court from the Diocese of Rochester, 1363–4', *English Historical Review* 106 (1991), 657. Belief in the curative properties of toads survived for a long time: in 1876 Thomas Hardy was told about an old Dorset man who had sold toads' legs in little bags as a cure for scrofula. Florence Hardy, *The Life of Thomas Hardy, 1840–1928* (1928, repr. London, 1962), p. 112.

26 K. Thomas, *Religion and the Decline of Magic* (London, 1971), p. 528.

which Lyndwood was to warn against. Alternatively, Russell's prosecution and those of later healers may have been the result of distrust on the part of either the ecclesiastical authorities or the defendant's neighbours. People who were able to cure by magic were often suspected of being able to use it to cause harm as well, so Russell may have been suspected of also bewitching people or animals to their detriment, or at least of having the potential to do so.

For his offence Philip Russell was publicly beaten three times in both the market place and the church. Sexual offenders whose punishment was recorded in the same document were sentenced to either two or three sessions of beating, so Russell's punishment was at the severe end of the spectrum, although not as severe as might be expected if he had really been believed to be exercising diabolical power. Later witchcraft cases, in the Canterbury ecclesiastical courts in the fifteenth and early sixteenth centuries, seem to have given rise to still less concern on the part of the authorities. Prosecutions were few. Many who confessed their crime were merely admonished not to repeat it; many others cleared themselves with the assistance of their neighbours' oaths, and little effort seems to have been expended on the pursuit of suspects who ignored the summons to court. Punishments, when they were prescribed at all, were relatively mild, often milder than the penalties for fornication or adultery.[27] In the diocese of Winchester around the same time, similarly small numbers of accused and lenient treatment are recorded.[28] The attitudes of the pre-Reformation English clergy towards witchcraft must have varied widely. Some, perhaps more at the higher echelons than the parish clergy, must have been aware of the idea that all witchcraft was effected by a pact with the devil. At the parish level, though, priests must have been aware of the harmlessness and even possibly beneficial effects of such folk traditions as healing with herbs and prayers. It has been suggested that most clergy understood and operated within the supernatural culture of their parishioners and that this may explain the infrequency of late medieval prosecutions for sorcery.[29] In fact, forms of magic which required literacy or the possession of books seem to have been something approaching a clerical monopoly, although priests claiming to be using supernatural power to unmask thieves may have been knowingly practising a form of deception on their parishioners (see below). From the point of view of the uneducated laity, the boundary between magic and religion was blurred, especially, it has been argued, in the fifteenth century when the Church, with its abundance of special feasts, rituals, relics and pilgrimages, tended to encourage superstitious attitudes.[30] The Canterbury evidence suggests that it was the unauthorised appropriation of aspects of Christian ritual and liturgy

27 For punishments for sexual offences, see K. Jones, *Gender and Petty Crime in Late Medieval England* (Woodbridge, 2006), chapter 5, passim.

28 Houlbrooke, 'Magic and Witchcraft', p. 138.

29 C. Marsh, *Popular Religion in Sixteenth-Century England* (London, 1998), p. 148.

30 Kieckhefer, *European Witch Trials*, p. 47. It is beyond the scope of this essay to elaborate on the controversy over the state of late medieval Catholicism. For an excellent brief outline, see P. J. P. Goldberg, *Medieval England: A Social History, 1250–1550* (London, 2004), pp. 221–33.

by lay people for their own 'magical' purposes, rather than any notion of a diabolical heresy, that was the pre-Reformation Church's main objection to witchcraft.

For offences involving magic, evidence survives of ninety-six citations of ninety-one individuals accused by the Canterbury ecclesiastical authorities between 1396 and 1543.[31] Twenty-two of the citations were of people from Canterbury, Dover, Folkestone, Hythe, Maidstone, Romney and Sandwich, the remainder being from rural parishes.[32] Only five cases predate 1450, but fewer records survive for the earlier part of the period. Since about a half to a third of the Church court office act books survive for the years from 1450 to 1550, it is likely that an annual average of two or three people per year were cited in the diocese for supernatural offences. This is negligible compared to the number of sexual delicts which constituted the bread and butter of the courts' disciplinary business.[33] Nevertheless, this scattering of cases includes examples of almost every kind of magical practice that was being prosecuted elsewhere in England and on the continent, so they must have been part of a popular culture common to Western Europe. If the traditional methods of harnessing supernatural power were so well-known, it is unlikely that they were not also very widely used, in which case there must have been many more practising 'witches' in Kent than the handful who were prosecuted.

The pre-Reformation act books provide little information about the accused. In about a third of the cases recorded, only the defendant's name, parish and alleged offence, such as *sortilegium* or *incantationes* were recorded. In the rest, there is enough information to allow most to be roughly classified as either beneficial or malevolent. The 'white' magic consisted mainly of the same practices as were carried out throughout Europe, by both elite magicians and local sorcerers or witches: healing, recovering lost goods and unmasking thieves.[34] Folk healers' remedies generally combined the use of medicinal herbs with prayers, charms or rituals likely to be construed by the Church as *sortilegium*, the sort of practices Lyndwood warned against. In late medieval herbal compendiums, the preparation

31 Two cases are from printed records of archiepiscopal visitations; the rest are from the act books. In scanning these for witchcraft cases, it is possible that I may have missed some. After 1543 there were no more prosecutions for witchcraft recorded in the act books till 1557.

32 This proportion of townspeople to country dwellers is very similar to witchcraft cases at the Kent assizes from 1560 to 1700, where twenty-seven per cent of the accused were town-dwellers, a proportion which roughly reflects the distribution of the population: A. Pollock, 'Social and Economic Characteristics of Witchcraft Accusations in Sixteenth and Seventeenth-Century Kent', *Arch. Cant.* 95 (1979), 44.

33 Witchcraft cases seem to have been comparatively rare and sexual misconduct the commonest offence in the pre-Reformation Church courts: R. H. Helmholz, 'Crime, Compurgation and the Courts of the Medieval Church', *Law and History Review* 1 (1983), 9; R. Wunderli, *London Church Courts and Society on the Eve of the Reformation* (Cambridge, MA, 1981), p. 123.

34 Beneficent magic has received comparatively little scholarly attention, but for recent studies, see K. Macpherson Bardell, 'Beyond Pendle', in *The Lancashire Witches*, ed. R. Poole (Manchester, 2002), pp. 105–22; O. Davies, *Cunning-Folk: Popular Religion in English History* (London, 2003).

or application of herbal remedies was sometimes accompanied by ritual actions or verbal formulae: this indicates a belief shared by the Germanic, Christian and classical traditions that natural objects possessed hidden 'virtues' which could be activated by rituals or forms of words.[35] As Karen Jolly has observed, it is because of the now discredited belief in the power of words to effect changes in the material world that much medieval medicine is classified as magic rather than science.[36] A charm used by one of the celebrated witches of Pendle in Lancashire in 1612 included the words:

> Five pater-nosters,
> Five Aves and a Creede
> In worship of five wounds
> Of our Lord

A similar formula was included in a London woman's healing ritual in 1528.[37] Juliana Tanner of Lympne used the same prayers, though in greater quantity; she confessed in 1522 to administering herbs to the sick 'with sixty Lord's Prayers, the same number of Angelic Salutations and five Creeds'. A year earlier, Alice Johnson of Westgate, Canterbury was said to have 'collected herbs saying fifty paternosters and Ave, etc, for the sick'.[38] Neither of these women seems to have been punished, though Tanner was ordered to omit the prayers, and Johnson to stop altogether. Despite the prevailing belief that healers could also cause sickness, it is noteworthy that none of the healers denied the charge against them, so they themselves (and probably their clients) cannot have viewed their activities as anything other than beneficial.

The gender of folk healers seems to have varied according to region and time, though it has been claimed that they were mainly women.[39] In Kent up to the mid-sixteenth century, women were apparently only marginally more likely than men to be healers: the accused consist of two men, four women and a married couple, but at least one of the women was acting only in an ancillary capacity. The most prominent healer in the records was John Byng of Harbledown. He was cited four times during the 1520s, and was also accused of using magic to find lost goods. He reportedly effected his cures by praying over his patients' clothes. Katherine Burgrove of Canterbury was cited for taking sick people's clothes to

35 Kieckhefer, *Magic in the Middle Ages*, p. 68; Jolly, 'Medieval Magic', pp. 33, 31.

36 Jolly, 'Medieval Magic', p. 36.

37 Bardell, 'Beyond Pendle', p. 112; W. H. Hale, *A Series of Precedents and Proceedings ... from the Act-books of Ecclesiatical Courts in the Diocese of London* (1847), pp. 107–8.

38 MS CKS PRC 3.5, fol. 32; PRC 3.4, fol. 162.

39 W. de Blécourt, 'Cunning Women, from Healers to Fortune Tellers', in *Curing and Insuring: Essays on Illness in Past Times*, ed. H. Binnefeld and R. Dekker (Hilversum, 1993), p. 48; R. Briggs, *Witches and Neighbours: The Social and Cultural Context of European Witchcraft* (London, 1996), p. 71; B. Ehrenreich and D. English, *Witches, Midwives and Nurses: A History of Women Healers* (London, 1973).

him for them to be cured.[40] The same method was reported at York in 1481.[41] It was not only verbal formulae that were appropriated from the Church for healing rituals. John Markes of St Dunstan's in Canterbury used a lighted candle when giving medicine for toothache.[42] The burning of candles, for example before statues and altars, played a large part in fifteenth- and early sixteenth-century worship. Alice Dyne of Stone in Oxney was reported at Archbishop Warham's visitation in 1511 because she 'hath a stick she calleth Moses yard, and with that she blesseth beasts and children from worms'.[43] Moses, like other biblical heroes, was thought to have been a magician, and 'Moses' rods' or rings were widely used for magic: for example, in 1634 the astrologer William Lilly used 'Mosaical Rods' of hazel during a treasure hunt in the cloisters of Westminster Abbey.[44] Worms, along with bleeding and childbirth, have been noted as the three most common medical problems for which supernatural remedies were sought.[45] It is possible that some of the prosecutions which were nominally for witchcraft, particularly the earlier ones, were in reality directed against fraud or incompetence. Prosecutions for fraudulent practice were very uncommon, but around 1400 Thomas Forster, priest of Tenterden, was cited, not for any form of witchcraft but for claiming to be a doctor (*medicus*) and having killed a mare he was treating for galls with arsenic powder.[46] Possibly if he had used prayers or holy water he would have been cited for witchcraft.

If spoken words could effect cures, the written (or later, printed) word was still more powerful. Although there are no examples of this in the Canterbury records, biblical texts could be ingested, or worn as protective amulets to ward off danger or sickness.[47] Innate power was thought to reside not only in liturgical books, Bibles and biblical texts, but also in books of magic or necromancy.[48] One of the earliest and most obscure surviving Canterbury cases concerns Robert Emery of Harrietsham, his wife Johanna and William, the priest of Harrietsham. In the shop of John Herworthe and in the presence of the rector of Boughton Malherbe, Johanna issued a warning to the priest William to 'beware of that art'. The warning was somehow connected with 'A boke of consecrates' and resulted in Robert and Johanna being charged with sorcery 'as it appears from obscure words in a certain document under the seal of the Commissary'.[49] It is unclear why the

40 MS CKS PRC 3.4, fols 147, 162; PRC 3.6, fols 28, 73, 76v, 29v.

41 C. Rawcliffe, *Medicine and Society in Later Medieval England* (Stroud, 1995), p. 99.

42 MS CKS PRC 3.1, fol. 132v (1499).

43 K. L. Wood-Legh, ed., *Kentish Visitations of Archbishop William Warham and his Deputies, 1511–12* (Gloucester, 1984), pp. 149–50.

44 Kittredge, *Witchcraft in Old and New England*, p. 105; Thomas, *Religion and Decline of Magic*, pp. 218, 280, 323; Davies, *Cunning-Folk*, p. 95.

45 Jolly, 'Medieval Magic', p. 35.

46 MS CCAL X.8.1, fol. 9v.

47 Jolly, 'Medieval Magic', pp. 41–2.

48 Peters, 'Medieval Church and State', p. 230.

49 MS CCAL X.8.1, fol. 44v (c. 1408). Possibly the book was the one later translated as the *Book of Secrets* of Albertus Magnus; Davies, *Cunning Folk*, p. 121.

lay couple, and not either of the priests, should have been accused, but the church courts seem, on the whole, to have been inclined to let clergy off more lightly than lay people for all kinds of offences.[50]

Priests would have been the most likely possessors of books, and James Rowe, parish priest of St Peter's, Dover, was accused in 1473 of using a book and key to reveal thefts.[51] The book and key (or psalter and key) method of detecting thieves was known at least as early as the thirteenth century. Reginald Scot in the late sixteenth century described the method. The name of each suspect was written on a slip of paper and each paper in turn put into the hollow end of a key. The diviner would lay the key on verse eighteen of Psalm fifteen ('When thou sawest a thief ...') and read some of the psalm. If the name in the key was the thief's, the book and key would turn and might fall to the ground.[52] A case of this was recorded in the London commissary court in 1497, and in 1549 a London defendant examined for 'conjuring' said he had lost count of the number of times he had used it.[53] It is not difficult to imagine how a 'conjurer' who already had a strong suspicion as to the identity of a thief could surreptitiously cause the book to move when the chief suspect's name was inserted. Although the unmasking of thieves was not limited to clergy (those accused in the Canterbury ecclesiastical courts were three women, three priests and two laymen), it seems to have been a clerical speciality. In a very unusual example of a magician being charged in a secular court, at a time when the practice of magic was not a secular offence, 'Frier William of the Blake Freres of the Cite' was presented in a Canterbury city court, probably for fraud rather than witchcraft, 'for that he take[s] uppon [himself] to conyour for menes goodes, to the grete disseipte of the kynges people'.[54] In addition to the awe inspired by their office and its trappings, priests were probably often in a good position to detect thieves, because they had access to inside information. Keith Thomas describes priests acting as agents for the detection of theft and the recovery of stolen goods, by using knowledge acquired through confession, and emphasises the possible efficacy of thief-magic in intimidating the guilty into confessions.[55]

The fullest picture of a priest's allegedly supernatural practices emerges in the case of William Dardus, vicar of Patrixbourne, who in 1473 was accused of adultery with the widow of John Clement of Patrixbourne. It was noted at the same time that he had told his parishioners that he could summon the souls of the dead to communicate with the living. A few weeks later, it was reported that he had spent the nights in Juliana Clement's room 'for seven whole weeks' and that he had taken the Eucharist home 'to conjure for some linen belonging to Nicholas Byng', and of 'ordering Byng's wife to close all the windows except one, and the

50 Jones, *Gender and Petty Crime*, pp. 148–51.
51 MS CCAL Y.1.10, fol. 50v.
52 Scot, *Discoverie of Witchcraft*, p. 277.
53 Kittredge, *Witchcraft in Old and New England*, pp. 196–7.
54 MS CCAL CC/J/Q/307/xiv, fol. 20 (1508).
55 Thomas, *Religion and Decline of Magic*, pp. 184, 259–60.

linen was put through that open window and recovered'.[56] The linen had presumably been stolen from Byng and Dardus was attempting to persuade the thief to return it. He must have threatened to raise the spirit of one of his parishioners who had died, implying (to the living parishioners) that the ghost would reveal the thief's identity.[57] When this failed, he must have made a show of conjuring with the sacrament to recover the cloth; the stratagem of closing the (shuttered) windows would have enabled the thief to return the stolen goods without being seen. Dardus seems not to have been asked whether he had claimed the ability to raise the souls of the dead. He denied the other charges, except for a subsidiary one of allowing Byng's wife to handle his private parts, and succeeded in compurgation, both for the conjuring and the adultery, with lay compurgators rather than the fellow priests who were usually required for clerical defendants. The court presumably waived the normal regulations to allow lay compurgation, tacitly recognising that if Dardus had broken the rules, he had done so to good purpose. Rowe, the other thief-detecting priest, was treated even more leniently: he was allowed to purge himself with his own oath alone. These two priests were charged with very similar offences in the same year, both were also accused of sexual delicts (Rowe was accused of 'keeping' Agnes Kent of Dover and was allowed to purge himself for this offence with only two laymen) and normal rules for clerical compurgation were waived in both cases. It seems unlikely that this is all coincidence. In both cases the charge of sexual misbehaviour was entered in the act book first, with the conjuring charge added as an apparent afterthought. It is possible that if Rowe and Dardus had not been suspected of sexual offences, their conjuring activities, which, after all, had produced socially beneficial results, might not have been brought to the court's attention, perhaps by an over-zealous court official. If this was the case, many parish priests may in fact have practised thief-detection among their parishioners when the need arose, and the Church may have turned a blind eye to what was in fact a useful complement to an inadequate system of law-enforcement.

Unskilful thief-detection was a different matter: it could involve defaming the innocent. The last pre-Reformation citation of a cleric for *sortilegium* in the surviving Canterbury act books was in 1491. Thomas Morgan, chaplain of Eastchurch, was accused at the instigation of Mr Dalton of Faversham of having told another priest, William Grere, that he had used sorcery to show that Dalton was a thief. Morgan's punishment was the very unusual one of being ordered to leave the court's jurisdiction.[58] Agnes Steveday of Hythe was accused of attributing thefts and other crimes to various people 'to their great scandal and

56 MS CCAL Y.1.11, fols 223, 229.

57 For ghosts performing this and similar functions, see Thomas, *Religion and Decline of Magic*, pp. 713–19.

58 MS CKS PRC 3.1, fol. 26v. The severity of the sentence might be an indication of a tougher line being taken by the Church against clerical use of magic, which could explain the absence of any later prosecutions. Alternatively, it might be because Morgan had slandered a person of higher status than himself.

grievance'. She admitted 'that she had revealed several thefts and other crimes, from information given her by a spirit of *le Fayrye*'.[59] This 'fairy' was the only reference to anything supernatural that was not derived from Christianity. Apart from the priests, nearly all the thief-detectors used witchcraft for other purposes as well. Elizabeth Edmund of Appledore and John Byng of Harbledown were also healers, while Alice Havyn of Brabourne was accused of using witchcraft for more nefarious practices.[60] Two Chartham men testified that Richard Draper of Bridge 'uses the art of sorcery for lost things' and did not claim that he had any other magical skills, but his case seems not to have been followed up.[61]

Table 6: Citations for sorcery, incantations and using magic, 1396–1543

Category	Men	Women	Totals
Obscure/no details	6	26	32
Cursing, fasting for revenge, harm to neighbours' goods or persons	0	15	15
Curing sick, finding lost goods, detecting thieves, fertility rites	9	9	18
Involvement with ghosts	3	1	4
Fortelling future	1	4	5
Treasure-seeking	15	1	16
Other	1	5	6
Totals	35	61	96

Note: Thirty-one men cited, one four times and one twice; sixty women cited, one twice.

An activity closely associated with finding lost goods was digging for treasure, either under crosses or in consecrated ground. As Table 6 shows, this was an almost exclusively male activity, as it continued to be in the early modern period.[62] The only woman accused in these Canterbury records was the wife of Robert Edyng of Warehorne, who had helped her husband.[63] Since digging was heavy work, treasure-seeking was often a group activity. It has been observed that participants in early sixteenth-century treasure-seeking ventures often included a priest but those in the Canterbury ecclesiastical courts were all lay people.[64] Thomas Downe, Henry Lyte, Robert Whitton and the tinker Richard Garold, all of Pluckley, spent the Easter of 1523 'digging around the cross at Shortar's Cross

59 MS CCAL Y.1.10, fol. 231 (1475).

60 MS CCAL Y.1.10, fols 116, 122 for Edmund; see above n. 40 for Byng; below for Havyn.

61 MS CKS PRC 3.6, fol. 37v (1525).

62 E. J. Kent, 'Masculinity and Male Witches in Old and New England, 1593–1680', *History Workshop Journal* 60 (2005), 71.

63 MS CKS PRC 3.2., fol. 112 (1509).

64 Thomas, *Religion and Decline of Magic*, p. 327.

for money'.[65] In what seems to have been a small epidemic of digging for treasure in the countryside around Ashford in 1523 and 1524, Thomas Chapman and Richard Hunt of Mersham were reported to have actually found and removed treasure from beneath the bell-tower at Bilsington. Hunt denied the charges but admitted that his wife had gossiped about this hidden treasure and that he himself had publicised the information.[66] Such rumours may have been common. The two men from River accused in consecutive sessions of the archdeaconry court were probably collaborators. One of them, John Crayer, had his case remitted to the commissary: in addition to failing to observe the sabbath, he was reported to have said that anyone who refused to hear Mass for three Sundays, or obtained the gospel of St John and holy bread and water could gain as much wealth as he desired. It was presumably in attempting to demonstrate the truth of his claims that he embarked on his excavations.[67] Other cases were also close together in both time and place: four men from Ewell were all accused of digging in the cemetery at night for treasure in 1529, and in 1527 and 1530 men from the nearby parishes of Folkestone and Denton were charged with digging up crosses. The chances of finding buried wealth were not necessarily entirely illusory, as Keith Thomas has pointed out.[68] But any rich man wanting to keep his valuables in a safe place would probably have avoided the vicinity of wayside crosses, because of the widespread belief, possibly connected with the legend of St Helena finding the True Cross buried in the ground that treasure could be found under crosses.[69] It was considered helpful to enlist supernatural aid to identify the right place to dig, and to have a magician to exorcise the demon who was expected to be guarding the treasure. The pronouncement of the theological faculty of the University of Paris in 1398, which emphasised the diabolic pact, referred to using demons to find hidden treasure.[70] The overturning of crosses and the use of magic or the invocation of spirits to find treasure were identified in the preamble to the first English witchcraft statute of 1542 as matters of particular concern, while the 1563 statute made using witchcraft to find hidden treasure an offence, though not a capital one.[71] Seeking hidden treasure, like finding lost goods, was not an activity limited to credulous peasants: a number of elite Englishmen engaged in it.[72] The striking points about these Kentish cases, though, are the indications that action was taken on rumours of buried treasure which had spread from neighbour to neighbour and from parish to neighbouring parish, and the fact that all these cases were prosecuted between the years 1503 and 1530. Despite the urgency of

65 MS CKS PRC 3.5, fols 49, 69v.
66 MS CKS PRC 3.5, fol. 63 (1524).
67 MS CKS PRC 3.1, fols 180v, 182. (1503/4).
68 Thomas, *Religion and Decline of Magic*, p. 279.
69 Compare Kieckhefer, *Magic in the Middle Ages*, pp. 89–90.
70 Peters, *Magician*, pp. 143–4.
71 33 Henry VIII, cap. 8, *Statutes of the Realm* 3, p. 837.
72 Thomas, *Religion and Decline of Magic*, pp. 280, 320 n. 53; Kittredge, *Witchcraft in Old and New England*, pp. 67–8.

the problem as evinced in the 1542 act, there were no further cases in the surviving records for this diocese between 1531 and 1563.

The identification of witches as female may be connected to fear of the power attaching to female gender roles. A few cases suggest such fear. Thomasyne Dunnyng of St Mildred's parish in Canterbury was accused of sorcery and administering herbs to procure an abortion.[73] Another case centred on the mundane female task of washing clothes: Joan Squyer of Woodchurch denied the charge that she had advised a female neighbour to follow her example in washing her husband's shirt in holy water, which would make him 'humble and obedient to her will'.[74] This might be categorised as something akin to 'love-magic', of which I found no other instance. Holy water, like other sacramentals such as holy candles, was widely believed to be capable of producing all kinds of desired effects: the 1547 Royal Articles ordered enquiry into superstitious abuse of the customs of the Church 'as in casting holy water upon their beds'.[75] Elizabeth Emerson of Sandwich took holy water from the font and washed her eyes and forehead with it,[76] perhaps in the hope of healing some ailment.

Early medieval evidence of pre-Christian Scandinavian and Germanic practices often associates women with special powers of knowing or finding information, as with the norns who weave fates.[77] Citations for fortune telling in late medieval Kent suggest that this remained a mainly female speciality. Agnes Sharpe of Molash and Agnes Aportyngale of Folkestone were cited for 'auguries', which probably means they foretold the future.[78] Johanna Mores of East Langdon, described as *auspicatrix*, used the croaking of frogs to predict the future.[79] The only man who was involved in foretelling the future was Gilbert Leche of Hythe, cited in 1469 for practising palmistry; his surname suggests that he may have combined this with medical practice.[80] Since her citation described her as *auspicatrix seu divinatrix*, perhaps Juliana Tanner of Lympne told fortunes as well as healing.[81] In the later sixteenth century, a Maidstone surgeon, John Halle, wrote a book inveighing against quack healers; three of the men he denounced were also fortune tellers.[82] A worrying aspect of foretelling the future was prophesying how long people would live. In 1472 a Dover woman identified only as Violet 'says she was made pregnant with the Holy Cross of the Maison Dieu in Dover, and that she prophesies the lives of certain people, who should live

[73] MS CKS PRC 3.4, fol. 17 (1513).
[74] MS CCAL Y.1.10, fol. 209v (1474).
[75] Thomas, *Religion and Decline of Magic*, pp. 32–3; W. Frere and W. Kennedy, ed., *Visitation Articles and Injunctions of the Period of the Reformation* (London, 1910) 2, p. 110.
[76] MS CCAL Y.4.4, fol. 104v (1530).
[77] Jolly, 'Medieval Magic', p. 58.
[78] MS CKS PRC 3.4, fols 81v, 82 (1517).
[79] MS CCAL Y.4.4, fol. 77 (1525).
[80] MS CCAL Y.1.10, fol. 21v.
[81] 'A predicter or diviner', see above, n. 38.
[82] J. Halle, *An Historiall Expostulation* (1565), ed. T. Pettigrew (London, 1844), pp. 6, 8, 11.

long and who should die'.[83] Nearly a century later, women consulted one of John Halle's rogues about 'whether they should burie their husbandes then lyving'.[84] Such prophecies had alarming implications and could even be associated with murder. Keith Thomas reports a wise woman being asked to poison a husband whose wife had previously enquired about his life expectancy.[85] Fortune-telling could produce other undesirable results. In a particularly bizarre case, Alice Breede of Whitstable seems to have been accused of hanging her child in order to avoid another sort of hanging foretold by witchcraft. Presumably a fortune-teller had predicted that the child would end up by hanging (that is, as a criminal), and the mother attempted to forestall fate by hanging it herself and then taking it down before it was killed. As a penance, Alice was ordered to walk through Canterbury, leading the child and carrying the halter in which she had suspended it.[86]

It has been noted that stories of revenants (reanimated corpses) and ghosts multiplied in the late Middle Ages.[87] The pre-Reformation Church taught that the souls of those trapped in purgatory might return to earth, and it was an offence to persuade a dying person to return to give an account of the afterlife, for the living to attempt to get in touch with the departed, or to report the walking of specific ghosts.[88] The few such cases in the Canterbury ecclesiastical courts seem to have involved mainly men, especially priests. William Dardus has already been encountered (see above). In 1396, John Northwych, priest of Egerton was accused of encouraging John Reynold, who allegedly defamed a dead man by claiming that he had made a pact with him to appear on the third night after his death.[89] Agnes Taylor of Westcliff, the only woman cited in connection with ghosts, reportedly claimed 'that the spirit of Ralf Tooke's wife walked at night'.[90] It may be significant that, like those involving priests, all these cases were well before 1500.

None of the activities discussed so far was directly intended to cause harm to others, and, except for treasure-seeking and possibly fortune-telling, none was very strongly identified with male or female defendants. When the accusations of 'black' magic are isolated from the rest, there is a marked difference in the gender distribution of the defendants. In the years up to 1543, fifteen women can be traced who were accused of causing, or attempting to cause, various forms of harm to their neighbours by supernatural means. Not a single man was accused of such offences. Cicely Maldon of Aldington and Joan Roo of Sittingbourne

83 MS CCAL Y.1.10, fol. 129 (1472).
84 Halle, *Expostulation*, p. 9.
85 Thomas, *Religion and Decline of Magic*, p. 287.
86 MS CKS PRC 3.1, fol. 30 (1492).
87 Jolly, 'Medieval Magic', p. 51.
88 *Dives and Pauper*, pp. 169–70; Thomas, *Religion and Decline of Magic*, p. 702.
89 MS CCAL X.8.1, fol. 3v.
90 MS CCAL Y.1.10, fol. 328 (1477).

allegedly spoiled their neighbours' ale, a common accusation against English witches.[91] All the remaining thirteen were accused of harming, or intending to harm, either their neighbours' persons or their livestock. A marked difference between these cases and a later cluster of witchcraft accusations in the Church courts, dating from 1557 to 1563 is that, although the later cases include many uninformative citations where the accusation is merely that the defendant uses *ars magica* or is 'suspected of witchcraft', they do not include any charges where the offence is specifically using witchcraft *with an intention* to cause harm. Among the earlier, late medieval, cases there are several such instances. The use of human excrement in witchcraft was common to both European and non-European societies.[92] Two Canterbury women were accused of burning it with a holy candle, with a view to causing harm to their neighbours. Joanna Meriwether of St Mildred's parish in Canterbury was reported at Cranmer's visitation in 1543, 'for displeasure that she bore towards a young maid named Elizabeth Celsay and her mother, made a fire upon the dung of the said Elizabeth; and took a holy candle, and dropt upon the said dung. And she told her neighbours that the said enchantment would make the cule of the said maid [that is, her bottom] to divide into two parts.'[93] Over seventy years earlier, Alice Duraunt of Northgate performed the same ritual, reportedly *in noctis silencio*; 'the silence of the night' was also when Alice Ralfis of Chartham was accused of 'making a prayer with an image called in the vulgar [tongue] *a Mandrake*'.[94] Any kind of nocturnal activity was immediately suspect in this period, and night was the proverbial time for witches' activities throughout Europe and elsewhere.[95] The aim of this ritual with the mandrake is not specified, but mandrake could be used for spells to avenge injuries, some of which appear in the *Liber Iuratus* (c. 1300).[96] Vengeance was the commonest alleged motive for witchcraft in the Early Modern period, and is almost the only specified motive in the few Canterbury cases where any reason for doing harm is given. Joan Glover of Bethersden was accused of 'offering candles with prayers for vengeance on her neighbours', presumably with the same objective as in a London case of 1490, when a woman was said to have used a candle in the anticipation that 'as the candle consumes, so the man must waste away'.[97] According to *Dives and Pauper*, it was common for witches to drop holy candle in an enemy's footsteps

91 MS CCAL X.8.3, fol. 55 (1464); Y.1.11, fol. 38 (1469); Kittredge, *Witchcraft in Old and New England*, pp. 34–5, 170.

92 Russell, *Witchcraft*, pp. 13–14; Kieckhefer, *Witch Trials*, p. 53.

93 J. Strype, *Memorials of Archbishop Cranmer*, I (1694) (Oxford, 1848), p. 232.

94 MS CCAL Y.1.11, fols 204 and 173v (both 1472).

95 A. Macfarlane, *Witchcraft in Tudor and Stuart England* (London, 1970), p. 21; Russell, *Witchcraft*, p. 23.

96 R. Kieckhefer, 'The Devil's Contemplatives: the *Liber Iuratus*, the *Liber Visionum* and Christian Appropriation of Jewish Occultism', in *Conjuring Spirits: Texts and Traditions of Medieval Ritual Magic*, ed. C. Fanger (Stroud, 1998), p. 255.

97 Briggs, *Witches and Neighbours*, p. 137; MS CKS PRC 3.7, fol. 11v (1525); Kittredge, *Witchcraft in Old and New England*, p. 85.

to make his feet rot off.[98] A Folkestone woman, Elizabeth at See, in 1507 denied that she was guilty of 'fasting a certain fast called *a blakke fast* for vengeance against enemies'.[99] The 'Black Fast' was said to have been practised by a woman in Lancashire in 1519, and the practice of fasting either to raise demons or to procure the death of an enemy was widespread.[100] Alice Havyn of Brabourne was accused of 'celebrating the fasts of Saints Ninian and George'; St Ninian's fast was according to Kittredge an alternative name for the black fast, though Havyn may have used it for finding lost goods.[101] But elaborate rituals were not necessary as proof of evil intent: the power of the spoken word was enough. Joan Dundys of St Mary's, Dover, was cited for habitual cursing, and predicting that those she cursed would suffer.[102]

In fact cursing seems to have been thought the most effective way to cause actual harm to one's neighbours. Five women, all in the late fifteenth century, were accused of killing or harming humans or livestock. Agnes Broke of Sandhurst was accused of killing her neighbours' cattle; Juliana Bartholomew of Adisham of killing livestock and hurting humans; Joan Cotyne (St Mary Bredin, Canterbury) of causing those already ill to die; Joan Newey (Whitstable) of harming and killing people and animals; and Elizabeth Woddis (St Clement, Sandwich) of killing 'diverse people'. Bartholomew, Cotyne and Newey were all reported to have cursed their victims; the other two were simply said to have used *ars magica*.[103] No man was accused of cursing, or of any malevolent ritual. That female cursing was the only specified means whereby women were believed to have actually killed or injured might simply indicate that cursing required no preparation, was often the result of a momentary outburst of temper in the course of a confrontation, and so was public, while fasting or performing rituals with excrement or candles involved premeditation, and might be done in secret. Alternatively, the power attributed to women's cursing might be taken to demonstrate fear of 'the unruly female tongue', like prosecutions for scolding and defaming, two other offences of which women were accused disproportionately often (see Plate 12).[104]

The expectation that 'bad' witches would be female is sometimes reinforced by the difference in the language used in the act books for male and female

98 *Dives and Pauper*, 1, p. 162.

99 MS CKS PRC 3.2, fol. 55v.

100 Thomas, *Religion and Decline of Magic*, pp. 611–12; C. Fanger, 'Medieval Ritual Magic', in *Conjuring Spirits: Texts and Traditions of Medieval Ritual Magic*, ed. C. Fanger (Stroud, 1998), p. viii; Kittredge, *Witchcraft in Old and New England*, pp. 129–30; Russell, *Witchcraft*, p. 208.

101 MS CKS PRC 3.1, fol. 130 (1499); Kittredge, *Witchcraft in Old and New England*, pp. 129–30.

102 MS CCAL Y.1.10, fol. 132 (1472).

103 MS CCAL Y.1.11, fol. 209v, 210v (both 1473); MS CKS PRC 3.1, fol. 20 (1490), PRC 3.1, fol. 73 (1496); MS CCAL Y.4.2, fol. 130 (1496).

104 For discussion of this, see J. Barry, 'Introduction', in *Witchcraft in Early Modern Europe: Studies in Culture and Belief*, ed. J. Barry, M. Hester and G. Roberts (Cambridge, 1996), pp. 37–8. For scolds in this period, see S. Bardsley, *Venomous Tongues: Speech and Gender in Late Medieval England* (Philadelphia, 2006); Jones, *Gender and Petty Crime*, pp. 94–128.

defendants. The citation usually mentions an offence, even if it is only a very general one such as 'sorcery' or 'enchantments', both for men and women. But a few women (and no men) were described as *being* a practitioner of magic. Johanna Mores and Juliana Tanner were both described as *auspicatrix* (see above). Johanna Sadeler of Bridge was described in 1450 as an enchantress of children by means of sorcery.[105] Johanna Yong of Fordwich was described as *sortilega*, which might be translated as either 'sorceress' or 'witch'.[106] This tendency to accuse women of being deviant people, while men were almost always accused of having committed a specific offence, is noticeable in secular as well as ecclesiastical jurisdictions and is not limited to accusations of witchcraft.[107] But its use in witchcraft cases does suggest that women, and only women, were beginning to be thought of as potential witches.

This identification of women as witches has been seen as a corollary of the diabolic pact, yet the Canterbury ecclesiastical courts cannot have seriously entertained the notion that the 'magic' effected or attempted by the defendants cited before them was the result of intercourse with the devil, otherwise they would have treated them more severely.[108] An alternative explanation sees the feminisation of witchcraft in England as an aspect of growing misogyny in the later fifteenth century, when various charges against women began to feature more prominently in local secular courts. It has been suggested that in the aftermath of the Black Death women enjoyed improved employment opportunities and greater independence, and that recession in the later fifteenth century may have produced a male backlash against this, of which harsher treatment of women in the courts was a manifestation.[109] As well as becoming anxious to control more mundane forms of female misbehaviour, men may have been more disposed to believe women guilty of malevolent witchcraft. But this is all rather conjectural, at a time when economic conditions varied considerably from place to place. Meanwhile, in the diocese of Canterbury at least, the idea of black magic as largely or exclusively the preserve of women seems to have been established by

105 '*Carminatrix puerorum arte sortilegii*'; MS CCAL X.1.1, fol. 7.

106 MS CKS PRC 3.6, fol. 61v (1527). The same woman was charged in her local borough court the same year as a scold and a curser, 'with other ill conditions'; MS CCAL U 4/3, fol. 220v.

107 Women in local secular courts were often described as, for example, 'a common scold' or 'common hedgebreaker'. Such descriptions were very occasionally applied to men; Jones, *Gender and Petty Crime*, pp. 206–7. R. M. Karras, 'The Latin Vocabulary of Illicit Sex in English Ecclesiastical Court Records', *Journal of Medieval Latin* 2 (1992), 16–17.

108 Of the fifteen women who were cited for causing or intending harm, only two were recorded as having been ordered to perform public penance; three more succeeded in compurgation and one was dismissed. If the remaining cases reached any conclusion it was not recorded in the surviving act books.

109 C. Barron, 'The "Golden Age" of Women in Medieval London', *Reading Medieval Studies* 15 (1989), 47–8; P. J. P. Goldberg, *Women, Work and Lifecycle in a Medieval Economy: Women in York and Yorkshire, c. 1300–1520* (Oxford, 1992), p. 7; A. Kettle, 'Ruined Maids: Prostitutes and Servant Girls in Later Medieval England', in *Matrons and Marginal Women in Medieval Society*, ed. R. Edwards and V. Ziegler (Woodbridge, 1995), p. 20; M. K. McIntosh, *Controlling Misbehavior in England, 1370–1600* (Cambridge, 1998), p. 13.

the middle of the fifteenth century, a little too early for the hypothetical male backlash.[110] Misogynist attitudes, whenever they came, almost certainly came from laymen, because the late medieval Church courts were on the whole protective towards women, as is clear in their treatment of women cited for other offences besides witchcraft.[111] It is to be hoped that research in the other dioceses which have surviving late medieval Church court records will eventually establish whether the identification of women as 'bad' witches was a general trend in England in the first half of the fifteenth century. What is already clear is that inhabitants of the diocese of Canterbury in the century or so before the Reformation shared many 'magical' beliefs and practices which had long been, and would long continue to be, common to the rest of England and the continent.

110 Indeed, as no Canterbury office books survive for the period 1411–49, for all we can tell it might have begun even earlier.

111 Jones, *Gender and Petty Crime*, p. 147; P. Mills, 'Spiritual Correction in the Medieval Church Courts of Canterbury' (unpublished PhD thesis, University of Rochester, NY, 1980), pp. 113–14.

10

The Landed Elite, 1300–1500*

PETER FLEMING

Part One: Overview

Ecclesiastical Landholding

The Church held between 30 and 40 per cent of the county's land, and the most substantial single landowner was the archbishop of Canterbury, followed by Christ Church Priory and St Augustine's Abbey, both in Canterbury. At the beginning of our period the archbishop held forty-five of the county's approximately 1348 manors, giving him a total annual income from his temporalities alone (mostly from rent) of £2616. Christ Church held thirty-one manors and enjoyed an annual income of £2062, while the figures for St Augustine's were twenty-one and £1233 respectively. By contrast with the archdiocese of Canterbury, the bishop of Rochester's annual income from temporalities was a mere £132.[1] The relative positions of these ecclesiastical landholders remained the same up to the Dissolution. In total, the Church may have held 27.5 per cent of the county's manors; by comparison, the gentry held 60 per cent, leaving the titled nobility with 4.5 per cent and the Crown with 3.6 per cent.[2]

The Landed Wealth of the Lay Elite

Assessing Kentish landowners' actual wealth with any degree of certainty is extremely difficult. Before experiments on taxing land, such as the subsidies of 1412, 1431 and 1450, and the 'Tudor subsidies' levied from 1513, our main evidence for assessing wealth are the subsidies on moveable property, usually

* I am grateful to the anonymous reader of the first draft of this chapter, David Grummitt and Malcolm Mercer for, variously, their comments, advice and encouragement.

1 J. Quick, 'Government and Society in Kent, 1232 to 1280' (unpublished D.Phil. thesis, University of Oxford, 1986), pp. 38–41. For a discussion of Kentish landholding from 1540 to 1640, see M. L. Zell, 'Landholding and the Land Market', in *Early Modern Kent, 1540–1640*, ed. M. L. Zell (Woodbridge, 2000), pp. 39–74.

2 F. R. H. Du Boulay, *The Lordship of Canterbury: An Essay on Medieval Society* (London, 1966), pp. 218–46, 114, 243, map 3; Zell, 'Landholding and the Land Market', pp. 49–51. Manors could vary considerably in extent and value, hence the disparity between annual income, acreage and the number of manors held. For the development of the later medieval English nobility and gentry, see C. Given Wilson, *The English Nobility in the Late Middle Ages* (London, 1987), pp. 29–83, and G. Harriss, *Shaping the Nation: England, 1360–1460* (Oxford, 2005), pp. 136–49.

levied at the rate of one-fifteenth of taxable property in the countryside and one-tenth in towns.[3] By its very nature this tax seriously under-assessed the income of the landed elites. The tax was originally assessed on individuals, but after 1334 it was frozen and collected communally, except in Kent. Here, the inhabitants of the Cinque Ports and the moneyers of Canterbury's immunity to county taxation necessitated continued individual assessment, thus providing a unique record of long-term economic trends.[4] The subsidy of 1334/5 can be supplemented by the assessment made in 1346/7 for the aid for the knighting of the Black Prince, levied on the basis of £2 for every knight's fee or any fraction thereof on a pro rata basis.[5] This covered all but four of Kent's hundreds. While it assessed only 367 individuals, as against the 11,016 names in the 1334/5 assessment (which itself does not represent the total population), and only counted knight's fees (the property deemed necessary to maintain and equip one knight), it probably includes most of the landed lay elite of the county (ecclesiastical property is seriously under-assessed).[6]

These assessments reveal the scale of the landed lay elite's wealth relative to the rest of the county's population. The wealthiest among those described in 1334/5 as knights, nobles or ladies (presumably the widows of knights or noblemen) were Sir Giles de Badlesmere (son of Sir Bartholomew), assessed at £5 16s 1.75d, Sir Henry de Cobham (£4 1s 10.5d), Sir Stephen de Cobham (£3 6s), and Sir Roger de Hegham (£5 10s 3.75d). Most gentry and nobles were assessed at under one pound, considerably less than the £3 14s 5d for which Roger Lapinus, 'moneyer', was assessed, or two Cinque Ports men, John Bouton, assessed at £3 3s 4d and William de Eghethorne, at £4 16s 1d. However, these sums represent a far higher proportion of the total wealth of individuals in this latter group than was the case for the landed gentry and nobility. The true relationship between landed and non-landed wealth is suggested by a comparison with the 1346/7 returns. The average figure for the twenty highest assessments of knightly or noble individuals in 1334/5 was £2 2s; the equivalent figure for the

3 R. E. Glasscock, ed., *The Lay Subsidy of 1334*, British Academy Records of Social and Economic History (London, 1975). The poll tax returns for Kent do not give sufficient detail to be useful for calculating the wealth of individuals; C. C. Fenwick, ed., *The Poll Taxes of 1377, 1379 and 1381, Part One: Bedfordshire to Leicestershire*, British Academy Records of Social and Economic History, new series 27 (Oxford, 1998).

4 H. A. Hanley and C. W. Chalklin, ed., 'The Kent Lay Subsidy Roll of 1334/5', *Documents Illustrative of Medieval Kent Society*, Kent Records 18, ed. F. R. H. Du Boulay (Ashford, 1964), pp. 58–170; R. E. Glasscock, 'The Distribution of Lay Wealth in Kent, Surrey, and Sussex, in the Early Fourteenth Century', *Arch. Cant.* 80 (1965), 61–8.

5 *FA* 3, pp. 20–53.

6 There is a surprisingly weak correlation between the two lists: only four knights of the same name are found in both lists, and there are only six instances were knights or ladies share the same family name between the two assessments. Neither is there a clear correlation between the two assessments in terms of relative wealth. While Sir William Septvans was the twelfth richest among the 1334/5 knights (assessed at £1 5s 4d), and the seventh richest individual in 1346/7 (£8), a reasonable degree of difference over the space of twelve years, Sir Maurice de Bruyn, the fourteenth richest in 1334/5 (£1), was the sixtieth richest in 1346/7 (£2). Even more striking, Sir Otto de Graundison was assessed in 1334/5 at only 6s 8d, in other words as holding less than a quarter of a knight's fee, but he was the fourth richest individual assessed in 1346/7 (£9 6s 8d).

twenty highest assessments in 1346/7 was £8, a ratio of one to four.[7] Therefore, the 1334/5 figures given for the gentry and nobility, whose wealth was vested largely in land, could be multiplied by four to give a figure that may come close to representing their true wealth. Accordingly, had the 1334/5 subsidy been based on the total wealth of Badlesmere, Sir Henry and Sir Stephen Cobham and Hegham it might have yielded sums in the region of, respectively, £23, £16, £12 and £15. The assessments made on the moveables of moneyers and merchants should be multiplied by a far smaller factor to represent the lesser proportion of landed property they probably held. This figure can only be guessed at, but it would be insufficient to put their total wealth at anything like the scale of the wealthiest landed individuals.[8] Even more striking is the immense gap between the wealth of the landed elite and that of the bulk of the county's population. The average assessment for the 1334/5 subsidy as a whole was around 3s 6d; as we have seen, the average for the twenty highest assessments of knightly or noble individuals was ten times this figure, but even this does not take into account the higher proportion of gentle wealth held as land, nor the fact that the assessors excluded the poorest from their lists.

Disparities in wealth were also considerable within the landed elite. Of the 367 individuals assessed in 1346/7, eighty-nine held the equivalent of one or more knight's fees, making 24 per cent of the total number assessed, but between them they had a total assessment of £336 17s, or 63 per cent of the assessor's figure for the whole county of £532 17s 1d. Only twenty-five were ecclesiastics (a major underestimate), whose aggregate assessment of £59 13s 4d amounts to only 11.18 per cent of the total assessment of the county as given by the assessors. Most of the rest, as holders of fractions of knight's fees, were probably lesser gentry: a century later they would have been described as esquires or gentlemen. Their average assessment of around 14s is dwarfed by the top eighty-nine who averaged £3 15s 8d.[9]

A similar picture is revealed by the fifteenth-century subsidy assessments. The 1412 subsidy on those holding land to the annual value of £20 or more provides the names of 174 Kentish landowners, of whom twenty were ecclesiastics, holding almost 14 per cent of the assessed landed wealth: again, the wealth of the Church is seriously underestimated.[10] The nobility held 11 per cent. The

7 A comparison between individuals' wealth assessed in fifteenth-century fifteenth and tenth subsidies on moveables on the one hand, with the 1431 and 1450 subsidies on land on the other for those members of the Kentish gentry who were assessed in both gave a ratio of one to three, which is not too far from the figure arrived at here; P. W. Fleming, 'The Character and Private Concerns of the Gentry of Kent, 1422–1509' (unpublished PhD thesis, University of Wales, 1985), pp. 51–2.

8 This would still be the case if the multiplier of three, derived from the fifteenth-century comparison, were used.

9 A similar pattern was found by Quick for thirteenth-century Kent, where of eighty-two knights identified between 1258 and 1272, twenty-five per cent held more than three manors, with the rest being lesser knights; Quick, 'Government and Society in Kent', pp. 56, 116–18.

10 The following discussion of the 1412 subsidy is based on B. Webster, 'The Community of Kent in the Reign of Richard II', *Arch. Cant.* 100 (1984), 217–29, and M. J. Barber, 'A Study of Landowners and

remaining 75 per cent of landed wealth was held by 141 individuals, most of whom were gentry. As in 1346/7, a steep wealth gradient is evident: eighty-eight held lands assessed at between £20 and £39; among the remaining fifty-three are individuals whose wealth was considerably greater than the average, such as John Ovedale, assessed at £66 13s 4d, Arnold Savage, assessed at £70, Sir Nicholas Haute, assessed at £122 6s 8d, and John Culpeper, assessed at £132.

The subsidy on land of 1450 reveals a similar pattern.[11] The extant Kentish returns cover Canterbury and thirty-seven of the county's sixty-six hundreds. The lower limit for assessment was set at an annual income of £1, and this included a greater range of sources of income than previously, thereby embracing a wider cross-section of society. Of the eighty-eight individuals assessed at £10 or more, sixty-four can be identified as Kentish gentry. Of the twenty-four who were not, most were assessed at below £15, but a few were assessed at relatively high levels, such as the draper, William Benet (£31) and the yeoman, Richard Knight (£20), and by contrast eight gentlemen were assessed at only £10. However, the twenty-one most highly assessed were all of gentle rank, and included all four of the assessed knights: Sir Thomas Brown, Sir Gervase Clifton, Sir John Scott, and Sir John Cheyne. The highest gentry assessment was that of Sir Thomas Brown, whose £200 was twice that of the next highest assessments, of Sir Gervase Clifton, Alexander Iden esquire, William Keen esquire and Sir John Scott, all at £100. There follows a gradual descent through the next twenty-five individuals, assessed at between £80 and £22, until the assessments plateau at £20 for the next sixteen, with another gradual descent to the final fourteen, assessed at £10.[12]

Inquisitions *post mortem*, taken on the property of deceased individuals thought to be tenants in chief of the Crown, supplement this picture. Between 1399 and 1413 inquisitions are extant for fifty Kentish property-holders. Of these, only the inquisitions for the duchess of Gloucester and her two daughters do not give valuations, and the rest give some sense of the relative value of their subjects' Kentish holdings.[13] The most valuable Kentish property was held by an outsider, William Heron, Lord Say, Henry IV's steward of the Household, valued at over £91. Next comes the property of Sir John (d. 1399) and Sir Reynold (d. 1403) Cobham, valued at nearly £80 and over £61 respectively, and Sir Arnold Savage (d. 1410), valued at £62. The next most valuable properties were held by non-resident nobility: Edmund, earl of Stafford and Maud, dowager countess of Oxford. Other non-resident noble property holders were the Scropes

their Estates in Essex, Kent, Surrey and Sussex at the Opening of the Fifteenth Century Based on the Land Tax Assessments of 1412' (unpublished B.Litt. thesis, University of Oxford, 1949), passim, both using material derived from *FA* 6, pp. 465–77.

11 MS TNA PRO E 179/124/218. The 1431 assessment has not been used since it survives for only sixteen of Kent's sixty-eight hundreds: *FA* 3, pp. 56–81. The 1436 assessment does not survive for Kent.

12 Fleming, 'Gentry of Kent', Appendix 4, pp. 475–6.

13 *IPM Henry IV* 18; 19. The unvalued assessments of the Gloucester holdings were probably substantial, and the likely distortion caused by their omission should be borne in mind throughout the following discussion.

of Masham, Philippa, widow of John, Lord Hastings; Alice, widow of Aubrey de Vere, earl of Oxford, and Joan, widow of Lord FitzWalter.[14] In addition, Edward, Lord Clinton (d. 1400) had Kentish property assessed at just over £12. The significant presence of non-resident magnates did not eclipse the landed wealth of the resident gentry: the latter accounted for fourteen of the top twenty valuations. Property held by outsiders tended to be in numerous, relatively small parcels. The total value of Kentish property held by the subjects of inquisitions was about £906 (again, not counting the Gloucester estates). Of this, at least £384 (over 42 per cent) was held by those with the most valuable part of their total landed estate located outside Kent, and therefore classified as non-resident. Another group held property elsewhere but had the majority of their landed wealth in Kent, where they held property to the total value of about £181 (20 per cent). The total value of property held by those without landed interests outside the county amounted to about £341 (37 per cent). So, in this period over one third of Kentish property held in chief was held by outsiders, and only a minority of tenants in chief held solely Kentish property. Of those tenants in chief resident in Kent, just over a third held property elsewhere. Of the twenty-six Kentish gentry whose inquisitions are extant from the reign of Henry VII (1485–1509), six held property outside the county. The total value of the Kentish property is about £1118. The total value of the non-Kentish property is about £112, or 10 per cent of the Kentish total.[15] In both samples, the proportion of property held outside the county increased with the overall wealth of the proprietor, suggesting the wider horizons of the wealthier gentry.

Tenure

Gavelkind, the Kentish form of partible inheritance, had originally been associated with the lower ranks of property holders, with the gentry and nobility holding by the military tenures (see Mate, this volume). However, by the later Middle Ages this distinction was fast disappearing. Of the fifty-two individuals who held land in Kent and who were the subjects of inquisitions post mortem between 1399 and 1413, sixteen held land by gavelkind; of these, Sir Reynold Cobham, who died in 1403, probably held the largest proportion of his lands by this tenure, with most of his Kentish property held in this way.[16] In 1431, in the areas for which subsidy returns survive, thirty-nine gavelkind properties were held by a total of twelve gentlemen and eleven esquires. While sometimes sizeable, the average value of these gentry-held gavelkind properties was less than half that of the average for the gentry's total assessed holdings (£3 19s 6d as against £8).[17]

14 These findings also suggest the importance of widows as property holders: they account for eighteen of the forty-seven inquisitions, not counting the duchess of Gloucester and her two daughters.

15 *IPM Henry VII*, 3 vols tabulated in Fleming, 'Gentry of Kent', Appendix 4, p. 477.

16 *IPM Henry IV* 18; 19. For a discussion of gavelkind and gentry landholding, see F. R. H. Du Boulay, 'Gavelkind and Knight's Fee in Medieval Kent', *English Historical Review* 77 (1962), 504–11.

17 *FA* 3, pp. 56–81.

The Nobility

Kent was not dominated by resident magnate families. The earldom of Kent was held by men whose main interests lay elsewhere. Edmund of Woodstock, half-brother of Edward II, was created earl in 1321, when he was also made keeper of Kent, of Tonbridge and Dover Castles and of the Cinque Ports, and was granted £30 per annum from the county. He was executed in 1330. His son, John, died without a male heir in 1352 and his sister carried the title to the Hollands of Buckinghamshire. With the Yorkist accession in 1461 they were deprived of the title in favour of William Neville, son of the earl of Westmoreland, but four years later it passed to the Greys of Ruthin. The earls continued to draw £20 to £30 from the county throughout this period, and occasionally appeared as JPs, but played little other part in Kentish affairs.[18]

The most significant secular lordship was that of the Lowy of Tonbridge, but ecclesiastical influence is once again apparent here, since it was held of the archbishop as feudal overlord. The Lowy was held by the Clares until their failure in the male line in 1314, when it passed by marriage to Hugh Audley, earl of Gloucester, and at his death in 1347, it passed, again by marriage, to Ralph de Stafford, created earl of Stafford four years later. Earl Ralph was buried at Tonbridge in 1372. The Lowy of Tonbridge comprised five manors and other lands centred on Tonbridge Castle, augmented in 1447 when the king granted Penshurst manor to Humphrey Stafford, duke of Buckingham.[19] However, the main interests of the Clares and the Staffords lay elsewhere, and for most of the later Middle Ages they were an influential, but not dominating, presence in the county. They were joined by several other magnates with Kentish lands. In the mid-fourteenth century, these included David Strathbogie, earl of Athol, William de Bohun, earl of Northampton, John Hastings and Aymer de Valence, earls of Pembroke, Robert Ufford, earl of Suffolk and the de Vere earls of Oxford.[20] The Staffords and de Veres appeared in the Kentish assessment for the subsidy on land of 1412, as did other noble families: the Fitzalans, Greys of Codnor, Hollands, Mortimers, Rooses and la Zouches.[21] Later in the century magnates with landed interests in the county included the dukes of Buckingham, John, duke of Bedford, Edmund, earl of March, Richard, duke of York, Ralph, Lord Cromwell, and Humphrey, duke of Gloucester.[22]

Resident Kentish nobility were few and usually of minor national importance, but locally they could be significant. At the beginning of the fourteenth century they included William, Lord Leybourne (d. 1310) and John, Lord Northwood (d. 1319). Leybourne's heir was his grand-daughter, but Northwood founded a

[18] G. E. Cokayne, *The Complete Peerage ...*, new edn revised by V. Gibbs et al. 7, pp. 142–66.

[19] C. Rawcliffe, *The Staffords, Earls of Stafford and Dukes of Buckingham, 1394–1521* (Cambridge, 1978), pp. 8, 10, 191–2, 194; Quick, 'Government and Society in Kent', pp. 46–8; Cokayne, *Complete Peerage* 12, pt 1, pp. 174–7.

[20] Based on the 1334 subsidy and the 1346/7 aid for knighting the Black Prince: see above, nn. 8–9.

[21] Webster, 'The Community of Kent', 219.

[22] Fleming, 'Gentry of Kent', p. 91.

baronial family in Kent that lasted until 1379, when it descended into the ranks of the gentry, and then, in 1416, died out in the male line.[23] Geoffrey, Lord Saye (d. 1322), founded a minor noble family seated at Codham and Birling, but his line became extinct when his grandson William died without surviving heirs in 1375. The title passed to John, Lord Clinton (d. 1399) through his marriage to Lord Saye's sister. Leading the Kentish list of those contributing towards the knighting of the Black Prince in 1346/7 was William de Clinton, earl of Huntingdon, with an assessment of over £21 8s 4d.[24] The younger son of Lord Clinton of Warwickshire, he acquired his Kentish properties through marriage to Juliana, the twice-widowed grand-daughter and heir of Lord Leybourne. He was constable of Dover Castle and warden of the Cinque Ports from 1330 to 1343, and was created earl of Huntingdon in 1337. He died in 1354.[25] The interests of his descendants became increasingly focused on Kent as their fortunes steadily declined. The fifteenth-century history of the family is in stark contrast to the glory days of the earl. In 1436 Lord John and Lady Clinton were assessed at a mere £112, making theirs among the poorest of noble families. Disaster struck in 1441 when Clinton was captured in France. His ransom of 6000 marks was crippling, and for much of his life he was too poor to be summoned to the Lords. In 1448 he was persuaded to renounce his right to the Saye title by the recently ennobled and ambitious James Fiennes, henceforth Lord Saye and Sele. In 1457/8 Lord Clinton had still not been knighted, suggesting that he had been unable to bear the attendant costs.[26] Of comparable national importance in the fourteenth century, but like the Clintons eclipsed by the fifteenth, were the Cobhams. There were three branches of the family among the fourteenth-century nobility, descended from John Cobham (d. c. 1251). The Lords Cobham of Cobham became extinct in the male line with the death of John in 1407, leaving only a daughter, through whom the title passed to the Brookes of Somerset and Devon. The Cobhams of Rundale and Allington were not summoned as peers after 1332, and hence took their place among the gentry; they died out in the male line by 1429. The third branch were not Kentish, being of Sterborough in Surrey, and they ceased to be summoned as peers after 1372.[27] The lords Poynings were

23 K. Faulkner, 'Leybourne, Sir Roger of (c.1215–1271)'; W. M. Ormrod, 'Leybourne, Juliana, Countess of Huntingdon (1303/4–67)'; C. L. Kingsford, 'Northwood, John, First Lord (1254–1319)', *ODNB*; Quick, 'Government and Society in Kent', chapter 5.

24 He was also assessed at £3 6s in moveable goods in 1334/5: see above, nn. 8–9.

25 Cokayne, *Complete Peerage* 6, pp. 648–50; W. M. Ormrod, 'Clinton, William, Earl of Huntingdon (d.1354)', *ODNB*.

26 J. C. Stanford & M. Townsend, *The Great Governing Families of England* 1 (London, 1865), pp. 195–201; J. C. Wedgwood, *History of Parliament: Biographies of the Members of the Commons House, 1439–1509* (London, 1936), pp. 196, 322–4; Hasted, *History* 5, p. 149; Cokayne, *Complete Peerage* 3, p. 315; 11, pp. 478–9; MS BL Additional 5485/47.

27 Cokayne, *Complete Peerage* 3, pp. 338–55; P. Fleming, 'Cobham Family (per. c.1250–c.1530)'; R. Allen, 'Cobham, John, third Baron Cobham of Cobham (c.1320–1408)', *ODNB*. N. Saul, *Death, Art and Memory in Medieval England: The Cobham Family and their Monuments, 1300–1500* (Oxford, 2001), chapter 1.

essentially a Sussex family, but failure in the male line thrust one branch into the Kentish gentry. When Robert, Lord Poynings died in 1446, his heir by common law and entail was his grand-daughter Eleanor, the wife of Henry Percy, earl of Northumberland. Lord Poynings's eldest son, Sir Richard, had died in 1429, leaving Eleanor as his sole heir. However, Sir Richard's two brothers, Robert and Edward, pressed their claim as heirs by gavelkind, in which tenure several of the Kentish estates were held. They were unsuccessful, and together with the two generations that followed, remained mere gentry of Kent and Sussex.[28] In the second half of the fifteenth century the Neville Lords Bergavenny were prominent in Kent, with their seat at Birling. While holding a Welsh title (from Abergavenny), their land came from the Hastings earls of Pembroke. George, third Lord Bergavenny (d. 1535) married as his second wife Margaret, daughter of the Kentish Brent family, who at this time were of merely gentlemanly rank, suggesting that this may have been a love match.[29]

Part Two: The Gentry

Lay society in Kent was dominated by its gentry, albeit with important absentee magnate landlords, and within the gentry there was a steep hierarchy of wealth. There were a large number of substantial gentry families, many of them considerably wealthier than their counterparts outside the south-east, but, while they might occasionally have been able to lord it over their neighbours, few were as wealthy as even the minor nobility. The estimated average baronial income in 1436 was £865, four times greater than the highest assessment made in 1450 on a member of the Kentish gentry, Sir Thomas Brown.[30] The absence of resident lay magnates meant that the greater gentry were able to dominate the county, but none of the resident dynasties had the necessary landed resources to maintain a monopoly of power over long periods, and in any case, their position was to varying degrees dependent on Crown favour. Royal administration gave the gentry the means to dominate their county.

County Administration

The machinery of Kent's county administration and law enforcement was largely in the hands of its gentry.[31] Before the fourteenth century the most important of

28 R. M. Jeffs, 'The Poynings-Percy Dispute: An Example of the Interplay of Open Strife and Legal Action in the Fifteenth Century', *Bulletin Institute Historical Research* 34 (1961), 148–64; P. Fleming, 'Poynings, Michael, first Lord Poynings (c.1318–69)', *ODNB*.

29 George seems to have been of a romantic disposition, since he later married his mistress; T. B. Pugh, 'Neville, Edward, first Baron Bergavenny (d.1476)'; A. Hawkyard, 'Neville, George, third Baron Bergavenny (c.1469–1535)', *ODNB*.

30 H. L. Gray, 'Incomes from Land in England in 1436', *English Historical Review* 49 (1934), 607–39; T. B. Pugh and C. D. Ross, 'The English Baronage and the Income Tax of 1436', *Bulletin Institute Historical Research* 26 (1953), 1–28; Fleming, 'Gentry of Kent', p. 63.

31 For medieval local administration, see H. M. Jewell, *English Local Administration in the Middle Ages*

the county officers had been the sheriff, almost autonomous within his shire as the Crown's representative. The sheriff presided over the most important institution of local government, the county court, which was then at the centre of county society, and as the regular venue for visitations by justices of assize and for parliamentary elections it was a major channel of communication between Crown and county. However, during the course of the fourteenth century both the sheriff and his court lost much of their authority to the central court of King's Bench and to justices, both local and itinerant, operating under the authority of royal commissions.[32]

A similar eclipse was suffered by another local judicial institution, the eyre. This was a visitation by Crown judges, who heard various criminal and civil pleas and investigated financial and administrative matters. By the early fourteenth century they had acquired the reputation of being more the means of royal coercion and extortion than of the dispensation of justice. The final eyre to be held in Kent, in 1313/4, perfectly fits this pattern, having been despatched to put pressure on the monks of Christ Church, who had elected Thomas Cobham as the next archbishop rather than Walter Reynolds, bishop of Worcester, Edward II's preferred candidate. The eyre scrutinised the archbishop's liberties, among others, and demanded justifications for local customs such as gavelkind. The cost of bribes and amercements ran into several hundred pounds. Under Edward III (1327–77) a familiar pattern emerged whereby an eyre was threatened during each episcopal vacancy, only to be bought off by the community of Kent. This pattern lasted until 1381, after which no further eyres were threatened.[33] By then, experiments in the organisation of county justice and administration had resulted in the appearance of the county bench of justices of the peace (JPs). During the succeeding century the power of the JPs eclipsed that of the sheriff, taking over most of his judicial and policing roles.[34] Of rather lesser consequence than the sheriff and JP in the personnel of county administration was the escheator, responsible for protecting the king's feudal rights. Kent shared its escheator with Middlesex.

The presence of the Cinque Ports liberty, in Kent covering New Romney,

(Newton Abbot, 1972); A. L. Brown, *The Governance of Late Medieval England, 1272–1461* (London, 1989), pp. 116–28, 141–55; A. Musson and W. M. Ormrod, *The Evolution of English Justice: Law, Politics and Society in the Fourteenth Century* (Houndmills, 1999), chapter 3; the gentry's role in county administration is summarised in P. W. Fleming, 'Politics', in *Gentry Culture in Late Medieval England*, ed. R. Radulescu and A. Truelove (Manchester, 2005), pp. 5–62.

32 Quick, 'Government and Society in Kent', pp. 98–9, 186, 200, 337; R. Gorski, *The Fourteenth-Century Sheriff: English Local Administration in the Late Middle Ages* (Woodbridge, 2003).

33 F. W. Maitland, L. W. V. Harcourt and W. C. Bolland, ed., *The Year Books of Edward II: The Eyre of Kent, 6 and 7 Edward II, 1313–14*, 3 vols., Selden Society 24, 27, 29, Year Books Series 5, 7, 8 (1910–13); D. Crook, 'The Later Eyres', *English Historical Review* 97 (1982), 241–68; F. J. Pegues, 'A Monastic Society at Law in the Kent Eyre of 1313–1314', *English Historical Review* 87 (1972), 548–64.

34 B. H. Putnam, ed., *Kent Keepers of the Peace, 1316–1317*, Kent Archaeological Society 13 (1933); Putnam, 'The Transformation of the Keepers of the Peace into the Justices of the Peace, 1327–1380', *Transactions Royal Historical Society* 4th series 12 (1929), 19–48.

Hythe, Dover and Sandwich, complicated matters since it had its own mechanisms for the enforcement of royal justice and governance, overseen by the warden, and county officials had no authority within its bounds. In addition, major private franchises, which also enjoyed certain judicial, administrative and financial privileges giving them limited autonomy, such as the right to return royal writs, were held by the archbishop, the bishop of Rochester, the prior of Christ Church, the abbot of St Augustine's, the abbot of Battle Abbey in his hundred of Wye, and by the holders of the Lowy of Tonbridge. As well as their symbolic value, such privileges could be lucrative: in the fifteenth century the archbishop received between £40 and £50 net from such sources.[35]

Bruce Webster has analysed Kent's county office-holding under Richard II (1377–1399).[36] He found that a group of twenty-five men dominated the shrievalty, bench of JPs and the county's parliamentary representation, each holding at least two of these positions, while twelve of them held all three. While these tended to come from the more substantial gentry families, and to have been knights or esquires, there is no exact correlation between wealth and office-holding: the most prestigious county offices did not simply go to the richest men. Royal favour played a part, but doubtless so did personal inclination and ability. Royal influence did not extend to forcing unsuitable or unqualified men on the county. Even through the crises of Richard's reign, including his usurpation, the impact of national politics on the personnel of local government was minimal. The stability of the administrative elite is noteworthy. Webster's conclusions are generally borne out by an analysis of county office-holders from 1422 to 1509. Since the fourteenth century, sheriffs were supposed to be worth at least £20 per annum in landed income – the assumption therefore being that they should be of knightly or esquiral rank – and to be resident in their shire. Of the sixty-nine men who held this office in Kent in this period, all but two were knights or esquires. The exceptions were Stephen Slegge, sheriff in 1448–49 as a result of Lord Saye and Sele's influence, and Henry Fane, a gentleman of Hadlow, sheriff in 1508 and 1525, who probably owed his appointments to his position as gentleman usher of the Chamber.[37] Most sheriffs had long been resident, and exceptions can again be accounted for by royal influence: Sir Robert Brackenbury, for example, appointed by Richard III in 1485, was among those northern favourites implanted in the south; under Richard he also sat on the Kentish bench and was the archbishop's steward.[38] Most of the sheriffs, then,

[35] Quick, 'Government and Society in Kent', pp. 161–5; Du Boulay, *Lordship of Canterbury*, pp. 284–6, 292–6.

[36] Webster, 'The County Community of Kent', 217–29.

[37] Sandford and Townsend, *Great Governing Families of England* 1, pp. 66–9; O. Barron, 'The Fanes', *The Ancestor* 12 (1905), 4–17; Hasted, *History* 5, p. 75; S. T. Bindoff, *The House of Commons, 1509 to 1558* (London, 1982), 3, p. 513; *CPR 1494–1509,* p. 589. Wedgwood, *Biographies of the Commons*, pp. 774–5.

[38] R. Horrox, *Richard III: A Study of Service* (Cambridge, 1989), pp. 190–1; R. Horrox, 'Brackenbury, Sir Robert (d.1485), *ODNB*.

were substantial local gentry; as royal appointees, they were also people in whom the Crown reposed trust. They tended to be drawn from a small group of families: just fourteen supplied half of Kent's sheriffs between 1422 and 1509. The Browns, Cheynes, Cliffords, Guildfords, Pecches and Scotts each provided three sheriffs, while four Culpepers filled the office; one of them, Alexander, did so twice.[39]

The commissions to the county bench were headed by a small number of magnates – usually including the warden of the Cinque Ports – and included a stiffening of circuit judges. Political influence is naturally apparent in some of these appointments, but with the exception of the judges and, possibly, the warden, the extent to which these great men actually participated in county administration was usually very limited. Excluding these gives us 126 Kentish JPs appointed between 1422 and 1509. Most were Kentish gentry, and while nearly a quarter of them were gentlemen, the bench was still dominated by knights and esquires; indeed, probably every Kentish knight sat at least once on the county bench. As with Richard II's JPs, there is little evidence of political manipulation, with the exception of a purge of the bench after the 1483 rebellion (see Mercer, this volume).[40] Of considerably less importance were the escheators, and this is reflected in the social composition of those for Kent and Middlesex in this period. There were no knights, fewer than half were esquires and the rest were gentlemen and four men of non-gentle rank. The residence requirement was not so closely observed, and Surrey and Essex each provided two escheators, while one other came from Northamptonshire.[41]

The county was represented in Parliament by two MPs, and between 1422 and 1509 thirty-seven men are known to have sat for Kent. While nearly half of these were esquires, fourteen were knights.[42] The only gentlemen were John Dreylond of Faversham, MP in 1425, John Pirie, a Canterbury lawyer, MP in 1433, and John Bamburgh, MP in 1427 and 1431, who was also a JP. Bamburgh probably owed his election in part to his Stafford connection: he had been a Stafford annuitant since at least 1428, and was steward of the family's Kentish lands in the 1440s.[43] As his case illustrates, magnate influence could help decide the county's

39 *List of Sheriffs for England and Wales*, PRO Lists and Index Society 9 (London, 1898), pp. 12–13.

40 Horrox, *Richard III*, pp. 188, 190–1; A. E. Conway, 'The Maidstone Sector of Buckingham's Rebellion, October 18 1483', *Arch. Cant.* 37 (1925), 97–120.

41 *List of Escheators for England and Wales*, PRO Lists and Index Society 72 (London, 1971), pp. 66–8; Fleming, 'Gentry of Kent', pp. 77–8.

42 *Members of Parliament* (House of Commons, 1878), pp. 303f; J. C. Wedgwood, *History of Parliament: Registers of the Ministers and of the Members of Both Houses, 1439–1509* (London, 1938), p. 650. This proportion represents a slight increase in the number of knights compared to the period 1386–1421; J. S. Roskell et al., *The History of Parliament: The House of Commons, 1386–1421* (Stroud, 1993), 1, p. 455.

43 Rawcliffe, *Staffords, Earls of Stafford and Dukes of Buckingham*, pp. 212, 235; History of Parliament Trust, London, unpublished articles on John Pirie and John Dreylond for 1422–1508 section by David Grummitt. I am grateful to the History of Parliament Trust for allowing me to see these articles in draft.

representation. Indeed, it was probably accepted practice that the warden of the Cinque Ports and, occasionally, the archbishop, would promote his own candidate, but promotion did not inevitably lead to election, and this was not systematic manipulation of parliamentary representation. At least fourteen MPs were members of the royal affinity, court or household, but it is again doubtful if this amounts to the control of elections: none of these appear to have been unsuitable candidates, and it would be reasonable for a man who had made his mark in county society to find himself a niche at court. At the same time, it would be a foolish electorate that returned a man known to be out of royal favour.[44]

The Gentry Community

Over the period from 1422 to 1509, 272 families have been identified of which at least one member bore the title of knight, esquire or gentleman and had his principal residence in Kent.[45] Of these, calculated according to the highest rank attained by a family member during this period, 62.8 per cent were gentlemen, 26.8 per cent esquires and 10.2 per cent knights. The profile of the gentry in terms of titular rank would thus appear as a broadly based but sharply pointed pyramid. These 272 families can be divided into four groups in terms of their tenure of public or seigniorial office. The first is made up of twenty families supplying at least two members as both sheriffs and JPs; second come those seventy-five families which also supplied members to at least one of these offices; third are the forty-six families which supplied only lesser offices, such as escheators; and the final group, of 131, held none of these offices. Table 7 relates these groups to the highest titular rank attained by a family member in the period, and to the average wealth of these families, as derived from the 1450 subsidy assessment and inquisitions post mortem.

There is a broad, not exact, correlation between rank, office-holding and wealth. The groups determined by office-holding do not match neatly with the three titular gentry ranks, nor do the wealth levels have much correspondence with the theoretical thresholds for knights, esquires and gentlemen of £40, £20 and £10, respectively. However, there was clearly a significant division between groups 1 and 2 on the one hand and groups 3 and 4 on the other. The groups either side of this division may appropriately be called the county gentry and the parish gentry. The former contained all of the knights, over half of the esquires but fewer than 15 per cent of the gentlemen; its ninety-five member families dominated the more prestigious county offices, and enjoyed average annual incomes about three times greater than those of the parish gentry, of whom the majority were gentlemen who never held important county office. This group of 177 parish

44 Fleming, 'Gentry of Kent', pp. 82–90. Roskell, *The Commons, 1386–1421* 1, pp. 455–7 generally confirms this view for the period 1386 to 1421, concluding that, 'there is nothing to indicate that the government ever interfered in elections to obtain a politically satisfactory outcome' (p. 456), and 'No hint of influence from magnates, lay or ecclesiastical, is to be found in the electoral indentures' (p. 457).

45 For this paragraph, see Fleming, 'Gentry of Kent', pp. 95–9.

Table 7: Kentish Gentry

Group (£)	Knights	Esquires	Gentlemen	Av. annual landed income (£)
	No. (%*)	No. (%*)	No. (%*)	
1	11 (55)	9 (45)	0 (0)	74
2	17 (22.6)	33 (44)	25 (33.3)	47
1 + 2	*28 (29.4)*	*42 (44.2)*	*25 (26.3)*	*60*
3	0 (0)	9 (19.5)	37 (80.4)	20
4	0 (0)	22 (16.6)	109 (83.2)	19
3 + 4	*0 (0)*	*31 (17.5)*	*146 (82.4)*	*19.5*
Total	28 (10.2)	73 (26.8)	171 (62.8)	

* percentage of group totals or, for final row, of the total number of 272 familes

gentry families constituted 65 per cent of the total number of gentry families in the period. The political history of later medieval Kent inevitably focuses on the minority of county gentry, since the majority were only marginally involved in politics and their county's governance.

A County Community?

Clearly, there was not one undifferentiated class of landowners in Kent: the greater gentry had more in common with the minor titled nobility than with the mere gentlemen, who in turn led lives not very different from the non-gentle yeomen immediately beneath them. Nor should one necessarily assume that all of these felt part of one county community.[46] Differentiated vertically, there may also have been important horizontal distinctions: Kent may not have been one county community, but a county of regional sub-communities. The areas of highest concentration of gentry residences were the environs of London and in the Stour valley; next came the Medway valley, followed by the central and eastern parts of north Kent. The areas of lower density were Romney Marsh and the vale of Kent, while the Downs and the High Weald were the most sparsely populated by the gentry. Within this broad pattern are variations dependent on rank. There was a greater preponderance of county gentry seats in the fertile arable lands of east Kent, particularly the Stour valley and the northern lowlands. Here were also concentrated the great ecclesiastical estates, in which a number of the gentry found employment and patronage, and here too were many of the landed

46 For a recent summary of the debate over the existence of 'county community' in later medieval England, see Harriss, *Shaping the Nation*, pp. 187–95.

investments of the moneyers of Canterbury and the merchants of the Cinque Ports. The area around London had a large number of lesser gentry, many of them with London connections, either as scions of metropolitan families or through employment or business interests. The High Weald was largely the preserve of lesser gentlemen, but to the west the archiepiscopal and Stafford lordships seem to have encouraged settlement of some of the greater gentry, such as the Culpepers and Pympes. The London fringe and High Weald appear to have constituted sub- communities, whose inhabitants had relatively fewer contacts with the rest of the county's gentry, and relatively more contact with outsiders, respectively, Londoners and other Wealden folk, either Sussex gentry or those of non-gentle status in both counties.[47]

There is a correlation between socio-economic rank and the geographical spread of connections and interests. The greater gentry had more extensive business interests (buying or selling property or acting as feoffees) and family connections outside the county, and outside the south-east, than their lesser cousins. For example, during the period 1422 to 1509, the Scotts, Hautes and Culpepers were between them involved with the residents of twenty-five counties, ranging from Northumberland to Cornwall to Calais, either in business deals or in marriage.[48] By contrast, lesser families like the Alfeghs, Hexstalls, Ellises and Brents had only a handful of business contacts outside the south-east, and only the Brents held property outside this area.[49] While the greater gentry might have identified more readily with their county as a whole, particularly since they were most heavily involved in its governance and representation, their mental horizons would also have extended far beyond its borders, perhaps diluting any exclusive county loyalty. The parish gentry would have ventured much less frequently beyond their locality (and for those living near the border this would necessarily have extended into other counties or into London) and so their sense of 'Kent' as a whole, as a focus for loyalty and sentiment, is again debatable. Nevertheless, there was a sense of Kentish solidarity among some of the gentry, as is demonstrated by Sir John Fogge's foundation of a chantry in 1462 for the souls of Kentish men who had died fighting for Edward IV.[50]

To address the temporal dimension, we may ask to what extent this was a stable community over time: how deep-rooted were these gentry families? The rates of depletion and recruitment into the gentry can be assessed by sampling

47 Fleming, 'Gentry of Kent', pp. 111–17, 148–54; summarised with additions in S. Pearson, *The Medieval Houses of Kent: An Historical Analysis* (London, 1994), pp. 16–17.

48 Fleming, 'Gentry of Kent', pp. 111–17; idem, 'Culpeper Family (per. c.1400–1540)'; idem, 'Haute Family (per. c.1350–1530)'; idem, 'Scott Family (per. c.1400–c.1525)', *ODNB*; Roskell, *The Commons, 1386–1421* 3, pp. 323–4.

49 Fleming, 'Gentry of Kent', pp. 113, 122–7, Appendix 3, Map A, pp. 465–6. In her will of 1516 Amy, widow of William Brent esquire, left her properties in Devon and Cornwall to her son John; MS CKS PRC 32/12, fol. 7.

50 *CPR 1461–67*, p. 76; *1467–77*, p. 42; see Mercer, this volume. Quick, 'Government and Society in Kent', pp. 100–5, provides further indications of a sense of community among the Kentish gentry.

two generations. Each sample is made up of resident families of gentry rank (classed according to the highest rank attained within the period by a family member): the first comprises 177 families present from 1422 to 1437; the second comprises 190 families from 1494 to 1509, about two generations later. Of the first, 83 per cent were still represented in the second group, so displaying a very respectable level of survival for this period.[51] Many of Kent's fifteenth-century gentry were of long-standing. Kent had been home to the Freninghams, Peckhams and Savages since the twelfth century.[52] The Appulderfields, Cheynes, Northwoods, Hautes and Kyriels had been among the county's gentry in the 1290s.[53] The Auger, Cobham, Culpeper and Septvans families could trace their Kentish roots to at least the reign of Edward II.[54] Only slightly less impressive, fifteenth-century members of the Pympe, Malmayns and Seynt Nicholas families could claim Kentish ancestors in the male line from at least the reign of Edward III.[55]

External Influences

The county's proximity to London, and hence to the royal court and central administration, and to the English Channel, had important consequences for the character of its landed society. The property market in London's Kentish environs was unusually active. The availability of many small properties provided a relatively easy toe-hold for outsiders, particularly Londoners.[56] These probably made up the largest single group of outsiders with whom the Kentish gentry were involved in property transactions.[57] As the most populous city in England, the country's most important trading centre, and increasingly the focus of the court and royal household, government and the law, London inevitably exerted a major influence throughout the county, not just in north-west Kent. Of two hundred pardons taken out between 1437 and 1494 by individuals describing themselves as of gentle rank and resident – though not necessarily exclusively resident – in Kent, nineteen (9.5 per cent) described themselves as 'late of London', as against only seven (3.5 per cent) who described themselves as formerly of another county.[58] Londoners, or those whose careers brought them to London, provided many new recruits into the Kentish gentry.

Prominent courtiers sometimes found the county a convenient place to settle.

51 Fleming, 'Gentry of Kent', pp. 129–31.

52 Roskell, *The Commons, 1386–1421* 3, p. 128; 4, pp. 37, 306.

53 MS TNA PRO E 198/1/9, m 2; C 47/1/4; Roskell, *The Commons, 1386–1421* 2, p. 557.

54 MS TNA PRO C 47/1/8, 9, 12; F. W. T. Attree and J. H. L. Booker, 'The Sussex Colepepers', *Sussex Archaeological Collections* 47 (1904), 47–81; 48 (1905), 65–98.

55 MS TNA PRO C 47/1/13, 16.

56 A. Brown, 'London and North-West Kent in the Later Middle Ages: The Development of a Land Market', *Arch. Cant.* 92 (1976), 145–55; see also W. Lambarde, *A Perambulation of Kent, Conteining the Description, Hystorie and Customes of the Shyre (1576)*, ed. R. Church (Bath, 1970), p. 6.

57 Fleming, 'Gentry of Kent', p. 112.

58 Fleming, 'Gentry of Kent', pp. 131–2.

The Yorkshireman Sir Henry Wyatt was treasurer of the Chamber and councillor to Henry VII, and these offices made residence near London a necessity. Accordingly, in 1492 he purchased Allington Castle, near Maidstone. Sir Henry subsequently made other purchases around Allington. He worked his way firmly into Kentish society, and was associated with the Cheyne, Scott and Crowmer families.[59] The royal household provided careers for a number of Kentish gentry, such as the two Sir Arnold Savages, father and son, and John de Cobham (d. 1399), and in turn the Crown was able to us them to extend its influence into the county.[60]

Personnel of the royal administration occasionally settled in Kent. Nicholas Lathel was clerk of the Exchequer from at least 1469/70, and baron from at least 1489. From the 1460s he resided and bought land in the Orpington, Chelsfield and St Mary's Cray area, by which time he was describing himself as a gentleman of Kent. Despite this, most of his associates appear to have been Londoners or Kentish yeomen, rather than his fellow gentry.[61] The Westminster law courts provided further recruits. Sir Robert Rede, chief justice of common pleas from 1506 until his death in 1518/9, came from a Norfolk and Lincolnshire mercantile family. By 1476 he had married Margaret, the daughter of John Alfegh of Chiddingstone, which probably brought him into the county: in a pardon of 1482 he described himself as a gentleman of Chiddingstone, late of London. In addition to land at Chiddingstone and Hever, acquired after his father-in-law's death in 1488, Rede, like Lathel, purchased land in the Orpington area. Unlike Lathel, Rede was deeply immersed in the affairs of his gentry neighbours: perhaps a rising lawyer and future chief justice was a more useful person to cultivate than a mere clerk and future baron of the Exchequer.[62]

Kent was attractive to rich London merchants looking for a country retreat. Among the wealthiest of these was the draper and lord mayor, Sir John Pultney (d. 1349), for whom Penshurst Place was built.[63] Marriage into the gentry was fairly common, and sometimes led to the transition from merchant to gentleman. William Whetnall, the son of a London grocer and alderman, married Margaret, the daughter of William Hexstall esquire, in or shortly before 1457. Their son, William junior, inherited the extensive Hexstall property around Tonbridge, and in 1501/2 enjoyed an annual landed income of a hundred marks. He seems to have

59 K. Muir, *The Life and Letters of Sir Thomas Wyatt* (Liverpool, 1963), pp. 1–3; Hasted, *History* 4, p. 450; W. Martin-Conway, 'Allington Castle', *Arch. Cant.* 28 (1909), 354–5; *CCR 1500–09*, nos 819, 953.

60 Roskell, *The Commons, 1386–1421* 2, pp. 607–8, 4, pp. 306–10. This point is examined in detail by Grummitt and Mercer, this volume.

61 MS TNA PRO C 67/47, 55; C 146/121, 125, 10117, 2792, 4466; *CCR 1485–1500*, nos 368, 768.

62 MS TNA PRO C 67/50, C 146/1157, 1160–1, 2219, 1334, 3941, 98880/3, 9929; E 179/124/218; E 210/960; E 326/877, 879, 1119; PROB 11/8 fol. 18; *CPR 1446–52*, p. 480; J. H. Baker, 'Rede, Sir Robert (d.1519)', *ODNB*. Other examples include Sir William Rickhill (d. 1407), justice of common pleas, and Sir Robert Bealknap (d. 1401), chief justice of common pleas: A. Tuck, 'Rickhill, Sir William (d.1407)', *ODNB*; Roskell, *The Commons, 1386–1421* 4, pp. 210–11; J. L. Leland, 'Bealknap, Sir Robert (d.1401)', *ODNB*.

63 S. L. Thrupp, *The Merchant Class of Medieval London* (Chicago, 1948), p. 121, and 120–1 for other Londoners with Kentish property interests.

fitted well into gentry society, marrying Jane, the daughter of Sir William Crowmer.[64] Crowmer's own forebears were Londoners. His namesake, a draper, alderman and several times lord mayor of London, purchased several manors and properties in Kent in the first half of the fifteenth century.[65] The son and grandson of the London alderman Sir Richard Lee (d. 1472), both named Richard, established themselves as Kentish esquires, but both chose to be buried with Sir Richard in London.[66]

The standing of another London merchant family – the Boleyns – rose spectacularly after they had made the transition. Geoffrey Boleyn, a mercer and alderman of London, already had some Kentish property by the time of his death in 1463, but it was his son and grandson who established the family as resident county gentry. Geoffrey's son, Sir William, claimed the Hoo estates through his mother, daughter of Thomas, Lord Hoo and Hastings, and this inheritance provided him with a substantial stake in the county. He died in 1490 leaving two sons. The younger, Sir William II, sat on the Kentish bench between 1502 and 1505, but it was the elder who made the biggest impression. This was Thomas, earl of Wiltshire and Ormond (d. 1538), Henry VIII's father-in-law. In four generations his family had climbed each rung of the social ladder from mere merchant to the second highest in the land.[67]

The nexus of court and commerce is also apparent in the case of John Pecche (d. 1380). Pecche, London fishmonger, mayor and MP, had connections with the court circle, which led to his impeachment before the Good Parliament of 1376. He was also connected with John of Gaunt. He acquired Kentish estates, but these were just one part of a property portfolio covering half a dozen counties. His son, Sir William Pecche, inherited the Kentish properties and settled at Lullingstone, but the Pecches never completely severed their metropolitan links.[68]

The other end of the county looked towards mainland Europe, and particularly, after its conquest in 1347, Calais. A number of the Kentish gentry served in the Calais garrison or administration, such as Sir William Pecche (d. 1399), Thomas Brockhill (d. 1411), Richard Clitheroe (d. 1420), Sir Gervase Clifton, Sir John Cheyne and William Haute (d. 1462).[69] On the Kentish side of the Channel, the

64 Thrupp, *The Merchant Class*, pp. 373–4; Hasted, *History* 5, pp. 101, 227, 287, 318; 9, p. 456; MS TNA PRO C 146/353; Wedgwood, *Biographies of the Commons*, pp. 450–1; *CPR 1485–94*, p. 271; W. Berry, *County Genealogies: Kent* (London, 1830), pp. 77–9.

65 Hasted, *History* 6 pp. 86, 146, 273. Richard Lovelace provides another example: P. W. Fleming, 'The Lovelace Dispute: Concepts of Property and Inheritance in Fifteenth-Century Kent', *Southern History* 11 (1991), 1–18.

66 MS TNA PRO C 67/53; CP 25 (i) 117a/345/12027; E 210/10; PROB 11/8 fol. 15, 22 fol. 15; Thrupp, *Merchant Class*, p. 353; Wedgwood, *Biographies of the Commons*, pp. 530–1.

67 Hasted, *History* 3, p. 38; MS TNA PRO C 140/10; *IPM Henry VII* 3, no. 404; Cokayne, *Complete Peerage* 10, pp. 137–40; 12, p. 739; J. Hughes, 'Boleyn, Thomas, earl of Wiltshire and earl of Ormond (1476/7–1539)', *ODNB*.

68 Roskell, *The Commons, 1386–1421*, 4, pp. 32–3; R. L. Axworthy, 'Pecche, John (d. 1380)', *ODNB*. Nicholas Potyn (d. 1398), provides another example; Roskell, *The Commons, 1386–1421* 4, pp. 125–7.

69 Roskell, *The Commons, 1386–1421* 2, pp. 364–5, 598–602; 3, pp. 324–7; 4, pp. 32–3; Wedgwood, *Biographies of the Commons*, pp. 181, 194–5.

Cinque Ports brought recruits into the ranks of the gentry. During the later fourteenth century John Monyn of Dover acquired substantial property in the area and in Canterbury and, most importantly, a landed estate in Buckland. By the time of his death, sometime after 1417, he had been known as an esquire for many years.[70]

Service in the Cinque Ports administration brought newcomers into the county. Geoffrey Louther, the younger son of a Cumberland gentry family, came to Kent as lieutenant to Humphrey, duke of Gloucester, warden of the Cinque Ports.[71] Opportunities at Dover Castle also opened up for local landowners, the most prominent example – and also one of the most short-lived – being James Fiennes, Lord Saye and Sele, appointed constable of Dover Castle and warden of the Cinque Ports in 1447, three years before his execution by the Cade rebels. His lieutenant was the Nottinghamshire-born Sir Gervase Clifton.[72] From 1450 the wardenship was held by the duke of Buckingham, who utilised his Kentish connection to fill posts in the Dover administration. Among them was Thomas Hexstall. Originally from Staffordshire, he had followed his brother William south in Stafford service. By 1454 he had been appointed Buckingham's receiver at Dover, where he established himself as a prominent gentleman-merchant. Both Thomas and his son Edward served as mayor. Hexstall's superior as receiver was Sir Thomas Kyriel, Buckingham's lieutenant of Dover.[73]

Lordship

Kent was not impervious to the influence of magnate patronage, affinities and retaining, the so-called 'bastard feudalism' characteristic of later medieval English society. Like Louther, Thomas Town of Throwley, MP for Kent in 1420, belonged to the duke of Gloucester's affinity.[74] In the later fourteenth century both John of Gaunt and the Black Prince had Kentish followers: Sir John Culpeper was one of Gaunt's retainers, while Sir Arnold Savage (d. 1375) was a member of the Black Prince's household, and died at the Prince's manor of Wallingford.[75] Nicholas Potyn (d. 1398) was closely connected with John, Lord Devereux, warden of the Cinque Ports in the 1390s, but their acquaintance seems

70 Roskell, *The Commons, 1386–1421* 3, pp. 764–5. Similar examples of Cinque Ports men entering the gentry include John Adam of New Romney (d.1440), and Thomas Loveryk of Sandwich: ibid. 2, pp. 10–11; 3, pp. 637–8.

71 J. S. Roskell, *The Commons in the Parliament of 1422* (Manchester, 1954), pp. 201–3; History of Parliament Trust, article on Geoffrey Lowther by D. Grummitt.

72 J. A. Nigota, 'Fiennes, James, first Baron Saye and Sele (c.1390–1450), *ODNB*; Rawcliffe, *Staffords, Earls of Stafford and Dukes of Buckingham*, p. 24.

73 *CCR 1447–54*, p. 175; *CFR 1485–1509*, p. 91; *CPR 1485–94*, p. 172; F. Hull, ed., *A Calendar of the White and Black Books of the Cinque Ports, 1432–1955* (London, 1966), pp. 30, 117 ff.; Wedgwood, *Biographies of the Commons*, p. 449–51; Rawcliffe, *Staffords, Earls of Stafford and Dukes of Buckingham*, pp. 72, 82, 212, 222; MS TNA PRO C 146/3720. For William, see below.

74 Roskell, *The Commons, 1386–1421* 4, p. 636.

75 P. Fleming, 'Culpeper Family (per. c.1400–c.1540)'; J. L. Kirby, 'Savage, Sir Arnold (1358–1410)', *ODNB*.

to have brought him little preferment, and may have been an instance of friendship, rather than a patron–client relationship.[76] Friendship and patronage appear to have co-existed in the case of John Freningham (d. 1410) and Hugh, earl of Stafford. He was appointed as Stafford's attorney, executor and guardian of his property before the earl departed on pilgrimage in 1386, and the connection continued under his successor. Freningham was also a client of Archbishop Courtenay and had close links with John, Lord Cobham, which may have persuaded him to join Bolingbroke in 1399.[77] His brother, Sir Ralph Freningham, married his daughter to his neighbour Reynold Pympe, who was a tenant and had probably been a ward of Earl Hugh.[78]

Prelates also retained members of the gentry. Richard Waller was a retainer of Cardinal Beaufort, and by 1439 had become master of his household, later becoming steward for life of the episcopal lands and executor of Beaufort's will.[79] However, the major ecclesiastical presence in the county was the archbishop, and a substantial number of the gentry were archiepiscopal clients, many finding preferment in the administration of the temporalities. The most important office was that of steward of the lands. In the fifteenth century this was filled by, among others, John Darell (1423–37), James Fiennes, later Lord Saye and Sele (1443–50) and Sir Robert Brackenbury (1484–85).[80] One characteristic linking all four is their connection, either with the warden of the Cinque Ports (in Darell's case), or with the royal household: it was deliberate policy to appoint to this post men who would have influence with the powerful.[81] Other posts in the archiepiscopal administration occasionally attracted prominent gentry. Sir Nicholas Haute was Archbishop Arundel's reeve of Reculver in 1396/7; this, and his acquaintance with John, Lord Cobham, may have rendered him suspect in the later 1390s, since after his shrievalty in 1396/7 he was not again given official employment under Richard II.[82] There were ample opportunities for less well-connected men among the Kentish gentry, such as John Freningham, a client of Archbishop Courtenay, Stephen Bettenham (d. 1415), Chichele's bailiff of Maidstone, and Roger Rye, Chichele's bailiff of Wingham and steward of the archiepiscopal liberty. This connection probably promoted him into county office: he was MP for Kent in 1417, three years after he first appears as the archbishop's servant.[83]

76 Potyn had moved in high circles as an associate of Alice Perrers before 1377, despite being no more than a citizen and draper of London at the time, and so such a relationship between one of the middle-ranking Kentish gentry and a lord is not necessarily unlikely; Roskell, *The Commons, 1386–1421* 4, pp. 125–7.

77 Roskell, *The Commons, 1386–1421* 3, pp. 128–30.

78 Roskell, *The Commons, 1386–1421* 4, pp. 151–2.

79 A. F. Pollard, 'Waller, Richard (c.1395–c.1462)', rev. E. L. O'Brien, *ODNB*.

80 Du Boulay, *Lordship of Canterbury*, pp. 269–70, 290–1, 395. For Darell and Brackenbury, see below. Close links between the gentry and the Church were evident in the thirteenth century; Quick, 'Government and Society in Kent', pp. 42–3.

81 Du Boulay, *Lordship of Canterbury*, pp. 112–13, 251–64, 286–7.

82 Roskell, *The Commons, 1386–1421* 3, pp. 323–4.

83 Roskell, *The Commons, 1386–1421* 2, pp. 219, 456–7; 4, pp. 264–5. Archiepiscopal service could also

Rye's position as MP is somewhat unusual for a steward of the liberty. Lesser men tended to be employed in this post, since it was probably expected that it be discharged in person, whereas the steward of the lands generally appointed a deputy. Stewards of the liberty may often have been professional administrators. Thus, Richard Bruyn, steward of the liberty in 1442, was variously described as gentleman or esquire, and never appeared among the gentry elite. He was from Staffordshire, and like the Hexstalls came south in Stafford service, being employed as the duke of Buckingham's steward of Kent.[84] Of slightly less significance than the stewards were the receivers. Men who filled these posts in the fifteenth century included William Palmer, Robert Est, Robert Tottisherst, and Roger Shelley, receiver-general from 1489 to 1490. All were gentlemen.[85] Chichele made particular use of family connections among the Kentish gentry. His steward of the lands, John Darell, was married to a daughter of his brother, William Chichele. In 1432 John Tattershal of Woolwich, the son of a London draper, married Agnes, the fourteen-year-old daughter of John Chichele and thus a kinswoman of the archbishop; either by the time of his marriage or shortly after he was the steward of the archiepiscopal liberties.[86]

Assimilation

Newcomers sometimes found it hard to win acceptance from longer established gentry families. The Hexstall brothers had many associates from outside the Kentish gentry, particularly Londoners and Kentish yeomen and merchants, but their links with their fellow gentry were few. Their status as new arrivals, and their urban and mercantile interests, may have counted against them.[87] The same seems to have held true for the Lovelace family, of London origins, who settled in Kent in the 1460s.[88] Such was not the experience of all new arrivals. Sir Thomas Fogge seems to have been the first member of his family to settle in Kent, brought there by his marriage to Joan, daughter of Sir Stephen de Valoignes; his standing owed much to his successful war service in the retinue of Henry of Lancaster, and he went on to represent his adopted county in Parliament throughout much of the 1370s and 1380s.[89]

bring newcomers into Kent, as appears to have been the case with John Butler and Roger Honyton; ibid. 2, pp. 456–7; 3, pp. 408–9.

84 Du Boulay, *Lordship of Canterbury*, p. 396; Rawcliffe, *Staffords, Earls of Stafford and Dukes of Buckingham*, p. 212; Wedgwood, *Biographies of the Commons*, pp. 120–1; MS TNA PRO C 67/39.

85 Du Boulay, *Lordship of Canterbury*, pp. 154, 272–3, 307n, 339–400; MS TNA PRO PROB 11/17 fol. 8.

86 MS TNA PRO C 1/185/71; KB 27/702 m 42v. See below for the case of William Keen, and F. R. H. Du Boulay, 'The Assembling of an Estate: Knole in Sevenoaks, c.1275 to c.1525', *Arch. Cant.* 89 (1974), 1–10 at 5–6 for earlier examples of men rising into the gentry through service to the archbishop.

87 U. V. Lambert, *Bletchingley: A Parish History* (London, 1921), p. 244.

88 Fleming, 'Lovelace Dispute', 2–4.

89 Roskell, *The Commons, 1386–1421*, 3, pp. 95–7. Sir Reginald Braybrooke (d. 1405), from a major Bedfordshire and Buckinghamshire family, similarly seems to have found few problems settling in Kent: ibid. 3, pp. 349–50.

Those who had successfully established themselves did not necessarily forget their origins. William Keen was a West Countryman who was brought to Kent through his marriage to Agnes, the daughter of John Chichele. The couple settled in Woolwich. William went on to serve as sheriff, and from 1456 to 1460 he sat on the county bench and on various commissions. He died in 1467, and in his will he left bequests not only to Woolwich and Eltham churches, but also to churches in Somerset and Dorset.[90] Also of West Country origin was the judge, Sir Walter Moyle, the third son of Thomas Moyle of Bodmin in Cornwall. By 1454 he had settled at Eastwell in Kent. In that same year he was appointed justice of King's Bench. He was knighted in 1465. His son, John, built on these foundations, and his inquisition post mortem of 1501 shows him to have been one of the wealthiest of the county's gentry. While his feet were firmly planted in Eastwell, John maintained links with his ancestral home, and sat for Bodmin in the 1467–68 Parliament.[91]

The examples given so far of newcomers could be repeated several times over, and they reveal varying degrees of success in assimilating. Kinship often played a crucial part in this process. Rede, Whetnall and Keen married their way into the gentry, and all three of these families, including the relatively humble Whetnalls, came to be accepted by the Kentish elite. Although the Boleyns made their first foray into Kent by purchasing land, it was through kinship, in the shape of the Hoo inheritance, that they became established. Moyle and Wyatt appear to have bought themselves in without relying on marriage alliances, but they were already of gentle birth and substantial means before they moved. By contrast, lesser men like Lathel and the Lovelaces may have met resistance. Londoners of aldermanic rank found ready acceptance, but perhaps it was a different story for less substantial city immigrants. On the other hand, continued contact with London does not necessarily imply a lack of successful integration with landed society: the Pecches of Lullingstone maintained their membership of London companies throughout the fifteenth century.[92] Not surprisingly then, pre-existing wealth and status helped ease the passage into Kentish gentry society.

The network of Clitheroe, Darell, Louther and Clifford shows how successfully even migrants from the far north of England could forge careers in Kent. Richard Clitheroe (d. 1420) was probably the younger son of a Lancashire gentry family who made his fortune in London and then moved out to Kent. He rendered valuable service to Richard II and Gaunt as an expert in military logistics and, as we have seen, also held office in Calais. In 1412 his Kentish property was valued at £141 13s 4d, amassed largely through purchase with the profits of royal service. Kent would have provided a convenient base for his interests in London

90 MS TNA PRO C 1/185/69; *CPR 1494–1509*, pp. 162–3; Wedgwood, *Biographies of the Commons*, pp. 183–4; E. F. Jacob, ed., *The Register of Henry Chichele, Archbishop of Canterbury, 1414–43*, 4 vols (Oxford, 1938–47), 1, pp. xvi–lviii.

91 Hasted, *History* 5, p. 455; 7, pp. 134 f.; Wedgwood, *Biographies of the Commons*, pp. 616–17; Bindoff, *History of Parliament*, 2, pp. 642–4.

92 Thrupp, *Merchant Class*, pp. 279f.

and Calais. His success encouraged other members of his family to settle in Kent: his brother, William, and nephew Richard Clitheroe II became prominent burgesses of New Romney, while the latter's son William was a burgess of Hythe.[93] John Darell was the younger son of a Yorkshire gentry family. He came south and married into the Kentish family of Baret when his elder brother inherited. He supplemented his wife's property through purchase, and by 1412 was assessed at £50 in Kent, and his second marriage around 1418 to Florence, the niece of Archbishop Chichele, brought him Scotney Castle. By the time of his second marriage he had already been associated with the archbishop for at least two years and he was also in the circle of Ralph Neville, earl of Westmoreland and his brother, Lord Furnivall. John's brother, William Darell, also came south, and was sheriff of Kent in 1416/7.[94] Geoffrey Louther of Cumberland, who arrived in Gloucester's service, became a central figure in the county as a JP and MP, and held property in and around Canterbury.[95] Robert Clifford's brother, Richard, bishop of London, was probably instrumental in bringing him south from their family home in Northumberland. By 1399 he had established himself in Kent, and by 1412 his lands in the county, largely acquired through purchase, were valued at £54 6s 8d. He sat as one of the county MPs in the 1406 Parliament, but also acted as proxy to the other Kent MP, his fellow northerner Richard Clitheroe, absent as admiral of the fleet; Clifford later acted as Clitheroe's feoffee.[96] This group demonstrates the importance of family links in introducing newcomers into the county, but its members also associated with each other in business and in their public lives. In particular, Lowther, John Darell, and both Richard Clitheroes worked together as members of the governing council of Rochester Bridge. In this capacity they were joined by another arrival from north-west England, James Hopwode, a lawyer who had been brought into the county by his marriage to Joan, grand-daughter of the Kentish judge Sir William Rickhill. Rickhill was another bridge patron, as was Hopewood's uncle, Thomas Langley, bishop of Durham: their association probably made possible Hopwode's marriage, and hence his move to Kent.[97] This network of readily identifiable – and perhaps self identifying – northerners in early fifteenth-century Kent can be compared with that other group of northerners settled in Kent under

93 Roskell, *The Commons, 1386–1421*, 2, pp. 598–604; History of Parliament Trust, articles on Richard I and William Clitheroe by D. Grummitt.

94 Roskell, *The Commons, 1386–1421* 2, pp. 752–5; History of Parliament Trust, article on John Darell I by D. Grummitt; W. A. Scott Robertson, 'Pedigree of Darell of Scotney', *Arch. Cant.* 17 (1887), 46–8; R. Griffin, 'An Inscription in Little Chart Church', *Arch. Cant.* 36 (1923), 131–42; MS BL Additional 33,920 fol. 193.

95 Roskell, *The Commons in the Parliament of 1422*, pp. 201–3.

96 Roskell, *The Commons, 1386–1421* 2, pp. 590–2.

97 History of Parliament Trust, articles on Richard Clitheroe I, John Darell I, Geoffrey Louther, and James Hopwode by D. Grummitt, to whom I am grateful for pointing out the Rochester Bridge connection. For the bridge in this period, see R. H. Britnell, 'Rochester Bridge, 1381–1530', in *Traffic and Politics: The Construction and Management of Rochester Bridge, AD 43–1993*, ed. N. Yates and J. M. Gibson (Woodbridge, 1994), pp. 41–106.

Richard III: the former's acceptance, while perhaps maintaining a separate identity, contrasts markedly with the hostility aroused by the latter (see Mercer, this volume).

There was some movement into the gentry from below. Richard Champney provides an intriguing case. In a heraldic visitation of Kent probably made soon after 1499 he is described as a herald, Gloucester King of Arms, but in a pardon he described himself as a gentleman of Selling, alias a franklin of Kent, alias late a yeoman, alias late a gentleman of London.[98] The use of the term 'franklin' is unusual by the early Tudor period, and may indicate a herald's interest in matters antiquarian, but seems to be in line with Champney's description of himself as once of yeoman status, and indicates that he was of non-gentle origins. He was nevertheless still of sufficient rank to marry into the Kentish gentry family of Dreyland.[99] A less secure entrant into gentry society was John Sharp. In his pardon of 1470 he described himself as a gentleman of Benenden, late a yeoman, and lately undersheriff to Sir John Culpeper (sheriff in 1466/7). His association with the Culpepers predated his appointment: in 1458 he was a feoffee of Walter Culpeper esquire, and in 1463 John Sharp, 'yeoman', was a feoffee of Nicholas Culpeper. The John Sharp who was escheator in 1500 may well have been the son of the undersheriff, in which case neatly indicating, through his tenure of a more prestigious office than that of his father, their family's rising status.[100] Others near the lower edge of gentry society included John Roberts, who in his pardon of 1458 described himself as a gentleman of Cranbrook, alias yeoman, alias draper.[101] Such descriptions do not indicate if the subject was upwardly or downwardly mobile, or even just in a long-term marginal state. In the case of John Aldy, the direction of movement was unmistakeably upward. In his pardon of 1470 he described himself as a Sandwich merchant and one-time London grocer; by 1483 that description had changed to gentleman of Ash-next-Sandwich, alias merchant, and lately mayor of Sandwich. In addition to the mayoralty, which he held in 1468 and 1476, he was also victualler of the Cinque Ports' fleet from 1461 to 1463, and MP for Sandwich from 1463 to 1465 and from 1472 to 1475. Thomas Aldy, parliamentary burgess for Sandwich in 1504, and probably John's grandson, described himself, unequivocally, as a gentleman in his will of 1534.[102]

Clearly, the barrier between gentle and non-gentle was permeable. The general

98 J. Greenstreet, ed., 'List of the Gentry of Kent in the Time of Henry VII', *Arch. Cant.* 11 (1877), 394–7; MS TNA PRO C 67/53.

99 MS TNA PRO C 1/124/27; CP 40/850 m 92; *CPR 1476–85*, p. 465; A. R. Wagner, *English Genealogy*, 2nd edn (Oxford, 1972), pp. 141–5; idem, *Heralds and Heraldry in the Middle Ages*, 2nd edn (Oxford, 1956), pp. 43–4; N. Saul, 'The Social Status of Chaucer's Franklin: A Reconsideration', *Medium Aevum* 52 (1983), 10–26.

100 MS TNA PRO C 67/47; CP 25(i)/117A/345/145, 147; MS BL Harleian Charters 76/G/56, 76/H/8, 77/F/36; MS CKS U 47/11/8; *CPR 1467–77*, p. 301.

101 MS TNA PRO C 67/42.

102 MS TNA PRO C 67/44, 51; PROB 11/19 fol. 10; 25 fol. 14; Wedgwood, *Biographies of the Commons*, p. 5.

prosperity of much of the region, the comparative personal freedom of the non-gentle population, gavelkind and the freedom to buy and sell all combined to produce a yeomanry that – while doubtless deferential to its social superiors – was in no way servile.[103] The gentry regularly did business with those below them. Around a third of fifteenth-century gentry partners in property transactions were yeomen. While their supervisors and most of their executors were of gentry or noble rank, many feoffees and executors of gentry wills were drawn from their lesser, non-gentle neighbours.

Family Structure

Social permeability may have been further facilitated by the structure of many Kentish gentry families. Several had branches that spanned the strata of the ranks of gentility and, sometimes, beyond. The family of Bettenham included esquires, gentlemen and at least one yeoman. They took their name from the village of Bettenham, near Cranbrook, where they had been resident since at least the mid-fourteenth century. The most prominent Bettenham was Stephen, an esquire and lord of the manors of Throwley and Sheerland in Pluckley and a county JP from 1389 to 1414, the year before he died. The other fifteenth-century male Bettenhams appear to have been gentlemen, with one exception, another Stephen, but a yeoman; in the 1480s he, and his gentlemanly namesake (Stephen the JP's grandson), were both tenants of the Roberts' manor of Glassenbury, near Cranbrook.[104] Examples of landowning families of several branches are provided by the Cobhams and the Culpepers.[105] The Bayhall and Preston Culpepers divided in the reign of Edward II, and by the early sixteenth century it was possible for two Culpeper branches to be allied by marriage without falling within the prohibited degrees of consanguinity.[106]

Kinship networks were sometimes tightly woven, and it was fairly common for two families to be related several times over by marriages contracted within the space of two or three generations. In addition to the Culpepers, the marriages of the Guildfords of Tenterden and Rolvenden in the Weald provide further examples. They married twice into the Pympes of Nettlestead, near Maidstone, and three times into the Hautes of Bishopsbourne in the Stour valley. Likewise,

103 Zell, 'Landholding and the Land Market', pp. 39–49.

104 L. B. Larking, 'Note on the Birthplace of Caxton', *Arch. Cant.* 5 (1863), 324–5; Jacob, ed., *Register of Henry Chichele* 2, p. 641; MS BL Harleian Charters 76/G/57, 77/F/15; MS TNA PRO C 1/41/48; MS CKS U 47/11/8; Roskell, *The Commons, 1386–1421*, 2, p. 219.

105 For the Cobhams, see above.

106 Thomas Culpeper esquire (d. 1515), of the Aylesford branch, was the husband of Margaret, daughter of Thomas Culpeper of Bedgebury. The couple shared a common ancestor in Sir John Culpeper, who died in 1413, but they were separated by five degrees of kinship, one degree beyond the most distant relationship; Hasted, *History* 4, pp. 436–7; Attree and Booker, 'The Sussex Colepepers'; E. Foss, *A Biographical Dictionary of the Judges of England* (London, 1870), pp. 180–1; P. Fleming, 'Culpeper family (per. c.1400–c.1540)', *ODNB*.

the Martyns of Graveney and the Appletons of Dartford were twice related by marriage.[107]

It is tempting to see gavelkind tenure as having been a major factor in the development of such characteristics. While the freedom to buy and sell land probably meant that repeated sub-division of estates was avoided, the compensation given to younger brothers and other co-parceners may have allowed them to found families close to the patrimonial holding, thereby encouraging the establishment of cadet branches (see Mate, this volume). However, the extent to which such factors operated among the gentry is debatable. The influence of gavelkind tenure was being lessened by two factors. The later Middle Ages saw the widespread employment of the use and other legal measures designed to give the landowner freedom to dispose of his property as he wished, regardless of the formal constraints implicit in its tenure. Second, a small number of prominent early Tudor landowners began to secure private acts of Parliament to disgavel their properties.[108] Another influence in family development may have been Kent's geography: the long coastline and relatively isolated regions such as the Weald may have encouraged repeated inter-marriage within a relatively small area.

Conclusions

Landed society in later medieval Kent shared many characteristics with its equivalents in many other counties, but there were also particular local characteristics that set it apart. The county's geography, forming a peninsula with land boundaries with only three other counties (including London), may have encouraged a certain insularity among its population, but this can easily be over-estimated. The Thames provided ready access to Essex, and Kent's links with continental Europe, the county's many ports, the London–Dover road and, of course, its proximity to London, ensured that its broad elite, at least, could not ignore the outside world. The contrasting geographical and agricultural regions within the county probably generated different regional cultures, which, in the case of the Downs, Weald and south-eastern marshes, did not respect county borders. The lack of resident magnate families, together with the importance of the Church and the gentry, meant that its political society could not conform to the classic 'bastard feudal' pattern based on magnate affinities, except insofar as the Crown generally acted as the greatest magnate of them all. While gavelkind and widespread personal freedom had some effect on elite society, they would have been more significant further down the social hierarchy, although the former at least may have played its part in creating distinctive family structures among the landed elite. Many of these factors are further explored elsewhere in this volume.

107 Fleming, 'Gentry of Kent', pp. 126–7.

108 For example, S. Cunningham, 'Guildord, Sir Richard (c.1450–1506)', *ODNB*.

11

Kent and National Politics 1399–1461*

DAVID GRUMMITT

In many ways Kent stood closer to the heart of the late-medieval English polity than any other county. Its proximity to the administrative and judicial centre of English government at Westminster; the presence within the county or close by of the king and his household for long periods; the importance of international trade, either through Sandwich or by the county's connexions to London; and, of central importance during the Lancastrian period, its strategic importance in the prosecution of the Hundred Years War, all ensured that events in Kent were inextricably linked with those wider political dramas played out on the national stage. It is the purpose of this essay to explore the relationship between local and national politics during the reigns of the Lancastrian kings. To what extent was the pattern of Kentish politics shaped by events in Westminster, the battlefields of France and elsewhere, and, in turn, how did local factors influence the outcome of national political struggles? I have divided the essay into four parts: first, the establishment and consolidation of the Lancastrian regime in Kent during the reigns of Henry IV and Henry V; second, Henry VI's minority and the struggle between the duke of Gloucester and Cardinal Beaufort; third, the rise of James Fiennes, later Lord Saye and Sele and the events surrounding Cade's Rebellion of 1450; and, finally, the 1450s and the collapse of the Lancastrian regime.

Although the internal politics of Kent were closely bound up with those of the wider polity, the county also had a strong sense and history of independence. Several factors contributed towards this, but principal among them must have been Kent's peculiar pattern of landholding. Throughout the late Middle Ages the county's largest landholder was the archbishop of Canterbury. Although often a major figure in national politics, the archbishop did not command the same kind of following as a lay magnate and his affinity did not exercise the same military or political cohesion as that of a magnate like John of Gaunt. This meant that the political community of Kent was more heterogeneous than in those of other counties, such as Devon where the Courtenay earls usually dominated local justice,

* This essay is indebted to the unpublished work of Peter Fleming and Malcolm Mercer. I am also grateful to the Trustees of the History of Parliament Trust for allowing me to draw upon my own unpublished work ahead of its publication in *The History of Parliament: The Commons, 1422–1461*.

lordship and politics.[1] Although several parliamentary peers held lands in Kent in 1400, none dominated its affairs or offered effective noble leadership of a gentry affinity within the county. In fact, it was leading members of the gentry, such as the Savages of Bobbing or Peckhams of Yalding in the fourteenth century or the Pecches of Lullingstone and Pympes of Pympe's Court in East Farleigh in the fifteenth century, who were the largest secular landlords. The practice of gavelkind (a Kentish customary tenure based upon partible inheritance) also militated against the accumulation of large estates (see Fleming, this volume).

Another important internal factor in shaping Kentish politics in the late Middle Ages was the confederation of the Cinque Ports. Although by 1400 the Kentish Ports (Dover, Hythe, New Romney, Sandwich and their members) had seen their economic and military importance wane from its thirteenth-century heyday, they still played a vital role in the relationship between local and national affairs. First, the office of warden and constable of Dover Castle, in the Crown's gift, afforded the opportunity for its incumbent to play a major role in the county's affairs. Second, control of the Ports, particularly Dover and Sandwich, was vital to the prosecution of the Hundred Years War, and, during the critical period 1459–60, was decisive in determining the fates of the Lancastrian and Yorkist claims to the throne. Dover, according to the author of *The Lybelle of Englysche Polycye*, was (along with its cross-channel neighbour English-held Calais) one of the 'two eyes' of the kingdom, while Sandwich was still a port of international significance. Finally, the influence of the Ports was felt by the widespread practice of admitting members of the Kentish political elite to their liberties so individuals might enjoy the barons' exemption from parliamentary taxation.[2]

The Establishment of the Lancastrian Regime 1399–1422

The accession of Henry Bolingbroke to the throne as Henry IV on 30 September 1399 did not lead to wholesale and immediate changes in Kent's political complexion.[3] Naturally, Richard II's partisans, Edward, duke of Aumerle, and Thomas, duke of Surrey, were removed from the county bench and replaced with the Lancastrian stalwarts, John, 3rd Lord Cobham (d. 1407), Bolingbroke's companion in exile, and Sir Thomas Erpingham, a Norfolk knight and chamberlain of the new king's household who was also appointed warden of the Cinque Ports.[4] Other members of the local elite, however, passed seamlessly from Ricardian to Lancastrian service. Sir Arnold Savage, perhaps the leading member

1 For the extent of the archbishop's landholding in the county, see F. R. H. Du Boulay, *The Lordship of Canterbury: An Essay on Medieval Society* (London, 1966). For Devon, see M. Cherry, 'The Courtenay Earls of Devon: The Formation and Disintegration of a Late Medieval Aristocratic Affinity', *Southern History* 1 (1971), 71–97.

2 K. M. E. Murray, *The Constitutional History of the Cinque Ports* (Manchester, 1935).

3 For Kent in Richard II's reign, see B. Webster, 'The Community of Kent in the Reign of Richard II', *Arch. Cant.* 100 (1984), 217–29.

4 *CPR 1399–1401*, p. 560; M. Mercer, 'The Administration of the Cinque Ports in the Early Lancastrian

of Richard's knightly affinity in the county, who had served as lieutenant of Dover Castle from at least 1397, was appointed to the first commission of the peace of the new reign and, by 1402, had become a member of the king's council. Another former member of Richard's household, John Freningham, was similarly appointed to the bench, represented the county in the first Parliament of the new reign after an absence from parliamentary affairs of eighteen years, and almost immediately became a member of Henry's council. In both cases, however, connexions with the Cobham family explain the apparent ease with which Freningham and Savage were accommodated within the new regime. Other members of the county elite had existing ties with the Lancastrian royal family: William Brenchley, Richard Clitheroe and John Culpepper, for example, had been members of John of Gaunt's affinity, although Clitheroe at least had also served Richard II. Indeed, of the Ricardian elite, only Sir William Burcester appears to have unable to accommodate himself to the new regime. Nevertheless, there are signs that Henry thought it necessary to secure the strategic military positions in the county. As well as Erpingham's appointment as warden of the Cinque Ports, Queenborough Castle was placed in the custody of Gaunt's former retainer, Sir Hugh Waterton, while the lieutenancy of Dover Castle (in effect the acting warden of the Ports during Epringham's long absences at court and council) was given to another Norfolk knight, Sir Robert Berney.[5]

During the first years of Lancastrian rule, however, the principal danger facing Kent was not unrest stirred by Ricardian loyalists; rather it was the threat of French raids and invasions that galvanised the local political community. Invasion threats occurred almost annually between 1400 and 1407, prompting commissions of array in 1399, 1402, 1403, 1405, 1406 and 1407 and the provisioning of Sandwich with royal artillery in 1404. The threat of French piracy in the Channel was also very real and in November 1405 the king himself was almost captured while making the journey between Queenborough and Leigh in Essex.[6] This external threat probably had the effect of militating against any possible tensions within the political community arising from the Lancastrian usurpation. In the commissions of array and the organisation of the county levies, local men worked alongside outsiders appointed to positions of local importance by the Crown, such as Erpingham and Berney, and recent arrivals in the county, such as Sir Thomas Clinton and William Rickhill.

Another factor which assisted in the creation of a politically stable Lancastrian elite in Kent was the disappearance, principally through their failure in the male line, of many established fourteenth-century gentry families and the emergence of new members of the gentry elite with strong connexions to the Lancastrian

Period', in *Peoples, Places and Perspectives: Essays on Later Medieval and Early Tudor England in Honour of Ralph A. Griffiths*, ed. K. Dockray and P. Fleming (Stroud, 2005), pp. 51–4.

5 Full biographical details on many of the individuals mentioned in this essay can be found in *The History of Parliament: The Commons, 1386–1421*, ed. J. S. Roskell, L. Clark and C. Rawcliffe, 4 vols (Stroud, 1993). For Waterton and Berney, see Mercer, 'Cinque Ports', pp. 52–3.

6 *CPR 1399–1401*, p. 211; *1401–05*, pp. 109, 115, 290–1, 478, 539; *1405–08*, pp. 231, 303; *CCR 1405–08*, pp. 359, 478; HMC IX, p. 138; Mercer, 'Cinque Ports', p. 52.

regime. The disappearance, during the first decade of the fifteenth century, of the Freninghams, Brenchelseas and Savages from an effective role in the affairs of the county opened the way for relative newcomers to take the lead. These men came to Kent from various places, from London to Devon, and for a variety of reasons, but a significant group came from the north of England and were linked together by friendship and service. Important among this group were the Lancashireman, Richard Clitheroe, John Darell from Yorkshire and Geoffrey Lowther from Cumberland. Three important connexions linked these individuals. The first was Lancastrian service, either to the king or to members of the royal family such as Humphrey, duke of Gloucester. The second was service to the archbishops of Canterbury. The final connexion, and one which drew them into a wider nexus with other members of the county's elite, was their involvement in the affairs of Rochester Bridge.[7]

The extent of this reordering of local political society in the first decade of the fifteenth century is apparent from the pattern of Kent's parliamentary representation. Twelve of the thirty-two known MPs who served in Henry IV and Henry V's Parliaments were the first generation of their families to have settled in Kent; for Richard II's reign the ratio had been three to twenty-two. Similarly, the proportion of knights to esquires serving as MPs for the county diminished, reflecting the influence of new families and those men with Lancastrian connexions: in Richard II's reign the ratio of knights to esquires elected was nine to thirteen; in Henry IV's reign five to eleven; and in Henry V's one to seven. Nevertheless, it would be wrong to assume royal interference in Kent's parliamentary affairs. The new men who rose to prominence in early Lancastrian Kent were fully integrated into local society, through marriage and through acting as feoffees and executors. There is no evidence of any royal (or, for that matter, magnate) interference in the process of election and the conclusion must be that by the end of Henry IV's reign Kentish political society was united in its support of the Lancastrian regime.[8]

The cohesion of the Kent political elite during the reigns of the first two Lancastrian kings is apparent in the county's apparent freedom from the rebellions and disorders that characterised other parts of the realm. Kentishmen were not involved in the pro-Ricardian rebellions early in Henry IV's reign and, perhaps surprisingly, there is no evidence that the Lollard rebellion led by Sir John Oldcastle in January 1414 enjoyed significant support in the county. Oldcastle had married in 1407–08 Joan, grand-daughter of John, 3rd Lord Cobham, and their seat at Cooling Castle had become a centre of local Lollardy. However, only three of the 162 known rebels were from Kent and the alleged conspiracy to seize the king and his brothers on Twelfth Night was revealed by a government spy.[9] Both the bishop of Rochester and archbishop of Canterbury

7 Roskell, *The Commons, 1386–1421* 2, pp. 598–601, 752–4. For Lowther, see L. Clark, ed., *The History of Parliament: The Commons, 1422–1461* (forthcoming).

8 Roskell, *The Commons, 1386–1421*, 1, pp. 453–7.

9 E. Powell, *Kingship, Law, and Society: Criminal Justice in the Reign of Henry V* (Oxford, 1989), pp. 149–61.

could apparently count on the support of local elites for the suppression of Lollardy within their dioceses. Although a commission of inquiry into treasons and felonies had to be issued in June 1404 and further commissions of *oyer et terminer* in 1408 and 1411, Kent appears to have been a relatively peaceful county in the opening years of the fifteenth century.[10]

The exception to this was piracy in the Channel carried out by the men of the Cinque Ports. This appears to have increased in scale and political consequence following the appointment of Henry, Prince of Wales, to the wardenship of the Ports in February 1409. First, it threatened to complicate England's position with regard to the ongoing struggle in France between the Burgundian and Armagnac factions, and, second, it challenged the Prince's drive at both a local and a national level to enforce royal justice. The prosecution of local men involved in piracy may have caused tensions between the elites of Dover and Sandwich and the prince's administration, but it appears that the Ports were fully reconciled to the Crown because of the renewal of the Hundred Years War once the Prince had acceded to the throne as Henry V. Successive wardens, Thomas, earl of Arundel and the king's brother, Humphrey, duke of Gloucester, were able to mobilise the men and resources of the Ports effectively in support of the king's campaigns.[11] In this the Ports mirrored the rest of Kentish society which was similarly mobilised in the royal war enterprise. Despite increasingly high levels of taxation and the continued predations of royal purveyors, by the end of Henry V's reign Kent's political elites had played a pivotal role in the success of the Lancastrian dynasty.

Gloucester, Beaufort and the Early Years of Henry VI

Henry V's premature death in August 1422 saw the accession of his nine-month-old son, Henry VI. During his lifetime Henry V had named his brother, Humphrey, duke of Gloucester '*tutelam et defensionem nostri filii carissimi principales*' and while Gloucester had interpreted this to mean the governance of the kingdom during the young king's minority, the council, led by his elder brother and regent of France, John, duke of Bedford, had refused to grant him this power. Duke Humphrey was forced to accept the lesser title of protector and defender of the realm and pre-eminence among the councillors. As Henry Beaufort, bishop of Winchester, an older and abler politician than Gloucester, built up a following in the council, Duke Humphrey saw his power and influence wane. Until the king came of age in 1437 domestic English politics were dominated by the efforts of Gloucester to secure the power and influence he thought rightfully his in the face of opposition from the Beauforts and Bedford.[12] As Gloucester was

10 *CPR 1401–05*, p. 431; *1405–08*, p. 417; *1408–13*, p. 318; M. Aston, *Lollards and Reformers* (London, 1984), pp. 78–81.

11 Mercer, 'Cinque Ports', pp. 55–62.

12 R. A. Griffiths, *The Reign of Henry VI* (London, 1981), pp. 28–45; J. Watts, *Henry VI and the Politics of Kingship* (Cambridge, 1996), pp. 112–22.

the most powerful lay figure in Kent at the beginning of the new reign, the county elite inevitably felt the repercussions of these national struggles.

Gloucester's position in Kent depended, above all, on his office of warden of the Cinque Ports. On his return from the Agincourt campaign in 1415 he had been appointed to command at Dover and in the following year the wardenship was confirmed to him for life. His landed base in the county was small: he acquired the lordship of Marden and Milton in 1406, the manor of Greenwich by 1426, and Bedford's manors of Penshurst, Havendencourt and Yenesfeld in 1438.[13] Nevertheless, Gloucester had an identifiable affinity within Kent, bound together principally through ties of military service. The most important member of Gloucester's Kentish affinity was probably Geoffrey Lowther, who served alongside him at Agincourt and was his deputy at Dover from 1417 until 1440. The French wars allowed Gloucester to develop further connexions among the Kent gentry, tapping into pre-existing networks of marriage and friendship. By 1422 the duke could count the Pympes, the Hautes, the Culpeppers, the Guildfords, the Brockhills, the Rickhills, Sir Reynold Cobham of Sterborough and William Clifford among his following in the county.[14] Gloucester's influence in Kent was most apparent in parliamentary elections. In politically sensitive Parliaments, like those of 1422, 1426 and 1432, the return of knights of the shire with close ties to Gloucester cannot have been coincidental. In February 1432 Gloucester demonstrated the opportunities that his position in Kent and the Cinque Ports afforded him to influence national politics when he seized Cardinal Beaufort's treasure at Sandwich en route to Calais. Beaufort had not secured a licence to export the treasure and Gloucester used the incident to attack the Cardinal on charges of *praemunire*. The Parliament which met between May and July that year saw the charges against Beaufort dropped, but the Cardinal agreed to enter into a bond for £6000 for the return of his treasure and temporarily returned to his diocese.[15]

It would be wrong, however, to present Gloucester as a dominant force within Kentish politics during Henry VI's minority, able to monopolise either parliamentary affairs or the dispensation of local justice. Other lords, notably Archbishop Chichele, also had influential followings and local connexions, such as those individuals involved in the administration of Rochester Bridge, militated against political polarisation.[16] Chichele's servants appears to have worked closely alongside Gloucester's, although it is not clear whether this was, as Roskell argued, because of the political affinity between the archbishop and the duke or because their servants were already connected locally. John Darell, for example, Chichele's steward and

[13] M. Mercer, 'Kent and National Politics, 1437–1534: The Royal Affinity and a County Elite' (unpublished PhD thesis, University of London, 1995), pp. 3–4.

[14] Roskell, *The Commons, 1386–1421* 3, pp. 254–5, 324–7; 4, pp. 151–2; Mercer, 'Kent', pp. 5–6.

[15] G. L. Harriss, *Cardinal Beaufort: A Study of Lancastrian Ascendancy and Decline* (Oxford, 1988), pp. 215–22.

[16] R. H. Britnell, 'Rochester Bridge, 1381–1530', in *Traffic and Politics: The Construction and Management of Rochester Bridge, AD 43–1993*, ed. N. Yates and J. M. Gibson (Woodbridge, 1994), pp. 93–106.

kinsman by marriage and the sheriff who returned Lowther and Reynold Pympe to Westminster in 1422, was already close friends with the former. Similarly, Nicholas Brockhill who had served with Gloucester in Normandy in 1417 had, by the early 1420s, entered archiepiscopal service. Chichele's servants, like Gloucester's, played an important role in county affairs. John Darrell was sheriff in 1422–23 and sat in the Parliaments of 1425, 1427 and 1429; William Burys of Halstead, a member of Chichele's council, sat in the Parliament of 1423 and served as sheriff in 1432–33; while Roger Honyton of Goudhurst, another servant of the archbishop since 1414, was appointed to the commission of peace in February 1422 and remained a member of the bench until March 1432.[17]

Equally, however, Gloucester's erstwhile enemies, the Beauforts, and his brother, Bedford, had their servants among the county elite. Beaufort's own property in the county was negligible (only the manors of Brabourne and Langley in Henry VI's reign). Nevertheless, by the late 1420s the Cardinal did have an identifiable affinity within Kent. It was of a similar nature to his affinity in other counties and was administrative rather than political. Thus during the 1420s and early 1430s there is no evidence that his servants clashed with Gloucester's or Chichele's men at a local level. The Beaufort affinity in Kent depended, like that of Gloucester, partly on connexions forged during the French wars. The Cardinal's associates, Richard Frogenhale, John Yerde, Richard Waller (later master of his household) and Sir Thomas Kyriell, had all served in Beaufort retinues in France.[18] This too gave them common ground with many of Gloucester's affinity and in times of military crisis, as in 1435–36, the gentry presented a united front serving together on commissions of array and in the election of parliamentary knights. Beaufort also developed important connexions with Canterbury, interceding on the city's behalf on more than one occasion during the 1430s.[19]

The years 1433–34 saw the partial eclipse of Gloucester's national political position, as Bedford returned from France and backed Beaufort's role in council and in the king's household, while in 1437 the king formally attained his majority, rendering obsolete any arguments over the duke's formal role on the council. In that year, Gloucester lost further influence by resigning as captain of Calais and the period between 1439 and 1441 witnessed his collapse as a force in local and national politics. In 1440 he incurred the king's wrath by openly opposing the release of the duke of Orleans and in the following year his wife, Eleanor Cobham (daughter of Sir Reynold) was accused of witchcraft and convicted of 'imagining' the king's death.[20] Even this, however, does not seem to have polarised Kentish politics. The 1430s had witnessed a gradual disintegration of Gloucester's local affinity. Bedford's chamberlain, Richard Wydeville, a Northamptonshire man

[17] Roskell, *The Commons, 1386–1421*, 2, pp. 752–5; 3, pp. 408–9. Biographies of Brockhill and Burys will appear in Clark, ed., *The Commons, 1422–1461*.

[18] Mercer, 'Kent', pp. 7–10.

[19] MS CCAL CC FA 1, fols 230, 250.

[20] R. A. Griffiths, *King and Country: England and Wales in the Fifteenth Century* (London, 1991), pp. 233–52.

who had purchased the manor of Mote near Maidstone, was appointed sheriff in November 1433 and served briefly as a JP, but as a man with long-standing local connexions (most importantly to the Hautes) and an impeccable military record he was more than acceptable to the rest of the Kentish political elite. Similarly, men not aligned with any great lord came to prominence in the county. The Londoner, Thomas Brown, appointed to the bench in 1436 and serving as MP and sheriff during the 1440s, had purchased the manor of Eythorne in 1427 and was a servant of the treasurer of England, Walter, Lord Hungerford. Similarly, Gervase Clifton, the illegitimate son of a wealthy Nottinghamshire landowner, had served in France before marrying Isabel, widow of the important Kentish landowner William Scott of Brabourne in 1433. This was due to the intervention of Isabel's kinsman Archbishop Kemp, a local man who had served previously as bishop of Rochester as well as chancellor of Normandy (where he had probably met Clifton). Clifton became a JP in 1437, served as sheriff in 1439–40 and sat in Parliament in 1439. More significantly, however, in 1444 he became Gloucester's deputy at Dover Castle and, two years later, the treasurer of the duke's household. Clifton is a good example, therefore, of the fluidity of political affiliations in Kent during the 1430s. Between 1433 and 1444 he was associated in turn with Kemp, the duke of York and Gloucester (as well as being chosen as knight of the shire in 1439 alongside Sir James Fiennes, a prominent member of the king's household); at a local level his connexions included the Cobhams, the Scotts and their Sussex relations, the Finches and Lewkenors.[21]

In some ways Kent political society during the first twenty years of Henry VI's reign reflected the wider national position. The two leading magnate connexions in the county were those of Gloucester and Chichele on one hand and the Beauforts and Bedford on the other. At times, in 1422, 1426 and 1432, national politics impacted directly upon affairs in Kent. However, despite this, there is no evidence of disorder at the parliamentary hustings or of major gentry quarrels which mirrored national political rivalries. Throughout the 1420s and 1430s Kent political society remained relatively harmonious and the county peaceful. The principal concern remained local stability and order, the defence of the county from the French and the prosecution of the war, a concern reflected in the number of prominent Kentishmen who had themselves played an active role in affairs across the Channel. The apparent harmony of Kentish politics into the mid-1440s makes Cade's Rebellion and its aftermath all the more extraordinary.

James Fiennes, the Household Circle and Cade's Rebellion

In the summer of 1450 the commons of Kent rose in rebellion. Led by Jack Cade, it has usually been presented as a particularly Kentish expression of wider national grievances: the domination of the king's government by a corrupt coterie

21 Biographies of Brown, Clifton and Wydeville will appear in Clark, ed., *The Commons, 1422–1461*.

of household officials led by William de la Pole, duke of Suffolk; high taxation to fund the war in France; and the subsequent sense of betrayal felt by the loss of Normandy. Contemporaries and more modern commentators have argued over whether the rising was spontaneous or engineered by Suffolk's political enemies, most notably Richard, duke of York. Attention has focused upon the activities of James Fiennes of Knole, from 1447 Lord Saye and Sele, warden of the Cinque Ports and the king's chamberlain, and of those of his affinity as indicative of the way in which 'normal' patterns of local government were displaced under the ineffective rule of Henry VI and self interest and 'covetise' replaced notions of 'commonweal' as the basis of political action. Assessments of Fiennes have been almost universally hostile. Since his summary execution at Cade's hands in London on 4 July 1450, he has been accused of extortion, of filling the shrievalty and other county offices with his servants and friends, of dominating the parliamentary elections in Kent and the Cinque Ports, of playing a part both in the murder of the duke of Gloucester at the Bury Parliament of 1447 and in the loss of Normandy. Indeed, the traditional account of the events of 1450 rests upon the malign influence both nationally and locally of Fiennes and his supposed patron Suffolk.[22]

James was the younger son of the Sussex landowner, Sir William Fiennes. With his elder brother, Sir Roger, he served in the French campaigns of Henry V and was present at the battle of Agincourt. By 1430 he had entered Henry VI's household and in 1438 became one of the esquires of the body in personal and intimate contact with the king. Meanwhile, he had purchased property in Kent and in 1433 he had been appointed to the county bench, first serving as sheriff three years later. Although not a native of the county, Fiennes and his family had close connexions with the Kentish political elite. The stained glass windows put into Nettlestead church by Reynold Pympe, probably sometime in the late 1420s, testify to the ties of kinship between the Fiennes and many of the leading Kentish families. As we have seen, local elites were willing to incorporate newly arrived men and there is no evidence that Fiennes encountered any opposition in his new responsibilities. In 1439 he was elected as knight of the shire for the first time and he was returned to every subsequent Parliament until 1447. More local office followed in the 1440s: in 1442–43 he briefly held the custody of Rochester Castle; in April 1443 he was granted the bailiffship of the archiepiscopal manor of Otford and the following year Archbishop Stafford confirmed him in this office; on 24 February 1447, immediately following Gloucester's sudden death, he was ennobled as Lord Saye and Sele and became warden of the Cinque Ports, underlining his position as the most powerful individual in Kent. At court he was associated with Suffolk regarding the king's foundations at Eton and King's College, Cambridge, but his position in the household was independent of Suffolk and he

22 I. W. M. Harvey, *Jack Cade's Rebellion of 1450* (Oxford, 1991), supplemented by Griffiths, *Henry VI*, pp. 610–49.

appears to have played no part in the negotiations, led by the duke, concerning the king's marriage and the truce of Tours.[23]

Fiennes, it is argued, stood at the apex of an identifiable court-based affinity in the county. According to Isabel Harvey, under his leadership 'the sheriffs and their underlings were corrupt, the choice of the county MPs managed, and the operation of the JPs grossly partial'.[24] In fact there is little evidence from the 1440s that this was the case; Harvey and other scholars' assessments are based mainly upon the indictments made in the aftermath of Cade's Rebellion.[25] The nature of the relationship between Fiennes and those individuals who allegedly comprised his circle – William Isle, Stephen Slegge, William Cromer, Robert Est and others – is far more elusive and there is little sign that these men incurred the hostility of their fellow gentry at the time. William Isle of Sundridge was a member of an established gentry family who was connected through marriage with the Freninghams, Pympes and Warners and who was also involved in the affairs of Rochester Bridge. His service as a JP from 1438 pre-dated any connexion with Fiennes, and his election as MP (in 1442) and his appointment to the shrievalty (in 1446) were to be expected for a man of his standing. William Cromer, on the other hand, clearly rose to prominence at a young age, serving as sheriff and MP while still in his early twenties, as an outcome of his marriage to Fiennes's daughter. While he may have been somewhat incompetent as a sheriff, there is no evidence that he deliberately exploited his position for his own benefit. It was, as the chroniclers noted, his kinship with Fiennes rather than his actions as sheriff of Kent that led to his murder in London on the same day as his father-in-law's execution. Of the four men mentioned above (all identified as 'great extorcioners and oppressors' by Cade), only Stephen Slegge, an Inns of Court-educated lawyer from Wouldham and Fiennes's closest associate, rose to enjoy office during the 1440s which was out of keeping with his social standing. Despite previously serving as undersheriff and escheator, he was an unusual choice as sheriff during the critical year from November 1448, a year in which he presided over the parliamentary elections in February 1449 when Cromer was returned to Westminster for a second time and he was himself elected as MP for Dover in a flagrant breach of the law which restricted serving sheriffs from sitting in the Commons. Indeed, 1448–49 may have witnessed the beginnings of the county elite's disenchantment with the regime in Westminster, of which Fiennes was an obvious representative, and this may have been exacerbated in November 1449 by the appointment of Cromer to his second shrievalty.[26]

Even if Cade's Rebellion did not represent the culmination of nearly a decade

23 A biography of Fiennes will appear in Clark, ed., *The Commons, 1422–1461*.

24 Harvey, *Cade*, p. 43.

25 R. Virgoe, 'Some Ancient Indictments in the King's Bench Referring to Kent, 1450–1452', in *Documents Illustrative of Medieval Kentish Society*, ed. F. R. H. Du Boulay, Kent Record Society 18 (Ashford, 1964), pp. 220–43.

26 Biographies of Cromer, Isle and Slegge will appear in Clark, ed., *The Commons, 1422–1461*. For Est's offices, see Harvey, *Cade*, pp. 40–1.

of grievances directed against Fiennes and his court clique, in 1450 Kent was clearly seething with discontent. The rebels' manifestos contain specifically local complaints, as well as those more general national ones relating to the processes of counsel and government. Two national events, however, had particular importance for the county. In April 1449 a fleet had been set forth for 'rebukyng of the robbeurs and privaters' then in the Channel, under the command of two Kentishmen, Gervase Clifton and Alexander Iden, and the Dartmouth man, Robert Wenyngton. Despite employing manpower and ships from the Cinque Ports, the fleet relied on two household esquires, Thomas Daniel and John Trevelyan, to provide much of the shipping. The expedition did not go as planned, however, and its actions became synonymous with the self-interest of the king's household men. Within a month of taking to the seas this fleet had captured the hundred-strong Bay fleet, comprising neutral Hanseatic, Flemish and Dutch vessels, off the Isle of Wight in a spectacular act of piracy. Wenyngton boastfully recorded his exploits in a letter to Daniel, but it seems that Iden and Clifton took no part in the venture. In any case, it was deeply unpopular in Kent and especially in the Cinque Ports and formed part of the rebels' complaints the following year.[27] The second event, acutely felt in Kent and across the south-east, was the worsening situation in the Hundred Years War. In November 1449 Parliament had assembled at Westminster determined to bring the duke of Suffolk to account for his alleged treason in the surrender of Maine and French successes in Normandy. Saved by the king's intervention, Suffolk was banished, but while en route to the continent he was seized and summarily beheaded on 2 May 1450, his body thrown ashore on Dover sands. Just two weeks earlier news had been received of Sir Thomas Kyriell's defeat at Formingny, and on 21 April the French had raided Queenborough Castle. When Caen capitulated on 24 June, the end was in sight for English-held Normandy. Before long Kent was awash with disaffected soldiers returning from France; popular verses circulated which linked Suffolk, Saye, Daniel and other household men with the defeat in France; and by the beginning of June the commons of Kent were organising themselves in military fashion for a march on London.[28]

It is easy to see why the loss of Normandy had so profound an effect on Kent. First, service in the Hundred Years War had been a defining feature of Kent's political elite since the beginning of Henry V's reign. The generation that had served at Agincourt and in the Norman garrisons of the 1420s appear to have passed this sense of military identity to the wider political community. Thus Sir William Pecche of Lullingstone was the first generation of his family to take an active role in the war when he accompanied Kyriell to Normandy in 1449, while

27 J. Gairdner, ed., *The Paston Letters*, 6 vols (London, 1904) 2, pp. 103–5; Harvey, *Cade*, pp. 56–7; G. von der Ropp, ed., *Hanserecesse von 1431–1476*, 3 vols (Leipzig, 1881), 3, pp. 402–6.

28 R. Virgoe, 'The Death of William de la Pole, Duke of Suffolk', in *East Anglian Society and the Political Community in Late Medieval England*, ed. C. Barron, C. Rawcliffe and J. T. Rosenthal (Norwich, 1997), pp. 247–58; M. Bhona, 'Armed Force and Civic Legitimacy in Jack Cade's Revolt, 1450', *English Historical Review* 118 (2003), 563–82.

the Beaufort associate Sir John Cheyne of the Isle of Sheppey accepted the difficult position of victualler of Calais in October 1451.[29] Second, the implication in the popular imagination of Suffolk and Fiennes in the death of Duke Humphrey and the surrender of Maine may have had the effect of alienating them and their closest followers from the mainstream of Kentish political society, many of whom had served Gloucester in Kent and in France.[30] Finally, Kent, like other south-eastern counties, suffered from the effects of returning soldiers and contemporary litigation includes numerous references to 'soldiers' acting as hired thugs and common criminals.[31]

Nevertheless, the Kentish political elite, if the pardons issued to the rebels on 6 and 7 July are a reliable guide, was conspicuous by its lack of active involvement in Cade's Rebellion. Sir John Cheyne was the only man of knightly rank to sue out a pardon and that probably on behalf of his tenants on the Isle of Sheppey, while only a handful of the squirearchy were pardoned.[32] Despite the difficulties of interpreting the evidence of the pardons, it seems clear that the majority of Cade's supporters were lesser gentry, yeomen, artisans and husbandmen. In fact, the rebellion was essentially popular and one in which the commons of Kent demonstrated an acute awareness of the realm's political problems and suggested remedies. This is clear from the language of the political poems and ballads in circulation around 1450 and from the rebels' petitions. If Suffolk's murderers really did state that 'they knew well the crown of England, saying that the aforesaid Crown was the community of the realm and that the community of the realm was the Crown of that realm' before decapitating the hapless duke, then they revealed the political consciousness that energised the Kentish commons on their march to London. Suffolk's murder was the spark that kindled the flames of rebellion (and William Cromer's ill-judged threat to destroy the county and turn it into a 'wylde fforest' in retribution must also have had a galvanising effect), but Cade's Rebellion was primarily a protest against the government of an ineffective king, dominated by corrupt counsel, that had led England to shameful defeat and directly threatened the security and livelihood of the men of Kent.[33]

The rebels' petitions reveal a combination of local and national political grievances. Three petitions are extant, all of them in contemporary hands. The prominence given to national issues, however, reveals that the uprising stemmed principally from perceived failures at Westminster, rather than the local corruption of Fiennes and his friends. In the earliest petition, royal debts and excessive taxation, the operation of counsel, the king's household and the loss of Normandy

29 Biographies of Cheyne, Kyriell and Pecche will appear in Clark, ed., *The Commons, 1422–1461*.

30 Harvey, *Cade*, pp. 48–52; MS TNA PRO KB 27/755, rex rot. 3.

31 A. Curry, 'The Loss of Lancastrian Normandy: An Administrative Nightmare?', in *The English Experience in France c.1450–1558: War, Diplomacy and Cultural Exchange* (Aldershot, 2002), pp. 44–5.

32 *CPR 1446–52*, pp. 338–74.

33 Virgoe, 'Suffolk', p. 253; D. Grummitt, 'Deconstructing Cade's Rebellion: Discourse and Politics in the Mid Fifteenth Century', in *The Fifteenth Century VI: Identity and Insurgency in the Late Middle Ages*, ed. L. Clark (Woodbridge, 2006), pp. 110–11.

provided the context for local complaints over purveyance, parliamentary elections, farms of royal land in the county, and the privileges of the Cinque Ports. In the second petition it was the nature of royal government, the murder of Gloucester and the return of the duke of York to political influence that made up the bulk of the grievances; there is nothing specifically Kentish about the document now in Magdalen College, Oxford. The final petition demanded the punishment of the 'fals traitours' and Suffolk's 'false progeny and afynyte' who murdered Gloucester and subverted the commonwealth. The charge of extortion levelled against Slegge, Cromer, Isle and Est was made specifically with regard to purveyance and the Statute of Labourers, rather than as a generalised indictment of local government in the county during the 1440s.[34]

Cade's rebels entered London on 3 July. They soon began to pillage and on the night of 5 July the citizens forced them to withdraw after a fierce battle on London Bridge. Five days later Cade was proclaimed a traitor (while his followers were pardoned) and he was captured and died of his wounds two days later. Royal commissioners sat in several Kentish towns during the summer, hearing indictments against Fiennes and his followers as well as a host of unrelated charges, but no punishment, it seems, was meted out to the 'great extorcioners' and their followers. The rebellion, and the return from Ireland of Richard, duke of York, dominated the Parliament which assembled at Westminster in November, but already the Crown was seeking to shape the memory and meaning of the rebellion.[35] Cade's name remained a powerful force in the popular Kentish imagination and there were further outbreaks of trouble, resurrecting his appeal (and those of rebels of 1381), throughout the early 1450s. It did not, however, result in a politically polarised county; indeed, the elite cooperated with the Crown against the rebels in restoring order at a local level. When the king made a judicial visitation to the county in the summer of 1451, he was met at Blackheath by a group of Kentishmen, stripped to the waist with halters around their necks, in a symbolic act of submittal and reconciliation to the royal will. While one chronicler referred to the 'harvyste of hedys' visited upon the county that summer, in reality retribution was limited, highlighting the fact that Cade's Rebellion had been a spontaneous, popular reaction to the loss of Normandy and not a more general challenge to local elite politics and culture.[36]

Richard, Duke of York and the Collapse of the Lancastrian Regime

By the end of 1450 Cade's rebellion had taken on a new significance in the developing struggle between the Crown and its leading critic, Richard, duke of York, which transformed its original purpose and aims. Because of the importance of

34 Harvey, *Cade*, pp. 186–91.

35 Grummitt, 'Deconstructing Cade', pp. 115–16.

36 J. Gairdner, ed., *The Historical Collections of a Citizen of London in the Fifteenth Century*, Camden Society, new series 17 (London, 1876), p. 197; Harvey, *Cade*, pp. 152–3.

the rebellion in shaping York's opposition to the Crown and the county's strategic position, Kent played an important role in the events leading to the Yorkist victory in 1461. York's enemies would claim that he had incited the uprising to further his own political gaols and the rebels had indeed called for a greater role for him in royal government. Nevertheless, there is no independent evidence to suggest that the duke was involved in raising the commons of Kent in the summer of 1450. York did, however, soon seek to use the rebellion to his own ends and, as early as September 1450, one of his bills presented to the king bemoaned the lack of punishment of the royal servants indicted before the Kentish commissioners. York held little land in the county, but in early 1452 his campaign to remove his rival, Edmund Beaufort, duke of Somerset, from court was partly directed towards a Kentish audience. It seems likely that York sought to exploit lingering disquiet over the loss of Normandy and perhaps appeal to those who had served in France. In the letters he sent to Canterbury, Maidstone and Sandwich in February he emphasised Somerset's disastrous handling of the final campaigns in Normandy and the restoration of good government both locally and nationally. If the duke's intention was to raise the political community of Kent behind him he failed. When he drew up his host at Brent Heath near Dartford on 1 March the only important local landowners to join him were Edward, Lord Cobham, and Sir William Pecche. York was forced into a humiliating submission which left him disengaged from national politics for some two years, Cobham was imprisoned in Berkhamstead Castle, while Pecche chose to redeem himself through military service in Gascony.[37]

The mid-1450s witnessed a period of consolidation among the Kentish elite after the turmoil of 1449–52. One of the most important figures in this was Humphrey Stafford, duke of Buckingham, who became warden of the Cinque Ports in 1451. Buckingham was already a landowner in the county with estates around Tonbridge and used his position at Dover to incorporate important local figures such as Gervase Clifton and Sir Thomas Kyriell into his service. He also brought some of his own servants from the midlands into the county and men with pre-existing Stafford connexions, like Thomas and William Hexstall, Richard Witherton, Walter Moyle and Richard Bruyn, became important figures both in the administration of the county and the Cinque Ports.[38] York's two protectorates seem to have had little impact on the government of the shire or Ports and there is little evidence of any Yorkist–Lancastrian rivalry in Kent before 1459. One incident which has been interpreted as symptomatic of national conflicts is the disputed parliamentary election of 1455. On 5 July that year the council instructed

37 J. L. Watts, 'Polemic and Politics in the 1450s', in *The Politics of Fifteenth-Century England: John Vale's Book*, ed. M. L. Kekewich, C. Richmond, A. F. Sutton, L. Visser-Fuchs and J. L. Watts (Stroud, 1995), pp. 12–15, 17–20; Grummitt, 'Deconstructing Cade', pp. 112–14; P. Johnson, *Duke Richard of York, 1411–1460* (Oxford, 1988), pp. 107–24.

38 *CPR 1446–52*, pp. 331, 473; C. Rawcliffe, *The Staffords, Earls of Stafford and Dukes of Buckingham 1394–1521* (Cambridge, 1978), pp. 191, 223, 235. Biographies of the Hextalls, Moyle and Bruyn will appear in Clark, ed., *The Commons, 1422–1461*.

the sheriff, Sir John Cheyne, to insure the 'said shire have theire free election' to Parliament. Cheyne, it was later alleged, returned the names of Sir Thomas Kyriell and Sir Gervase Clifton having erased that of the rightfully-elected knight of the shire, Richard Culpepper. In reality, rather than being an attempt to insure MPs favourable to York at the forthcoming Parliament, Cheyne's actions were probably motivated by his desire to see the finances of Calais settled. Cheyne, victualler of Calais, and Clifton, treasurer there, had both fallen foul of the recent ordinance requiring them to render account for their Calais offices. The large debts owed to them in their official capacity and the sums they themselves owed to their creditors had prevented them from so doing and both men were anxious to secure parliamentary pardons and the settlement of the garrison's arrears.[39]

In the crisis years 1459–61 Kent would play a vital role: Richard Neville, earl of Warwick, who had been captain of Calais from 1455, built up a following in the Cinque Ports and when the Yorkist earls landed at Sandwich on 26 June 1460 they were unimpeded by the men of Kent during their march on London. Several factors explain the county's acceptance of the Yorkist earls' political programme and the eventual accession of Edward, earl of March, to the throne as Edward IV in March 1461. Probably the most important of these was the failure of the Lancastrian regime to defend the county. In August 1457 a French force had raided Sandwich, killing the mayor and causing widespread damage. The invaders were eventually repelled by Kyriell and the county levies, but the event encouraged local men, especially the barons of the Cinque Ports, to look to Warwick for protection. Warwick's campaign of piracy from his Calais base in 1458–59 clearly proved popular among the Portsmen.[40] Second, Yorkist propaganda continued the familiar themes voiced by the rebels of 1450 and sought to identify their programme with the grievances of the Kentish political community in the broadest terms. Warwick's Calais manifesto in the autumn of 1459 argued that the disorder caused by Lancastrian misgovernment would encourage the French to attack, an implicit reference to the raid on Sandwich two years before. More explicitly, in June 1460, the Yorkists resurrected one of Cade's petitions and published it as the 'Articles of the commons of Kent at the coming of the Yorkist lords'. The anti-Lancastrian ballad pinned to the gates of Canterbury at the same time reveals the support the Yorkist earls enjoyed among the political community of Kent and that this support arose principally from the same dissatisfaction with the Lancastrian regime at a national level which had formed the core of Cade's grievances.[41] But unlike in 1450, in 1460 the county elite supported the popular opposition to the government. In June the earls had been guaranteed safe passage to London by the defection of Robert Horne, John Scott and John Fogg at

39 MS TNA PRO E 13/146, rots. 11–11d, 36–36d, 43, 46d; Johnson, *York*, p. 161; Griffiths, *Henry VI*, p. 749.

40 M. Hicks, *Warwick the Kingmaker* (Oxford, 1998), pp. 138–48; Griffiths, *Henry VI*, pp. 815–16.

41 Watts, 'Politics and Polemic', pp. 26–31; W. Marx, ed., *An English Chronicle 1377–1461: A New Edition* (Woodbridge, 2003).

Canterbury. Other leading figures to join the Yorkist ranks were Lords Cobham, Abergavenney and Saye and Sele, Sir Thomas Kyriell and Fogg's father-in-law, William Haute, Sir William Pecche and John Guildford. Only a handful remained loyal to the Crown: Sir Gervase Clifton and Sir Thomas Brown joined the defence of the Tower of London against the Yorkists in July, the latter losing his life for his efforts, while Sir John Cheyne apparently retained his Beaufort loyalties and was removed from the Yorkist-dominated commission of the peace in December. It is clear that Kent was a Yorkist stronghold in 1460–61, a fact not lost on contemporary commentators.[42]

Why had Kent's political elite deserted the Lancastrian crown in 1460 when they had so steadfastly stood against Cade's rebels ten years earlier? From the late 1430s the Crown had developed close links with the Kentish gentry, establishing itself, in a way, as a surrogate noble presence within the county. The household connexions of James Fiennes are well known, but other important local figures, outside Fiennes's immediate circle, had similar close ties to the king and his household. Sir John Cheyne, John Warner, Thomas Brown, William Say and Thomas Walter (both MPs for Canterbury in the 1440s) and Stephen Knight, a Faversham man who was escheator in 1449–50, had all become members of the royal household by 1450.[43] In 1450 these men had supported Henry VI despite perhaps sympathising with some of the grievances expressed by Cade. In 1460, however, the Kent elite deserted the Crown. Deprived of effective royal leadership at both a local and national level and with the effects of Henry VI's misgovernment made manifest by the raid on Sandwich, they turned to the Yorkist earls and their programme of reform, accepting their noble leadership of Kentish political society. Under Edward IV this was transformed into an effective royal affinity within the county.

The Lancastrian period demonstrated the importance of Kent within the national polity and the dynamic relationship between local and national politics. The proximity of the centre of political and governmental power at Westminster combined with the county's strategic position, especially after the renewal of the Hundred Years War by Henry V, to ensure that Kent and its political community was intimately involved in the major events of the early fifteenth century. The particular nature of Kentish political society, especially the lack of dominant noble leadership for much of the period, also ensured that the county's reaction to events was less predictable and potentially more volatile than for those areas of the country in which local society was effectively constrained by a strong royal or magnate presence. In 1450 and 1460 Kent's political society in its broadest sense made its voice heard in national politics in ways that determined the fate of the Lancastrian dynasty.

42 Harvey, *Cade*, pp. 183–5; Mercer, 'Kent', pp. 68–70; Griffiths, *Henry VI*, pp. 859–62.

43 Mercer, 'Kent', pp. 19, 21–3. Biographies of Knight, Say, Walter and Warner will appear in Clark, ed., *The Commons, 1422–1461*.

12

Kent and National Politics, 1461–1509*

MALCOLM MERCER

On 22 February 1462 a royal grant was made to the vicar of Ashford for the provision of two chaplains and two secular clerks to celebrate divine service for those who had lost their lives at the battles of Northampton, St Albans and Towton. Amongst the ranks of the dead were numbered many Kentishmen. The prime mover behind this act of remembrance was Sir John Fogg of Repton in Ashford, one of the most influential men in Yorkist Kent.[1] Fogg had been amongst the first men to join the Yorkist earls when they arrived in Kent in the summer of 1460. Now, less than a year after Edward IV's dramatic victory at Towton, peace had largely returned to southern England and Fogg took time to reflect on recent events and to remember friends and kinsmen who had fallen in battle. Kentishmen had played a fundamental part in securing the Yorkist victory in 1461 and figured prominently on the national stage thereafter.[2] As David Grummitt has shown in the previous essay, Kentish politics during the first half of the fifteenth century reflected trends on the national stage very closely. This essay will take the story a stage further by exploring political events within the shire during the Yorkist, Ricardian and early Tudor periods. Did those trends identified in the early fifteenth century continue to impact on local affairs thereafter? With this in mind, this essay has been divided into five sections: first, the establishment of the Yorkist regime in Kent, 1461–69; second, Edward IV, Warwick the Kingmaker and the restoration of Henry VI, 1470–71; third, the consolidation of royal authority, 1471–83; fourth, the usurpation of Richard III, 1483–85; and finally, the battle of Bosworth and the creation of the Tudor regime, 1485–1509.

* I would like to thank Peter Fleming and David Grummitt for all their advice and assistance with this essay as well as the Trustees of the History of Parliament Trust for being able to cite a number of their unpublished biographies.

1 *CPR 1461–67*, p. 76.

2 For example, J. S. Davies, ed., *An English Chronicle of the Reigns of Richard II, Henry IV, Henry V, and Henry VI*, Camden Society, original series 64 (1856), pp. 90–1, 95; J. Gardiner, ed., *Historical Collections of a Citizen of London*, Camden Society, new series 17 (1876), p. 206; J. A. Giles, ed., *Chronicles of the White Rose of York* (London, 1845), p. 7.

The Establishment of the Yorkist Regime 1461–71

In the short-term, the political settlement in Kent reflected the Yorkist regime at the centre where the new dynasty and their principal supporter, Richard Neville, earl of Warwick, worked closely together. In an astute move Edward IV appointed Warwick constable of Dover and warden of the Cinque Ports in May 1461. The earl already enjoyed widespread popular support in the county and his role in bringing over the Kentishmen had been instrumental in securing a Yorkist victory.[3] During the course of the decade Warwick was probably able to benefit from this popularity by recruiting a section of the local gentry into his service. The earl already enjoyed a close association with Henry Aucher of Newenden. Amongst those he now employed was John Guildford of Rolvenden, who became his lieutenant of Dover Castle from about 1465.[4] Since Warwick's uncle, Edward Neville, Lord Abergavenny, was already a force in Kent, the Nevilles now formed an influential power bloc in this strategically important region of the county.[5]

Political leadership within the county, however, fell to Sir John Fogg and Sir John Scott. Along with Robert Horne, a casualty at Towton, they had defected to the Yorkist earls at Canterbury at the end of June 1460. This had signalled a widespread desertion by the Kentish elite of the Lancastrian regime as many leading figures swelled the ranks of Yorkist forces as they made their way to London (see Grummitt, this volume).[6] Within a short space of time Fogg and Scott rose to prominence within the Yorkist establishment as treasurer and controller of the royal household respectively. The benefits of being on the winning side became obvious as each received various grants of royal patronage inside and outside the county. Fogg, already emerging as the senior partner, obtained the lion's share. He received the constableship of Rochester Castle, the manors of Tonford and Dane that had formerly belonged to the Lancastrian loyalist, Sir Thomas Brown, and the keeping of Hothfield manor. Meanwhile Scott secured the reversion of Chilham Castle and the keeping of the royal manor of Huntingfield.[7]

In the years immediately after 1461 a significant group of Kentishmen also found employment within the royal household, many of whom had no identifiable traditions of service to the Crown. Some had been early supporters of the Yorkists like Sir William Pecche. Pecche's sympathies towards Richard, duke of York had

3 *CPR 1461–67*, p. 45. See also M. Hicks, *Warwick the Kingmaker* (Oxford, 1998), pp. 193–5.

4 M. Mercer, 'Kent and National Politics, 1437–1534: The Royal Affinity and a County Elite' (unpublished PhD thesis, University of London, 1995). For further reflections on Guildford, see M. Mercer, 'A Forgotten Kentish Rebellion, September–October, 1470', *Arch. Cant.* 122 (2002), 145. Warwick's attitude towards the Ports is not done justice in Hicks, *Warwick*, p. 248. It is more likely that he took a keen interest in connections between the Ports and his base at Calais.

5 Mercer, 'Kent and National Politics, 1437–1534', p. 90.

6 W. G. Searle, ed., *Christ Church, Canterbury, I. The Chronicle of John Stone, Monk of Christ Church 1415–1471, II. Lists of the Deans, Priors and Monks of Christ Church, Canterbury*, Cambridge Antiquarian Society 34 (Cambridge, 1902), p. 79; C. L. Schofield, *The Life and Reign of Edward IV*, 2 vols (London, 1923) 1, pp. 76–7.

7 Mercer, 'Kent and National Politics, 1437–1534', pp. 91–2.

been evident as early as 1452 when he had turned out in support of the duke at Dartford. He now became one of the king's carvers and was granted an annuity of £40 from the revenues of Kent.[8] A key development in Kentish politics, however, was the creation of a large body of royal annuitants between 1461 and 1463. There is no evidence that a similar number of annuitants had existed during the Lancastrian era.[9] It was an interesting, but short-lived, experiment in local political management. Elsewhere in the country, the king's need to win over former Lancastrian enemies to his cause had already limited the number of attainders and forfeitures in comparison to other areas of the country. Such had been the support in Kent that there had been no obvious enemies to win over. Nevertheless, Edward still recognised the need to reward those who had supported his cause. Among those who received grants were a cross-section of the leading families including Sir William Haute, Thomas and Ralph St Leger, John Guildford, John Digges and John Isaak.[10]

Members of this newly-created royal affinity dominated the local administrative machinery from the very beginning of Edward's reign. The royal affinity was appointed wholesale to the commission of the peace, although after 1464 the size of the bench was systematically reduced with Fogg, Scott, Pecche and Haute remaining its most important members.[11] Similarly, sheriffs during the 1460s included Sir John Scott, Sir William Pecche and Sir William Haute.[12] The reliance on a pool of key supporters is most evident in the appointment of Pecche. In November 1461 he was selected as sheriff of Kent, and then, most unusually, in September the following year he was formally granted the office, along with the custody of Canterbury Castle, with £40 per annum until such times as lands to the same value should be entailed upon him. This broke with established practice. Sheriffs were normally replaced every year. It would appear that Kent remained unsettled and that Edward regarded Pecche as the best person to enforce royal rule.

For much of the 1460s the Yorkist royal affinity within the county avoided popular criticism.[13] The petition brought during the early years of this decade against Pecche by Thomas Waren, citizen and armourer of London, was typical of the complaints made against local officials. Waren complained that Pecche had falsely accused him of breaking into Pecche's residence at Lullingstone and stealing his goods, in particular a helmet inlaid with 'precious stones and pearls set in silver to the value of £40'. Such was the 'might of the said Sir William' that

8 Ibid., pp. 92–3. A full biography of Pecche will appear in L. Clark, ed., *The History of Parliament: The Commons, 1422–1461* (forthcoming).

9 Mercer, 'Kent and National Politics, 1437–1534', pp. 92–5.

10 C. Ross, *Edward IV* (London, 1974), pp. 64–71; C. Carpenter, *The Wars of the Roses: Politics and the Constitution, c.1437–1509* (Cambridge, 1997), pp. 158–63; *CPR 1461–67*, pp. 49, 215.

11 *CPR 1461–67*, p. 566: *CPR 1467–77*, pp. 617–18.

12 *List of Sheriffs for England and Wales*, PRO Lists and Indexes 9 (1898), p. 68.

13 For popular criticism levelled against Lancastrian servants, see D. Grummitt, 'Deconstructing Cade's Rebellion: Discourse and Politics in the Mid Fifteenth Century', in *The Fifteenth Century VI: Identity and Insurgency in the Late Middle Ages*, ed. L. Clark (Woodbridge, 2006), pp. 107–22.

Waren had been unable to receive justice.[14] However, the effectiveness of Pecche was soon brought into question after he was unable to catch the gang who had murdered William Isle in September 1463. It may be this failure that explained his replacement as sheriff the following month by John Digges and by the king's personal visit to the county.[15]

In 1464 the structure of Kentish politics was fundamentally altered by the king's marriage to Elizabeth Wydeville, daughter of the former Lancastrian dissident, Richard Wydeville, Lord Rivers. Although remaining loyal to the Lancastrian cause until the battle of Towton in March 1461, Rivers and his sons had grown weary of their Scottish exile after the Lancastrian defeat and quickly made their peace with Edward IV. This had paved the way for their political rehabilitation. A royal marriage cannot have been anticipated, however, even by Lord Rivers. Nevertheless, its repercussions were to be felt until Henry Tudor seized the throne in 1485.[16] The Wydevilles were kinsmen of the Hautes and Foggs and already enjoyed long-established ties within Kent. Their prominence at court now served to shift the balance of power in Kent increasingly in the direction of the Wydeville, Fogg and Haute families. Having chosen wisely in 1460–61 and followed Fogg's example, the Hautes were able to capitalise even further on their status as the queen's cousins. Sir William Haute was created a knight of the Bath in 1465 along with his cousins, Richard and John Wydeville. Towards the end of the decade, Haute's brothers, James and Richard, emerged as leading officials within the queen's household and that of her daughter, Princess Elizabeth.[17] Unfortunately for the Wydevilles, their growing political prominence coincided with an increasing sense of disillusionment with Edward IV's government. In many respects 1465–66 was the high point of his first reign. To some extent he had been learning on the job as stability was gradually restored to the kingdom. By 1467, though, Parliament was drawing the king's attention to an increase in general lawlessness. Disagreements between his leading supporters, and the 'heavy lordship' of his supporters in certain regions had begun to fuel popular unrest. Disturbances were reported as far apart as Yorkshire, the midlands, the Isle of Wight and Kent.[18]

14 MS TNA PRO C 1/45/291. The date of this case could be between 1460 and 1465 for Pecche received a pardon on 3 February 1465; *CPR 1461–67*, p. 423.

15 MS TNA PRO KB 9/50, m. 12.

16 J. R. Lander, 'Marriage and Politics in the Fifteenth Century: The Nevilles and the Wydevilles', *Bulletin of the Institute of Historical Research* 36 (1963), 119–52; M. A. Hicks, 'The Changing Role of the Wydevilles in Yorkist Politics to 1483', in *Patronage, Pedigree and Power in Later Medieval England*, ed. C. D. Ross (Gloucester, 1979), pp. 60–86.

17 'Annales rerum anglicarum', in J. Stevenson, ed., *Letters and Papers Illustrative of the Wars of the English in France*, Rolls Series, 2 vols (1864) 2 (2), p. 784; *CPR 1467–77*, p. 86; A. R. Myers, 'The Household of Queen Elizabeth Wydeville, 1466–7', *Bulletin of the John Rylands Library* 1 (1967–68), 450; R. Somerville, *History of the Duchy of Lancaster*, 2 vols (1953–70) 1, p. 604. A. F. Sutton, 'The Hautes of Kent', *The Ricardian* 6 (1982), 54–5; P. W. Fleming, 'The Hautes and their "Circle": Culture and the English Gentry', in *England in the Fifteenth Century: Proceedings of the 1986 Harlaxton Symposium*, ed. D. Williams (Woodbridge, 1987), pp. 85–102.

18 Ross, *Edward IV*, pp. 119–20.

That Kent, a bastion of the Yorkist crown, now found itself thrust into the political limelight might at first seem puzzling. The answer, however, lies within the context of the deteriorating relationship between Edward IV and Warwick, coupled with an upsurge in Lancastrian plotting from abroad. At what point Warwick turned against Edward IV is unclear. As the Wydevilles' star had waxed, so Warwick's had waned. Nevertheless, his increasing resentment found one outlet in Kent where Neville tenants, probably from Lord Abergavenny's estates at Birling and Mereworth, attacked Rivers's residence at the Mote in Maidstone in January 1468. Warwick might also have been behind a minor insurrection in Sandwich that same year.[19] To add to the increasing uncertainity, a Lancastrian agent called John Cornelius was captured in June 1468 at Queenborough on the Isle of Sheppey, just off the north Kent coast. He was found to be carrying letters from Queen Margaret to potential sympathisers. After an investigation, a number of arrests were made, including Sir Gervase Clifton, Sir John Scott's step-father.[20]

In late June 1469 Warwick and the king's ambitious but unreliable brother, George, duke of Clarence were briefly able to seize power. Having successfully appealed to anti-Wydeville and anti-court sentiments in Kent they were able to gather together a substantial force of lesser gentry and yeomanry and detain Edward IV. Their hold on the reins of power was short-lived and within the space of a couple of months the king had been released. Although they had controlled the king's person, they could not maintain law and order. Undeterred, Warwick and Clarence were again implicated in rebellion in 1470. After being linked to Sir Robert Welles's Lincolnshire rising they fled across the Channel and made their way to the court of King Louis XI of France. Louis engineered a reconciliation between Warwick and Margaret of Anjou in which they entered into an agreement to restore Henry VI to the throne. On 17 September Warwick, Clarence, and the Lancastrian partisans, John de Vere, earl of Oxford, and Jasper Tudor, earl of Pembroke, landed in Devon. Kent was by now in a state of political turmoil. Edward was clearly unsure upon whom he could rely. No instructions were issued to the sheriff, John Brumston. Instead, they were apparently sent directly to local gentry to resist any rebel landing. Their effectiveness can only be doubted.[21] In fact, news of the landing in the West Country provoked violent unrest across the shire and there are hints that two of Warwick's supporters there, John Guildford and Henry Aucher, were part of a co-ordinated attempt by the earl of Warwick to

19 Jean De Waurin, *Anchiennes Cronicques d'Engleterre*, ed. E. Dupont, Societe de l'Histoire de France, 3 vols (Paris, 1858–63), 3, pp. 193–4; Ross, *Edward IV*, pp. 119, 124–5. For some of those tried in the summer and autumn of 1468, see MS TNA PRO KB 27/829 rex rot. 16; 830 rex rot. 11d.

20 'Annales rerum anglicarum', pp. 789–90; Schofield, *Edward IV* 1, pp. 454–62; M. A. Hicks, 'The Case of Sir Thomas Cook, 1468', *English Historical Review* 93 (1978), 82–96; A. F. Sutton, 'Sir Thomas Cook and his "Troubles": An Investigation', *Guildhall Studies in London History* 3 (1978), 85–108; P. Holland, 'Cook's Case in History and Myth', *Historical Research* 61 (1988), 21–35; K. Dockray, 'The Yorkshire Rebellions of 1469', *The Ricardian* 85 (1983), 246–57.

21 P. Holland, 'The Lincolnshire Rebellion of March 1470', *English Historical Review* 103 (1988), 849–69; Schofield, *Edward IV*, 1, pp. 511–39; Mercer, 'Forgotten Kentish Rebellion', 143–51.

exert pressure on London's governors. A large force of Kentishmen spearheaded by Aucher broke into Southwark and the surrounding suburbs, allegedly stole the goods of Sir William Brandon, marshal of the Marshelsea prison, and ransacked the property of Dutch and Flemish merchants. In the meantime, Edward IV had been in Yorkshire suppressing uprisings there. After discovering that John Neville, marquess of Montagu, had deserted the king's cause for that of his brother, Warwick, the king abandoned his troops, narrowly avoided capture by the marquess at Doncaster, and escaped by ship from Bishop's Lynn to the Netherlands. It is likely that a small band of followers, including Fogg, accompanied Edward into exile.

Edward IV, Warwick the Kingmaker and the Restoration of Henry VI

Warwick entered London in triumph on 6 October 1470, assuming the position of lieutenant of the realm. From the outset the restored regime of Henry VI, known as the Readeption, was fatally flawed. It depended on an uneasy and fragile grouping of Warwick's supporters, former Lancastrians and moderate Yorkists. In Kent, Warwick relied on the Guildford connection to manage affairs. John Guildford had been Warwick's lieutenant at Dover Castle since about 1465 and despite his temporary replacement by Sir John Scott in April 1470, appears to have exercised the office during the Readeption as well. Guildford had been in close communication with the earl during 1469 and 1470.[22] Henry Aucher was appointed sheriff in November 1470. Two benches of JPs were commissioned during the Readeption, on 21 December 1470 and 28 January 1471.[23] Sir William Haute, Sir Thomas Vaughan, Sir William Pecche, Sir John Fogg and Sir John Scott were removed. Archbishop Bourchier was retained, the only concession to Yorkist sentiment. As the greatest landowner in Kent his removal would only have served to de-stablise local structures of power. The most significant members of the bench were Sir John Guildford, Sir Richard Frogenhale and George Brown. Guildford's appointment was self-evident. The inclusion of the veteran soldier, Frogenhale, a former lieutenant of Edmund Beaufort, duke of Somerset, reflected the narrowness of local support as the regime looked to exploit residual Lancastrian sentiment. Brown clearly hoped for the restoration of his lands and position in local society. He was the son of Sir Thomas Brown who had been executed for his role in the Lancastrian defence of the Tower of London in 1460. He was a man with a grudge whose actions were largely governed by a feeling that his father's death and attainder had been the result of malice. Excluded from local affairs throughout the 1460s, his lands were in the control of

22 Guildford was present when the earl's great ship, the 'Trinity', was commissioned at Sandwich in June 1469: Hicks, *Warwick*, p. 232, Gervase Horne, a relative of John Guildford, joined Warwick and Clarence when they had landed in Kent in July 1469; *CPR 1467–77*, pp. 206, 218.

23 *CPR 1467–77*, pp. 617–18.

his mother and Yorkist stepfather, Sir Thomas Vaughan. To a desperate man, the Readeption offered a measure of hope.[24]

Edward IV launched his bid to recover the Crown in March 1471. Victories at Barnet on 14 April and Tewkesbury on 4 May proved decisive. Kentish participation at Barnet remains uncertain, although Rivers was present with the Yorkist forces. Kentishmen were more visible at Tewkesbury. Some, like George Brown, who was knighted on the eve of the battle, were eager to atone for their previous errors and demonstrate their new-found commitment to Edward IV by fighting under Clarence's banner. Other Kentishmen like James Cromer, one of the commissioners of array appointed on 18 April 1471, was also knighted. Together, they possibly led a contingent from Clarence's lordship of Milton and Marden. Few Kentishmen probably felt committed enough to fight with Queen Margaret's forces for the continued survival of the Lancastrian dynasty. The only notable supporter was Sir Gervase Clifton, who had long ceased to be resident in the county.[25] The county remained in some turmoil in the wake of Barnet and Tewkesbury. Immediately after the battle, reports reached Edward of a rising in Kent by Thomas Neville, bastard of Fauconberg. Too late had Fauconberg brought over ships and men from the Calais garrison to assist Warwick. Despite news of these setbacks, he continued with his plan to seize control of London. Having gathered together a significant force of lesser gentry, yeomanry and townsmen including Nicholas Faunt, mayor of Canterbury, he marched on the capital. Rivers, the earls of Essex and Arundel, and Sir John Scott had been left in charge of London's defence while Edward had moved north to suppress delayed uprisings in support of Queen Margaret and Henry VI. During the course of Fauconberg's attempt to force the gate of the tower at the south end of London Bridge, somewhere between thirteen and seventeen houses in the vicinity were destroyed by 'Kentish mariners'.[26] When his forces showed no signs of breaking through Fauconberg abandoned them and made good his escape to Sandwich. Although he was pardoned by the king on 10 June, Faunconberg did not escape Yorkist retribution for long. He was executed by Richard, duke of Gloucester, in the north in September 1471 on what were probably trumped-up charges.

After reaching London on 21 May, Edward headed into Kent. On 29 May Faunt was executed at the Bullstake in Canterbury. Most of the judicial business was then conducted by a commission appointed on 15 July.[27] In addition to the many fines and executions, Canterbury and the Cinque Ports were briefly deprived of their liberties, suggesting the involvement of certain leading citizens

[24] Mercer, 'Kent and National Politics, 1437–1534', pp. 109, 113, 121–2; M. Mercer, 'Winners and Losers after the Battle of Towton: Structural Changes to the Royal Affinity, 1461–85', paper presented at the International Congress on Medieval Studies, Western Michigan University (2006).

[25] *CPR 1467–77*, pp. 283–4. For a detailed biography of Clifton, see Clark, ed., *The Commons, 1422–1461* (forthcoming).

[26] J. Stow, *The Survey of London* (London, 1987), pp. 40, 56.

[27] *CPR 1467–77*, pp. 287–8; C. Richmond, 'Fauconberg's Kentish Rising of May 1471', *English Historical Review* 85 (1970), 673–92.

from among the various civic authorities.[28] Amongst those implicated in Fauconberg's rising was Sir John Guildford and Sir George Brown. City of Canterbury records show Guildford enjoyed good relations with Nicholas Faunt. He, along with his kinsman, Henry Aucher, were in close communication with the city's authorities around the time of the rising. Guildford had enjoyed a business relationship with Faunt since at least the middle part of the 1460s.[29] Guildford, however, managed to convince the Council of his innocence and secured a pardon on 18 May, just three days before Edward IV returned to London. He thus avoided an appearance before the commissioners.[30] Brown, it was later alleged, managed to obtain a list of Warwick's supporters in Canterbury that had been found in Faunt's pocket. In an attempt to suppress the document, and possibly his own involvement too, he allegedly sent it down to Canterbury's authorities. On balance this story is probably apocryphal.[31]

The Consolidation of Royal Authority, 1471–83

It has been suggested that Edward IV adopted a new management policy for the localities after 1471, concentrating power and authority in the hands of a more compact group of followers drawn from the immediate royal family and royal household.[32] What emerged in Kent reflected this trend. The idea of a broadly based affinity was rejected in favour of one centred primarily around Wydeville connections. Fogg and Scott no longer exercised household office, but Fogg remained a king's councillor, and in 1473 both he and Scott were appointed two of Prince Edward's tutors and councillors. Fogg's kinsman, Anthony Wydeville, Earl Rivers, was the Prince's governor.[33] Fogg's Haute kinsmen also continued to rise in royal service. Richard Haute had also been appointed one of Prince Edward's tutors and councillors in 1473 and by 1483 he was controller of his household. Richard Haute's brother, James Haute, had became one of Edward IV's esquires of the body by 1480.[34] There were few additions to the political elite after 1471. Only those with the correct credentials were admitted to the ranks of the elite. One new figure was Sir Henry Ferrers, nephew of the king's chamber-

[28] *CPR 1467–77*, pp. 260, 276, 296. D. Gardiner, *Historic Haven: The Story of Sandwich* (Derby, 1954), pp. 143–4.

[29] MS CCAL CC FA 5 fol. 112; HMC IX, p. 141; Hicks, *Warwick*, p. 251. For a detailed biography of Faunt see Clark, ed., *The Commons, 1422–1461* (forthcoming).

[30] MS TNA PRO C 67/47 m. 5.

[31] HMC IX, p. 142; Schofield, *Edward IV*, 2, p. 1; MS CCAL CC FA 5 fol. 113.

[32] D. A. L. Morgan, 'The King's Affinity in the Polity of Yorkist England', *Transactions of the Royal Historical Society* 5th series 23 (1973), 11–25. Aspects of his analysis have been argued against in C. Carpenter, *Locality and Polity: A Study of Warwickshire Landed Society, 1401–99* (Cambridge, 1992), chapter 14 and R. Horrox, *Richard III: A Study in Service* (Cambridge, 1989), chapter 1.

[33] J. R. Lander, 'Council, Administration and Councillors, 1461–85', *Bulletin of the Institute of Historical Research* 32 (1959), 173; *CPR 1467–77*, p. 366.

[34] *CPR 1476–85*, p. 169; *CPR 1467–77*, p. 366; N. Orme, 'The Education of Edward V', *Bulletin of the Institute of Historical Research* 57 (1984), 124.

lain, William, Lord Hastings. He had been a squire of the chamber and household in the 1460s.[35] Following his knighthood at Tewkesbury in 1471 he became a knight of the chamber. By September 1481 he was a knight of the body.[36] His incorporation within Kentish circles was the result of his marriage in 1468 to Margaret, widow of William Whetenhall and daughter of William Hexstall of East Peckham.[37] Of greater significance to the Edwardian affinity was the re-admittance of Sir George Brown into county society. Brown's kinship connections tied him firmly to the new regime at the centre and in Kent. Brown had married Elizabeth Paston, the widow of Robert Poynings. This made him step-father to Edward Poynings, already Sir John Scott's son-in-law. Moreover, his niece was also married to Thomas Fogg, son of Sir John Fogg.[38] Such connections no doubt worked in his favour in the long run. Initially, however, he was forced to pay for his poor judgement during the Readeption. He had to return the manors of Southfrith, Tong, Swanscombe, formerly possessed by Richard, duke of York, to his widow, Cecily, duchess of York, in 1472.[39] Yet, he managed to successfully petition the king in the Parliament of 1472–75 for the judgements against his father to be cancelled. This paved his way back into royal favour, and in 1478 Brown was appointed steward of the queen's lordship of Milton and Marden. In November 1479 it was reported to Margaret Paston that Brown was waiting on the king and sleeping at night in his chamber.[40]

The Usurpation of Richard III

This settled state of affairs looked set to continue until disaster struck in April 1483. On 9 April, after a brief illness lasting about ten days, Edward IV died. Soon afterwards, his brother, Richard, duke of Gloucester, launched his bid for power. On 30 April, at Stony Stratford in Northamptonshire, Gloucester and his ally, Henry Stafford, duke of Buckingham, seized the prince and arrested Earl Rivers, the prince's step-brother, Sir Richard Grey, his chamberlain, Sir Thomas Vaughan, and his controller, Richard Haute. About the middle of May Gloucester set about neutralising the power and influence of the Wydevilles and their allies. Kent was an obvious target. At first, the only Wydeville associate to suffer confiscation of his lands was Richard Haute of Ightham Mote.[41] On 14 May Gloucester

35 MS TNA PRO E 101/411/13 fol. 36; E 101/411/15 fol. 23; E 101/412/2 fol. 36.

36 J. Gardiner, ed., *The Paston Letters* 5 (Gloucester, 1986), p. 105; A. R. Myers, *The Household of Edward IV* (Manchester, 1959), p. 199; MS TNA PRO C 146/431.

37 *Catalogue of Ancient Deeds* 1, nos C 425, 431; *CPR 1467–77*, pp. 18–19.

38 Mercer, 'Kent and National Politics, 1437–1534', p. 121.

39 *CCR 1468–76*, no. 947. These had been granted in 1449 to Sir Thomas Brown by Richard, duke of York, in an attempt to secure his assistance at the exchequer with redeeming tallies: P. Johnson, *Duke Richard of York, 1411–60* (Oxford, 1988), pp. 60–1.

40 *CPR 1476–85*, p. 92; J. Strachey et al., ed., *Rotuli Parliamentorum, 1278–1504*, 6 vols (1767) 6, pp 19–20; Gardiner, *Paston Letters* 6, p. 29.

41 Horrox, *Richard III*, pp. 96–7; R. Horrox and P. W. Hammond, ed., *British Library Harleian Manuscript 433*, 4 vols (Gloucester, 1979–83) 3, p. 2.

ordered one of his northern knights, Sir Thomas Wortley, to seize Haute's residence. For the time being, other members of the political elite were permitted to hold onto their positions. In keeping with his anti-Wydeville policy, though, Gloucester made some minor adjustments to Kentish local administration. The sheriff, Sir William Haute, was dismissed and replaced by Hastings's nephew, Ferrers.[42] A new commission of the peace was appointed on 26 June. Although Sir William Haute and Richard Haute were removed, Sir John Fogg, Sir John Scott and Sir Thomas Bourchier the elder were allowed to remain.[43] However, Gloucester attempted to introduce alternative elements onto the county bench like Sir Thomas Bourchier the younger and Sir John Guildford, neither of whom enjoyed strong links to the Wydevilles. The appointment of Sir John Guildford was perhaps an attempt to appeal to former Neville connections, as well as to those excluded from county affairs during the 1470s. In addition to Guildford and Bourchier, Buckingham and John, Lord Howard, were added to the bench. The Staffords had strong links with Kent and Buckingham's appointment re-established the family's contact with the county. Yet the duke showed little interest in Kent and Richard used him instead to replace the Wydeville influence in the Welsh Marches. Howard was better positioned to act as Gloucester's representative in the south-east, enjoying some personal connections within the shire. His sister had married Edward Neville, Lord Abergavenny, making Howard step-uncle to the present Lord Abergavenny.[44]

Gloucester's seizure of the throne, and his coronation as Richard III on 6 July, had a dramatic impact on Kentish politics. Although over seventy knights attended the occasion, Sir John Guildford and Sir George Brown were the only Kentish knights known to have done so.[45] There is no evidence that Brown remained in the royal household. His later execution would suggest that he did not. Nevertheless, Sir William Pecche probably supported the change of regime for Richard soon renewed his annuity of £40.[46] Furthermore, his son, John, married Elizabeth, the niece of one of Richard's northern supporters, Lord Scrope of Bolton.[47] Richard seemed content to leave the county much as it was. Despite Hastings's execution, his nephew, Sir Henry Ferrers, remained sheriff until November 1483. Richard made relatively few changes to the membership of the county bench, introducing just three new men in July 1483: Robert Rede, a lawyer

42 *Sheriffs*, p. 68.

43 *CPR 1476–85*, pp. 562–3.

44 *CPR 1461–7*, p. 379; MS TNA E 404/74/1/55; *CPR 1476–85*, p. 333; G. E. Cokayne, *The Complete Peerage* ... new edn revised by V. Gibbs et al. 1, p. 31; W. Rye, ed., *The Visitation of Norffolk; Made and Taken by William Hervey, Clarenceux ... 1563, Enlarged with Another Visitation made by Clarenceux Cooke ... and also the Visitation made by John Raven, Richmond,1613*, Harleian Society 32 (1891), p. 162. Mercer, 'Kent and National Politics, 1437–1534', pp. 130–1.

45 A. F. Sutton and P. W. Hammond, ed., *The Coronation of Richard III: The Extant Documents* (Gloucester, 1983), pp. 271–2; L. Wickham-Legg, ed., *English Coronation Records* (1901), pp. 194–5.

46 *Harleian 433* 1, p. 141; *CPR 1476–85*, p. 416.

47 C. Norcliffe, ed., *The Visitation of Yorkshire in the Years 1563 and 1564*, Harleian Society 16 (1881), p. 280.

from Chiddingstone, Richard Fiennes, Lord Dacre, a minor Sussex nobleman, and Sir Ralph Ashton, a knight of the body from Yorkshire who had recently re-located to Westenhanger after marrying Elizabeth, widow of John Kyriell.[48]

As the shock of recent events began to fade, it soon became apparent that Richard's usurpation had not been accepted without question by the Yorkist affinity. Towards the end of July the first rumours of discontent emerged in London and a plot to rescue the princes from the Tower was uncovered.[49] It was probably at the beginning of September 1483 that Richard decided to murder Edward V and his brother, Richard, duke of York, perhaps hoping to remove any reason for further conspiracies. In the short-term this policy seemed to succeed. However, details of a newer, more widespread plot emerged at the beginning of October centred around Henry Tudor, earl of Richmond. The chronicles emphasise a core of conspirators comprising Tudor's mother, Margaret Beaufort, John Morton, bishop of Ely, Reginald Bray, Margaret Beaufort's steward, and Richard Guildford, son of Sir John.[50] It was through Morton that the ambitious, and unstable duke of Buckingham was recruited into the conspiracy.[51] Margaret Beaufort's group had apparently been in contact with other disaffected elements within the Yorkist establishment. This was no Lancastrian rising. Tudor was, in fact, the best rival candidate selected by Edward IV's former affinity.[52] The Act of Attainder of 1484 portrayed the rebellion as a series of inter-connected risings with rebels from each sector advancing on the capital with military precision.[53] In reality, of course, the organisation was undoubtedly much vaguer. In Kent, Richard Guildford was instrumental in organising an apparently successful rising. The Kentish rebels were drawn from all the major gentry circles within the shire with the exception of the Scotts and St Legers.[54] Richard was in Lincoln preparing to march against a rising organised by Buckingham in Wales when news of the Kentish rising reached him. He started to head back to London, but changed his mind and resumed his march against Buckingham, presumably relying on Norfolk and Lord Cobham to defend London. Norfolk quickly instructed the loyal Sir William Pecche to lead an advance party into the county on 10 October. The following day Norfolk dispatched another force. On 13

48 *Sheriffs*, p. 68; *CPR 1476–85*, p. 563. Rede had married Margaret, daughter of John Alfegh: MS TNA PRO PROB 11/8 fols 144v–145; J. R. Dunlop, 'Pedigree of the Family of Crioll, or Kyriell, of co. Kent', *Miscellanea, Genealogica et Heraldica*, 5th series 6 (1916–31), 257; MS TNA PRO C 67/52 m. 7; 53 m. 12; Horrox, *Richard III*, pp. 41, 42, 43, 45, 47.

49 J. Stow, *The Annales of England* (1592), p. 762.

50 E. Hall, *Hall's Chronicle*, ed. H. Ellis (1809), pp. 391–2; Polydore Vergil, *Three Books of English History*, ed. H. Ellis, Camden Society, original series 29 (1844), pp. 196–7; Raphael Holinshed, *Chronicles of England, Scotland and Ireland*, 6 vols (1807–8) 3, p. 414.

51 Sir Thomas More, *The History of King Richard III and selections from the English and Latin Poems*, ed. R. Sylvester (Yale, 1976), pp. 92–6.

52 C. Carpenter, *The Wars of the Roses*, p. 215.

53 *Rotuli Parliamentorum* 6, p. 245.

54 Mercer, 'Kent and National Politics, 1437–1534', pp. 135, 141.

October there was even a small skirmish at the Gravesend fair when a rebel called Bountayne murdered 'master Mowbray'.[55]

Events did not favour the rebels in Kent. Lord Cobham mobilised a large force and successfully prevented them from crossing the Thames. Although the Kentish rebels managed to join up with other groups from Essex, London remained untroubled.[56] Unable to proceed any further, the rebellion rapidly collapsed. Rebels scattered in all directions, anxious to avoid capture and possible execution. Edward Poynings and Richard Guildford were fortunate. They managed to join Henry Tudor in Brittany.[57] The remainder were not so fortunate. Sir George Brown, Poynings's stepfather, had suffered a variety of misfortunes during the course of his life. Why he decided to rebel is unclear, although it does not seem to have been out of a deep-rooted sense of loyalty to the Yorkist dynasty. Nevertheless, his luck finally ran out in 1483. He was captured and executed on 3 December. Sir John Guildford was also captured, having been hidden for a time by his close neighbour, Walter Roberts of Cranbrook. Unlike Brown, however, Guildford was lucky to escape with his life.[58] So great was the feeling of suspicion surrounding many rebels that many of their relatives secured pardons in order to protect themselves from official reprisals.[59]

The rebellion signalled the end of Richard's attempt to maintain the status quo in Kent and the south. The region was now largely hostile to the new king. He therefore had little option but to remove Kentish rebels from local office, in the process destroying the crucial link between the centre and the locality. The new round of shrieval appointments in November 1483 provided him with his first opportunity to select a more reliable figure than Sir Henry Ferrers. Yet the lack of available candidates is shown in his selection of John Bamme of Gillingham and Dartford, bailiff and steward of the courts of the hundreds of Milton and Marden under Edward IV. Bamme was an unusually humble choice but had been one of Richard's few Kentish associates when duke of Gloucester.[60] Shortly after the new round of shrieval appointments moves were made to purge the commission of the peace. Sir John Fogg, Sir Henry Ferrers, Sir Thomas Bourchier the younger and Sir John Guildford were all sacked. Sir John Scott and a handful of others remained on the bench appointed on 5 December.[61] The Scotts and their associates

55 J. P. Collier, ed., *Household Books of John, Duke of Norfolk and Thomas, Earl of Surrey temp. 1481–90* (1844), pp. 470–1; P. W. Hammond, ed., *Richard III: Loyalty, Lordship and Law* (London, 1986), pp. 15, 199 n. 62; Richard Kilburne, *A Topographie or Survey of the County of Kent* (1659), pp. 113–14; Stow, *Annales*, p. 775.

56 *CPR 1476–85*, p. 535.

57 Stow, *Annales*, p. 774; *The Crowland Chronicle*, p. 181; Shaw, *Knights of England*, 2, p. 22.

58 *Rotuli Parliamentorum* 6, p. 251.

59 Mercer, 'Kent and National Politics, 1437–1534', p. 139. For a general discussion on the granting of pardons, see L. Gill, *Richard III and Buckingham's Rebellion* (Stroud, 1999), pp. 95–101.

60 *Sheriffs*, p. 68; P. H. Reaney and M. Fitch, ed., *Feet of Fines for Essex, 1423–1547* (Colchester, 1964), 4, p. 73.

61 *CPR 1476–85*, pp. 562–3. Gill suggests that Scott was under suspicion although his presence on the bench suggests that any involvement was judged to be minimal; Gill, *Buckingham's Rebellion*, p. 88.

had been used to besiege the Sussex rebels sheltering in Bodiam Castle. By remaining loyal they avoided the subsequent Ricardian reprisals. Sir John Scott's loyalty to the Ricardian regime continues to remain unexplained. So, too, has James Haute's. As a former servant of Edward IV and kinsman of Queen Elizabeth his apparent support for Richard III is puzzling. Perhaps he was simply trying to protect the family's local position. Alternatively he might have retained an underlying sense of loyalty to the Crown, whoever the incumbent. Either way, Haute was granted his brother's manor of Ightham Mote in March 1484 and survived the purges conducted across the county.[62]

With so few Kentishmen to help run the county, Richard was forced to rely on members of his former ducal affinity to run local affairs at the highest level. The rebellion had released patronage in the south-east with which to do this. Most lands had been granted away to his servants before the passing of the Act of Attainder in 1484. Richard used eight men in Kent: Sir Ralph Ashton, Robert Brackenbury, Sir Edward Stanley, Sir William Harrington, Sir John Savage, Sir Marmaduke Constable, Sir Ralph Bigod and William Malyverer. Richard was particularly keen to extend the influence of these northerners who already had southern interests. Sir Ralph Ashton was the only one of his newly created royal affinity with a pre-existing landed base in the county. To boost Ashton's local position he received additional lands forfeited by Sir George Brown, Sir John Fogg and Richard Guildford.[63] Ashton probably became Richard's man of affairs in the county where he was active throughout the remainder of the reign. A soldier who had fought under Gloucester in Scotland, and known as the Black Knight by virtue of the armour he wore, he was a tough and unscrupulous individual. Ashton had been appointed vice-constable of England in the wake of Buckingham's rebellion and in 1484 he was also made lieutenant of Dover Castle. The aged earl of Arundel, warden of the Cinque Ports, remained little more than a figurehead.[64]

Unlike Ashton, Richard's remaining northeners had no Kentish interests. Initially Sir Marmaduke Constable, knight of the body, looked set to become Ashton's deputy. Between December 1483 and January 1484 he was made steward and constable of Tonbridge Castle and given control of the honour of Tonbridge and the Stafford lordships of Penshurst, Brasted, Hadlow and Yalding. It is perhaps no surprise that Constable was met by considerable local hostility when he settled into west Kent, but he seemed to achieve a measure of success in restoring law and order.[65] However, by March 1484 Constable had been moved up to Leicestershire and Robert Brackenbury from Selaby in Durham, an esquire

62 *CPR 1476–85*, pp. 370, 458; MS TNA PRO PROB 11/16 fol. 28v; MS TNA PRO DL 29/637/10360A; Sutton, 'The Hautes of Kent', 54–5; Fleming, 'The Hautes and their "Circle"', pp. 87–8.

63 *Harleian 433* 2, p. 55; *CPR 1476–85*, pp. 445, 482–3.

64 *CPR 1476–85*, pp. 368, 397; R. Horrox, 'Ashton, Sir Ralph (c. 1425–1487–90)', *ODNB*.

65 *Harleian 433* 2, p. 60; Gill, *Buckingham's Rebellion*, p. 107; K. Dockray, 'Richard III and the Yorkshire Gentry c.1471–85', *Richard III: Loyalty, Lordship and Law*, ed. P. W. Hammond (London, 1986), pp. 61–3.

of the body, had become Ashton's second-in-command.[66] In March 1484 he was granted the receivership of the lordships of Tonbridge, Hadlow, Penshurst and Milton and Marden, and lands forfeited by Earl Rivers, Walter Roberts and the Cheynes; in May 1484 he was appointed surveyor of Tonbridge, Hadlow and Penshurst; and in January 1485 he was made constable of Tonbridge Castle.[67] Brackenbury was also appointed steward of the archbishop of Canterbury's lands in 1484.[68] Richard provided more modest grants to his other appointees. Sir William Harrington acquired the Darell manor of Calehill; Sir John Savage was granted the Pympe manor of Nettlestead and the marriage and custody of the lands of Thomas Culpeper, son of Richard Culpeper; Sir Edward Stanley, younger son of the earl of Derby, and therefore Margaret Beaufort's step-son, was granted the Guildfords' manor of Rolvenden; and William Malyverer was granted certain lands forfeited by Fogg. He was also commissioned to receive the issues from some of Sir George Brown's lands.[69] Richard's northern affinity played a prominent role in Kentish local government: Brackenbury was appointed sheriff in November 1484 and William Malyverer was escheator between 1483 and 1485. However, the main instrument used in the rapid take-over of power in Kent was the commission of the peace. Brackenbury, Ashton, Harrington, Savage and Constable were all active participants on the bench.[70] Richard had re-created a following in Kent that was a crude parody of Edward IV's post-1471 political settlement.

This plantation policy caused widespread friction throughout the south. According to the *Crowland Chronicle*, Richard distributed the forfeited lands 'amongst his northerners whom he had planted in every part of his dominions, to the shame of all the southern people who murmured ceaselessly and longed more each day for the return of their old lords in the place of the tyranny of the present ones'.[71] While the writer of the *Crowland Chronicle* might have been using hindsight to explain Richard's deposition, public opinion at the time was undoubtedly offended. Local gentry accepted newcomers into their ranks through the traditional avenues of inheritance, marriage or purchase. They were less willing to accept the imposition of outsiders for reasons of political expediency. Perhaps in time Richard hoped that they would become integrated into southern society but the Ricardian regime did not last long enough for this to happen. Instead the county elite seemed to witness a breakdown in law and order. In part this was due

66 Horrox, *Richard III*, p. 286; *CPR 1476–85*, p. 383. Robert Brackenbury had moved south in July 1483 after becoming constable of the Tower of London: *CPR 1476–85*, p. 364.

67 *CPR 1476–85*, pp. 383, 385, 433, 521, 546.

68 F. R. H. Du Boulay, *The Lordship of Canterbury: An Essay on Medieval Society* (London, 1966), p. 395.

69 *Harleian 433* 2, pp. 54, 55, 116; *CPR 1476–85*, pp. 515–16, 534. The grant of the Guildford manor of Rolvenden was perhaps an attempt to place their principal residence in favourable hands.

70 *Sheriffs*, p. 68; *List of Escheators for England and Wales*, PRO Lists and Indexes 72 (1971), p. 68; *CPR 1476–85*, pp. 387, 562–3; MS TNA PRO KB 9/51/28, 60; KB 9/366/32; KB 9/ 950/18.

71 *The Crowland Chronicle*, pp. 169–71; A. J. Pollard, 'The Tyranny of Richard III', *Journal of Medieval History* 3 (1977), 157–8; Gill, *Buckingham's Rebellion*, pp. 105–6.

to in-fighting between the newcomers. Brackenbury, for example, had his servants expelled from Dymchurch manor by Ashton's sons who were claiming it as part of the Kyriell inheritance.[72] Elsewhere there were clashes with the traditional local elites themselves. It is very likely that these would have happened at some point. Landed disputes were endemic within gentry and magnate society. Nevertheless, the Ricardian disruption of local society gave them an added dimension. Ashton, for example, also found himself in conflict with Sir John Fogg. Fogg's first wife had been Alice Kyriell, co-heiress of Sir Thomas Kyriell and niece of John and Elizabeth Kyriell. Kyriell had settled his manors of Westenhanger, Great Mongeham and Walmer on Elizabeth for life with Fogg as a feoffee. Fogg, however, had refused to hand over the deeds. Richard intervened on Ashton's behalf by forcing the prior of Christ Church to surrender the documents Fogg had placed in his keeping.[73] In another incident, William Malyverer, who had married Joan, widow of William Langley of Knolton seized custody of Langley's heir and lands.[74] This brought him into conflict with the Guildfords. After William Langley died on 20 February 1483, Richard Guildford occupied Langley's lands because of his appointment as John Langley's guardian. He held the lands until the following All Hallows (1 November). He was then expelled by Malyverer who continued in possession until 30 August 1485, eight days after the battle of Bosworth.[75]

Richard continued to be plagued by hints of unrest throughout 1484 and 1485 which prompted him to attempt a lasting peace with the Wydevilles by suggesting a marriage alliance with his niece, Princess Elizabeth. This caused so much unrest among his closest supporters that the idea was quickly dropped.[76] Nevertheless, Richard continued to make overtures to those he judged most useful to the survival of his regime. On 12 January 1485, Sir John Fogg and Sir Richard Wydeville bound themselves in the sum of a thousand marks to remain loyal to the king.[77] In February Fogg was pardoned and even had some of his lands restored. Wydeville was pardoned in March. So, too, was his kinsman, Richard Haute of Ightham Mote.[78] However, Richard was not prepared to re-integrate these men into local political structures and his limited efforts at conciliation could not halt the steady erosion of loyalty to the Ricardian regime. The county's political elite for the most part remained stubbornly set against him until Tudor's dramatic victory at Bosworth on 22 August 1485 settled matters once and for all.[79]

72 MS TNA PRO KB 9/951/28.

73 MS TNA PRO C 1/76/3–5, 79/2; J. B. Sheppard, ed., *Christ Church Letters*, Camden Society, new series 19 (1877), p. 47; *CFR 1471–85*, no. 668; *CCR 1476–85*, nos 1013, 1113.

74 For Malyverer, see Norcliffe, *Visitation of Yorkshire*, p. 201.

75 *IPM Henry VII* 1, no. 362; *Harleian 433* 1, pp. 18–19; *Sheriffs*, p. 68; Horrox, *Richard III*, p. 286.

76 MS TNA PRO C 67/51 mm. 3, 27; *Harleian 433* 1, pp. 195, 268; *CPR 1476–85*, pp. 382, 418.

77 MS TNA PRO C 244/136/130, 132.

78 *CPR 1476–85*, p. 511.

79 MS TNA PRO C 244/136/27, 28, 30; MS TNA PRO E 405/74; *CCR 1476–85*, no. 1456.

Early Tudor Kent

Not surprisingly, the new king, Henry VII, preferred to draw his closest companions and associates from those who had supported his cause while he was a pretender. His experiences before 1485 served to shape his particular style of kingship. During the early Tudor period the relative positions of the nobility and the royal affinity underwent a further shift in favour of the latter.[80] This, however, had relatively little impact on Kent where there was no dominant magnate. Nevertheless, there was a structural shift within the ranks of the royal affinity as the Guildfords emerged as the leading royal servants within the shire. Sir Richard Guildford had been intimately involved in Buckingham's rebellion and had joined Henry Tudor in exile after its failure. He was prominent at court from the moment of Henry's accession and quickly became one of the king's chief military and security advisors. In 1485 Guildford was made a king's knight; in 1486 he was appointed joint-master of the ordnance and keeper of the armoury in the Tower with his son, Edward; by 1487 he had become master of the horse and a king's councillor; in 1488 he was one of Henry's knights of the body, and by 1493–94 he had been appointed controller of the royal household. He remained controller until his disgrace and resignation in 1505–06.[81] In addition to Guildford, a significant number of Kentishmen were also recruited into royal service between 1485 and 1504. Some like Sir John Guildford and Sir John Fogg had now passed their political prime but were appointed king's councillors. Henry was not a man to ignore the political and administrative experience of others, nor the need to work within existing structures at the start of the reign.[82] Other less experienced men also joined the royal household. Principal among these were Sir Edward Poynings, Sir Anthony Brown, brother of Sir George Brown, John Darell and John Pecche.[83]

Throughout this period Guildford's prominence rested on a combination of his position within the royal household and the use of his private networks in the county. The structure of power in early Tudor Kent differed little from the late Lancastrian or Yorkist periods. Guildford received few grants of royal patronage

80 S. Gunn, *Early Tudor Government 1485–1558* (Basingstoke, 1995), pp. 30–2, 34–5, 38–40; D. Grummitt, 'The Establishment of the Tudor Dynasty', in *A Companion to Tudor Britain*, ed. R. Tittler and N. Leslie (Oxford, 2004), pp. 13–28. As the events of 1495 demonstrate, however, events during his reign also helped determine his kingship; D. Starkey, 'Intimacy and Innovation: The Rise of the Privy Chamber, 1485–1547', in D. Starkey et al., *The English Court from the Wars of the Roses to the Civil War*, 2nd edn (Harlow, 1992), pp. 73–6.

81 *CPR 1485–94*, pp. 18, 467; MS TNA PRO E 404/79/176; J. R. Hooker, 'Some Cautionary Notes on Henry VII's Household and Chamber System', *Speculum* 33 (1958), 74–5. In 1500 Guildford was made a knight of the Garter; Shaw, *Knights of England* 1, p. 19. When he was pardoned in 1506 he remained a knight of the body; *CPR 1494–1509*, p. 453.

82 *CPR 1485–94*, pp. 150, 257; C. G. Bayne and W. H. Dunham, ed., *Select Cases in the Council of Henry VII*, Selden Society 75 (1958), pp. 11, 12, 13, 19, 20. Fogg died in 1490; MS CKS PRC 32/3/280; Guildford died in 1493; MS TNA PRO PROB 11/9 fols 223–3v.

83 Mercer, 'Kent and National Politics, 1437–1534', pp. 156–7. Sir William Pecche's Ricardian associations did not count against the recruitment of his son, John, into the royal affinity; MS TNA PRO E 404/82/47; E 101/415/7/84.

in the locality, although his appointment as steward of Duchess Cecily of York's lands in Kent, Sussex and Surrey in 1496 was a useful enhancement to his local position.[84] His closest ally was Sir Edward Poynings who acted as his deputy. The two men enjoyed a close public and private relationship. Poynings was probably appointed lieutenant of Dover Castle about 1493 and also became steward of the lands of the archbishop of Canterbury in 1505.[85] Guildford connections quickly became the dominant force in the county. His daughters married within the county gentry, drawing them more closely into his network. The marriage of the eldest son, Edward Guildford to Eleanor, daughter of Thomas West, Lord de la Warre, however, reflected the increased status of the Guildford family on the national stage as well. This alliance made him brother-in-law to Sir Henry Owen, son of Henry VII's half-uncle and carver, Sir David Owen of Midhurst in Sussex.[86] The Scotts also re-established strong connections with the royal affinity once again. Any previous associations with Richard III were forgotten. Sir John Scott died soon after Henry's accession but his son, Sir William, brother-in-law to Sir Edward Poynings, became part of the new royal affinity. This personal connection would explain his temporary appointment acting as lieutenant of Dover Castle in 1495.

Guildford and this network of royal servants dominated local administation for most of the reign. The first sheriff of Kent was William Cheyne of Sheppey who had also shared the new king's exile.[87] Sir Richard Guildford, Sir William Scott, John Darell and John Pecche all served as sheriff during the crucial first decade of Henry VII's reign.[88] Sir John and Sir Richard Guildford, Sir Edward Poynings, John Pympe, John Darell and Sir William Scott also sat on the bench for all or part of the period from 1485 to 1504.[89] It also seems the royal affinity monopolised shire representation in Parliament. Parliamentary returns for Henry VII's reign are rare and are largely the result of guesswork. Nevertheless, it has been suggested that Richard Guildford represented Kent in 1487, 1489/90, 1491, 1495, 1496/7 and 1503. His father, Sir John, was knight of the shire in 1485, while Sir William Scott was Sir Richard's partner in 1495.[90] Each of these families enjoyed

84 Fleming, 'The Hautes and their "Circle" ', p. 99; M. Gregory, 'Wickham Court and the Heydons', *Arch. Cant.* 78 (1963), 12; J. G. Nichols and J Bruce, ed., *Wills from Doctor's Commons*, Camden Society, original series 83 (1863), p. 8. For other examples of this delegated authority, see Carpenter, *Wars of the Roses*, pp. 228–30.

85 F. Hull, ed., *A Calendar of the White and Black Books of the Cinque Ports, 1432–1955*, Kent Records 19/HMC Joint Publications 5 (1966), pp. 115, 118, 119–20; *CPR 1485–94*, p. 400; HMC IX, p. 120.

86 R. C. Jenkins, 'The Family of Guldeford', *Arch. Cant.* 14 (1882), 4–5; W. H. Rylands, ed., *Pedigrees from the Visitation of Hampshire made by Thomas Benolte, Clarenceux, 1530 ...*, Harleian Society 64 (1913), p. 59. Sir Richard Guildford participated in two enfeoffments made by Lord de la Warre in 1499; *CCR 1485–1500*, nos 1182–3.

87 S. B. Wyatt, *Cheneys and Wyatts: A Brief History in Two Parts* (London, 1960), pp. 27–30.

88 *Sheriffs*, pp. 68–9.

89 *CPR 1485–94*, pp. 489–90; *CPR 1494–1509*, pp. 644–5.

90 J. C. Wedgwood and A. D. Holt, *History of Parliament: Register of the Members the House of Commons, 1439–1509* (1938), pp. 507, 523, 538, 555, 577, 593, 609; W. Jay, 'List of Members of the Fourth Parliament of Henry VII', *Bulletin of the Institute of Historical Research* 3 (1925–26), 169.

long histories of bureaucratic and parliamentary service for the county. Henry was working firmly within existing structures of power in the county.

The national and local prominence of Sir Richard Guildford and Sir Edward Poynings made them the natural enforcers of royal peace and justice in the county. In about 1487 Guildford wrote to Scott offering to arbitrate in a dispute between him and the prior of Horton. Sir Edward Poynings had no doubt briefed him on the details of the case. Guildford assured Scott that 'you may be sure I will not see your hurt nor dishonour, but will do for you as I would you should do for me'.[91] On another occasion, Poynings intervened in a dispute between Scott and James Isaak over Fleet manor. In an exemplification lodged in Chancery in 1497, it was agreed that Poynings was to hold the manor subject to certain provisos. This agreement was ratified by Guildford and the archbishop of Canterbury.[92] Guildford and the Tudor royal affinity faced few serious challenges to their authority. In 1495 Perkin Warbeck's attempted landing at Sandwich was easily fended off by the sheriff, John Pecche, and his local levies. Pecche was already gaining a reputation for martial prowess. Just nine months previously, in November 1494, he had taken part in the jousts at Westminster Palace and won himself a ruby ring in recognition of his achievements. Still only in his early twenties when he tackled Warbeck he succeeded in capturing 140–160 of his followers. He then conveyed them to London roped together like cart-horses.[93] It is possible that one of those captured was Guildford's cousin, Gervase Horne, who was accused of treason around about this time. However, through his influence, Horne was pardoned shortly after Warbeck's landing was thwarted.[94]

The royal affinity's management of Kentish political life remained uncontested until George Neville, 3rd Lord Abergavenny began to attract royal favour in the later 1490s. He had succeeded to his title in 1492 and was granted livery of his lands the following year.[95] Abergavenny first started to participate in county affairs by recruiting his own personal following in 1495 to oppose Warbeck. Two years later he raised additional forces to face the Cornish insurgents at Blackheath. These fought alongside levies from Kent and other counties.[96] In 1498 he was sworn onto the king's council and in 1500 his local position in Kent was enhanced further by a grant of the keepership of Southfrith Park.[97]

There are indications that Henry had started to become concerned about increasing tensions within Kent by 1502. He had specifically sent a copy of a royal proclamation prohibiting retaining to Guildford, Thomas Iden, bailiff of

91 MS CKS U 1115/C1 (Scott of Scott's Hall).
92 *CPR 1494–1509*, p. 107.
93 Holinshed, *Chronicles* 3, p. 511; *Hall's Chronicle*, p. 472; Canon Scott Robertson, 'Pecche of Lullingstone', *Arch. Cant.* 16 (1886), 232–3.
94 *CPR 1494–1509*, p. 352.
95 *CPR 1485–94*, pp. 409–10.
96 Holinshed, *Chronicles* 3, p. 514; *Hall's Chronicle*, p. 478.
97 Bayne and Dunham, *Select Cases*, p. 30; *CPR 1494–1509*, p. 200.

Milton and Marden, and to Sir Richard Carew, sheriff of Surrey and Sussex.[98] Trouble broke out in one potential flash-point at Aylesford in the Medway valley. The Guildfords and Abergavenny both had connections in the area: George Guildford was steward of Aylesford manor and Abergavenny had family ties in Aylesford village.[99] In 1503 the conflict was stepped up when George Guildford initiated proceedings in the council against Abergavenny's retainer, Robert Gaynesford of Allington.[100] As a result of this tussle the Guildfords came out on top. The king was not willing to sacrifice the power of his leading servants within Kent. Indictments before the court of king's bench at Westminster in 1503 alleged that Abergavenny had been retaining in the very heart of Guildford territory.[101] Abergavenny was undoubtedly fined for this offence although the precise sum is unknown. Nevertheless, it seems to have led him to sell some lands in Lincolnshire and Nottinghamshire. However, the Guildfords did not escape punishment completely. George Guildford and associates were required to enter into recognisances for their good behaviour in 1505.[102]

Sir Richard Guildford's successful defence of his family's supremacy in Kent was short-lived. By 1503 Henry's health was failing steadily and the succession was playing on his mind. At much the same time disturbing rumours from Calais had reached his ears which raised questions in his mind over the loyalty of members of the royal affinity. Guildford appears to have become a victim of the king's wider doubts concerning the loyalty of his own servants. In 1505 he was disgraced, ostensibly for refusing to account properly for his offices of master of the ordnance and keeper of the armoury.[103] A more likely explanation is that he became the victim of a coup engineered by the leading figures on Henry VII's council-learned-at-law, Richard Empson and Edmund Dudley.[104] Henry's uncertainty about his closest servants and the destablising effect that the Abergavenny–Guildford dispute had had in Kent probably convinced him that Sir Richard was dispensable. The precise pattern of events which led to Guildford's demise are unclear. Nevertheless, the fact that he seems to have been constantly plagued by debt throughout the reign made him an easy target to his enemies.[105] These financial problems remained with him until the end and are clearly visible in his will. In 1506 he resigned his offices in disgrace and departed on a pilgrimage to the Holy Land where he died.[106]

98 *CPR 1494–1509*, p. 286; P. L. Hughes and J. F. Larkin, ed., *Tudor Royal Proclamations*, 3 vols (New Haven, CT, 1964–9) 1, pp. 55–6; *Sheriffs*, p. 137.

99 Hasted, *History* 4, pp. 435–6; Cokayne, *Complete Peerage* 1, p. 31.

100 *CPR 1485–94*, p. 419; MS TNA PRO PROB 11/11 fol. 216.

101 MS TNA PRO KB 9/430 mm. 48–69.

102 MS TNA PRO E 36/214 fol. 261v; *CCR 1500–9*, nos 340, 607.

103 MS TNA PRO E 159/284 mm. 36–6v.

104 Guildford's colleague, Daubeney fell victim to similar charges of embezzlement in 1506; S. Gunn, 'The Courtiers of Henry VII', *English Historical Review* 108 (1993), 47; D. Grummitt, '"For the Surety of the Towne and Marches": Early Tudor Policy towards Calais, 1485–1509', *Nottingham Medieval Studies* 44 (2000), 184–203.

105 MS TNA PRO PROB 11/17 fol. 225v.

106 H. Ellis, ed., *The Pylgrymage of Sir Richard Guylforde*, Camden Society, original series 51 (1851).

Abergavenny was unable to enjoy the downfall of his rival for long. His own disgrace followed immediately afterwards. In 1506 he was prosecuted for misprision of treason, that is, concealing knowledge of treason. Then, in 1507 he was prosecuted again for illegal retaining. Just as the precise circumstances of Guildford's downfall are unclear, the underlying reasons behind Abergavenny's fall from grace are equally uncertain. The charges against him in 1506 related to a case being conducted against the Yorkist pretender, the earl of Suffolk. Abergavenny was charged with concealing an incident which had taken place in 1497, just before the battle of Blackheath. Abergavenny and Suffolk had supposedly discussed the possibility of joining the Cornish rebels. For this offence Abergavenny spent a short spell in the Tower. On this occasion, Henry seemed willing to let bygones be bygones. Yet the following year Abergavenny was in trouble again for illegal retaining in contravention of the 1504 Act. Abergavenny had allegedly raised a substantial retinue from about eighty-six towns and villages in central Kent. Most of the gentry he recruited were from established, but relatively minor families. However, in some cases they had substantial county contacts. By far the most significant was Lewis Clifford. Clifford had served as sheriff in 1497–8 and a justice of the peace between 1500 and 1506. Not surprisingly, Abergavenny did not escape so lightly for this second offence. He was fined a crippling £70,650 and forced to find associates willing to enter into recognisances for his continued good behaviour.[107]

The Yorkist and Tudor periods demonstrated the continuing importance that Kent played in national events. Those families which had first appeared in early Lancastrian Kent remained intimately involved in county affairs throughout the second half of the fifteenth century. Yet this period also witnessed the increasing monopolisation of the structures of power by an expanding royal affinity recruited from these same families. However, the county did not readily abandon its potential for volatility and unpredictability. The apparent stability of the mid-to-late 1460s quickly evaporated when Edward IV's authority was challenged by Warwick in 1469 and 1470–71. Very few Kentishmen actively took up arms to oppose the Kingmaker. Indeed, the Cinque Ports provided one of the most important reserves of support for Warwick and the Lancastrians. During the brief restoration of Henry VI in 1470–71 the gentry remained quietly on the sidelines or supported the restored Lancastrian regime. The royal affinity's domination of local affairs remained open to challenge until Edward IV's victories at Barnet and Tewkesbury in April and May 1471 appeared to settle the dynastic question. After Edward IV emerged triumphant he was mindful of the perils of power-sharing in the localities. The royal affinity subsequently tightened its grip on power in Kent. Such was its supremacy that when Richard III seized the throne in 1483 the

[107] Mercer, 'Kent and National Politics, 1437–1534', pp. 173–4.

overwhelming majority of the gentry threw their backing behind Buckingham's ill-fated rebellion. Richard III's futile attempt to recreate royal authority from scratch with members of his northern retinue was a failure. The political community within the shire refused to cooperate. In the wake of Henry Tudor's victory at Bosworth, the relationship between Crown, nobility and gentry underwent a final shift in favour of the Crown. The Tudor court established a dominant position as the centre for personal advancement and political influence. The tentacles of the Tudor royal affinity now reached ever further into local political society. Noble power became an adjunct of royal power. The conflict between the Guildfords and Lord Abergavenny did not present a serious challenge to the long-term position of the royal affinity. When the young Henry VIII succeeded to the throne in 1509 he inherited a county in which service to the Crown had became the most sought after option for the gentry.

Bibliography

This extensive bibliography has been compiled to provide a resource for people interested in the medieval history of Kent, and for those who wish to investigate the county's history in the context of the wider history of England.

Printed Primary Sources

Barnum, P. H., ed., *Dives and Pauper*, Early English Text Society, 2 vols (Oxford, 1976).

Bateson, M., ed., *Borough Customs*, Seldon Society, 2 vols (London, 1904, 1906).

Bayne, C. G. and W. H. Dunham, ed., *Select Cases in the Council of Henry VII*, Selden Society 75 (London, 1958).

Boys, W., *Collections for an History of Sandwich in Kent, with Notices of the other Cinque Ports and Members and of Richborough* (Canterbury, 1792).

Brie, F. W., ed., *The Brut or The Chronicles of England,* Early English Text Society, original series 131, 2 vols (New York, 1906–8, repr. 1960).

Calendar of Chancery Warrants Preserved in the Public Record Office, 1244–1326 (London, 1927).

Calendar of Entries in the Papal Registers Relating to Great Britain and Ireland: Papal Letters, 17 vols (London, 1893–1994).

Calendar of Inquisitions Miscellaneous 1392–99 (London, 1963).

Catalogue of Ancient Deeds, 6 vols (London, 1890–1915).

Cokayne, G. E., *The Complete Peerage* ... new edn revised by V. Gibbs et al., 13 vols (1910–49).

Collier, J. P., ed., *Household Books of John, Duke of Norfolk and Thomas, Earl of Surrey temp. 1481–90* (1844).

Cowper, J. M., ed., *The Roll of the Freemen of the City of Canterbury from AD 1392 to 1800* (Canterbury, 1903).

Cowper, J. M., ed., *Intrantes: A List of Persons Admitted to Live and Trade within the City of Canterbury, 1392–1592* (Canterbury, 1904).

Davies, J. S., ed., *An English Chronicle of the Reigns of Richard II, Henry IV, Henry V, and Henry VI*, Camden Society, original series 64 (London, 1856).

Davis, A. H., trans., *William Thorne's Chronicle of Saint Augustine's Abbey, Canterbury* (Oxford, 1934).

Du Boulay, F. R. H., 'Calendar of Archbishopric Demesne Leases, 1503–1532', in *Documents Illustrative of Medieval Kentish Society*, Kent Records 18, ed. F. R. H. Du Boulay (Ashford, 1964), pp. 266–97.

Duncan, L. L., ed., *Testamenta Cantiana: West Kent* (London, 1906).

Duncombe, J. and N. Battely, *The History and Antiquities of the Three Archiepiscopal Hospitals at or near Canterbury viz. St Nicholas at Harbledown, St John, Northgate and St Thomas of Eastbridge, with some Account of the Priory of St Gregory, the Nunnery of St Sepulcre, the Hospitals of St James and St Laurence and Maynard Spittle* (London, 1785).

Ellis, H., ed., *The Pylgrymage of Sir Richard Guylforde*, Camden Society, original series 51 (London, 1851).

Emden, A., *A Bibliographical Register of the University of Oxford to AD 1500*, 3 vols (Oxford, 1957–59).

Emden, A., *A Biographical Register of the University of Oxford, AD 1501–1540* (Oxford, 1974).

Fenwick, C. C., ed., *The Poll Taxes of 1377, 1379, 1381, Part One: Bedfordshire to Leicestershire*, Records of Social and Economic History, new series 27 (Oxford, 1998).

Finn, A., *Records of Lydd* (Kent, 1911).

Foxe, J., *Actes and Monuments of these Latter and Perillous Dayes* (London, 1583).

Gairdner, J., ed., *The Historical Collections of a Citizen of London in the Fifteenth Century*, Camden Society, new series 17 (London, 1876).

Gairdner, J., ed., *The Paston Letters, 1422–1509*, 6 vols (London, 1904).

Gibson, J. M., ed., *Kent: Diocese of Canterbury*, Records of Early English Drama, 3 vols (Toronto and London, 2002).

Giles, J. A., ed., *Chronicles of the White Rose of York* (London, 1845).

Giraud, F. F., 'Faversham: Regulations for the Town Porters, 1448', *Arch. Cant.* 20 (1893), 219–21.

Giraud, F. F., 'Cinque Ports. Notes from Minute Books of the Corporation of Faversham', *Arch. Cant.* 28 (1909), 28–74.

Glasscock, R. E., ed., *The Lay Subsidy of 1334*, British Academy Records of Social and Economic History (London, 1975).

Graham, R., trans. and ed., *Registrum Roberti Winchelsey, Archiepiscopi Cantuariensis AD 1294–1313*, Canterbury and York Society, 2 vols (Oxford, 1952).

Greenstreet, J., ed., 'List of the Gentry of Kent in the Time of Henry VII', *Arch. Cant.* 11 (1877), 394–97.

Hale, W. H., *A Series of Precedents and Proceedings ... from the Act-books of Ecclesiastical Courts in the Diocese of London* (1847).

Hall, E., *Hall's Chronicle*, ed. H. Ellis (1809).

Halle, J., *An Historiall Expostulation* (1565), ed. T. Pettigrew (London, 1844).

Hanley, H. A. and C. W. Chalklin, 'The Kent Lay Subsidy Roll of 1334/5', in *Documents Illustrative of Medieval Kentish Society*, Kent Records 18, ed. F. R. H. Du Boulay (Ashford, 1964), pp. 71–172.

Hardy, Florence, *The Life of Thomas Hardy, 1840–1928* (1928, repr. London, 1962).

Harrington, D. and P. Hyde, *The Early Town Books of Faversham c.1251 to 1581* (Folkestone, 2008).

Holden, A. J., ed., *History of William Marshal*, Anglo-Norman Text Society, 3 vols, (Woodbridge, 2002–06).

Holinshed, Raphael, *Chronicles of England, Scotland and Ireland*, 6 vols (1807–08).

Holland, E., trans., *The Canterbury Chantries and Hospitals in 1546. A Supplement to Kent Chantries*, Kent Records 12 supplement (Ashford, 1934).

Horrox, R. and P. W. Hammond, ed., *British Library Harleian Manuscript 433*, 4 vols (Gloucester, 1979–83).

Hull, F., ed., *A Calendar of the White and Black Books of the Cinque Ports, 1432–1955*, Kent Records 19/HMC Joint Publications 5 (1966).

Hussey, A., ed., *Testamenta Cantiana: East Kent* (London, 1907).

Hussey, A., ed., *Kent Chantries*, Kent Records 12 (1932).

Jacob, E. F., ed., *Register of Henry Chichele, Archbishop of Canterbury AD 1414–1443*, Canterbury and York Society, 3 vols (Oxford, 1938–47)

Jean de Waurin, *Anchiennes Cronicques d'Engleterre*, ed. E. Dupont, Societe de l'Histoire de France, 3 vols (Paris, 1858–63).

Johnson, C., ed. and trans., *Registrum Hamonis Hethe Diocesis Roffensis AD 1319–1352* (Oxford, 1948).

Kilburne, Richard, *A Topographie or Survey of the County of Kent* (1659).

Kingsford, C. L., ed., *Chronicles of London* (Oxford, 1905).

Lambarde, W., *A Perambulation of Kent, Conteining the Description, Hystorie and Customes of the Shyre (1576)*, ed. R. Church (Bath, 1970).

Larkin, J. F., ed., *Tudor Royal Proclamations*, 3 vols (New Haven, CT, 1964–69).

List of Escheators for England and Wales, PRO Lists and Indexes 72 (1971).

List of Sheriffs for England and Wales, PRO Lists and Indexes 9 (1898).

Mackeson Mr and S. Robertson, 'Hythe Churchwardens' Accounts in the Time of Henry IV', *Arch. Cant.* 10 (1876), 242–9.

Maitland, F. W., L. W. V. Harcourt and W. C. Bolland, ed., *The Year Books of Edward II: The Eyre of Kent, 6 and 7 Edward II, 1313–14*, 3 vols, Selden Society 24, 27, 29, Year Books Series 5, 7, 8 (1910–13).

Marx, W., ed., *An English Chronicle 1377–1461: A New Edition* (Woodbridge, 2003).

Members of Parliament (House of Commons, 1878).

Morgan, P., ed., *Domesday Book: Kent* (Chichester, 1983).

Murray, K. M. E., trans. and ed., *The Register of Daniel Rough, Common Clerk of Romney 1353–1380*, Kent Records 16 (1945).

Myers, A. R., *The Household of Edward IV* (Manchester, 1959).

Nichols, J. G. and J Bruce, ed., *Wills from Doctor's Commons*, Camden Society, original series 83 (1863).

Norcliffe, C., ed., *The Visitation of Yorkshire in the Years 1563 and 1564*, Harleian Society 16 (1881).

Panton, W. A., ed., *Documents Illustrating the Activities of the General and Provincial Chapters of the English Black Monks, 1215–1540*, 3 vols, Camden Society, 3rd series 45; 47 (1931–37).

Pedrick, G., *Borough Seals of the Gothic Period* (London, 1904).

Pocock, R., *The History of the Incorporated Town and Parishes of Gravesend and Milton in the County of Kent, Selected with Accuracy from Topographical Writers and Enriched with Manuscripts hitherto un-noticed* (printed by R. Pocock, 1797).

Putnam, B. H., ed., *Kent Keepers of the Peace, 1316–1317*, Kent Archaeological Society 13 (1933).

Reaney, P. H. and M. Fitch, ed., *Feet of Fines for Essex, 1423–1547* (Colchester, 1964).

Ropp, G. von der, ed., *Hanserecesse von 1431–1476,* 3 vols (Leipzig, 1881).

Rowe, P., 'The Customary of the Shrine of St Thomas Becket, a Translation of the Customary with Notes' (unpublished M.A. dissertation, University of London, 1990).

Rule, M., ed., *Eademeri Historia Novorum in Anglia*, Rolls Series (London, 1884).

Rye, W., ed., *The Visitation of Norffolk; made and taken by William Hervey, Clarenceux ... 1563, enlarged with another visitation made by Clarenceux Cooke ... and also the visitation made by John Raven, Richmond, 1613*, Harleian Society 32 (1891).

Rylands, W. H., ed., *Pedigrees from the Visitation of Hampshire made by Thomas Benolte, Clarenceux, 1530 ...*, Harleian Society 64 (1913).

Scot, R., *The Discoverie of Witchcraft* (1584) (New York, 1972).

Searle, W. G., ed., *Christ Church, Canterbury, I. The Chronicle of John Stone, Monk of Christ Church 1415–1471, II. Lists of the Deans, Priors and Monks of Christ Church, Canterbury*, Cambridge Antiquarian Society 34 (1902).

Sheppard, J. B., ed., *Literae Cantuarienses: The Letter Books of the Monastery of Christ Church, Canterbury*, 3 vols (London, 1887).

Shirley, W. W., ed., *Fasciculi zizaniorum Magistri Johannis Wyclif cum tritico*, Rolls Series (1858).

Skeat, W., ed., *The Complete Works of Geoffrey Chaucer* (Oxford, 1954).

Smith, L. T., ed., *The Maire of Bristowe is Kalendar by Robert Ricart*, Camden Society, new series 5 (London, 1872).

Somner, W., *The Antiquities of Canterbury*, with an intro by W. Urry (1703, repr. Wakefield, 1977).

Stevenson, J., ed., *Letters and Papers Illustrative of the Wars of the English in France*, 2 vols, Rolls Series (London, 1864).

Stow, J., *The Annales of England* (1592).

Stow, J., *The Survey of London* (London, 1987).

Strachey, J. et al., ed., *Rotuli Parliamentorum, 1278–1504*, 6 vols (1767).

Strype, J., *Memorials of Archbishop Cranmer* I (1694) (Oxford, 1848).

Stubbs, W., ed., *The Historical Works of Gervase of Canterbury*, 2 vols (London, 1879–80).

Sutton, A. F. and P. W. Hammond, ed., *The Coronation of Richard III: The Extant Documents* (Gloucester, 1983).

Sylvester, R., ed., *The History of King Richard III and Selections from the English and Latin Poems* (New Haven, CT, 1976).

Tanner, N. P., ed., *Heresy Trials in the Diocese of Norwich, 1428–31*, Camden Society, 4th series 20 (London, 1977).

Tanner, N. P., ed., *Kent Heresy Proceedings, 1511–12*, Kent Records 26 (Stroud, 1997).

Taylor, A. H., 'The Municipal Records of Tenterden', *Arch. Cant.* 32 (1917), 283–302.

Teichman-Derville, M., 'The Annals of the Town and Port of New Romney: with Some Extracts from the Records of the Town', *Arch. Cant.* 41 (1929), 153–73.

Thomas, A. H. and I. D. Thornley, ed., *The Great Chronicle of London* (London, 1938).

Thorpe, J., ed., *Registrum Roffense* (London, 1769).

Three Chronicles of the Reign of Edward IV, with an Introduction by K. Dockray (Gloucester, 1988).

Vergil, Polydore, *Three Books of English History*, ed. H. Ellis, Camden Society, original series 29 (1844).

Virgoe, R., 'Some Ancient Indictments in the King's Bench referring to Kent, 1450–1452', in *Documents Illustrative of Medieval Kentish Society*, ed. F. R. H. Du Boulay, Kent Record Society 18 (Ashford, 1964), pp. 214–65.

Wedgwood, J. C. and A. D. Holt, *History of Parliament: Register of the Members of the House of Commons, 1439–1509* (1938).

Wickham-Legg, L., ed., *English Coronation Records* (1901).

Witney, K., ed., *The Survey of Archbishop Pecham's Manors, 1283–85*, Kent Records 28 (Maidstone, 2000).

Wood, A., trans. and ed., *Registrum Simonis Langham, Cantuariensis Archiepiscopi*, Canterbury and York Society (Oxford, 1956).

Wood-Legh, K. L., ed., *Kentish Visitations of Archbishop William Warham and his Deputies, 1511–12*, Kent Records 24 (Gloucester, 1984).

Woodruff, C. E., *A History of the Town and Port of Fordwich with a Transcription of the Fifteenth-Century Custumal* (Canterbury, 1895).

Woodruff, C. E., 'Some Early Visitation Rolls Preserved at Canterbury', *Arch. Cant.* 33 (1918), 71–90.

Secondary Sources

Acheson, R. J., 'The Development of Religious Separatism in the Diocese of Canterbury, 1590–1660' (unpublished PhD thesis, University of Kent, 1983).

Adair, J., *The Pilgrims Way: Shrines and Saints in Britain and Ireland* (London, 1978).

Adler, M., 'The Jews of Canterbury', *Jewish Historical Society Transactions* 7 (1915), 19–59.

Allen, T., 'Swine, Salt and Seafood: A Case Study of an Anglo-Saxon and Early Medieval Settlement in North-East Kent', *Arch. Cant.* 124 (2004), 115–36.

Andrewes, J., 'Industries in Kent, c.1500–1640', in *Early Modern Kent 1540–1640*, ed. M. L. Zell (Woodbridge, 2000), pp. 105–39.

Arnold, A., 'A Fourteenth-Century Court Roll of the Manor of Ambree, Rochester', *Arch. Cant.* 29 (1911), 89–153.

Arnold, J. H., 'Lollard Trials and Inquisitorial Discourse', in *Fourteenth-Century England*, 2, ed. C. Given Wilson (Woodbridge, 2002), pp. 81–94.

Arnold, J. H., 'Inquisition, Texts and Discourse', in *Texts and the Repression of Medieval Heresy*, ed. C. Bruschi and P. Biller (York, 2003), pp. 63–80.

Arnold, J. H., *Belief and Unbelief in Medieval Europe* (London, 2005).

Aston, M., 'Lollardy and Sedition, 1381–1431' (first published in *Past and Present* 17 (1960), 1–44), in Aston, *Lollards and Reformers: Images and Literacy in Late Medieval Religion* (London, 1984), pp. 1–47.

Aston, M., 'William White's Lollard Followers' (first published in *Catholic Historical Review* 68 (1982), 469–97) in Aston, *Lollards and Reformers*, pp. 71–100.

Aston, M., *Lollards and Reformers* (London, 1984).

Aston, M., 'Corpus Christi and Corpus Regni: Heresy and the Peasants' Revolt', *Past and Present* 143 (1994), 3–47.

Attree, F. W. T. and J. H. L. Booker, 'The Sussex Colepepers', *Sussex Archaeological Collections* 47 (1904), 47–81.

Attree, F. W. T. and J. H. L. Booker, 'The Sussex Colepepers', *Sussex Archaeological Collections* 48 (1905), 65–98.

Bailey, M., 'Peasant Welfare in England, 1290–1348', *Economic History Review* 2nd series 51 (1998), 223–51.

Baillie, M., *New Light on the Black Death: The Cosmic Connection* (Stroud, 2006).

Baker, A. R. H., 'Open Fields and Partible Inheritance on a Kent Manor', *Economic History Review* 2nd series 17 (1964), 1–23.

Baker, A. R. H., 'Some Fields and Farms in Medieval Kent', *Arch. Cant.* 80 (1965), 152–74.

Baker, A. R. H., 'Field Systems of Southeast England', in *Studies of Field Systems in the British Isles*, ed. A. R. H. Baker and R. H. Butlin (Cambridge, 1973), pp. 377–419.

Barber, L. and G. Priestley-Bell, *Medieval Adaptation, Settlement and Economy of a Coastal Wetland: The Evidence from around Lydd, Romney Marsh, Kent* (Oxford, 2008).

Barber, M. J., 'A Study of Landowners and their Estates in Essex, Kent, Surrey and Sussex at the Opening of the Fifteenth Century Based on the Land Tax Assessments of 1412' (unpublished B.Litt. thesis, University of Oxford, 1949).

Bardsley, S., *Venomous Tongues: Speech and Gender in Late Medieval England* (Philadelphia, 2006).

Barron, C., 'The "Golden Age" of Women in Medieval London', *Reading Medieval Studies* 15 (1989), 35–58.

Barron, O., 'The Fanes', *The Ancestor* 12 (1905), 4–17.

Barry, J., 'Introduction', in *Witchcraft in Early Modern Europe: Studies in Culture and Belief*, ed. J. Barry, M. Hester and G. Roberts (Cambridge, 1996), pp. 1–45.

Bartley, K. and B. M. S. Campbell, '*Inquisitiones Post Mortem*, G.I.S., and the Creation of a Land-Use Map of Pre Black Death England', *Transactions in G.I.S.* 2 (1997), 333–46.

Bellamy, P. and G. Milne, 'An Archaeological Evaluation of the Medieval Shipyard Facilities at Small Hythe', *Arch. Cant.* 123 (2003), 353–82.

Bennett, P., 'The Poor Priests' Hospital – the Chapel', *Arch. Cant.* 98 (1982), 216–20.

Bennett, P., 'St John's Hospital and St John's Nursery', *Arch. Cant.* 108 (1990), 226–31.

Beresford, M., *The Lost Villages of England* (London, 1954).

Berry, W., *County Genealogies: Kent* (London, 1830).

Bhona, M., 'Armed Force and Civic Legitimacy in Jack Cade's Revolt, 1450', *English Historical Review* 118 (2003), 563–82.

Biddick, K., 'Pig Husbandry on the Peterborough Abbey Estate from the Twelfth to the Fourteenth Century A.D.', in *Animals and Archaeology, Volume IV, Husbandry in Europe*, ed. J. Clutton-Brock and C. Grigson, BAR International Series 227 (Oxford, 1985), pp. 161–77.

Bindoff, S. T., *The House of Commons, 1509 to 1558* (London, 1982).

Birrell, J., 'Peasant Craftsmen in the Medieval Forest, *Agricultural History Review* 17 (1969), 91–106.

Bishop, B. and M. Bagwell, *Iwade: Occupation of a North Kent Village from the Mesolithic to the Medieval Period*, Pre-Construct Archaeology monograph 3 (London, 2005).

Bishop T. A. M., 'Monastic Demesnes and the Statute of Mortmain', *English Historical Review* 49 (1934), 301–6.

Bishop, T. A. M., 'The Rotation of Crops at Westerham, 1297–1350', *Economic History Review* 9 (1938), 38–44.

Blécourt, W. de, 'Cunning Women, from Healers to Fortune Tellers', in *Curing and Insuring: Essays on Illness in Past Times*, ed. H. Binnefeld and R. Dekker (Hilversum, 1993), pp. 43–57.

Bower, J., 'Kent Towns, 1540–1640', *Early Modern Kent 1540–1640*, ed. M. L. Zell (Woodbridge, 2000), pp. 141–76.

Brandon, P. F., 'Farming Techniques: South-Eastern England', in *The Agrarian History of England and Wales, Volume II, 1042–1350*, ed. H. E. Hallam (Cambridge, 1988), pp. 312–25.

Brauner, S., *Fearless Wives and Frightened Shrews: The Construction of the Witch in Early Modern Germany* (Amherst, MA, 1995).

Briggs, R., *Witches and Neighbours: The Social and Cultural Context of European Witchcraft* (London, 1996).

Briscall, W. R., 'The Ashford Cage', *Arch. Cant.* 101 (1984), 57–68.

Britnell, R. H., 'English Markets and Royal Administration before 1200', *Economic History Review* 2nd series 34 (1981), 209–21.

Britnell, R. H., 'Rochester Bridge, 1381–1530', in *Traffic and Politics: The Construction and Management of Rochester Bridge, AD 43–1993*, ed. N. Yates and J. M. Gibson (Woodbridge, 1994), pp. 93–106.

Brooks, N., 'Romney Marsh in the Early Middle Ages', in *The Evolution of Marshland Landscapes*, ed. T. Rowley (Oxford, 1987), pp. 24–94.

Brooks, N., 'Rochester Bridge, AD 43–1381', in *Traffic and Politics: The Construction *and Management of Rochester Bridge, AD 43–1993*, ed. N. Yates and J. Gibson (Woodbridge, 1994), pp. 3–40.

Brown, A., 'London and North-West Kent in the Later Middle Ages: The Development of a Land Market', *Arch. Cant.* 92 (1976), 145–55.

Brown, A. D., *Popular Piety in Late Medieval England: The Diocese of Salisbury, 1250–1550* (Oxford, 1995).

Brown, A. D., *Church and Society in England, 1000–1500* (Basingstoke, 2003).

Brown, A. L., *The Governance of Late Medieval England, 1272–1461* (London, 1989).

Brown, R. A., 'King Edward's Clocks', *Antiquaries Journal* 39 (1959), 283–6.

Bullough, V., 'A Note on Medical Care in Medieval English Hospitals', *Bulletin of the History of Medicine* 35 (1961), 74–7.

Burke, T., 'Wittersham Walk, 4 September 2004', *Romney Marsh Irregular* [the newsletter of the Romney Marsh Research Trust] 26 (2005), 21–2.

Burnham, P., *The College at Wye: A Historical Guide* (Wye, 2007).

Butcher, A. F., 'The Origins of Romney Freemen, 1433–1523', *Economic History Review* 2nd series 27 (1974), 16–27.

Butcher, A. F., 'Rent and the Urban Economy: Oxford and Canterbury in the Later Middle Ages', *Southern History* 1 (1979), 37–44.

Butcher, A. F., 'The Hospital of St Stephen and St Thomas, New Romney: The Documentary Evidence', *Arch. Cant.* 96 (1980), 17–26.

Butcher, A. F., 'English Urban Society and the Revolt of 1381', *The English Rising of 1381*, ed. R. H. Hilton and T. H. Aston (Cambridge, 1987), pp. 84–111.

Campbell, B. M. S., 'Agricultural Progress in Medieval England: Some Evidence from Eastern Norfolk', *Economic History Review* 2nd series 36 (1983), 26–46, reprinted in Campbell, *Medieval Antecedents*.

Campbell, B. M. S., 'The Diffusion of Vetches in Medieval England', *Economic History Review* 2nd series 41 (1988), 193–208.

Campbell, B. M. S., ed., *Before the Black Death: Studies in the 'Crisis' of the Early Fourteenth Century* (Manchester, 1989).

Campbell B. M. S. and M. Overton, 'A New Perspective on Medieval and Early Modern Agriculture: Six Centuries of Norfolk Farming *c.*1250–*c.*1850', *Past and Present* 141 (1993), 54–66.

Campbell, B. M. S., J. A. Galloway, D. J. Keene and M. Murphy, *A Medieval Capital and its Grain Supply: Agrarian Production and its Distribution in the London Region c.1300*, Historical Geography Research Series 30 (n.p., 1993).

Campbell, B. M. S., 'Measuring the Commercialisation of Seigniorial Agriculture *circa* 1300', in *A Commercialising Economy: England 1086–1300*, ed. R. H. Britnell and B. M. S. Campbell (Manchester, 1995), pp. 132–93.

Campbell, B. M. S., 'Economic Rent and the Intensification of English Agriculture, 1086–1350', in *Medieval Farming and Technology: The Impact of Agricultural Change in Northwest Europe*, ed. G. Astill and J. Langdon (Leiden, 1997), pp. 235–41.

Campbell, B. M. S., *English Seigniorial Agriculture 1250–1450* (Cambridge, 2000).

Campbell, B. M. S., 'The Sources of Tradable Surpluses: English Agricultural Exports 1250–1349', in *Cogs, Cargoes and Commerce: Maritime Bulk Trade in Northern Europe, 1150–1400*, ed. L. Berggren, N. Hybel and A. Landen (Toronto, 2002), pp. 6–10.

Campbell, B. M. S., 'The Agrarian Problem in the Early Fourteenth Century', *Past and Present* 188 (2005), 3–70.

Campbell B. M. S. and K. Bartley, *England on the Eve of the Black Death: An Atlas of Lay Lordship, Land and Wealth, 1300–49* (Manchester, 2006).

Campbell, B. M. S., 'Benchmarking Medieval Economic Development: England, Wales, Scotland, and Ireland, *circa* 1290', *Economic History Review* 2nd series 61 (2008), 896–945.

Cannon, H., 'The Battle of Sandwich and Eustace the Monk', *English Historical Review* 108 (1912), 649–70.

Carpenter, C., *Locality and Polity: A Study of Warwickshire Landed Society, 1401–99* (Cambridge, 1992).

Carpenter, C., *The Wars of the Roses: Politics and the Constitution, c.1437–1509* (Cambridge, 1997).

Carus-Wilson, E. M. and O. Coleman, *England's Export Trade, 1275–1547* (Oxford, 1963).

Cavello, S., 'The Motivations of Benefactors: An Overview of Approaches to the Study of Charity', in *Medicine and Charity Before the Welfare State*, ed. J. Barry and C. Jones (London and New York, 1991), pp. 46–62.

Cherry, M., 'The Courtenay Earls of Devon: The Formation and Disintegration of a Late Medieval Aristocratic Affinity', *Southern History* 1 (1971), 71–97.

Clanchy, M. T., *From Memory to Written Record, England 1066–1307*, 2nd edn (Oxford, 1993).

Clark, G., 'The Long March of History: Farm Wages, Population, and Economic Growth, England 1209–1869', *Economic History Review* 2nd series 60 (2007), 97–135.

Clark, J. G., 'The Religious Orders in Pre-Reformation England', in *The Religious Orders in Pre-Reformation England*, ed. J. G. Clark (Woodbridge, 2002), pp. 3–33.

Clark, J. G., 'Monasteries and Secular Education in Late Medieval England', in *Monasteries and Society in the British Isles in the Later Middle Ages*, ed. J. Burton and K. Stöber (Woodbridge, 2005), pp. 145–67.

Clark, L., ed., *The History of Parliament: The Commons, 1422–1461* (forthcoming).

Clark, P., *English Provincial Society from the Reformation to the Revolution: Religion, Politics and Society in Kent, 1500–1640* (Hassocks, 1977).

Clark, P. and L. Murfin, *The History of Maidstone: The Making of a Modern County Town* (Stroud, 1995).

Clarke D. and A. Stoyel, *Otford in Kent: A History* (Battle, 1975).

Clarke, H., 'Early Harbours Along the Rother', *Romney Marsh Irregular* 16 (2000), 11–13.

Clarke, H., S. Pearson and M. E. Mate, *Sandwich: 'The Completest Medieval Town in England'. A Study of the Town and Port from its Origins to 1600* (Oxford, 2010).

Clarke, H., 'The Liberty of Sandwich, Kent, c. 1300, and its implications for earlier topography', in *Early Medieval Art and Archaeology in the Northern World*, ed. S. Reynolds and L. Webster (forthcoming).

Clarke, R., *The Medieval Hospital of St John the Baptist, Sevenoaks* (Sevenoaks, 1971).

Clay, R. M., *The Medieval Hospitals of England* (London, 1909, repr. 1966).

Collinson, P., 'Cranbrook and the Fletchers: Popular and Unpopular Religion in the Kentish Weald', in P. Collinson, *Godly People: Essays in Protestantism and Puritanism* (London, 1983), pp. 399–428.

Collinson, P., 'Truth and Legend: The Veracity of John Foxe's Book of Martyrs', in *Clio's Mirror: Historiography in Britain and the Netherlands*, Britain and the Netherlands 8, ed. A. C. Duke and C. A. Tamse (Zutphen, 1985), pp. 31–54.

Collinson, P., 'Truth, Lies, and Fiction in Protestant Historiography', in *The Historical*

Imagination in Early Modern Britain: History, Rhetoric, and Fiction, 1500–1800, ed. D. R. Kelley and D. Harris Sacks (Cambridge, 1997), pp. 37–68.

Collinson, P., 'Night Schools, Conventicles and Churches', in *The Beginnings of English Protestantism*, ed. P. Marshall and A. Ryrie (Cambridge, 2002), pp. 209–35.

Connor, M., 'The Political Allegiances of Christ Church Priory 1400–1472: The Evidence of John Stone's Chronicle', *Arch. Cant.* 127 (2007), 383–406.

Conway, A. E., 'The Maidstone Sector of Buckingham's Rebellion, October 18 1483', *Arch. Cant.* 37 (1925), 97–120.

Coulson, C., 'Battlements and the Bourgeoisie: Municipal Status and the Apparatus of Urban Defence in Later Medieval England', *Medieval Knighthood* 5, Papers from the Sixth Strawberry Hill Conference 1994, ed. S. Church and R. Harvey (Woodbridge, 1995), pp. 119–95.

Creighton O. and R. Higham, *Medieval Town Walls: An Archaeology and Social History of Urban Defence* (Stroud, 2005).

Croft, J. P., 'Hythe MS 1061: The Making of an Urban Register' (unpublished M.A. dissertation, University of Kent, 1992).

Croft, J. P., 'The Custumals of the Cinque Ports c.1290–c.1599: Studies in the Cultural Production of the Urban Record' (unpublished PhD thesis, University of Kent, 1997).

Croft, J. P., 'An Assault on the Royal Justices at Ash and the Making of the Sandwich Custumal', *Arch. Cant.* 117 (1997), 13–36.

Crook, D., 'The Later Eyres', *English Historical Review* 97 (1982), 241–68.

Crossley, D., 'Iron and Glass Industries', in *An Historical Atlas of Sussex*, ed. K. Leslie and B. Short (Chichester, 1999), pp. 62–3.

Crumlin-Pedersen, O., 'The Vikings and the Hanseatic Merchants: 900–1450', in *A History of Seafaring, Based on Underwater Archaeology*, ed. G. Bass (London, 1972), pp. 181–204.

Cullum, P. H., 'Leperhouses and Borough Status in the Thirteenth Century', in *Thirteenth Century England* 3, proceedings of the Newcastle upon Tyne Conference 1989, ed. P. Coss and S. Lloyd (Woodbridge, 1989, 1991), pp. 37–46.

Cullum, P. H., 'Hospitals and Charitable Provision in Medieval Yorkshire' (unpublished D.Phil. thesis, University of York, 1990).

Cullum, P. H., ' "For Pore People Harberles": What was the Function of the Maisonsdieu?', in *Trade, Devotion and Governance: Papers in Later Medieval History*, ed. R. G. Davies and P. McNiven (Stroud, 1994), pp. 36–54.

Curry, A., 'The Loss of Lancastrian Normandy: An Administrative Nightmare?', in *The English Experience in France c.1450–1558: War, Diplomacy and Cultural Exchange*, ed. D. Grummitt (Aldershot, 2002), pp. 24–45.

Currie, C. R. J., 'Early Vetches: A Note', *Economic History Review* 2nd series 41 (1988), 114–16.

Daly, C., 'The Hospitals of London: Administration, Reformation and Benefaction, c.1500–1572' (unpublished D.Phil. thesis, University of Oxford, 1993).

Davies, O., *Cunning-Folk: Popular Religion in English History* (London, 2003).

Davies, R. G., 'Lollardy and Locality', *Transactions Royal Historical Society* 6th series 1 (1991), 193–7.

Davis, J. F., 'Lollard Survival and the Textile Industry in the South-East of England', *Studies in Church History* 3, ed. G. J. Cuming (1966), pp. 191–201.

Davis, J. F., 'Joan of Kent, Lollardy and the English Reformation', *Journal of Ecclesiastical History* 32 (1982), 225–33.

Davis, J. F., 'Lollardy and the Reformation in England', *Archiv für Reformationsgeschicte* 73 (1982), 227–32.

Davis, J. F., *Heresy and Reformation in the South-East of England, 1520–1529* (London, 1983).

Deighton, E., 'The Carmelite Friary in Sandwich', *Arch. Cant.* 114 (1994), 317–27.

Dimmock, S., 'English Small Towns and the Emergence of Capitalist Relations, c.1450–1550', *Urban History* 28 (2001), 5–24.

Dobson, R. B., *Durham Priory 1400–1450* (Cambridge, 1973).

Dobson, R. B., *The Peasants' Revolt of 1381*, 2nd edn (London, 1983).

Dobson, R. B., 'The English Monastic Cathedrals in the Fifteenth Century', *Transactions of the Royal Historical Society* 6th series 1 (1991), 151–72.

Dobson, R. B., 'The Monks of Canterbury in the Later Middle Ages', in *A History of Canterbury Cathedral*, ed. P. Collinson, N. Ramsay and M. Sparks (Oxford, 1995), pp. 69–153.

Dockray, K., 'The Yorkshire Rebellions of 1469', *The Ricardian* 85 (1983), 246–57.

Dohrn-van Rossum, G., *History of the Hour: Clocks and Modern Temporal Orders*, trans. T. Dunlap (Chicago and London, 1996).

Drake, C., 'The Hospital of St Mary of Ospringe Commonly called Maison Dieu', *Arch. Cant.* 30 (1914), 35–78.

Draper, G. M., ' "There hath not bene any grammar scole kepte, preacher maytened or pore people releved, other then … by the same chauntreye": Educational Provision and Piety in Kent, c.1400–1640', in *Pieties in Transition: Religious Practices and Experiences, c.1400–1640,* ed. R. Lutton and E. Salter (Aldershot, 2007), pp. 75–91.

Draper, G. M., with contributions by D. Martin, B. Martin and A. Tyler, *Rye: A History of a Sussex Cinque Port to 1660* (Chichester, 2009).

Draper, G. M. and F. Meddens, *The Sea and the Marsh: The Medieval Cinque Port of New Romney*, Pre-Construct Archaeology monograph 10 (London, 2009).

Du Boulay, F. R. H., 'Late Continued Demesne Farming at Otford', *Arch. Cant.* 73 (1959), 116–24.

Du Boulay, F. R. H., *Medieval Bexley* (Bexley, 1961).

Du Boulay, F. R. H., 'Gavelkind and Knight's Fee in Medieval Kent', *English Historical Review* 77 (1962), 504–11.

Du Boulay, F. R. H., 'Who were Farming the English Demesnes at the End of the Middle Ages?', *Economic History Review* 2nd series 17 (1964–65), 443–55.

Du Boulay, F. R. H., *The Lordship of Canterbury: An Essay on Medieval Society* (London, 1966).

Du Boulay, F. R. H., 'The Assembling of an Estate: Knole in Sevenoaks, c.1275 to c.1525', *Arch. Cant.* 89 (1974), 1–10.

Duffy, E., *The Stripping of the Altars: Traditional Religion in England, 1400–1580* (New Haven, CT and London, 1992).

Dunkin, J., *The History and Antiquities of Dartford with Topographical Notices of the Neighbourhood* (London, 1844).

Dunlop, J. R., 'Pedigree of the Family of Crioll, or Kyriell, of co. Kent', *Miscellanea, Genealogica et Heraldica* 5th series 6 (1916–31), 254–61.

Dyer, C., 'The Social and Economic Background to the Rural Revolt of 1381', in *The English Rising of 1381*, ed. R. H. Hilton and T. H. Aston (Cambridge, 1987), pp. 28–34.

Dyer, C., 'Small Towns 1270–1540', in *The Cambridge Urban History of Britain, 600–1540*, ed. D. M. Palliser (Cambridge, 2000), pp. 505–37.

Eddison, J., 'The Settlement of Romney Marsh: Some Aspects Reconsidered', *Arch. Cant.* 99 (1983), 47–58.

Egan, M., 'The Church in Medieval Greenwich', *Arch. Cant.* 123 (2003), 233–54.

Ehrenreich B. and D. English, *Witches, Midwives and Nurses: A History of Women Healers* (London, 1973).

Evans, N., 'The Descent of Dissenters in the Chiltern Hundreds', in *The World of Rural Dissenters, 1520–1725*, ed. M. Spufford (Cambridge, 1995), pp. 288–308.

Evans, R., 'Merton College's Control of its Tenants at Thorncroft 1270–1349', in *Medieval Society and the Manor Court*, ed. Z. Razi and R. Smith (Oxford, 1996), pp. 199–259.

Everitt, A., 'Nonconformity in Country Parishes', in *Land, Church and People, Essays Presented to Professor H. P. R. Finberg*, The Agricultural History Review 18, supplement, ed. J. Thirsk (1970), 178–99.

Everitt, A., 'The Making of the Agrarian Landscape of Kent', *Arch. Cant.* 92 (1976) 1–31.

Everitt, A., *Continuity and Colonization: The Evolution of Kentish Settlement* (Leicester, 1986).

Fanger, C., 'Medieval Ritual Magic: What it Is and Why We Need to Know More About It', in *Conjuring Spirits: Texts and Traditions of Medieval Ritual Magic*, ed. C. Fanger (Stroud, 1998), pp. vii–xviii.

Farmer, D. L., 'Prices and Wages, 1350–1500', in *Agrarian History of England and Wales, 1348–1500*, ed. E. Miller (Cambridge, 1991), pp. 431–525.

Filmer, R., *Kent Town Crafts* (Meresborough, 1982).

Flaherty, W. E., 'The Great Rebellion in Kent Illustrated from the Public Records', *Arch. Cant.* 3 (1860), 65–96.

Fleming, P. W., 'Charity, Faith, and the Gentry of Kent 1422–1529', in *Property and Politics: Essays in Later Medieval English History*, ed. A. Pollard (Gloucester, 1984), pp. 36–58.

Fleming, P. W., 'The Character and Private Concerns of the Gentry of Kent, 1422–1509' (unpublished PhD thesis, University of Wales, 1985).

Fleming, P. W., 'The Hautes and their "Circle": Culture and the English Gentry', in *England in the Fifteenth Century: Proceedings of the 1986 Harlaxton Symposium*, ed. D. Williams (Woodbridge, 1987), pp. 85–102.

Fleming, P. W., 'The Lovelace Dispute: Concepts of Property and Inheritance in Fifteenth-Century Kent', *Southern History* 11 (1991), 1–18.

Fleming, P. W., 'Conflict and Urban Government in Later Medieval England: St Augustine's Abbey and Bristol', *Urban History* 27 (2000), 321–43.

Fleming, P. W., 'Politics', *Gentry Culture in Late Medieval England*, ed. R. Radulescu and A. Truelove (Manchester, 2005), pp. 5–62.

Flight, C. and A. C. Harrison, 'The Southern Defences of Medieval Rochester', *Arch. Cant.* 103 (1986), 1–26.

Fordham, S. J. and R. D. Green, *Soils of Kent*, Soil Survey of Great Britain (England and Wales) (Harpenden, 1980).

Forrest, I., *The Detection of Heresy in Late Medieval England* (Oxford, 2005).

Foss, E., *A Biographical Dictionary of the Judges of England* (London, 1870).

Freeman, T., 'Dissenters from a Dissenting Church: The Challenge of the Freewillers, 1550–1558', in *Beginnings of Protestantism*, ed. P. Marshall and A. Ryrie, pp. 129–56.

Frere, W. and W. Kennedy, ed., *Visitation Articles and Injunctions of the Period of the Reformation* (London, 1910).

Frere, S., S. Stow, and P. Bennett, *Excavations on the Roman and Medieval Defences of Canterbury* (Canterbury, 1982).

Frohnsdorff, M., *The Maison Dieu and Medieval Faversham* (Faversham, 1997).

Galloway, J. A., M. Murphy, and O. Myhill, *Kentish Demesne Accounts up to 1350: A Catalogue* (London, 1993).

Galloway, J. A., 'London's Grain Supply: Changes in Production, Distribution and Consumption during the Fourteenth Century', *Franco-British Studies: Journal of the British Institute in Paris* 20 (1995), 23–34.

Gardiner, D., *Historic Haven: The Story of Sandwich* (Derby, 1954).

Geremek, B., *The Margins of Society in Late Medieval Paris*, trans. J. Birrell (Cambridge, 1987).

Gibson, J. M. and I. Harvey, 'A Sociological Study of the New Romney Passion Play', *Research Opportunities in Renaissance Drama* 39 (2000), 203–21.

Gibson, J. M., 'The Chantry College of Cobham', *Arch. Cant.* 125 (2005), 83–118.

Gilchrist, R., 'Medieval Bodies in the Material World: Gender, Stigma and the Body', in *Framing Medieval Bodies*, ed. S. Kay and M. Rubin (Manchester, 1994), pp. 43–61.

Gill, L., *Richard III and Buckingham's Rebellion* (Stroud, 1999).

Ginzburg, C., *The Cheese and the Worms: The Cosmos of a Sixteenth-Century Miller*, trans. J. and A. Tedeschi (London and Henley, 1980).

Glasscock, R. E., 'The Distribution of Lay Wealth in Kent, Surrey and Sussex in the Early Fourteenth Century', *Arch. Cant.* 80 (1965), 61–68.

Goldberg, P. J. P., *Women, Work and Lifecycle in a Medieval Economy: Women in York and Yorkshire, c. 1300–1520* (Oxford, 1992).

Goldberg, P. J. P., *Medieval England: A Social History, 1250–1550* (London, 2004).

Goodburn, D., 'Ship Construction and Breaking at the Southlands School Site', in G. Draper and F. Meddens, *The Sea and the Marsh; The Medieval Cinque Port of New Romney*, Pre-Construct Archaeology monograph (forthcoming).

Gorski, R., *The Fourteenth-Century Sheriff: English Local Administration in the Late Middle Ages* (Woodbridge, 2003).

Graham, R., 'The Conflict between Robert Winchelsey, Archbishop of Canterbury and the Abbot and Monks of St Augustine's, Canterbury', *Journal of Ecclesiastical History* 1 (1950), 37–50.

Gray, H. L., *English Field Systems* (Cambridge, MA, 1915).

Gray, H. L., 'Incomes from Land in England in 1436', *English Historical Review* 49 (1934), 607–39.

Greatrex, J., 'Recent Perspectives in Monastic History', in *The Religious Orders in Pre-Reformation England*, ed. J. G. Clark (Woodbridge, 2002), pp. 35–50.

Greenwood, E., *The Hospital of St Bartholomew, Rochester* (Rochester, 1962).

Gregory, M., 'Wickham Court and the Heydons', *Arch. Cant.* 78 (1963), 1–21.

Griffin, R., 'The Lepers' Hospital at Swainestrey', *Arch. Cant.* 34 (1920), 63–78.

Griffin, R., 'An Inscription in Little Chart Church', *Arch. Cant.* 36 (1923), 131–42.

Griffiths, R. A., *The Reign of Henry VI* (London, 1981).

Griffiths, R. A., *King and Country: England and Wales in the Fifteenth Century* (London, 1991).

Grummitt, D., ' "For the Surety of the Towne and Marches": Early Tudor Policy towards Calais, 1485–1509', *Nottingham Medieval Studies* 44 (2000), 184–203.

Grummitt, D., 'The Establishment of the Tudor Dynasty', in *A Companion to Tudor Britain,* ed. R. Tittler and N. Leslie (Oxford, 2004), pp. 13–28.

Grummitt, D., 'Deconstructing Cade's Rebellion: Discourse and Politics in the Mid

Fifteenth Century', in *The Fifteenth Century VI: Identity and Insurgency in the Late Middle Ages*, ed. L. Clark (Woodbridge, 2006), pp. 107–22.

Gunn, S., *Early Tudor Government 1485–1558* (Basingstoke, 1995).

Haines, C. R., *Dover Priory: A History of the Priory of St Mary the Virgin, and St Martin of the New Work* (Cambridge, 1930).

Hammond, E., 'Physicians in Medieval English Religious Houses', *Bulletin of the History of Medicine* 32 (1958), 105–20.

Hammond, P. W., ed., *Richard III: Loyalty, Lordship and Law* (London, 1986).

Harris, O., 'Marshmen at Work: Dover Harbour, 1583', *Romney Marsh Irregular* 28 (2006), 13–21.

Harrison, A., 'Excavations on the Site of St Mary's Hospital, Strood', *Arch. Cant.* 84 (1969), 139–60.

Harriss, G. L., *Cardinal Beaufort: A Study of Lancastrian Ascendancy and Decline* (Oxford, 1988).

Harriss, G. L., *Shaping the Nation: England, 1360–1460* (Oxford, 2005).

Harvey, B. F., *Westminster Abbey and its Estates in the Middle Ages* (Oxford, 1977).

Harvey, B. F., *Living and Dying in England 1100–1540: The Monastic Experience* (Oxford, 1993).

Harvey, I. W. M., *Jack Cade's Rebellion of 1450* (Oxford, 1991).

Hatcher, J., 'Mortality in the Fifteenth Century: Some New Evidence', *Economic History Review* 2nd series 10 (1986), 19–38.

Hatcher, J., 'The Great Slump of the Mid-Fifteenth Century', in *Progress and Problems in Medieval England*, ed. R. Britnell and J. Hatcher (Cambridge, 1996), pp. 237–72.

Hayes, J., D. Williams and P. Payne, 'Report of an Excavation in the Grounds of St Bartholomew's Chapel, Chatham', *Arch. Cant.* 98 (1982), 177–89.

Helmholz, R. H., 'Crime, Compurgation and the Courts of the Medieval Church', *Law and History Review* 1 (1983), 1–26.

Hewitt, H. J., *The Organization of War under Edward III, 1338–62* (Manchester, 1966).

Hicks, A. and M. Houliston, *The Whitefriars Excavation* (forthcoming).

Hicks, M. and A. Hicks, *St Gregory's Priory, Northgate, Canterbury: Excavations, 1988–1991* (Canterbury, 2001).

Hicks, M. A., 'The Case of Sir Thomas Cook, 1468', *English Historical Review* 93 (1978), 82–96.

Hicks, M. A., 'The Changing Role of the Wydevilles in Yorkist Politics to 1483', in *Patronage, Pedigree and Power in Later Medieval England*, ed. C. D. Ross (Gloucester, 1979), pp. 60–86.

Hicks, M. A., *Warwick the Kingmaker* (Oxford, 1998).

Hicks, M. A., 'The Rising Price of Piety in the Later Middle Ages', in *Monasteries and Society in the British Isles in the Later Middle Ages*, ed. J. Burton and K. Stöber (Woodbridge, 2005), pp. 95–112.

Hill, C., 'Lollards to Levellers', in C. Hill, *Collected Essays of Christopher Hill II: Religion and Politics in Seventeenth-Century England* (Brighton, 1986), pp. 89–116.

Hilton, R., *The English Peasantry in the Later Middle Ages* (Oxford, 1975).

Hogan, T. L., 'The Memorandum Book of Henry of Eastry', 2 vols (unpublished PhD thesis, London, 1966).

Holland, P., 'Cook's Case in History and Myth', *Historical Research* 61 (1988), 21–35.

Holland, P., 'The Lincolnshire Rebellion of March 1470', *English Historical Review* 103 (1988), 849–69.

Holt, R., *The Mills of Medieval England* (Oxford, 1988).

Hooker, J. R., 'Some Cautionary Notes on Henry VII's Household and Chamber System', *Speculum* 33 (1958), 69–75.

Hope, A., 'Martyrs of the Marsh: Elizabeth Barton, Joan Bocher and Trajectories of Martyrdom in Reformation Kent', in *Pieties in Transition: Religious Practices and Experiences, c.1400–1640*, ed. R. Lutton and E. Salter (Aldershot, 2007), pp. 41–55.

Horden, P., 'Small Beer? The Parish and the Poor and Sick in Later Medieval England', in *The Parish in Late Medieval England*, Harlaxton Medieval Studies 14, ed. C. Burgess and E. Duffy (Donington, 2006), pp. 339–64.

Horrox, R., *Richard III: A Study in Service* (Cambridge, 1989).

Houlbrooke, R., 'Magic and Witchcraft in the Diocese of Winchester, 1491–1570', in *Cross, Crown and Community: Religion, Government and Culture in Early Modern England*, ed. D. J. B. Trim and P. J. Balderstone (Oxford, 2004), pp. 113–41.

Howard, M., 'Tudor and Stuart Great Houses', in *An Historical Atlas of Sussex*, ed. K. Leslie and B. Short (Chichester, 1999), pp. 54–5.

Hull, F., *Ordnance Survey Historical Guides: Kent*, George Philip, London and the Ordnance Survey (Southampton, 1988).

Hudson, A., 'The Examination of Lollards', *Bulletin Institute Historical Research* 46 (1973), 145–59.

Hudson, A., *The Premature Reformation: Wycliffite Texts and Lollard History* (Oxford, 1988).

Hudson, A., ' "Laicus Litteratus": The Paradox of Lollardy', in *Heresy and Literacy, 1000–1530*, ed. P. Biller and A. Hudson (Cambridge, 1994), pp. 222–36.

Jacob, E., *The History of Faversham* (1774).

James, M. K., *Studies in the Medieval Wine Trade* (Oxford, 1971).

Jay, W., 'List of Members of the Fourth Parliament of Henry VII', *Bulletin of the Institute of Historical Research* 3 (1925–26), 168–75.

Jeffs, R. M., 'The Poynings-Percy Dispute: An Example of the Interplay of Open Strife and Legal Action in the Fifteenth Century', *Bulletin Institute Historical Research* 34 (1961), 148–64.

Jenkins, R. C., 'The Family of Guldeford', *Arch. Cant.* 14 (1882), 1–17.

Jewell, H. M., *English Local Administration in the Middle Ages* (Newton Abbot, 1972).

Johnson, P., *Duke Richard of York, 1411–1460* (Oxford, 1988).

Jolly, K., 'Medieval Magic: Definitions, Beliefs, Practices', in *Witchcraft and Magic in Europe: The Middle Ages*, ed. K. Jolly, C. Raudvere and E. Peters (London, 2002), pp. 6–71.

Jones, E. D., 'The Crown, Three Benedictine Houses, and the Statute of Mortmain, 1279–1348', *Journal of British Studies* 14 (1975), 1–28.

Jones, K., *Gender and Petty Crime in Late Medieval England: The Local Courts in Kent, 1460–1560* (Woodbridge, 2006).

Jordan, W. K., *Social Institutions of Kent 1480–1660: A Study of the Changing Pattern of Social Aspirations*, Kent Archaeological Society 75 (Ashford, 1961).

Jurkowski, M., 'Lollardy in Coventry and the Revolt of 1431', in *The Fifteenth Century VI: Identity and Insurgency in the Late Middle Ages*, ed. L. Clark (Woodbridge, 2006), pp. 145–63.

Jurkowski, M., 'Lollardy and Social Status in East Anglia', *Speculum* 82 (2007), 120–52.

Jurkowski, M. and N. Ramsay, ed., *English Monastic Estates, 1066–1540: A List of Manors, Churches and Chapels*, Part One, List and Index Society Special Series 40 (2007).

Karras, R. M., 'The Latin Vocabulary of Illicit Sex in English Ecclesiastical Court Records', *Journal of Medieval Latin* 2 (1992), 1–17.

Karras, R. M., *Common Women: Prostitution and Sexuality in Medieval England* (Oxford, 1996).

Keene, D. J., *Cheapside before the Great Fire* (London, 1985).

Keene, D. J., 'The South-East of England', in *The Cambridge Urban History of Britain, 600–1540*, ed. D. M. Palliser (Cambridge, 2000), pp. 545–82.

Kent, E. J., 'Masculinity and Male Witches in Old and New England, 1593–1680', *History Workshop Journal* 60 (2005), 69–72.

Kershaw, I., 'The Great Famine and Agrarian Crisis in England, 1315–22', *Past and Present* 59 (1973), 3–50.

Kettle, A., 'Ruined Maids: Prostitutes and Servant Girls in Later Medieval England', in *Matrons and Marginal Women in Medieval Society*, ed. R. Edwards and V. Ziegler (Woodbridge, 1995), pp. 19–31.

Kieckhefer, R., *European Witch Trials: Their Foundations in Popular and Learned Culture, 1300–1500* (London, 1979).

Kieckhefer, R., *Magic in the Middle Ages* (Cambridge, 1990).

Kieckhefer, R., 'The Devil's Contemplatives: The *Liber Iuratus*, the *Liber Visionum* and Christian Appropriation of Jewish Occultism', in *Conjuring Spirits: Texts and Traditions of Medieval Ritual Magic*, ed. C. Fanger (Stroud, 1998), pp. 250–65.

Kilby, K., *Coopers and Coopering* (Princes Risborough, 2004).

Kittredge, G. L., *Witchcraft in Old and New England* (Cambridge, MA, 1929).

Knowles, D., *The Religious Orders in England: The End of the Middle Ages*, 2 vols (Cambridge, repr. 1961).

Knowles, D. and R. N. Hadcock, 'Additions and Corrections to Medieval Houses: England and Wales [hospitals]', *English Historical Review* 72 (1957), 76–85.

Knowles, D. and R. N. Hadcock, *Medieval Religious Houses: England and Wales*, 2nd edn (London, 1971).

Kosminsky, E. A., *Studies in the Agrarian History of England in the Thirteenth Century*, trans. R. Kisch, ed. R. H. Hilton (Oxford, 1956).

Lambert, M. D., *Medieval Heresy: Popular Movements from the Gregorian Reform to the Reformation*, 3rd edn (Oxford, 2002).

Lambert, U. V., *Bletchingley: A Parish History* (London, 1921).

Lander, J. R., 'Council, Administration and Councillors, 1461–85', *Bulletin of the Institute of Historical Research* 32 (1959), 191–219.

Lander, J. R., 'Marriage and Politics in the Fifteenth Century: The Nevilles and the Wydevilles', *Bulletin of the Institute of Historical Research* 36 (1963), 119–52.

Langdon, J., *Horses and Oxen and Technological Innovation* (Cambridge, 1986).

Langdon, J., *Mills in the Medieval Economy* (Oxford, 2004).

Larking, L. B., 'Note on the Birthplace of Caxton', *Arch. Cant.* 5 (1863), 324–5.

Lawson, T., 'Maritime Kent 1500–1700, in *An Historical Atlas of Kent*, ed. T. Lawson and D. Killingray (Chichester, 2004), pp. 91–2.

Lawson, T., 'Markets in the Medieval Period', in *An Historical Atlas of Kent*, ed. T. Lawson and D. Killingray (Chichester, 2004), pp. 50–1.

Lee, P., 'Monastic and Secular Religion and Devotional Reading in Late Medieval Dartford and West Kent' (unpublished PhD thesis, University of Kent, 1998).

Lee, P., 'Orthodox Parish Religion and Chapels of Ease in Late Medieval England: the Case of St George's Chapel in Gravesend', *Arch. Cant.* 119 (1999), 55–70.

Lee, P., *Nunneries, Learning and Spirituality in Late Medieval English Society: The Dominican Priory of Dartford* (York, 2001).

Levack, B. P., *The Witch-hunt in Early Modern Europe* (London, 1987).

Lloyd, T. H., *Some Aspects of the Building Industry in Medieval Stratford upon Avon*, Dugdale Society Occasional Papers 14 (Oxford, 1961).

Lloyd, T. H., *The English Wool Trade in the Middle Ages* (Cambridge, 1977).

Lutton, R., *Lollardy and Orthodox Religion in Pre-Reformation England* (Woodbridge, 2006).

Lutton, R., 'Geographies and Materialities of Piety: Reconciling Competing Narratives of Religious Change in Pre-Reformation and Reformation England', in *Pieties in Transition: Religious Practices and Experiences, c.1400–1640*, ed. R. Lutton and E. Salter (Aldershot, 2007), pp. 11–39.

Lyle, M., 'Canterbury 1500–1700: Two Centuries of Upheaval', in *An Historical Atlas of Kent*, ed. T. Lawson and D. Killingray (Chichester, 2004), pp. 68–9.

Lyon, J., *The History of the Town and Port of Dover*, 2 vols (Dover, 1813–14).

Lyons, M., 'Weather, Famine, Pestilence and Plague in Ireland, 900–1500', in *Famine: the Irish Experience, 900–1900: Subsistence Crises and Famine in Ireland*, ed. E. M. Crawford (Edinburgh, 1989), pp. 321–74.

MacCulloch, D., *Tudor Church Militant: Edward VI and the Protestant Reformation* (London, 1999).

Macfarlane, A., *Witchcraft in Tudor and Stuart England* (London, 1970).

Macpherson Bardell, K., 'Beyond Pendle', in *The Lancashire Witches*, ed. R. Poole (Manchester, 2002), pp. 105–22.

Maddicott, J. R., 'The English Peasantry and the Demands of the Crown, 1294–1341', in *Past and Present Supplement* 1 (Oxford, 1975), reprinted in *Landlords, Peasants and Politics in Medieval England*, ed. T. H. Ashton (Cambridge, 1987), pp. 285–359.

Marsh, C., *Popular Religion in Sixteenth-Century England* (London, 1998).

Martin, G. H., 'The English Borough in the Thirteenth Century', in *The Medieval Town: A Reader in English Urban History 1200–1540*, ed. R. Holt and G. Rosser (London and New York, 1990), pp. 29–48.

Martin-Conway, W., 'Allington Castle', *Arch. Cant.* 28 (1909), 337–62.

Mate, M., 'High Prices in Early Fourteenth Century England, Causes and Consequences', *Economic History Review* 2nd series 28 (1973), 1–16.

Mate, M., 'The Role of Gold Coinage in the English Economy, 1338–1400', *Numismatic Chronicle* 7th series 18 (1978), 126–41.

Mate, M., 'The Impact of War on the Economy of Canterbury Cathedral Priory, 1294–1340', *Speculum* 57 (1982), 761–78.

Mate, M., 'The Farming out of Manors: A New Look at the Evidence from Canterbury Cathedral Priory', *Journal of Medieval History* 9 (1983), 331–43.

Mate, M., 'Property Investment by Canterbury Cathedral Priory, 1250–1400', *Journal of British Studies* 23 (1984), 1–21.

Mate, M., 'Agrarian Economy after the Black Death: The Manors of Canterbury Cathedral Priory, 1348–91', *Economic History Review* 2nd series 37 (1984), 341–54.

Mate, M., 'Labour and Labour Services on the Estates of Canterbury Cathedral Priory in the Fourteenth Century', *Southern History* 7 (1985), 55–68.

Mate, M., 'Medieval Agrarian Practices: The Determining Factors?', *Agricultural History Review* 33 (1985), 22–31.

Mate, M., 'The Estates of Canterbury Cathedral Priory before the Black Death, 1315–1348', *Studies in Medieval and Renaissance History* new series 8 (1986), 3–31.

Mate, M., 'Tenant Farming and Tenant Farmers: Kent and Sussex', in *The Agrarian History of England and Wales, Volume III, 1348–1500*, ed. E. Miller (Cambridge, 1991), pp. 680–703.

Mate, M., 'Farming Practice and Techniques: Kent and Sussex', in *The Agrarian History of England and Wales, Volume III, 1348–1500*, ed. E. Miller (Cambridge, 1991), pp. 268–85.

Mate, M., 'The Rise and Fall of Markets in Southeast England', *Canadian Journal of History* 31 (1996), 60–85.

Mate, M., *Trade and Economic Developments, 1450–1550: The Experience of Kent, Surrey and Sussex* (Woodbridge, 2006).

May, T., 'The Estates of the Cobham Family in the Later Thirteenth Century', *Arch. Cant.* 84 (1969), 211–29.

Maycock, A., *Malling Abbey: A History of St Mary's Abbey West Malling* (West Malling, 1975).

Mayhew, N. J., 'Numismatic Evidence and Falling Prices in the Fourteenth Century', *Economic History Review* 2nd series 27 (1974), 1–15.

McCloskey, D. N., 'The Persistence of the English Open Fields', in *European Peasants and Their Markets*, ed. W. N. Parker and E. C. Jones (Princeton, NJ, 1975), pp. 73–119.

McCloskey, D. N., 'English Open Fields as a Behavior towards Risk', *Research in Economic History* 1 (1976), 124–70.

McIntosh, M. K., 'Local Responses to the Poor in Late Medieval and Tudor England', *Continuity and Change* 3 (1988), 209–45.

McIntosh, M. K., *Controlling Misbehavior in England, 1370–1600* (Cambridge, 1998).

McLain, B. A., 'Factors in Market Establishment in Medieval England: The Evidence from Kent 1086–1350', *Arch. Cant.* 117 (1997), 83–103.

McNiven, P., *Heresy and Politics in the Reign of Henry IV* (Woodbridge, 1981).

McSheffrey, S., *Gender and Heresy: Women and Men in Lollard Communities* (Philadelphia, 1995).

Mercer, M., 'Kent and National Politics, 1437–1534: The Royal Affinity and a County Elite' (unpublished PhD thesis, University of London, 1995).

Mercer, M., 'A Forgotten Kentish Rebellion, September–October, 1470', *Arch. Cant.* 122 (2002), 143–52.

Mercer, M., 'The Administration of the Cinque Ports in the Early Lancastrian Period', in *Peoples, Places and Perspectives: Essays on Later Medieval and Early Tudor England in Honour of Ralph A. Griffiths*, ed. K. Dockray and P. Fleming (Stroud, 2005), pp. 47–67.

Merry, M., 'Ricart's *Kalender*: Urban Ideology and Fifteenth-Century Bristol' (unpublished M.A. dissertation, University of Kent, 1994).

Mills, J., 'The Priory at Lewisham' (unpublished Diploma in Local History dissertation, University of London, 1986).

Mills, P., 'Spiritual Correction in the Medieval Church Courts of Canterbury' (unpublished PhD thesis, University of Rochester, 1980).

Milne, G., 'Joining the Medieval Fleet', *British Archaeology Magazine* 61 (2001) [unpag].

Milne, G., *The Port of Medieval London* (Stroud, 2003).

Milne G. et al., 'The Fourteenth-Century Merchant Ship from Sandwich: A Study in Medieval Maritime Archaeology', *Arch. Cant.* 124 (2004), 227–64.

Moon, J. O., 'The Art of Managing Canterbury Cathedral Priory in the Middle Ages 1270–1414' (unpublished research paper, 2007).

Moon, J. O., 'The European Connection: Aspects of Canterbury Cathedral Priory's Temporalities Overseas', paper given to 'Canterbury: A Medieval City' conference at University of Le Havre (March 2009).

Morgan, D. A. L., 'The King's Affinity in the Polity of Yorkist England', *Transactions of the Royal Historical Society* 5th series 23 (1973), 11–25.

Muir, K., *The Life and Letters of Sir Thomas Wyatt* (Liverpool, 1963).

Murray, K. M. E., *The Constitutional History of the Cinque Ports* (Manchester, 1935).

Musson, A. and W. M. Ormrod, *The Evolution of English Justice: Law, Politics and Society in the Fourteenth Century* (Houndmills, 1999).

Myers, A. R., 'The Household of Queen Elizabeth Wydeville, 1466–7', *Bulletin of the John Rylands Library* 1 (1967–68), 207–35, 443–81.

Newfield, T. P., 'A Cattle Panzootic in Early Fourteenth-Century Europe', *Agricultural History Review* 57 (2009), 155–90.

Newman, E. I. and P. D. A. Harvey, 'Did Soil Fertility Decline in Medieval English Farms? Evidence from Cuxham, Oxfordshire, 1320–1340', *Agricultural History Review* 45 (1997), 119–36.

Nicholas, D., *Urban Europe 1100–1700* (Basingstoke, 2003).

Nilson, B., *Cathedral Shrines of Medieval England* (Woodbridge, 1998).

Oakley, A., 'Rochester Priory, 1185–1540', in *Faith and Fabric: A History of Rochester Cathedral 640–1994*, ed. N. Yates and P. Welsby (Woodbridge, 1996), pp. 29–56.

Orme, N., 'The Education of Edward V', *Bulletin of the Institute of Historical Research* 57 (1984), 119–30.

Orme, N., *Medieval Schools: From Roman Britain to Renaissance England* (London and New Haven, CT, 2006).

Orme, N. and M. Webster, *The English Hospital, 1070–1570* (New Haven, CT and London, 1995).

Ormrod, W. M., 'The Crown and the English Economy, 1290–1348', in *Before the Black Death: Studies in the 'Crisis' of the Early Fourteenth Century*, ed. B. M. S. Campbell (Manchester, 1991), pp. 149–83.

Palliser, D. M., 'Introduction', in *The Cambridge Urban History of Britain, 600–1540*, ed. D. M. Palliser (Cambridge, 2000), pp. 3–15.

Parfitt, K., 'St John's Hospital Reredorter, Canterbury', *Arch. Cant.* 109 (1991), 298–308.

Parfitt, K., B. Corke and J. Cotter, *Townwall Street, Dover: Excavations 1996*, Canterbury Archaeological Trust (Canterbury, 2006).

Parker, S. L. and L. R. Poos, 'A Consistory Court from the Diocese of Rochester, 1363–4', *English Historical Review* 106 (1991), 652–65.

Parkin, E. W., 'Wingham, a Market Town', *Arch. Cant.* 93 (1977), 61–79.

Parkin, E. W., 'The Old Court Hall, Lydd', *Arch. Cant.* 98 (1982), 107–20.

Parkin, E. W., 'The Medieval Origins of Wye College', *Arch. Cant.* 102 (1985), 209–31.

Pearson, S., *The Medieval Houses of Kent: An Historical Analysis* (London, 1994).

Pegues, J., 'A Monastic Society at Law in the Kent Eyre of 1313–1314', *English Historical Review* 87 (1972), 548–64.

Pelham, R., Some Aspects of the East Kent Wool Trade in the Thirteenth Century', *Arch. Cant.* 44 (1932), 218–28.

Peters, E., *The Magician, the Witch and the Law* (Pennsylvania, 1978).

Peters, E., 'The Medieval Church and State on Superstition, Magic and Witchcraft: From Augustine to the Sixteenth Century', in *Witchcraft and Magic in Europe: The Middle Ages*, ed. K. Jolly, C. Raudvere and E. Peters (London, 2002), pp. 173–86.

Philips, E. M., 'Charitable Institutions in Norfolk and Suffolk c.1350–1600' (unpublished PhD thesis, University of East Anglia, 2001).

Pidgeon, L., 'Antony Wydevile, Lord Scales and Rivers: Family, Friends and Affinity, Part 2', *The Ricardian* 16 (2006), 15–45.

Plumb, D., 'The Social and Economic Spread of Rural Lollardy: A Reappraisal', in *Voluntary Religion*, Studies in Church History 23, ed. W. J. Sheils and D. Wood (Oxford, 1986), pp. 111–29.

Plumb, D., 'A Gathered Church? Lollards and their Society', in *The World of Rural Dissenters, 1520–1725*, ed. M. Spufford (Cambridge, 1995), pp. 132–63.

Pollard, A. J., 'The Tyranny of Richard III', *Journal of Medieval History* 3 (1977), 147–65.

Pollock, A., 'Social and Economic Characteristics of Witchcraft Accusations in Sixteenth and Seventeenth-Century Kent', *Arch. Cant.* 95 (1979), 37–48.

Poos, L. R., 'The Rural Population of Essex in the Later Middle Ages', *Economic History Review* 2nd series 38 (1985), 515–30.

Powell, E., *Kingship, Law, and Society: Criminal Justice in the Reign of Henry V* (Oxford, 1989).

Power, E., *Medieval English Nunneries: c.1275 to 1535* (Cambridge, 1922).

Prescott, E., *The English Medieval Hospital 1050–1640* (Melksham, 1992).

Prestwich, M., *War, Politics and Finance under Edward I* (London, 1972).

Prestwich, M., 'Currency and the Economy of Early Fourteenth Century England', in *Edwardian Monetary Affairs, 1279–1341*, ed. N. J. Mayhew, British Archaeological Reports 36 (1977), pp. 45–58.

Pugh, T. B. and C. D. Ross, 'The English Baronage and the Income Tax of 1436', *Bulletin Institute Historical Research* 26 (1953), 1–28.

Putnam, B. H., 'The Transformation of the Keepers of the Peace into the Justices of the Peace, 1327–1380', *Transactions Royal Historical Society* 4th series 12 (1929), 19–48.

Quick, J., 'Government and Society in Kent, 1232 to 1280' (unpublished D.Phil. thesis, University of Oxford, 1986).

Raban, S., 'Mortmain in Medieval England', in *Landlords, Peasants and Politics in Medieval England*, ed. T. Aston (Cambridge, 1987), pp. 203–26.

Rawcliffe, C., *The Staffords, Earls of Stafford and Dukes of Buckingham 1394–1521* (Cambridge, 1978).

Rawcliffe, C., 'The Hospitals of Later Medieval London', *Medical History* 28 (1984), 1–21.

Rawcliffe, C., *The Hospitals of Medieval Norwich*, Studies in East Anglian History 2 (Norwich, 1995).

Rawcliffe, C., *Medicine and Society in Later Medieval England* (Stroud, 1995).

Rawcliffe, C., 'Curing Bodies and Healing Souls: Pilgrimage and the Sick in Medieval East Anglia', in *Pilgrimage: The English Experience from Becket to Bunyon*, ed. C. Morris and P. Roberts (Cambridge, 2002), pp. 108–40.

Rawcliffe, C., 'Written in the Book of Life: Building the Libraries of English Medieval Hospitals and Almshouses', *The Library* 7th series 3 (2002), 127–62.

Rawcliffe, C., 'The Earthly and Spiritual Topography of Suburban Hospitals', in *Town and Country in the Middle Ages: Contrasts, Contacts and Interconnections, 1100–1500*, ed. K. Giles and C. Dyer (Leeds, 2005), pp. 251–74.

Rawcliffe, C., *Leprosy in Medieval England* (Woodbridge, 2006).

Reeves, A., 'The Testimony of Trees', *Romney Marsh Irregular* 24 (2004), 21–4.

Renn, D., 'Refortification at Rochester in the 1220s: A Public/Private Partnership?', *Arch. Cant.* 124 (2004), 343–63.

Rex, R., *The Lollards* (Houndmills, 2002).

Reynolds, M., 'Religious Denominations in the 17th Century: The Compton Census', in *An Historical Atlas of Kent*, ed. T. Lawson and D. Killingray (Chichester, 2004), pp. 83–5.

Richards, P., *The Medieval Leper and his Northern Heirs* (Cambridge, 1977).

Richardson, C. T., 'Household Objects and Domestic Ties', in *The Medieval Household in Christian Europe, c.850–1550*, ed. C. Beatties et al. (Turnhout, Belgium, 2003), pp. 433–47.

Richardson, C. T., *Domestic Life and Domestic Tragedy in Early Modern England* (Manchester and New York, 2006).

Richardson, T. L. *Medieval Sandwich and its World* (Sandwich, 2004).

Richmond, C., 'Fauconberg's Kentish Rising of May 1471', *English Historical Review* 85 (1970), 673–92.

Roberts, H., *Tenterden: The First Thousand Years* (York, 1995).

Robertson, Canon Scott, 'Pecche of Lullingstone', *Arch. Cant.* 16 (1886), 227–40.

Röhrkasten, J., 'The Mendicant Orders in Urban Life and Society: The Case of London', in *Religious and Laity in Western Europe, 1000–1400: Interaction, Negotiation, and Power*, ed. E. Jamroziak and J. Burton (Turnhout, 2006), pp. 333–55.

Roskell, J. S., L. Clark and C. Rawcliffe, ed., *The History of the Parliament: The Commons, 1386–1421*, 4 vols (Stroud, 1993).

Ross, C., *Edward IV* (Berkeley, CA, 1974).

Rosser, G., 'Myth, Image and Social Process in the English Medieval Town', *Urban History* 23 (1996), 5–25.

Rosser, G., 'Urban Culture and the Church 1300–1540', in *The Cambridge Urban History of Britain, 600–1540*, ed. D. M. Palliser (Cambridge, 2000), pp. 335–69.

Rubin, M., *Charity and Community in Medieval Cambridge* (Cambridge, 1987).

Ruderman, A., *A History of Ashford* (Chichester, 1994).

Russell, J., *The History of Maidstone* (1881, repr. Rochester, 1978).

Russell, J. B., *Witchcraft in the Middle Ages* (London, 1972).

Ruual, M., 'Monks in the World: The Case of Gundulf of Rochester', in *Anglo-Norman Studies* 11, ed. R. A. Brown (Woodbridge, 1989), pp. 245–60.

Ryrie, A., *The Gospel and Henry VIII: Evangelicals in the Early English Reformation* (Cambridge, 2003).

Salter, E. E., 'Some Differences in the Cultural Production of Household Consumption in Three North Kent Communities', in *The Medieval Household in Christian Europe, c.850–1550*, ed. C. Beatties et al. (Turnhout, Belgium, 2003), pp. 391–407.

Satchell, A. E. M., 'The Emergence of Leper-Houses in England' (unpublished D.Phil. thesis, University of Oxford, 1998).

Saul, N., 'The Social Status of Chaucer's Franklin: A Reconsideration', *Medium Aevum* 52 (1983), 10–26.

Saul, N., *Death, Art and Memory in Medieval England: The Cobham Family and their Monuments, 1300–1500* (Oxford, 2001).

Schofield, C. L., *The Life and Reign of Edward IV*, 2 vols (London, 1923).

Schofield, R. S., 'The Geographical Distribution of Wealth in England, 1334–1649', *Economic History Review* 2nd series 18 (1965), 483–510.

Searle, E., *Lordship and Community: Battle Abbey and its Banlieu, 1066–1538* (Toronto, 1974).

Seymour, M., 'The Organisation, Personnel and Functions of the Medieval Hospital in the Later Middle Ages' (unpublished M.A. thesis, University of London, 1946).

Shagan, E. H., *Popular Politics and the English Reformation*, Cambridge Studies in Early Modern British History (Cambridge, 2003).

Shiel, R. S., 'Improving Soil Fertility in the Pre-Fertiliser Era', in *Land, Labour and Livestock: Historical Studies in European Agricultural Productivity*, ed. B. M. S. Campbell and M. Overton (Manchester, 1991), pp. 51–77.

Shrubsole, W., *The History and Antiquities of Rochester and its Environs* (printed and sold by T. Fisher, 1772).

Simpson, P., 'The Continuum of Resistance to Tithe, *c*.1400–1600', in *Pieties in Transition: Religious Practices and Experiences, c.1400–1640*, ed. R. Lutton and E. Salter (Aldershot, 2007), pp. 93–108.

Sinclair Williams, C., 'Maritime East Malling', *Arch. Cant.* 88 (1973), 51–5.

Smetham, H., *History of Strood* (Chatham, 1899, repr. 1978).

Smith, A., 'Regional Differences in Crop Production in Medieval Kent', *Arch. Cant.* 78 (1964 for 1963), 147–60.

Smith, F., *A History of Rochester* (1928, repr. Rochester, 1976).

Smith, R. A. L., *Canterbury Cathedral Priory: A Study in Monastic Administration* (Cambridge, 1943).

Somerville, R., *History of the Duchy of Lancaster*, 2 vols (1953–70).

Spain, R., 'Medieval Watermills', in *An Historical Atlas of Kent*, ed. T. Lawson and D. Killingray (Chichester, 2004), pp. 62–3.

Sparks, M., 'St Gregory's Priory, Canterbury: A Re-assessment', *Arch. Cant.* 118 (1998), 77–90.

Spufford, M., 'The Importance of Religion in the Sixteenth and Seventeenth Centuries', in *The World of Rural Dissenters, 1520–1725*, ed. M. Spufford (Cambridge, 1995), pp. 1–102.

Stanford, J. C. and M. Townsend, *The Great Governing Families of England*, 1 (London, 1865).

Starkey, D., 'Intimacy and Innovation: The Rise of the Privy Chamber, 1485–1547', in D. Starkey et al., *The English Court from the Wars of the Roses to the Civil War*, 2nd edn (Harlow, 1992), pp. 71–118.

Steane, J. M., *The Archaeology of Power: England and Northern Europe AD 800–1600* (Stroud, 2001).

Sutton, A. F., 'Sir Thomas Cook and his "Troubles": An Investigation', *Guildhall Studies in London History* 3 (1978), 85–108.

Sutton, A. F., 'The Hautes of Kent', *The Ricardian* 6 (1982), 54–5.

Swanson, R. N., 'Literacy, Heresy, History and Orthodoxy: Perspectives and Permutations for the Later Middle Ages', in *Heresy and Literacy, 1000–1530*, ed. P. Biller and A. Hudson (Cambridge, 1994), pp. 279–93.

Sweetinburgh, S., 'Women, Household and Community: Appledore and Hythe c.1400–1470' (unpublished M.A. dissertation, University of Kent, 1993).

Sweetinburgh, S., 'The Role of the Hospital in Medieval Kent, c.1080–c.1560' (unpublished PhD thesis, University of Kent, 1998).

Sweetinburgh, S., 'Supporting the Canterbury Hospitals: Benefaction and the Language of Charity in the Twelfth and Thirteenth Centuries', *Arch. Cant.* 122 (2002), 237–58.

Sweetinburgh, S., 'Joining the Sisters: Female Inmates of the Late Medieval Hospitals in East Kent', *Arch. Cant.* 123 (2003), 17–39.

Sweetinburgh, S., *The Role of the Hospital in Medieval England: Gift Giving and the Spiritual Economy* (Dublin, 2004).

Sweetinburgh, S., 'Monastic Houses', in *An Historical Atlas of Kent*, ed. T. Lawson and D. Killingray (Chichester, 2004), pp. 42–3.

Sweetinburgh, S., 'Medieval Hospitals and Almshouses', in *An Historical Atlas of Kent*, ed. T. Lawson and D. Killingray (Chichester, 2004), pp. 44–5.

Sweetinburgh, S., 'The Austin Friars in Late Medieval Canterbury: Negotiating Spaces', in *Monasteries and Society in the British Isles in the Later Middle Ages*, ed. J. Burton and K. Stöber (Woodbridge, 2005), pp. 197–212.

Sweetinburgh, S., 'Strategies of Inheritance among Kentish Fishing Families in the Later Middle Ages', *The History of the Family* 11 (2006), 93–105.

Sweetinburgh, S., 'Mayor-Making and Other Ceremonies: Shared Uses of Sacred Space among the Kentish Cinque Ports', in *The Use and Abuse of Sacred Spaces in Late Medieval Towns*, ed. P. Trio and M. de Smet (Leuven, 2006), pp. 165–88.

Sweetinburgh, S., 'Royal Patrons and Local Benefactors: The Experiences of the Hospitals of St Mary at Ospringe and Dover in the Thirteenth Century', in *Religious and Laity in Northern Europe 1000–1400: Interaction, Negotiation and Power*, Europa Sacra 2, ed. E. Jamroziak and J. Burton (Turnhout, 2007), pp. 111–29.

Sweetinburgh, S., 'The Poor, Hospitals and Charity in Sixteenth-Century Canterbury', in *Pieties in Transition: Religious Practices and Experiences, c.1400–1640*, ed. R. Lutton and E. Salter (Aldershot, 2007), pp. 59–73.

Sylvester, D., 'Shaping the Urban Landscape of Maritime England: The Interests of the King and Barons in the 1292 Founding of New Winchelsea', in *Maritime Topography and the Medieval Town*, Studies in Archaeology and History 4, ed. J. Bill and B. Clausen (Copenhagen 1999), pp. 155–79.

Sylvester, D., 'The Development of Winchelsea and its Maritime Economy', in D. and B. Martin, *New Winchelsea, Sussex: A Medieval Port Town*, Field Archaeology Unit Monograph 2, Institute of Archaeology, University College London (London, 2004), pp. 7–19.

Tanner, N. P., *The Church in Late Medieval Norwich* (Toronto, 1984).

Tanner, N. P., 'Penances Imposed on Kentish Lollards by Archbishop Warham, 1511–12', in *Lollardy and the Gentry in the Later Middle Ages*, ed. M. Aston and C. Richmond (Stroud, 1997), pp. 229–49.

Tanner, N. P., *The Ages of Faith: Popular Religion in Late Medieval England* (London, 2009).

Tanner, T., *Saint Edmund's Chapel, Dover, and its Restoration* (Dover, 1968).

Tatton-Brown, T., 'The Churches of the Canterbury Diocese in the Eleventh Century', in *Minsters and Parish Churches: The Local Church in Transition*, ed. J. Blair (Oxford, 1988), pp. 105–18.

Tatton-Brown, T., 'Medieval Parishes and Parish Churches in Canterbury', in *The Church in the Town*, ed. T. R. Slater and G. Rosser (Aldershot, 1998), pp. 236–71.

Taylor, T. and M. Aston, *Time Team 99: The Site Reports* (London, 1999).

Thirsk, J., 'Industries in the Countryside', in *Essays in the Economic and Social History of Tudor and Stuart England*, ed. F. J. Fisher (Cambridge, 1961), pp. 70–88.

Thirsk, J., 'The Farming Regions of England', in *The Agrarian History of England and Wales, Volume IV, 1500–1640*, ed. J. Thirsk (Cambridge, 1986), pp. 1–112.

Thirsk, J., ed., *Hadlow: Life, Land and People in a Wealden Parish 1460–1600* (Maidstone, 2007).

Thomas, K., *Religion and the Decline of Magic* (London, 1971).

Thomson, J. A. F., 'A Lollard Rising in Kent: 1431 or 1438?', *Bulletin Institute Historical Research* 37 (1964), 100–2.

Thomson, J. A. F., *The Later Lollards, 1414–1520* (Oxford, 1965).

Thornhill, P., 'A Lower Thames Ford and the Campaigns of 54 B.C. and A.D. 43', *Arch. Cant.* 92 (1976), 119–28.

Thornton, C., 'The Level of Arable Productivity on the Bishop of Winchester's Estate in the Early Fourteenth Century', in *The Winchester Pipe Rolls and Medieval English Society*, ed. R. H. Britnell (Woodbridge, 2003), pp. 115–21.

Thrupp, S. L., *The Merchant Class of Medieval London* (Chicago, 1948).

Titow, J. Z., *Winchester Yields: A Study in Medieval Agricultural Productivity* (Cambridge, 1972).

Tittler, R., *Architecture and Power: The Town Hall and the English Urban Community c.1500–1640* (Oxford, 1991).

Turner, H., *Town Defences in England and Wales: An Architectural and Documentary Study AD 900–1500* (London, 1971).

Underdown, D., *Revel, Riot and Rebellion: Popular Politics and Culture in England, 1603–1660* (Oxford, 1985).

Urry, W., 'The Jubilee of St Thomas, 1420: Billeting and Rationing Problems in the Fifteenth Century', *Canterbury Cathedral Chronicle* 42 (1947), 23–7.

Urry, W., *Canterbury under the Angevin Kings* (London, 1967).

Velden, H. van der, *The Donor's Image: Gerard Leyet and the Votive Portraits of Charles the Bold* (Turnhout, 2000).

Vincent, N., 'English Monasteries and their French Possessions' (unpublished paper).

Virgoe, R., 'The Death of William de la Pole, Duke of Suffolk', in *East Anglian Society and the Political Community in Late Medieval England*, ed. C. Barron, C. Rawcliffe and J. T. Rosenthal (Norwich, 1997), pp. 247–58.

Wadmore, J. F., 'Tonbridge Castle and its Lords', *Arch. Cant.* 16 (1886), 12–57.

Wagner, A. R., *Heralds and Heraldry in the Middle Ages*, 2nd edn (Oxford, 1956)

Wagner, A. R., *English Genealogy*, 2nd edn (Oxford, 1972).

Walcott, M., 'Inventories of (i) St Mary's Hospital or Maison Dieu, Dover, (ii) the Benedictine Priory of St Martin New-Work, Dover, for Monks, (iii) the Benedictine Priory of SS Mary and Sexburga, in the Island of Sheppey, for Nuns', *Arch. Cant.* 7 (1868), 272–306.

Wallace, J., 'The Overseas Trade of Sandwich, 1400–1520' (unpublished M.Phil. thesis, University of London, 1974).

Ward, A., 'Castles and other Defensive Sites', in *An Historical Atlas of Kent*, ed. T. Lawson and D. Killingray (Chichester, 2004), pp. 53–5.

Watts, J. L., 'Polemic and Politics in the 1450s', in *The Politics of Fifteenth-Century England: John Vale's Book*, ed. M. L. Kekewich, C. Richmond, A. F. Sutton, L. Visser-Fuchs and J. L. Watts (Stroud, 1995), pp. 3–42.

Watts, J., *Henry VI and the Politics of Kingship* (Cambridge, 1996).

Webb, D., *Pilgrimage in Medieval England* (London and New York, 2000).

Webb, D., 'Pilgrimage', in *An Historical Atlas of Kent*, ed. T. Lawson and D. Killingray (Chichester, 2004), pp. 46–7.

Webster, B., 'The Community of Kent in the Reign of Richard II', *Arch. Cant.* 100 (1984), 217–29.

Wedgwood, J. C., *History of Parliament: Biographies of the Members of the Commons House, 1439–1509* (London, 1936).

Wilson, C. G., *The English Nobility in the Late Middle Ages* (London, 1987).

Witney, K. P., *The Jutish Forest* (London, 1976).

Witney, K. P., 'The Woodland Economy of Kent, 1066–1348', *Agricultural History Review* 38 (1990), 20–39.

Woodcock, B. L., *Medieval Ecclesiastical Courts in the Diocese of Canterbury* (Oxford, 1952).

Woodruff, C. E., 'Financial Aspects of the Cult of St Thomas of Canterbury', *Arch. Cant.* 44 (1932), 13–32.

Wooldridge, S. W. and D. L. Linton, 'Some Aspects of the Saxon Settlement in South-East England Considered in Relation to the Geographical Background', *Geography* 20 (1935), 161–75.

Wooldridge, S. W., 'The Anglo-Saxon Settlement', in *An Historical Geography of England before A.D. 1800: Fourteen Studies*, ed. H. C. Darby (Cambridge, 1936), pp. 88–132.

Wragg, E., C. Jarrett and J. Haslam, 'The Development of Medieval Tonbridge Reviewed in the Light of Recent Excavations at Lyons, East Street', *Arch. Cant.* 125 (2005), 119–50.

Wunderli, R., *London Church Courts and Society on the Eve of the Reformation* (Cambridge, MA, 1981).

Wyatt, S. B., *Cheneys and Wyatts: A Brief History in Two Parts* (London, 1960).

Zell, M. L., *Industry in the Countryside: Wealden Society in the Sixteenth Century* (Cambridge, 1994).

Zell, M. L., 'The Establishment of a Protestant Church', in *Early Modern Kent, 1540–1640*, ed. M. L. Zell (Woodbridge, 2000), pp. 207–44.

Zell, M. L., 'The Coming of Religious Reform', in *Early Modern Kent 1540–1640*, ed. M. L. Zell (Woodbridge, 2000), pp. 177–206.

Zell, M. L. 'Landholding and the Land Market', in *Early Modern Kent, 1540–1640*, ed. M. L. Zell (Woodbridge, 2000), pp. 39–74.

Ziegler, P., *The Black Death* (New York, 1971).

Index

Note: Page references in **bold** denote figures, tables and maps. *Italicised* references prefaced with *pl* indicate plate numbers.
Individual religious houses are listed under "religious houses" and individual hospitals under "hospitals".